International Management:
A Reader

International Management:
A Reader

Edited by

Pervez N Ghauri and S Benjamin Prasad

The Dryden Press
Harcourt Brace & Company Limited
London Fort Worth New York Orlando
Philadelphia San Diego Toronto Sydney Tokyo

The Dryden Press
24/28 Oval Road
London NW1 7DX

Copyright © 1995 by
Harcourt Brace & Company, Limited for the collection.
Copyright for individual pages – various, see title pages.

All rights reserved

No part of this book may be reproduced in any form by photostat,
microfilm or other means, without permission from the publishers.

A catalogue for this book is available from the British Library
ISBN 0–03–099015–7

Typeset by Input Ltd, London
Printed in Great Britain by WBC Book Manufacturers, Bridgend, Mid Glamorgan

Contents

Introduction and Overview
P. N. Ghauri and S. B. Prasad ... ix

PART I: TOWARD GLOBAL STRATEGIZING: THEORETICAL FRAMEWORKS AND COMPANY APPROACHES ... 1

1. The tortuous evolution of the multinational corporation ... 3
   Howard V. Perlmutter
   Columbia Journal of World Business, **4**, 9–18 (1969)
2. A theory of international operations ... 15
   Peter J. Buckley and Mark Casson
   In *European Research in International Business*, Elsevier–North-Holland, 45–50 (1979)
3. The globalization of markets ... 21
   Theodore. Levitt
   Harvard Business Review, May–June, 92–102 (1983)
4. Global strategy: an organizing framework ... 33
   Sumantra Ghoshal
   Strategic Management Journal, **8**, 425–440 (1987)
5. New structures in MNCs based in small countries: a network approach ... 51
   Pervez Ghauri
   European Management Journal, **10**(3), 357–364 (1992)
6. The hypermodern MNC—a heterarchy? ... 64
   Gunnar Hedlund
   Human Resource Management, **25**(1), 9–35 (1986)
7. Managing across borders: an empirical test of the Bartlett and Ghoshal (1989) organizational typology ... 85
   Siew Meng Leong and Chin Tiong Tan
   Journal of International Business Studies, **24**(3), 449–464 (1993)
8. Bridgestone's quest for leadership in the global tire industry ... 100
   S. Benjamin Prasad
   The Review of Business Studies, **2**(1), 17–34 (1993)

PART II: COOPERATIVE INTERNATIONAL COMPETITION ... 115

9. Cooperate to compete globally ... 117
   Howard V. Perlmutter and David A. Heenan
   Harvard Business Review, March–April, 136–152 (1986)
10. A theory of cooperation in international business ... 126
    Peter J. Buckley and Mark Casson
    In F. J. Contractor and P. Lorange (eds) *Cooperative Strategies in International Business*, Lexington, Mass. (1988)

11. Collaborate with your competitors—and win 146
    Gary Hamel, Yves L. Doz and C. K. Prahalad
    Harvard Business Review, January–February, 133–139 (1989)
12. Interfirm diversity, organizational learning, and longevity in global
    strategic alliances 155
    Arvind Parkhe
    Journal of International Business Studies, Fourth Quarter, 579–601 (1991)
13. Towards a theory of business alliance formation 174
    Jagdish N. Sheth and Atul Parvatiyar
    Scandinavian International Business Review, 1(3), 71–87 (1992)

PART III: UNDERSTANDING NON-WESTERN STRUCTURES 189

14. Eastern Asian enterprise structures and comparative analysis of forms
    and business organization 191
    Richard D. Whitley
    Organization Studies, 11(1), 47–74 (1990)
15. The nature and competitiveness of Japan's *Keiretsu* 213
    Angelina Helou
    Journal of World Trade, 25, 99–131 (1991)
16. The Japanese corporate network: a blockmodel analysis 244
    Michael L. Gerlach
    Administrative Science Quarterly, 37, March, 105–139 (1992)
17. The worldwide web of Chinese business 274
    John Kao
    Harvard Business Review, March–April, 24–36 (1993)
18. A network approach to probing Asia's invisible business structures 285
    S. Benjamin Prasad and Pervez N. Ghauri
    In *Proceedings of Southern Management Association*, M. Schenke (ed.),
    Atlanta, Georgia, 371–374 (1993)

PART IV: DEVELOPING GLOBAL MANAGERS 293

19. Human resource planning in Japanese multinationals: a model for US firms? 295
    Rosalie Tung
    Journal of International Business Studies, 15(2), 139–149 (1984)
20. The cross-cultural puzzle of international human resource management 308
    André Laurent
    Journal of Human Resource Management, Spring, 91–102 (1986)
21. Developing leaders for the global enterprise 317
    Stephen H. Rhinesmith, John N. Williamson, David M. Ehlen and Denise S. Maxwell
    Training and Development Journal, April, 25–34 (1989)

22. Toward a comprehensive model of international adjustment: an integration of multiple theoretical perspectives 327
J. Stewart Black, Mark Mendenhall and Gary Oddou
Academy of Management Review, **16**, 291–317 (1991)
23. Managing globally competent people 350
Nancy J. Adler and Susan Bartholomew
Academy of Management Executive, **6**(3), 52–65 (1992)
24. Initial examination of a model of intercultural adjustment 365
Barbara Parker and Glenn M. McEvoy
International Journal of Intercultural Relations, **17**, 355–379 (1993)
Index 385

Introduction and Overview

P. N. Ghauri and S. B. Prasad

In the 1960s and the 1970s international management was rather narrowly defined either as a framework for comparing and contrasting typical national management systems or, alternatively, as that of managing a company's foreign subsidiaries. Comparing and contrasting management concepts and principles formulated in the US context with those of Europe was part of the academic interest. More fashionable in the 1980s were comparative themes that focused upon the Japanese management,[1] in contrast with the American or the European management. As is known, part of the impetus came from Theory Z (Ouchi, 1980), and the other part flowed from the Toyota System that ushered in the 'lean manufacturing' paradigm.

The international business environment of the 1980s was dynamic and turbulent enough to reinforce some of the earlier insights, such as, the globalization of many consumer products and markets (Levitt, 1983) on the one hand, as well as a fairly high degree of harmonization of managing firms across national political boundaries. This is not to assert that there are no differences in the country contexts or the philosophical bases of management structures, but merely to contend that the 'convergence' hypothesis advanced more than 35 years ago (Harbison and Myers, 1959) appears to have been reinforced by the globalization process itself, especially in manufacturing industries such as automotive and consumer electronics, and in service industries such as banking, hospitality, and insurance.

The term 'international management' has had no single meaning or interpretation. In a broad sense, 'international management' would entail *managing* multinational assets and resources (Prasad and Shetty, 1976) of a company, or as more recently phrased, 'organizing cross-border activities to produce a set of products at the lowest production and transaction cost' (Dunning, 1993). The transactions cost approach, as Nooteboom (1993, p. 283) argues, does consider the effects of scale and scope in costs of production, and to a limited degree their effects in costs of organization, but hardly their effects in costs of transactions. Our view of the multinational corporation (MNC), among its other salient features, is that of a firm that is constantly engaged in many transactions in many countries and at many levels concurrently.

One way to clarify the content of the subject matter of international management is perhaps to examine the contents of books titled *International Management*. We cite two of them, one by Negandhi (1987); the other by Beamish *et al.* (1994). (See Appendix A for a list of topics treated in these two books.) In both of them about 10 topics are covered. We consider about half of them in each case to be what we consider as international management topics; the other topics (such as international corporation and government, export marketing, international marketing, financial management in the Negandhi book as well as international trade, managing exports, international business environment, impact of globalization, and political risk in the Beamish *et al.* volume) are relevant to the operations of any modern firm including the MNC. Both of these books take a very broad perspective of international management. Our volume, with a narrower focus, is aimed at the advanced undergraduate and postgraduate students.

Our narrower view of 'international management' can be interpreted as follows: cross-border or multinational business/economic activities of a firm may entail various types of transactions and managerial functions. All of these can be classified into two, not necessarily mutually exclusive, dimensions:

(1) Activities and functions that result from business decisions, other than foreign direct investment (FDI), aimed at the basic corporate objectives of survival and growth. Examples would include exporting products, importing/sourcing inputs, licensing proprietary rights, adhering to government rules and regulations, managing financial assets and liabilities, and so forth.

(2) Those management functions and activities that can be regarded as the direct consequence of FDI decisions. We consider such topics as organization design and structure, headquarter-subsidiary relations, human resource management, international production, long range/strategic planning covered by Negandhi (1987) as well as such topics, covered by Beamish *et al.* (1994), as global sourcing, global strategy formulation, international joint ventures, developing global managers as constituting the core of international management.

We have dealt with these two perspectives with a managerial perspective.

Others, espousing an organizational behavioural orientation (e.g. Lane and DiStefano, 1992) address and discuss questions involving people, culture, and the corporation. In short, such a focus allows one to examine the implications of alternative, or combinatorial, approaches to managing people, a vital resource of MNCs. In contrast to these two approaches—Negandhi's/Beamish's and Lane and DiStefano's—we prefer to take a mid-range position, and refer to managing international assets and resources as the core of international management and, in so doing, we focus on issues that are germane to managing for global effectiveness.

The international assets that result from the FDI decisions of companies will normally take the shape and substance of tangible factories, distribution facilities, research laboratories as well as the intangible systems, networks, and relationships. What propels a company's FDI decisions is a set of factors including the company's growth objective given its organizational life stage, product market-scope, organizational and management competence, rivals' intentions, foreign market opportunities and the like. Some of the firm-specific factors that played a role in the case of Europe's mature MNCs (e.g. Nestlé, Philips, Unilever) were their size, proprietary brand names, market knowledge, and access to the less developed parts of the world. Some have characterized these companies as 'multidomestic' meaning that such an MNC comprises and manages many foreign subsidiaries in ways similar to managing the domestic subsidiaries.

The role of the headquarters was prominent in the international management of subsidiaries. US-based MNCs such as General Electric[2] extended its products/services to the developed parts of the world first much like other US firms. The domestic market was large enough, and grew steadily for nearly two decades after World War II, and hence until about mid-1960s, only a small number of US firms actively deployed and managed their assets abroad. The 1980s marked a series of developments that have compelled both the European and the US companies to rethink their corporate strategies, and hence their management approaches, because the external environmental forces, exemplified by the rapid success of Japanese multinationals, demanded higher levels of global efficiency and effectiveness. This development spawned the maxim of managing for global efficiency.

From an analytical perspective, Bartlett and Ghoshal (1992, p. 105) argue that what transformed the structures of many industries from national to global have been 'three principal economic forces': economies of scale, economies of scope, and the national differences in the availability and cost of productive resources. They argue that 'MNCs must build the capability to learn from many environments to which they are exposed and to appropriate benefits of such learning throughout their global operations' (p. 199)

In theory, global efficiency results from global integration of production, distribution, and innovation as well as from (product-market) differentiation (Bartlett and Ghoshal, 1992, pp. 284-287). Yet, it is useful to recognize that economies of scale flow primarily from internal activities, while the economies of scope flow mainly from product-market differentiation. Interfacing these two are national or regional 'market imperfections' which can be seen as differences in the availability and cost of such factors as human, capital, and technical resources.

Furthermore, if one subscribes to the notion that 'efficiency' is a *necessary* condition for a company to survive in the competitive context, then 'managing for global efficiency' can only be a significant part of international management. The other part is represented by 'effectiveness', the *sufficiency* condition, suggesting that 'managing for global effectiveness' should also be a part of the topic.

In order to explicate the notion of 'managing for global effectiveness', we shall briefly sketch two Asian examples. One is that of Minebea, a lesser-known Japanese MNC; the other is that of ELGI Ltd., a small family-controlled Indian company. The purpose of these sketches is merely to illustrate that the goal of managing for global effectiveness can be achieved in numerous ways, and at various points on the globalization continuum. ELGI is evidently to the far left of Minebea which is far left of Toyota on the continuum of globalization. In short, we believe that internationalization or globalization are matters of degree, not kind.

INTERNATIONAL EXPANSION OF MINEBEA

Minebea is a miniature multinational that comprises 50 factories, 52 subsidiaries, 16 affiliated companies, and some 30 000 employees scattered around the globe. Its sales revenue in 1992 was US$1.2 billion. A glass jar in the company's boardroom contains the firm's entire product range, hundreds of ballbearings ranging from 30 mm in diameter all the way down to just 3 mm. It is one of the largest firms in its industry in the world. Much of the growth and diversification of Minebea is attributed to the 'non-traditional leadership of its chief executive, Takami Takahashi' (*The Economist*, 1992).

Among the three avenues that Takahashi took, the decision to engage in offshore production (the other two being vertical integration and diversification) contributed more to the profitability of the firm. The production facilities to make ballbearings and electrical components were initially established in Singapore, then in Taiwan, and more recently in Thailand. At present, more than 60% of Minebea's ballbearing production is international. As if to reward Takahashi's adroit management behaviour there came the trend toward miniaturization in consumer electronics. While we have no knowledge of how Takahashi managed Minebea's foreign subsidiaries, it can be assumed that not only did he organize these cross-border activities with an eye to minimizing production and transaction costs, he also managed them to meet his corporate objective of minimizing wage costs. This undertaking was long before other Japanese automotive, electronics, and tyre companies started overseas production.

The second example is illustrative not of offshore production but of the case of a small company in southern India—ELGI—developing core competence to make compressors that meet current European quality standards.

TECHNICAL PARITY OF ELGI

ELGI is an old metallurgical company that has operated as a rather paternalistic firm in southern India. At present, it employs some 2000 workers and can be described as a multiplant operation. Among the various metal products it makes, its screw compressors meet global efficiency standards. From a plant (1995) visit, one could roughly sketch the international context in which such an accomplishment was possible. We identify four key variables:

(a) the equipment was German, fully automated and robotized;
(b) the raw material was an alloy (which any metallurgical firm could procure);
(c) the technical operator skills were learned by Indian nationals who had undergone training in Germany;
(d) the quality standards, set to meet ISO 9000, were embedded in the machinery subject to operator skills.

One may consider the case of ELGI as a firm that is pursuing a niche strategy; however, in terms of managing the operations the question of whether the firm was managing for global efficiency or for global effectiveness remains blurred. ELGI is actively engaged in exporting part of its output that meets global standards to the emerging economies in the Middle East and Africa, but unlike Minebea, its management is unlikely ever to consider FDI. Yet, it is noteworthy that the executives of ELGI had grasped the portents of the Single European Act (1987) which ushered in the European Union (EU) early enough to position their tiny firm on a par with manufacturing firms in the G-7 nations. Although ELGI is not yet an MNC, one could consider it as 'possessing' the ability to scan 'worldwide intelligence' (Bartlett and Ghoshal, 1992, pp. 783-784).

* * *

Consistent with our mid-range stance on international management, we identified several theoretical and empirical writings. The published articles included in this volume cover the following management themes that are not only germane to an understanding of the complexity and dynamics of managing for global effectiveness but also can be a knowledge-source from which to formulate fresh hypotheses. The themes are:

I. Toward Global Strategizing;
II. Cooperative International Competition;
III. Understanding Non-Western Structures;
IV. Developing Global Managers.

An overview of the articles included in each theme follows.

I. TOWARD GLOBAL STRATEGIZING

The first five papers (Perlmutter, 1969; Buckley and Casson, 1979; Levitt, 1983; Ghoshal, 1987; Ghauri 1992), offer rich theoretical or normative frameworks. The article by Hedlund (1986) (Reading 6) provides a rather new framework to identify organizational properties of MNCs. The article by Leong and Tan (1993) (Reading 7) discusses the empirical validity of Bartlett and Ghoshal's (1989) former study, mentioned in an earlier section. And the last article (Prasad, 1993) (Reading 8) in this section provides a detailed study of the global approach of a large regional MNC.

Perlmutter (Reading 1) not only offers a concise, yet insightful, typology of management orientation (ethnocentric, polycentric, and geocentric) but also formulated two hypothetical foundations upon which many other postulates rest. The propositions are: (1) the MNC is a new kind of an institution; (2) the degree of multinationality of an enterprise is positively related to the firm's long-term viability. He advocates the geocentrism as an ideal for the MNC, and suggests that 'The ultimate goal of geocentricism is a worldwide or global approach in both headquarters and subsidiaries.'

A theoretical framework for explaining and predicting methods of servicing markets by MNCs is offered by Buckley and Casson (Reading 2). The premise they develop is that both the intermediate and the final goods are subject to location and ownership effects. 'The division between exports and local servicing is largely the result of the economics of location'. Regarding the latter, the authors discuss the five main types of market imperfections that pave the way for the 'internalization' benefits to the MNC. Furthermore, they contend that the strategy of the MNCs can be explained by a combination of the knowledge of locational influences with the opportunities for internalizing markets profitably. (Valuable insights can be found in Kogut, 1985.)

The theme of standardization permeates Levitt's article (Reading 3). In his powerful essay, the author asserts that well-managed companies have moved from emphasis on customizing items to offering globally standardized products. Whereas Buzzel (1968) outlines a number of significant impediments (such as market characteristics including cultural nuances, industry conditions, marketing institutions, and legal restrictions), Levitt's initial, and enduring premise is that the force driving 'the world toward a converging commonality' is technology, his first vector. While he does not deny that the barriers to standardization, as enumerated by Buzzel (1968) exist, he focuses more on global imagination or the mind-set that is essential to engage in creative analysis of market conditions on a global basis. He also considers globalization itself as the second vector.

Ghoshal (Reading 4), taking stock of the writings of the previous decade, is convinced 'that there is a great deal of conceptual ambiguity about what a global strategy really means ... the concept has been linked almost exclusively with how the firm structures the flow of tasks within its worldwide value-adding system'. Hence, he sets out to provide an organizing framework within which different perspectives and prescriptions can be assimilated. The framework he proposes relates to an integrated analysis of the different means and ends which can be of value to both MNC managers and researchers in analysing the content of global strategies. While this contribution is not a blueprint for formulating global strategies, as Ghoshal himself recognizes, it offers 'a synthesis of existing ideas and techniques'.

Much of the literature on MNCs either illustrates or draws from the past management decisions and organizational processes of MNCs based in the United Kingdom or the United

States, there are several MNCs that are based in smaller, yet industrially advanced, nations. Ghauri (Reading 5), using data on the processes fostered by Swedish MNCs, especially in their Southeast Asian operations, examines the rather novel phenomenon, namely, the tendency of the parent firms to spawn subsidiaries which could not only become as large in their activities as the parent but also be quite autonomous. He uses the Swedish network approach to help explain this unfolding phenomenon.

Hedlund (Reading 6) offers an extension of Perlmutter's insightful treatment of the evolution of the MNC and employs the notion of heterarchy, not simple as anti-hierarchy but, as the logical framework within which the organizational properties of the modern MNC can be identified. In so doing, he draws on several theoretical strands such as the sociologist's interdependence, social integration, transaction cost economics, and typologies of organizational environments. In the final section, he identifies a number of properties of the MNC many of which demonstrate how his view goes far beyond those of internalization economists.

Leong and Tan (Reading 7) empirically test the Bartlett and Ghoshal (1989) organizational typology. They asked 131 senior executives to classify their companies as multinational, global, international or transnational. Their results provide partial support for the typology. However, the 'transnational', as suggested by Bartlett and Ghoshal, was least frequently reported. They also report that differences in the characteristics suggested across the four organizational types were not very clear for the executives. Generally, the firms are trying to 'think global' and 'act local'. The authors thus suggest that reformation of the Bartlett and Ghoshal typology is needed. It is, perhaps, more apparent now than in 1993 that there is a lack of understanding in the differences in activities between 'transnational' and other types of organizations. This may also be due to new drives such as 'back to core business' and 're-engineering'.

At a more detailed and a theoretical level, Prasad (Reading 8) focuses on the forces that moulded a Japanese regional multinational into a global firm. The paper is organized into five related sections: (a) Expansion of Bridgestone as a regional MNC, (b) Planning for the initial FDI in the United States; (c) New management thinking; (d) Acquisition of the US company (Firestone Tire); (e) Emergence of Bridgestone as a formidable rival (to Goodyear and Michelin) in the global tyre industry.

II. COOPERATIVE INTERNATIONAL COMPETITION

Although earlier theoretical frameworks and insights, which form the mainstream theorizing about the causes and consequences of the multinational phenomenon, have been influenced to a large extent by the industrial organization theories, much of the literature dealt with the fundamental question of how a single MNC can achieve sustained performance in an intensely competitive global marketplace. In the late 1980s, a supplementary source of a firm's competitive advantage, namely through one form or level of cooperation, or another, with a rival, came to the fore. The term 'strategic alliances' does not replace 'global competition'; rather it can be viewed as an offspring of global competition. It is more common in the literature to include the entire gamut of cooperative arrangements under 'strategic alliances than to differentiate between involuntary joint ventures and voluntary joint ventures on the one hand, and, on the other, between a joint venture and a strategic alliance'.[3] Finer distinctions notwithstanding, the five papers (Readings 9-13, by Perlmutter and Heenan, 1986; Buckley and Casson, 1988; Hamel et al., 1989; Parkhe, 1991; Sheth and Parvatiyar, 1992) included in this section capture the substance of strategic alliances that have been ascribed to such factors as decreasing product life cycle spans and increasing costs of innovation (or R&D). We regard this phenomenon as the (relatively) new cooperative dimension in global competition.

The focus of the paper by Perlmutter and Heenan (Reading 9) is upon 'global strategic partnerships' (GSPs), or strategic alliances. The authors construe that forging such partnerships as a strategic option 'that touches every sector of the world economy, from sunrise (emerging) to sunset (maturing/declining) industries'. They specify the distinguishing feature of GSPs thus: two, or more, firms developing a long-term strategy aimed at world leadership either as low-cost producers or as differentiated marketers. Yet, the partners retain their national, or philosophical, identity. Sketching the GSP portfolio of Philips (the Dutch MNC), the authors discuss a number of prerequisites to successful partnering, a form of cooperation.

Buckley and Casson (Reading 10) delve into the question of how cooperative the collaborative arrangements—any alternative to 100% equity ownership of a foreign affiliate—are really cooperative. They offer a stringent definition of cooperation as 'coordination effected through mutual forbearance', and proceed to elaborate coordination to sketch the 'Economic Theory of Joint Ventures'. Joint ventures, as Buckley and Casson characterize, are primarily a mechanism or a device to mitigate the worst consequences of mistrust (between business partners). They also hint at several empirical questions of immense relevance to researchers in international business management. (For further discussion see Buckley and Ghauri, 1993.)

Hamel, Doz and Prahalad (Reading 11) contend that 'the case for collaboration is stronger than ever'. They base their observation on detailed examinations of fifteen strategic alliances among American, European and Japanese MNCs. Their data appear to indicate that the US MNCs, in their sample, have yet to learn the sum total about collaborating, particularly, with Asian firms. Their advice: companies in Europe and the United States must become good borrowers—much like the Asian companies did in the 1960s and 1970s. We also think, as premised in Part III, that knowledge about and a historical perspective of non-Western firms could be of immense value to MNCs in constructing new competitive relationships.

Parkhe's paper (Reading 12) develops a multilevel typology of interfirm diversity, and concentrates on organizational learning and adaptation in the realm of global strategic alliances (GSAs). GSAs are becoming an essential feature of (multinational) companies' organization structure. More important, that the firm's competitive advantage depends not only on the company's internal capabilities but also on the types of alliances with other companies is the author's initial premise. While the author's contributions can be seen in terms of an argument for inductive theory-building to which end he advances a set of propositions, the delineation of GSA's properties (mixed motive, international scope, high significance to partners) is of immense relevance to future research. While there is much by way of theorizing how an MNC can go about (or internalize) its internal resourcefulness, Parkhe underscores the potential significance of external corporate relationship-building.

A complementary theory of strategic alliance is offered by Sheth and Parvatiyar (Reading 13). The authors alert that the term strategic alliance is borrowed from military and political science wherein it has the connotation of a formal association of two sovereign states for the deployment of military or non-military forces against a specific third state. Thus, their effort is expended to develop a theory of competitive and collaborative alliances based on a fusion of behavioural and economic constructs that underlie and determine the formation, governance, and the properties (and consequences) of business alliances. In other words, the authors draw upon four established strands (transaction costs theory, agency theory, rational contracting, and resource-dependence) to design a theory of business alliance.

III. UNDERSTANDING NON-WESTERN STRUCTURES

The linchpin of international management until the 1990s was thought to be only within the 'triad' (Ohmae, 1985). The triad power concept underscored the need for MNCs to develop sustainable positions in the three significant markets, namely the United States, Western Europe, and Japan. The depth of economic recessions in the late 1980s and the early 1990s in these major markets and the burgeoning economic growth[4] in China and in South East Asia during the same time has broadened the international management horizons beyond the 'triad'. Because of the growing importance of the Asian region for products and services, multinational manufacturing companies (such as US, Japanese, and European automotive firms), multinational service companies (such as the large US-based WMX Technologies or the small Holland-based Victron) are vying to develop sustainable market positions at the earliest.

In mapping out corporate strategies, western managers in particular often tended to assume that the management values they espouse are essentially the same as others—rivals and partners—in the Asian region. To put it another way, we think MNCs should attempt to understand, not merely the cultural milieu and the nuances,[5] but the institutional makeup and the enterprise structures *ex-ante*. As Hamilton and Biggart (1988) have cogently argued, economic organization varies considerably across national boundaries, and there is no *a priori* reason why they should converge and constitute a uniform mode. The business success of different forms of organizations in the Asian region, particularly in East Asian countries, demonstrate the viability of various enterprise structures.

Of particular relevance to international management is the group concept including different forms of network structures. An endeavour to fathom the depths of such enterprise structures contributes to enhanced knowledge on the part of international managers. Some of the main issues and challenges (Prahalad, 1990) that are likely to face the western-MNC managers include: integrating acquisitions, understanding the meaning of performance and accountability, developing country-specific strategies, and balancing the pressures for global integration and local independence. We concur with his notions, and hasten to add that a thorough understanding of the different business structures almost always leads to sound analysis whether such analysis serves as a base to formulate either new research hypotheses or prudent business strategies. The five articles (Readings 14-18, by Whitley, 1990; Helou, 1991; Gerlach, 1992; Kao, 1993; Prasad and Ghauri, 1993) included in this section painstakingly highlight a few of the structures in Japan and in a few spots on the changing landscape of Asia.

Whitley (Reading 14) cogently prefaces that not only does the archetypal Japanese company differ considerably from the integrated and diversified US corporation (Chandler, 1977), but successful South Korean business groups (*chaebol*) and expatriate Chinese family businesses markedly differ from both the US and Japanese models of enterprise. The author's basic thesis is that not only do institutional variations affect management systems, but there is also no dominant technical rationality in economic markets which inexorably leads to a single mode of organizing and managing economic (human) resources. The enterprise structures that he subjects to comparative examination are the large Japanese company, the Korean *chaebol*, and the Chinese family business in Taiwan and Hong Kong. His analysis leads him to identify eight distinct dimensions by which different types of enterprise structures can be compared and contrasted. Together, these dimensions describe distinct business processes. The factors that affect these processes include both specific institutional structures (such as the financial and political systems) as well as the general phenomena such as cultural milieu, patterns of dependence, and the foundation of social identities.

While Whitley's paper treats the large firm in Japan as the exemplar of the Japanese business structure, Helou (Reading 15) focuses on Japan's economic institution, *keiretsu*. To the author, the institution originates from a state of mind and can take effect, in some form, in any market where the Japanese have economic and business interests. The initial premise of the author is that understanding the Japanese *keiretsu* is to understand the Japanese way of bringing parts together and finding out what is involved in their own concept of what Japanese normally interpret as 'cohesion'. The (Asian) 'economics of cohesion' can be thought of as being parallel to (American) 'global integration'. Yet, the very mechanics of the *keiretsu* have been exposed to winds of change brought about by technological developments and globalization. Helou also interprets the challenges to *keiretsu* that arise in the concerns in regard to 'competitiveness' of global industries.

The theoretical and conceptual perspectives that can be gleaned from Helou's article can also be seen, in rich detail, in Gerlach's article (Reading 16). Gerlach examines Japanese interfirm relationships in terms of three structures of interactions: (a) interfirm alliances including *keiretsu* groupings; (b) financial centrality, the cardinal role of banks in terms of capital allocation within the network; and (c) industrial interdependence, the mechanisms of coordination with rivals and allies by which business firms manage environmental uncertainty. Using macro-network block modelling analysis, he tests the significance of each of these structures with the aid of data on 40 largest Japanese industrial firms, and 20 largest Japanese financial firms. With respect to the latter, one of his empirical questions is: do Japanese banks and other financial institutions play the same kind of central role in networks of directorships, stockownership, and corporate control as they do in the United States? We surmise that this question has equal relevance in the European context.

Kao (Reading 17) makes the initial assertion that Chinese businesses—many of which are functioning outside of China—make up the world's fourth economic power. For many centuries, emigrant Chinese entrepreneurs have been operating successfully in a network of family and clan in many parts of the globe—the Chinese network. This network and Japan, according to the author, 'represent two different integrating forces in Asia'. In contrast to the Japanese *keiretsu*, the Chinese network is interconnected, yet an open system providing a new market mechanism for conducting global business. Kao states that countries with Chinese-based economies have large capital surpluses. Invariably, capital abundance leads to greater business flexibility and mobility facilitating 'knowledge arbitrage'.

Dealing with Asia's invisible structures, Prasad and Ghauri (Reading 18) provide an insight into '*Keiretsu*' in Japan, '*Chaebols*' in South Korea and 'Groups' in India. These structures are often invisible impediments to Western multinationals. These structures are of a relational (not contractual) nature and the authors compare these within the Scandinavian network perspective. The paper also discusses the useful implications of relational structures for Western firms planning to enter or expand in the emerging markets of Asia.

IV. DEVELOPING GLOBAL MANAGERS

More than two decades ago Negandhi and Prasad (1971) isolated the human resource management challenges facing MNCs into two components: managing the workforce, and managing the managers. Cross-national research interest in the former can be traced back to Schultz's (1951) notion of 'human capital' which imputed equal importance to people working for a company. From an MNC perspective, the challenge of managing the workforce has been at the level of its subsidiaries captured in the phrase 'managing cultural diversity'. While it is true that FDI is also influenced by differing wage rates, theoretically referred to as a factor market imperfection, the challenges to managing diverse workforces stem from sociocultural or ideological differences between foreign financial/technical capital and domestic human capital.

Our interest, however, is in the latter component—managing the managers. We equate this phrase with developing global managers, that is educating, training, and developing the 'social skills' of both home-country (or expatriate) and host-country managers for the global enterprise. The six articles included in this section (Readings 19–24, by Tung, 1984; Laurent, 1986; Rhinesmith *et al.* 1989; Black *et al.*, 1991; Adler and Bartholomew, 1992; Parker and McEvoy, 1993) highlight the research, during the last ten years, on many dimensions of developing MNC managers with a global mind-set.

Stressing human resource, Tung (Reading 19) argues that human power is the most important resource for successful operations of multinationals. It is considered most important because without this resource other resources such as technology, capital and know-how cannot be efficiently and effectively utilized. It is also important for the transfer of these resources from head offices to subsidiaries. Hence, she suggests that MNCs should devote more attention to human resource planning, and development. She compares human resource management and development between Japanese and American firms and concludes that if American MNCs could emulate the positive aspects of the human resource development programmes of their Japanese counterparts, the incidence of ineffective or poor performance overseas could be reduced.

The paper on international human resource management by Andre Laurent (Reading 20) claims that the field of cross-cultural management is still in its infancy. He builds upon Tichy's (1983) paper which concluded that the human resource field is going through a process of gradual and uneven transformation. He goes as far as questioning, 'Is there such a field?' and stresses the importance of cultural phenomena and their influence on international human resource management because of the national differences in management preferences. The issues such as hierarchy, centralization, power, structure and instrumentalization are discussed in this context. The paper concludes with the statement that a truly international conception of human resource management requires a number of critical and painful steps that have not occurred yet. This is a very useful and thought-provoking paper which can lead to some sort of consistency in policies and practices in international human resource management.

Rhinesmith *et al.* (Reading 21) start their paper by stating that a global company is not just a company with some offshore operations; it takes more than some frequent flyer miles to become a global leader. They claim that due to several new developments, the global enterprise is rapidly becoming a competitive behaviour in many industries. They profess that an enterprise goes through four complex but distinct phases as it evolves from domestic to international organization: domestic enterprise; exporter; MNC; global enterprise. The global enterprise is relatively more proactive in looking for new products, business and markets. Moreover, it delivers from the most cost efficient position and with the most appropriate management resources. It reaches and penetrates marketplaces before its competitors and even before the local companies. Building on Ohmae's triad power, they stress that the most important issue in a global enterprise is to organize, integrate and manage their activities to become a global company. In spite of this, they believe, little attention is given to management and human-development needs of global enterprises. They provide a global leadership development agenda arguing for the needs of a global enterprise. They raise important issues that should be taken seriously by academics as well as by practitioners. Some of their strongest arguments are that, 'They need to recognize that the new game will not be played or driven by the US business models', 'Multinational companies cannot submerge the individuality of different cultures' and that 'Human resources need to reflect the same capacity for adaptation and flexibility as technology and financial resources'.

Even though Black *et al.* (Reading 22) make an initial reference to American managers living and working abroad, we should note that their effort is to provide a comprehensive framework which would further the understanding of why expatriate managers often do not succeed in international assignments. In this copious paper, the authors delineate the major variables bearing upon domestic as well as international adjustment (by expatriates) and integrate the various approaches and develop an extensive framework of international adjustment. Furthermore, they deduce 19 propositions that have significance in future research and on policy-making in the area of human resources in multinational corporations. They conclude that, although 'uncertainty reduction' is common both to domestic and international adjustment, there are several contextual differences that introduce variation in the common thread.

Adler and Bartholomew (Reading 23) contend that the contemporary human resource strategies of multinational firms are less global than their corporate strategies, and proceed to identify some of the underlying reasons for such a corporate neglect. Based on their survey findings, the authors emphasize that globally competent managers require a broader range of skills than traditional international managers. Even though they identify seven different skills that presumably differentiate the global and the traditional international manager, the differences could be one of degree rather than one of kind. Also, the differences may be more pronounced in the case of US-based MNCs than in the case of Europe-based MNCs.

A case in point: in January 1992, Unilever Arabia (as a new organizational unit of Unilever Middle East) opened for business in the Gulf Cooperation Council countries. Although Unilever Arabia was a new organization, Unilever, the parent firm, had established trading contacts as early as the 1930s after which the peninsula was treated as an export market territory. The chief executive of the new Unilever Arabia is neither European nor an Arab national. He is a globally competent third-country national. It may be that Unilever is much more global than most MNCs, or at least as global as Citicorp whose CEO stated, as cited by Adler and Bartholomew (1992), 'Our global human capital may be as important as a resource, if not more important, than our financial capital'. The article contains many insights valuable to human resource managers and to researchers in the arena of international management.

Parker and McEvoy (Reading 24) focus primarily on the issue of (staff and managerial) employee adjustment to foreign cultures. With a view to replicate Black's (1988) findings regarding the multidimensionality of the adjustment concept, they test selected aspects of the model of intercultural adjustment using a sample of 169 employees working in a total of 12 countries. Their empirical results strongly suggest that 'culture novelty' plays a significant role in explaining the variance. To put it another way, the organization (MNC) can contribute much toward its expatriate manger's adjustment abroad but there is something beyond that can be characterized as culture-general rather than culture-specific.

In the past, firms and countries became profitable and wealthy if they possessed technological or natural resources. This has no longer been true since the 1970s with the recognition of the emergence of global industries. As Lester Thurow (1992) cogently puts it: 'New technologies and institutions are combining to substantially alter the traditional resources of competitive advantage ... And in the twenty-first century, the education and skills of the work force will be the dominant competitive weapon' (p. 6).

NOTES

1. The 1980s witnessed numerous expressions—academic, journalistic, and popular—of Japan's meteoric rise to the top among the Group of Seven (G-7) industrialized nations. Japan as the Land of the Rising Sun was not only widespread, but deservedly so. Ezra Vogel's *Japan as Number One* (1979) was one of the best selling books in Japan. That theme prevailed for some time, and entered the popular stream when fiction-writer Michael Crichton came out with his novel, *Rising Sun* (1992).

However, recent developments within the past 24 months, appear to have turned the table in favour of the United States. That, at least, is the perception. Increasingly, in Japan, there is reportedly a widely-held view, that things have improved in the United States; things such as managing for efficiency, and managing for effectiveness are perceived as having improved so much so that the United States has regained its pre-eminent position among the G-7. One Japanese theme gaining widespread popularity in 1994 has been that of 'Rising Sam' (referring to 'Uncle Sam', a term for the United States that became popular during the Second World War).

2. Based on their detailed analysis of the question whether General Electric has truly become a global enterprise, they conclude that it has. They arrive at this conclusion after tracing numerous developments within the GE organization. The milestones in the transformation include the setting up, after World War II, of a subsidiary called International General Electric (IGE) which handled the company's export business and corporate issues relating to GE's foreign subsidiaries; a distinction between 'domestic' and 'global' products and markets which surfaced as a result of a 1973-74 study by IGE which serve as a basis for forging a few joint ventures between IGE and a few of GE's strategic business units (SBUs) as a way of internationalizing the SBUs; and more prominently, since 1981 under the leadership of Jack Welch the expression of GE's strategic intent which provided management focus on areas where an SBU intended to be either number one or two in the market leadership by 1990. The instrumental role of the CEO in the globalization process looms large in this research study.

3. We noted earlier that, for analytical purposes, a firm's decisions can be classified as those coming under FDI and the rest. In a similar vein, it is possible to draw a distinction between a 'joint venture' and a 'strategic alliance' thus: In a joint venture, firms A and B, through equity, create an operating firm C. The classic example in the US context is Dow-Corning (C), a 50:50 joint venture between Dow Chemical (A) and Corning Glass (B). All other forms of non-equity collaborations and cooperations can be included under business alliances. Even though Sheth and Parvatiyar (Reading 13) are correct in saying that the term 'strategic alliances', has had its origin in the geopolitical sense, there are many concrete examples of alliances formed by two MNCs; for example, General Mills and Nestlé have forged an alliance to compete with vigour against, if not annihilate, General Mills' rival, namely Kellogg, in the European Union.

4. China's GDP and industrial production, expressed as percentage change on the previous year, were 12.1 and 29.8 respectively (*Economist*, 1994).

5. Understanding cultural milieu, of course, is not just a matter of Western managers learning about Eastern cultures. It may also include, for example, a German firm trying to become familiar with the culture of a small town in the United States. Mercedez, a unit of Daimler-Benz, decided in 1993 to make a foreign direct investment in the United States. The location it chose was Vance (population 350) in Alabama. In Stuttgart, about 40 German engineers and managers are assiduously studying the culture of Alabama with help from some native Alabamans flown to Stuttgart for a 'cross-cultural encounter group' (see Atkinson, 1994).

REFERENCES

Atkinson, R. (1994) 'Mercedez Immerses Executives in 'Bama'. *International Herald Tribune* (No. 34,512), The Hague, 15 February: 1,4.
Bartlett, C. A. and Ghoshal, S. (1992) *Transnational Management*, Richard D. Irwin, Homewood, IL.
Beamish, P. W., Killing, J. P., Lecraw, D. J. and Morrison, A. J. (1994) *International Management*, 2nd edn. Richard D. Irwin, Burr Ridge, IL.
Black, J. S. (1988) 'Work Role Transitions: A Study of American Expatriate Managers in Japan'. *Journal of International Business Studies*, **19**: 277-294.
Buckley, P. J. and Ghauri, P. N. (eds) (1993) *The Internationalization of the Firm: a Reader*. Academic Press, London.
Buzzel, R. D. (1968) 'Can you Standardize Multinational Marketing?' Harvard Business Review (Nov–Dec.): 98–104.
Chandler, A. D. (1977) *The Visible Hand, The Management Revolution in American Business*. Harvard University Press, Cambridge, MA.
Crichton, M. (1992) *Rising Sun*. Knopf, New York.
Dunning, J. H. (1993) *The Globalization of Business*. Routledge, London.
Economist (1992) 'The Nonconformist'. *The Economist*, 22 August: 61-62.
Hamilton, G. G. and Biggart, N. W. (1988) 'Market, Culture and Authority: A Comparative Analysis of Management and Organization in the Far East'. *American Journal of Sociology* (special supplement on the sociology of economics), **94**: 852-894.
Harbison, F. and Myers, C. A. (1959) *Management in the Industrial World*. McGraw-Hill, New York.
Kogut, B. (1985) 'Designing Global Strategies: Profiting from Operational Flexibility'. *Sloan Management Review*, **26** (Fall): 27–38.
Lane, H. and J. DiStefano (1992) *International Management Behaviour*, 2nd edn. PWS-Kent.
Levitt, T. (1983) 'The Globalization of Markets'. *Harvard Business Review*, May–June: 92-102.
Neghandi, A. R. (1987) *International Management*. Allyn & Bacon, Boston.
Neghandi, A. R. and S. B. Prasad (1971) *Comparative Management*. Appleton-Century-Crofts, New York.
Nooteboom, B. (1993) 'Firm Size Effects on Transaction Costs'. *Small Business Economics*, **5**: 283-295.
Ohmae, K. (1985) *Triad Power: The Coming Shape of Global Competition*. The Free Press, New York.
Ouchi, W. G. (1981) *Theory Z*. Addison-Wesley, Reading, MA.
Prahalad, C. K. (1990) 'Globalization: the Intellectual and Managerial Challenges'. *Human Resource Management*, Spring: 29-40.
Prasad, S. B. and Shetty, Y. K. (1976) *Introduction to Multinational Management*. Prentice Hall, Englewood Cliffs, NJ.
Schultz, T. W. (1951) 'Investment in Human Capital'. *American Economic Review*, **51**:1-17.
Thurow, L. (1992) *Head to Head: the Coming Economic Battle among Japan, Europe and America*. Morrow Corp., New York.
Tichy (1983) *Managing Strategic Change*. John Wiley & Sons, New York.
Vogel, E. (1979) *Japan as Number One*. Harvard University Press, Cambridge, MA.

Appendix A

Contents of Negandhi, A. R. (1987) *International Management* (first edition) compared with Beamish, P. W. *et al.* (1994) *International Management* (second edition).

Negandhi	Beamish *et al.*
1 World of International Business	1 Internationalization Process
2 International Corporation	2 Global Business Environment
3 Organization Design and Structure	3 International Trade
4 Policy Making and Control	4 Managing Exports
5 Headquarters-Subsidiary Relationships	5 Global Servicing
6 Long-Range Planning	6 Licensing
7 Human Resource Management	7 International Joint Ventures
8 International Production	8 Global Strategy Formulation
9 Export Marketing	9 Impact of Globalization
10 International Marketing	10 Global Manager
11 Financial Management	11 Political Risk

Note: We find the contents of the following chapters to be similar in the two books:

Negandhi	Beamish *et al.*
2	11
3	9
4	8
8	5
9	4

Part I

Toward Global Strategizing: Theoretical Frameworks and Company Approaches

CONTENTS

1. The tortuous evolution of the multinational corporation 3
   HOWARD V. PERLMUTTER, *Columbia Journal of World Business* (1969) **4**, 9–18

2. A theory of international operations 15
   PETER J. BUCKLEY AND MARK CASSON, In *European Research in International Business* (1979), 45-50, Elsevier–North-Holland.

3. The globalization of markets 21
   THEODORE LEVITT, *Harvard Business Review* (1983), May–June, 92–102

4. Global strategy: an organizing framework 33
   SUMANTRA GHOSHAL, *Strategic Management Journal* (1987), **8**, 425–440

5. New structures in MNCs based in small countries: a network approach 51
   PERVEZ GHAURI, *European Management Journal* (1992), **10**(3), 357–364

6. The hypermodern MNC—a heterarchy? 64
   GUNNAR HEDLUND, *Human Resource Management* (1986), **25**(1), 9–35

7. Managing across borders: an empirical test of the Bartlett and Ghoshal (1989) organizational typology 85
   SIEW MENG LEONG AND CHIN TIONG TAN, *Journal of International Business Studies* (1993), **24**(3), 449–464

8. Bridgestone's quest for leadership in the global tire industry 100
   S. BENJAMIN PRASAD, *The Review of Business Studies* (1993), **2**(1), 17–34

1

The Tortuous Evolution of the Multinational Corporation

Howard V. Perlmutter

Four senior executives of the world's largest firms with extensive holdings outside the home country, speak:

Company A: 'We are a multinational firm. We distribute our products in about 100 countries. We manufacture in over 17 countries and do research and development in three countries. We look at all new investment projects—both domestic and overseas—using exactly the same criteria'.

Company B: 'We are a multinational firm. Only 1% of the personnel in our affiliate companies are non-nationals. Most of these are US executives on temporary assignments. In all major markets, the affiliate's managing director is of the local nationality'.

Company C: 'We are a multinational firm. Our product division executives have worldwide profit responsibility. As our organizational chart shows, the United States is just one region on a par with Europe, Latin America, Africa, etc., in each product division'.

Company D (non-American): 'We are a multinational firm. We have at least 18 nationalities represented at our headquarters. Most senior executives speak at least two languages. About 30% of our staff at headquarters are foreigners'.

While a claim to multinationality, based on their years of experience and the significant proportion of sales generated overseas, is justified in each of these four companies, a more penetrating analysis changes the image.

The executive from Company A tells us that most of the key posts in Company A's subsidiaries are held by home-country nationals. Whenever replacements for these men are sought, it is the practice, if not the policy, to 'look next to you at the head office' and 'pick someone (usually a home-country national) you know and trust'.

The executive from Company B does not hide the fact that there are very few non-Americans in the key posts at headquarters. The few who are there are 'so Americanized' that their foreign nationality literally has no meaning. His explanation for this paucity of non-Americans seems reasonable enough: 'You can't find good foreigners who are willing to live in the United States, where our headquarters is located. American executives are more mobile.

Reprinted from *Columbia Journal of World Business*, Vol. 4, pp. 9–18.
Copyright © 1969 Columbia Journal of World Business. Reprinted with permission.

In addition, Americans have the drive and initiative we like. In fact, the European nationals would prefer to report to an American rather than to some other European'.

The executive from Company C goes on to explain that the worldwide product division concept is rather difficult to implement. The senior executives in charge of these divisions have little overseas experience. They have been promoted from domestic posts and tend to view foreign consumer needs 'as really basically the same as ours'. Also, product division executives tend to focus on the domestic market because the domestic market is larger and generates more revenue than the fragmented European markets. The rewards are for global performance, but the strategy is to focus on domestic. His colleagues say 'one pays attention to what one understands—and our senior executives simply do not understand what happens overseas and really do not trust foreign executives in key positions here or overseas.

The executive from the European Company D begins by explaining that since the voting shareholders must by law come from the home country, the home country's interest must be given careful consideration. In the final analysis he insists: 'We are proud of our nationality; we shouldn't be ashamed of it'. He cites examples of the previous reluctance of headquarters to use home-country ideas overseas, to their detriment, especially in their US subsidiary. 'Our country produces good executives, who tend to stay with us a long time. It is harder to keep executives from the United States'.

A ROSE BY ANY OTHER NAME

Why quibble about how multinational a firm is? To these executives, apparently being multinational is prestigious. They know that multinational firms tend to be regarded as more progressive, dynamic, geared to the future than provincial companies which avoid foreign frontiers and their attendant risks and opportunities.

It is natural that these senior executives would want to justify the multinationality of their enterprise, even if they use different yardsticks: ownership criteria, organizational structure, nationality of senior executives, percent of investment overseas, etc.

Two hypotheses seem to be forming in the minds of executives from international firms that make the extent of their firm's multinationality of real interest. The first hypothesis is that the degree of multinationality of an enterprise is positively related to the firm's long-term viability. The 'multinational' category makes sense for executives if it means a quality of decision making which leads to survival, growth and profitability in our evolving world economy.

The second hypothesis stems from the proposition that the multinational corporation is a new kind of institution—a new type of industrial social architecture particularly suitable for the latter third of the twentieth century. This type of institution could make a valuable contribution to world order and conceivably exercise a constructive impact on the nation-state. Some executives want to understand how to create an institution whose presence is considered legitimate and valuable in each nation-state. They want to prove that the greater the degree of multinationality of a firm, the greater its total constructive impact will be on host and home nation-states as well as other institutions. Since multinational firms may produce a significant proportion of the world's GNP, both hypotheses justify a more precise analysis of the varieties and degrees of multinationality (Perlmutter, 1968). However, the confirming evidence is limited.

STATE OF MIND

Part of the difficulty in defining the degree of multinationality comes from the variety of parameters along which a firm doing business overseas can be described. The examples from the four companies argue that (1) no single criterion of multinationality such as ownership or the number of nationals overseas is sufficient, and that (2) external and quantifiable measures such as the percentage of investment overseas or the distribution of equity by nationality are useful but not enough. The more one penetrates into the living reality of an international firm, the more one finds it is necessary to give serious weight to the way executives think about doing business around the world. The orientation toward 'foreign people, ideas, resources', in headquarters and subsidiaries, and in host and home environments, becomes crucial in estimating the multinationality of a firm. To be sure, such external indices as the proportion of nationals in different countries holding equity and the number of foreign nationals who have reached top positions, including president, are good indices of multinationality. But one can still behave with a home-country orientation despite foreign shareholders, and one can have a few home-country nationals overseas but still pick those local executives who are home-country oriented or who are provincial and chauvinistic. The attitudes men hold are clearly more relevant than their passports.

Three primary attitudes among international executives toward building a multinational enterprise are identifiable. These attitudes can be inferred from the assumptions upon which key product, functional and geographical decisions were made.

These states of mind or attitudes may be described as ethnocentric (or home-country oriented), polycentric (or host-country oriented) and geocentric (or world-oriented) (Perlmutter, 1965). While they never appear in pure form, they are clearly distinguishable. There is some degree of ethnocentricity, polycentricity or geocentricity in all firms, but management's analysis does not usually correlate with public pronouncements about the firm's multinationality.

HOME-COUNTRY ATTITUDES

The ethnocentric attitude can be found in companies of any nationality with extensive overseas holdings. The attitude, revealed in executive actions and experienced by foreign subsidiary managers, is: 'We, the home nationals of X company, are superior to, more trustworthy and more reliable than any foreigners in headquarters or subsidiaries. We will be willing to build facilities in your country if you acknowledge our inherent superiority and accept our methods and conditions for doing the job'.

Of course, such attitudes are never so crudely expressed, but often determine how a certain type of 'multinational' firm is designed. Table 1 illustrates how ethnocentric attitudes are expressed in determining the managerial process at home and overseas. For example, the ethnocentric executive is more apt to say: 'Let us manufacture the simple products overseas. Those foreign nationals are not yet ready or reliable. We should manufacture the complex products in our country and keep the secrets among our trusted home-country nationals'.

In a firm where ethnocentric attitudes prevailed, the performance criteria for men and products are 'home-made'. 'We have found that a salesman should make 12 calls per day in Hoboken, New Jersey (the headquarters location) and therefore we apply these criteria

Table 1. Three types of headquarters orientation toward subsidiaries in an international enterprise

Organization design	Ethnocentric	Polycentric	Geocentric
Complexity of organization	Complex in home country, simple in subsidiaries	Varied and independent	Increasingly complex and interdependent
Authority; decision making	High in headquarters	Relatively low in headquarters	Aim for a collaborative approach between headquarters and subsidiaries
Evaluation and control	Home standards applied for persons and performance	Determined locally	Find standards which are universal and local
Rewards and punishments, incentives	High in headquarters, low in subsidiaries	Wide variation; can be high or low rewards for subsidiary performance	International and local executives rewarded for reaching local and worldwide objectives
Communication; information flow	High volume to subsidiaries orders, commands, advice	Little to and from headquarters. Little between subsidiaries	Both ways and between subsidiaries. Heads of subsidiaries part of management team
Identification	Nationality of owner	Nationality of host country	Truly international company but identifying with national interests
Perpetuation (recruiting, staffing, development)	Recruit and develop people of home country for key positions everywhere in the world	Develop people of local nationality for key positions in their own country	Develop best men everywhere in the world for key positions everywhere in the world

everywhere in the world. The salesman in Brazzaville is naturally lazy, unmotivated. He shows little drive because he makes only two calls per day (despite the Congolese salesman's explanation that it takes time to reach customers by boat)'.

Ethnocentric attitudes are revealed in the communication process where 'advice', 'counsel', and directives flow from headquarters to the subsidiary in a steady stream, bearing this message: 'This works at home; therefore, it must work in your country'.

Executives in both headquarters and affiliates express the national identity of the firm by associating the company with the nationality of the headquarters: this is 'a Swedish company', 'a Swiss company', 'an American company', depending on the location of headquarters. 'You have to accept the fact that the only way to reach a senior post in our firm', an English executive in a US firm said, 'is to take out an American passport'.

Crucial to the ethnocentric concept is the current policy that men of the home nationality are recruited and trained for key positions everywhere in the world. Foreigners feel like 'second-class' citizens.

There is no international firm today whose executives will say that ethnocentrism is absent in their company. In the firms whose multinational investment began a decade ago, one is more likely to hear, 'We are still in the transitional stage from our ethnocentric era. The traces are still around! But we are making progress'.

HOST-COUNTRY ORIENTATION

Polycentric firms are those which, by experience or by inclination of a top executive (usually one of the founders), begin with the assumption that host-country cultures are different and that foreigners are difficult to understand. Local people know what is best for them, and the part of the firm which is located in the host country should be as 'local in identity' as possible. The senior executives at headquarters believe that their multinational enterprise can be held together by good financial controls. A polycentric firm, literally, is a loosely connected group with quasi-independent subsidiaries as centres—more akin to a confederation.

European multinational firms tend to follow this pattern, using a top local executive who is strong and trustworthy of the 'right' family and who has an intimate understanding of the workings of the host government. This policy seems to have worked until the advent of the Common Market.

Executives in the headquarters of such a company are apt to say: 'Let the Romans do it their way. We really don't understand what is going on there, but we have to have confidence in them. As long as they can earn a profit, we want to remain in the background'. They assume that since people are different in each country, standards for performance, incentives and training methods must be different. Local environmental factors are given greater weight (see Table 1).

Many senior executives mistakenly equate polycentrism with multinationalism. This is evidenced in the legalistic definition of a multinational enterprise as a cluster of corporations of diverse nationality joined together by ties of common ownership. It is no accident that many senior executives in headquarters take pride in the absence of non-nationals in their subsidiaries, especially people from the head office. The implication is clearly that each subsidiary is a distinct national entity, since it is incorporated in a different sovereign state. Lonely senior executives in the subsidiaries of polycentric companies complain that: 'The home office never tells us anything'.

Polycentrism is not the ultimate form of multinationalism. It is a landmark on a highway. Polycentrism is encouraged by local marketing managers who contend that: 'Headquarters will never understand us, our people, our consumer needs, our laws, our distribution, etc…'.

Headquarters takes pride in the fact that few outsiders know that the firm is foreign-owned. 'We want to be a good local company. How many Americans know that Shell and Lever Brothers are foreign-owned?'

But the polycentric personnel policy is also revealed in the fact that no local manager can seriously aspire to a senior position at headquarters. 'You know the French are so provincial; it is better to keep them in France. Uproot them and you are in trouble,' a senior executive says to justify the paucity of non-Americans at headquarters.

One consequence (and perhaps cause) of polycentrism is a virulent ethnocentrism among the country managers.

A WORLD-ORIENTED CONCEPT

The third attitude which is beginning to emerge at an accelerated rate is geocentrism. Senior executives with this orientation do not equate superiority with nationality. Within legal and political limits, they seek the best men, regardless of nationality, to solve the company's problems anywhere in the world. The senior executives attempt to build an organization in which the subsidiary is not only a good citizen of the host nation but is a leading exporter from this nation in the international community and contributes such benefits as (1) an increasing supply of hard currency, (2) new skills and (3) a knowledge of advanced technology. Geocentrism is summed up in a Unilever board chairman's statement of objectives: 'We want to Unileverize our Indians and Indianize our Unileverans'.

The ultimate goal of geocentrism is a worldwide approach in both headquarters and subsidiaries. The firm's subsidiaries are thus neither satellites nor independent city states, but parts of a whole whose focus is on worldwide objectives as well as local objectives, each part making its unique contribution with its unique competence. Geocentrism is expressed by function, product and geography. The question asked in headquarters and the subsidiaries is: 'Where in the world shall we raise money, build our plant, conduct R&D, get and launch new ideas to serve our present and future customers?'

This conception of geocentrism involves a collaborative effort between subsidiaries and headquarters to establish universal standards and permissible local variations, to make key allocational decisions on new products, new plants, new laboratories. The international management team includes the affiliate heads.

Subsidiary managers must ask: 'Where in the world can I get the help to serve my customers best in this country?' 'Where in the world can I export products developed in this country—products which meet worldwide standards as opposed to purely local standards?'

Geocentrism, furthermore, requires a reward system for subsidiary managers which motivates them to work for worldwide objectives, not just to defend country objectives. In firms where geocentrism prevails, it is not uncommon to hear a subsidiary manager say, 'While I am paid to defend our interests in this country and to get the best resources for this affiliate, I must still ask myself the question "Where in the world (instead of where in my country) should we build this plant?"' This approach is still rare today.

In contrast to the ethnocentric and polycentric patterns, communication is encouraged among subsidiaries in geocentric-oriented firms. 'It is your duty to help us solve problems anywhere in the world', one chief executive continually reminds the heads of his company's affiliates. (See Table 1.)

The geocentric firm identifies with local company needs. 'We aim to be not just a good local company but the best local company in terms of the quality of management and the worldwide (not local) standards we establish in domestic and export production'. 'If we were only as good as local companies, we would deserve to be nationalized'.

The geocentric personnel policy is based on the belief that we should bring in the best man in the world regardless of his nationality. His passport should not be the criterion for promotion.

THE EPG PROFILE

Executives can draw their firm's profile in ethnocentric (E), polycentric (P) and geocentric (G) dimensions. They are called EPG profiles. The degree of ethnocentrism, polycentrism and geocentrism by product, function and geography can be established. Typically R&D often turns out to be more geocentric (truth is universal, perhaps) and less ethnocentric than finance. Financial managers are likely to see their decisions as ethnocentric. The marketing function is more polycentric, particularly in the advanced economies and in the larger affiliate markets.

The tendency toward ethnocentrism in relations with subsidiaries in the developing countries is marked. Polycentric attitudes develop in consumer goods divisions, and ethnocentrism appears to be greater in industrial product divisions. The agreement is almost unanimous in both US and European-based international firms that their companies are at various stages on a route toward geocentrism but none has reached this state of affairs. Their executives would agree, however, that:

(1) a description of their firms as multinational obscures more than it illuminates the state of affairs;
(2) the EPG mix, once defined, is a more precise way to describe the point they have reached;
(3) the present profile is not static but a landmark along a difficult road to genuine geocentrism;
(4) there are forces both to change and to maintain the present attitudinal 'mix', some of which are under their control.

FORCES TOWARD AND AGAINST

What are the forces that determine the EPG mix of a firm? 'You must think of the struggle toward functioning as a worldwide firm as just a beginning—a few steps forward and a step backward', a chief executive put it. 'It is a painful process, and every firm is different'.

Executives of some of the world's largest multinational firms have been able to identify a series of external and internal factors that contribute to or hinder the growth of geocentric

Table 2. 'International executives' view of forces and obstacles toward geocentrism in their firms

Forces toward geocentrism		Obstacles toward geocentrism	
Environmental	Intra-organizational	Environmental	Intra-organizational
1. Technological and managerial know-how increasing in availability in different countries	1. Desire to use human vs. material resources optimally	1. Economic nationalism in host and home countries	1. Management inexperience in overseas markets
2. International customers	2. Observed lowering of morale in affiliates of an ethnocentric company	2. Political nationalism in host and home contries	2. Nation-centred reward and punishment structure
3. Local customers' demand for best product at fair price	3. Evidence of waste and duplication in polycentrism	3. Military secrecy associated with research in home country	3. Mutual distrust between home country people and foreign executives
4. Host country's desire to increase balance of payments	4. Increasing awareness and respect for good men of other than home nationality	4. Distrust of big international firms by host country political leaders	4. Resistance to letting foreigners into the power structure
5. Growing world markets	5. Risk diversification in having a worldwide production and distribution system	5. Lack of international monetray system	5. Anticipated costs and risks of geocentrism
6. Global competition among international firms for scarce human and material resources	6. Need for recruitment of good men on a worldwide basis	6. Growing differences between the rich and poor countries	6. Nationalistic tendencies in staff
7. Major advances in integration of international transport and telecommunications	7. Need for worldwide information system	7. Host country belief that home countries get disproportionate benefits of international firms' profits	7. Increasing immobility of staff
8. Regional supranational economic and political communities	8. Worldwide appeal of products	8. Home country political leaders' attempts to control firms' policy	8. Linguistic problems and different cultural backgrounds
	9. Senior management's long term commitment to geocentrism as related to survival and growth		9. Centralization tendencies in headquarters

attitudes and decision. Table 2 summarizes the factors most frequently mentioned by over 500 executives from at least 17 countries and 20 firms.

From the external environmental side, the growing world markets, the increase in availability of managerial and technological know-how in different countries, global competition and international customers, advances in telecommunications, regional political and economic communities are positive factors, as is the host countries desire to increase its balance of payments surplus through the location of export-oriented subsidiaries of international firms within its borders.

In different firms, senior executives see in various degrees these positive factors toward geocentrism: top management's increasing desire to use human and material resources optimally, the observed lowering of morale after decades of ethnocentric practices, the evidence of waste and duplication under polycentric thinking, the increased awareness and respect for good men of other than the home nationality, and, most importantly, top management's own commitment to building a geocentric firm as evidenced in policies, practices and procedures.

The obstacles toward geocentrism from the environment stem largely from the rising political and economic nationalism in the world today, the suspicions of political leaders of the aims and increasing power of the multinational firm. On the internal side, the obstacles cited most frequently in US-based multinational firms were management's inexperience in overseas markets, mutual distrust between home-country people and foreign executives, the resistance to participation by foreigners in the power structure at headquarters, the increasing difficulty of getting good men overseas to move, nationalistic tendencies in staff, and the linguistic and other communication difficulties of a cultural nature.

Any given firm is seen as moving toward geocentrism at a rate determined by its capacities to build on the positive internal factors over which it has control and to change the negative internal factors which are controllable. In some firms the geocentric goal is openly discussed among executives of different nationalities and from different subsidiaries as well as headquarters. There is a consequent improvement in the climate of trust and acceptance of each other's views.

Programmes are instituted to assure greater experience in foreign markets, task forces of executives are upgraded, international careers for executives of all nationalities are being designed.

But the seriousness of the obstacles cannot be underestimated. A world of rising nationalism is hardly a pre-condition for geocentrism; and overcoming distrust of foreigners even within one's own firm is not accomplished in a short span of time. The route to pervasive geocentric thinking is long and tortuous.

COSTS, RISKS, PAYOFFS

What conclusions will executives from multinational firms draw from the balance sheet of advantages and disadvantages of maintaining one's present state of ethnocentrism, polycentrism or geocentrism? Not too surprisingly, the costs and risks of ethnocentrism are seen to out-balance the payoffs in the long run. The costs of ethnocentrism are ineffective planning because of a lack of good feed-back, the departure of the best men in the subsidiaries, fewer innovations and an inability to build a high calibre local organization. The risks are political and social repercussions and a less flexible response to local changes.

The payoffs of ethnocentrism are real enough in the short term, they say. Organization is simpler. There is a higher rate of communication of know-how from headquarters to new markets. There is more control over appointments to senior posts in subsidiaries.

Polycentrism's costs are waste due to duplication, to decisions to make products for local use but which could be universal, and to inefficient use of home-country experience. The risks include an excessive regard for local traditions and local growth at the expense of global growth. The main advantages are an intensive exploitation of local markets, better sales since local management is often better informed, more local initiative for new products, more host-government support, and good local managers with high morale.

Geocentrism's costs are largely related to communication and travel expenses, educational costs at all levels, time spent in decision-making because consensus seeking among more people is required, and an international headquarters bureaucracy. Risks include those due to too wide a distribution of power, personnel problems and those of re-entry of international executives. The payoffs are a more powerful total company throughout, a better quality of products and service, worldwide utilization of best resources, improvement of local company management, a greater sense of commitment to worldwide objectives, and last, but not least, more profit.

Jaques Maisonrouge, the French-born president of IBM World Trade, understands the geocentric concept and its benefits. He wrote recently:

> The first step to a geocentric organization is when a corporation, faced with the choice of whether to grow and expand or decline, realizes the need to mobilize its resources on a world scale. It will sooner or later have to face the issue that the home country does not have a monopoly of either men or ideas ...
>
> I strongly believe that the future belongs to geocentric companies ... What is of fundamental importance is the attitude of the company's top management. If it is dedicated to 'geocentrism', good international management will be possible. If not, the best men of different nations will soon understand that they do not belong to the '*race des seigneurs*' and will leave the business (Maisonrouge, 1967).

Geocentrism is not inevitable in any given firm. Some companies have experienced a 'regression' to ethnocentrism after trying a long period of polycentrism, of letting subsidiaries do it 'their way'. The local directors built little empires and did not train successors from their own country. Headquarters had to send home-country nationals to take over. A period of home-country thinking took over.

There appears to be evidence of a need for evolutionary movement from ethnocentrism to polycentrism to geocentrism. The polycentric stage is likened to an adolescent protest period during which subsidiary managers gain their confidence as equals by fighting headquarters and proving 'their manhood', after a long period of being under headquarters' ethnocentric thumb.

'It is hard to move from a period of headquarters domination to a worldwide management team quickly. A period of letting affiliates make mistakes may be necessary', said one executive.

WINDOW DRESSING

In the rush toward appearing geocentric, many US firms have found it necessary to emphasize progress by appointing one or two non-nationals to senior posts—even on occasion to headquarters. The foreigner is often effectively counteracted by the number of nationals around him, and his influence is really small. Tokenism does have some positive effects, but it does not mean geocentrism has arrived.

Window dressing is also a temptation. Here an attempt is made to demonstrate influence by appointing a number of incompetent 'foreigners' to key positions. The results are not impressive for either the individuals or the company.

Too often what is called 'the multinational view' is really a screen for ethnocentrism. Foreign affiliate managers must, in order to succeed, take on the traits and behaviour of the ruling nationality. In short, in a US-owned firm the foreigner must 'Americanize'—not only in attitude but in dress and speech—in order to be accepted.

A GEOCENTRIC MAN—?

The geocentric enterprise depends on having an adequate supply of men who are geocentrically oriented. It would be a mistake to underestimate the human stress which a geocentric career creates. Moving where the company needs an executive involves major adjustments for families, wives and children. The sacrifices are often great and, for some families, outweigh the rewards forthcoming—at least in personal terms. Many executives find it difficult to learn new languages and overcome their cultural superiority complexes, national pride and discomfort with foreigners. Furthermore, international careers can be hazardous when ethnocentrism prevails at headquarters. 'It is easy to get lost in the world of the subsidiaries and to be "out of sight, out of mind" when promotions come up at headquarters', as one executive expressed it following a visit to headquarters after five years overseas. To his disappointment, he knew few senior executives. And fewer knew him!

The economic rewards, the challenge of new countries, the personal and professional development that comes from working in a variety of countries and cultures are surely incentives, but companies have not solved by any means the human costs of international mobility to executives and their families.

A firm's multinationality may be judged by the pervasiveness with which executives think geocentrically—by function, marketing, finance, production, R&D, etc., by product division and by country. The takeoff to geocentrism may begin with executives in one function, say marketing, seeking to find a truly worldwide product line. Only when this worldwide attitude extends throughout the firm, in headquarters and subsidiaries, can executives feel that it is becoming genuinely geocentric.

But no single yardstick, such as the number of foreign nationals in key positions, is sufficient to establish a firm's multinationality. The multinational firm's route to geocentrism is still long because political and economic nationalism is on the rise, and, more importantly, since within the firm ethnocentrism and polycentrism are not easy to overcome. Building trust between persons of different nationality is a central obstacle. Indeed, if we are to judge men, as Paul Weiss put it, by the kind of world they are trying to build, the senior executives engaged in building the geocentric enterprise could well be the most important social architects of the last third of the twentieth century. For the institution they are trying to erect promises a greater universal sharing of wealth and a consequent control of the explosive centrifugal tendencies of our evolving world community.

The geocentric enterprise offers an institutional and supranational framework which could conceivably make war less likely, on the assumption that bombing customers, suppliers and employees is in nobody's interest. The difficulty of the task is thus matched by its worthiness.

A clearer image of the features of genuine geocentricity is thus indispensable both as a guideline and as an inviting prospect.

REFERENCES

Perlmutter, H.V. (1968) 'Super-Giant Firms in the Future'. *Wharton Quarterly*, Winter.
Perlmutter, H.V. (1965) 'Three Conceptions of a World Enterprise'. *Revue Economique et Sociale*, May.
Maisonrouge, J. (1967) 'The Education of International Managers'. *The Quarterly Journal of AIESEC International*, February.

2

A Theory of International Operations

Peter J. Buckley and Mark Casson

This chapter provides a theoretical framework for the explanation and prediction of the methods of market servicing (or 'sourcing policies') of multinational enterprises (MNEs).

1. THE DIVISION OF NATIONAL MARKETS

A national market for a final product can be served in four main ways: by indigenous firms, by subsidiaries of MNEs located in the market, by exports to the market from foreign locally owned firms and by exports from foreign plants owned by MNEs. The first two methods are distinguished from the second two by the 'location effect': the market is served by local production rather than export. The first method is distinguished from the second and the third method from the fourth by the 'ownership effect': production is owned and controlled by domestic nationals rather than by a foreign-owned international corporation.

Final goods markets cannot, however be considered in isolation from the markets for the intermediate goods involved in the production process. Intermediate goods too are subject to ownership and location effects. In order to service a final product market it may be advantageous to locate different stages of production in different locations. Also the ownership of 'the good' may change as we move through the process—an example of this is licensing where essential proprietary knowledge to produce the final good is licensed from one producer to another.

In order to examine these factors in detail the following sections deal firstly with location effects and then with ownership effects.

2. THE LOCATION OF PRODUCTION FACILITIES

Production in a multi-stage process can be characterized as a sequence of distinct activities linked by the transport of semi-processed materials. The orthodox theory of location assumes constant returns to scale, freely available and therefore standardized technology and that firms are price takers in all factor markets. Given such assumptions, a firm chooses its optimal location for each stage of production by evaluating regional production costs and choosing the

This article was first published in *European Research in International Business*, edited by Gherman, Michel and Leontiades, James, Elsevier–North-Holland, 1979, pp. 45–50. Copyright © 1978 the editors.

set of locations for which the overall average cost of production is minimized. Regional production costs vary only according to regional differentials in non-tradeable goods (the price of tradeables is standardized by trade), the relative prices of tradeables and non-tradeables and elasticities of substitution between pairs of non-tradeables and between tradeables and non-tradeables. Overall average production costs are minimized by the correct choice of the least cost 'route' from the location of raw materials through to the final destination.[1]

This location strategy is complicated in practice by a number of factors.

First, there are increasing returns to scale in many activities. Where only one destination is to be serviced, increasing returns means that location strategy may change in response to a change in the size of market. Where more than one destination is to be serviced, increasing returns in either production or transportation create an incentive to concentrate each stage of production at just a few locations. Increasing returns at any one stage of production or in the transport of any one semi-processed material may be diffused through the entire process, leading to the relocation of plants involved in quite remote stages of production, and to the reorganization of the entire network of trade.

The second major factor is that modern businesses perform many activities other than routine production. Such activities require different inputs from production, but need to be integrated with the production process. They have a twofold influence on location: their own least cost location will differ from that of routine production because of their differing input requirements and secondly they will exercise a locational 'pull' on routine production. Two important non-production activities are marketing and research and development (R&D).[2] Both these functions represent an integral set of activities. Marketing has three main constituents: stockholding, distribution and advertising. The location of stockholding depends on the interplay between the better quality of service provided by decentralized stockholding and the declining costs of large, centralized warehouses. Only above a certain market size is local stockholding efficient. Routine advertising and distribution are generally located in the final market. The location of R&D will depend largely on the regional differentials in the price of the most important non-traded input—skilled labour. However, this will be modified by information costs which play the same role as transport costs in routine production. Where a firm relies on the creation and internal use of productive knowledge from its own R&D department, there are strong reasons for centralizing this creative function and integrating it closely with the more creative aspects of marketing and production.[3] Constant reworking of ideas through teamwork is necessary for least cost innovation and the importance of information flows will encourage the centralization of these activities. However, the more routine development work may be much more diffused: the communications problem is not so great and local knowledge and inputs are more important. We conclude that the location strategy of a firm which integrates production marketing and R&D is highly complex. The activities are normally interdependent and information flows as well as transport cost must be considered. Information costs which increase with distance encourage the centralization of activities where exchanges of knowledge through teamwork are of the essence. Such activities are the 'high level' ones of basic research, innovative production and the development marketing strategy; they require large inputs of skilled labour, and the availability of skilled labour will therefore exert a significant influence on the location strategy of such firms.[4]

The third factor which complicates the location strategies of firms is that in practice they operate largely in imperfectly competitive markets. This means that, in many cases, MNEs cannot be considered as price takers in intermediate and factor markets. Consequently, a firm which can force down input or factor prices in a particular region will tend to concentrate the production processes which are intensive in these inputs in that region. It has been argued that the explanation of monopsony power may also exert a significant influence on a firm's choice of production technique in a particular region.[5]

The fourth factor is government intervention. The influence of taxes and tariffs and other regulations such as preferential duties has been shown by many analysts to affect location[6] and it is unnecessary to elaborate on this here.

Finally, location decisions will be influenced by the ownership effect, or the extent to which the internalization of markets in the firm modify the above considerations. This is examined in detail in the following section.

To sum up, the location decisions of firms in the international economy will in practice differ considerably from the predictions of the theory of the location of production under ideal competitive conditions where transport costs are the only barrier to trade. The possibilities of economies of scale in certain activities, the complexities of the activities, the extent of their integration, the type of market structure and the extent of government intervention will all influence location strategy. We now examine ownership effects and the extent to which location strategy is dependent on the replacement of external markets by internal markets within the firm.

3. THE OWNERSHIP OF PRODUCTION

Having considered location effects in some detail, we can now turn our attention to the ownership of production, considering production locations unchanged. A strong case can be made for the contention that the major dynamic of the world economy is changing *ownership* effects which influence the pattern of distribution of production between MNEs and national firms. Resource endowments are to a large extent geographically fixed: copper, bauxite and oil reserves for instance. The question at issue is why US-owned copper companies, US and Canadian aluminium producers and US and UK oil companies should dominate their markets. We argue here that the essence of the ownership effect can be explained in terms of the internalization of key intermediate goods markets within firms of particular nationalities.

In a situation where firms are attempting to maximize profits in a world of imperfect markets, there will often exist an incentive to bypass imperfect markets in intermediate products. Their activities which were previously linked by the market mechanism are brought under common ownership and control in a 'market' internal to the firm. Where markets are internalized across national boundaries, MNEs are created.[7]

Benefits of internalization arise from the avoidance of imperfections in the external market, but there are also costs. The optimum size of firm is set where the costs and benefits of further internalization are equalized at the margin. We now go on to examine these costs and benefits and to consider how they apply in practice.

Benefits from 'internalization' arise from five main types of market imperfection. Firstly, production takes time. Often activities linked by the market involve significant time lags and the relevant futures markets required for their co-ordination are inadequate or completely lacking. This creates a strong incentive for the creation of an internal future market. Secondly, the efficient explanation of market power may require discriminating pricing of a type not feasible in an external market—this will encourage the monopolist to integrate forwards and the monopsonist to integrate backwards. Thirdly, internal markets remove—or prevent the growth of—bilateral concentrations of market power, and thus reduce the likelihood of unstable bargaining situations. The fourth type of imperfection occurs where there is inequality between buyer and seller with respect to the evaluation of a product. 'Buyer uncertainty' is prevalent where the product in question is a type of knowledge, which cannot be properly valued unless the valuer is in full possession of it. Buyer uncertainty is eliminated when buyer and seller are part of the same organization. Fifth, internalization may be a way of avoiding government intervention. Prices reported in an organization are much more difficult to monitor than those in an external market. Consequently government evaluation of tax and tariff payments and its enforcement of exchange control regulations becomes difficult, and the firm is able to exploit this through transfer pricing.

There are also costs of internalization which may offset the benefits. Firstly, some of the costs of operating a market—whether internal or external—are fixed independently of the volume of transactions, so that if a single external market is split up and internalized within a number of distinct firms the costs of market organization for each firm will tend to rise. Secondly, when a single external market is replaced by several internal ones it may be necessary for firms to adjust the scales of the activities linked by the markets to make them compatible; this may mean that some activities have to be operated on a less efficient scale than would be possible with a larger external market. Thirdly, there may be increased communication costs. In an external market only price and quantity information is exchanged, but the demands of an internal market are normally greater because of the additional flows of accounting and control information. Finally, internalization costs have an international dimension arising from problems associated with foreign ownership and control. It should be noted that such problems can, in varying degrees, be reduced or eliminated by *partially* internalizing a market; for instance disposing of excess output on the open market or subcontracting outside the firm.

Having set out the general theory of the costs and benefits of internalizing markets, we now turn to the application of the theory. It can be argued that the benefits of internalization are particularly large in two cases. Firstly in industries where firms need to receive future supplies of vital raw materials and secondly in industries where flows of technical and marketing knowledge are important. The first phase of the growth of MNEs (up to the end of World War I) was concerned with maintaining and developing raw material supplies through vertical integration. However the major force in the world economy at the present time arises from the special advantages of internalizing flows of knowledge. It is this factor to which we look to account for the continued strength of the ownership effect.

The production of knowledge (through R&D) is a lengthy process which requires careful synchronization with other activities within the firm. Knowledge is a (temporary) 'natural monopoly' which is best exploited through discriminatory pricing. The buyers of knowledge are in many cases monopsonists, by virtue of control of regional distribution outlets, and so bilateral monopoly is likely if knowledge is licensed through an external market. Buyer uncertainty applies with particular force, for knowledge cannot be valued until it is in full possession of the valuer. Finally, because of difficulties of evaluation, knowledge flows provide an excellent basis for transfer pricing.

Internalization across national boundaries of markets in knowledge-based products is clearly of great importance in accounting for overseas production by MNEs. Subsidiaries of MNEs are likely to be successful in taking a large share of foreign markets because of the 'branch plant effect' arising from subsidiary unit's access to the internal markets of MNEs. This access gives it a great advantage over those firms which have access only to (often inadequate) external markets. The greater the market imperfections. the more disadvantaged are 'national' firms in competing with MNEs.

Branch plant effect—the fact that subsidiaries of MNEs can out-perform national firms arise not from multinationality but from access to internal markets. This has two main aspects. Firstly, subsidiaries can obtain inputs which are simply not available in external markets. Most important among such inputs are proprietary knowledge (the output of past R&D), marketing know-how (arising from a worldwide intelligence system) and production experience. Secondly, branch plants can often obtain inputs more cheaply within the firm than their competitors can on the open market. This price differential arises, not from plant economies, but from access to the firm's internal futures markets, and from tax savings arising from transfer pricing.

Ownership effects may impinge on the location policies of MNEs. Firstly efficient transfer pricing normally involves giving the highest mark-up to operations in the lowest tax area. This policy may imply, a complete change of location strategy within the scheme of Section 2. Secondly, internalization involves increased communication costs in the form of accounting and control information. As communication costs increase with geographical, social and linguistic 'distance', this will bias the location of internally co-ordinated activities towards a central region.

4. THE DIVISION OF NATIONAL MARKETS EXPLAINED

Combining both ownership and location effects allows us to give the reasons for the division of particular markets between domestic producers, local subsidiaries of MNEs, exports from foreign-owned plants and exports from MNEs. The division between exports and local servicing is largely the result of the economics of location. Least cost location, influenced by regional price differentials and by barriers to trade largely governs the proportion of a market serviced by exports. This, however, is modified by the economics of internalizing a market, for not only can this affect the least cost location of any stage of production but the strategy of a MNE after having internalized a market may differ from that which external market forces would dictate. Consequently, the question of servicing a final market is inextricably bound up with the nature and ownership of internal markets—which will be dictated by the costs of benefits of internalization.

In order to predict the division of national markets between the above groups we must have information relating to the following variables.

(1) *Industry-specific factors*: the nature of the product, the structure of the external market and the relation between the optimal scales of the activities linked by the market.
(2) *Region-specific factors*: factor costs in different regions, intermediate and raw material availability, the geographical and social distance between the regions involved.
(3) *Nation-specific factors*: the political and fiscal structures particularly of the nations involved.
(4) *Firm-specific factors*: in particular the ability of management to communicate internally across national boundaries, and to cope with the legal and accounting complexities of international ownership.

From the above, the strategy of MNEs can be explained by combining our knowledge of locational influences with the opportunities of internalizing markets profitably. Location and ownership effects are interdependent for the least cost location of an activity is at least partly determined by the ownership of the activities integrated with it.

NOTES

1. For a full exposition see Peter J. Buckley and Mark Casson, *The Future of the Multinational Enterprise*, Macmillan, London 1976. Chapter II, Section 3.
2. R&D includes the innovative aspects of advertising.
3. Note the similarity of this argument with Raymond Vernon, 'International Investment and International Trade in the Product Cycle', *Journal of Economics*, **80** (1966): 190–207.
4. This agrees with Hymer's 'Law of Uneven Development': the centralization of 'higher order activities' in the parent. See S. Hymer 'The Multinational Corporation and the Law of Uneven Development', in J. N. Bhagwati (ed.), *Economics and World Order*, Macmillan, 1972.
5. See e.g. D. E. de Meza. 'Multinationals' Choice of Technique', *mimeo*, Reading, 1975.
6. Notably T. Horst, 'The Theory of the Multinational Firm: Optimal Behaviour under Different Tariff and Tax Rates', *Journal of Political Economy*, **79** (1971): 1059–1072.
7. Note the similarity of this argument with Stephen H. Hymer, *The International Operations of National Firms*, MIT Press, Cambridge, Mass., 1976.

3

The Globalization of Markets

Theodore Levitt

A powerful force drives the world toward a converging commonality, and that force is technology. It has proletarianized communication, transport, and travel. It has made isolated places and impoverished peoples eager for modernity's allurements. Almost everyone everywhere wants all the things they have heard about, seen, or experienced via the new technologies.

The result is a new commercial reality—the emergence of global markets for standardized consumer products on a previously unimagined scale of magnitude. Corporations geared to this new reality benefit from enormous economies of scale in production, distribution, marketing, and management. By translating these benefits into reduced world prices, they can decimate competitors that still live in the disabling grip of old assumptions about how the world works.

Gone are accustomed differences in national or regional preference. Gone are the days when a company could sell last year's models—or lesser versions of advanced products—in the less-developed world. And gone are the days when prices, margins, and profits abroad were generally higher than at home.

The globalization of markets is at hand. With that, the multinational commercial world nears its end, and so does the multinational corporation.

The multinational and the global corporation are not the same thing. The multinational corporation operates in a number of countries and adjusts its products and practices in each—at high relative costs. The global corporation operates with resolute constancy—at low relative cost—as if the entire world (or major regions of it) were a single entity; it sells the same things in the same way everywhere.

Which strategy is better is not a matter of opinion but of necessity. Worldwide communications carry everywhere the constant drumbeat of modern possibilities to lighten and enhance work, raise living standards, divert, and entertain. The same countries that ask the world to recognize and respect the individuality of their cultures insist on the wholesale transfer to them of modern goods, services, and technologies. Modernity is not just a wish but also a widespread practice among those who cling, with unyielding passion or religious fervour, to ancient attitudes and and heritages.

Who can forget the televised scenes during the 1979 Iranian uprisings of young men in fashionable French-cut trousers and silky body shirts thirsting with raised modern weapons for blood in the name of Islamic fundamentalism?

Reprinted by permission of *Harvard Business Review*. 'The Globalization of Markets', by Theodore Levitt, May–June, pp. 92–102. Copyright © 1983 by the President and Fellows of Harvard College; all rights reserved.

In Brazil, thousands swarm daily from pre-industrial Bahian darkness into exploding coastal cities, there quickly to install television sets in crowded corrugated huts and, next to battered Volkswagens, make sacrificial offerings of fruit and fresh-killed chickens to Macumban spirits by candlelight.

During Biafra's fratricidal war against the Ibos, daily televised reports showed soldiers carrying bloodstained swords and listening to transistor radios while drinking Coca-Cola.

In the isolated Siberian city of Krasnoyarsk, with no paved streets and censored news, occasional Western travellers are stealthily propositioned for cigarettes, digital watches, and even the clothes off their backs.

The organized smuggling of electronic equipment, used automobiles, western clothing, cosmetics, and pirated movies into primitive places exceeds even the thriving underground trade in modern weapons and their military mercenaries.

A thousand suggestive ways attest to the ubiquity of the desire for the most advanced things that the world makes and sells — goods of the best quality and reliability at the lowest price. The world's needs and desires have been irrevocably homogenized. This makes the multinational corporation obsolete and the global corporation absolute.

LIVING IN THE REPUBLIC OF TECHNOLOGY

Daniel J. Boorstin, author of the monumental trilogy *The Americans*, characterized our age as driven by 'the Republic of Technology [whose] supreme law... is convergence, the tendency for everything to become more like everything else'.

In business, this trend has pushed markets toward global commonality. Corporations sell standardized products in the same way everywhere—autos, steel, chemicals, petroleum, cement, agricultural commodities and equipment, industrial and commercial construction, banking and insurance services, computers, semiconductors, transport, electronic instruments, pharmaceuticals, and telecommunications, to mention some of the obvious.

Nor is the sweeping gale of globalization confined to these raw material or high-tec products, where the universal language of customers and users facilitates standardization. The transforming winds whipped up by the proletarianization of communication and travel enter every crevice of life.

Commercially, nothing confirms this as much as the success of McDonald's from the Champs Elysées to the Ginza, of Coca-Cola in Bahrain and Pepsi-Cola in Moscow and of rock music, Greek salad, Hollywood movies, Revlon cosmetics, Sony televisions, and Levi jeans everywhere. 'High-touch' products are as ubiquitous as high-tech.

Starting from opposing sides, the high-tech and the high-touch ends of the commercial spectrum gradually consume the undistributed middle in their cosmopolitan orbit. No one is exempt and nothing can stop the process. Everywhere everything gets more and more like everything else as the world's preference structure is relentlessly homogenized.

Consider the cases of Coca-Cola and Pepsi-Cola, which are globally standardized products sold everywhere and welcomed by everyone. Both successfully cross multitudes of national, regional, and ethnic taste buds trained to a variety of deeply ingrained local preferences of taste, flavour, consistency, effervescence, and aftertaste. Everywhere both sell well. Cigarettes, too, especially American-made, make year-to-year global inroads on territories previously held in the firm grip of other, mostly local, blends.

These are not exceptional examples. (Indeed their global reach would be even greater were it not for artificial trade barriers.) They exemplify a general drift toward the homogenization of the world and how companies distribute, finance, and price products.[1] Nothing is exempt. The products and methods of the industrialized world play a single tune for all the world, and all the world eagerly dances to it.

Ancient differences in national taste or modes of doing business disappear. The commonality of preference leads inescapably to the standardization of products, manufacturing, and institutions of trade and commerce. Small nation-based markets transmogrify and expand. Success in world competition turns on efficiency in production, distribution, marketing, and management, and inevitably becomes focused on price.

The most effective world competitors incorporate superior quality and reliability into their cost structures. They sell in all national markets the same kind of products sold at home or in their largest export market. They compete on the basis of appropriate value—the best combinations of price, quality, reliability, and delivery for products that are globally identical with respect to design, function, and even fashion.

That, and little else, explains the surging success of Japanese companies dealing worldwide in a vast variety of products—both tangible products like steel, cars, motorcycles, hi-fi equipment, farm machinery, robots, microprocessors, carbon fibres, and now even textiles, and intangibles like banking, shipping, general contracting, and soon computer software. Nor are high-quality and low-cost operations incompatible, as a host of consulting organizations and data engineers argue with vigorous vacuity. The reported data are incomplete, wrongly analysed, and contradictory. The truth is that low-cost operations are the hallmark of corporate cultures that require and produce quality in all that they do. High quality and low costs are not opposing postures. They are compatible, twin identities of superior practice.[2]

To say that Japan's companies are not global because they export cars with left-side drives to the United States and the European continent, while those in Japan have right-side drives, or because they sell office machines through distributors in the United States but directly at home, or speak Portuguese in Brazil is to mistake a difference for a distinction. The same is true of Safeway and Southland retail chains operating effectively in the Middle East, and to not only native but also imported populations from Korea, the Philippines, Pakistan, India, Thailand, Britain, and the United States. National rules of the road differ, and so do distribution channels and languages. Japan's distinction is its unrelenting push for economy and value enhancement. That translates into a drive for standardization at high quality levels.

Vindication of the Model T

If a company forces costs and prices down and pushes quality and reliability up—while maintaining reasonable concern for suitability—customers will prefer its world-standardized products. The theory holds, at this stage in the evolution of globalization, no matter what conventional market research and even common sense may suggest about different national and regional tastes, preferences, needs, and institutions. The Japanese have repeatedly vindicated this theory, as did Henry Ford with the Model T. Most important, so have their imitators, including companies from South Korea (television sets and heavy construction), Malaysia (personal calculators and microcomputers), Brazil (auto parts and tools), Colombia (apparel), Singapore (optical equipment), and yes, even from the United States (office copiers, computers, bicycles, castings), Western Europe (automatic washing machines), Rumania (housewares), Hungary (apparel), Yugoslavia (furniture), and Israel (pagination equipment).

Of course, large companies operating in a single nation or even a single city don't standardize everything they make, sell, or do. They have product lines instead of a single product version, and multiple distribution channels. There are neighbourhood, local, regional, ethnic, and institutional differences, even within metropolitan areas. But although companies customize products for particular market segments, they know that success in a world with homogenized demand requires a search for sales opportunities in similar segments across the globe in order to achieve the economies of scale necessary to compete.

Such a search works because a market segment in one country is seldom unique; it has close cousins everywhere precisely because technology has homogenized the globe. Even small local segments have their global equivalents everywhere and become subject to global competition, especially on price.

The global competitor will seek constantly to standardize his offering everywhere. He will digress from this standardization only after exhausting all possibilities to retain it, and he will push for reinstatement of standardization whenever digression and divergence have occurred. He will never assume that the customer is a king who knows his own wishes.

Trouble increasingly stalks companies that lack clarified global focus and remain inattentive to the economics of simplicity and standardization. The most endangered companies in the rapidly evolving world tend to be those that dominate rather small domestic markets with high value-added products for which there are smaller markets elsewhere. With transportation costs proportionately low, distant competitors will enter the now-sheltered markets of those companies with goods produced more cheaply under scale-efficient conditions. Global competition spells the end of domestic territoriality, no matter how diminutive the territory may be.

When the global producer offers his lower costs internationally, his patronage expands exponentially. He not only reaches into distant markets, but also attracts customers who previously held to local preferences and now capitulate to the attractions of lesser prices. The strategy of standardization not only responds to worldwide homogenized markets but also expands those markets with aggressive low pricing. The new technological juggernaut taps an ancient motivation—to make one's money go as far as possible. This is universal not simply a motivation but actually a need.

THE HEDGEHOG KNOWS

The difference between the hedgehog and the fox, wrote Sir Isaiah Berlin in distinguishing between Dostoevski and Tolstoy, is that the fox knows a lot about a great many things, but the hedgehog knows everything about one great thing. The multinational corporation knows a lot about a great many countries and congenially adapts to supposed differences. It willingly accepts vestigial national differences, not questioning the possibility of their transformation, not recognizing how the world is ready and eager for the benefit of modernity, especially when the price is right. The multinational corporation's accommodating mode to visible national differences is medieval.

By contrast, the global corporation knows everything about one great thing. It knows about the need to be competitive on a worldwide basis as well as nationally and seeks constantly to drive down prices by standardizing what it sells and how it operates. It treats the world as composed of few standardized markets rather than many customized markets. It actively seeks and vigorously works toward global convergence. Its mission is modernity and its mode, price competition, even when it sells top-of the-line, high-end products. It knows about one great thing all nations and people have in common: scarcity.

Nobody takes scarcity lying down; everyone wants more. This is in part explains division of labour and specialization of production. They enable people and nations to optimize their conditions through trade. The median is usually money.

Experience teaches that money has three special qualities: scarcity, difficulty of acquisition, and transience. People understandably treat it with respect. Everyone in the increasingly homogenized world market wants products and features that everybody else wants. If the price is low enough, they will take highly standardized world products, even if these aren't exactly what mother said was suitable, what immemorial custom decreed was right, or what market-research fabulists asserted was preferred.

The implacable truth of all modern production—whether of tangible or intangible goods—is that large-scale production of standardized items is generally cheaper within a wide range of volume than small-scale production. Some argue that CAD/CAM will allow companies to manufacture customized products on a small scale—but cheaply. But the argument misses the point. If a company treats the world as one or two distinctive product markets, it can serve the world more economically than if it treats it as three, four, or five product markets.

Why remaining differences?

Different cultural preferences, national tastes and standards, and business institutions are vestiges of the past. Some inheritances die gradually; others prosper and expand into mainstream global preferences. So-called ethnic markets are a good example. Chinese food, pita bread, country and western music, pizza, and jazz are everywhere. They are market segments that exist in worldwide proportions. They don't deny or contradict global homogenization but confirm it.

Many of today's differences among nations as to products and their features actually reflect the respectful accommodation of multinational corporations to what they believe are fixed local preferences. They *believe* preferences are fixed, not because they are but because of rigid habits of thinking about what actually is. Most executives in multinational corporations are thoughtlessly accommodating. They falsely presume that marketing means giving the customer what he says he wants rather than trying to understand exactly what he'd like. So they persist with high-cost, customized multinational products and practices instead of pressing hard and pressing properly for global standardization.

I do not advocate the systematic disregard of local or national differences. But a company's sensitivity to such differences does not require that it ignore the possibilities of doing things differently or better.

There are, for example, enormous differences among Middle Eastern countries. Some are socialist, some monarchies, some republics. Some take their legal heritage from the Napoleonic Code, some from the Ottoman Empire, and some from the British common law; except for Israel, all are influenced by Islam. Doing business means personalizing the business relationship in an obsessively intimate fashion. During the month of Ramadan, business discussions can start only after 10 o'clock at night, when people are tired and full of food after a day of fasting. A company must almost certainly have a local partner; a local lawyer is required (as, say, in New York), and irrevocable Letters of credit are essential. Yet, as Coca-Cola's Senior

Vice President Sam Ayoub noted, 'Arabs are much more capable of making distinctions between cultural and religious purposes on the one hand and economic realities on the other than is generally assumed. Islam is compatible with science and modern times'.

Barriers to globalization are not confined to the Middle East. The free transfer of technology and data across the boundaries of the European Common Market countries are hampered by Legal and financial impediments. And there is resistance to radio and television interference ('pollution') among neighbouring European countries.

But the past is a good guide to the future. With persistence and appropriate means, barriers against superior technologies and economics have always fallen. There is no recorded exception where reasonable effort has been made to overcome them. It is very much a matter of time and effort.

A FAILURE IN GLOBAL IMAGINATION

Many companies have tried to standardize world practice by exporting domestic products and processes without accommodation or change—and have failed miserably. Their deficiencies have been seized on as evidence of bovine stupidity in the face of abject impossibility. Advocates of global standardization see them as examples of failures in execution.

In fact, poor execution is often an important cause. More important, however, is failure of nerve—failure of imagination.

Consider the case for the introduction of fully automatic home laundry equipment in Western Europe at a time when few homes had even semiautomatic machines. Hoover Ltd., whose parent company's headquarters were in North Canton, Ohio, had a prominent presence in Britain as a producer of vacuum cleaners and washing machines. Due to insufficient

Table 1. Consumer preferences as to automatic washing machine features in the 1960s

Features	Great Britain	Italy	West Germany	France	Sweden
Shell dimensions†	34 inches and narrow	Low and narrow	34 inches and wide	34 inches and narrow	34 inches and wide
Drum material	Enamel	Enamel	Stainless steel	Enamel	Stainless steel
Loading	Top	Front	Front	Front	Front
Front porthole	Yes/No	Yes	Yes	Yes	Yes
Capacity	5 kilos	4 kilos	6 kilos	5 kilos	6 kilos
Spin speed	700 rpm	400 rpm	850 rpm	600 rpm	800 rpm
Water heating system	No*	Yes	Yes**	Yes	No*
Washing action	Agitator	Tumble	Tumble	Agitator	Tumble
Styling features	Inconspicuous appearance	Brightly coloured	Indestructible appearance	Elegant appearance	Strong appearance

† 34 inches height was (in the process of being adopted as) a standard work-surface height in Europe
* Most British and Swedish homes had centrally heated hot water.
** West Germans preferred to launder at temperatures higher than generally provided centrally.

demand in the home market and low exports to the European continent, the large washing machine plant in England operated far below capacity. The company needed to sell more of its semiautomatic or automatic machines.

Because it had a 'proper' marketing orientation, Hoover conducted consumer preference studies in Britain and each major continental country. The results showed feature preferences clearly enough among several countries (see Table 1).

The incremental unit variable costs (in pounds sterling) of customizing to meet just a few of the national preferences were as shown in Table 2. Considerable plant investment was needed to meet other preferences.

Table 2. Incremental unit variable costs of customization

	£	s	d
Stainless steel vs. enamel drum	1	0	0
Porthole window		10	0
Spin speed of 800 rpm vs. 700 rpm		15	0
Water heater	2	15	0
6 vs. 5 kg capacity	1	10	0
Total	£6	10s	0d

Total equivalent to $18.20 at the exchange rate at that time.

The lowest retail prices (in pounds sterling) of leading locally produced brands in the various countries were approximately:

UK	110
France	114
West Germany	113
Sweden	134
Italy	57

Product customization in each country would have put Hoover in a poor competitive position on the basis of price, mostly due to the higher manufacturing costs incurred by short production runs for separate features. Because Common Market tariff reduction programmes were then incomplete, Hoover also paid tariff duties in each continental country.

How to make a creative analysis

In the Hoover case, an imaginative analysis of automatic washing machine sales in each country would have revealed that:

(1) Italian automatics, small in capacity and size, low-powered, without built-in heaters, with porcelain enamel tubs, were priced aggressively low and were gaining large market shares in all countries, including West Germany.
(2) The best-selling automatics in West Germany were heavily advertised (three times more than the next most promoted brand), were ideally suited to national tastes, and were also by far the highest priced machines available in that country.
(3) Italy, with the lowest penetration of washing machines of any kind (manual, semiautomatic, or automatic) was rapidly going directly to automatics, skipping the pattern of first buying handwringer, manually assisted machines and then semiautomatics.

(4) Detergent manufacturers were just beginning to promote the technique of cold-water and tepid-water laundering then used in the United States.

The growing success of small, low-powered, low-speed, low-capacity, low-priced Italian machines, even against the preferred but highly priced and highly promoted brand in West Germany, was significant. It contained a powerful message that was lost on managers confidently wedded to a distorted version of the marketing concept according to which you give the customer what he says he wants. In fact the customers *said* they wanted certain features, but their behaviour demonstrated that they would take other features provided the price and the promotion were right.

In this case it was obvious that, under prevailing conditions, people preferred a low-priced automatic over any kind of manual or semiautomatic machine and certainly over higher priced automatics, even though the low-priced automatics failed to fulfil all their expressed preferences. The supposedly meticulous and demanding German consumers violated all expectations by buying the simple, low-priced Italian machines.

It was equally clear that people were profoundly influenced by promotions of automatic washers; in West Germany, the most heavily promoted ideal machine also had the largest market share despite its high price. Two things clearly influenced customers to buy: low price regardless of feature preferences and heavy promotion regardless of price. Both factors helped homemakers get what they most wanted—the superior benefits bestowed by fully automatic machines.

Hoover should have aggressively sold a simple, standardized high-quality machine at a low price (afforded by the 17% variable cost reduction that the elimination of £6-10-0 worth of extra features made possible). The suggested retail prices could have been somewhat less than £100. The extra funds 'saved' by avoiding unnecessary plant modifications would have supported an extended service network and aggressive media promotions.

Hoover's media message should have been: *this* is the machine that you, the homemaker, *deserve* to have to reduce the repetitive heavy daily household burdens, so that *you* may have more constructive time to spend with your children and your husband. The promotion should also have targeted the husband to give him, preferably in the presence of his wife, a sense of obligation to provide an automatic washer for her even before he bought an automobile for himself. An aggressively low price, combined with heavy promotion of this kind, would have overcome previously expressed preferences for particular features.

The Hoover case illustrates how the perverse practice of the marketing concept and the absence of any kind of marketing imagination let multinational attitudes survive when customers actually want the benefits of global standardization. The whole project got off on the wrong foot. It asked people what features they wanted in a washing machine rather than what they wanted out of life. Selling a line of products individually tailored to each nation is thoughtless. Managers who took pride in practising the marketing concept to the fullest did not, in fact, practice it at all. Hoover asked the wrong questions then applied neither thought nor imagination to the answers. Such companies are like the ethnocentricists in the Middle Ages who saw with everyday clarity the sun revolving around the earth and offered it as Truth. With no additional data but a more searching mind, Copernicus, like the hedgehog, interpreted a more compelling and accurate reality. Data do not yield information except with the intervention of the mind. Information does not yield meaning except with the intervention of imagination.

ACCEPTING THE INEVITABLE

The global corporation accepts for better or for worse that technology drives consumers relentlessly toward the same common goals—alleviation of life's burdens and the expansion of discretionary time and spending power. Its role is profoundly different from what it has been for the ordinary corporation during its brief, turbulent, and, remarkably protean history. It orchestrates the twin vectors of technology and globalization for the world's benefit. Neither fate, nor nature, nor God but rather the necessity of commerce created this role.

In the United States two industries became global long before they were consciously aware of it. After over a generation of persistent and acrimonious labour shutdowns, the United Steelworkers of America have not called an industrywide strike since 1959; the United Auto Workers have not shut down General Motors since 1970. Both unions realize that they have become global—shutting down all or most of US manufacturing would not shut out US customers. Overseas suppliers are there to supply the market.

Cracking the code of Western markets

Since the theory of the marketing concept emerged a quarter of a century ago, the more managerially advanced corporations have been eager to offer what customers clearly wanted rather than what was merely convenient. They have created marketing departments supported by professional market researchers of awesome and often costly proportions. And they have proliferated extraordinary numbers of operations and product lines—highly tailored products and delivery systems for many different markets, market segments, and nations. Significantly, Japanese companies operate almost entirely without marketing departments or market research of the kind so prevalent in the West. Yet, in the colourful words of General Electric's chairman John F. Welch, Jr., the Japanese, coming from a small cluster of resource-poor islands, with an entirely alien culture and an almost impenetrably complex language, have cracked the code of Western markets. They have done it not by looking with mechanistic thoroughness at the way markets are different but rather by searching for meaning with a deeper wisdom. They have discovered the one great thing all markets have in common—an overwhelming desire for dependable, world-standard modernity in all things, at aggressively low prices. In response, they deliver irresistible value everywhere, attracting people with products that market-research technocrats described with superficial certainty as being unsuitable and uncompetitive.

The wider a company's global reach, the greater the number of regional and national preferences it will encounter for certain product features, distribution systems, or promotional media. There will always need to be some accommodation to differences. But the widely prevailing and often unthinking belief in the immutability of these differences is generally mistaken. Evidence of business failure because of lack of accommodation is often evidence of other shortcomings.

Take the case of Revlon in Japan. The company unnecessarily alienated retailers and confused customers by selling world-standardized cosmetics only in elite outlets; then it tried to recover with low-priced world-standardized products in broader distribution, followed by a change in the company president and cutbacks in distribution as costs rose faster than sales. The problem was not that Revlon didn't understand the Japanese market; it didn't do the job right, wavered in its programmes, and was impatient to boot.

By contrast, the Outboard Marine Corporation, with imagination, push, and persistence, collapsed long-established three-tiered distribution channels in Europe into a more focused and controllable two-step system—and did so despite the vociferous warnings of local trade groups. It also reduced the number and types of retail outlets. The result was greater improvement in credit and product-installation service to customers, major cost reductions, and sales advances.

In its highly successful introduction of Contac 600 (the timed-release decongestant) into Japan, SmithKline Corporation used 35 wholesalers instead of the 1000-plus that established practice required. Daily contacts with the wholesalers and key retailers, also in violation of established practice, supplemented the plan, and it worked.

Denied access to established distribution institutions in the United States, Komatsu, the Japanese manufacturer of lightweight farm machinery, entered the market through over-the-road construction equipment dealers in rural areas of the Sunbelt, where farms are smaller, the soil sandier and easier to work. Here inexperienced distributors were able to attract customers on the basis of Komatsu's product and price appropriateness.

In cases of successful challenge to prevailing institutions and practices, a combination of product reliability and quality, strong and sustained support systems, aggressively low prices, and sales-compensation packages, as well as audacity and implacability, circumvented, shattered, and transformed very different distribution systems. Instead of resentment there was admiration.

Still, some differences between nations are unyielding, even in a world of microprocessors. In the United States almost all manufacturers of microprocessors check them for reliability through a so-called parallel system of testing. Japan prefers the totally different sequential testing system. So Teradyne Corporation, the world's largest producer of microprocessor test equipment, makes one line for the United States and one for Japan. That's easy.

What's not so easy for Teradyne is to know how best to organize and manage, in this instance, its marketing effort. Companies can organize by product, region, function, or by using some combination of these. A company can have separate marketing organizations for Japan and for the United States, or it can have separate product groups, one working largely in Japan and the other in the United States. A single manufacturing facility or marketing operation might service both markets, or a company might use separate marketing operations for each.

Questions arise if the company organizes by product. In the case of Teradyne, should the group handling the parallel system, whose major market is the United States, sell in Japan and compete with the group focused on the Japanese market? If the company organizes regionally, how do regional groups divide their efforts between promoting the parallel vs. the sequential system? If the company organizes in terms of function, how does it get commitment in marketing, for example, for one line instead of the other?

There is no one reliably right answer—no one formula by which to get it. There isn't even a satisfactory contingent answer.[3] What works well for one company or one place may fail for another in precisely the same place, depending on the capabilities, histories, reputations, resources, and even the cultures of both.

THE EARTH IS FLAT

The differences that persist throughout the world despite its globalization affirm an ancient dictum of economics—that things are driven by what happens at the margin, not at the core.

Thus, in ordinary competitiveness analysis, what's important is not the average price but the marginal price; what happens not in the usual case but at the interface of newly erupting conditions. What counts in commercial affairs is what happens at the cutting edge. What are most striking today are the underlying similarities of what is happening now to national preferences at the margin. These similarities at the cutting edge cumulatively form an overwhelming, predominant commonality everywhere.

To refer to the persistence of economic nationalism (protective and subsidized trade practices, special tax aids, or restrictions for home market producers) as a barrier to the globalization of markets is to make a valid point. Economic nationalism does have a powerful persistence. But, as with the present almost totally smooth internationalization of investment capital, the past alone does not shape or predict the future.

Reality is not a fixed paradigm, dominated by immemorial customs and derived attitudes, heedless of powerful and abundant new forces. The world is becoming increasingly informed about the liberating and enhancing possibilities of modernity. The persistence of the inherited varieties of national preferences rests uneasily on increasing evidence of, and restlessness regarding, their inefficiency, costliness, and confinement. The historic past, and the national differences respecting commerce and industry it spawned and fostered everywhere, is now subject to relatively easy transformation.

Cosmopolitanism is no longer the monopoly of the intellectual and leisure classes; it is becoming the established property and defining characteristic of all sectors everywhere in the world. Gradually and irresistibly it breaks down the walls of economic insularity, nationalism, and chauvinism. What we see today as escalating commercial nationalism is simply the last violent death rattle of an obsolete institution.

Companies that adapt to and capitalize on economic convergence can still make distinctions and adjustments in different markets. Persistent differences in the world are consistent with fundamental underlying commonalities; they often complement rather than oppose each other—in business as they do in physics. There is, in physics, simultaneously matter and anti-matter working in symbiotic harmony.

The earth is round, but for most purposes it's sensible to treat it as flat. Space is curved, but not much for everyday life here on earth.

Divergence from established practice happens all the time. But the multinational mind, warped into circumspection and timidity by years of stumbles and transnational troubles, now rarely challenges existing overseas practices. More often it considers any departure from inherited domestic routines as mindless, disrespectful, or impossible. It is the mind of a bygone day.

The successful global corporation does not abjure customization or differentiation for the requirements of markets that differ in product preferences, spending patterns, shopping preferences, and institutional or legal arrangements. But the global corporation accepts and adjusts to these differences only reluctantly, only after relentlessly testing their immutability, after trying in various ways to circumvent and reshape them as we saw in the cases of Outboard Marine in Europe, SmithKline in Japan, and Komatsu in the United States.

There is only one significant respect in which a company's activities around the world are important, and this is in what it produces and how it sells. Everything else derives from, and is subsidiary to, these activities.

The purpose of business is to get and keep a customer. Or, to use Peter Drucker's more refined construction, to *create* and keep a customer. A company must be wedded to the ideal of innovation—offering better or more preferred products in such combinations of ways, means, places, and at such prices that prospects *prefer* doing business with the company rather than with others.

Preferences are constantly shaped and reshaped. Within our global commonality enormous variety constantly asserts itself and thrives, as can be seen within the world's single largest domestic market the United States. But in the process of world homogenization, modern markets expand to reach cost-reducing global proportions. With better and cheaper communication and transport, even small local market segments hitherto protected from distant competitors now feel the pressure of their presence. Nobody is safe from global reach and the irresistible economies of scale.

Two vectors shape the world—technology and globalization. The first helps determine human preferences; the second, economic realities. Regardless of how much preferences evolve and diverge, they also gradually converge and form markets where economies of scale lead to reduction of costs and prices.

The modern global corporation contrasts powerfully with the ageing multinational corporation. Instead of adapting to superficial and even entrenched differences within and between nations, it will seek sensibly to force suitably standardized products and practices on the entire globe. They are exactly what the world will take, if they come also with low prices, high quality, and blessed reliability. The global company will operate, in this regard, precisely as Henry Kissinger wrote in *Years of Upheaval* about the continuing Japanese economic success—'voracious in its collection of information, impervious to pressure, and implacable in execution'.

Given what is everywhere the purpose of commerce, the global company will shape the vectors of technology and globalization into its great strategic fecundity. It will systematically push these vectors toward their own convergence, offering everyone simultaneously high-quality, more or less standardized products at optimally low prices, thereby achieving for itself vastly expanded markets and profits. Companies that do not adapt to the new global realities will become victims of those that do.

NOTES

1. In a landmark article, Robert D. Buzzell pointed out the rapidity with which barriers to standardization were falling. In all cases they succumbed to more and cheaper advanced ways of doing things. See 'Can You Standardize Multinational Marketing?' *Harvard Business Review*, November–December 1968: 102.
2. There is powerful new evidence for this, even though the opposite has been urged by analysts of PIMS data for nearly a decade. See Lynn W. Phillips, Dae Chang and Robert D. Buzzell, 'Product Quality: Cost Production and Business Performance—A Test of Some Key Hypotheses', Harvard Business School Working Paper No. 83-13.
3. For a discussion of multinational reorganization, see Christopher A. Bartlett, 'MNCs: Get Off the Reorganization Merry-Go-Round'. *Harvard Business Review*, March-April 1983: 138.

4

Global strategy: an organizing framework

Sumantra Ghoshal

Over the past few years the concept of global strategy has taken the world of multinational corporations (MNCs) by storm. Scores of articles in the *Harvard Business Review, Fortune, The Economist* and other popular journals have urged multinationals to 'go global' in their strategies. The topic has clearly captured the attention of MNC managers. Conferences on global strategy, whether organized by the Conference Board in New York, *The Financial Times* in London, or Nomura Securities in Tokyo, have invariably attracted enthusiastic corporate support and sizeable audiences. Even in the relatively slow-moving world of academe the issue of globalization of industries and companies has emerged as a new bandwagon, as manifest in the large number of papers on the topic presented at recent meetings of the Academy of Management, the Academy of International Business and the Strategic Management Society. 'Manage globally' appears to be the latest battlecry in the world of international business.

MULTIPLE PERSPECTIVES, MANY PRESCRIPTIONS

This enthusiasm notwithstanding, there is a great deal of conceptual ambiguity about what a 'global' strategy really means. As pointed out by Hamel and Prahalad (1985), the distinction among a global industry, a global firm, and a global strategy is somewhat blurred in the literature. According to Hout, Porter and Rudden (1982), a global strategy is appropriate for global industries which are defined as those in which a firm's competitive position in one national market is significantly affected by its competitive position in other national markets. Such interactions between a firm's positions in different markets may arise from scale benefits or from the potential of synergies or sharing of costs and resources across markets. However, as argued by Bartlett (1985), Kogut (1984) and many others, those scale and synergy benefits may often be created by strategic actions of individual firms and may not be 'given' in any *a priori* sense. For some industries, such as aeroframes or aeroengines, the economies of scale may be large enough to make the need for global integration of activities obvious. However, in a large number of cases industries may not be born global but may have globalness thrust upon them by the entrepreneurship of a company such as Yoshida Kagyo KK (YKK) or Procter and Gamble.

'Global Strategy: an Organizing Framework', by S. Ghoshal, *Strategic Management Journal*, Vol. 8, pp. 425–440.
Copyright © 1987 by John Wiley & Sons, Ltd. Reprinted by permission.

In such cases the global industry—global strategy link may be more useful for ex-post explanation of outcomes than for ex-ante predictions or strategizing.

Further, the concept of a global strategy is not as new as some of the recent authors on the topic have assumed it to be. It was stated quite explicitly about 20 years ago by Perlmutter (1969) when he distinguished between the geocentric, polycentric, and ethnocentric approaches to multinational management. The starting point for Perlmutter's categorization scheme was the world-view of a firm, which was seen as the driving force behind its management processes and the way it structured its world-wide activities (see Robinson, 1978 and Rutenberg, 1982 for detailed reviews and expositions). In much of the current literature, in contrast, the focus has been narrowed and the concept of global strategy has been linked almost exclusively with how the firm structures the flow of tasks within its world-wide value-adding system. The more integrated and rationalized the flow of tasks appears to be, the more global the firm's strategy is assumed to be (e.g. Leontiades, 1984). On the one hand, this focus has led to improved understanding of the fact that different tasks offer different degrees of advantages from global integration and national differentiation and that, optimally, a firm must configure its value chain to obtain the best possible advantages from both (Porter, 1984). But, on the other hand, it has also led to certain dysfunctional simplifications. The complexities of managing large, world-wide organizations have been obscured by creating polar alternatives between centralization and decentralization, or between global and multidomestic strategies (e.g. Hout et al., 1982). Complex management tasks have been seen as composites of simple global and local components. By emphasizing the importance of rationalizing the flow of components and final products within a multinational system, the importance of internal flows of people, technology, information, and values has been de-emphasized.

Differences among authors writing on the topic of global strategy are not limited to concepts and perspectives. Their prescriptions on how to manage globally have also been very different, and often contradictory.

(1) Levitt (1983) has argued that effective global strategy is not a bag of many tricks but the successful practice of just one: product standardization. According to him, the core of a global strategy lies in developing a standardized product to be produced and sold the same way throughout the world.

(2) According to Hout et al. (1982), on the other hand, effective global strategy requires the approach not of a hedgehog, who knows only one trick, but that of a fox, who knows many. Exploiting economies of scale through global volume, taking pre-emptive positions through quick and large investments, and managing interdependently to achieve synergies across different activities are, according to these authors, some of the more important moves that a winning global strategist must muster.

(3) Hamel and Prahalad's (1985) prescription for a global strategy contradicts that of Levitt (1983) even more sharply. Instead of a single standardized product, they recommend a broad product portfolio, with many product varieties, so that investments on technologies and distribution channels can be shared. Cross-subsidization across products and markets, and the development of a strong world-wide distribution system, are the two moves that find the pride of place in these authors' views on how to succeed in the game of global chess.

(4) If Hout et al.'s (1982) global strategist is the heavyweight champion who knocks out opponents with scale and pre-emptive investments, Kogut's (1985b) global strategist is the nimble-footed athlete who wins through flexibility and arbitrage. He creates options so as to

turn the uncertainties of an increasingly volatile global economy to his own advantage. Multiple sourcing, production shifting to benefit from changing factor costs and exchange rates, and arbitrage to exploit imperfections in financial and information markets are, according to Kogut, some of the hallmarks of a superior global strategy.

These are only a few of the many prescriptions available to MNC managers about how to build a global strategy for their firms. All these suggestions have been derived from rich and insightful analyses of real-life situations. They are all reasonable and intuitively appealing, but their managerial implications are not easy to reconcile.

THE NEED FOR AN ORGANIZING FRAMEWORK

The difficulty for both practitioners and researchers in dealing with the small but rich literature on global strategies is that there is no organizing framework within which the different perspectives and prescriptions can be assimilated. An unfortunate fact of corporate life is that any particular strategic action is rarely an unmixed blessing. Corporate objectives are multi-dimensional, and often mutually contradictory. Contrary to received wisdom, it is also usually difficult to prioritize them. Actions to achieve a particular objective often impede another equally important objective. Each of these prescriptions is aimed at achieving certain objectives of a global strategy. An overall framework can be particularly useful in identifying the trade-offs between those objectives and therefore in understanding not only the benefits but also the potential costs associated with the different strategic alternatives.

The objective of this paper is to suggest such an organizing framework which may help managers and academics in formulating the various issues that arise in global strategic management. The underlying premise is that simple categorization schemes such as the distinction between global and multidomestic strategies are not very helpful in understanding the complexities of corporate-level strategy in large multinational corporations. Instead, what may be more useful is to understand what the key strategic objectives of an MNC are, and the tools that it possesses for achieving them. An integrated analysis of the different means and the different ends can help both managers and researchers in formulating, describing, classifying and analysing the content of global strategies. Besides, such a framework can relate academic research, that is often partial, to the totality of real life that managers must deal with.

THE FRAMEWORK: MAPPING MEANS AND ENDS

The proposed framework is shown in Table 1. While the specific construct may be new, the conceptual foundation on which it is built is derived from a synthesis of existing literature.

The basic argument is simple. The goals of a multinational—as indeed of any organization—can be classified into three broad categories. The firm must achieve efficiency in its current activities; it must manage the risks that it assumes in carrying out those activities; and it must develop internal learning capabilities so as to be able to innovate and adapt to future changes. Competitive advantage is developed by taking strategic actions that optimize the firm's achievement of these different and, at times, conflicting goals.

A multinational has three sets of tools for developing such competitive advantage. It can exploit the differences in input and output markets among the many countries in which it operates. It can benefit from scale economies in its different activities. It can also exploit synergies or economies of scope that may be available because of the diversity of its activities and organization.

The strategic task of managing globally is to use all three sources of competitive advantage to optimize efficiency, risk and learning simultaneously in a world-wide business. The key to a successful global strategy is to manage the interactions between these different goals and means. That, in essence, is the organizing framework. Viewing the tasks of global strategy this way can be helpful to both managers and academics in a number of ways. For example, it can help managers in generating a comprehensive checklist of factors and issues that must be considered in reviewing different strategic alternatives. Such a checklist can serve as a basis for mapping the overall strategies of their own companies and those of their competitors so as to understand the comparative strengths and vulnerabilities of both. Table 1 shows some illustrative examples of factors that must be considered while carrying out such comprehensive strategic audits. Another practical utility of the framework is that it can highlight the contradictions between the different goals and between the different means, and thereby make salient the strategic dilemmas that may otherwise get resolved through omission.

Table 1. Global strategy: an organizing framework

Strategic objectives	Sources of competitive advantage		
	National differences	Scale economies	Scope economies
Achieving efficiency in current operations	Benefiting from differences in factor costs—wages and cost of capital	Expanding and exploiting potential scale economies in each activity	Sharing of investments and costs across products, markets and businesses
Managing risks	Managing different kinds of risks arising from market or policy-induced changes in comparative advantages of different countries	Balancing scale with strategic and operational flexibility	Portfolio diversification of risks and creation of options and side-bets
Innovation learning and adaptation	Learning from societal differences in organizational and managerial processes and systems	Benefiting from experience—cost reduction and innovation	Shared learning across organizational components in different products, markets or businesses

In the next two sections the framework is explained more fully by describing the two dimensions of its construct, viz. the strategic objectives of the firm and the sources of competitive advantage available to a multinational corporation. Subsequent sections show how selected articles contribute to the literature and fit within the overall framework. The paper concludes with a brief discussion of the trade-offs that are implicit in some of the more recent prescriptions on global strategic management.

THE GOALS: STRATEGIC OBJECTIVES

Achieving efficiency

A general premise in the literature on strategic management is that the concept of strategy is relevant only when the actions of one firm can affect the actions or performance of another. Firms competing in imperfect markets earn different 'efficiency rents' from the use of their resources (Caves, 1980). The objective of strategy, given this perspective, is to enhance such efficiency rents.

Viewing a firm broadly as an input–output system, the overall efficiency of the firm can be defined as the ratio of the value of its outputs to the costs of all its inputs. It is by maximizing this ratio that the firm obtains the surplus resources required to secure its own future. Thus it differentiates its products to enhance the exchange value of its outputs, and seeks low cost factors to minimize the costs of its inputs. It also tries to enhance the efficiency of its throughput processes by achieving higher scale economies or by finding more efficient production processes.

The field of strategic management is currently dominated by this efficiency perspective. The generic strategies of Porter (1980), different versions of the portfolio model, as well as overall strategic management frameworks such as those proposed by Hofer and Schendel (1978) and Hax and Majluf (1984) are all based on the underlying notion of maximizing efficiency rents of the different resources available to the firm.

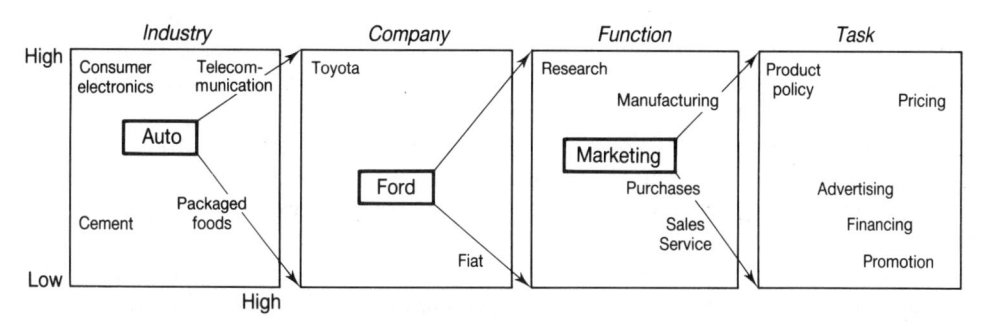

Figure 1. The Integration-Responsiveness Framework. (Reproduced from Bartlett, 1985.)

In the field of global strategy this efficiency perspective has been reflected in the widespread use of the integration-responsiveness framework originally proposed by Prahalad (1975) and subsequently developed and applied by a number of authors including Doz, Bartlett and Prahalad (1981) and Porter (1984). In essence, the framework is a conceptual lens for visualizing the cost advantages of global integration of certain tasks *vis-à-vis* the differentiation benefits of responding to national differences in tastes, industry structures, distribution systems, and government regulations. As suggested by Bartlett (1985), the same framework can be used to understand differences in the benefits of integration and responsiveness at the aggregate level of industries, at the level of individual companies within an industry, or even at the level of different functions within a company (see Figure 1, reproduced from Bartlett, 1985). Thus the consumer electronics industry may be characterized by low differentiation benefits and high integration advantages, while the position of the packaged foods industry may be quite the opposite. In the telecommunications switching industry, in contrast, both local and global forces may be strong, while in the automobile industry both may be of moderate and comparable importance.

Within an industry (say, automobile), the strategy of one firm (such as Toyota) may be based on exploiting the advantages of global integration through centralized production and decision-making, while that of another (such as Fiat) may aim at exploiting the benefits of national differentiation by creating integrated and autonomous subsidiaries which can exploit strong links with local stakeholders to defend themselves against more efficient global competitors. Within a firm, research may offer greater efficiency benefits of integration, while sales and service may provide greater differentiation advantages. One can, as illustrated in Figure 1, apply the framework to even lower levels of analysis, right down to the level of individual tasks. Based on such analysis, a multinational firm can determine the optimum way to configure its value chain so as to achieve the highest overall efficiency in the use of its resources (Porter, 1984).

However, while efficiency is clearly an important strategic objective, it is not the only one. As argued recently by a number of authors, the broader objective of strategic management is to create value which is determined not only by the returns that specific assets are expected to generate, but also by the risks that are assumed in the process (see Woo and Cool (1985) for a review). This leads to the second strategic objective of firms—that of managing risks.[1]

Managing risks

A multinational corporation (MNC) faces many different kinds of risks, some of which are endemic to all firms and some others are unique to organizations operating across national boundaries. For analytical simplicity these different kinds of risks may be collapsed into four broad categories.

First, an MNC faces certain *macroeconomic risks* which are completely outside its control. These include cataclysmic events such as wars and natural calamities, and also equilibrium-seeking or even random movements in wage rates, interest rates, exchange rates, commodity prices, and so on.

Second, the MNC faces what are usually referred to in the literature as political risks but may be more appropriately called *policy risks* to emphasize that they arise from policy actions of national governments and not from either long-term equilibrium-seeking forces of global markets, nor from short-term random fluctuations in economic variables arising out of stickiness or unpredictability of market mechanisms. The net effect of such policy actions may often be indistinguishable from the effect of macroeconomic forces; for example, both may lead to changes in the exchange rate of a particular currency. But from a management perspective the two must be distinguished, since the former is uncontrollable but the latter is at least partially controllable.

Third, a firm also faces certain *competitive risks* arising from the uncertainties of competitors' responses to its own strategies (including the strategy of doing nothing and trying to maintain the status quo). While all companies face such risks to varying extents (since both monopolies and perfect competition are rare), their implications are particularly complex in the context of global strategies since the responses of competitors may take place in many different forms and in many different markets. Further, technological risk can also be considered as a part of com-

---

1. In the interest of simplicity the distinction between risk and uncertainty is ignored, as is the distinction between systematic and unsystematic risks.

petitive risk since a new technology can adversely affect a firm only when it is adopted by a competitor, and not otherwise.[2]

Finally, a firm also faces what may be called *resource risks*. This is the risk that the adopted strategy will require resources that the firm does not have, cannot acquire, or cannot spare. A key scarce resource for most firms is managerial talent. But resource risks can also arise from lack of appropriate technology, or even capital (if managers, for reasons of control, do not want to use capital markets, or if the market is less efficient than finance theorists would have us believe).

One important issue with regard to risks is that they change over time. Vernon (1977) has highlighted this issue in the context of policy risks, but the same is true of the others. Consider resource risks as an example. Often the strategy of a multinational will assume that appropriate resources will be acquired as the strategy unfolds. Yet the initial conditions on which the plans for on-going resource acquisition and development have been based may change over time. Nissan, for instance, based its aggressive internationalization strategy on the expectation of developing technological, financial, and managerial resources out of its home base. Changing competitive positions among local car manufacturers in Japan have affected these resource development plans of the company, and its internationalizing strategy has been threatened significantly. A more careful analysis of alternative competitive scenarios, and of their effects on the resource allocation plans of the company, may have led Nissan to either a slower pace of internationalization, or to a more aggressive process of resource acquisition at an earlier stage of implementing its strategy.

The strategic task, with regard to management of risks, is to consider these different kinds of risks *jointly* in the context of particular strategic decisions. However, not all forms of risk are strategic since some risks can be easily diversified, shifted, or shared through routine market transactions. It is only those risks which cannot be diversified through a readily available external market that are of concern at the strategic level.

As an example, consider the case of currency risks. These can be classified as contractual, semicontractual and operating risks (Lessard and Lightstone, 1983). Contractual risks arise when a firm enters into a contract for which costs and revenues are expected to be generated in different currencies: for example a Japanese firm entering into a contract for supplying an item to be made in Japan to an American customer at a price fixed in dollars. Semicontractual risks are assumed when a firm offers an option denominated in foreign currencies, such as a British company quoting a firm rate in guilders. Operating risks, on the other hand, refer to exchange rate-related changes in the firm's competitiveness arising out of long-term commitments of revenues or costs in different currencies. For example, to compete with a Korean firm, an American firm may set up production facilities in Singapore for supplying its customers in the United States and Europe. A gradual strengthening of the Singapore dollar, in comparison with the Korean won, can erode the overall competitiveness of the Singapore plant.

Both contractual and semicontractual currency risks can be easily shifted or diversified, at relatively low cost, through various hedging mechanisms. If a firm does not so hedge these risks, it is essentially operating as a currency speculator and the risks must be associated with the speculation business and not to its product-market operations. Operating risks, on the other hand, cannot be hedged so easily,[3] and must be considered at the strategic rather than the operational level.

2. This assumes that the firm has defined its business correctly and has identified as competitors all the firms whose offerings are aimed at meeting the same set of market needs that the firm meets.
3. Some market mechanisms such as long-term currency swaps are now available which can allow at least partial hedging of operating risks.

Analysis of strategic risks will have significant implications for a firm's decisions regarding the structures and locations of its cost and revenue streams. It will lead to more explicit analysis of the effects of environmental uncertainties on the configuration of its value chain. There may be a shift from ownership to rental of resources; from fixed to variable costs. Output and activity distributions may be broadened to achieve the benefits of diversification. Incrementalism and opportunism may be given greater emphasis in its strategy in comparison to pre-emptive resource commitments and long-term planning. Overall strategies may be formulated in more general and flexible terms, so as to be robust to different environmental scenarios. In addition, side-bets may be laid to cover contingencies and to create strategic options which may or may not be exercised in the future (see Kogut, 1985b; Aaker and Mascarenhas, 1984; Mascarenhas, 1982).

Innovation, learning and adaptation

Most existing theories of the multinational corporation view it as an instrument to extract additional rents from capabilities internalized by the firm (see Calvet, 1981, for a review). A firm goes abroad to make more profits by exploiting its technology, or brand name, or management capabilities in different countries around the world. It is assumed that the key competencies of the multinational always reside at the centre.

While the search for additional profits or the desire to protect existing revenues may explain why multinationals come to exist, they may not provide an equally complete explanation of why some of them continue to grow and flourish. An alternative view may well be that a key asset of the multinational is the diversity of environments in which it operates. This diversity exposes it to multiple stimuli, allows it to develop diverse capabilities, and provides it with a broader learning opportunity than is available to a purely domestic firm. The enhanced organizational learning that results from the diversity internalized by the multinational may be a key explanator of its ongoing success, while its initial stock of knowledge may well be the strength that allows it to create such organizational diversity in the first place (Bartlett and Ghoshal, 1985).

Internal diversity may lead to strategic advantages for a firm in many different ways. In an unpredictable environment it may not be possible, ex ante, to predict the competencies that will be required in the future. Diversity of internal capabilities, following the logic of population ecologists (e.g. Hannan and Freeman, 1977; Aldrich, 1979), will enhance the probability of the firm's survival by enhancing the chances that it will be in possession of the capabilities required to cope with an uncertain future state. Similarly, diversity of resources and competencies may also enhance the firm's ability to create joint innovations, and to exploit them in multiple locations. One example of such benefits of diversity was recently described in the *Wall Street Journal* (April 29, 1985):

> P&G [Procter and Gamble Co.] recently introduced its new Liquid Tide, but the product has a distinctly international heritage. A new ingredient that helps suspend dirt in wash water came from the company's research centre near P&G's Cincinnati headquarters. But the formula for Liquid Tide's surfactants, or cleaning agents, was developed by P&G technicians in Japan. The ingredients that fight mineral salts present in hard water came from P&G's scientists in Brussels.

As discussed in the same *WSJ* article, P&G's research centre in Brussels has developed a special capability in water softening technology due, in part, to the fact that water in Europe contains more than twice the level of mineral content compared to wash water available in the

United States. Similarly, surfactant technology is particularly advanced in Japan because Japanese consumers wash their clothes in colder waters compared to consumers in the US or Europe, and this makes greater demands on the cleaning ability of the surfactants. The advantage of P&G as a multinational is that it is exposed to these different operating environments and has learned, in each environment, the skills and knowledge that coping with that environment specially requires. Liquid Tide is an example of the strategic advantages that accrue from such diverse learning.

The mere existence of diversity, however, does not enhance learning. It only creates the potential for learning. To exploit this potential, the organization must consider learning as an explicit objective, and must create mechanisms and systems for such learning to take place. In the absence of explicit intention and appropriate mechanisms, the learning potential may be lost. In some companies, where all organizational resources are centralized and where the national subsidiaries are seen as mere delivery pipelines to supply the organization's value-added to different countries, diverse learning may not take place either because the subsidiaries may not possess appropriate sensing, analysing, and responding capabilities to learn from their local environments, or because the centralized decision processes may be insensitive to knowledge accumulated outside the corporate headquarters. Other companies, in which the subsidiaries may enjoy very high levels of local resources and autonomy, may similarly fail to exploit global learning benefits because of their inability to transfer and synthesize knowledge and expertise developed in different organizational components. Local loyalties, turf protection, and the 'not invented here' (NIH) syndrome—the three handmaidens of decentralization—may restrict internal flow of information across national boundaries which is essential for global learning to occur. In other words, both centralization and decentralization may impede learning.

THE MEANS: SOURCES OF COMPETITIVE ADVANTAGE

Most recent articles on global strategy have been aimed at identifying generic strategies (such as global cost leadership, focus or niche) and advocating particular strategic moves (such as cross-subsidy or pre-emptive investments). Underlying these concepts, however, are three fundamental tools for building global competitive advantage: exploiting differences in input and output markets in different countries, exploiting economies of scale, and exploiting economies of scope (Porter, 1985).

National differences

The comparative advantage of locations in terms of differences in factor costs is perhaps the most discussed, and also the best understood, source of competitive advantage in international business.

Different nations have different factor endowments, and in the absence of efficient markets this leads to inter-country differences in factor costs. Different activities of the firm, such as R&D, production, marketing, etc., have different factor intensities. A firm can therefore gain cost advantages by configuring its value-chain so that each activity is located in the country which has the least cost for the factor that the activity uses most intensely. This is the core concept of comparative advantage-based competitive advantage—a concept for which highly developed analytical tools are available from the discipline of international economics. Kogut (1985a) provides an excellent managerial overview of this concept.

National differences may also exist in output markets. Customer tastes and preferences may be different in different countries, as may be distribution systems, government regulations applicable to the concerned product-markets, or the effectiveness of different promotion strategies and other marketing techniques. A firm can augment the exchange value of its output by tailoring its offerings to fit the unique requirements in each national market. This, in essence, is the strategy of national differentiation, and it lies at the core of what has come to be referred to as the multidomestic approach in multinational management (Hout *et al.*, 1982).

From a strategic perspective, however, this static and purely economic view of national differences may not be adequate. What may be more useful is to take a dynamic view of comparative advantage and to broaden the concept to include both societal and economic factors.

In the traditional economics view, comparative advantages of countries are determined by their relative factor endowments and they do not change. However, in reality one lesson of the past four decades is that comparative advantages change and a prime objective of the industrial policies of many nations is to effect such changes. Thus, for any nation, the availability and cost of capital change, as do the availability of technical manpower and the wages of skilled and unskilled labour. Such changes take place, in the long run, to accommodate different levels of economic and social performance of nations, and in the short run they occur in response to specific policies and regulations of governments.

This dynamic aspect of comparative advantages adds considerable complexity to the strategic considerations of the firm. There is a first-order effect of such changes—such as possible increases in wage rates, interest rates or currency exchange rates for particular countries that can affect future viability of a strategy that has been based on the current levels of these economic variables. There can also be a more intriguing second-order effect. If an activity is located in an economically inefficient environment, and if the firm is able to achieve a higher level of efficiency in its own operations compared to the rest of the local economy, its competitive advantage may actually increase as the local economy slips lower and lower. This is because the macroeconomic variables such as wage or exchange rates may change to reflect the overall performance of the economy relative to the rest of the world and, to the extent that the firm's performance is better than this national aggregate, it may benefit from these macro-level changes (Kiechel, 1981).

Consistent with the discipline that gave birth to the concept, the usual view of comparative advantage is limited to factors that an economist admits into the production function, such as the costs of labour and capital. However, from a managerial perspective it may be more appropriate to take a broader view of societal comparative advantages to include 'all the relative advantages conferred on a society by the quality, quantity and configuration of its material, human and institutional resources, including 'soft' resources such as inter-organizational linkages, the nature of its educational system, and organizational and managerial know-how' (Westney, 1985, p.4). As argued by Westney, these 'soft' societal factors, if absorbed in the overall organizational system, can provide benefits as real to a multinational as those provided by such economic factors as cheap labour or low-cost capital.

While the concept of comparative advantage is quite clear, available evidence on its actual effect on the overall competitiveness of firms is weak and conflicting. For example, it has often been claimed that one source of competitive advantage for Japanese firms is the lower cost of capital in Japan (Hatsopoulos, 1983). However, more systematic studies have shown that there is practically no difference in the risk-adjusted cost of capital in the United States and Japan, and that capital cost advantages of Japanese firms, if any, arise from complex interactions between government subsidies and corporate ownership structures (Flaherty and Itami, 1984). Similarly, relatively low wage rates in Japan have been suggested by some authors as the primary reason for the success of Japanese companies in the US market (Itami, 1978). However, recently, companies such as Honda and Nissan have commissioned plants in the USA and have been able to retain practically the same levels of cost advantages over US manufacturers as they had for their production in Japan (Allen, 1985). Overall, there is increasing evidence that while comparative advantages of countries can provide competitive advantages to firms, the realization of such benefits is not automatic but depends on complex organizational factors and processes.

Scale economies

Scale economies, again, is a fairly well established concept, and its implications for competitive advantage are quite well understood. Microeconomic theory provides a strong theoretical and empirical basis for evaluating the effect of scale on cost reduction, and the use of scale as a competitive tool is common in practice. Its primary implication for strategy is that a firm must expand the volume of its output so as to achieve available scale benefits. Otherwise a competitor who can achieve such volume can build cost advantages, and this can lead to a vicious cycle in which the low-volume firm can progressively lose its competitive viability.

While scale, by itself, is a static concept, there may be dynamic benefits of scale through what has been variously described as the experience or learning effect. The higher volume that helps a firm to exploit scale benefits also allows it to accumulate learning, and this leads to progressive cost reduction as the firm moves down its learning curve.

The concept of the value-added chain recently popularized by Porter (1985) adds considerable richness to the analysis of scale as a source of competitive advantage. This conceptual apparatus allows a disaggregated analysis of scale benefits in different value-creating activities of the firm. The efficient scale may vary widely by activity—being higher for component production say, than for assembly. In contrast to a unitary view of scale, this disaggregated view permits the firm to configure different elements of its value chain to attain optimum scale economies in each.

Traditionally, scale has been seen as an unmixed blessing—something that always helps and never hurts. Recently, however, many researchers have argued otherwise (e.g. Evans, 1982). It has been suggested that scale efficiencies are obtained through increased specialization and through creation of dedicated assets and systems. The same processes cause inflexibilities and limit the firm's ability to cope with change. As environmental turbulence has increased, so has the need for strategic and operational flexibility (Mascarenhas, 1982). At the extreme, this line of argument has led to predictions of a re-emergence of the craft form of production to replace the scale-dominated assembly form (Piore and Sabel, 1984). A more typical argument has been to emphasize the need to balance scale and flexibility, through the use of modern technologies such as CAD/CAM and flexible manufacturing systems (Gold, 1982).

Scope economies

Relatively speaking, the concept of scope economies is both new and not very well understood. It is based on the notion that certain economies arise from the fact that the cost of the joint production of two or more products can be less than the cost of producing them separately. Such cost reductions can take place due to many reasons—for example resources such as information or technologies, once acquired for use in producing one item, may be available costlessly for production of other items (Baumol, Panzer and Willig, 1982).

The strategic importance of scope economies arise from a diversified firm's ability to share investments and costs across the same or different value chains that competitors, not possessing such internal and external diversity, cannot. Such sharing can take place across segments, products, or markets (Porter, 1985) and may involve joint use of different kinds of assets (see Table 2).

Table 2. Scope economies in product and market diversification

	Sources of scope economies	
	Product diversification	Market diversification
Shared physical assets	Factory automation with flexibility to produce multiple products (Ford)	Global brand name (Coca-Cola)
Shared external relations	Using common distribution channel for multiple products (Matsushita)	Servicing multinational customers world-wide (Citibank)
Shared learning	Sharing R&D in computer and communications businesses (NEC)	Pooling knowledge developed in different markets (Procter and Gamble)

A diversified firm may share physical assets such as production equipment, cash, or brand names across different businesses and markets. Flexible manufacturing systems using robots, which can be used for production of different items, is one example of how a firm can exploit such scope benefits. Cross-subsidization of markets and exploitation of a global brand name are other examples of sharing a tangible asset across different components of a firm's product and market portfolios.

A second important source of scope economies is shared external relations: with customers, suppliers, distributors, governments, and other institutions. A multinational bank like Citibank can provide relatively more effective service to a multinational customer than can a bank that operates in a single country (see Terpstra, 1982). Similarly, as argued by Hamel and Prahalad (1985), companies such as Matsushita have benefited considerably from their ability to market a diverse range of products through the same distribution channel. In another variation, Japanese trading companies have expanded into new businesses to meet different requirements of their existing customers.

Finally, shared knowledge is the third important component of scope economies. The fundamental thrust of NEC's global strategy is 'C&C'—computers and communication. The company firmly believes that its even strengths in the two technologies and resulting capabilities of merging them in-house to create new products gives it a competitive edge over global giants such as IBM and AT&T, who have technological strength in only one of these two areas. Another example of the scope advantages of shared learning is the case of Liquid Tide described earlier in this paper.

Even scope economies, however, may not be costless. Different segments, products or markets of a diversified company face different environmental demands. To succeed, a firm needs to differentiate its management systems and processes so that each of its activities can develop *external consistency* with the requirements of its own environment. The search for scope economies, on the other hand, is a search for *internal consistencies* within the firm and across its different activities. The effort to create such synergies may invariably result in some compromise with the objective of external consistency in each activity.

Further, the search for internal synergies also enhances the complexities in a firm's management processes. In the extreme, such complexities can overwhelm the organization, as it did in the case of EMI, the UK-based music, electronics, and leisure products company which attempted to manage its new CT scanner business within the framework of its existing organizational structure and processes (see EMI and the CT scanner, ICCH case 9–383–194). Certain parts of a company's portfolio of businesses or markets may be inherently very different from some others. and it may be best not to look for economies of scope across them. For example, in the soft drinks industry, bottling and distribution are intensely local in scope while the tasks of creating and maintaining a brand image, or that of designing efficient bottling plants, may offer significant benefits from global integration. Carrying out both these sets of functions in-house would clearly lead to internalizing enormous differences within the company with regard to the organizing, coordinating, and controlling tasks. Instead of trying to cope with these complexities, Coca-Cola has externalized those functions which are purely local in scope (in all but some key strategic markets). In a variation of the same theme, IBM has 'externalized' the PC business by setting up an almost stand-alone organization, instead of trying to exploit scope benefits by integrating this business within the structure of its existing organization (for a more detailed discussion on multinational scope economies and on the conflicts between internal and external consistencies, see Lorange, Scott Morton and Ghoshal, 1986).

PRESCRIPTIONS IN PERSPECTIVE

Existing literature on global strategy offers analytical insights and helpful prescriptions for almost all the different issues indicated in Table 1. Table 3 shows a selective list of relevant publications, categorized on the basis of issues that, according to this author's interpretations, the pieces primarily focus on.[4]

Pigeon-holing academic contributions into different parts of a conceptual framework tends to be unfair to their authors. In highlighting what the authors focus on, such categorization often amounts to an implicit criticism for what they did not write. Besides, most publications cover a broader range of issues and ideas than can be reflected in any such categorization scheme. Table 3 suffers from all these deficiencies. At the same time, however, it suggests how the proposed framework can be helpful in integrating the literature and in relating the individual pieces to each other.

4. From an academic point of view, strategy of the multinational corporation is a specialized and highly applied field of study. It is built on the broader field of business policy and strategy which, in turn, rests on the foundation of a number of academic disciplines such as economics, organization theory, finance theory, operations research, etc. A number of publications in those underlying disciplines, and a significant body of research carried out in the field of strategy, in general, provide interesting insights on the different issues highlighted in Table 1. However, given the objective of suggesting a limited list of further readings that managers may find useful, such publications have not been included in Table 3. Further, even for the more applied and prescriptive literature on global strategy, the list is only illustrative and not exhaustive.

Table 3. Selected references for further reading

Strategic objectives	Sources of competitive advantage		
	National differences	Scale economies	Scope economies
Achieving efficiency in current operations	Kogut (1985a); Itami (1978); Okimoto, Sugano and Weinstein (1984)	Hout, Porter and Rudden (1982); Levitt (1983): Doz (1978); Leontiades (1984); Gluck (1983)	Hamel and Prahalad (1985); Hout, Porter and Rudden (1982); Porter (1985); Ohmae (1985)
Managing risks	Kiechel (1981); Kobrin (1982); Poynter (1985); Lessard and Lightstone (1983); Srinivasula (1981); Herring (1983)	Evans (1982); Piore and Sabel (1984); Gold (1982); Aaker and Mascarenhas (1984)	Kogut (1985b); Lorange, Scott Morton and Ghoshal (1986)
Innovation, learning and adaption	Westney (1985); Terpstra (1977); Ronstadt and Krammer (1982)	BCG (1982); Rapp (1978)	Bartlett and Ghoshal (1985)

From parts to the whole

For managers, the advantage of such synthesis is that it allows them to combine a set of insightful but often partial analyses to address the totality of a multidimensional and complex phenomenon. Consider, for example, a topic that has been the staple for academics interested in international management: explaining and drawing normative conclusions from the global successes of many Japanese companies. Based on detailed comparisons across a set of matched pairs of US and Japanese firms, Itami concludes that the relative successes of the Japanese firms can be wholly explained as due to the advantages of lower wage rates and higher labour productivity. In the context of a specific industry, on the other hand, Toder (1978) shows that manufacturing scale is the single most important source of the Japanese competitive advantage. In the small car business, for example, the minimum efficient scale requires an annual production level of about 400 000 units. In the late 1970s no US auto manufacturer produced even 200 000 units of any subcompact configuration vehicle, while Toyota produced around 500 000 Corollas and Nissan produced between 300 000 and 400 000 B210s per year. Toder estimates that US manufacturers, suffered a cost disadvantage of between 9% and 17% on account of inefficient scale alone. Add to it the effects of wage rate differentials and exchange rate movements, and Japanese success in the US auto market may not require any further explanation. Yet process-orientated scholars such as Hamel and Prahalad suggest a much more complex explanation of the Japanese tidal wave. They see it as arising out of a dynamic process of strategic evolution that exploits scope economies as a crucial weapon in the final stages. All these authors provide compelling arguments to support their own explanations, but do not consider or refute each other's hypotheses.

This multiplicity of explanations only shows the complexity of global strategic management. However, though different, these explanations and prescriptions are not always mutually exclusive. The manager's task is to find how these insights can be combined to build a multidimensional and flexible strategy that is robust to the different assumptions and explanations.

The strategic trade-offs

This, however, is not always possible because there are certain inherent contradictions between the different strategic objectives and between the different sources of competitive advantage. Consider, for instance, the popular distinction between a global and a multidomestic strategy described by Hout *et al.* (1982). A global strategy requires that the firm should carefully separate different value elements, and should locate each activity at the most efficient level of scale in the location where the activity can be carried out at the cheapest cost. Each activity should then be integrated and managed interdependently so as to exploit available scope economies. In essence, it is a strategy to maximize efficiency of current operations.

Such a strategy may, however, increase both endogenous and exogenous risks for the firm. Global scale of certain activities such as R&D and manufacturing may result in the firm's costs being concentrated in a few countries, while its revenues accrue globally, from sales in many different countries. This increases the operating exposure of the firm to the vicissitudes of exchange rate movements because of the mismatch between the currencies in which revenues are obtained and those in which costs are incurred. Similarly, the search for efficiency in a global business may lead to greater amounts of intra-company but inter-country, flows of goods, capital, information and other resources. These flows are visible, salient and tend to attract policy interventions from different host governments. Organizationally, such an integrated system requires a high degree of coordination, which enhances the risks of management failures. These are lessons that many Japanese companies have learned well recently.

Similarly, consideration of the learning objective will again contradict some of the proclaimed benefits of a global strategy. The implementation of a global strategy tends to enhance the forces of centralization and to shift organizational power from the subsidiaries to the headquarters. This may result in demotivation of subsidiary managers and may erode one key asset of the MNC—the potential for learning from its many environments. The experiences of Caterpillar is a case in point. An exemplary practitioner of global strategy, Cat has recently spilled a lot of red ink on its balance sheet and has lost ground steadily to its archrival, Komatsu. Many factors contributed to Caterpillar's woes, not the least of which was the inability of its centralized management processes to benefit from the experiences of its foreign subsidiaries.

On the flipside of the coin, strategies aimed at optimizing risk or learning may compromise current efficiency. Poynter (1985) has recommended 'upgrade', i.e. increasing commitment of technology and resources in subsidiaries, as a way to overcome risk of policy interventions by host governments. Kogut (1985b), Mascarenhas (1982) and many others have suggested creating strategic and operational flexibility as a mechanism for coping with macroenvironmental risks. Bartlett and Ghoshal (1985) have proposed the differentiated network model of multinational organizations as a way to operationalize the benefits of global learning. All these recommendations carry certain efficiency penalties, which the authors have ignored.

Similar trade-offs exist between the different sources of competitive advantages. Trying to make the most of factor cost economies may prevent scale efficiency, and may impede benefiting from synergies across products or functions. Trying to benefit from scope through product diversification may affect scale, and so on. In effect these contradictions between the different strategic objectives, and between the different means for achieving them, lead to trade-offs between each cell in the framework and practically all others.

These trade-offs imply that to formulate and implement a global strategy, MNC managers must consider all the issues suggested in Table 1, and must evaluate the implications of different strategic alternatives on each of these issues. Under a particular set of circumstances a particular strategic objective may dominate and a particular source of competitive advantage may play a more important role than the others (Fayerweather, 1981). The complexity of global strategic management arises from the need to understand those situational contingencies, and to adopt a strategy after evaluating the trade-offs it implies. Existing prescriptions can sensitize MNC managers to the different factors they must consider, but cannot provide ready-made and standardized solutions for them to adopt.

CONCLUSION

This paper has proposed a framework that can help MNC managers in reviewing and analysing the strategies of their firms. It is not a blueprint for formulating strategies; it is a road map for reviewing them. Irrespective of whether strategies are analytically formulated or organizationally formed (Mintzberg, 1978), every firm has a realized strategy. To the extent that the realized strategy may differ from the intended one, managers need to review what the strategies of their firms really are. The paper suggests a scheme for such a review which can be an effective instrument for exercising strategic control.

Three arguments underlie the construct of the framework. First, in the global strategy literature, a kind of industry determinism has come to prevail not unlike the technological determinism that dominated management literature in the 1960s. The structures of industries may often have important influences on the appropriateness of corporate strategy, but they are only one of many such influences. Besides, corporate strategy may influence industry structure just as much as be influenced by it.

Second, simple schemes for categorizing strategies of firms under different labels tend to hide more than they reveal. A map for more detailed comparison of the content of strategies can be more helpful to managers in understanding and improving the competitive positions of their companies.

Third, the issues of risk and learning have not been given adequate importance in the strategy literature in general, and in the area of global strategies in particular. Both these are important strategic objectives and must be explicitly considered while evaluating or reviewing the strategic positions of companies.

The proposed framework is not a replacement of existing analytical tools but an enhancement that incorporates these beliefs. It does not present any new concepts or solutions, but only a synthesis of existing ideas and techniques. The benefit of such synthesis is that it can help managers in integrating an array of strategic moves into an overall strategic thrust by revealing the consistencies and contradictions among those moves.

For academics this brief view of the existing literature on global strategy will clearly reveal the need for more empirically grounded and systematic research to test and validate the hypotheses which currently appear in the literature as prescriptions and research conclusions. For partial analyses to lead to valid conclusions, excluded variables must be controlled for, and rival hypotheses must be considered and eliminated. The existing body of descriptive and normative research is rich enough to allow future researchers to adopt a more rigorous and systematic approach to enhance the reliability and validity of their findings and suggestions. The proposed framework, it is hoped, may be of value to some researchers in thinking about appropriate research issues and designs for furthering the field of global strategic management.

ACKNOWLEDGEMENTS

The ideas presented in this paper emerged in the course of discussions with many friends and colleagues. Don Lessard, Eleanor Westney, Bruce Kogut, Chris Bartlett and Nitin Nohria were particularly helpful. I also benefited greatly from the comments and suggestions of the two anonymous referees from the *Strategic Management Journal*.

REFERENCES

Aaker, D. A. and Mascarenhas, B. (1984) 'The need for strategic flexibility'. *Journal of Business Strategy*, 5(2): 74–82.
Aldrich, H. E. (1979) *Organizations and Environments*. Prentice-Hall, Englewood Cliffs, NJ.
Allen, M. K. (1985) 'Japanese companies in the United States: the success of Nissan and Honda'. Unpublished manuscript, Sloan School of Management, MIT, November.
Bartlett C. A. (1985) 'Global competition and MNC managers'. ICCH Note No. 0-385-287, Harvard Business School, Boston.
Bartlett, C. A. and Ghoshal, S. (1985) 'The new global organization: differentiated roles and dispersed responsibilities'. Working Paper No. 9-786-013, Harvard Business School, Boston, October.
Baumol, W. J., Panzer, J. C. and Willig, R. D. (1982) *Contestable Markets and the Theory of Industry Structure*. Harcourt Brace Jovanovich, New York.
Boston Consulting Group (1982) *Perspectives on Experience*, BCG, Boston, MA.
Calvet, A. L. (1981) 'A synthesis of foreign direct investment theories and theories of the multinational firm', *Journal of International Business Studies*, Spring-Summer, pp. 43–60.
Caves, R. E. (1980) 'Industrial organization, corporate strategy and structure', *Journal of Economic Literature*, **XVIII** (March): 64–92.
Doz, Y. (1978) 'Managing manufacturing rationalization within multinational companies', *Columbia Journal of World Business*, Fall, pp. 82–94.
Doz, Y. L., Bartlett, C. A. and Prahalad, C. K. (1981) 'Global competitive pressures and host country demands: managing tensions in MNC's', *California Management Review*, Spring, pp. 63–74.
Evans, J. S. (1982) *Strategic Flexibility in Business*, Report No. 678, SRI International, December.
Fayerweather, J. (1981) 'Four winning strategies for the international corporation', *Journal of Business Strategy*, Fall, pp. 25–36.
Flaherty, M. T. and Itami, H. (1984) 'Finance', in Okimoto, D.I., T. Sugano and F. B. Weinstein (Eds), *Competitive Edge*, Stanford University Press, Stanford, CA.
Gluck, F. (1983) 'Global competition in the 1980's' *Journal of Business Strategy*, Spring, pp. 22–27.
Gold, B. (1982) 'Robotics, programmable automation, and international competitiveness', *IEEE Transactions on Engineering Management*, November.
Hamel, G. and Prahalad, C. K. (1985) 'Do you really have a global strategy?'. *Harvard Business Review*, July–August, pp. 139–148.
Hannan, M. T. and Freeman, J. (1977) 'The population ecology of organizations', *American Journal of Sociology*, **82**: 929–964.
Hatsopoulos, G. N. (1983) 'High cost of capital: handicap of American industry'. Report sponsored by the American Business Conference and Thermo-Electron Corporation, April.
Hax, A. C. and Majluf, N. S. (1984) *Strategic Management: an Integrative Perspective*. Prentice-Hall, Englewood Cliffs, NJ.
Herring, R. J. (ed.) (1983) *Managing International Risk*. Cambridge University Press, Cambridge.
Hofer, C. W. and Schendel, D. (1978) *Strategy Formulation: Analytical Concepts*. West Publishing Co., St Paul, MN.
Hout, T., Porter, M. E. and Rudden, E. (1982) 'How global companies win out'. *Harvard Business Review*, September–October, pp. 98–108.
Itami, H. (1978) 'Japanese–U.S. comparison of managerial productivity' *Japanese Economic Studies*, Fall.
Kiechel, W. (1981) 'Playing the global game'. *Fortune*, November 16, pp. 111–126.

Kobrin, S. J. (1982) *Managing Political Risk Assessment*. University of California Press, Los Angeles, CA.
Kogut, B. (1984) 'Normative observations on the international value-added chain and strategic groups'. *Journal of International Business Studies*, Fall, p. 151–167.
Kogut, B. (1985a) 'Designing global strategies: comparative and competitive value added chains'. *Sloan Management Review*, **26**(4): 15–28.
Kogut, B. (1985b) 'Designing global strategies: profiting from operational flexibility'. *Sloan Management Review*, Fall, pp. 27–38.
Leontiades, J. (1984) 'Market share and corporate strategy in international industries'. *Journal of Business Strategy*, **5**(1): pp. 30–37.
Lessard, D. and Lightstone, J. (1983) 'The impact of exchange rates on operating profits: new business and financial responses'. Mimeo, Lightstone-Lessard Associates.
Levitt, T. (1983) 'The globalization of markets'. *Harvard Business Review*, May–June, pp. 92–102.
Lorange, P., Scott Morton, M. S. and Ghoshal, S. (1986) *Strategic Control*. West Publishing Co., St Paul MN.
Mascarenhas, B. (1982) 'Coping with uncertainty in international business'. *Journal of International Business Studies*, Fall, pp. 87–98.
Mintzberg, H. (1978) 'Patterns in strategic formation'. *Management Science*, **24**: 934–948.
Ohmae, K. (1985) *Triad Power: The Coming Shape of Global Competition*. Free Press, New York.
Okimoto, D. I., Sugano, T. and Weinstein, F. B. (eds). (1984) *Competitive Edge*. Stanford University Press, Stanford, CA.
Perlmutter, H. V. (1969) 'The tortuous evolution of the multinational corporation'. *Columbia Journal of World Business*, January–February, pp. 9–18.
Piore, M. J. and Sabel, C. (1984) *The Second Industrial Divide: Possibilities and Prospects*. Basic Books, New York.
Porter, M. E. (1980) *Competitive Strategy*. Basic Books, New York.
Porter, M. E. (1984) 'Competition in global industries: a conceptual framework'. Paper presented to the Colloquium on Competition in Global Industries, Harvard Business School.
Porter, M. E. (1985) *Competitive Advantage*. Free Press, New York.
Poynter, T. A. (1985) *International Enterprises and Government Intervention*. Croom Helm, London.
Prahalad, C. K. (1975) 'The strategic process in a multinational corporation'. Unpublished doctoral dissertation, Graduate School of Business Administration, Harvard University.
Rapp, W. V. (1983) 'Strategy formulation and international competition'. *Columbia Journal of World Business*, Summer, pp. 98–112.
Robinson, R. D. (1978) *International Business Management: A Guide to Decision Making*. Dryden Press, Illinois.
Ronstadt, R. and Krammer, R. J. (1982) 'Getting the most out of innovations abroad'. *Harvard Business Review*, March–April, pp. 94–99.
Rutenberg, D. P. (1982) *Multinational Management*. Little, Brown, Boston, MA.
Srinivasula, S. (1981) 'Strategic response to foreign exchange risks'. *Columbia Journal of World Business*, Spring, pp. 13–23.
Terpstra, V. (1977) 'International product policy: the role of foreign R&D'. *Columbia Journal of World Business*, Winter, pp. 24–32.
Terpstra, V. (1982) *International Dimensions of Marketing*. Kent, Boston, MA.
Toder, E. J. (1978) *Trade Policy and the US Automobile Industry*. Praeger Special Studies, New York.
Vernon, R. (1977) *Storm Over the Multinationals*. Harvard University Press, Cambridge, MA.
The Wall Street Journal (1985) April 29, p. 1.
Westney, D. E. (1985) 'International dimensions of information and communications technology'. Unpublished manuscript, Sloan School of Management, MIT.
Woo, C. Y. and Cool, K. O. (1985) 'The impact of strategic management of systematic risk'. Mimeo, Krannert Graduate School of Management, Purdue University.

5

New Structures in MNCs Based in Small Countries: a Network Approach

Pervez Ghauri

INTRODUCTION

Much of the literature on multinationals deals with structural development of MNCs from domestic to global structure. Stopford and Wells (1972) introduced a 'stage model' for organizational structure for international firms. Their study of 187 US-based international companies states that international companies typically adapt different structures at different levels of their internationalization (Figure 1). They use two variables, 'foreign product diversity' and 'foreign sales as percentage of total sales'.

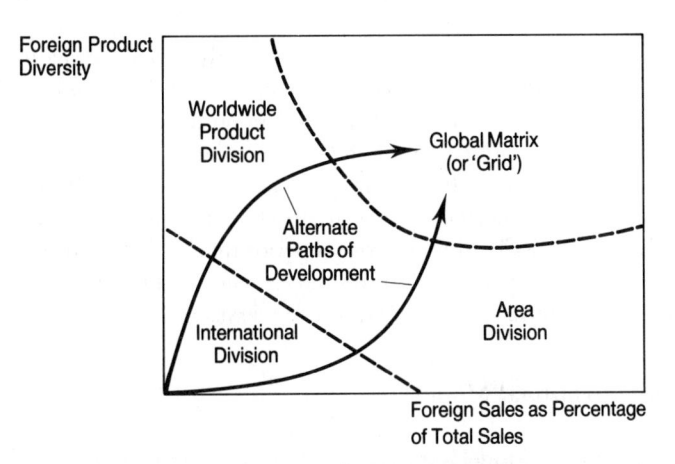

Figure 1. Stopford and Wells' (1972) International Structure Stage Model.

The model states that at an early stage of foreign expansion, companies manage foreign operations through an international division. If a company decides to expand abroad by increasing its foreign sales in different markets, it manages its foreign operations through area division, while a company that expands through product diversity manages through a worldwide product division structure. However, if the company expands through both foreign sales

This article is reprinted with kind permission of *European Management Journal*, Vol. 10 No. 3, pp.357–364.
Copyright © 1992 European Management Journal.

and foreign product diversity, it manages through a global matrix. In other words, this study leads to discussion on product- or geography-based structures and centralization or decentralization. In the past it was thought that global structure was the right form of structure for an international company, where line managers report simultaneously to another group of managers. e.g. product or area. But companies which adapted to this solution faced more conflict than cooperation within their organization and barriers of distance, language, time and culture were unhelpful (Bartlett and Ghoshal, 1989).

In a recent study, Bartlett and Ghoshal (1989) presented their 'transnational solution'. They believe that until now there have been three main types of business or structure. They present characteristics of these three under multinational, international and global structures, considering that these are both chronological and specific for companies coming from different continents.

The Multinational Organizational Model

The Multinational Organizational Model is the classic model used by prewar companies; these companies allowed their foreign offices (subsidiaries) to manage economic, political and social issues in their respective markets.

In other words 'decentralized federation'. This form was often considered a European management style, where control was exercised through personal relationships and informal contacts rather than formal structure and reporting systems. It was a decentralized system which was controlled through financial control systems as well as personal coordination.

The International Organizational Model

The International Organizational Model is a typically early postwar structure where international companies were supposed to transfer knowledge and technologies to foreign markets. The foreign offices (subsidiaries) were more dependent on their head office for development, new products and processes. More control and coordination was exercised by the head office than in multinational structures. It was classified as a 'coordinated federation'. This was, according to Bartlett and Ghoshal, a typical structure for American international firms. The head office always considered itself more superior than its international offices as it was the head office which had capabilities and resources. The subsidiaries were more dependent on the head office and control was exercised by formal systems.

The Global Organizational Model

The Global Organizational Model is the earliest global corporate form, where companies produce standard products to be shipped worldwide with a very 'tightly controlled central strategy'. It was adapted by Henry Ford, John Rockefeller, and later by the Japanese in the 1970s and 1980s. The model states that resources and capabilities are centralized at head offices while foreign offices (subsidiaries) are opened to access markets. Their role is limited to sales and service. Although in some countries, economic and political issues forced these companies to start assembly plants, the purpose is still sales and service. They do not have any freedom to develop or modify products. The term is 'central hub'. Decision-making and control are central and overseas subsidiaries depend on the centre for resources and directions. The flow of goods, resources and support is one way. This is typically a Japanese organizational structure.

The Transnational Model

According to Bartlett and Ghoshal (1989) today's companies, instead of demanding efficiency, or responsiveness, or ability to develop and exploit knowledge for success, should have all three capabilities. To achieve this, they must adopt the transnational organizational model. Innovations can be generated at several places so the company can make selective decisions, instead of being centralized or decentralized. For example, resources and capabilities can be centralized abroad. This kind of centralization would lead to scale economics.

A transnational distributes and centralizes some resources at home and some abroad, in different national operations. The company 'integrates dispersed resources through strong interdependencies', which are reciprocal. The distribution of transnational assets and resources are represented as an 'integrated network' (Figure 2).

This is an over-simplification of a complex issue. First, it is unrealistic to relate structures as different as European, American and Japanese; we can find firms from Europe following the international or global model, and many Japanese firms following the international or multi-national model. Second, by the 1970s and 1980s, several firms were adopting the 'transnational solution', i.e. different resources and capabilities centralized at different places. Firms like Philips, Shell and Unilever are good examples. The 'integrated network' is rather misleading. The network approach, developed at Uppsala, is used in a different context than the above. It is more a question of a network of relationship between the firm and its environment, e.g. suppliers, distributors, competitors, etc., then a network relationship between the head office and its subsidiaries. This 'integrated network' or 'transnational model' does not include responsiveness to the local market (network) which is one of the three capabilities a firm managing across borders should have. To understand the complex problem of managing across borders,

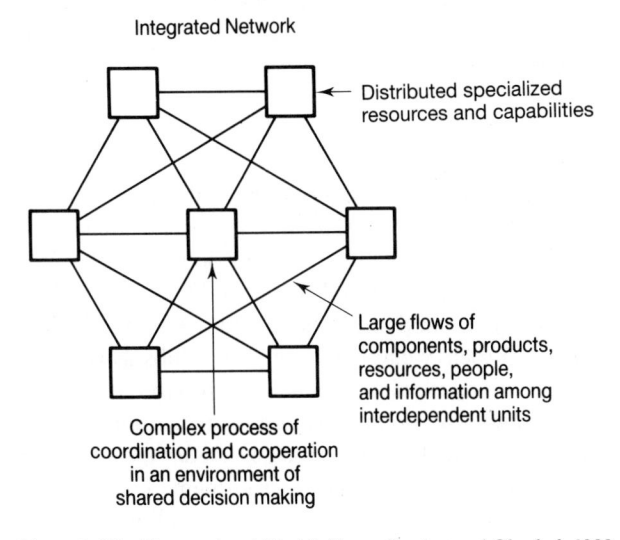

Figure 2. The Transnational Model. (*Source*: Bartlett and Ghoshal, 1989, p 89.)

one should take into consideration other issues and complexities faced by international or multinational companies.

Here, we consider an evolutionary phenomenon where foreign subsidiaries become more prominent than the parent firm. Using a network approach, it is assumed that a foreign subsidiary has a three-dimensional relationship: (1) with the head office; (2) with local authorities; (3) with the local network. Data on Swedish firms operating in Southeast Asia support the assumption that a new form of MNC structure is emerging: foreign subsidiaries are becoming more influential and independent than the parent firm. Furthermore, the emergence of a 'centre–centre' relationship suggests that some regional subsidiaries become the centre for a number of subsidiaries around them.

Here, we attempt to understand and analyse how the subsidiaries are dealing with these three-dimensional relationships and to see if there is any factual basis for this behaviour. We try to explain how subsidiaries are dealing with issues and policies of the head office which conflict with demands of the local network.

The study is based on primary data gathered from all Swedish firms having wholly- or partly-owned subsidiaries in Thailand, The Philippines and Indonesia. The data were collected through personal interviews with area managers at the head office of each firm in Sweden and with the managing director of each subsidiary in the respective foreign country. In some cases, the marketing managers of the subsidiaries were also interviewed. Firms such as Atlas Copco, Electrolux, Nitro Nobel, Swedish Match, Sandvik, ASEA (now Asea Brown Boveri) and Volvo are included. We believe that our conclusions regarding the independence of foreign subsidiaries/affiliates of Swedish MNCs are likely to be conservative, as they are based on data for Asian subsidiaries. Subsidiaries in large economies like the US are likely be even more independent.

THE SWEDISH MODEL

The involvement of Swedish firms in international markets dates as far back as the 1870s. By the 1890s, several firms such as AGA, Alfa Laval, Nitroglycerin, and Ericsson, were manufacturing abroad. The decades immediately after World War II were a golden era for Swedish international business activities and by the 1960s most of them were involved in international marketing. Innovation capabilities and a well-established network of relationships have been important factors in their success.

The literature on multinational firms focuses on traditional firms from large countries such as the US (Franko, 1976; Kindleberger, 1979; Aggarwal, 1988). Research on Swedish firms and their international marketing activities is rather limited (Johanson and Wiedersheim-Paul, 1975, for the internationalization process; and (Kaynak and Ghauri, 1987, for export behaviour). There have been some studies on Swedish firms and their activities in Western Europe (Jagren and Horwitz, 1984). In them it has been stated that subsidiaries of major European multinationals (e.g. Siemens, Philips, Nestlé) overwhelm their parent firms (Eliasson, 1988).

The phenomenon of subsidiaries becoming more influential and independent has not been systematically studied. In the early 1980s there was a government committee report (1983) on the impact of inward and outward foreign direct investment. Hedlund and Aman (1984) following Stopford and Wells (1972) and Franko (1976) looked at the structural development of multinational companies and explained how the structure of these firms developed from domestic to global. Hedlund and Aman (1984) presented a 'Swedish model' of managing foreign subsidiaries, containing the following key strategic and structural components:

- Swedish firms were competing on the basis of advanced technology, superior products, and premium prices.
- They had been producing for industrial buyers.
- Early internationalization.
- Low product diversity, expansion only in related areas.
- International expansion through 'green-field' investments.
- Mother–daughter structure, with subsidiaries reporting directly to the president of the parent company.
- More autonomy for subsidiary managers as compared to subsidiaries from other countries.
- Extended personal networks of close contacts between headquarters, and important foreign subsidiaries.
- Informal personalized control through information sharing and common experience.
- Strong position of managers with a technical/manufacturing background.

INTERNATIONAL GROWTH OF SWEDISH FIRMS

Initially, Swedish firms found an early market in Europe where countries needed Swedish raw materials and other products to rebuild their infrastructure after the Second World War. This was not the only factor in the success of Swedish firms abroad, however. Strong demand in the European market and abolition of trade restrictions after the war, helped Swedish firms expand internationally.

In 1965, 82 Swedish firms had 800 overseas manufacturing and sales subsidiaries with 170 000 employees. However, in the growth of Swedish multinationals, the 1970s and 1980s were crucial. Their ability to serve foreign markets through exports alone declined, and they had to increase activities involving FDI to protect these markets. In terms of expansion, there were two groups of firms: (1) those that started international activity long before the two World Wars, such as AGA, Alfa Laval, SKF, ASEA, and Swedish Match (Johanson and Wiedersheim-Paul, 1975); (2) those which began after World War II, such as Volvo, Electrolux, and Saab.

Most Swedish firms, such as ASEA, Atlas Copco, Sandvik, Nitro Nobel, and Volvo, became international in a traditional way. They started their activities first in the adjacent markets of Europe and later on went to Southeast Asia. They followed traditional modes of internationalization, starting first with an agent which was then converted into a sales subsidiary and only later into a manufacturing subsidiary. Swedish firms are generally among the world leaders in their product areas. Evidence from our studies reveals that the firms' knowledge of the market and relationship with all the actors are more important elements of competitive strategies than low cost production (Swedenborg, 1982).

The foreign operation of larger Swedish firms, even in the 1970s, illustrates the above point. Table 1 provides a list of the 30 largest Swedish firms ranked in terms of their total sales and the part/percentage of sales derived from foreign markets.

These firms are large compared to other international firms. Most of them produce special products for relatively small international market niches where a network of relationships is more important than the price.

Table 1. Largest Swedish firms in terms of 1986 sales

Rank	Name	Sales	Foreign Sales	% FS
		(Millions of SEK)		
1	Volvo	84 090	70 604	84
2	Electrolux	53 090	43 434	82
3	ASEA	46 031	33 447	73
4	Saab-Scania	35 222	23 247	66
5	Ericsson	32 278	25 177	78
6	KF	29 476	4 185	14
7	ICA	28 469	na	—
8	Televerket	26 340	na	—
9	Carnegie	20 411	na	—
10	SKF	20 232	19 220	95
11	SJ	16 431	na	—
12	Skanska	16 103	2 632	16
13	SCA	15 303	10 406	68
14	Procordia	15 299	4 950	32
15	Nordstjernan	15 251	7 000	46
16	Vattenfall	15 207	na	—
17	Stora	13 238	6 863	52
18	SSAB	13 010	5 204	40
19	Sandvik	12 721	11 652	92
20	Boliden	12 384	6 232	50
21	Postverket	11 956	na	—
22	Systembolaget	11 922	na	—
23	A. Johanson & Co.	11 543	na	—
24	Nobel Industries	11 535	6 865	60
25	Esselte	11 251	7 421	66
26	Swedish Match	10 912	7 976	73
27	Flakt (Asea)	10 352	8 075	78
28	Atlas Copco	10 351	na	—
29	Alfa-Laval	10 300	na	—
30	ABV	9 661	1 700	18

Notes: na: not available; %FS: foreign sales as a percentage of total sales; SEK: Swedish krona.
Source: Veckans Affärer No. 38/17 (September 1987 and Company Annual Reports).

The major part of Swedish FDI is undertaken by larger firms with more than 500 employees abroad. The 30 largest firms have between 2 000 and 60 000 employees outside Sweden. According to Swedenborg (1982), approximately one-third of the 118 Swedish firms having manufacturing abroad, accounted for 90% of the employees of these firms outside of Sweden. Table 2 shows the 1965–1985 trend in employment by Swedish affiliates abroad.

Table 2. Employment abroad in foreign subsidiaries of Swedish firms.

Year	1965	1970	1978	1981	1985
Number of employees (thousands)	171	122	301	326	329
Percentage of employment in manufacturing industry in Sweden	1	24	33	39	43

Source: Government Proposition 1986/1987, Central Bank of Sweden, 74, app. 3, p. 299.

There has been considerable growth in Swedish FDI. These firms have expanded their activities abroad and at home.

THE NETWORK APPROACH

Here, we examine the operating characteristics and recent evolution of Swedish MNCs using a framework based on the network approach. According to this approach, a firm has to develop various relationships to acquire raw material, components, and other factors of production. It also has to sell and distribute its products. These relationships have to be developed and nurtured, both before and after the firm operates in the production chain, with subcontractors, suppliers, distributors, and wholesalers. The firm also has to develop relationships (liaison) with other organizations in the same network, such as competitors, local authorities and other third parties working in the same industry (Johanson and Mattsson, 1988; Ghauri, 1988).

In the existing literature, multinationals (MNCs) are portrayed as working with a strong head office that controls and coordinates its subsidiaries around the globe (Swedenborg, 1982; Hedlund and Aman, 1984). Top management in these firms is, therefore, assumed to formulate an overall strategy and control for all the units. According to this view the MNC functions with a strong head office, 'centre', and a number of subsidiaries, 'peripheries', as illustrated by Figure 3.

A new stage of multinational structure is emerging after the global stage, as noted by Stopford and Wells (1972) and also the head office/subsidiary relationship is changing. This is contrary to Bartlett and Ghoshal (1989). The changing relationship is a step further in the internationalization process of the firm. The concept was introduced earlier by Ghauri (1990) and Aggarwal and Ghauri (1989), and we can see the emergence of a number of centres within the same firm. Due to their size and importance some regional subsidiaries have started functioning as centres. However, this picture is also changing, as illustrated by Figure 4.

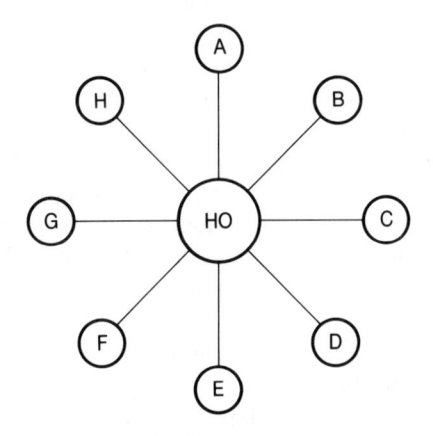

HO = Head Office
A–H = Subsidiaries in different foreign markets

Figure 3. Traditional Head Office/Subsidiary Relationship.

```
                    ┌─────┐
                    │  E  │
                    └──┬──┘  ┌───┐
              ┌───┐  ┌─┴─┐   │ F │
              │ D ├──┤SC ├───┘
              └───┘  └─┬─┘──┐
       ┌───┐           │    │ G │
       │ M │           │    └───┘
       └─┬─┘           │
  ┌───┐ ┌┴──┐      ┌───┴──┐
  │ L ├─┤SB ├──────┤  HO  ├─────┐ H
  └───┘ └┬──┘      └───┬──┘     
         │             │ ╲    
         │ K         ╱SA╲
                    ╱    ╲
                   J      I
```

          ———————   = Strong relationship
          ------- = Moderate relationship
          HO   = Head Office
          SA   = Subsidiary A in a foreign market
          SB   = Subsidiary B in a foreign market
          SC   = Subsidiary C in a foreign market
          D–M   = Different subsidiaries in foreign markets

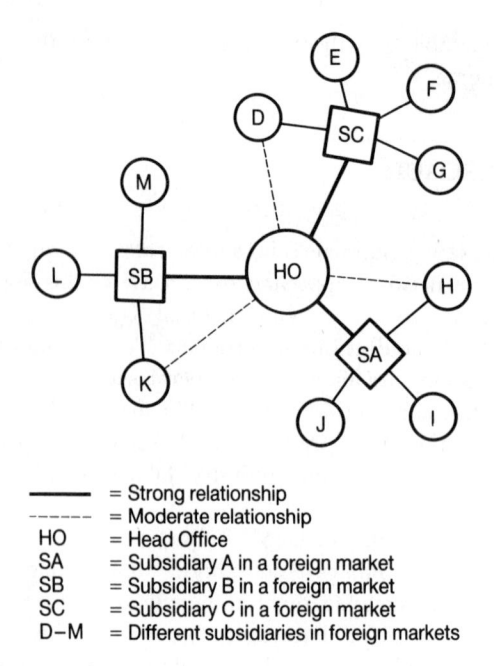

Figure 4. 'Centre–Centre' Relationship in Multinational Firms.

The phenomenon is different from regional headquarters, where the head office itself delegates some of its decision-making to regional headquarters to encourage better coordination (Eliasson, 1988). It is a further step in the internationalization process, which may not be initiated according to the policies of headquarters.

Here, a number of subsidiaries such as A, B and C, are functioning as centres for other subsidiaries. In some cases the subsidiaries may or may not have contacts with the head office. As a result, a 'centre–centre' structure is emerging. Hedlund and Aman (1984) also concluded that interdependencies vary among the head office and its subsidiaries, depending upon the degree and experience of different markets. The subsidiaries, through adaptation to local markets, acquire a prominent position in the local network.

In the case of MNCs, the subsidiaries in the foreign markets are a part of the parent company's network as well as having their own network in the local market. These subsidiaries have to function and survive in the local market and must comply with the demands of the local network. At times, these demands may be counter to the policies of the parent company. Subsidiaries thus come to have a three-dimensional relationship: (1) there is the hierarchical relationship with the head office; (2) their activities are limited by the rules and regulations of the local government; (3) they have to comply with the demands of other actors in the local network. This is illustrated by Figure 5.

The traditional head office/subsidiary relationship is strong, while the local network is weak. In the early stages of establishing the subsidiary, the head office directs the subsidiary in all matters, including how it manages its relationship with local government and the local network. However, as the subsidiary gains more experience in the local market, it may acquire a stronger position in the local network. It may also become resourceful enough to cope with the rules and regulations of local government, and eventually, its relationship priorities tend to change as illustrated by Figure 6.

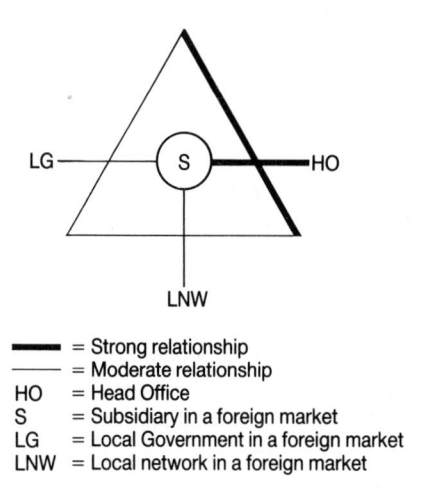

TOWARD GLOBAL STRATEGIZING: THEORETICAL FRAMEWORKS AND COMPANY APPROACHES   59

```
         = Strong relationship
         = Moderate relationship
HO   = Head Office
S    = Subsidiary in a foreign market
LG   = Local Government in a foreign market
LNW  = Local network in a foreign market
```

Figure 5. The Three-Dimensional Relationships for a Foreign Subsidiary.

The most important relationship for the subsidiary at this stage, is with other organizations in the local network; it has to abide by the rules and regulations of local government. The relationship with head office becomes less important. According to the network approach, the most important relationship for the subsidiary is the local network in which it has to operate. It is interesting to see how these firms are dealing with the issues and policies of the head office which conflict with the demands of the local network. We assume here that the subsidiary takes care of its own interests (i.e. the demands of the local network) and acts contrary to the policies of the head office This depends upon several factors such as the size of the local market and the position of the subsidiary in the local network.

The stronger the position, the more inclined it is to have its own policies, and not consider itself dependent on head office. Similarly, the bigger the size of the market (bigger than the parent company's market) the greater the chances are that the subsidiary becomes independent. These inferences are based on data gathered from Swedish firms having wholly- or partly-owned subsidiaries in Thailand, the Philippines, and Indonesia.

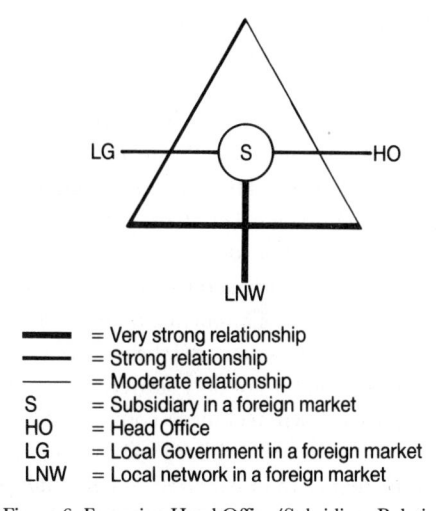

```
         = Very strong relationship
         = Strong relationship
         = Moderate relationship
S    = Subsidiary in a foreign market
HO   = Head Office
LG   = Local Government in a foreign market
LNW  = Local network in a foreign market
```

Figure 6. Emerging Head Office/Subsidiary Relationship.

HEAD OFFICE/SUBSIDIARY RELATIONSHIP

Importance of Regional Centres

There are several examples where subsidiaries have become larger than the parent firm in terms of sales and number of employees. Considering the size of the home market, it appears to be natural in the case of Swedish firms. They now have their own R&D as well as product development programmes. In some cases, a number of subsidiaries have been grouped together into regional networks. This mode has been popular in the case of Swedish firms in Southeast Asia, with Singapore being the regional headquarters. These regional offices work as independent firms which are many times more powerful than head office.

For example, Sandvik's subsidiary in the Philippines although, all the components emanate from Sweden, always sends its requisitions to Singapore. All the materials are channelled through Singapore. Some of the components used are not available from Sandvik group firms and are bought from other foreign firms; even so, these components are bought and delivered by the regional office in Singapore. The payments for all these components are also made to Singapore, not to head office or the suppliers. Singapore has jurisdiction over the Southeast Asia region, that is, Sandvik subsidiaries in Thailand, Malaysia, Singapore, Indonesia, the Philippines, Hong Kong, and Taiwan. All financial reports are sent to the regional office which later on consolidates all the returns and reports to head office. For head office, it is the performance of the regional office that counts, not the individual subsidiary.

Subsidiaries that grow through foreign operations meet problems, as illustrated by a Danish study (Rørsted, 1985). The largest farm equipment company established ten sales subsidiaries in major overseas markets during the 1970s as outlets for its home production. Soon, these sales subsidiaries began to modify the parent company products in order to adapt them to local demands. This eventually evolved into local production. In some cases, the production facility even led to facilities for the development and manufacturing of new products. Most of these subsidiaries started buying parts and components from local suppliers in order to compete successfully with other international companies such as Massey Ferguson, John Deere, International Harvester, and Caterpillar. One subsidiary in England was buying 65% of its components and parts from local suppliers, which was a clear violation of head office policy.

These developments eventually led to conflicts between the parent company and its overseas subsidiaries over sourcing and the optimal product mix. The parent company believed that the affiliates should purchase from each other. Some of the products offered by competitors were at prices and in quality hard to beat. Head office wanted to focus resources and know-how on product lines with higher technological content. Yet, purchasing policies and product mix strategies of subsidiaries were dictated by local networks and not by head office.

The head office/subsidiary conflict is illustrated by the Electrolux subsidiary in the Philippines. During 1979/1980, the subsidiary was importing all of its components from the parent company, and from affiliated sister companies around the world. As it gained more experience and a better position in the local network, it not only started buying from local suppliers but it helped local suppliers develop their own technical competence so they could supply to Electrolux's specification. In 1987, the local subsidiary was buying more than 85% of its components locally and the vacuum cleaner manufactured in the Philippines was quite different from the one Electrolux was manufacturing at its subsidiaries in Europe. Another example of how the product mix adapted to the local market is illustrated by the Philippines water purifiers which were not even sold in the home market.

It is the same with the Nobel Industries subsidiary in the Philippines. The local firm purchases almost all of its components and raw materials from the local (Japanese and American) suppliers; only a small portion of the material being bought from Sweden. In 1984, the subsidiary started its own R&D department. As far as marketing was concerned, in 1984 when the market was shrinking in the Philippines, the subsidiary started exporting to nearby countries. This conflicted with sister firms from countries where the subsidiary wanted to export. Head office decided to establish a common sales subsidiary to sell to Indonesia and Thailand, countries where Nobel had no subsidiary.

Tetra Pak, which sells machines and raw materials for liquid packings, is another example. its Philippine subsidiary imported all the machines and tools from Sweden and leased these machines to four different packers of milk and juices. Tetra Pak Philippines has a leasing contract for the service and maintenance of machines. The producers using Tetra Pak's machines are not allowed to use any materials other than those supplied by Tetra Pak. The subsidiary is nonetheless importing all the material they sell in the Philippines from Singapore where Tetra Pak has a manufacturing subsidiary. Here too, we see the emergence of a strong regional office—Tetra Pak, Singapore, supplying the material to all subsidiaries in Southeast Asia. The development was not anticipated by head office.

Swedish Match, which wholly or partly owns 150 subsidiaries in about 40 countries, has 73% of its total sales and 55% of its production outside Sweden. It started international production with manufacturing subsidiaries in markets in India, Thailand, and the Philippines as early as the 1920s and 1930s. Although they are wholly-owned by Swedish Match, they work autonomously, purchasing their material from local suppliers and even the imported material is not necessarily bought from parent or sister firms. Most of the imported material comes from Germany, Japan, China, and Finland, often from competitors of Swedish Match. In the Philippines the subsidiary had two factories at two different locations, one in Cebu and one in Manila. In 1977, it sold one and bought 50 per cent shares of one of the suppliers of raw materials. It was considered more important to have a secure local supply of raw materials than to have a greater market share, although this goal was clearly against the policy of the head office.

CONCLUSION

The concept of centre and periphery, and the interdependence between the two are diminishing in importance in MNCs. In many cases, several centres in the same company have emerged, as for Tetra Pak and Sandvik, the Singapore unit is emerging as a centre for subsidiaries in Southeast Asia. The 'centre' or head office for these subsidiaries is Singapore, and not the parent company located in Sweden. The Electrolux subsidiary in the Philippines is working independently has excellent manufacturing facilities, and exports to other Electrolux subsidiaries operating in the region—Thailand and Indonesia. Knowing the independent status of the Philippines subsidiary, and also accepting the fact that it is one of the most successful subsidiaries for the whole concern, the parent company has chosen not to have any say in their business with other regional companies and in their purchasing policies. For Electrolux subsidiaries in that geographical area, the Philippines subsidiary is the resource 'centre'. The product manufactured in that subsidiary is more suitable for them than the products manufactured in Sweden, or in any other European subsidiary.

We may conclude that changes in head office/subsidiary relationships are gradual. Our evidence suggests that this relationship changes with time and depends upon the position of the subsidiary in the local network. These changes can be shown, in theory, as going through three different stages (Figure 7).

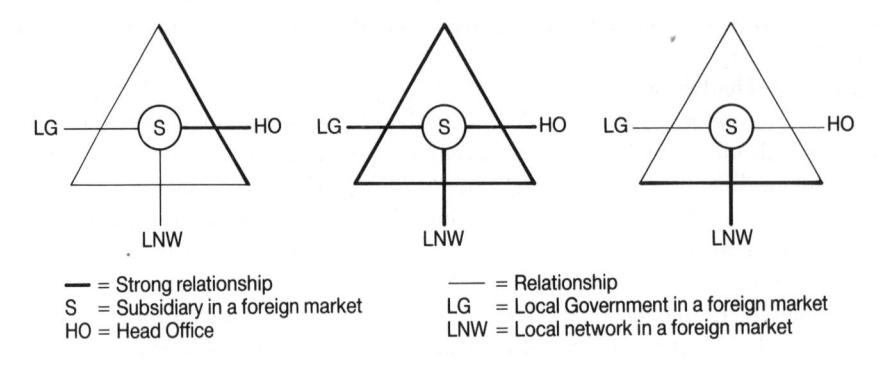

―― = Strong relationship
―― = Relationship
S = Subsidiary in a foreign market
LG = Local Government in a foreign market
HO = Head Office
LNW = Local network in a foreign market

Figure 7. The Process of Changing Head Office/Subsidiary Relationship.

The first stage is at the start of internationalization, which is the most important relationship with head office. In the second, the subsidiary gives equal importance to head office, the local network, and local government. Finally, in the third, the subsidiary gains in experience, knowledge, and power in the local network and the relationship becomes pivotal. In some cases, the subsidiary's relationship with head office is replaced by its relationship with a regional office (centre). We believe it is not easy to control or enforce different structures from head office. In practice, it would be difficult for MNCs, especially those coming from small economies, to adapt the 'transnational solution' advocated by Bartlett and Ghoshal (1989). The three capabilities a transnational should have—efficiency, responsiveness to the local market and innovation, are best met by our network approach. In fact the transnational model ignores responsiveness to the local market.

We highlight the emerging concept of regional centres in MNCs based in small economies like Sweden. Foreign units are likely to become independent, or regional 'centre'-oriented as they overtake the parent firm in size and influence. Swedish cases from Southeast Asia are consistent with recent developments in foreign direct investment. We hope that more practical work will throw light on this intriguing developing and changing relationship between head office and its subsidiaries.

ACKNOWLEDGEMENT

The author thanks 'Handelsbankens Forskningsstiftelser', Sweden, for financing the study and travel to Southeast Asia for data collection.

REFERENCES

Aggarwal, R. (1988) 'Multinationals of the South'. *Journal of International Business Studies*, **19**(1): 140–143.

Aggarwal, R., and Ghauri, P. N. (1989) 'The Evolution of Multinationals from Small Economies: A Study of Swedish Firms in Asia'. Paper presented in UK meeting of Academy of International Business, University of Bath, 7–8 April.

Bartlett, C. A., and Ghoshal, S. (1989) *Managing Across Borders: The Transnational Solution*. Hutchinson Business Books, Boston.

Eliasson, G. (1988) *De Utomlandsetablerade Foretagen och den Svenska Ekonomin, Förskningsrapport nt. 26*, IUI. Almquist & Wiksell, Stockholm.

Franko, L. G. (1976) *Joint Venture Survival in Multinational Enterprise*. Praeger, New York.

Ghauri, P. N. (1988) 'Marketing Strategies: Swedish Firms in South-East Asia'. In Varaldo, R. (ed.), *International Marketing Cooperation*. Editirce, Pisa, Est.

Ghauri, P. N. (1990) 'Emergence of New Structures in Swedish Multinationals'. In Prasad, S. B. (ed.) *Advances in International Comparative Management*, Vol. 5, pp. 227–243. JAI Press.

Hedlund, G. and Aman, P. (1984) *Managing Relationships with Foreign Subsidiaries*, Vastervik: Severiges Mekan Forbund.

Jagren, L., and Horwitz, E. C. (1984) *Svenska Marknadshandelar* (Swedish Marketing) (Working Paper). IUI, Stockholm.

Johanson, J. and Wiedersheim-Paul, F. (1975) 'The Internationalization of the Firm. Four Swedish Cases'. *Journal of Management Studies*, October: 205–231.

Johanson, J. and Mattson, L. G. (1988) Internationalization in Industrial Systems—A Network Approach. In Hood, N. and Vahlne, J. E. (eds), *Strategies in Global Competition* pp. 287–314, Croom Helm, London.

Kaynak, E. and Ghauri, P. N. (1987) 'Export Behaviour of Smaller Swedish Firms'. *Journal of Small Business Management*, **25**(2): 26–32.

Kindleberger, C. P. (1979) *American Business Abroad*. Yale University Press, New Haven, CT.

Rørsted, B. (1985) 'Defining, Planning and Evaluating Subsidiary Competitive Profiles—an Empirical Investigation'. Conference Paper at the Fifth Annual Strategic Management Society Conference, Barcelona.

Stopford, J. M. and Wells, L. T. (1972) *Managing the Multinational Enterprise*. Basic Books, New York.

Swedenborg, B. (1982) *Svensk Industri i Utlandet*. (Swedish Industries Abroad). IUI, Stockholm.

6

The Hypermodern MNC—A Heterarchy?

Gunnar Hedlund

Commenting upon an early b7–b6 (or, in an alternative notation, PQKn2–Kn3 as black), Aron Nimzowitsch advertised his move as one of 'hypermodern daring'. The exaggeration contained in the expression served two purposes. It helped selling Nimzowitsch's pathbreaking books on chess strategy. It focused attention on the novelty of his ideas and thus inspired attempts to refute his conclusions.

The present paper is restricted to the second goal. The term 'hypermodern MNC' is meant to convey the suspicion that some crucial aspects of developments of and in multinational corporations (MNCs) cannot be grasped by notions in the merely 'modern' schools of thought. Even more than in the case of the grandmaster's rallying calls for the 'hypermodern school', 'my system', etc., the departure from supposedly conventional views is bound to be exaggerated. However, some polarization of issues is desirable in order to arrive at greater conceptual clarity. In addition, it seems that concepts and theories older than present variations on the theme of 'global strategy' and sometimes not used by protagonists of the said theme, can usefully be applied.

The other word in the title—heterarchy—is no less problematical. It was used in a recent study by the Stanford Research Institute to describe a shift of perspective in a wide range of sciences. (See also Ogilvy, 1977.) A key idea is that of reality being organized non-hierarchically. A special case is holographic coding where entire systems are represented and, as it were, 'known' at each component of the system. (As in a hologram, each part contains information sufficient to reproduce the whole original image, albeit somewhat blurred.)

The concept of heterarchy does not seem to have been used much, if at all, in discussing MNCs. Nor has it inspired more than passing allusions in organization studies in general. Sjöstrand (1985) uses the concept in contrast to hierarchy, but he does not give any definition, nor does the notion figure much in his discussion. The holographic paradigm is encountered more frequently (Mitroff, 1983; El Sawy, 1985). The discussion in Faucheux and Laurent (1980) about integrating others' roles and vantage point, and about 'internalizing the environment' in decision-making in a more direct way touches on many of the issues brought up below concerning heterarchy; so do contributions on self-referential systems, such as Varela (1975). Also Laurent (1978) discusses the concept of hierarchy.

As the previous discussion indicates, there are no strict definitions to hold on to. As always, consultation of the *Oxford English Dictionary* gives food for thought. The only direct reference to 'heterarchy' gives the meaning 'the rule of an alien'. This is exactly what heterarchy in the present use of the term is not. This use, as well as SRI's and Ogilvy's, builds on putting 'homo', rather than 'auto', as the opposite of 'hetero'. It is not easy to arrive at a simple definition, for example by contradistinction in relation to 'hierarchy'. The apparent superiority of this latter term as to clarity of meaning derives mostly from the dulling effects of old habits. We have become so accustomed to the concept of hierarchy that we forget exactly what it is that we want to conceive of with it. For example, the etymological meaning of 'ruling through the sacred' or 'rule of the episcopate' is rather alien to transaction cost analyses of markets and 'hierarchies'. Certainly it would not make much sense to define heterarchy as non-hierarchy, meaning ruling through the profane. The abstruseness of novelty in 'heterarchy' thus partly derives from the abstruseness of convention in 'hierarchy'. Many authors hail hierarchy as the dominant or even only stable form of organization of human as well as other systems. Space limitations do not permit a thorough discussion of this strain of thought. One contribution will, however, be briefly mentioned. Koestler (1978, p. 290) puts the argument for hierarchy very strongly:

> All complex structures and processes of a relatively stable character display hierarchic organization, and this applies regardless whether we are considering inanimate systems, living organisms, social organizations, or patterns of behaviour.

Koestler himself mentions the suspicion that the hierarchic model's universal applicability may originate in the model being logically empty, or merely a reflection of the way in which a perceiver approaches an object or situation. He rejects these possibilities but does not discuss them at length. The pervasiveness of hierarchical thinking models is treated by Ogilvy (1977) and Bouvier (1984), who support the view that hierarchy to a large extent is in the eye of the beholder. Some other comments should also be made in relation to Koestler's arguments.

A key idea with Koestler is the existence of parts which are self-regulating, relatively autonomous, and which exhibit properties not deducible from lower units. At the same time, they are parts of larger wholes. Koestler calls these units 'holons'. This is not inconsistent with the hierarchy notion. However, he also discusses more complex networks, where 'vertical' and 'horizontal' connections intertwine. We are warned, however, not to forget the primacy of the vertical, hierarchical, dimension (ibid., p. 298):

> It is as if the sight of the foliage of the entwined branches in a forest made us forget that the branches originate in separate trees. The trees are vertical structures. The meeting points of branches from neighbouring trees form horizontal networks at several levels. Without the trees there could be no entwining, and no network. Without the networks, each tree would be isolated, and there would be no integration of functions. Arborization and reticulation seem to be complementary principles in the architecture of organisms. In symbolic universes of discourse arborization is reflected in the 'vertical' denotation (definition) of concepts, reticulation in their 'horizontal' connotations in associative networks.

The last paragraph indicates a tendency to define whatever cannot be captured in a hierarchical order as only a looser kind of 'association'. Another example is the discussion of 'abstract' and 'spotlight' memory. The latter—very vivid, almost photographic images resembling total recall of past situations—seems not to fit the hypothesis of hierarchic storing of information. Koestler (ibid., p. 48 ff, 296–297) 'solves' this problem by assuming that there is something he calls 'emotional relevance', which leads to lack of schematization in hierarchies. He also regards spotlight memory as more 'primitive' (ibid., p. 53), and possibly phylogenetically older than abstractive memory.

Koestler even regards the supposedly older principles of storing and managing information in the human brain as harmful. He suggests to initiate (ibid., p. 103):

> Not an amputation, but a process of harmonization which assigns each level of the mind, from visceral impulses to abstract thought, its appropriate place in the hierarchy. This implies reinforcing the new brain's power of veto against that type of emotive behaviour—and that type only—which cannot be reconciled with reason, such as the 'blind' passions of the group-mind.

The 'process of harmonization' cannot be achieved by education. 'It can be done only by 'tempering' with human nature itself to correct its endemic schizopsychological disposition', (p. 104). He expects 'the laboratories to succeed in producing an immunizing substance conferring mental stability' (p. 105).

To the present author, this line of reasoning seems like trying to expurge and, if possible, eradicate thought patterns which do not fit a hierarchical model. The tree metaphor also hides an important aspect of much social organization. Any given unit may be a member of several systems, which each may be conceived of as a hierarchy. In a tree, every branch obviously primarily 'belongs' to one tree. However, is it equally clear to what 'arborizing structure' a US citizen, born by Jewish parents, working for a French company in Spain belongs? Koestler quotes Hyden (1961), who suggests that in the same neuron may be a member of several functional 'clubs', as support for the distinction between arborizing and reticulating structures. However, it seems that this could rather be taken as an example of non-hierarchy. (Below, a heterarchy will be endowed with the attributes of having many centers of different kinds. This seems to fit the neuronal clubs better.)

Also on the empirical level, some of Koestler's examples of hierarchic organization may be questioned. Later research on memory, and on the entire functioning of the brain, does not appear to fit the hierarchic model (McCulloch, 1965; Pribram, 1971). Organizations, in their actual functioning, are far less hierarchic than their organization charts would imply. Action systems do not always work as hierarchy of strategies transformed into action programmes and simple final acts (Allison, 1971; Mintzberg, 1978).

The 'holon property' of Koestler is fully consistent with the heterarchy model outlined below. The supposed inevitability of hierarchy, however, seems to be a Procrustean bed in describing life in real organizations. Therefore, rather than continuing the conceptual discussion, I will try to sketch some developments in MNCs, illustrating the need for a concept covering these developments. Thereafter, a tentative delimitation of the concept of a heterarchical MNC will be provided.

A pioneer in reviewing the development of different kinds of MNCs was Howard V. Perlmutter (1965). His original scheme of an evolution of, or at least a distinction between, ethnocentric, polycentric, and geocentric MNCs has hardly been improved upon. Therefore, this is a natural starting point to discuss tendencies of change in the nature of multinational business.

ETHNOCENTRISM

Almost all existing firms started on a national basis and only gradually developed international ties. Foreign business was initially only marginal, more so for companies from large nations than for those with small 'home markets'. Internationalization was often based on monopolistic advantages which could be exploited by internalizing transactions within the firm. (See Hymer (1976) and Dunning (1977) for early and representative statements of theories of foreign direct investment based on 'firm-specific advantages'.) These advantages, in terms of, for example, proprietary technology were exploited in a slow, gradual process, by moving concentrically to markets further away from the home country, and by investing in increasingly committing forms. From sales outlets in the neighboring country, the firm cautiously moved towards manufacturing plants on alien continents (Vernon (1966) Stopford and Wells (1972) and Johanson and Vahlne (1977) are good examples of gradual learning theories of foreign direct investment.)

Ethnocentric companies are managed by home country people, and with time there is a lot of rotation between HQ and subsidiaries. The control style will vary in accordance with practice in the parent company and parent country. For example, Swedish firms transferred a reliance on normative control (Etzioni, 1961) to their international operations. US companies used relatively more of calculative and coercive control, with less autonomy for the subsidiaries (Hedlund, 1980,1984; Hedlund and Åman, 1983).

The role of a foreign subsidiary in such a company is operational rather than strategic. Strategies are derived from the prospects of extending the geographical scope of firm-specific advantages and formulated at the centre. The subsidiaries implement, but there is also an entrepreneurial element to early stages of internationalization, which is lost as the firm gets used to going to foreign lands.

The environment of the MNC—as far as aspects of internationalization are concerned—could be characterized as Type 1 (placid random) or Type 2 (placid clustered) in the Emery and Trist (1965) classification. That is, opportunities and problems are either randomly distributed (Type 1) or clustered (Type 2), but competitive relations are not primary as in Type 3, nor is drastic environmental turbulence the main issue (Type 4). The absence of strategy in a Type 1 situation is particularly apparent in the subsidiary. The best strategy is to do as well as possible on a purely local and perhaps also short-term basis.

Interdependencies between the centre and the subsidiaries in the enterprise are primarily sequential (Thompson, 1967). Products, know how, and money for investment are sent from the center to the periphery. There is a vertical division of labor, so that activities up-stream the value-added chain are conducted at the center and down-stream operations at the periphery. (This is, of course, does not hold for raw materials-based MNCs.) The novelty and uncertainty of foreign operations favor hierarchy rather than market or federation solutions (Williamson, 1975; Daems, 1980). That is, subsidiaries are controlled rather tightly, either through orders or shared outlooks; for example, by transferring people between units in the firm (Edström and Galbraith, 1977).

POLYCENTRISM

As time goes by, foreign business may become dominant rather than marginal, the subsidiaries get more activities and become more self-sufficient, management becomes more host-country oriented and consisting of host-country nationals. The MNC becomes an assemblage of semi-independent units. There is less rotation of personnel, and in a way, the polycentric MNC is less trans- or international than the ethnocentric version. Indeed, the term *multinational* fits better for the polycentric firm than for the other archetypes.

The competitive strengths move from proprietary technology to access to distribution channels, brand name, international experience, and finance. Economies of scale and scope become important. New investments are sought worldwide, almost as in a portfolio placement strategy. As long as the firm stays in the original line of business, the size of the host market will be an important criterion for the decision on where to invest. The ethnocentric stage of confinement to near and familiar abodes loses in significance. (See Vernon (1979) and Hedlund and Kverneland (1984) for a discussion and some empirical support. Some of the results reported have to do with changes in the environment of MNCs, allowing 'instant polycentrism', rather than with firm-specific developments.)

Subsidiaries are operationally independent and increasingly forced to take strategic decisions with respect to their operations in their market ('Disturbed reactive' local environment for the subsidiary). HQ control moves towards calculative, based on financial results rather than on influencing the substance of decisions. The extreme is reached when the parent company acts only as a holding company, buying and selling assets internationally, with no view to anything but the financial outcomes of its dispositions.

Interdependence between subsidiaries and center is *pooled*. Financial resources and some specialist competence are kept at the centre, whereas product and technology flows are less pronounced. Activities are duplicated internationally, so that manufacturing, for example, is undertaken in most subsidiaries.

The tendency in terms of control mode is to move toward looser coupling between units and from the hierarchy (in this case also somewhat in the etymological sense) of ethnocentrism to market solutions. Transfer pricing based on market prices rather than internal costs, freedom to choose external suppliers, rewards and punishment in monetary terms, and elaborate bonus payment systems accompany greater turnover rates of personnel and organizational units being sold off and bought. Internationalization is more and more conducted through acquisitions rather than green-field ventures. The tendency to market solutions could be interpreted in terms of increased routinization of international transactions, with consequent reduction of uncertainty. Also, the idiosyncracy of assets (technology, people, etc.) is not as pronounced as in the initial stages. According to Williamson (1975), this should lead to markets rather than hierarchies.

GEOCENTRISM

Perlmutter's (1965) original classification defines the various 'centrisms' primarily according to the attitudes of management. Above, such aspects have been linked to strategic situations, stages in the 'life cycle of internationalization', types of interdependence between parts of the firm, types of environment facing the company, etc. It becomes even more necessary to discuss these other aspects when describing a geocentric firm. One reason for this is that 'geocentric strategies' may be accompanied by ethnocentric attitudes. Indeed, the shift from poly- to geocentric strategic focus is often perceived by host country management as a shift back to HQ and home country attitudes.

Writers on 'global strategy' mostly mention interdependence between units in the firm as a distinguishing characteristic. (See, for example, Porter, 1980, 1984.) The actions of a subsidiary in country A influence prospects for the subsidiary in country B, perhaps because they face the same competitor, who has to divide his resources between the two markets. Thus, competition is not confined within each national market, but system-wide. The MNC exploits systems advantages, subsidiaries, and country-specific advantages being considered the parts of the system. Thus, at the extreme, subsidiaries specialize and operate globally in limited fields. The MNC in this way *internalizes the exploitation of (country) comparative advantages*. This is very important from the point of view of theories of international trade and investment. Ricardo never thought that the same agent would produce both wine and cloth. Assumptions that the MNC is a reflection of firm-specific advantages à la Hymer must confront a very peculiar type of advantage, that is *multinationality in itself*. To say that the MNC exists because it exploits the advantages of being an MNC is tautological, so the convenient theoretical starting point in monopolistic advantages dissolves when applied to the geocentric firm. As Vernon (1979) himself has noted, the product life cycle theory of international trade and investment becomes less useful as the international spread of companies is extended.

Global competition, where a firm faces the same rivals on most markets, means that gradual internationalization strategies pose problems. Hedlund and Kverneland (1984) and Lundren and Hedlund (1983) show how market entry by Swedish firms into Japan and South-East Asia respectively is faster and more committing than theories of gradualism would lead one to expect. Firms do not follow a neat sequence from agent over sales subsidiary and some local manufacturing to large-scale local production. Instead, the pattern is one of jumping steps in the chain and building up positions very rapidly. International strategy is increasingly driven by considerations of rivals', and sometimes actual or potential cooperators', behavior, rather than by the exploitation of FSAs (firm-specific advantages) as in the ethnocentric firm, or by the attractiveness of markets one by one as in the polycentric firm. Oligopolistic reaction, in terms of *imitating* competitors' moves (Knickerbocker, 1973) as well as *avoiding* competitors and building up *mutual hostage positions*, becomes common.

Perlmutter saw the use of third country nationals (TCNs) in management as a sign of geocentricity. Other aspects concerning the management process are reliance on global profitability goals and increased rotation of personnel. Probably a shift back to less calculative and more normative and coercive control is required in order for global strategies to work. The subsidiaries have to implement strategies formulated according to a global logic, they have to be able to act quickly in response to competitive conditions, they must be encouraged to look at a wider picture. Most writings on global strategy give the subsidiaries a less independent role than that implied in a polycentric MNC. A recentralization of authority to HQ often follows, and is recommended to follow, a globalization of competition. (See, for example, Channon and Jalland, 1979; Hedlund and Åman, 1983.) Often, global divisions structured around products, technologies, or customer types are created to coordinate activities in specific competitive niches. The business environment can be characterized as a global disturbed reactive one in the terms of Emery and Trist (1965).

Interdependence between parts of the firm moves from the polycentric pooling of resources at the center to sequential and *reciprocal*. Products, know-how, money, and people flow in increasingly complex patterns, and not as in the ethnocentric firm from one core to the periphery. (See also Bartlett (1984) and his discussion of the 'integrated network model' of an MNC. His other concepts of 'centralized hub' and 'decentralized federation' can be compared with ethnocentrism and polycentrism, respectively.) Particularly reciprocal interdependence is expected to lead to internalization in a hierarchy (cf. Thompson, 1967), so the trend towards markets in the polycentric MNC is reversed. Also reversed is the tendency to duplicate activities in various subsidiaries.

The discussion so far is summarized in Table 1. Obviously, it ignores many complexities and gives a very simple picture of the range of possibilities. For example, there certainly exist geocentric MNCs which build primarily upon sequential interdependencies between center and

Table 1.

	Ethnocentrism	Polycentrism	Geocentrism
Importance of foreign business	Marginal	Substantial/dominant	Dominant
Basis for international strategy	Exploit firm-specific advantages	Market size, scale and scope economies, finance	Competition, multinationality as such
Expansion mode	Gradual, concentric, green-field	Market-driven, acquisitions, cash-constrained	Quick, direct competition-driven
Organization structure	Mother/daughter international division	Mother/daughter, international division, holding company	Global divisions or matrix organization
Type of interdependence	Sequential centre-subsidiary	Pooled centre-subsidiary	System of sequential and reciprocal
Governance mode	Hierarchy	Market	Hierarchy, 'hierarchy'
Specialization in value-added chain	Specialization up–downstream HQ–subsidiaries	Duplication	Specialization up–downstream, between subsidiaries
Control style	HQ-derived, coercive, normative	Calculative	Normative, coercive
MNC internationalization environment	Placid–random Type I	Placid–clustered Type II	Disturbed–reactive, turbulent Type III → IV
Subsidiary environment	Type I, II	Type I, II, III	Type III → IV
Autonomy of subsidiary	Low–medium	High	Low–medium
Strategic role of subsidiary	Implement local strategy	Formulate and implement local strategy	Implement and adapt to global strategy
Recruitment and rotation	Home-country managers, much rotation	Local managers, little rotation	Mixed, TCNs, much rotation

periphery. A clear example would be mining companies in highly concentrated industries. Nevertheless, one can better understand the character of most geocentricity and globality of competition if several strains of—in this context—often forgotten theoretical heritage are applied:

- Thompson's (1967) classification of various types of interdependence, and his hypotheses of mechanisms of integration related to those types.
- Transaction cost theorists' (Coase, 1937; Williamson, 1975) notions of alternative governance modes and the determinants of effective solutions to the governance problem.
- Classification of mechanisms of social integration such as Etzioni's (1961).
- Typologies of organizational environments (Emery and Trist, 1965) and hypotheses about behavioural implications of those environments.

Three entries in Table 1 have not been adequately foreshadowed in the discussion above. Organization structure has been added, using the results of Stopford and Wells (1972), Franko (1976) and others linking strategy to the structure of the international organization. 'Hierarchy' as one governance mode in geocentric firms will be explained in the next section. I believe that pure hierarchy will be detrimental to many global strategies, and that there nevertheless is a strong possibility that this is what will happen in many firms. Emery and Trist's type 4 environment—the turbulent one—has been introduced as a likely development for both the entire geocentric MNC and its subsidiaries. This will also be discussed in the next section.

STRAINS ON THE GEOCENTRIC MNC

A radical view concerning geocentrism and globality is that we are witnessing the disappearance of the international dimension of business. For commercial and practical purposes, the nations do not exist, and the relevant business arena becomes something like a big unified 'home market'. Business action as well as concepts to describe firms and the situations they face will be similar to the case of a company working in one national market.

However, there are a number of difficulties facing the MNC, which wants to act as if the world was one big market and competitive arena, to be adapted to in a scaled-up version of 'ordinary', national strategy.

- In spite of proclaimed increased homogenization of demand (Vernon, 1979), there are still strong differences between nations and regions. Protectionism is furthermore on the increase rather than the other way around. The loyalty of many employees is still primarily with their home country. (See Doz, 1979; Doz and Prahalad, 1980.)
- The need for cooperation, in joint ventures or in other forms, characteristic of many branches of industry, makes unilateral strategy making problematical.
- Cultural differences in management style makes one at least question the viability of uniform, worldwide control systems and other management practices.
- Economizing by sharing resources between different lines of business, with different customers and competitors, mitigates against totally subduing the local country dimension in organization and strategy.
- Size itself may be a severe problem in coordinating operations globally in the same way as one would coordinate national business. The complexity and variability of environmental circumstances compound the size of problems. Response times may be too long to keep up

with changes in markets. The cognitive limitations of integrating information are very real. Particularly at the strategic level, advances in information technology may not be sufficient, although no doubt be of value.
- The supply of managers able to carry out ambitious global strategies already is a bottleneck today for most firms. If strategy making is recentralized to the HQ 'brain', it will become even more difficult to fill positions, since this requires more transfer of personnel.
- With the development of specialization between subsidiaries, these will become so large and important that it will be detrimental to assign narrow strategic roles to them. For example, a research centre in India serving the whole network of an MNC would probably, with time, develop ideas and products which do not fit the prevailing strategies of the group, but which could well be a basis for a new line of business. It would be wasteful not to entertain a capacity to utilize the creativity and entrepreneurship of people at all nodes of the network. Besides, those people would probably resign if they did not get such opportunities.
- Finally, centrally guided global strategies for given products aimed at beating given competitors, looking at the world as one market, may lead to neglect of opportunities to exploit existing differences between nations. If the global thrust is combined with a re-emphasis on HQ and home-country guidance, the company may return to ethnocentrism, only being able to exploit ideas originating at home. Advantage seeking and advantage development will not be main concerns, but only the exploitation of existing advantages. In the long run, such a firm may become sterile. The results in Davidson and Haspeslagh (1982) indicate that the global product division as an organizational solution may indeed entail such risks.

Most of the points illustrate the danger of seeing geocentricity just as the scaling up of the national corporation, thereby getting rid of the international dimension of business and reestablishing central strategic direction from a center, which is at the apex of one, big global hierarchy. Even if this characterization of global strategy is a caricature and may seem to be set up as a straw-man, I believe that both academic discussion and—but less so—practice in large MNCs are affected by outlooks, philosophies, strategies, and management practices similar to the ones described.

Perlmutter's original conception of geocentricity was not as restricted as the 'mononational' version sketched above. He sketched a situation where subsidiaries were 'parts of a whole whose focus is on worldwide objectives as well as local objectives, each part making its unique contribution with its unique competence'. These lines do not clearly denote the attributes of geocentricity, but their connotative meaning is very rich. I believe one can usefully single out some of those connotations and specify a special case of geocentricity, an option which is still not fully developed in actuality but towards which many companies probably will, and should, move. This is the hypermodern MNC, and one of its distinguishing marks is its heterarchical nature.

THE HETERARCHICAL MNC

The heterarchical MNC differs from the standard geocentric one both in terms of strategy and in terms of structure. *Strategically*, the main dividing line is between exploiting competitive advantages derived from a home country base on the one hand, and actively seeking advantages originating in the global spread of the firm on the other. In its most extreme form, this would mean that one could not assign the company to any particular industry. Any opportunity which activates the potential inherent in broad geographical coverage would be a

Industry Characteristics
Global Integration/National Responsiveness Grid

	Lo	Hi
Hi	Consumer Electronics	Telecommunications
Lo	Cement	Branded Packaged Goods

(Y-axis: Forces for Global Coordination/Integration; X-axis: Forces for National Responsiveness/Differentiation)

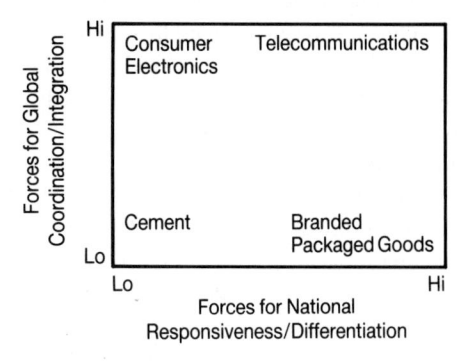

Figure 1. (*Source*: Bartlett, 1984.)

candidate for inclusion in the company's repertoire of products and services. Obviously, no MNC would like to go to this extreme. Specialization benefits apply also to information search, and in many contexts existing barriers to entry into a global industry would be prohibitively restrictive.

However, the concept of exploiting the advantage of multinationality as such also applies within a rather limited field of business. Information on competition, technological trends, developments in related fields, aspects of national environments, etc. lead to opportunities not easily identified by purely local firms, or by polycentric MNCs, or even by ethnocentrically tainted global MNCs. The difference between the latter and the heterarchy is most pronounced when it comes to the *structure* of the enterprise and the processes of managing it. Indeed, it may be that the idea of structure determining strategy (see Hall and Saias, 1980) is a fundamental one for the heterarchical MNC. Rather than identifying properties of the industry in which it competes and then adapting its structure to the demands thus established, the hypermodern MNC first defines its structural properties and then looks for strategic options following from these properties. In actual life, of course, every candidate for heterarchy will have come from a history in a given set of industries, regions, etc. The MNCs most likely to face the indeterminacy of strategically relatively open vistas are probably those described by Bartlett (1984) as 'transnational'. Such firms are active in industries where it is important both to achieve global integration and local differentiation, for example, adaptation to host government demands (see Figure 1).

Thus, strategic imperatives of dual focus force some MNCs to adopt structural solutions and management practices in consonance with these task demands. These adaptations then constitute an opportunity for sometimes much wider and diverse strategic options, or at least more intensive utilizations of the global spread of the company. In order to achieve this, further development of structural traits are desirable. Their archetypical expressions will be enumerated below.

(1) First, the heterarchical MNC has *many centers*. One could speak of a polyarchical rather than monarchical MNC, were it not for the lack of integration implied in the former term. The main idea is that the foundations of competitive advantage no longer reside in any one country, but in many. New ideas and products may come up in many different countries and later be exploited on a global scale. A geographically diffused pattern of expertise is built up,

corresponding to unique abilities in each node of the network. These abilities may be a reflection of dissimilarities between countries as in 'demand theories' of international trade (Burenstam-Linder, 1961) or simply expressions of spatially distributed talents for technological development within the firm. At the extreme, each 'subsidiary' is at the same time a center for and perhaps a global coordinator of activities within one field (such as for one product), and a more peripheral agent for local distribution in another.

In diversified firms it is obviously easier to find examples of such international specialization. For example, the Swedish company Atlas Copco has the headquarters for its Air Power division located in Belgium, whereas the other divisions' headquarters are in Sweden. Esselte (office equipment) has put the center of its largest division in London.

However, even within one product division there is scope for multi-centredness. The dangers of the global product division undiluted by geographical considerations have been discussed by Davidson and Haspeslagh (1982). Relations are restricted to those between one center and units in the periphery. Relations within the supposed periphery are not exploited, and information overload on the centre and lack of motivation in subsidiaries create grave problems. Hedlund (1980) documents the strategic alienation of subsidiary managers in Swedish MNCs, and gives some suggestions of how to involve the subsidiaries more in strategy formulation. In this case, the mother–daughter structure, rather than global product divisions, is the organizational background. This seems to support the views of Bartlett (1981,1984) that the importance of the formal organization structure is easily exaggerated. Simmonds (1985), reviewing the literature and discussing various ways to 'achieve the geocentric ideal', concludes that other management systems, such as the planning, accounting, and reporting systems, are important obstacles.

(2) A key idea in the conception of a heterarchical MNC is that *subsidiary managers are also given a strategic role, not only for their 'own' company, but for the MNC as a whole*. The notions of 'headquarters', 'center', 'home country', and 'corporate level' dissolve and are not synonymous. Corporate level strategy has to be implemented *and* formulated in a geographically scattered network.

(3) Heterarchy implies *different kinds of centers*. There is not only a set of global divisions and subdivisions, or only a set of geographical divisions further split up in national and regional subunits. A heterarchy consists of a mix of organizing principles. There may be an R&D center in Holland with global responsibilities for coordinating product development, product division headquarters in Germany responsible for the main product, a marketing centre for Asia in Singapore, and a centre for dealing with global purchases in London. The multidimensionality of organizing principles (functions, products, geography, customer type, etc.) reflects the need to coordinate activities along each and all of those dimensions. In a heterarchy, *there is not one overriding dimension superordinate to the rest*.

All this may seem an unduly complicated way of describing a matrix organization. Recognizing the probability of muddled thinking and expression, I still believe that there are important differences between what I call a heterarchy and a matrix structure, for example:

(i) In a matrix, all units are coordinated along all the dimensions of the matrix in a heterarchy, the pattern is more mixed and flexible. The R&D center in the example above may not have all other R&D departments reporting to it or have the right to give them orders Rather, it may have a 'softer' coordinating role. Furthermore, not all units in the firm would fall within its direct sphere of interest.

(ii) A matrix implies stability in the criticality of the dimensions included in the matrix. Mostly, not more than two dimensions can be formally included; for example, products and geography. If functional coordination, such as for the global logistical system, is suddenly required, the matrix is ill-equipped to handle the problem.

(iii) The matrix ends in an apex, so that conflicts between, for example, product and country perspectives, are resolved by a corporate officer. The heterarchy would not rely much on this mechanism, but more on conflict resolution through negotiations based on shared perspectives and sometimes arms-length bargaining.

Admittedly, most writers on matrix organization would stress that the formal matrix is only a small part of the 'matrix way of life'. They stress the need for shift of focus over time, flexibility in applying dual reporting relationships, and care in not overloading the arbiter role of top management.

(4) A further characteristic of a heterarchy concerns the degree of coupling between organizational units. In many cases, there would be a de-integration of relationships. A subsidiary will be given increased freedom to purchase components externally, and to sell to customers outside the corporation. Joint ventures and other types of cooperation with other firms will be more prevalent than in the tightly controlled global firm. If such freedom is not given, there will be little chance of really profiting from the opportunities provided by global reach.

Of course, negative effects on the rest of the operations of the MNC must be considered also. An important subset of global opportunities consist exactly in *internalizing* flows of information, products, and money within the bounds of the firm, saving on transaction costs associated with market solutions. Perhaps it is more appropriate to speak of *flexibility in the selection of governance mode*, rather than reintegration. A heterarchical MNC will have no problem in entering joint ventures, externalizing production and handling internal transactions according to arms-length principles in one business area, and insisting on unitary control, internalization, and governance by management fiat in another context. Full exploitation of global scanning and information processing capabilities will lead to a range of opportunities, some best handled in hierarchies, others rather suited to market-like governance. The heterarchical MNC could be seen as a *meta-institution*, which continuously creates new institutional arrangements, in the light of expertise concerning what works best for each specific purpose. This, assuming that choices are rational, speeds up the process of institutional evolution in comparison with a 'Darwinian' process of selection. A 'Lamarckian' development, where experience is accumulated, experiments fully exploited and memory over 'generations' kept intact, guides the choice of governance forms.

Thus, it may be correct to speak of de-integration for firms coming from a tradition of strict global control from one centre. For firms with a polycentric past, the tendency may be the opposite. Common to both is that the range of types of relationships between units in the company, as well as in relation to outside actors, will increase.

(5) Another attribute of heterarchy is that *integration is achieved primarily through normative control*, and only secondarily through calculative and coercive/bureaucratic regulations. 'Corporate culture', 'management ethos' (Bartlett, 1984), 'management style', 'cultural control' (Jaeger and Baliga, 1985), etc. become critical. This is the only way to assure coordination in the diverse, extended, and fluctuating environment and activities of a heterarchical MNC. Pure bureaucratic control breaks down because of cognitive overload and motivational problems. Pure calculative control, which may serve well in the polycentric MNC, will not establish the

mutual trust, the ability to 'sacrifice' the local for the global and the short term for the long term, and the shared code of communication necessary for rapid action in a coordinated fashion. Thus, and paradoxically so, a heterarchy may contain more of hierarchy, in its etymological sense, than does bureaucratic hierarchy itself. This is the reason for 'hierarchy' in Table 1.

(6) It was mentioned above that the hologram is a special type of heterarchy, *where information about the whole is contained in each part*. This is a critical characteristic of the heterarchical MNC. Every member of the company will in the extreme case be aware of all aspects of the firm's operations. Obviously, this is only a theoretical ideal. However, widely shared awareness of central goals and strategies, and of critical interdependencies between units in the firm, is not an impossibility. Some remarkable corporate turnarounds recently are no doubt partly attributable to initiatives in this direction. In Sweden, the cases of SAS and ASEA are particularly striking.

The distribution of information in every part of a hologram is possible because of laser technology. One could say that the corporate ethos is the analogue of the laser light. By sharing certain conceptions about the firm, and certain ways of acting in relation to other members of the firm, it becomes possible to rapidly share information, interpret the meaning of events in and outside the organization in similar ways, and see opportunities for local action in the interest of the global good. The laser beam effect of corporate culture is the unifying element of a heterarchical organization. It is crucial to support the formation of such a culture, since the risks of anarchy are otherwise very great.

Pessimism regarding the efficiency and integrity of non-hierarchical and unified control is less warranted on empirical than on 'theoretical' grounds. Ogilvy (1977) discusses how ambitions to organize societies and polities hierarchically are influenced by and influence modes of thought and even the structure of the personality. The fact that a phenomenon may be hard to grasp and explain in terms familiar to the grasper does not mean, however, that the phenomenon does not exist. Ogilvy quotes McCulloch (1965) on heterarchical patterns of preference in neural networks.

> Circularities in preference instead of indicating inconsistencies, actually demonstrate consistency of a higher order than had been dreamed of in our philosophy. An organism possessed of this nervous system—six neurons—is sufficiently endowed to be unpredictable from any theory founded on a scale of values. It has a heterarchy of values, and is thus internectively too rich to submit to a summum bonum (McCulloch, 1965, p. 43).

Yet, although we cannot explain how we are able to walk, for example, we still do. It is worth quoting McCulloch again, for some clues about the properties of heterarchies and possible analogies (no more but also no less) with a discussion on organization and control in human institutions. (Emphases added by the present author.)

> The details of its (the brain) neurons and their specific connections need not concern us here. In general, you may think of it as a computer *to any part* of which come signals from many parts of the body and from other parts of the brain and spinal cord. It is *only one cell deep* on the path from input to output, but it can set the filters on all of its inputs and can control the behaviour of the programmed activity, the half-centres, and the reflexes. It gets a *substitute for depth by its intrinsic fore-and-aft connections*. Its business, given its *knowledge of the state* of the whole organism and the world impingent upon it, is to decide whether the rule is one requiring fighting, fleeing, eating, sleeping, etc. It must do it with millisecond component action and conduction velocities of usually less than 100 meters per second, and *do it in real time*, say, in a third of a second. That it has worked so well throughout evolution, without itself evolving, points to its structure as the natural solution of the organization of appropriate

behavior. We know much experimentally of the behavior of the components but still have no theory worthy of the name to explain its circuit actions (McCulloch, 1965, p. 397).

(7) The foregoing discussion on the heterarchical nature of the nervous system leads to another, perhaps hair-raising, analogy. The metaphor underlying much thought on corporate strategy is one of the firm consisting of a brain and a body. The strategy makers in the center are the brain, and the implementors in the periphery are the body. Thinking and acting take place at different locations. Books like *The Brain of the Firm* (Beer, 1972) testify to the forcefulness of the metaphor. However, the dangers of separating thinking and acting too much in an organization have been well illustrated by the decline and often fall of formal long-range planning departments in companies. One way of describing the heterarchical MNC is to say that *thinking is not only restricted to one exclusive center, but goes on in the whole enterprise.* Thus, an appropriate metaphor for discussing a heterarchical firm would be a '*firm as a brain*' model rather than a 'brain of the firm' model.

A weakness of the metaphor is that it may lead one to see the firm as only a cognitive entity. However, the core of the idea is that not only does thinking take place also in the periphery, but it *goes together with and directly informs action.*

(8) *Coalitions with other companies and also other types of actors* are frequent in the heterarchical MNC. Exploiting global reach will often mean to serve as a catalyst, bringing together elements with synergistic potential, perhaps firms from different continents previously not known to one another. It may be of interest to note that Emery and Trist (1965) saw as two primary ways of coping with turbulence:

(i) The creation of common values, binding people and organizations together and enabling them to respond quickly to environmental change. This corresponds to the emergence of corporate culture as a binding element discussed above.
(ii) Cooperation between heterogenous elements rather than competition between homogenous elements (as in 'Type 3') as the primary occupation of top leaders.

The latter point includes things such as joint ventures and cooperation between firms and governments. A heterarchical MNC will share and pool its power with other actors in order to benefit maximally from its global capabilities. This does not mean that it will do so in all fields of business. Again, it is the *multitude* of governance forms and degrees of internalization which characterizes a heterarchy.

(9) Finally, and returning to the strategic ambitions rather than the structural properties of heterarchy, this type of MNC would be fit to attack the most difficult global problems of today. This may seem naive and even ridiculous to managers busy surviving producing and selling a narrow line of products or services. However, assuming a type of company that sees the exploitation of globality as such as its main source of strength, it does not seem that far-fetched to consider *radical problem-orientation* as guiding strategy formulation. (Rather than starting from existing physical or human resources, or from competitive positions in narrow fields of business.)

HUMAN RESOURCE MANAGEMENT IN A HETERARCHICAL MNC

No full discussion of human resource management in the context of a heterarchy will be attempted here. Instead, a few important points will be brought up, without pretence of exhaustive treatment.

(1) Concerning *organization structure*, many models will be simultaneously used in a heterarchical MNC. The flexibility and multidimensionality of the structure defy easy categorization. Change of the formal organization will not give rise to heterarchy. Subtler changes in management processes are required. However, the formal organization may stop a movement towards heterarchy.

One consequence of breaking down (up?) a large hierarchy is that it is *no longer possible to promote people mainly by giving them jobs 'higher up'*. Movement between centers will be more common, and movement from periphery towards centre in the same unit will be less common. Also, the need to build up the 'nervous system' of the heterarchy is of importance here, as is the need to use personal competence wherever it pays off best.

(2) The core of a heterarchical enterprise will consist of *people with a long experience in it*. A firm invests considerably in the employee, and vice versa. The latter is a part of the communication system of the firm, and the history of the human system in the company may be its most strategic resource. This is often said and may sound like a platitude. However, it is less so in an organization which builds its strategy on advantage seeking and using its global coverage, rather than on advantage exploitation on the basis of known and stable assets.

This communication network is not easily imitable by other firms. Much less so can a small part of it be used by others. In a limited sense, the employee is of value to competitors as a source of information, since he has a lot of it, also of a strategic nature. After having interrogated and 'emptied' the unfaithful soul, however, it is of little use. Thus, from the point of view of the employee, the idiosyncracy of his relation with the firm is very great. This is also true the other way around, since it takes a long time to find and train a replacement. However, the 'hologram quality' makes the firm *more* robust than in a hierarchy. Many employees will share the same information and be able to support or replace each other. This does not mean that the firm can easily fire the employee, since such behaviour would undermine the mutual trust necessary to encourage investment in the long-term future of the MNC. Idiosyncratic assets should lead to internalization, according to Williamson (1975), so one can expect *more encompassing and long-term contracts* with employees. Another possibility is participation in the ownership of the company.

One can exaggerate the need for permanence, however. There is considerable flux in the activities of the heterarchical MNC, and this requires flexibility also concerning personnel. Joint ventures and other forms of cooperation, sometimes on a project basis, by definition mean that new members continuously enter and leave the system. Perhaps one can speak of a *dual career system*, just as one speaks of dual labor markets in some countries. There will be a limited but still numerous core of almost life-time employees, and a much larger number of people with more fleeting association with the firm. In the debate on the Japanese labor system, it is often pointed out that the core enjoying life-time employment and other marvels of the Japanese employment system is rather small. What has surprised most analysts is that the duality of the labor market has not disappeared with modernization. Perhaps the solution with an integrated core surrounded by quasi-integrated satellites (which themselves might constitute cores in other systems) is a good combination of stability and flexibility?

The core provides the memory and the information infrastructure necessary to grasp opportunities on a global scale. The looser links to the outside help against rigidification of response by establishing channels for the communication of new ideas. In this context, the *balance between young and old members* of the organization is probably critical. (See the discussion by Lorenz, 1971) on the balance between processes of acquiring, retaining, and dismantling cultural knowledge, and the importance of age in this respect.) Company demography needs to be planned more systematically than when the firm is a system of roles which can be easily communicated and learnt. Not allowing steady recruitment of 'new blood', or dismantling of knowledge by early retirement, are traps in this area. However, much more research is needed on company demography before any strong statements can be made.

(3) In order for internalization of norms to take place, *a lot of rotation of personnel* and international travel and postings are necessary. The tendency to man purportedly global firms with home country managers—and more so than in polycentric firms—will not work in a heterarchical MNC. Advances in information technology may help the formation of the nervous system of the firm, but this will not be enough for building strong internal cultures.

The problems on the practical level of international transfers of people are well known. The solutions are less well known, apart from obvious hints such as paying well, giving spouses jobs, and being aware of re-entry problems. Perhaps recruitment of candidates for the core should be very selective, with a strong emphasis on willingness to travel and change function in the company. Sending people abroad very early is probably a good idea, possibly even before they have formed families. (Would the best be to have the new employee swear to chastity and keep unmarried, like in the very successful international operations of some ecclesiastical organizations such as the Jesuit Order?)

(4) A much *broader range of people in the firm must develop capacity for strategic thinking and action*. This implies open communication of strategies and plans, decentralization of strategic tasks, using task forces on strategic issues actively, and providing early opportunities for development of 'top management capabilities' also for 'subsidiary' employees. (The words 'subsidiary' and even 'manager' sound a bit funny in the context of a heterarchical MNC. There is less obvious subordination, and the clear distinction between managing and operational functions is less relevant than in a clear hierarchy. Heterarchy may mean the beginning of the decline of the professional manager as a species within the organizational zoo.)

Control systems which measure performance along many dimensions (products, regions, short and long term, etc.) are necessary. This is also almost a platitude, but in actual practice many companies who claim they do this really do not. Even if the systems are there, they are not used for more than very limited purposes. (Hedlund and Zander (1985) report on the economic control systems of Swedish MNCs. See also Czechowics *et al.* (1982).)

(5) *Reward and punishment systems are critical.* Carriers of bad news must not be killed. Kobrin (1984) shows how MNCs neglect to use the expertise of host country managers for the assessment of political risk. The long term must not be sacrificed. Perhaps a bonus should be given on the basis of profitability in the unit where the employee served five years ago? Particularly at very high levels, an effective career strategy is to turn 'star' and 'question mark' jobs into 'cash cow' jobs, and leave just before they start looking like 'dogs'. Top managers are rather

adept at taking credit for other people's work and avoiding criticism for their own, and temporal extension of the review period may counter the tendency to misuse such talents.

Similarly, the global aspects may be supported by rewarding people for global rather than local profits, or whatever the objective is. The difficulty lies in matching responsibility with authority. Probably, a heterarchical MNC has to refrain from mechanical compensation formulae to a large extent. It is not possible to construct perfect equations for the distribution of bonuses, for example, particularly when circumstances change often and drastically. Paying employees partly on the basis of the performance of the entire firm is one possibility. SAB-Nife, a small Swedish MNC, has a large bonus element in its system for paying subsidiary managers. Half of the bonus is based on the performance of the entire company (90% of sales are abroad), and half depends on the results of the individual subsidiary.

Shareholding by employees may be a very potent instrument to stimulate action in the interest of the total company, and to encourage normative integration. Would it not be better to have the employees in, say, the Indian subsidiary own shares in the parent company than the Indian government forcing the subsidiary to joint ventures with local partners, some more sleeping than others? Not that the former would stop the latter, but in the long run this would constitute an important change in the identity of the MNC.

Global mentality may be required far 'down' in the organization. Starting up new and closing down old activities is helped by understanding of the reasons for change. Technological developments are turning many workers into technicians, and to technicians needing to know a lot about customers. Global competition is changing the rules of the game for all employees. Some examples of action in Swedish firms in the direction indicated is given by:

- Volvo's gigantic program for improving substantially the technical know-how at all levels in the company.
- SAS' focus on foreign competition in mobilizing for turnaround, and the very public nature of its corporate strategy.
- SKF Steel's program to import steel technology from Japan and teach its employees about competitive facts (and, of course, technical matters) by sending workers on assignments with the Japanese licensor. (An informal race on productivity ensued, and the Swedes caught up with their teachers in Japan.)

(6) It is hard to tell what the *personality type best suited to heterarchy* is. Ogilvy (1977) argues that a sort of 'polytheistic' personality, and acceptance of such Protean prospects, go together with more decentralized organizations and societies. Speculating on this, one could argue that people from polytheistic or atheistic cultures would be most comfortable in such situations. Old Greeks, Vikings, Hindus, and Japanese would do well. Christians (particularly protestants), Moslems, Jews, communists, and people affected by 'scientism' would do worse. The representatives of western culture included in the former list are all dead, so many firms would do well to look around a bit for new managers.

Such speculation aside, it seems clear that a heterarchical MNC would require many employees with the following qualities:

- Aptitude for *searching for and combining elements* in new ways. Probably good knowledge in several fields of science and technology is one precondition for this.
- Skill in *communicating ideas* and rapidly *turning them into action*.

- Very good *command of several languages* and knowledge of and sympathy for several cultures. (Steiner (1975) argues that bilingualism is *qualitatively* different from monolingualism, in that it gives a 'stereo quality' to perception and interpretation. See also Maruyama (1978).)
- *Honesty and personal integrity.* These old fashioned ideals are critical for heterarchy not to turn into chaos.
- *Willingness to take risks and to experiment.* Advantage seeking is much more risky than advantage exploitation. The organization must support such learning from failures. The heterarchical MNC would mean an attempt to innovate from the basis of a large firm, working across national boundaries at very early stages in the innovation process. As in all entrepreneurial activity, a high failure rate is to be expected. Therefore, in practice, every company needs *also* a part which makes money in more stable and predictable ways. The theoretical alternative of a perfect external capital market can be ignored for the moment, because of agency cost considerations (Jensen and Meckling, 1976). It would be very difficult for anonymous shareholders, as well as for lenders, to assess ex ante, monitor constantly, and even evaluate ex post, the activities of a genuinely and entirely heterarchical MNC. This also means that the financial strength of a well-run, fairly large traditional MNC makes it the *only* realistic candidate for heterarchy on an international level. Neither small firms on their own or together through market relationships nor governments, for various reasons but in both cases having to do with agency cost problems, are likely to succeed.
- *'Faith' in the company* and its activities. Enthusiasm for the company need not go to the etymological limits of the word, but genuine appreciation of the company and its culture is valuable. Perhaps this means that the widely admired sceptical thinking type of person is of less interest than the person able to form strong attachments?

(7) *Management development activities* (in the more restricted sense) *should be seen as a primary instrument to build a corporate culture*, formulate and disseminate strategies, and establish links in the communication system of the firm. Its role for acquiring skills and for learning facts and methods is perhaps only subsidiary.

CONCLUSION

The heterarchical MNC is, so far, a loosely defined concept. It covers a particular brand of geocentric company, which differs significantly from a version that is likely to develop more rapidly in the immediate future. The importance in bringing up and further outlining the demands of and possibilities inherent in heterarchy lies in the risk of the purely global company regressing into a sized-up model of the large national firm. An ethnocentric backlash is a clear possibility, but mostly unnecessarily so. Therefore, firms should actively explore the dangers of recentralization, even if and when such moves are desirable, and find ways of compensating for those dangers. Only the broad outlines of response can be drawn without much experimentation and accumulation of experience. The MNC is a crucial arena for such institutional innovation, since it is uniquely powered to address some of the most urgent problems of a global scale.

Where should one look for signs of heterarchy? In terms of industries, probable fields are those characterized by the use of many different technologies, high but not maximum global homogeneity of demand, fast rate of technical and market change, non-trivial scale economies (but not necessarily in manufacturing), and absence of strong local barriers to entry. This means that information technology and biotechnology come to mind, which should make the reader (and writer) suspicious, since this seems too obvious (and boring). However, also the automobile industry, building and construction, and many services fit many, but not all, of the criteria.

In terms of geographical and corporate origins, heterarchical MNCs are more likely to evolve from less than gigantic firms. and from contexts with a history of rather autonomous and entrepreneurial subsidiaries. This may give European firms an advantage over US ones. In a larger picture, MNCs from newly modernizing nations may stand an even better chance. Chandler and Daems (1980) show how institutional inertia and established forms of corporate organization in Europe delayed the formation of the large, managerially run firm, compared to in the USA. Olsen (1982) has discussed how the same mechanisms may make whole nations rise and fall. The heterarchical prospect may seem too remote, or even silly, to people in successful hierarchies likely to enjoy still some time of harvesting the fruits of investments in a powerful organization for the maximum utilization of existing physical assets and know-how. It may seem less remote for people who have little alternative but to directly exploit the amazing global fluidity of capital, technology, and people to develop *new* products, markets, and competences.

REFERENCES

Allison, G. T. (1971) *Essence of Decision: Explaining the Cuban Missile Crisis*. Little, Brown.
Bartlett, C. A. (1981) 'Multinational Structural Change: Evolution Versus Reorganization'. In Otterbeck, L. (ed.), *The Management of Headquarters-Subsidiary Relationships in Multinational Corporations*. Gower Publishing Company Limited.
Bartlett, C. A. (1984) Organization and Control of Global Enterprises: Influences, Characteristics and Guidelines'. Harvard Business School, Boston.
Beer, S. (1972) *The Brain of the Firm*. Allen Lane.
Bouvier, P. L. (1984) 'Subjectivity and the Concept of Hierarchy: the Dominant Paradigm and the Prevailing Work System'. In *Proceedings from the International Conference of Society for General Systems Research*, New York, June.
Burenstam-Linder, S. (1961) *Essays on Trade and Transportation*. Wiley, New York.
Chandler, A. D. Jr. and Daems, H. (eds) (1980) *Managerial Hierarchies*. Harvard University Press, Cambridge, MA and London, England.
Channon, D. F. and Jalland, M. (1979) *Multinational Planning*. Basingstoke, London.
Coase, R. H. (1937) 'Nature of the Firm'. *Economica* N.S. 4: 386–405.
Czechowics, I. J., Choi, F. D. S. and Bashivi, V. B. (1982) *Assessing Foreign Subsidiary Performance*. Business International Corporation.
Daems, H. (1980) 'The Rise of the Modern Industrial Enterprise: A New Perspective'. In Chandler, A. D. and Daems, H. (eds), *Managerial Hierarchies*. Harvard University Press, Cambridge MA and London.
Davidson, W. H. and Haspeslagh, P. (1982) 'Shaping a Global Product Organization'. *Harvard Business Review*, July–August.
Doz, Y. L. (1979) *Government Control and Multinational Strategic Management: Power Systems and Telecommunications Equipment*. Praeger.
Doz, Y. L. and Prahalad, C. K. (1980) 'How MNCs Cope with Host Government Intervention'. *Harvard Business Review*, March–April.
Dunning, J. H. (1977) 'Trade, Location of Economic Activity and the Multinational Enterprise. A Search for an Eclectic Approach'. In Ohlin, B., Hesselbom, P. O. and Wiskman, P. J. (eds.), *The International Allocation of Economic Activity*. Macmillan, London.
Edström, A. and Galbraith, J. R. (1977) 'Transfers of Managers as a Coordination and Control Strategy in Multinational Organizations'. *Administrative Science Quarterly*, June: 248–263.

El Sawy, O. A. (1985) 'From Separation to Holographic Enfolding'. Paper presented to TIMS meeting, May, Boston.
Emery, F. E. and Trist, E. L. (1965) 'The Causal Texture of Organizational Environments'. *Human Relations*, 18: pp. 21–32.
Etzioni, A. (1961) *A Comparative Analysis of Complex Organizations*. Free Press, New York.
Faucheux, C. and Laurent, A. (1980) 'Significance of the Epistemological Revolution for a Management Science'. In *Proceedings from the Workshop on the Epistemology of Management*, EIASM.
Franko, L. G. (1976) *The European Multinationals*. Greylock Press, Greenwich, CT.
Hall, D. and Saias, M. (1980) 'Strategy Follows Structure'. *Strategic Management Journal*, 1(2).
Hedlund, G. (1980) 'The Role of Foreign Subsidiaries in Strategic Decision-Making in Swedish Multinational Corporations'. *Strategic Management Journal* 9: 23–26.
Hedlund, G.(1984) 'Organization In-Between: The Evolution of the Mother–Daughter Structure of Managing Foreign Subsidiaries in Swedish MNCs'. *Journal of International Business Studies*, Fall.
Hedlund, G. and Åman, P. (1983) *Managing Relationships with Foreign Subsidiaries—Organization and Control in Swedish MNCs*. Sveriges Mekanförbund, Stockholm.
Hedlund, G. and Kverneland, Å. (1984) *Investing in Japan—the Experience of Swedish Firms*. Institute of International Business, Stockholm School of Economics, Stockholm.
Hedlund, G. and Zander, U. (1985) *Formulation of Goals and Follow up of Performance for Foreign Subsidiaries in Swedish MNCs*. Working Paper 85/4, Institute of International Business, Stockholm School of Economics, Stockholm.
Hyden, H. 'Control of the Mind'. In Farber, S. M. and Wilson, R H. L. (eds) *Control of the Mind*. New York.
Hymer, S. (1976) *The International Operations of National Firms: A Study of Direct Foreign Investment*. MIT Press. (Originally published as doctoral dissertation in 1960).
Jaeger, A. M. and Baliga, B. R. (1985) 'Control Systems and Strategic Adaptation: Lessons from the Japanese Experience'. *Strategic Management Journal*, 6(2).
Jensen, M. C. and Meckling, W. H. (1976) 'Theory of the Firm: Managerial Behaviour, Agency Costs and Ownership Structure'. *Journal of Financial Economics*, October: 305–360.
Johanson, J. and Vahlne, J-E. (1977) 'The Internationalization Process of the Firm—A Model of Knowledge Development and Increasing Foreign Market Commitment'. *Journal of Management Studies*, **12**(3).
Knickerbocker, F. T. (1973) *Oligopolistic Reaction and Multinational Enterprise*. Harvard Business School, Boston.
Kobrin, S. J. (1984) *Managing Political Risk Assessment*. University of California Press.
Koestler, A. (1978) *Janus—a Summing up*. Random House, New York.
Laurent, A. (1978) 'Managerial Subordinacy'. *Academy of Management Review*, 220–230.
Lorenz, K. (1971) 'Knowledge, Belief and Freedom'. In Weiss, P. H. (ed.), *Hierarchically Organized Systems in Theory and Practice*. Hafner Publishing Company.
Lundgren, S. and Hedlund, G. (1983) *Svenska Företag i Sydostasien*. Institute of International Business, Stockholm School of Economics, Stockholm.
Maruyama, M. (1978) 'The Epistemological Revolution'. *Futures*, June: 240–242.
McCulloch, W. (1965) *Embodiments of Mind*. Cambridge, MA.
Mintzberg, H. (1978) 'Patterns in Strategy Formation'. *Management Science*, 934–948.
Mitroff, I. (1983) *Why Our Old Pictures of the World Don't Work Anymore*. Research Paper, University of Southern California.
Ogilvy, J. (1977) *Multidimensional Man*. Oxford University Press.
Ohlin, B., Hesselbom, P. O. and Wiskman, P. J. (eds) (1977) *The International Allocation of Economic Activity*. Macmillan, London.
Olsen, M. *The Rise and Decline of Nations*. Yale University Press, New Haven and London.
Perlmutter, H. V. (1965) 'L'enterprise Internationale—Trois Conceptions'. *Revue Economique et Sociale*, **23**.
Porter, M. E. (1980) *Competitive Strategy*. Free Press, New York.
Porter, M. E. (1984) *Competition in Global Industries—A Conceptual Framework*. Harvard Business School, New York.
Pribram, K. (1971) *Languages of the Brain*. Prentice-Hall, Englewood Cliffs, NJ.
Simmonds, K. (1985) 'Global Strategy: Achieving the Geocentric Ideal'. *International Marketing Review*, Spring.
Sjöstrand, S-E. (1985) *Samhällsorganisation*. Doxa, Stockholm.

Steiner, G. (1975) *After Babel*. Oxford University Press.
Stopford, J. M. and Wells, L. T. (1972) *Managing the Multinational Enterprise*. Basic Books, New York.
Thompson, J. D. (1967) *Organizations in Action*. McGraw-Hill, New York.
Varela, F. (1975) 'A Calculus for Self-Reference'. *International Journal of General Systems*, **2**, 5–24.
Vernon, R. (1966) 'International Investment and International Trade in the Product Cycle'. *Quarterly Journal of Economics*, May.
Vernon, R. (1979) 'The Product Cycle Hypothesis in a New International Environment'. *Oxford Bulletin of Economics and Statistics*, **41**.
Williamson, O. E. (1975) *Markets and Hierarchies: Analysis and Antitrust Implications*. New York, Free Press.

7

Managing Across Borders: An Empirical Test of the Bartlett and Ghoshal (1989) Organizational Typology

Siew Meng Leong and Chin Tiong Tan

The multinational of the 1970s is obsolete. Global companies must be more than just a bunch of overseas subsidiaries with executive decisions made at headquarters. Instead, a new type of company is evolving. It does research wherever necessary, develops products in several countries, and promotes key executives regardless of nationality (*Business Week*, 1990, front cover).

Several recent conceptualizations of global business management seem to suggest the emergence of stateless organizations operating in a borderless world. Accelerating this trend has been the lowering of transportation costs and the advent of modern communications networks (Reich, 1991). Such developments have encouraged businesses to get the most value from the least cost for their output. This shift in focus from volume to value production can be observed worldwide and across products and industries. Indeed, Ohmae (1989, 1990) has documented that successful corporations were those with such global-minded management.

However, many of these arguments have been founded on the observations and views of business people, academics, and management consultants. There has been a relative scarcity of empirical work verifying the extent of globalization among corporations. A major exception to this has been the stream of research by Bartlett and Ghoshal (1986, 1987a, b, 1989). Using a clinical approach, they conducted an in-depth study of nine companies from three countries operating in three industries with worldwide interests. Both personal interviews and survey questionnaires of key personnel were employed to develop a typology of organizations operating in the international business environment. Based on their results, these scholars identified four forms of organizations used to manage international businesses. They labelled these the multinational, global, international, and transnational corporations. Specific characteristics associated with the four forms of international organizational structures that differentiated their management practices were also proposed. Further, it was argued that businesses with a transnational structure and mindset would be most effective and efficient in future. This thesis is thus consistent with the view that a new, stateless corporate identity with a network of systems and activities in different parts of the world, deriving value from whichever location provides it at the lowest cost, is emerging (cf. Hedlund, 1986; Perlmutter and Twist, 1986; Prahalad and Doz, 1986).

Reprinted with permission from *Journal of International Business Studies*, Vol. 24, No. 3, pp.449–464.
Copyright © 1993 Journal of International Business Studies.

Bartlett and Ghoshal's (1989) typology represents a significant contribution to the literature in international business. These scholars furnished a more fine-grained delineation of the evolution, structure, and orientation of the four organizational types not heretofore accomplished. The typology also offered prescriptive insights for a transnationalistic perspective for future international business organization. Clearly, it also provides propositions for empirical testing necessary for theory building and extension.

We address two issues pertaining to the typology in this article from an international sample of executives of corporations with worldwide interests. These include: (1) the prevalence of the transnational corporation in contemporary international business relative to the other three organization types identified in it; and (2) whether the characteristics purported by it to distinguish one organization type from the others are demarcations employed by executives managing such enterprises. Empirical evidence on these issues would furnish some tentative insights regarding the relevance of the typology for international business organization and perhaps suggest aspects of it that require additional conceptual attention. In addition, the larger sample studied here would augment the empirical basis for the typology by incorporating companies from a wider array of national origins operating in a more diverse range of industries than those investigated by Bartlett and Ghoshal (1989).

In the remainder of this article, we first discuss the evolution of corporate structure in the international business context. In particular, the Bartlett and Ghoshal (1989) organizational typology, which forms the foundation for our empirical investigation, will be described.[1] Based on this literature review, hypotheses are advanced to examine the extent to which (1) the four organizational structures are adopted among companies, and (2) the various characteristics noted by Bartlett and Ghoshal (1989) correspond to their respective organizational types. The research method employed is then detailed, followed by the presentation of our survey results. Finally, we discuss the implications of the findings and provide some directions for future research.

EVOLUTION OF INTERNATIONAL CORPORATE STRUCTURE

Corporations are constantly seeking better ways of managing their businesses. Over time, every company is likely to evolve an organizational structure that facilitates its growth and international expansion (see, e.g., Stopford and Wells, 1972). According to Bartlett and Ghoshal (1989), different types of organizational structure evolve as a function of two key determinants. The first factor is the need for firms to match their capabilities to the strategic demands of their businesses. Hence, companies that manage a portfolio of multiple national entities perform well when the key strategic requirement is a high degree of responsiveness to differences in national environments around the world. Where global efficiency is vital, more centralized strategic and operational decision-making and the treatment of the world market as an integrated whole appeared most suitable. Finally, where transfer of knowledge is crucial, a structure that levered learning by adapting the parent company's expertise to foreign markets was preferred.

Bartlett and Ghoshal (1989) labelled these three types of organizations that operate in the international business environment as: (1) multinational companies, which build a strong local presence through sensitivity and responsiveness to national differences; (2) global companies, which build cost advantages through centralized global-scaled operations; and (3) international companies, which exploit parent company knowledge and capabilities through worldwide diffusion and adaptation.

The second factor influencing the organization of worldwide operations is the company's administrative heritage. Defined as its existing organizational attributes and way of doing things, it is shaped by the company's founder or key executive, the norms, values, and behaviours of managers in its national companies, and its historical context. Bartlett and Ghoshal (1989, p.33) argue that a company's administrative heritage can be a major asset, the underlying source of its key competencies, as well as a significant liability, since it resists change and thereby prevents realignment or broadening of the firm's strategic capabilities. They further detail how this internal force produces strategic and organizational consequences in a firm's expansion overseas (Bartlett and Ghoshal, 1989, pp.48–52).

Briefly, a multinational company reflects a decentralized federation with distributed resources and delegated responsibilities. Such structures are impacted by the enduring influence of family ownership, personal relationships, and informal contacts upon which organizational processes are built. Rather than relying on formal structures and systems, such processes reinforce the delegation of operating independence to trusted appointees in offshore subsidiaries. In contrast, the global organization can be construed as a centralized hub, a structural configuration based on group-oriented behaviour requiring intensive communication and a complex system of personal interdependencies and commitments. This in turn produces a dependence of overseas subsidiaries on the parent headquarters for resources and direction. The international form may be described as a coordinated federation suiting companies with a reputation for professional management. This implies a willingness to delegate responsibility while retaining overall control via sophisticated management systems and specialist corporate staffs.

Bartlett and Ghoshal (1989) caution that no particular organization type is best suited for specific industries or countries. Rather, they propose that the three organizational forms vary based on their (1) configuration of assets and capabilities, (2) role of overseas operations, and (3) development and diffusion of knowledge. Specifically, multinational corporations are seen to (1) be decentralized and nationally self-sufficient, (2) have their overseas operations sense and exploit local opportunities, and (3) develop and retain knowledge within each individual unit. In contrast, global corporations are those that (1) are centralized and globally scaled, (2) have their overseas operations as implementing tools of parent company strategies, and (3) develop and retain knowledge at headquarters level. International corporations are characterized by (1) having some of their sources of core competencies centralized, others decentralized, (2) adapting and levering parent company competencies, and (3) developing knowledge at parent level and transferring it to overseas units.

Beyond these organizational types, Bartlett and Ghoshal (1989) go further in arguing that with the growing complexities of conducting international business, such traditional management modes cannot effectively respond to the multidimensional and dynamic demands of contemporary industries and markets. They propose a fourth model based on the notion of a transnational corporation. Such companies seek to be globally competitive through multinational flexibility and worldwide learning capability. Their organizational characteristics include (1) being dispersed, interdependent, and specialized, (2) having differentiated contributions by national units to integrated worldwide operations, and (3) developing knowledge jointly and sharing it worldwide.

HYPOTHESES

The Bartlett and Ghoshal (1989) framework thus offers some interesting propositions for empirical testing. To the extent that the transnational structure is considered a new form and ideal structure for international business management, it can be predicted that it would be the least prevalent form observed in the marketplace today. Hence, H1 states:

H1. Relative to other organizational types, the transnational corporation will be the least prevalent form for organizing international business activities.

The other predictions stated in H2, H3, and H4 arise directly from the assertions of their framework concerning the practices associated with each type of organization. These hypotheses compare characteristics of organizing international activities among the three other types of structures—multinational, global, and international.

H2. Relative to global and international organizations, multinational corporations are more likely to (a) be decentralized and nationally self-sufficient, (b) have their overseas operations sense and exploit local opportunities, and (c) develop and retain knowledge within each individual unit.

H3. Relative to multinational and international organizations, global corporations are more likely to (a) be centralized and globally scaled, (b) have their overseas operations as implementing tools of parent company strategies, and (c) develop and retain knowledge at headquarters level.

H4. Relative to multinational and global corporations, international corporations are more likely to (a) have sources of core competencies centralized and others decentralized, (b) adapt and lever parent company competencies, and (c) develop knowledge at parent level and transfer it to overseas units.

Given its special status in the Bartlett and Ghoshal (1989) typology, the transnational structure should be assessed against all the other organizational types. Thus, a final test of the typology is that:

H5. Relative to all other types of organizations, transnational corporations are more likely to (a) be dispersed, interdependent, and specialized, (b) have differentiated contributions by national units to integrated worldwide operations, and (c) develop knowledge jointly and share it worldwide.

METHOD

Sample

A major consideration in research of this nature is that respondents be willing and able to provide the necessary information (cf. Campbell, 1955). Clearly, respondents should be executives of sufficiently high corporate standing to possess the likely expertise and bird's eye view required to furnish an informed perspective of their organization's international management structure. Moreover, they should represent companies with worldwide interests. Finally, they should provide input almost simultaneously so that enhanced comparability is possible within a given time frame (Sekaran, 1983).

One opportunity presented itself that enabled these criteria to be satisfied. A Global Strategies Conference was organized in 1990 by the Singapore Economic Development Board. Top officers of MNCs around the world were invited to participate in the seminar. Some 151 executives participated at the meeting and formed the sample for this study. Of these, 131 provided complete and usable returns for the analyses. The modal designation of respondents was managing director (38.4%). Of the remainder, such titles as president, director, chairman, and CEO were common. Their companies were engaged in a wide range of operations, with electronics, computers, and chemical industries most frequently mentioned (45.7%). The large scale of their operations was reflected in annual parent company sales exceeding US$10 billion for 78.5% of the respondents' organizations. All but 22.2% also had at least 1000 employees worldwide.

In summary, these statistics seem to suggest that respondents were well qualified to make informed judgments in the survey and represented large corporations with worldwide interests. The sample profile seems to fit well with the four organizational types posited by Bartlett and Ghoshal (1989) to be tested in this study. However, as the sample does not include domestic and probably just-internationalizing firms, more comprehensive validity assessment of the typology is precluded. To the extent that such firms can be shown not to possess the characteristics associated with the four corporate forms in the typology, greater evidence of discriminant validity can be accorded to it.

Measurement

A survey questionnaire was designed that required respondents to (1) categorize the international management structure of their organization into one of four types as defined by Bartlett and Ghoshal (1989), and (2) indicate the extent of agreement with 12 statements on 5 point scales regarding the three dimensions of configuration of assets and capabilities, role of overseas operations, and development and diffusion of knowledge in their organizations.

Specifically, respondents were asked to indicate how their company achieved competitiveness in the global market on one of four forced choices: (a) by building a strong local presence through sensitivity and responsiveness to national differences among countries; (b) by building cost advantages through global-scaled operations; (c) by exploiting their parent company's knowledge and capabilities through worldwide implementation and adaptation; or (d) by building interdependent resources with specialized subsidiary roles while maintaining flexible and joint operations among countries. Each option reflected one of four international management structures in the Bartlett and Ghoshal (1989) framework. In particular, options (a), (b), (c), and (d) reflected the typical multinational, global, international, and transnational type of organization, respectively.

Note that the self-typing approach used by respondents in this study to classify their organizations is not without shortcomings (cf. Snow and Hambrick, 1980). Managers may be reluctant to categorize their own organizations. However, the number who did not do so in this study was a mere 13%. There may be possible variance among managers' perceptions within the same organization. However, this possibility can be discounted given that only one respondent per organization provided the classification in this research. The approach used also lacks external confirmation of the respondents' categorization. However, by using key informants

Table 1. Mean Agreement Scores of International Organizational Structures[a]

Statement	Overall	Multinational	Global	International	Transnational
1. The skills and resources of my organization are located around the world, but each overseas unit conducts its own operations without relying on the expertise of other units located elsewhere.	2.75 (1.16)	2.72 (1.10)	2.73 (1.15)	2.69 (1.17)	2.81 (1.33)
2. The main role of our overseas operation is to implement parent company strategies.	3.49 (0.88)	3.41 (0.76)	3.81 (0.63)	3.63 (0.93)	3.00 (1.14)
3. New knowledge (e.g., product improvements) is developed at the parent company and then transferred to overseas units.	3.43 (0.89)	3.36 (0.85)	3.42 (0.86)	3.45 (0.96)	3.48 (0.93)
4. The most vital and strategic skills and resources of my organization tend to be located at parent company headquarters, while less important activities are located in our overseas units.	2.91 (1.04)	2.75 (1.06)	3.12 (1.07)	3.24 (0.87)	2.50 (1.06)
5. The primary role of our overseas units is to find out and take advantage of opportunities within the countries in which they operate.	3.94 (0.86)	4.09 (0.83)	3.72 (1.06)	3.80 (0.71)	4.05 (0.84)
6. Research and development activities are conducted, and the results retained, at parent company headquarters with little dissemination to our overseas units.	2.45 (0.97)	2.20 (0.87)	2.67 (1.01)	2.66 (1.04)	2.45 (1.00)
7. Our skills and resources are centralized and globally scaled.	3.04 (0.94)	2.68 (0.86)	3.48 (0.99)	3.25 (0.89)	3.00 (0.89)

Table 1 (continued)

	Statement	Overall	Multinational	Global	International	Transnational
8.	Research and development activities are typically conducted jointly by parent company and overseas units with the knowledge gained shared worldwide in my organization.	3.68 (0.87)	3.74 (0.88)	3.79 (0.72)	3.52 (0.99)	3.68 (0.89)
9.	Our overseas operations receive and adapt products and services offered by our parent company to the best advantage in the countries in which they operate.	3.92 (0.66)	3.95 (0.68)	3.68 (0.69)	4.03 (0.50)	3.89 (0.74)
10.	My organization locates specialized skills and resources around the world, but our overseas units often cooperate with and depend upon each other.	3.64 (0.82)	3.70 (0.88)	3.58 (0.72)	3.48 (0.87)	3.84 (0.76)
11.	The new knowledge (e.g., product improvements) developed in our overseas units tends not to be transferred to other locations in which my organization operates.	2.38 (0.82)	2.09 (0.60)	2.83 (0.96)	2.52 (0.74)	2.26 (0.81)
12.	My organization is integrated worldwide and our overseas units play an important role by contributing their individual strengths and know-how towards its operation.	3.95 (0.77)	4.02 (0.79)	3.75 (0.68)	4.00 (0.85)	4.00 (0.56)

[a] Standard deviations in parentheses.

who were willing and able to furnish their perceptions, this possibility is also minimized. Another limitation of this method is executives' tendency to report their organizations' intended rather than realized international management structure. Most serious is that if none existed, an arbitrary one may be created for the benefit of the researchers. However, this is a common problem in the social sciences (Nisbett and Wilson, 1977), although use of an 'other' category to allow respondents to fill in their own classification could have alleviated it somewhat.[2]

Given four organizational types to be evaluated on three dimensions, the minimum of 12 statements was created to assess the individual characteristics of respondents' organizations. These were modified from Bartlett and Ghoshal's (1989, p.65) summary table, the conclusions of which were reported in the literature review. The modifications to improve comprehension were based on a pre-test with 12 specialists working in the area of global investment and business. All items were also consistent with the group's views of operations of the various types of organizations.

RESULTS

H1 stated that relative to other organizational types, the transnational corporation will be the least prevalent form for organizing international business activities. Consistent with expectations, only 23 respondents considered their organizations as being transnational in character. Of the remainder, some 51 respondents considered their organizations as being multinational in nature, 26 deemed theirs as being global, and 31 classified their organizations as international corporations. The observed frequencies differed statistically from a uniform distribution of firms across the four organizational forms (*chi square*=14.55, df=3, $p<0.01$). More importantly, the actual proportion of transnational firms (17.6%) was significantly lower than the 25% expected under the null hypothesis of an equal proportion of firms in each category ($z=-1.97, p<0.05$). Hence, the evidence appears to support H1 as transnational corporations were observed to be the least prevalent organizational structure in international business management. Furthermore, the 38.9% of multinational firms significantly exceeded the 25% level ($z=3.67, p<0.01$). This bears out Bartlett and Ghoshal's (1989) observation that most worldwide operations are of the multinational organization type.

Descriptive statistics concerning respondents' evaluation of the hypothesized practices of the four organizational forms are contained in Table 1. On the average, respondents most strongly agreed with the statements concerning (1) the primary role of overseas units is to find and take advantage of opportunities within the countries in which they operate, and (2) their organization being integrated worldwide, with overseas units playing an important role by contributing their individual strengths and know-how towards their operations. In contrast, they most strongly disagreed with the statements regarding (1) new knowledge developed in overseas units tending not to be transferred to other locations in which their organization operates, and (2) R&D activities conducted and retained at parent company level without being disseminated to overseas units.

To test H2–H5, the mean agreement score for the target organizational type in each hypothesis was compared against the average score of the other organizations of concern for each of the three characteristics (statements) with which it was associated.[3] Given the *a priori* non-orthogonal nature of the contrasts, *t*-tests were performed using the Dunnett procedure (see Kirk, 1982, for details). Table 2 reports the results.

H2 stated that relative to global and international corporations, multinational organizations are more likely to be decentralized and nationally self-sufficient, have their overseas operations sense and exploit local opportunities, and develop and retain knowledge within each unit. As Table 2 shows, multinational corporations differed from their global and international counterparts on two of the three hypothesized characteristics. These included: viewing the role of overseas operations as uncovering and exploiting local opportunities, as well as new knowledge developed overseas tending not to be transferred elsewhere. On the remaining item regarding the autonomy of overseas units and their non-reliance on expertise from other units, the difference in agreement was in the predicted direction but was not statistically significant. Considered collectively, these results furnished some support for H2.

H3 posited that relative to multinational and international organizations, global corporations are more likely to be centralized and globally scaled, have their overseas operations as implementing tools of parent company strategies, and develop and retain knowledge at headquarters level. The survey findings also provided support for H3. Executives of global corporations more strongly agreed with the three statements concerning the characteristics of their organizational type *vis-à-vis* those from multinational and international corporations. Specifically, they held more strongly to the view that the role of overseas operations was to implement parent company strategies, that results from research and development activities were retained at headquarters, and that their companies' skills and resources were centralized and globally scaled.

H4 proposed that relative to multinational and global corporations, international organizations are more likely to have sources of core competencies centralized and others decentralized, adapt and lever parent company competencies, and develop knowledge at parent level and transfer it to overseas units. Executives from international organizations also reported stronger agreement (than those of multinational and global corporations) on all three hypothesized characteristics regarding their categorization. However, only one such difference—that pertaining to the most strategic skills and resources being maintained at parent company level while less important activities were located overseas—was found to be statistically significant.[4] Overall, the results do not furnish much support for H4.

H5 stated that, relative to all other types of organizations, transnational corporations are more likely to be dispersed, interdependent, and specialized, have differentiated contributions by national units to integrated worldwide operations, and develop knowledge jointly and share it worldwide. Even less empirical evidence was obtained supporting H5. In no case did executives from transnational corporations differ from their counterparts in the other three organizational types on the hypothesized characteristics. In two cases, however, differences obtained were in the predicted direction. These included location of specialized skills and resources worldwide and overseas units contributing their individual strengths and know-how towards their operations. On the remaining item of joint conduct of research and development, the difference was in the direction opposite to that hypothesized.[5]

Table 2. Results of hypotheses testing (t-statistics)

Statement	H2 MNC vs GC & IC	H3 GC vs MNC & IC	H4 IC vs MNC & GC	H5 TC vs Others
1. The skills and resources of my organization are located around the world but each overseas unit conducts its own operations without relying on the expertise of other units located elsewhere.	0.064	—	—	—
2. The main role of our overseas operation is to implement parent company strategies.	—	1.775[b]	—	—
3. New knowledge (e.g., product improvements) is developed at the parent company and then transferred to overseas units.	—	—	0.360	—
4. The most vital and strategic skills and resources of my organization tend to be located at parent company headquarters, while less important activities are located in our overseas units.	—	—	1.632[c]	—
5. The primary role of our overseas units is to find out and take advantage of opportunities within the countries in which they operate.	1.898[b]	—	—	—
6. Research and development activities are conducted and the results retained at parent company headquarters with little dissemination to our overseas units.	—	1.285[c]	—	—
7. Our skills and resources are centralized and globally scaled.	—	2.671[a]	—	—

Table 2 (continued)

Statement	H2 MNC vs GC & IC	H3 GC vs MNC & IC	H4 IC vs MNC & GC	H5 TC vs Others
8. Research and development activities are typically conducted jointly by parent company and overseas units with the knowledge gained shared worldwide in my organization.	—	—	—	−0.024
9. Our overseas operations receive and adapt products and services offered by our parent company to the best advantage in the countries in which they operate.	—	—	1.277	—
10. My organization locates specialized skills and resources around the world, but our overseas units often cooperate with and depend upon each other.	—	—	—	1.130
11. The new knowledge (e.g., product improvements) developed in our overseas units tends not to be transferred to other locations in which my organization operates.	3.763[a]	—	—	—
12. My organization is integrated worldwide and our overseas units play an important role by contributing their individual strengths and know-how towards its operation.	—	—	—	0.272

[a] significant at 0.01.
[b] significant at 0.05.
[c] significant at 0.10.

DISCUSSION

This study produced two principal findings. First, the results showed that executives perceived their companies to vary in international organization type. Multinational corporations dominated, followed by the international and global forms. The transnational form, as expected, was found to be the least evident structure. Second, the evidence in general furnished partial support for the differences in characteristics predicted across the four organization types of Bartlett and Ghoshal (1989). In particular, the demarcations between multinationally and especially globally organized corporations relative to other organizational types were more evident than those expected for international and transnational corporations. Prior to discussing these results, due qualification must again be made of the sample and questionnaire limitations in this research.

Implications

In general, corporations appeared to be trying to 'think global' and 'act local'. The strong levels of agreement towards the expanded and proactive role of overseas units coupled with worldwide integration of activities and free transfer of knowledge to all locations tended to support this contention. More interestingly, the results suggested variations existed in the practice of managing across national borders. Specifically, it was found that multinational and global corporations seemingly followed a particular mode of organization for managing their international operations by adopting practices consistent with those stipulated by Bartlett and Ghoshal (1989). However, it was found that executives who typed their organizations as being international and transnational in nature did not appear to endorse many of the behaviours predicted by the typology.

Our findings thus indicate that a reformulation of the Bartlett and Ghoshal (1989) typology appears necessary. Specifically, they imply that the practices of international and transnational forms may be distinguished from other organizational types as well as from each other on a more selective basis than previously conceptualized. Hence, international corporations may differ from multinational and global organizations on the role accorded to their overseas operations. Transnational corporations seem to be marginally differentiated from international organizations on their configuration of assets and capabilities, and from global enterprises on the role of their overseas operations.

In addition, the minimal differences obtained regarding the characteristics of transnationals versus the other organization types in the framework seem disturbing. Several explanations may be advanced to refute the inference that this represents a critical contradiction of the typology. One rationale may be that executives from the three other types of organizations have misclassified their corporations. This appears unlikely given the generally consistent differences obtained from examination of characteristics reflective of their respective types relative to others.

A more possible explanation concerns the finding that the transnational organization category received the fewest proportion (18%) of mentions. Bartlett and Ghoshal (1989), by comparison, noted that *none* of the companies they surveyed had reached this ideal. This may imply respondents misclassifying their organization as being transnational. It may also suggest that simply deeming one's organization as being transnational does not necessarily result in its adopting the characteristics normatively prescribed to such an entity. Potentially, the desired mindset of their executives may be one that has not truly absorbed the underlying managerial mentality of transnational organizations. If so, more effort is needed to cultivate this perspective to enhance the global competitiveness of their organizations.

The lack of differences in activities between the transnational and other types of organizations also may be due to the evolving nature of corporate structures in international business. Being the preferred option in the competitive global environment, the transnational structure is likely to be the one most companies are attempting to adopt. Given that they are likely to be operating in the multinational, global, or international mode, they are likely to resemble these existing organizational types. Moreover, the path towards transnationalism appears to be a difficult one. Indeed, Hu (1992) argues that international organization forms were mainly national firms with international operations.[6] Using secondary data, he found that the geographic spread and scope, ownership and control, management and workforce, and legal nationality and tax domicile of several well-known companies with worldwide operations were concentrated in their home countries.

FUTURE RESEARCH

Several useful directions for future research emanate from this study. First, only single-item measures were employed here given the limited time the participants had to complete the questionnaire. The development of multi-item, internally consistent measures would allow for a more complete explication of these complex constructs in future research. As alluded to earlier, it would also be instructive to include domestic and just-internationalizing firms in future samples to more completely assess the typology's discriminant validity.

Third, it may be beneficial to perform a study using customers of the organizations. This will provide an external validation of the findings. Moreover, factors other than those suggested by Bartlett and Ghoshal (1989) accounting for differences in organizational types may be theorized and tested (cf. Egelhoff, 1991; Hu, 1992). Indeed, such research may lead to the uncovering of omissions and misrepresentations of the typology, possibly leading to added conceptual refinement and extension. In a similar vein, added effort may be directed towards furthering the conceptual development of the transnational and international organization types as well as more precisely delineating them from other structural configurations.

Perhaps the most important area meriting research attention is whether transnationals do indeed outperform the other organizational types across countries and industries over time. Such an analysis would require longitudinal, rather than the present cross-sectional, data to empirically examine how differences in customer requirements and key success factors have an impact upon the movement towards transnationalism.

ACKNOWLEDGEMENTS

The authors thank the Singapore Economic Development Board for its assistance in data collection, the National University of Singapore for funding this research, and the three anonymous *JIBS* reviewers for their helpful comments.

NOTES

1. This exposition is necessarily brief for economy of presentation. Interested readers may find a more detailed and comprehensive account of the framework directly from Bartlett and Ghoshal (1989).
2. Nonetheless, using more open-ended categories is not without drawbacks. Errors may arise in researcher classification of such responses unless appropriate coding schemes are developed to categorize them reliably.
3. While from a strict psychometric perspective. the dependent variables were measured on ordinal scales, the Likert-type items employed here have been treated as though they were interval in nature in most social science research (cf. Guilford, 1954). One exception would be when *gross* inequality of the intervals exists (Kerlinger, 1973, p.441, his emphasis), a possibility that does not appear to hold here. Consequently our data have been subjected to parametric tests to extract the most information from them.
4. A one-tailed t-test showed that it was the difference between executives of international corporations and those from multinational enterprises ($t=2.57$, $p<0.01$) that accounted for this result. Another test revealed that executives of international corporations also more strongly agreed that their overseas operations received and adapted products and services to the best advantage where they operated relative to those from global corporations ($t=2.22$, $p<0.05$). All other pairwise comparisons were not significant (t's< 1, p's>0.10).
5. Pairwise comparisons using one-tailed t-tests revealed only two marginally significant findings (p's<0.10). Transnational managers agreed more strongly than those of international corporations that they located specialized skills and resources worldwide, with overseas units often cooperating and depending on each other ($t=1.59$). They also agreed more strongly than those of global enterprises that their organizations were integrated worldwide with overseas units playing an important role by contributing their individual strengths and know-how in operations ($t=1.39$). All other pairwise comparisons were not significant (t's<1.23, p's>0.10).
6. The two exceptions cited were binational companies that were owned, controlled, and staffed in two home nations and firms from small nations, for which the home nation accounts for a small percentage of total assets and operations (Hu, 1992, pp.121–122).

REFERENCES

Bartlett, C. A. and Ghoshal, S. (1986) 'Tap Your Subsidiaries for Global Reach'. *Harvard Business Review*, **64**: 87–94.
Bartlett, C. A. and Ghoshal, S. (1987a) 'Managing Across Borders: New Strategic Requirements'. *Sloan Management Review*, **28**:7–18.
Bartlett, C. A. and Ghoshal, S. (1987b) 'Managing Across Borders: New Organizational Responses'. *Sloan Management Review*, **29**:43–54.
Bartlett, C. A. and Ghoshal, S. (1989) *Managing Across Borders: The Transnational Solution*. Harvard Business School Press, Boston, MA.
Business Week (1990) 'The Stateless Corporation'. May 14: 52–60.
Campbell, D. T. (1955) 'The Informant in Quantitative Research'. *American Journal of Sociology*, **60**: 339–342.
Egelhoff, W. G. (1991) 'Information-Processing Theory and the Multinational Enterprise'. *Journal of International Business Studies*, **22**(3): 341–368.
Guilford, J. P. (1954) *Psychometric Methods*, 2nd edn. McGraw–Hill, New York.
Hedlund, G. (1986) 'The Hypermodern MNC: A Heterarchy?' *Human Resource Management*, Spring: 9–35.
Hu, Y. S. (1992) 'Global or Stateless Corporations are National Firms with International Operations'. *California Management Review*, Winter: 107–126.
Kerlinger, F. N. (1973) *Foundations of Behavioral Research*. Holt, Rinehart and Winston, New York.
Kirk, R. E. (1982) *Experimental Design*, 2nd edn. Brooks/Cole Publishing, Monterey, CA.
Nisbett, R. E. and Wilson, T. D. (1977) 'Telling More Than We Know: Verbal Reports on Mental Processes'. *Psychological Review*, **84**: 231–259.
Ohmae, K. (1989) 'The Global Logic of Strategic Alliances'. *Harvard Business Review*, **67**: 143–154.

Ohmae, K. (1990) 'The Borderless World'. *Harvard Business Review*, **68**: 32–42.
Perlmutter, H. and Twist, E. (1986) 'Paradigms for Social Transition'. *Human Relations*, **39**(1), 1–27.
Prahalad, C. K. and Doz, Y. (1986) *The Multinational Mission: Balancing Local Demands and Global Vision*. Free Press, New York.
Reich, R. B. (1991) *The Work of Nations*. Knopf, New York.
Sekaran, U. (1983) 'Methodological and Theoretical Issues and Advancements In Cross-Cultural Research'. *Journal of International Business Studies*, **14**(2): 61–74.
Snow, C. C. and Hambrick, D. C. (1980) 'Measuring Organizational Strategies: Some Theoretical and Methodological Problems'. *Academy of Management Review*, **5**: 527–538.
Stopford, J. M. and Wells, L. T. Jr. (1972) *Managing the Multinational Enterprise*. Basic Books, New York.

8

Bridgestone's Quest for Leadership in the Global Tire Industry

S. Benjamin Prasad

INTRODUCTION

In February 1982, Bridgestone acquired a single tire plant from the venerable US tire maker Firestone. Six years later, in 1988, it acquired the entire Firestone Tire & Rubber Company for $2.6 billion by topping Pirelli's takeover bid for Firestone. This foreign direct investment (FDI) decision by Bridgestone is construed in this paper as a bold quest for leadership in the global tire industry, which has been racked by overcapacity and intense struggle for market shares.

Elucidated as a case study, this paper focuses upon Bridgestone's FDI decisions in the 1980s and its competitive stance in the North American car and truck tire 'oligopoly'—that is, its competitive position *vis-à-vis* Groupe Michelin of France and Goodyear of the United States. This approach is consistent with the notion that 'each foreign subsidiary arises out of a particular set of circumstances which needs to be assessed in the context of the business strategy of the individual multinational companies' (Teichova, 1986, p.367).

Details here pertain mostly to the 1980–1989 time frame, although references to earlier time periods are essential to one's understanding the decision of the Japanese firm and its senior management. A large part of the data included here is drawn from published sources; a small portion is from the author's personal interview notes in Tokyo in 1982 and 1986. The paper is organized as follows: (a) Expansion of Bridgestone as a regional Japanese multinational; (b) Planning for the initial FDI decision in the United States; (c) New management at Bridgestone; (d) Acquisition of Firestone; and (e) Emergence of Bridgestone as a formidable rival in the global tire industry.

EXPANSION OF BRIDGESTONE AS A REGIONAL MULTINATIONAL

Until 1980, few Americans had ever heard the name Bridgestone. Even a few years later, many would not know that it was a Japanese tire company. However, as early as 1932, the US subsidiaries of Chrysler, Ford, and GM in Asia put Bridgestone tires on their cars and trucks.

In 1933, Firestone sued Bridgestone alleging brand name infraction, but Bridgestone 'won the case when its founder, Ishibashi Shojiro, demonstrated that "bridgestone" was a literal translation of his family name' (Johnson, 1982, p.211).

Bridgestone is named after the founder, Ishibashi, whose name means 'stone bridge'. 'In 1906, on the southern Japanese island of Kyushu, Shojiro Ishibashi and his brother assumed control of the family business—making *tabi*' (Bridgestone, 1983–85, p.1), the traditional Japanese footwear. The technology of mass producing *tabi* led to the formation of a tire plant. Shojiro Ishibashi formed Bridgestone in 1931 in Kurume, Japan, to produce tires with domestic capital and technology. In the 1930s, Bridgestone began producing car tires, airplane tires and golf balls. The company followed the Japanese military to occupied territories and built plants there. Although Bridgestone lost all of its overseas plants in World War II, the domestic plants escaped damage and thus became the foundation for later expansion (ibid., p.3). As is the case with all tire companies the demand for whose products is 'derived', Bridgestone's growth until the 1970s paralleled that of the Japanese automotive industry.

In the ensuing years, two principles[1] consistently guided the conduct of Bridgestone's business in both tires and chemical industrial products. The first has been a genuine commitment to 'enhancing the quality of life', a commitment served by the second: 'serving society with products of superior quality' (Bridgestone, 1981–90). These two maxims were the basis of founder Ishibashi's business philosophy; they constitute the guiding forces of Bridgestone during the first fifty years of its existence. Milestones in the 50-year history of Bridgestone (1931–1980), which are sketched in Table 1, provide a glimpse of the growth of this Japanese multinational.

Table 1. Milestones in the History of Bridgestone, 1931–1980

1931	Bridgestone Tire Company was founded by Shojiro Ishibashi who had established a tire division at Nippon Rubber Co. to study tire production. In 1930, the first tire was produced.
1932	Japanese subsidiaries of Chrysler, Ford, and GM selected Bridgestone tires.
1934	The factory at Kurume, established in 1931, began production of bias and radial tires.
1948	Bridgestone relocated its headquarters to its current location in Kyobashi, Tokyo.
1951	Sojiro Ishibashi reached an agreement to share technology with Goodyear.
1961	Bridgestone went public. Until then, ownership remained in the family, which started out in the clothing business, focusing on making *tabi*, the traditional Japanese footwear, and in 1923 began work on rubber soles.
1964	Bridgestone ranked tenth among world's rubber product producers.
1968	Bridgestone was awarded the coveted Deming Prize for quality achievements.
1971	Bridgestone produced the world's largest tire at its Shimonoseki factory.
1974	First orders from overseas OEM for truck and bus tires from British Leyland and Volvo.
1977	Proving ground completed in Kuroiso City, Japan.
1980	Bridgestone becomes the sixth largest company among world's rubber products producers. Total sales exceed Y500 billion.

Source: Bridgestone 50th Anniversary Report 1985.

In 1978, Bridgestone reached a landmark: total production topped 500 million tires, a first for any Japanese tire maker. In 1980, Bridgestone became the only Japanese tire maker to manufacture tires abroad with four overseas plants located in Australia, Indonesia, Taiwan, and Thailand. In short, Bridgestone emerged as a regional multinational. It led the Japanese rubber industry in sales and climbed to the sixth place (as of 1978) among rubber-product firms around the world (Bridgestone, 1983–85).

In 1979, the Japanese economy faced rising costs of raw materials due to sharply higher crude oil prices and the lower exchange value of the yen. Even so, strong personal consumption and public sector investment boosted the gross national product (GNP) by a healthy measure. In this climate, Bridgestone intensified its marketing efforts in order to lift overall corporate performance. The company also pursued ongoing programs to develop innovative products, raise productivity, and contain mounting energy costs.

The results were noteworthy. Total consolidated sales rose to Y579.7 billion (US $645.1 million), up 16% over 1978. Before-tax income amounted to Y69.9 billion (US $318.9 million), 68% over 1978; and net earnings reached Y29.1 billion (US $132.9 million), a 72% advance (Bridgestone, 1983–85). These returns far exceeded the targets for the year. Higher demand in Japan and abroad contributed to this phenomenal growth of tire sales.

The company stepped up its marketing activities and introduced new products (such as the Super Filler Radial tire RD-207 STEEL), to achieve gains in both the original-equipment and replacement-tire markets. Sales of truck tires also advanced. Also, Bridgestone's exports increased significantly as the company focused on sales of steel radials and large tires for mining and construction vehicles. The drop in the value of the yen had a significant positive effect on Bridgestone's exports at the time.

There is evidence (Bridgestone, 1981–90, 1983–85) to suggest that the company actively cultivated international markets. It marketed the Super Filler Radial in West Germany and Australia. Eastern Airlines and Frontier Airlines in the United States adopted Bridgestone aircraft tires. Exports accounted for more than 23% of total sales, with the Overseas Division reporting its highest sale. The vigorous overseas demand and the decline of the yen by nearly 10% were the major contributing factors. Among overseas factories, Thai Bridgestone Co. hailed the tenth anniversary of its founding by expanding its production facilities.

Since its founding, technological process and innovation have been central aims of Bridgestone. The company has always wanted its processes, materials, and products to remain in the technological vanguard. The company's research and development (R&D) strategy focused on the developments of new products and technologies of the diverse needs of today's society. In addition, efforts over the years to find ways to recycle discarded tires culminated in a highly efficient recycling system.

Bridgestone's Technical Center in Tokyo employs over 1000 engineers and technicians. The world's largest tire for heavy mining vehicles, the mammoth 200-ton trucks, was designed by a team at the Technical Center. The Center has created tires for the linear motor car, the ground transportation system developed by the Japan National Railways as a successor to the Shinkansen high-speed bullet trains.

Kuroiso City, in Tochigi Prefecture, is the home of Japan's largest tire testing ground. Here, Bridgestone has had some of the most up-to-date facilities in the world. Thirty types of road surfaces, including cobblestone pavement imported from Belgium, reproduce road conditions that are found throughout the world, permitting comprehensive, meticulous testing for every Bridgestone tire design. Testing data go to the Technical Center, a feedback process essential to Bridgestone's product strategy for providing unsurpassed tire quality. Because materials and the construction of new products are becoming even more complex, Bridgestone continued its efforts to maintain productivity superior to that of its major international 'competitor actors' (Zajac and Baderman, 1991, p.37) particularly Goodyear, Michelin and Pirelli. Table 2 summarizes financial data, expressed in yen, from December 1979 to December 1989 and indicates a healthy growth in assets, revenues and earnings through 1987.

Table 2. Bridgestone financial data 1979–1988

Millions of Yen

	1979	1980	1981	1982	1983	1984	1985	1986	1987	1988
Net sales	579 737	680 812	724 397	712 162	761 619	801 759	864 285	792 708	820 419	1191 229
Tires	428 131	510 556	535 025	514 539	564 768	585 344	631 136	561 557	57 419	876 817
Non-tire products	151 606	170 256	189 372	197 623	196 851	216 415	233 149	231 151	246 000	314 412
Earnings before income taxes	74 033	67 923	50 076	38 531	53 761	51 014	60 621	61 178	91 371	108 713
Net earnings	29 105	28 446	15 844	13 002	18 524	15 673	21 084	21 006	36 001	39 960
Total assets	523 121	604 539	607 274	626 804	662 390	716 672	757 165	753 998	856 473	1399 841
Total shareholders' equity	171 608	205 833	217 100	233 843	250 075	259 136	277 850	310 701	345 356	377 931
(Ratio of total shareholders' equity to total assets)	(32.8%)	(34.0%)	(35.7%)	(37.3%)	(37.8%)	(36.2%)	(36.7%)	(41.2%)	(40.3%)	(27.0%)
Purchases of property plant and equipment	40 150	72 943	55 934	32 001	48 955	60 722	67 325	43 005	43 835	96 884
Depreciation and amortization	26 473	32 133	37 929	37 684	37 379	39 553	45 878	48 645	46 353	58 527
Number of employees	30 059	30 911	33 498	32 350	32 308	32 577	32 834	33 425	34 061	88 148

Source: Bridgestone Annual Report, 1989 p.25.

PLANNING FOR FDI IN THE US

Senior executives at Bridgestone recognized that they had to consider five salient managerial issues that surrounded the company's FDI intentions in the US in the early 1980s. The issues included:

(1) The size, location, and capacity of the production plant(s).
(2) A decision to build a new plant or acquire an existing plant. (Most US tire companies, except Goodyear, were following a retrenchment strategy in the early 1980s).
(3) The need for highly specialized labour, since radial tire making represents a fine art. More important, US workers having such skills would invariably be members of United Rubber Workers (URW).[2] Although Bridgestone has had production facilities in four countries in the Pacific Rim, this would be the first time that Bridgestone would have to deal with an American union—the URW.
(4) A strategic option whether to start production first and then make US consumers aware of Bridgestone products made in the United States, or to bring about consumer awareness first with production to follow.
(5) Ability to maintain the (perceived) high quality of Bridgestone radial tires manufactured in the United States.

These issues and other concerns warranted a need for a preliminary strategic analysis of manufacturing both car and truck tires in the United States. This was a major challenge to Bridgestone management. On the one hand, unlike its American counterparts, Bridgestone would not have extensively studied the North American market structure and conditions. Speed was a paramount criterion in the FDI decision, as expressed by a knowledgeable Japanese person. On the other, the conceptual models of the strategic management process were found to be helpful to senior management in that they could recognize the three types of analysis suggested therein. From the standpoint of Bridgestone, the analytical questions would have been framed approximately as follows:

(1) What factors in the United States would have an important bearing on Bridgestone's consideration about its direct investment in the United States?
(2) Although Bridgestone was resourceful enough to invest directly in the United States, what other distinct advantages does it have or does it need?
(3) With which major tire companies would Bridgestone have to compete, and on what basis?

Thus, the external analysis would call for an assessment of market opportunities for Bridgestone tires in the 1980s, that is, 1982 and beyond. The competitor analysis would call for an assessment of market share, market standing, and the distribution networks of at least two major multinational competitors, namely, Goodyear and Groupe Michelin. As senior executives contemplated further, they would realize that they would have to redefine Bridgestone's corporate objectives and strategic intent in global terms. The broad framework for that daunting task (*Business Week*, 1980a, p.14) had already been sketched out in 1980 by Chairman Kanichiro Ishibashi (founder's son) (Bridgestone, 1983–85).

The company's records (Bridgestone, 1981–90, 1983–85) showed that, more than being alert to market demand for tires and other rubber products, Bridgestone had anticipated and developed entirely new technologies. Foreign expansion of production facilities had, through 1979, followed a pattern of organizing an entirely new company and constructing a plant—

Greenfield Investment—on an available site. Major subsidiaries of Bridgestone can be gleaned from Appendix A. However, acquisitions—in contrast to greenfield investments—of existing manufacturing plants was being preferred in the 1980s. In retrospect, there was both an initiative from top management and a sense of exigency to transform Bridgestone into a global business organization. As coincidence would have it, John Nevin (CEO of Firestone) had made some initial overtures to Bridgestone Chairman Ishibashi through a mutual friend, Akio Morita of Sony Corporation. This approach was part of Nevin's turnaround strategy at the time for Firestone. In describing this strategy, Vernon and Welles (1991, p.326) note that 'In 1981, Nevin presented the board with a plan... Businesses which did not have the potential to meet 15 percent ROE, which equated to an 18 percent operating profit on capital employed would be liquidated or sold. A bellwether example was his proposal to withdraw from the manufacture of radial truck tires in North America'.

In mid-May 1981, Bridgestone sent a team of its specialists to visit a Firestone plant near Nashville, Tennessee. Designed to produce radial truck tires, this plant opened in 1972. It was touted as Firestone's most modern truck-tire manufacturing facility. During the late 1970s, Firestone had fallen on bad times. In 1978, it lost nearly $148 million. The arrival of John Nevin in 1980 as the new CEO clearly suggested a 'turnaround strategy' as the only viable option for Firestone. Such a strategy called for cost-cutting and down-sizing by means of selling off assets to bolster the balance-sheet conditions.

Firestone had decided to sell one or more of its operating tire plants including the La Vergne, Tennessee, plant. Bridgestone's interest in this La Vergne plant continued, and so did negotiations culminating in a meeting of Mr Kunio Hattori, President of Bridgestone, and Mr John Nevin, CEO of Firestone. In February 1982, Bridgestone signed a letter of intent with Firestone Tire Company regarding the purchase of the plant in Tennessee.

Specifically, Bridgestone agreed to acquire the Firestone plant for $52 million and to continue producing truck and bus tires, as before, for Firestone. However, plans and programs were well underway to shift gears by 1984. New machinery and equipment would be introduced at the time and truck tires of Bridgestone design would be manufactured bearing Bridgestone and Firestone brand names. Plant remodelling began in January 1983.

Table 3. Tire companies sales figures, 1980–1984

	US Dollars				
	1980	1981	1982	1983	1984
Goodyear	8 444 015	9 152 905	8 688 700	9 735 800	10 240 800
Michelin	7 731 084	6 227 783	5 567 205	5 390 093	5 075 763
Firestone	4 850 500	4 361 000	3 869 000	3 866 000	4 161 000
Pirelli	7 511 430[a]	4 450 000	4 209 533	3 730 231	3 497 646
B. F. Goodrich	3 079 597	3 184 600	3 005 300	3 191 700	3 415 700
Bridgestone	3 015 997	3 296 006	2 859 505	3 207 559	3 374 584
GenCorp	2 215 206	2 524 309	2 061 659	2 184 351	2 727 062
Uniroyal	2 299 463	2 260 100	1 967 221	2 040 285	2 209 974
Dunlop	—	2 951 006	2 667 942	2 429 957	2 112 867
Continental	1 740 727	1 434 037	1 337 992	1 325 978	1 240 761

[a] Net sales in 1980 were combined totals for Dunlop and Pirelli. In 1981 Dunlop and Pirelli became separate entities.
Source: *Fortune 500* outside USA. The above figures were calculated using exchange rates determined by *Fortune*.

The URW issue had been given plenty of thought. Bridgestone executives had a continuing dialogue with the URW in an effort to reach a satisfactory agreement that stipulates 'full' employment with URW members and a boost in plant productivity. What Bridgestone managers found at the La Vergne plant and how they augmented plant productivity is detailed by Ishikure (1991, pp.221–234) who stated: 'We compared the Tennessee plant in the first half of 1983 with a similar plant in Japan ... [and found] that the productivity level was less than one-third that of the Japanese plant ... We used the 4M approach—Machine, Material, Method and Manpower—in order to produce the highest quality tires'.

Bridgestone Tire Co., Ltd., announced a change in its corporate name, to Bridgestone Corporation, effective 1 April 1984. As of 1984, Bridgestone had become the sixth largest tire company in the world (Table 3). In announcing the new name, Chairman Ishabashi and President Hattori said that tires would remain as the company's principal business (Bridgestone, 1983–85).

The Tennessee plant, now dubbed Bridgestone Tire Company (USA), Inc., began production of steel radial truck and bus tires in January 1983. To respond more fully to demand from varied segments, it began expanding the range of tires. As noted earlier, for a short time this plant would make tires to keep the production line active. However, the first American-made Bridgestone-brand tire came off the line on 1 March 1984. By 1985, Bridgestone's total investment in the Tennessee plant was about $80 million, including the purchase price and it was agreed that Bridgestone would re-employ the displaced Firestone workers.

By 1985, most of the 441 workers laid off by the financially troubled Firestone in 1980 had been recalled[3] by Bridgestone. The plant was being run at full capacity. In January 1985, Bridgestone Tire (USA) celebrated the production of its one millionth truck radial tire with a 'Thanks a Million' observance for employees at the La Vergne plant. The commemorative ceremony involved the company officials and employees and the distribution of over 1000 'Thanks a Million' T-shirts to workers at the plant. Arthur Eggert, director of manufacturing, noted that 'the Tennessee-produced tires are now as good as those produced in any Bridgestone plant in Japan' (Bridgestone, 1983–85).

NEW MANAGEMENT AT THE PARENT

Bridgestone Corporation announced a change in the company's top management, effective 15 February 1985. Teiji Eguchi, 58, became Bridgestone's new Chairman. Akira Yeiri, 56, was named its new President. Kanichiro Ishibashi, 64, who had been Chairman since 1973, and Kunio Hattori, 62, President since 1981, agreed to step aside. The company entered a new era in the sense it came under non-family management.

Citing an aggressive program, aimed at strengthening its international sales network, developing new technology and new products, and streamlining management system as reason for its success, Bridgestone Corporation announced record sales of $6.5 billion for 1984, a 6% increase over 1983. The 1984 performance also showed that, while Bridgestone's primary business was still in tires, the company's efforts to diversify further into non-tire products bore fruit. The ratio between tire and non-tire products showed that non-tire products accounted for 17.6% of the company's sales, up by 1% over 1983. Bridgestone's leading market position in Japan is shown in Table 4.

Table 4. Bridgestone's 1984 market position in Japan

	Production of tires and tubes in Japan (%)	Tire and tube exports from Japan (%)
Bridgestone	46.5	48.6
Rival A	19.1	16.6
Rival B	14.7	13.7
Rival C	12.0	13.1
Rival D	4.8	4.1
Others	2.9	3.9

Source: Bridgestone, Summary of Activities, 1985.

Foreign operations and export sales also continued to show increases for Bridgestone. Although export sales accounted for 31.6% of the company's revenues, down 0.41% from 1983, the $689 million (Y172.8 billion) in export sales were up 5% over 1983 figures. These were in large part assisted by several factors. The first was an unusually large shipment of tires to the Middle East during the first half of the year. The second was improved market conditions in the United States, primarily due to the popularity of Bridgestone's new all-season passenger radials and the m711 and m716 truck and bus tires.

Of vital significance to Bridgestone was the consolidation of its US manufacturing company and its sales and marketing subsidiary. The new company, Bridgestone (USA), Inc., has its headquarters in Torrance, California. Bridgestone, by 1985, had become the world's fourth largest tire manufacturer.

The year 1987 emerged as a second FDI point. According to *Business Week* (1980a), Bridgestone officials denied that Bridgestone would soon decide to build a US plant to make car tires.

However, the opinion of Mr Akio Mino, general manager of the international tire sales, was that 'if we want to sell tires to the Japanese car industry in the US, Bridgestone must make a decision quickly' (Bridgestone, 1983–85). Again, a sense of urgency is discernible.

There was the obvious negative impact on the export of car tires to the United States because of the appreciation of the yen. In 1980, as we noted at the outset, a decision to invest in the United States was carefully deliberated by Bridgestone. The choice to acquire a plant from Firestone, rather than to build one from ground up, was evidently sound in terms of organizational learning—operating a subsidiary in the United States—as well as in terms of being close to the vast North American market. The decision was to acquire Firestone.

ACQUISITION OF FIRESTONE

In the spring of 1988, Bridgestone acquired Firestone Tire and emerged as one of the world's leading tire manufacturers with consolidated sales of about $11.7 billion at the end of 1989. In terms of 1989 consolidated sales per employee, Bridgestone was the most productive among the three largest tire manufacturers, at US $132 833 per employee, followed by Goodyear at US $99 083 (Hoover *et al.*, 1991). Although it is generally known in the tire industry circles that while Bridgestone desired to foster a joint-venture relationship with Firestone, Pirelli of Italy made a bid to buy up Firestone at $58 a share. Reacting to the move by Pirelli, Bridgestone decided to acquire Firestone and paid $80 a share. In a candid account, Nevin (1989), CEO of Firestone, provides a behind-the-scene look at the events that led to the acquisition of Firestone by Bridgestone.

Nevin's account can be paraphrased as follows. The Board of Directors of Firestone asked CEO Nevin in 1984 to explore the possibilities of joint-venturing with a foreign (European or Japanese) tire company. Nevin discussed the possibilities with several companies during 1984 and 1988. In February 1988, the two companies agreed to form a joint venture. 'Firestone and Bridgestone would jointly manage Firestone's tire business, with Bridgestone paying $1.25 billion and buying 75 percent interest'—that is, equity interest in Firestone (Nevin, 1989). Soon after this agreement, Pirelli made the tender offer.

At that critical point, states Nevin (1989): 'There were only three possible outcomes: Firestone could have been sold to Pirelli at $58 [per share]; some other buyer could make a better offer than Pirelli; or some of our management could have taken Firestone private in a leveraged buyout'. From Firestone's perspective, accepting Pirelli's offer would negate the joint venture possibility. 'We said to Bridgestone that we could not proceed with the joint venture, if we were owned by Pirelli. That led Bridgestone to make the $80 offer' (Nevin, 1989). In short, Italy's Pirelli and Japan's Bridgestone fought a duel. Bridgestone countered with $80 a share, 38% higher than what Pirelli had bid. Not surprisingly, Bridgestone won.

EMERGENCE AS A MAJOR PLAYER

'Our business and financial results for the year marked an important new stage in our quest for leadership in the global tire industry', claimed Bridgestone's 1989 Annual Report (Bridgestone, 1981–1990). Underscoring that international tire operations had been crucial to the pursuit of the leadership position in the global tire industry, the Report (Bridgestone, 1981–1990) went on to say that 'we took substantive measures during 1989 to improve the efficiency of those operations'. These measures included beginning a major investment program for raising productivity and quality at Firestone facilities worldwide.

Most of Bridgestone sales in the replacement market in North America are through independent dealers, though the MasterCare network of more than 1550 tire and car service centers is also an important sales channel for passenger car tires. The company markets Bridgestone as well as Firestone brand tires through this network. Also, the company supplied a growing volume of Firestone and Bridgestone tires to Japanese transplants in the US. However, in May 1988, General Motors decided to discontinue Firestone as a supplier.

Sales in North America increased only very slightly in 1989, as gains achieved in market share were insufficient to compensate for a downturn in demand. Business was sluggish in the US and the Canadian replacement markets for passenger car tires and for truck and bus tires. New car sales tailed off from their strong pace of the previous year, dampening demand in the original equipment market. Demands for automobile tires worldwide rose only 2.4% in 1989. Table 5 shows the ten-year comparative performance of Bridgestone, Goodyear, and Michelin.

In 1990, Bridgestone ranked third, measured in terms of volume of car, truck, and bus tires worldwide (Table 6).

Table 5. Ten-year comparative performance of three largest tire makers

	1980	1981	1982	1983	1984	1985	1986	1987	1988	1989	1990
Bridgestone											
Sales (Y bil)	681	724	712	762	802	864	793	820	1191	1689	1784
Net Income (Y mil)	28.4	15.8	13.0	18.5	15.7	21.1	21.0	36.0	39.9	9.7	5.0
Sales index	100	106	104	112	118	127	116	120	175	248	261
Income index	100	56	45	65	55	74	74	127	140	34	17
Income as % of sales	4.2	2.2	1.8	2.4	2.0	2.4	2.6	4.4	3.4	0.6	0.3
Earnings per share (Y)	39	23	20	28	24	32	30	54	59	13	6
Goodyear											
Sales ($ bil)	8.45	9.15	8.69	9.73	10.24	9.58	9.10	9.90	10.81	10.87	NA
Net income ($ bil)	207	244	248	270	411	301	101	51	350	189	NA
Sales index	100	108	103	115	121	113	107	117	128	129	NA
Income index	100	117	119	130	198	145	49	248	169	91	NA
Income as % of sales	2.4	2.7	2.9	2.8	4.0	3.1	1.1	5.2	3.2	1.7	NA
Earnings per share ($)	2.85	3.36	3.35	2.71	3.87	2.8	1.94	8.49	6.05	3.28	NA
Michelin											
Sales (FF bil)	29.8	33.65	36.61	41.08	44.38	46.64	46.32	46.93	51.28	55.26	62.73
Net income (FF mil)	815	(290)	(4169)	(2145)	(2242)	1040	1908	2647	3519	2653	(4811)
Sales index	100	112	122	138	149	156	155	157	172	185	210
Income index	100	NM	NM	NM	NM	127	234	324	440	325	NM
Income as % of sales	2.7	−0.9	−11.4	−5.2	−5.1	2.2	4.1	5.6	5.0	4.8	NM
Earnings per share (FF)	19	−9	−101	−52	−55	19	28	34	29	22	(45)

Note: Sales revenue and income are shown in domestic currencies (Y: yen; FF: French francs). Indices shown are more meaningful for comparative purposes.
Source: Hoover et al. (1991, 1992).

Table 6. Share of worldwide tire market by volume, 1990 (car, truck, and bus tires)

	Percentage
Groupe Michelin	21.5
Goodyear	19.0
Bridgestone/Firestone	16.5
Continental/General	7.0
Pirelli/Armstrong	6.0
Sumitono/Dunlop	6.0
Yokohama	4.5
Toyo	2.0
Cooper	1.5
Others	16.0
	100.0

Source: Fundamental Research, Inc. (UK), 1991.

DISCUSSION AND CONCLUDING REMARKS

Analogous to any competitive race, there are several rounds in the quest for the number one position in the global tire industry. About 40% of the global tire industry is made up of tire sales in North America. 'A dogfight over market dominance in North America is shaping up between Goodyear and its archcompetitor, France's Michelin Group' (Elias, 1990). That is an apt description of the competitive context.

Unlike Bridgestone, Michelin entered the North American market with its presence in Nova Scotia, Canada. The story of Michelin's entry into Canada, in 1969, has been characterized as 'one of intrigue and political manoeuvring on a complex, international scale' (Harkleroad, 1982). Michelin received a patent for radial tires in 1946. Since then, and especially in the 1970s, Michelin enjoyed worldwide growth in radial tire sales. Even though Michelin and radial tires are most often synonyms in the minds of the consumer, both Goodyear and Bridgestone have laid claims to the original development of the radial tire. 'When France's Michelin invented the radial tire in the late 1960s, it expanded in North America by building eight new factories'(*Economist*, 1991). This organic, or greenfield, approach to global expansion included the first US plant in Greenville, South Carolina, in 1975. According to Browning (1990) 'Michelin is a rarity. Paternalistic, secretive and obsessed with a single product, it has succeeded at something that most European companies never manage'. Michelin acquired Uniroyal Goodrich Tire Company for $1.5 billion in 1980 (*Business Week*, 1980b), a strategic move that appears similar to the acquisition by Bridgestone. Currently it holds about 25% of the US market and about 35% of the European market. As of the first quarter of 1991, however, Michelin announced layoffs of 15 000 employees worldwide. In 1990, it lost about $895 million. Goodyear, in 1986, became a takeover target. To stave off the takeover attempt, it borrowed heavily, adding $2.6 billion to its long-term debt, and has retained its independence. 'Goodyear's problems—or opportunities—crystallized in 1986 when Sir James Goldsmith threatened to take over the company' (Weiner, 1991).

Although Goodyear's diversification effort has been an embarrassing corporate strategy, it has sold off tire plants and invested nearly $1.4 billion to upgrade its remaining plants and has demonstrated some OEM market savvy in mounting its premium brand tire on to Audi and Lexus. However, Goodyear's market capitalization had been less than $1 billion. It was speculated that this figure would attract suitors from abroad. That did not happen. Tables appear to have turned for the better.

Goodyear is now being led by Stanley Gault—ex-V.P. of GE and the recently retired CEO of Rubbermaid—much to the pleasure of the investment community. Its stock traded at about $24 (31 May 1991) jumped to about $44 within a span of four-and-a-half months, partly due to price increases of replacement tires, expected new products, and partly to Mr Gault's stature as one who could uplift organizational morale. In an aggressive bid to pare its $3.7 billion debt, Mr Gault has crafted a divestment strategy. Compared to 1990, in 1991 Goodyear is expected to show earnings of $45 million to $55 million. 'The expected results affirmed the favourable impression of a turnaround at the once-troubled company' (*Wall Street Journal*, 1991; Weiner, 1991).

This shift in Goodyear's stature as well as Michelin's losses and layoffs do not augur well for Bridgestone since its focus is currently fixed on its attempt to consolidate Firestone operations. *Business Week* (1990) noted that 'Reaching the top depends on solving Firestone's many problems'. The significance of solving these problems could be gauged by Chairman Teiji Eguchi's unprecedented physical move to Akron, Ohio (*Business Week*, 1990). However, Eguchi decided in 1991 to retire and at the helm of Bridgestone is the new Chairman Y. Kaizaki dispatched from Tokyo to Akron to spur, among other things, the productivity of its Firestone plants, said to be only 60% of Bridgestone plants in Japan. One can only surmise that this move represents possibly a change in top management's 'strategic intent' (Chakravarthy and Lorange, 1991).

Above all, it would appear that the significant OEM market for tires has matured.[4] What little room for growth there is, remains in the replacement market, which has taken a curious turn too in light of oil prices—e.g., making the retread skin is said to require one gallon of oil compared to seven gallons to make an entire tire. It also appears that the industry's attempt to differentiate the product has had its successful days. Nonetheless, mature companies in general tend to introduce new products often at the higher end of the price scale generally to convince investors that the innovative spirit is alive and well. (Goodyear's Aquatread, Michelin's 80 000-miler, and Chrysler's Viper are examples.)

Because tires are thought of as an automotive part, tiremakers depend heavily upon the automotive industry. Despite their 1990 and 1991 losses, in the US, the Big Three automotive firms remain a formidable global force. As Forbes put it, 'Contrary to popular opinion, the big three haven't lost their war against the Japanese . . . Detroit still makes three-fourths of all trucks and cars sold in America' (Flint, 1991). Both GM and Ford have new CEOs and Chrysler will also have one in 1992. As long as the automotive industry is dormant, the struggle among the top three tire companies will be virulent.

Whether Bridgestone can climb to the top spot from its 1990 number three position and stay there for a while depends upon a number of critical factors. Upgrading the quality of Firestone plants is the obvious challenge. At the theoretical level, some strategy akin to 'tight integration' (Leontiades, 1991) is needed to cement the two 'Stones' into a solid block. Logic would suggest that the company has to place its marketing thrust on a single family brand name for the radial tires. The history of Firestone radial tires makes it less than desirable. Bridgestone may be perceived as a Japanese product. BFS is a possibility, at least in the North American market. (Other multinationals such as Philips or Matsushita excel in marketing their ware in the North American market employing such names as Norelco or Panasonic.)

From the demand side, manufacturers need to recognize that their tire products are now a commodity just like low- and medium-priced autos and personal computers. Given this, exacerbated by economic downturns, price competition should not come as a surprise. Bridgestone claims 'that Michelin, for all its heavy losses, has cut prices sharply in Europe to keep the Japanese company from increasing its share of the market there... Goodyear says both Michelin and Bridgestone have been cutting prices in America' (O'Boyle, 1991; *Wall Street Journal*, 1991).

All tire makers also face the challenge that the greening of the tire business also means that companies must also pay more attention to how their products are disposed of or recycled. For a multinational such as Bridgestone, it is as important to think about this issue, consistent with founder Ishibashi's own philosophy of 'enhancing the quality of life', as it is to resolve the so-called 'culture clash' between a Japanese parent firm and its acquired American subsidiary.

APPENDIX A. EXPANDING DIVERSIFICATION AT BRIDGESTONE

Major companies have been established to add talent and ability to the corporate family. These subsidiaries produce liquid propane gas (LPG), bicycles, golf balls, and other products that mesh with Bridgestone's main products and technology.[5]

Bridgestone Liquefied Gas Company, Ltd. Bridgestone has undertaken a significant role in transporting and supplying liquid propane gas by launching the 'S.S. Bridgestone', the world's first giant LPG tanker.

Bridgestone Cycle Company, Ltd. Japan's leading bicycle maker, with an annual capacity of 1.5 million units, is rated as one of the three largest bicycle manufacturers in the world.

Japan Synthetic Rubber Company. This company was established originally by joint investments from the rubber industry, especially Bridgestone Tire Company, Ltd., the petrochemical industry, and the government. Today it is a private firm, the top producer in Japan, and the third largest in the world.

Bridgestone Boshingomo Company, Ltd. Specializing in vibration-damping rubber parts, this company is producing extra durable bushings, engine mounts, shock absorbers, and other components for safe, comfortable riding in the age of high-speed transportation.

Bridgestone Bekaert Steel Cord Company, Ltd. Bekaert of Belgium is the world's largest steel cord manufacturers. In a joint venture with Bridgestone, its steel cord is used extensively in tires and conveyer belts and is sold to other tire manufacturers as well. Construction of a second factory in Saga Prefecture to augment the output of Tochigi factor was on schedule in 1980.

Fukuda Industries Company, Ltd. Established in 1972, this company has received praise for its recovery of the 'good life' and preservation of the natural environment. It supplies trees and shrubs for the reforestation project. The company also aids private and public corporations and local governments in preserving and beautifying the landscape.

Bridgestone Machinery Company, Ltd. This company is a natural outgrowth of Bridgestone's acknowledged leadership in machinery for processing rubber for industry.

Bridgestone Sports Company, Ltd. Specializing in the manufacture of golf clubs bearing the world-famous 'Spaulding' name, this company also produces other golfing items and apparel. It is branching out to import and sell a wide variety of sports and recreational products.

Bridgestone Imperial Company, Ltd. This company, a joint venture with Gould, Inc., produces and sells oil pressure hoses such as high pressure rubber hoses, plastic hoses, and metal parts.

NOTES

1. 'Serving society with superior products' has served as an enduring guiding principle in the case of Bridgestone and other Japanese enterprises. Interested readers may refer to *Watashi no Ayumi* (in Japanese) by Shojiro Ishibashi, founder of Bridgestone. The philosophy of Konosuke Matsushita, the founder of Matsushita Industrial Electric Company, can be discerned from Gould (1970).
2. It should be noted that Bridgestone's concern in dealing with the URW stemmed not only from the URW being an American labor union, but also from the fact that, in February 1947, Bridgestone had a strike in Japan. The labor union *Asahi Rengokai* organized the strike and demanded that wages be doubled and that there be changes in the decision-making process relative to labor matters. Founder Ishibashi staunchly opposed the union demand for power-sharing even though he was receptive to wage demands. (See *Watashi no Ayumi* by Shojiro Ishibashi, in Japanese, 1960.)
3. Lex McCarthy began work at the Firestone plant in La Vergne, Tennessee, directly out of high school and worked there for about nine months before he was laid off in April 1980 (URW 1055 News Release, July 1985).
4. Cooper Tire & Rubber is said to ignore the original equipment market and, instead, concentrate on being a low-cost producer of car tires. Bandag (Iowa) whose stock price hovered around $85 compared with $17 for Goodyear's (1990–91), is the major retreader of truck tires in the United States.
5. Source: Bridgestone 50th Anniversary Report, 1985.

REFERENCES

Bridgestone (1981–90) Bridgestone Annual Reports.
Bridgestone (1983–85) Bridgestone News Release, various issues.
Browning, E. S. (1990) 'Long-Term Thinking and Paternalistic Ways Carry Michelin to Top'. *The Wall Street Journal*, February 5.
Business Week (1980a) 'Why a Tiremaker wants a U.S. base'. January 14: 40.
Business Week (1980b) 'Michelin: The High Cost of being a Big Wheel'. November 5: 66.
Business Week (1990) 'Why Bridgestone's Chairman is Making Tracks to Akron'. November 20: 32–33.
Chakravarthy, B.S. and Lorange P. (1991) *Managing the Strategy Process*, p.300. Prentice Hall, Englewood Cliffs, NJ.
Elias, C. (1990) 'Goodyear Race with Michelin: Burning Rubber to be No. 1.' *Insight*, May 7: 36–39.
Flint, J. (1991) 'Consumer Durables'. *Forbes*, January 7: 130 ff.
Gould, R. (1970) *The Matsushita Phenomenon*. Diamond-sha, Tokyo.
Harkleroad, D. (1982) 'Pneumatiques Michelin 1B', in Davidson, W. H. and de la Torre, J. (eds), *Managing the Global Corporation*. McGraw-Hill, New York.
Hoover, G., Campbell, A. and Spain, P.J. (1991, 1992) *Hoover's Handbook*. The Reference Press, Austin, TX.
Ishikure, K. (1991) 'Achieving Japanese Productivity and Quality Levels at a US Plant'. In Taylor, B. and Harrison, J. (eds) *The Managers' Casebook of Business Strategy*, pp.221–234. Butterworth-Heinemann, Oxford.
Johnson, C. (1982) *MITI and the Japanese Miracle*. Stanford University Press, Stanford.
Leontiades, M. (1991) 'The Japanese Art of Managing Diversity'. *The Journal of Business Strategy*, March/April: 30–33.

Nevin, J. J. (1989) 'The Bridgestone-Firestone Merger: An Insider's Account'. *Journal of Business Strategy*, July/August, 26–30.

O'Boyle, T. F. (1991) 'Spinning Wheels: Bridgestone Discovers Purchase of US Firm Creates Big Problems'. *The Wall Street Journal*, April 4.

Teichova, A. (ed) (1986) *Multinational Enterprise in Historical Perspective*. Cambridge University Press, London.

Wall Street Journal (1991) 'Goodyear Tire and Rubber Co'. *The Wall Street Journal*, December 5: B3.

Vernon, R. and Welles, L.T. Jr. (1991) *The Manager in the International Economy*. Prentice Hall, Englewood Cliffs, NJ.

Weiner, S. (1991), 'Debt focusses the mind'. *Forbes*, January 7: 40–41.

Zajac, E.J. and Baderman, M.H. (1991) 'Blind Spots in Industry and Competitor Analysis'. *Academy of Management Review*, **16**(1).

Part II

Cooperative International Competition

CONTENTS

9. Cooperate to compete globally   117

    HOWARD V. PERLMUTTER and DAVID. A. HEENAN, *Harvard Business Review* (1986), March–April, 136–152

10. A theory of cooperation in international business   126

    PETER J. BUCKLEY and MARK CASSON, *Cooperative Strategies in International Business* (1988), Lexington Books, Lexington, Mass.

11. Collaborate with your competitors—and win   146

    GARY HAMEL, YVES. L. DOZ and C. K. PRAHALAD
    Harvard Business Review (1989), January–February, 133–139

12. Interfirm diversity, organizational learning, and longevity in global strategic alliances   155

    ARVIND PARKHE, *Journal of International Business Studies* (1991), Fourth Quarter, 579–601

13. Towards a theory of business alliance formation   174

    JAGDISH N. SHETH and ATUL PARVATIYAR, *Scandinavian International Business Review*, (1992) **1**(3), 71–87

9

Cooperate to Compete Globally

Howard V. Perlmutter and David A. Heenan

Increasingly, to be globally competitive, multinational corporations must be globally cooperative. This necessity is reflected in the acceleration of global strategic partnerships (GSPs) among companies large and small. GSPs have become an important new strategic option that touches every sector of the world economy, from sunrise to sunset industries, from manufacturing to services.

For smaller companies, these global partnerships with both peers and giants represent the most profitable route to future opportunities. Few companies will achieve international leadership and few nations will prosper in the world economy without some set of GSPs in their portfolios. Some examples:

- AMC's link with Renault seven years ago both gave the US automaker an infusion of capital and experience with front-wheel-drive cars, and opened up the US market to the French company. Since then, Ford, GM, and Chrysler have consummated production deals with Mazda, Toyota, Suzuki, Isuzu, and Mitsubishi, as well as emerging South Korean automakers.
- AT&T signed twin accords with Europe's leaders in information technology, Olivetti and Philips. By combining corporate expertise, AT&T hopes to gain a foothold first in Europe and then around the world.
- Through its alliance with France's state-owned SNECMA, General Electric produces a low-pollution engine for high-performance aircraft. In coming together, both sides agreed to share the estimated $800 million development cost, an amount neither company was prepared to commit on its own.
- Madison Avenue has seen a wave of international ventures, triggered in 1981 by Young & Rubicam's linkup with Tokyo's Dentsu, the world's largest advertising agency. The American agency further plans to merge its Marsteller Advertising unit with Havas Conseil and the other European affiliates of Eurocom, the French market leader.
- The number of East–West ventures is growing. A recent example is the venture between North Korea and two Japanese trade companies, Asahi Corporation and Ryuko Trading Company, to set up a chain of 31 stores in North Korea to sell goods from Japan and the Communist bloc.

Reprinted by permission of *Harvard Business Review*. 'Cooperate to Compete Globally', by Howard V. Perlmutter and David A. Heenan, March April 1986, pp.136 152
Copyright © 1986 by the President and Fellows of Harvard College; all rights reserved.

- American high-tech companies formed two coalitions, the Microelectronics and Computer Cooperative and the Semiconductor Research Cooperative, to buffer the competitive shocks of similar groups from Japan, the 'second Japans' and Western Europe.

While these specific examples show giants teaming with giants, GSPs are not the exclusive province of large MNCs. Enormous companies will frequently combine with smaller ones to exploit their entrepreneurial capabilities and market niches. This was the case when IBM teamed up with Microsoft to exploit the latter's growing expertise in software for desktop computers. The smaller companies, like Microsoft, benefit by gaining access to global markets and the resource strength of their bigger partners.

In another case, an American multinational that buys plastic moulds from a number of suppliers has changed the nature of its relationship with the smaller companies and now encourages them to go overseas as part of a shared global strategy. The pattern holds in retailing as well, where thousands of small companies supplying everything from corduroy suits to kitchen appliances strike deals with retailers all over the world for global distribution of their products. Other industries are also initiating global partnerships. Some of these industries include: furniture, hand tools, insurance, toys, and apparel.

The idea of GSPs, however, may not be easily accepted. Many US managers still adhere to the traditional competitive model of the corporation, where cooperation is regarded with scepticism and suspicion. These tenets generally act as a barrier against collaboration. So it is important to investigate what GSPs are and why some companies need them.

WHAT IS A GSP?

Not all the efforts to mould international coalitions are either global or strategic; some are mere extensions of traditional joint ventures—localized partnerships with a focus on a single market. One example of a localized partnership is GM's venture with China to coproduce diesel engines and transmissions in that country. Neither the product nor the market is global. Other partnerships are loose amalgams of companies from different countries with little intention of attacking world markets systematically; these alliances usually want a short-term, tactical edge in manufacturing or marketing. A few partnerships widen their scope in order to focus their energies on a geographic region, such as the European Economic Community.

More important, but still not global, are those ventures aimed at the tricentres of economic power: the United States, Western Europe, and Japan. Even these ventures, however, are not global strategic partnerships by our definition. GSPs are those alliances in which:

(1) Two or more companies develop a common, long-term strategy aimed at world leadership as low-cost suppliers, differentiated marketers, or both, in an international arena.
(2) The relationship is reciprocal. The partners possess specific strengths that they are prepared to share with their colleagues.
(3) The partners' efforts are global, extending beyond a few developed countries to include nations of the newly industrializing, less developed, and socialist world.
(4) The relationship is organized along horizontal, not vertical, lines; technology exchanges, resource pooling, and other 'soft' forms of combination are the rule.
(5) The participating companies retain their international and ideological identities while competing in those markets excluded from the partnership.

Philips's GSP portfolio

The number of new coalitions that meet these five criteria is growing. Holland's Philips is one of several MNCs well on its way to developing a portfolio of GSPs. The Dutch electronic giant is discarding a corporate culture based on 94 years of self-sufficiency for one relying heavily on multiple ventures with outsiders. (See Table 1 for a partial list of Philips's partnerships.)

Philips's chairman, Wisse Dekker, sees GSPs as serving two aims: blunting the forces of American, Japanese, and, more recently, Taiwanese and Korean competition in high-quality electronics; and reducing the company's dependence on Europe, where one-half of its sales and almost two-thirds of its work force and assets are located. Philips has recharted its world into three 'competence centres': Europe, North America, and the Pacific Basin. In the next five to ten years the company plans to reposition itself to do 30% of its business in each of these centres with the balance going to newly industrializing countries. (*Economist*, 1985).

Philips is teaming up with its neighbour Siemens in West Germany to take on the United States and Japan in advanced microtechnology. This undertaking, which carries $140 million in grants from the Dutch and German governments in addition to the partners' $435 million investment, will pool 500 researchers in an effort to develop superchips that each company will market separately. 'These projects are so large', claims one company spokesperson, 'you have to take a European approach'.

But in keeping with the GSP philosophy, Philips's ambitions go beyond Europe. 'We are aware that what we do has to have global dimensions—world products and world systems', says Gerrit Jeelof, the management board member in charge of telecommunications and computers (*Tagliabue*, 1984). The Dutch MNC is keen to exploit its current relationship with Matsushita beyond the Japanese market, while continuing to press ahead with other coproduction agreements in Hong Kong, Taiwan, and Singapore. In the developing countries Philips is joining forces with other MNCs. One example is its recent pact with AT&T and France's CIT-Alcatel to improve the Venezuelan telephone system.

Even more important is Philips's partnership with AT&T, an agreement designed to strengthen Philips's hold on the North American market, which generates 27% of its sales, and to gain access to, AT&T's vaunted technology in light and electronic components. AT&T, a neophyte to the world of international business, can borrow heavily from Philips's comprehensive overseas network. The Dutch company is trading its geographical expertise for its partner's state-of-the-art technology.

Philips and other MNCs have long recognized that joining forces can lead to large-scale economies, technology and resource pooling, improved access to foreign markets, and avoidance of national regulations. But Philips more recent ventures have the makings of GSPs—they represent a systematic effort to fuse the principles of competitive advantage with global strategy.

The company's partnership with Du Pont in compact laser-disc products, for instance, links Philips's leadership in consumer markets with the US company's expertise in developing high-density optical discs for data storage. Their coming together represents the first attempt to supply the entire range of optical discs on a worldwide basis. Moreover, every Philips alliance has cost leadership and/or differentiated product superiority in at least one national market as its objective. This goal of strategic mutual advantage is prompting Philips and other MNCs to restructure their global portfolios along more cooperative lines.

GSPs also allow multinationals to join together in specific products or markets while retaining autonomy in others. The companies involved, therefore, do not sacrifice their national or ideological identities. In this respect, they are quite different from earlier coventures such as Royal Dutch/Shell, Unilever, and Scandinavian Airline Systems—long-standing multinational corporations that manage global strategy from a single or, occasionally, a dual headquarters. A GSP preserves its national and corporate roots and so prepares the ground for future cooperation and competition.

Table 1. Partial list of Philips's partnerships

Industry	Participating companies	Country of incorporation
Advanced telephone systems	AT&T	USA
Compact discs	Sony	Japan
Electronic credit cards	Compagnie des Machines Bull	France
Lighting and electronic components	Matsushita Electronic Devices	Japan Hong Kong
Minicomputer software	Compagnie des Machines Bull ICL PLC Siemens Nixdorf Computer Olivetti	France Britain West Germany West Germany Italy
Mobile communications	CIT-Alcatel Thomson Siemens	France France West Germany
Personal memory systems	Control Data	USA
Personal computers	Corona Data Systems Siemens	USA West Germany
Semiconductors and microchips	Intel Siemens Advanced Semiconductor Materials International	USA West Germany Holland
Video recorders	Grundig Victor Company	West Germany Japan
Videotex software and systems	Enidata	Italy

OBSTACLES ON THE ROAD

GSPs are not achieved without hardship. Companies that want the edge a GSP can provide must cope with a host of constraints—from nationalism to cultural differences to antitrust attitudes.

Since the days of Senator Sherman, US companies have been wary of cooperation. Today America's ideological position shows little sign of changing; even well-structured, 'safe' combinations still proceed with caution. Because of the careful drafting of the GM-Toyota venture, both parties were confident that they would not stumble over an antitrust technicality. 'But let's face it', admitted one GM official, 'the idea of even talking to each other is bound to be a little scary to some people' (Koten, 1983). Those people include the Federal Trade Commission's 'trust busters'. Only after extended deliberations and negotiation of the venture's limited 12-year pact did the FTC bless the proposal. In an era of GSPs, America's antiquated concepts of antitrust will need rethinking if our GSPs are to emerge as a major competitive force.

Inevitable problems from within are as challenging as the outside obstacles. History has shown that companies have a hard time sustaining long-term relationships. Cultural differences, poor communication, and political infighting can lead to the demise of a potential GSP. For example:

- One of the first cross-border mergers, the union of two large European tyre makers, Britain's Dunlop Holdings and Italy's Pirelli & Company, broke up in 1981. A combination of nationalism and sick home economies made profitability difficult. Also, top management was unable to shape an Anglo-Italian corporate culture.
- In the early 1970s, Dutch, French, and German computer makers sent off hundreds of their top engineers to a multinational venture called Unidata, Europe's would-be answer to IBM. But Unidata dissolved in 1975 without developing a single global product. The Dutch accused the French of not cooperating and the Germans had great difficulty making machines that were compatible with anyone else's.
- London-based consortium banks also fell apart. In 1982, Den Norske Creditbank of Norway bought out its Swedish, Danish, and Finnish partners in the Nordic Banking Group. Previously, Standard Chartered Bank had followed the same course with London's oldest consortium bank, Midland and International Banks. In March 1981, the Orion Bank, whose members included Chase Manhattan, National Westminster, Credito Italiano, Mitsubishi, and Westdeutsche Landesbank, folded. Conflicts of interest, political infighting, inadequate financial controls, and the inability to develop a global strategy undermined the venture.

Corporate collaboration is difficult to achieve, especially where it involves diverse backgrounds and cultures. Our research on GSPs shows that an atmosphere of mutual distrust and domination by one partner jeopardizes the stability of the alliance (Heenan and Perlmutter, 1979). To overcome these obstacles, top executives need to focus on the elements that promote successful GSPs.

SIX SIGNS OF SUCCESS

The health of GSPs depends on the participating companies learning and sharing their abilities. Joint management seminars and multipartner international task forces can accelerate the learning process. Here are six areas that deserve special attention:

(1) *Mission*. Participants in a potential GSP must be committed to a 'win–win' sense of mission—that is, each partner must believe the other has something it needs. Top executives and divisional managers must convince middle managers and affiliates on both sides to build on strengths and reduce weaknesses. An example of this is the pact between AT&T and Olivetti.

Their collective mission is to capture a major share of the global information processing and communications market. Olivetti gives AT&T access to the lucrative European market. AT&T gives Olivetti a much needed $260 million cash infusion, technical support in microprocessors and telecommunications, and muscle in the US market. By coming together both AT&T and Olivetti should win.

In contrast, AT&T's other efforts to attract Italian and British partners have failed because the American company could not demonstrate mutual advantage. Its discussions with STET, Italy's state-owned telecommunications company, broke down because AT&T would not allow STET to export its wares to attractive foreign markets. Inmos, the British government's semiconductor manufacturer, rejected an alliance with the American multinational for public policy reasons thinking that a GSP could destroy the British company's national identity.

(2) *Strategy*. MNCs sometimes rush into a partnership, hoping that a synergistic plan will somehow evolve. But strategy must come first. Partners must avoid 'niche collision'. It occurs when separate deals produce untenable overlap between cooperation and competition. For instance, when Philips established its pact with AT&T to market the American multinational's digital telephone-switching systems, the Dutch company hoped that the relationship would extend to other products. AT&T then teamed up with Olivetti, a major Philips competitor in the office machine market, and prospects for wider cooperation vanished.

Prospective partners can avoid colliding by carefully analysing what each can contribute in various national, regional and world markets, then they must craft their GSPs with these niches in mind.

Balancing cooperation with competition is crucial to achieving strategic synergy. Far too often the accords fall apart as once friendly colleagues revert to hostile competitors. In the Ricoh–Savin, Pentax–Honeywell and Canon–Bell & Howell alliances, Japanese colleagues took advantage of valuable US technology and marketing know-how only to discard their American partners. Similarly, South Korea's Lucky-Goldstar Group. a $7 billion multinational, ended several ventures with Japanese companies because the Japanese were unwilling to transfer vital technology to a potential competitor.

On the other hand, Rolls-Royce, the state-owned British aircraft engine manufacturer, is staking its future on pacts with two American competitors, Pratt &Whitney and General Electric. The Pratt partnership is an admission that neither company dares to develop a new jet engine without the other. In the GE case, Rolls hopes to exploit the US company's weakness in medium-sized engines while joining forces in the upper end of the market. Despite the risks, Rolls remains convinced that teaming with the enemy is a must.

The tricky balancing of cooperation and competition is especially troublesome in resource allocation decisions. Several sponsoring companies, for example, have balked at surrendering their sharpest minds to a venture that might help the opposition. Some MNCs have gone so far as to offer raises and bonuses to their key people if they promise not to join the partnership.

Some potential GSPs solve this problem by using 'nonaligned personnel', individuals not associated with any of the participating companies, to manage the venture. At DMS Laboratories, a diagnostic testing venture linking FCS Industries of New Jersey with France's API Systems Inc., all sales and marketing people as well as top management will be outsiders. Similarly, the Microelectronics and Computer Technology Corporation has chosen to appoint six of its seven major project directors and more than half of its research staff form companies totally removed from the 20-member consortium. Using inside people, however, is usually a better strategy since they are more likely to have the loyalty an alliance needs to survive.

(3) *Governance*. Americans have historically harboured the belief that power, not parity, should govern collaborative ventures. In contrast, the Europeans and Japanese often consider partners as equals, subscribe to management by consensus, and rely on lengthy discussion to secure stronger commitment to shared enterprises.

During the Renault–AMC negotiations, some US executives feared a French takeover. It never materialized. Instead, the French multinational has tried to support, not control, its American partner, and Americans are doing the same. Only four of AMC's top 24 officers and six of its 15 board members are from Renault. Also, AMC enjoys equal status in making key model changes. In the Alliance's design, for instance, Americans rejected the allegedly inferior French air-conditioning system and expressed their dissatisfaction with Renault's ideas on rear-wheel openings on the four-door cars. Eventually these disputes were settled by 'arm wrestling over a bottle of wine', according to one insider. In our view, any prospective GSP that resorts to dominance is inherently weak. Its chances for success are slim.

(4) *Culture.* The most important factor in the endurance of a global alliance is chemistry. The partners must be willing to mould a common set of values, style, and culture while retaining their national identities. This missing dimension in the Dunlop–Pirelli venture led to its demise.

Cultural incompatibility can produce enormous operational difficulties. Consider the problems confronted by Pittsburgh's Alcoa and Japan's NEC. Because of language differences, Alcoa and NEC each thought the other was responsible for a part called a 'feed horn' on their jointly manufactured satellite television receiver. But when they finished the first prototype, they discovered this vital item was missing. Eventually the partners rectified the problem and avoided further misunderstandings.

In contrast, the GSP formed by the advertising giants, Young & Rubicam and Dentsu, seems well on its way to developing corporate themes that combine both cultures. 'In the West I say, 'Go out and buy it',' explains Alexander Brody, president and CEO of DYR, the holding company. 'In the East I talk about the sea and the stars ... I create a feeling', (Galante, 1984). Simply stated, DYR is telling its clients that it can give them either the American hard-sell technique or Japan's more low-key approach.

This flexible approach may not work in every instance. One Japanese executive we interviewed is doubtful that MNCs from the East and West can fashion a common culture. 'The best we can, or should, do', he argues, 'is foster a shared appreciation for the cultural strengths and weaknesses of each partner'.

(5) *Organization.* The new approach to partnerships mandates new organizational patterns. Mindful of the lessons of the ill-fated Concorde, Airbus Industrie (AI) is shaping its own version of a composite organization in part because of the logistical complexities of multicountry management. Assembly of its A300 and A310 wide-body aircraft takes place in Toulouse, with the Germans responsible for the main fuselage; the British, the wings; the French, the cockpit; and the Spanish, the tailfin.

Accordingly, AI's articles of incorporation include several features enabling the consortium to blend the talents of French Aerospatiale, Deutsche Airbus, British Aerospace, and elements of the Spanish aerospace industry with a minimum of organizational fragmentation. For example:

- The alliance was formed under French law as a 'groupement d'intérêt économique', which permits a group of companies to create a single structure. Under this arrangement, the partners must act as mutual guarantors for all of AI's commitments to third parties.
- A supervisory board acts as a buffer between AI's operating management and the respective aircraft manufacturers. It controls all the consortium's strategic decisions.
- A 'convention cadre' is singularly responsible for generating common solutions to partnership disputes in areas ranging from aircraft design changes to amortization of development costs.

While some conflicts inevitably persist, these and other provisions have reduced tension among the members. To compete effectively with its US rivals, Boeing and McDonnell Douglas, the consortium needs to maintain these new organizational methods within the international partnership.

(6) *Management.* A GSP changes the nature of daily decision making and places new pressures on an enterprise. Before formalizing any coalition, MNCs must identify those operational issues—from transfer pricing to personnel matters—that are most likely to cause friction, and must then set up unitary management processes where one decision point has the authority to commit all the partners. Far too often, however, managers neglect this important step. As a result, the new venture suffers from unclear lines of authority, poor communication, and slow decision making.

Look at TRW and Japan's Fujitsu—a potential GSP that got bogged down in bureaucratic red tape. A 'double management system' requiring dual approvals interfered, and the coalition ended with Fujitsu reorganizing the business as a much simpler, wholly owned subsidiary.

Besides adopting unitary management methods, MNCs must develop an ongoing surveillance system to sense potential disputes between the partners. Progress reports on the partnership, which analyse growing or declining mutual trust and respect, should supplement operational progress and performance reports. Invariably, many of the initial expectations of the participating companies prove to be unrealistic. Disillusionment sets in and the partnership eventually dissolves. Building mutual trust and respect is the key to forging a long-term GSP; the partnership depends on both sides sharing their expertise for mutual gain. This requires an in-depth understanding of the strengths and weaknesses of each partner and a commitment to build on the plusses while reducing the minuses.

These are the six main elements in operating a GSP. Both sides must be committed to the alliance: they must share an appreciation for what makes a mutually beneficial partnership. Top executives ready to forge these new values and beliefs will possess a much different perspective on international business than their predecessors ever did.

In the traditional view, competitive advantage is a product of a home-country orientation, proprietary technology, centralized decision making, vertical planning systems, and market dominance. The new global model, on the other hand, is more flexible about ownership and managerial control. It encourages joint decision making, vertical and horizontal planning, and the fusion of competent allies from around the world despite cultural differences. Managers who want to implement GSPs must be ready to make fundamental philosophical changes. Without a new mind-set GSPs are bound to fail.

LOOKING AHEAD

Consider just one recent week's worth of multinational joint venture announcements. In Washington, the Pentagon disclosed its agreement to exchange proprietary radar technology for Japanese expertise in missile-guidance systems, opening the door for further US–Japan cooperation in defence. In Madrid, Telefónica, Spain's semiprivate telephone monopoly with $7.8 billion in sales, announced its plans to go multinational through alliances with prospective competitors: AT&T, Philips, Fujitsu, and the Pacific Telesis Group. In Detroit, Ford was negotiating with a European rival, Fiat, while in New York, IBM announced that it had acquired a major interest in MCI. This hectic partnering is becoming commonplace today as MNCs search frantically for the best set of corporate colleagues.

Negotiating and implementing this slew of new partnerships requires a new, global orientation. MNCs are vying for strategic position in a global chess game. And as GSPs proliferate, strategic issues will become even more complicated, and the boundaries between companies will become blurred. It is unlikely, for instance, that the global planning process can be conducted exclusively from a single Corporation. Furthermore, if single companies no longer set strategy, and if groups of companies negotiate common interests with the government—at the government's initiative—the international political arena is bound to change.

GSPs may challenge our traditional concept of national sovereignty. Notions about economic competitiveness, based on the competitive model of the nation, may be rendered obsolete. No country can afford to be excluded from partnering just as no company can avoid the shifting patterns of global supply and demand. Indeed, the nation-states that prosper in the years ahead will be those that nurture a series of GSPs that stress the values of parity and mutual benefit.

We are, of course, a long way from shaping multilateral industrial policies at the national level. But at the corporate level we are already at the stage where such policies are in force. The automobile and advanced electronics industries are two such examples; over time, agriculture, textiles, and other mature, low-growth industries may follow suit.

Building GSPs represents a tremendous challenge for the multinationals of the future. Companies must learn to join forces in some areas, while pursuing independent courses in others. These trade-offs require managers to think of their companies almost as if they were living entities, seeking to compete and to survive.

The noted biologist Lewis Thomas expressed it best when he argued that survival of the fittest does not mean that nature is red in the tooth and claw—as nineteenth century evolutionary theory argued. Nor does it mean that only the strongest, shrewdest, and most dominating will win. The fittest—those who survive—Thomas suggested, are those who cooperate best with other living things.

REFERENCES

Economist (1985) 'Philips in a New Light'. *Economist*, January 5: p. 60
Galante, S. P. (1984) 'Japan-US Ad Agency Attempts to Go Global', *Wall Street Journal*, April 20.
Heenan, D. A. and Perlmutter, H. V. (1979) *Multinational Organization Development: A Social Architectural Perspective*, Chapter 5. Addison-Wesley, Reading, MA.
Koten, J. (1983) 'GM-Toyota Venture Stirs Antitrust and Labour Problems', *Wall Street Journal*, June 10.
Tagliabue, J. (1984) 'The New Philips Strategy in Electronics'. *New York Times*, January 15.

10
A Theory of Cooperation in International Business

Peter J. Buckley and Mark Casson

THE CONCEPT OF COOPERATION

To what extent are cooperative ventures really cooperative? What exactly is meant by *cooperation* in this context? In international business, the term *cooperative venture* is often used merely to signify some alternative to 100% equity ownership of a foreign affiliate: it may indicate a joint venture, an industrial collaboration agreement, licensing, franchising, subcontracting, or even a management contract or countertrade agreement. It is quite possible, of course, to regard such arrangements as cooperative by definition, but this fudges the substantive issue of just how cooperative these arrangements really are.

If not all cooperative ventures are truly cooperative, then what distinguishes the cooperative ones from the rest? To answer this question, it is necessary to provide a rigorous definition of cooperation. This chapter attempts to distil, from the common-sense notion of cooperation, those aspects of the greatest economic relevance. It is not intended, however, to preempt the use of the word *cooperation* for one specific concept. There is a spectrum of concepts—concepts variously known as cooperation, collaboration, copartnership, and so on—and a diversity of fields of application—employee-ownership of firms, intergovernment collaboration in economic policy, and so on; several different concepts will be needed to do full justice to the complex issues raised by cooperative behaviour in the broadest meaning of that term.

Because the manifestations of cooperative behaviour are so wide-ranging, it is desirable, within the scope of a single chapter, to restrict attention to a single case. The 50:50 equity joint venture a (JV) has been chosen. It is argued that while genuine cooperation is a feature of some JVs, adversarial elements can be present too and, in some cases, can dominate. The factors that govern the degree of cooperation are delineated. The organizational structure of the venture and the extent and nature of the other ventures in which the participants are involved turn out to be crucial. It is potentially misleading to analyse a joint venture in isolation from other ventures, for the extent of cooperation in any one venture is strongly influenced by the overall configuration of the ventures in which the parties are involved.

Reprinted with permission of Lexington Books, an imprint of The Free Press, a Division of Simon & Schuster, from *Cooperative Strategies in International Business* by Farok J. Contractor and Peter Lorange, editors.
Copyright © 1988 by Lexington Books.

Coordination

The definition of *cooperation* advocated here is 'coordination effected through mutual forbearance'. This identifies cooperation as a special type of coordination. *Coordination* is defined as effecting a Pareto-improvement in the allocation of resources, such that someone is made better off, and no one worse off, than they would otherwise be. Coordination is an appropriate basis upon which to build a concept of cooperation, for it articulates the idea that cooperation is of mutual benefit to the parties directly involved (Casson, 1982).

Coordination sounds as if it must always be a good thing, but the following points should be noted about the way that the concept is applied in practice.

The externality problem

Coordination is defined with respect to all parties who are in any way affected by a venture, and not just those who join in voluntarily. Those who join presumably expect to benefit, but others who do not join may lose as a result. Sometimes the losers have legal rights which can be used to block the venture, or they can organize themselves into a club to compensate the beneficiaries for not going ahead. But when there are many nonprivileged losers who have difficulty organizing themselves, it is quite possible that a venture may go ahead even though the losers, as a group, suffer more than the beneficiaries gain.

Coordination under duress

Coordination is defined with respect to an alternative position—namely, what would otherwise happen—so that what is assumed about this alternative position is crucial in determining whether coordination occurs. A voluntary participant may decide to join a venture simply because it is in such an adverse position that the alternative to joining would be absolute disaster.

In some cases, the adversity may be deliberately contrived by others—in particular, by other participants anxious to increase their bargaining power. Even where the adversity has not been contrived, other participants may still seek to take advantage of the unattractive nature of the alternatives available to the party concerned. A related point is that where adversity stems from a recent setback, the party may expect coordination to return it to a position as good as its original one, and it may regard as exploitative any terms that fail to do this.

Empty threats and disappointments

It is a party's perception of the outcome of a venture, and of the alternative position, that governs its decision concerning whether to join. These perceptions are subjective, in the sense that they depend upon the information available to the participant, and can vary, within the same situation, between one person and another. Expectations can be erroneous, so that a venture that effects coordination ex ante may turn out not to do so ex post. Astute individuals or managements may be able to influence the expectations of others to their own advantage. One participant may threaten another participant that if it does not join on onerous terms, the first participant will act to make the other participant's alternative position considerably worse than it would otherwise be. It is quite possible, therefore, for a participant to join a venture under a threat that subsequently turns out to have been empty and, either for this reason or for some other, to later regret having joined at all.

Autonomy of preferences

In conventional applications of the concept of coordination, it is assumed that a party's objectives are unchanged by involvement in a coordinating venture. This assumption is relaxed when introducing the concept of commitment later on. Many economists consider it methodologically unsound to introduce endogeneity of preferences in this way, but in the present context, there are good reasons for doing so. Not everyone is likely to be convinced of its necessity, however.

Interfirm coordination

Coordination applies first and foremost to people rather than to firms. In certain cases, however, a firm can be regarded as a person, as when it consists of a single individual who acts as owner, manager, and worker. In large firms, of course, these various functions are specialized with different individuals. The firm then becomes an institutional framework for coordinating the efforts of different people working together. This exemplifies *intrafirm* coordination. The focus of this chapter, however, is on *interfirm* coordination, in which one firm coordinates with another. It is analytically useful to separate the intrafirm and interfirm aspects of coordination by assuming that interfirm coordination takes place between single-person firms of the kind just described. Subject to this qualification, interfirm coordination may be defined as an increase in the profits of some firms that is achieved without a reduction in the profits of others.

It is also important to distinguish interfirm coordination from extrafirm coordination, which is coordination effected between firms on the one hand and households on the other. Extrafirm coordination is exemplified by trade in final product markets and factor markets. Because of externalities of the kind just described, certain types of interfirm coordination can damage extrafirm coordination to the point where coordination within the economy as a whole is reduced. It is well known, for example, that when firms collude to raise the price within an industry to a monopolist level, the additional profit accruing to the firms is less than the loss of consumer welfare caused by the higher prices and the associated curtailment of demand. Because the consumers are usually more numerous than the firms, it is difficult for them to organize effective opposition to this. Thus, when interfirm coordination is motivated by collusion, even though the firms gain, the economy as a whole may be a loser.

FORBEARANCE

All the parties involved in a venture have an inalienable de facto right to pursue their own interests at the expense of others. It is one of the hallmarks of institutional economics—and transaction cost economics in particular—that it recognizes the widespread implications of this. It can manifest itself in two main ways: aggression and neutrality. An aggressive party perpetrates some act that damages another party's interests, while a neutral party behaves more passively: it simply refrains from some act that would benefit someone else. In either case, the party is deemed to cheat; if it refrains from cheating, it is said to *forbear*. Often, both options are available: the party can either *commit* a damaging act or merely *omit* to perform a beneficial one. Under such conditions, neutrality is regarded as *weak cheating* and aggression as *strong cheating*.

Forbearance and cheating can take place between parties that have no formal connection with each other. They also occur in the establishment of a venture. To fix ideas, this chapter focuses on the problem of sustaining a venture once operations have commenced. It is assumed that at this stage each participant has accepted certain specific obligations. Typically, a minimal set of obligations will have been codified in a formal agreement, while a fuller set of obligations has been made informally. Failure to honour minimal obligations represents strong cheating, honouring only minimal obligations represents weak cheating, while honouring the full obligations represents forbearance. In the special case where the obligations relate to the supply of effort, strong cheating involves disruption, weak cheating involves supplying a minimal amount of effort, and forbearance involves providing maximum effort.

The incentive to forbear

When only the immediate consequences of an action are considered, it often seems best to cheat. But when the indirect effects are considered, forbearance may seem more desirable. This means, intuitively, that forbearance appeals most to those agents who take a long-term view of the situation.

A short-term view is likely to prevail when the agent expects the venture to fail because of cheating by others. The risk of prejudicing the venture through its *own* cheating is correspondingly low, and there may be considerable advantages in being the first to cheat because the richest pickings are available at this stage.

Knock-on effects arise principally because of the responses of others. Their perceived importance depends upon the *vulnerability* of the party. A party is vulnerable if some course of action that might be chosen by another party would significantly reduce its welfare. Vulnerability encourages a party to think through how its own actions affect the incentives facing others. The more vulnerable the party is, the more important it is to avoid stimulating an adverse response from other agents. Each party can, to some extent, induce long-term thinking in other parties by threats that emphasize their vulnerability to its own actions. Partly because of this, the likely pattern of response by others, in many cases, is to match forbearance with forbearance, but to punish cheating. Confronted with this pattern of response, the optimal strategy in most cases is to do the same. Specifically, it is to forbear at the outset and to continue forbearing as long as others do. The situation in which all parties forbear on a reciprocal basis is termed *mutual forbearance*. According to the earlier definition, coordination effected through this mechanism is the essence of cooperation.

If other parties cheat, the victim has a choice of punishment strategies. These strategies differ in both the nature of the evidence required and the severity of the punishment inflicted.

Recourse to the law

This method has very limited scope because many forms of cheating are perfectly legal. This is particularly true where weak cheating is concerned. Even where the law has been breached, the principle that the defendant is guilty until proven innocent, coupled with controls over what evidence is admissible in court, makes it costly, in many legal systems, for the victim to translate circumstantial information about cheating into convincing evidence.

Do-it-yourself punishment

This strategy is often much cheaper. The victim can rely upon its own assessment of the situation. It does not need to convince others of its case. There are two main problems with this strategy. First, the victim may have far more limited sanctions than the law and, indeed, in some cases (such as punishing theft), the victim may have lost, as a direct consequence of the crime, the very resources needed to inflict the punishment. Second, there may be a credibility problem. If the potential victim threatens to withhold promised bonuses, the threat will have little force if it is not trusted to pay them when they are deserved anyway. If it threatens to perform some seriously damaging action instead, it is possible that the victim may damage its own interests too—as when it threatens to undermine the entire venture—and this may create the belief that it will not actually do it. Despite these difficulties, do-it-yourself punishment is widely used. A common strategy is tit-for-tat, which matches acts of cheating with similar acts in kind. It has an appropriate incentive structure, is simple to implement, is not too costly, and is easily intelligible to other parties (Axelrod, 1981, 1984).

Residual risk sharing

In some cases, punishment is semiautomatic, when each participant requires each of the others to hold a share in the residual risks of the venture. If anyone cheats, the venture as a whole suffers, and the value of their equity stake diminishes as a result. This device is particularly appropriate in ventures calling for teamwork, when it is difficult to pinpoint the individuals who are cheating. This means that incentives must be based, not on the inputs (because they are difficult to observe), but upon the joint output instead. This principle works well for small teams, but not for large ones, where the link between individual performance and the share of the team rewards is relatively weak. It is also dependent on their being less likelihood of cheating in the sharing out of residual rewards than in the supply of inputs—which is a reasonable assumption in many cases.

Although these three methods are substitutes in dealing with any one type of cheating, most ventures provide opportunities for various types of cheating. In this respect, the methods are often drafted by professional lawyers to make them easy to enforce through the courts. The formalities typically refer to readily observable aspects of behaviour on which convincing evidence is easy to collect. The law provides an appropriate punishment mechanism in this case. But the formal aspect of a venture cannot usually guarantee much more than its survival. True success can only come if informal understandings between the parties are honoured as well (Williamson, 1985). In this context, legal processes are seriously deficient. A system of shared equity ownership provides a suitable incentive framework, but almost invariably needs to be supplemented by do-it-yourself rewards and punishments too.

Reputation effects

We have noted that do-it-yourself arrangements often suffer from a credibility problem. One way of resolving this problem is for the potential victim to gain a reputation for always carrying out threatened reprisals. Reputations can have other benefits too. A party with a reputation for never being first to abandon forbearance gives partners a greater incentive to forbear themselves, for it increases the likelihood that if they too forbear, then the venture as a whole will reach a successful conclusion. A reputation for forbearance also facilitates the formation of ventures in the first place; it makes it easier for the reputable party to find partners because prospective partners anticipate fewer problems in enforcing the arrangements (Blois, 1972; Richardson, 1972).

A reputation is an investment. It requires a party to forego certain short-term gains in order to save on future transaction costs. The most valuable reputation appears to be a reputation for reciprocating forbearance: never being the first to abandon it but always taking reprisals against others who do. The factors most conducive to investment in reputation are as follows:

(1) *The prospect of many future ventures in which the party expects to have an opportunity to be involved.* The number of ventures will be larger, the greater the party's range of contacts, the longer its remaining life expectancy, and the higher its expectation of the frequency with which new economic opportunities occur.

(2) *The conspicuous demonstration of forbearance in a public domain.* A high-profile venture, with a large number of observers, and a dense network of contacts spreading information about it, facilitates reputation building. Conspicuous forbearance is favoured by a cultural environment that is open rather than secretive. A dense network of contacts is most likely within a stable social group, in which few parties enter or leave.

(3) *A propensity for observers to predict the future behaviour of a party by extrapolating its past pattern of behaviour.* This governs the extent to which a party can signal future intentions through current behaviour. If peoples' attitudes are governed by prejudice based on superficial appearance rather than upon actual behaviour, acquiring a reputation that is at variance with prejudice may prove very difficult.

COOPERATION, COMMITMENT, AND TRUST

To what extent can it be said that one contractual arrangement is more cooperative than another? To answer this question, it is necessary to distinguish between cooperation as an input to a venture and cooperation as an output from it. An arrangement that gives all parties a strong incentive to cheat requires a great deal of mutual forbearance if it is to be successful. Loosely speaking, it requires a large input of cooperation. In one respect, this is a weakness rather than a strength of the arrangement, since it means that in practice the arrangement is quite likely to fail. This is important when considering joint ventures later, for it does seem that joint ventures that begin by being hailed extravagantly as a symbol of cooperation have a high propensity to fail.

Cooperation may be regarded as an output when an arrangement leads to greater trust between the parties, which reduces the transaction costs of subsequent ventures in which they are involved. Focusing on cooperation as an output gives a perspective that is closest to the common sense view that cooperative ventures are a 'good thing'.

There is a connection, however, between input and output. This is because an arrangement that calls for a considerable input of cooperation and then turns out successfully enhances the reputation of the parties. First and foremost, it enhances their reputations with each other, but, if there are spectators to the arrangement, then it enhances their reputations with them too.

The connection between input and output suggests that some arrangements may be more efficient than others in transforming an input of cooperation into an output. More precisely, cooperation is efficient when a given amount of mutual forbearance generates the largest possible amount of mutual trust. Efficiency is achieved by devising the arrangement of the venture so as to speed up the acquisition of reputation. One reason why reputation building may be slow is that cheating is often a covert practice—it is more viable if it goes undetected—and so it may be a long time before parties can be certain whether or not an agent has cheated. The importance of this factor varies from one venture to another, depending upon how easy it is for agents to make their own contributions and monitor and supervise their partners at the same time.

Reputation building

To speed up reputation building, it may be advantageous to create, within the arrangement itself, additional opportunities for agents to forbear reciprocally. Thus, a venture may provide for a sequence of decisions to be taken by different parties, in each of which the individual agent faces a degree of conflict between its own interests and those of others. Each agent (except the first-mover) has an opportunity to respond to the earlier moves of others. The essence of this reputation building mechanism is that, first, the decisions are open and overt, rather than secretive and covert, and second, there is some connection between the overt decisions made by agents and their covert ones. In other words, the mechanism rests on the view that what the agent does when observed is a reflection of the way it behaves when not observed. Because of bounded rationality and the persistence of habits, it is difficult for most agents to adjust their behaviour fully according to the conditions of observation. A sophisticated arrangement can set traps to catch agents off guard; provided agents do not face similar sequences of decisions too often, all but the cleverest and most alert are likely to unintentionally reveal something about the pattern of their unobserved behaviour as a result.

This device has certain dangers, however, not least of which is that it increases the amount of discretion accorded to each party. For it is the essence of the deferred decisions that agents have discretion over how they use the information at their disposal. If they were instructed to follow a decision rule prescribed at the outset, then their only discretionary decision would be whether to cheat on the rule. The situation would revert to one that encouraged covert rather than overt behaviour. To avoid creating excessive risks for the other parties, however, it is necessary to carefully control the amount of discretion by focusing the earliest decisions in the sequence upon issues that do not really matter. As the venture proceeds and trust grows, so the degree of real discretion can be increased. To start with, therefore, the situation may resemble a game in which only token gains and losses are made, and only as time passes does the game become fully integrated into the real world.

There are certain types of venture that naturally create game-playing situations. In long-term ventures in a volatile environment, for example, there is a very sound logic for deferring certain decisions until after the venture has begun—namely, that new information may subsequently become available that is relevant to how later parts of the venture are carried out.

It may well be appropriate to delegate these decisions to the individuals who are most likely to have this information at hand. It then becomes possible to fine-tune the degree of discretion to the amount of trust already present. Thus, it is quite common to observe that when a number of parties work together for the first time, a tight discipline is imposed to begin with, which is then progressively relaxed as the parties begin to trust each other more.

Commitment

Up to this point, it has been assumed that cooperation is encouraged by appealing to the agents' enlightened self-interest—their incentive to cooperate is strengthened by reducing the cost of building up a reputation for reciprocity. It is also possible, however, to encourage cooperation by changing an agent's preferences so that the successful completion of the venture receives a higher priority than it did before. One way of doing this is to encourage the agent to perceive cooperation not as a means but as an end in itself. Cooperation then ceases to be based on strategic considerations—considerations that recommend cooperation as an appropriate means—and becomes based on commitment to cooperation in its own right.

It is worth noting, in this connection, that many everyday situations call for forbearance to be shown to people whom it is unlikely that one will ever meet again, and where there is, as a result, little incentive to forbear so far as self-interest alone is concerned. A typical situation arises in connection with unanticipated congestion in the use of a facility. When there is insufficient time to negotiate agreements between the users, and when there is either no system of priorities or the system in force is an inappropriate one, coordination may depend upon spontaneous forbearance. Examples include moving out of other people's way when shopping and giving way to traffic entering from byroads. The reason many people forbear in these situations, it seems, is that they derive welfare directly from their constructive role in the encounter.

It is likely that participation in certain types of venture can affect parties in a similar way. Indeed, participation in a venture may leave an individual far more oriented toward spontaneous cooperation than it was before. The main reason for this is the role of information sharing in a venture. It is characteristic of many ventures that agents are asked to agree to share certain types of information with their partners. This is principally because the agents who possess certain types of information (or are in the best position to obtain it) are not necessarily those with the best judgement on how to use it. Another reason is that information provided by an agent may act as an early warning that, due to environmental changes, it (and perhaps others too) has a strong incentive to cheat, which can be reduced, in everyone's interests, by a limited renegotiation of their agreement.

In asking people to share information, however, it is likely that the response will divulge some of their more general beliefs and their moral values too. Thus, the sharing of information provides those who stand to gain most from the successful completion of the venture with an opportunity to disseminate—whether deliberately or quite subconsciously—a set of values conducive to cooperation. In this case, a venture can promote cooperation simply by providing a forum for the preaching of the cooperative ethic.

The degree of commitment to a venture is likely to be conditional upon certain characteristics of the venture. The commitment of the partners is likely to be higher, for example, the more socially meritorious or strategically important the output is deemed to be. Commitment will also tend to be higher if the distribution of rewards from the venture, when it is successfully completed, is deemed equitable by all parties. Envy of the share of gains appropriated by another partner cannot only diminish motivation, but can encourage cheating—which may be 'justified' as a means of generating a more equitable outcome. It is one of the characteristics of the JVs analysed in the next section that, superficially at least, the distribution of rewards seems fair because it is based on a 50:50 principle. As subsequent discussion indicates, however, such equity may be illusory, and once any such illusion is recognized, the degree of commitment may fall dramatically.

The psychology of commitment, if understood correctly, can be used by one party to manipulate another. But securing commitment through manipulation is a dangerous strategy for, once it is exposed, some form of reprisal or revenge is likely. The commitment previously channelled into the venture by the victim of manipulation may be transferred and channelled into punishing the manipulator instead.

From the standpoint of economic theory, these propositions are equivalent to a postulate that an agent's preferences depend not only upon material consumption (or profit), but also upon the characteristics of the ventures in which it is involved. These characteristics relate both to the nature of the venture itself and to the extent of mutual commitment shown by the parties concerned. This postulate provides the basis for further developments of the theory of cooperation, which lie beyond the scope of the present chapter.

THE ECONOMIC THEORY OF JOINT VENTURES

Analysis of the cooperative content of cooperative ventures must be based upon a rigorous theory of nonequity arrangements. Because nonequity arrangements can take so many different forms, it is useful to focus upon one particular type. The 50:50 equity joint venture (JV) seems appropriate because it is very much symbolic of the cooperative ethos. The main focus is on arrangements involving two private firms, for, although arrangements involving state-owned firms and government agencies are very important in practice (particularly in developing countries), they raise issues lying beyond the scope of this chapter. To the extent, however, that the state sector is primarily profit-motivated, the following analysis will still apply.

It is assumed that each partner in the JV already owns other facilities. It is also assumed that the JV is preplanned, and that the equity stakes are not readily tradeable in divisible units. This means, in particular, that the joint ownership of the venture cannot be explained by a 'mutual fund' effect—in other words, it is not the chance outcome of independent portfolio diversification decisions undertaken by the two firms.

Working under these assumptions, theory must address the following three key issues.

Why does each partner wish to own part of the JV rather than simply trade with it on an arm's-length basis? The answer is that there must be some net benefit from internalizing a market in one or more intermediate good and/or service flowing between the JV and the parties' other operations. A *symmetrically motivated* JV is defined as one in which each firm has the same motive for internalizing. This is the simplest form of JV to study, and it is the basis for the detailed discussion presented later. (See also Buckley and Casson, 1985, chapters 2–4.)

Why does each firm own half of the JV rather than all of another facility? The force of this question rests on an implicit judgement that joint ownership poses managerial problems of accountability that outright ownership avoids. To the extent that this is true, there must be some compensating advantage in not splitting up the jointly owned facility into two (or possibly more) separate facilities. In other words, there must be an element of economic indivisibility in the facility. The way this indivisibility manifests itself will depend upon how the JV is linked into the firms' other operations.

(1) If the JV generates a homogeneous output which is shared between the partners, or uses a homogeneous input which is sourced jointly by them, then the indivisibility is essentially an economy of scale.
(2) If the JV generates two distinct outputs, one of which is used by one partner and the other by the other, then the indivisibility is essentially an economy of scope.
(3) If the JV combines two different inputs, each of which is contributed by just one of the parties, then the indivisibility manifests itself simply as a technical complementarity between the inputs (a combination of a diminishing marginal rate of technical substitution and nondecreasing returns to scale).

Given that, in the light of the first two issues, each partner wishes to internalize the same indivisible facility, why do the partners not merge themselves, along with the JV, into a single corporate entity? The answer must be that there is some net disadvantage to such a merger. It may be managerial diseconomies arising from the scale and diversity of the resultant enterprise, legal obstacles stemming from antitrust policy or restrictions on foreign acquisitions, difficulties of financing because of stock market scepticism, and so on.

It is clear, therefore, that JV operation is to be explained in terms of a combination of three factors, namely internalization economies, indivisibilities, and obstacles to merger.

As noted in the introduction, there are many contractual alternatives to JV operation, but for policy purposes, particular interest centres on the question of when a JV will be preferred to outright ownership of a foreign subsidiary. Given that location factors, such as resource endowments, result in two interdependent facilities being located in different countries, the first of the three factors mentioned—internalization economies—militates in favour of outright ownership. It is the extent to which it is constrained by the other two factors—indivisibilities and obstacles to merger—that governs the strength of preference for a JV. The larger are indivisibilities, the greater the obstacles to merger; the smaller are internalization economies (relative to the other two factors), the more likely it is that the JV will be chosen (Casson, 1987, chapter 5). The interplay between these factors in governing the choice of contractual arrangements is illustrated by the following examples.

The configuration of a JV operation

The configuration of a JV operation is determined by whether it stands upstream or downstream with respect to each partner's other operations, and by the nature of the intermediate products that flow between them. A JV arrangement is said to be *symmetrically positioned* if each partner stands in exactly the same (upstream or downstream) relation to the JV operation as does the other. Figure 1 illustrates symmetric forward integration, and Figure 2 shows symmetric backward integration. Sometimes an operation may be integrated both backward and forward into the same partner's operations. Figure 3 illustrates a symmetric buyback arrangement in which each partner effectively subcontracts the processing of a product to the same jointly owned facility.

Some writers seem to suggest that JVs are inherently symmetric—presumably because of the 50:50 symmetry in the pattern of ownership—but this is far from actually being the case. JVs

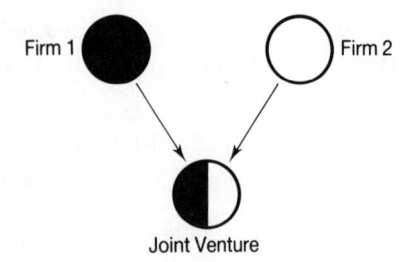

Figure 1. Forward Integration into a Joint Venture.

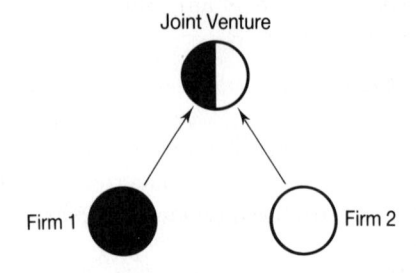

Figure 2. Backward Integration into a Joint Venture.

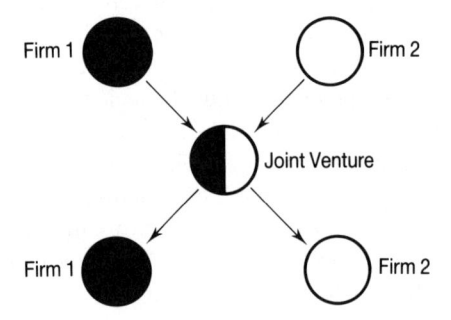

Figure 3. Buyback Arrangement.

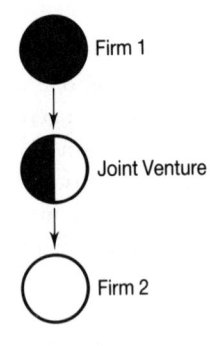

Figure 4. Multistage Arrangement.

may, for a start, be asymmetrically positioned with respect to the partners' operations. Figure 4 illustrates a multistage arrangement in which one partner integrates forward into the JV and the other integrates backward; such an arrangement is quite common in JVs formed to transfer proprietary technology to a foreign environment.

Even if a JV is symmetrically positioned, it does not follow that it is symmetrically configured, for the intermediate products flowing to and from the respective partners may be different. It is only when both the positioning is symmetric and the products are identical that the configuration is fully symmetric in the sense we defined.

The fact that the configuration is symmetric does not guarantee that the motivation for internalization is symmetric too. If each partner, for example, resells the JV output within a different market structure, then the motivation for internalization may differ in spite of the fact that the configuration is symmetric.

The symmetry properties illustrated in Figures 1–3 refer only to the immediate connections between the JV and the rest of the partners' operations. Each partner's operations may be differently configured from the others. This means that while the activities directly connected with the JV are symmetrically configured, the operations when considered as a whole may be asymmetric. Thus, the symmetry concept just used was essentially one of local symmetry, and not of global symmetry. While global symmetry implies local symmetry, the converse does not apply.

The distinction between local and global symmetry has an important bearing on the question of the distribution of economic power between the parties. It is important to appreciate that local symmetry does not guarantee that there is a balance of economic power between the parties to the JV. It is quite possible, for example, that one of the partners may own facilities that are potential substitutes for the jointly owned facility, while the other partner does not. This becomes important if the other partner could not easily gain access to an alternative facility should the first partner place some difficulty in its way. It may be, for example, that the first partner holds a monopoly of alternative facilities. This means that in bargaining over the use of the jointly owned facility, the first partner is likely to have the upper hand. It can use power either to secure priorities for itself through nonprice rationing or to insist on trading with the JV at more favourable prices. The fact that the JV is 50:50 owned implies only that residual income is divided equally between the partners; it does not guarantee that total income is divided equally. And, as we have argued, a locally symmetric configuration does not guarantee that total income will be divided equally. It is the symmetry of substitution possibilities that is crucial in this respect. Symmetry of substitution is likely to occur only with global symmetry, and this is a much less common type of configuration. One important consequence of this is considered below ('Networks of interlocking JVs').

JV operations motivated by lack of confidence in long-term arm's-length contracts

We now illustrate how different motives for internalization manifest themselves in various contexts. Readers familiar with the most recent literature on internalization theory may prefer to proceed directly to the section 'Building reputation and commitment', where the main line of argument is resumed.

This section presents three simple examples in which both the configuration of the JV and the motivations for it are symmetric. The examples are designed to illustrate a progression from internalization involving no day-to-day operational integration between the JV and the partners' operations to internalization involving very close operational integration indeed.

Hedging against intermediate product price movements in the absence of a long-term futures market

Consider the construction industry, in which main contractors have to quote fixed prices for long-term projects, some of which require a large input of cement, which is liable to vary in price over the life of the project. For obvious reasons, the cement cannot be stored, and there is no organized futures market either. Cement has to be purchased locally for each project, and because the sites are geographically dispersed, there is no one supplier that can economically supply all the projects. Nevertheless, prices of cement at different sites tend to vary in line with each other, so that ownership of a cement-making facility at any one location will still help to hedge against price fluctuations in the many different sources of supply that are used. There are two major contractors of equal size who specialize in cement-intensive projects. Because of economies of scale in cement production, however, a cement plant of efficient scale generates much more cement than either contractor uses. There is one plant whose output price varies most closely with the average price of cement paid by the contractors, and so they each acquire a half of the equity in this plant. This is the most efficient mechanism available for diversifying their risks relating to the price of cement. It involves no operational integration whatsoever between the cement facility and the site activities.

Avoiding recurrent negotiation under bilateral monopoly over the price of a differentiated intermediate product

Suppose there are two firms that are the only users of an intermediate product produced with economies of scale. It is difficult for either firm to switch away from the product, since it has no close substitutes. Upstream, therefore, there is natural monopoly, while downstream there is duopsony. Before any party incurs nonrecoverable setup costs through investment in specific capacity, it would be advantageous to negotiate once and for all long-term supply contracts for the product. Because of the difficulty of enforcing such contracts, however, the duopsonists may prefer to jointly acquire the upstream facility. This insures both of them against a strategic price rise initiated by an independent natural monopolist. The fact that both share in the residual risks also helps to discourage them from adversarial behaviour toward each other. A modest degree of operational integration is likely in this case.

Operational integration between upstream and downstream activities in the absence of efficient short-term forward markets

Extending the construction industry example, suppose that the two firms have long-term projects in hand at adjacent sites and require various types of form work to be supplied to mould the concrete foundations. The form work is customized and each piece has to be in place precisely on time. Both firms are sceptical about devising enforceable incentives for prompt supply by a subcontractor, as arms' length forward contracts are difficult to enforce in law. Because of the small scale of local demand relative to the capacity of an efficient-size team of workers, the two contractors may decide to secure quality of service through backward integration into a JV. Unlike the previous arrangements, this involves close day-to-day management of an intermediate product flow between the owners and the JV.

Quality uncertainty

Quality uncertainty can manifest itself in many different contexts. Four examples are given next to demonstrate the ubiquity of this phenomenon.

Insuring against defective quality in components

This example relates to forward integration involving two distinct flows of materials. Consider two components which are assembled to make a product. The quality of the components is difficult to assess by inspection, while other methods of assessment, such as testing to destruction, are expensive—not least in terms of wasted product. Reliable performance of the final product is crucial to the customer; failure of the final product is often difficult to diagnose and attribute to one particular component. Because of legal impediments, it is impossible to comprehensively integrate the assembly with the production of both components, and an independent assembler would lack confidence in subcontracted component supplies. If two independent component producers form a joint venture, however, then each can enjoy a measure of confidence in the other, since each knows that the other bears half the penalty incurred by the venture if it supplies a defective product to it. This is the JV analogue of the 'buyer uncertainty' argument emphasized in the internalization literature.

Adapting a product to an overseas market

This example involves the combination of two distinct but complementary types of know-how in the operation of an indivisible facility. The first type of know-how is technological and is typically embodied in the design of a sophisticated product developed in an industrialized country. The other is knowledge of an overseas market possessed by an indigenous foreign firm. The complementarity concerns their use in adapting the design and marketing strategy of the product to overseas conditions. The indivisible facility is the plant used to manufacture it overseas. Together, these elements make up the classic example of the use of a JV to commence overseas production of a maturing product.

Management training and the transfer of technology

In some cases, a JV may be chosen as a vehicle for training (Kojima, 1978). Employees of a technologically advanced firm are seconded to a JV to train other employees who will remain with the venture when it is later spun off to the currently technologically backward partner. Training involves two inputs, rather than just the one that is usually assumed. It requires not only the knowledge and teaching ability of the tutor, but also the tutee's time, attention, and willingness to learn. The tutee may be uncertain of the quality of the tutor's knowledge and ability, and may demand that the tutor bears all the commercial risks associated with the early stages of the venture. The tutor, on the other hand, may be uncertain of the effort supplied by the tutee, which could jeopardize the performance of the venture if it were poor, and so the tutor may require the tutee to bear some of the risks as well. These conflicting requirements are partially reconciled by a JV that requires both to bear some of the risks and thereby gives each an incentive to maintain a high quality of input. Those incentives can be further strengthened, in some cases, by a buyback arrangement—or production-sharing arrangement as it is sometimes called—which encourages each party to use the output that the newly trained labour has produced and thereby gives an additional incentive to each party to get the training right.

Buyback arrangements in collaborative R&D

Buyback arrangements, which combine backward and forward integration, are particularly common in collaborative research. In the research context, both the inputs to and the outputs from the JV are services derived from heterogeneous intangible assets (that is, they are flows of knowledge).

Consider two firms, each with a particular area of corporate expertise, who license their patents and personnel to a joint research project (the indivisible facility). The planned output—new knowledge—is a proprietary public good, which is licensed back to the two firms. Each firm may be suspicious of the quality of the input supplied by the other firm, but the fact that the other firm not only holds an equity stake in the project but also plans to use the product of the research for its own purposes serves to reassure the first firm that the quality will be good (though there still remains a risk that personnel and ideas of the very best quality will be held back). Likewise, the fact that the firm itself has partially contributed to the production of the new knowledge is a reassuring factor when it comes to implementing this knowledge in downstream production.

Collusion

The role of indivisibility facilities in the previous discussion can, in fact, be taken over by any arrangement that either reduces the costs of two plants by coordinating their input procurement or enhances the value of their outputs by coordinating their marketing. The former is relevant to backward integration by firms into a JV, while the latter pertains to forward integration instead. The forward integration case, to be discussed shortly, shows the JV to be an alternative to a cartel.

Consider two firms that have identified an opportunity for colluding in their sales policy. They may have independently discovered a new technology, territory, or mineral deposit and wish to avoid competition between them in its exploitation. They may, on the other hand, be established duopolists operating behind an entry barrier, who would benefit from fixing prices or quotas to maximize their joint profits from the industry. (The nature of the entry barrier is irrelevant to the argument. It may be based on technological advantage, brand names, statutory privilege, or exclusive access to inputs, and so on.)

The main problem with a sales cartel is the mutual incentive to cheat by undercutting the agreed price—for example, by selling heavily discounted items through unofficial outlets. This poses an acute monitoring problem for each party. Channelling sales through a JV reduces the incentive to cheat, since the gains from cheating are partially outweighed by the reduction in profits earned from the JV. Economies in monitoring costs may also be achieved if both parties specialize this function with the JV.

Hostages: internalizing the implementation of counterthreats

In an atmosphere of mutual distrust, an imbalance in the vulnerability of two parties to a breakdown of the venture can further undermine confidence in it. This suggests the possibility that instead of collaborating on a single venture, they should collaborate on two ventures instead. The function of the second venture is to counteract the imbalance in the first venture by giving the least vulnerable party in the first venture the greatest vulnerability in the second venture. Suppose, for example, that the two firms wished to collude in a product market where one firm has a much larger market share, coupled with much higher fixed costs, than the other. This is the firm that is most vulnerable to cheating by the other. To redress the balance, it may be advantageous for the two firms to agree on some other venture—say, collaborative research—to run in parallel with a collusive JV to give the weaker firm an effective sanction against the stronger one. In such a case, the primary motive for the second JV concerns nothing intrinsic to the venture itself, but simply its ability to support the other venture.

It should be clear from the preceding examples that there are an enormous number of different forms that a JV operation can take. Each of the three main factors the internalization motive, the indivisibility, and the obstacle to merger—can take several different forms. The internalization motive may differ between the firms. Add to this the considerable diversity of global configurations, and it can be seen that the permutations to which these aspects lend themselves make any simple typology of JV operations out of the question. While the economic principles governing the logic of JV operation are intrinsically quite straightforward, the way that environmental influences select the dominant factors in any one case is extremely complex.

BUILDING REPUTATION AND COMMITMENT

It was established in the first part of the chapter that almost all coordinating activity calls for some degree of mutual forbearance and that, therefore, most ventures—even simple trade or team activities—involve an element of cooperation. It was also established that extensive reliance on mutual forbearance was not necessarily a good thing. The essence of cooperative efficiency, it was suggested, is that as a result of a venture, a small amount of mutual forbearance is transformed into a large amount of trust. Cooperatively efficient ventures will tend to accord all parties an opportunity to reciprocate forbearance within a sequence of decisions, observable to the others, calling for increasing levels of loyalty. Ventures of this kind are likely to be followed by a succession of other ventures involving the same parties—perhaps in the same grouping or perhaps in other groupings involving other parties with whom the original participants have established a reputation. (Propositions of this kind are certainly testable, even if the propositions regarding 'quantities' of forbearance and trust, from which they derived, are not.)

Some ventures lend themselves naturally to an internal organizational structure that encourages participation. These ventures call for widespread decentralization of decision making, afford decisions of varying degrees of responsibility, and call for the sharing of information. They provide ample opportunity for overt behaviour and only limited opportunity for covert behaviour. These considerations suggest that certain motives for JV operation are far more conducive to cooperation than are others. It is, in fact, the combination of the motive and the main activity performed by the JV that seems to be crucial in this respect.

In the production sector, JVs that involve very little operational integration with the partners' other activities provide little opportunity for the partners to meet and interact on a regular basis. The greater the degree of operational integration, the greater is the regularity with which forbearance may have to be exercised when short-term holdups occur in production, and the greater are the opportunities for sharing information in the planning of production. Quality uncertainty provides a motive for both parties to open up their wholly owned operations to their JV partner once a certain degree of trust has been established, and so provides a natural route through which cooperation could progress to a point where it embraces production, product development, and basic research.

Joint R&D is naturally cooperative because it is based upon the sharing of information and, for reasons already noted, the sharing of information often leads to the emergence of shared values too. This may, perhaps, partly explain why collaborative R&D seems to enjoy a special mystique all of its own.

Of the various functional areas in which JV operations can occur, sales and procurement are the least promising so far as true cooperation is concerned. A dominant motive for JV operations in this area is collusion. Collusion affords large incentives to cheat and therefore requires a major input of cooperation. The maintenance of a high price in a static market environment—so characteristic of many collusive arrangements—does not, however, create much need for meetings at which open forbearance and reciprocity can be displayed. Collusion emphasizes the covert rather than overt dimensions of behaviour. It therefore generates little output of trust. The most promising area for cooperation in marketing arises when a proprietary product is transferred to a new country, for then both the source firm and the recipient firm need to share information. Since the demand is uncertain, but has considerable growth potential, the market environment is dynamic rather than static, and so, unlike the case of collusion, it provides opportunities for deferring key decisions and delegating in a way that allows both parties to demonstrate forbearance.

The International Dimension

So far, nothing has been said specifically about the international aspects of JV operation. To a certain extent, this is deliberate, since there are no reasons to believe that the familiar factors of international cost differentials, tariffs, transport costs, and variations in the size of regional markets are any different for JVs than they are for other international operations. It can, however, be argued that the political risks of expropriation, the blocking of profit repatriation, and so on, are lower in the case of a JV than in the case of a wholly owned operation, though empirical support for this view is very limited, to say the least. Tax-minimizing transfer pricing, though not impossible with JVs, is more difficult to administer because of the need to negotiate the prices with the partner and to find a subterfuge for paying any compensation involved.

So far as the general concept of cooperation is concerned, the international dimension is much less important than the intercultural dimension. In purely conventional analysis of transaction costs, the focus is on the legal enforcement of contracts, and so the role of the nation state is clearly paramount, in respect to both its legislation and its judicial procedures. The mechanism of cooperation, however, is trust rather than legal sanction, and trust depends much more on the unifying influence of the social group than on the coercive power of the state. Trust will normally be much stronger between members of the same extended family, ethnic group, or religious group, even though it transcends national boundaries, than between members of different groups within the same country.

This means that in comparing the behaviour of large firms legally domiciled in different countries, differences in behaviour are just as likely to reflect cultural differences in the attitudes of senior management as the influence of the fiscal and regulatory environment of the home country. Cultural attitudes are certainly likely to dominate in respect of the disposition to cooperate with other firms. In this context, it may be less important to know whether a corporation is British or Italian, say, than to know whether its senior management is predominantly Quaker or Jewish, Protestant or Catholic, Anglo-Saxon or Latin, and so on. National and cultural characteristics are correlated, but not perfectly so. In some instances, such as Japanese firms, it has proved extremely problematic to disentangle them.

In the light of these remarks, it is clear that JV operations involving firms with different cultural backgrounds are of particular long-term significance. Once established, they provide a mechanism for cultural exchange, particularly as regards attitudes to cooperation. The success of this mechanism will depend upon how receptive each firm is to ideas emanating from an alien culture. Where the firm is receptive, participation in international JVs may have lasting effects on its behaviour, not only in international operations, but in many other areas too.

Networks of Interlocking JVs

The recent proliferation of international JVs means that many firms are now involved in several JVs. Two JVs are said to interlock when the same firm is a partner in both. It is not always recognized as clearly as it should be that a set of interlocking JVs is an extremely effective way for a firm to develop monopoly power at minimal capital cost. By taking a part-interest in a number of parallel ventures, producing the same product with a different partner in each case, the firm can not only establish a strong market position against buyers of the product, but it can also create a strong bargaining position against each partner as well.

Once an individual partner is committed to a venture, it is vulnerable if the monopolist threatens to switch production to one of its other JVs instead. The partner has no similar option because the remaining facilities are all partly controlled by the monopolist. The

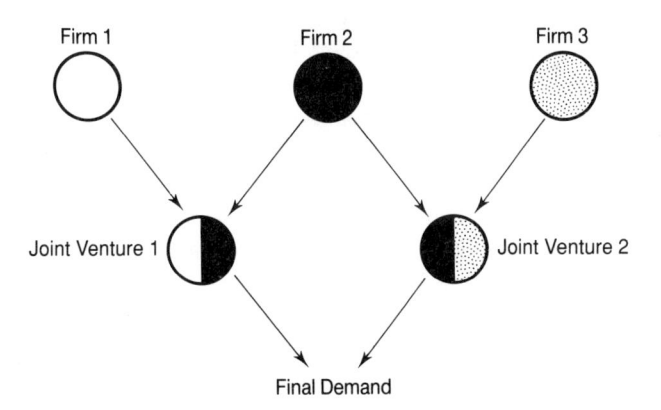

Figure 5. The Dominant Partner in Networks.

vulnerable firm may be obliged to renegotiate terms under duress. Although the monopolist may stand to lose by withdrawing production from one JV, it will be able to recover most of these losses from enhanced profits arising from the JVs to which production is switched.

A situation of this kind is illustrated in Figure 5. Firm 2 has the ability to switch production between the two downstream plants, but neither firm 1 nor firm 3 has this option because the only other plant is partly controlled by firm 2. Although each JV is symmetrically configured in a local sense, the overall situation is globally asymmetric. Superficially, it may seem that firm 2 is a 'good cooperator' because it is involved in more JVs than either of the other firms, but in reality its claim to cooperate may simply be a subterfuge. Firm 2 can, in fact, not only exercise monopoly power against the buyers of downstream output, but also play off its partners against each other. In this case, it is conflict (not cooperation) and deception (not trust) that is the driving force in firm 2's choice of JV operation.

CONCLUSION

Joint ventures are, first and foremost, a device for mitigating the worst consequences of mistrust. In the language of internalization theory, they represent a compromise contractual arrangement that minimizes transaction costs under certain environmental constraints. But some types of joint venture also provide a suitable context in which the parties can demonstrate mutual forbearance and thereby build up trust. This may open up possibilities for coordination that could not otherwise be entertained. The prospect of this encourages partners to take an unusually open-ended view of JV partnerships and gives JVs heir political and cultural mystique.

An important role of JVs, from the limited perspective of internalization economics, is to minimize the impact of quality uncertainty on collaborative research and training. From the more open-ended perspective of long-term cooperation, however, JVs designed to cope with quality uncertainty are also well adapted to help partners to reciprocate and also to learn the values that inspire the other partner to unreserved commitment to a venture. Without doubt, JVs of this type offer a way forward to genuine cooperation in international economic relations in the future.

The analysis also suggests, however, that a degree of cynicism may be warranted in respect of the claims advanced for JVs of certain kinds. A JV may be merely a subterfuge, luring partners into making commitments that leave them exposed to the risk of renegotiation under duress. It may be a device for enhancing collusion—a practice that may be warranted if it is necessary to recover the costs of technological or product innovation, but not otherwise. It may represent a pragmatic response to regulatory distortion—as when a misguided national competition policy outlaws a merger between the partners that would afford considerable efficiency gains; the JV, in this case, is better than nothing at all, but is only second best to a policy of removing the distortion itself.

One of the most topical applications of the theory of the JV is to industrial cooperation and production-sharing arrangements involving Japanese firms. To what extent, for example, can quality uncertainty in the training process support the argument that the Japanese JV is an appropriate vehicle for tutoring partners in developing countries? Are Japanese JV networks in Southeast Asia merely agglomerations of independent JV operations, or are they part of a wider strategy to play off one partner against another in an effort to maintain low prices for Japanese imports and thereby assure the competitiveness of Japanese reexports?

Other questions may be asked, for example, of Western corporations that seem anxious to cooperate with the Japanese. Are they really interested in long-term collaboration in the development of leading-edge technologies, or is it their hope that token research collaboration with the Japanese can open the door to short-term cartellike restrictions on international trade? Do Western collaborators really hope to learn something of a cooperative ethic (and perhaps even a new system of values) from the Japanese, or are they merely interested in cooperation as a mask to disguise the replacement of competition by collusion?

There do not seem to be any easy answers to these questions. More empirical evidence is required. It is hoped that the analysis presented in this chapter affords a framework within which such evidence can be interpreted. So far, it is only possible to clarify the questions, but eventually it should be possible to answer them.

ACKNOWLEDGEMENTS

A preliminary version of this chapter was presented to the joint seminar of the Swedish School of Business Administration, Helsinki, The Finnish School of Economics, and the University of Helsinki (kindly arranged by H.C. Blomqvist, T. Bergelund and I. Menzler-Hokkanen) and to the staff workshop at the University of Reading. Steve Nicholas provided considerable encouragement, mixed with healthy scepticism. We are grateful to Farok Contractor, Peter Lorange, Peter Gray, Kathryn Harrigan, Ingo Walter, and others for their constructive comments.

REFERENCES

Axelrod, R. (1981) 'The Evolution of Cooperation among Egoists'. *American Political Science Review*, **75**: 306–318.
Axelrod, R. (1984) *The Evolution of Cooperation*. Basic Books, New York.
Blois, K.J. (1972) 'Vertical Quasi-Integration'. *Journal of Industrial Economics*, **20**: 253–272.
Buckley, P. J. and Casson, M. C. (1985) *Economic Theory of the Multinational Enterprise: Selected Papers*. Macmillan, London.
Casson, M. C. (1982) *The Entrepreneur: An Economic Theory*. Blackwell, Oxford, England.
Casson, M. C. (1987) *The Firm and the Market*. MIT Press, Cambridge, MA.
Kojima, K. (1978) *Direct Foreign Investment*. Croom Helm, London.
Richardson, G. B. (1972) 'The Organisation of Industry'. *Economic Journal*, **82**: 883–896.
Williamson, O. E. (1985) *The Economic Institutions of Capitalism; Firms, Markets, Relational Contracting*. Free Press, New York.

11

Collaborate with Your Competitors—and Win

Gary Hamel, Yves L. Doz and C. K. Prahalad

Collaboration between competitors is in fashion. General Motors and Toyota assemble automobiles, Siemens and Philips develop semiconductors, Canon supplies photocopiers to Kodak, France's Thomson and Japan's JVC manufacture videocassette recorders. But the spread of what we call 'competitive collaboration'—joint ventures, outsourcing agreements, product licensings, cooperative research—has triggered unease about the long-term consequences. A strategic alliance can strengthen both companies against outsiders even as it weakens one partner *vis-à-vis* the other. In particular, alliances between Asian companies and Western rivals seem to work against the Western partner. Cooperation becomes a low-cost route for new competitors to gain technology and market access.[1]

Yet the case for collaboration is stronger than ever. It takes so much money to develop new products and to penetrate new markets that few companies can go it alone in every situation. ICL, the British computer company, could not have developed its current generation of mainframes without Fujitsu. Motorola needs Toshiba's distribution capacity to break into the Japanese semiconductor market. Time is another critical factor. Alliances can provide shortcuts for Western companies racing to improve their production efficiency and quality control.

We have spent more than five years studying the inner workings of 15 strategic alliances and monitoring scores of others. Our research[2] involves cooperative ventures between competitors from the United States and Japan, Europe and Japan, and the United States and Europe. We did not judge the success or failure of each partnership by its longevity—a common mistake when evaluating strategic alliances—but by the shifts in competitive strength on each side.

---

[1] For a vigorous warning about the perils of collaboration, see Robert B. Reich and Eric D. Mankin, 'Joint Ventures with Japan Give Away Our Future'. *Harvard Business Review*, March–April 1986: 78.

[2] We sought answers to a series of interrelated questions. What role have strategic alliances and outsourcing agreements played in the global success of Japanese and Korean companies? How do alliances change the competitive balance between partners? Does winning at collaboration mean different things to different companies? What factors determine who gains most from collaboration? To understand who won and who lost and why, we observed the interactions of the partners firsthand and at multiple levels in each organization. Our sample included four European–US alliances, two intra-European alliances, two European–Japanese alliances, and seven US–Japanese alliances. We gained access to both sides of the partnerships in about half the cases and studied each alliance for an average of three years. Confidentiality was a paramount concern. Where we did have access to both sides, we often wound up knowing more about who was doing what to whom than either of the partners. To preserve confidentiality, our article disguises many of the alliances that were part of the study.

Reprinted by permission of *Harvard Business Review*. 'Collaborate with Your Competitors—and Win', by Gary Hamel, Yves L. Doz and C. K. Prahalad, January–February 1989, pp. 133–139.
Copyright © 1989 by the President and Fellows of Harvard College; all rights reserved.

We focused on how companies use competitive collaboration to enhance their internal skills and technologies while they guard against transferring competitive advantages to ambitious partners.

There is no immutable law that strategic alliances *must* be a windfall for Japanese or Korean partners. Many Western companies do give away more than they gain—but that's because they enter partnerships without knowing what it takes to win. Companies that benefit most from competitive collaboration adhere to a set of simple but powerful principles.

Collaboration is competition in a different form. Successful companies never forget that their new partners may be out to disarm them. They enter alliances with clear strategic objectives, and they also understand how their partners' objectives will affect their success.

Harmony is not the most important measure of success. Indeed, occasional conflict may be the best evidence of mutually beneficial collaboration. Few alliances remain win–win undertakings forever. A partner may be content even as it unknowingly surrenders core skills.

Cooperation has limits. Companies must defend against competitive compromise. A strategic alliance is a constantly evolving bargain whose real terms go beyond the legal agreement or the aims of top management. What information gets traded is determined day to day, often by engineers and operating managers. Successful companies inform employees at all levels about what skills and technologies are off-limits to the partner and monitor what the partner requests and receives.

Learning from partners is paramount. Successful companies view each alliance as a window on their partners' broad capabilities. They use the alliance to build skills in areas outside the formal agreement and systematically diffuse new knowledge throughout their organizations.

WHY COLLABORATE?

Using an alliance with a competitor to acquire new technologies or skills is not devious. It reflects the commitment and capacity of each partner to absorb the skills of the other. We found that in every case in which a Japanese company emerged from an alliance stronger than its Western partner, the Japanese company had made a greater effort to learn.

Strategic intent is an essential ingredient in the commitment to learning. The willingness of Asian companies to enter alliances represents a change in competitive tactics, not competitive goals. NEC, for example, has used a series of collaborative ventures to enhance its technology and product competences. NEC is the only company in the world with a leading position in telecommunications, computers, and semiconductors—despite its investing less in R&D (as a percentage of revenues) than competitors like Texas Instruments, Northern Telecom, and L.M. Ericsson. Its string of partnerships, most notably with Honeywell, allowed NEC to lever its inhouse R&D over the last two decades.

Western companies, on the other hand, often enter alliances to avoid investments. They are more interested in reducing the costs and risks of entering new businesses or markets than in acquiring new skills. A senior US manager offered this analysis of his company's venture with a Japanese rival: 'We complement each other well—our distribution capability and their manufacturing skill. I see no reason to invest upstream if we can find a secure source of product. This is a comfortable relationship for us'.

An executive from this company's Japanese partner offered a different perspective: 'When it is necessary to collaborate, I go to my employees and say, "This is bad, I wish we had these skills ourselves. Collaboration is second best. But I will feel worse if after four years we do not know how to do what our partner knows how to do." We must digest their skills'.

The problem here is not that the US company wants to share investment risk (its Japanese partner does too) but that the US company has no ambition *beyond* avoidance. When the commitment to learning is so one-sided, collaboration invariably leads to competitive compromise.

Many so-called alliances between Western companies and their Asian rivals are little more than sophisticated outsourcing arrangements (see the Appendix 'Competition for Competence'). General Motors buys cars and components from Korea's Daewoo. Siemens buys computers from Fujitsu. Apple buys laser printer engines from Canon. The traffic is almost entirely one way. These OEM deals offer Asian partners a way to capture investment initiative from Western competitors and displace customer-competitors from value-creating activities. In many cases this goal meshes with that of the Western partner: to regain competitiveness quickly and with minimum effort.

Consider the joint venture between Rover, the British automaker, and Honda. Some 25 years ago, Rover's forerunners were world leaders in small car design. Honda had not even entered the automobile business. But in the mid-1970s, after failing to penetrate foreign markets, Rover turned to Honda for technology and product-development support. Rover has used the alliance to avoid investments to design and build new cars. Honda has cultivated skills in European styling and marketing as well as multinational manufacturing. There is little doubt which company will emerge stronger over the long term.

Troubled laggards like Rover often strike alliances with surging latecomers like Honda. Having fallen behind in a key skills area (in this case, manufacturing small cars), the laggard attempts to compensate for past failures. The latecomer uses the alliance to close a specific skills gap (in this case, learning to build cars for a regional market). But a laggard that forges a partnership for short-term gain may find itself in a dependency spiral: as it contributes fewer and fewer distinctive skills, it must reveal more and more of its internal operations to keep the partner interested. For the weaker company, the issue shifts from 'Should we collaborate?' to 'With whom should we collaborate?' to 'How do we keep our partner interested as we lose the advantages that made us attractive to them in the first place?'

There's a certain paradox here. When both partners are equally intent on internalizing the other's skills, distrust and conflict may spoil the alliance and threaten its very survival. That's one reason joint ventures between Korean and Japanese companies have been few and tempestuous. Neither side wants to 'open the kimono'. Alliances seem to run most smoothly when one partner is intent on learning and the other is intent on avoidance—in essence, when one partner is willing to grow dependent on the other. But running smoothly is not the point; the point is for a company to emerge from an alliance more competitive than when it entered it.

One partner does not always have to give up more than it gains to ensure the survival of an alliance. There are certain conditions under which mutual gain is possible, at least for a time:

The partners' strategic goals converge while their competitive goals diverge. That is, each partner allows for the other's continued prosperity in the shared business. Philips and Du Pont collaborate to develop and manufacture compact discs, but neither side invades the other's market. There is a clear upstream/downstream division of effort.

The size and market power of both partners is modest compared with industry leaders. This forces each side to accept that mutual dependence may have to continue for many years. Long-term collaboration may be so critical to both partners that neither will risk antagonizing the other by an overtly competitive bid to appropriate skills or competences. Fujitsu's 1 to 5 size disadvantage with IBM means it will be a long time, if ever, before Fujitsu can break away from its foreign partners and go it alone.

Each partner believes it can learn from the other and at the same time limit access to proprietary skills. JVC and Thomson, both of whom make VCRs, know that they are trading skills. But the two companies are looking for very different things. Thomson needs product technology and manufacturing prowess; JVC needs to learn how to succeed in the fragmented European market. Both sides believe there is an equitable chance for gain.

HOW TO BUILD SECURE DEFENCES

For collaboration to succeed, each partner must contribute something distinctive: basic research, product development skills, manufacturing capacity, access to distribution. The challenge is to share enough skills to create advantage *vis-à-vis* companies outside the alliance while preventing a wholesale transfer of core skills to the partner This is a very thin line to walk. Companies must carefully select what skills and technologies they pass to their partners. They must develop safeguards against unintended, informal transfers of information. The goal is to limit the transparency of their operations.

The type of skill a company contributes is an important factor in how easily its partner can internalize the skills. The potential for transfer is greatest when a partner's contribution is easily transported (in engineering drawings, on computer tapes, or in the heads of a few technical experts); easily interpreted (it can be reduced to commonly understood equations or symbols); and easily absorbed (the skill or competence is independent of any particular cultural context).

Western companies face an inherent disadvantage because their skills are generally more vulnerable to transfer. The magnet that attracts so many companies to alliances with Asian competitors is their manufacturing excellence—a competence that is less transferable than most. Just-in-time inventory systems and quality circles can be imitated, but this is like pulling a few threads out of an oriental carpet. Manufacturing excellence is a complex web of employee training, integration with suppliers, statistical process controls, employee involvement, value engineering, and design for manufacture. It is difficult to extract such a subtle competence in any way but a piecemeal fashion.

There is an important distinction between technology and competence. A discrete, stand-alone technology (for example, the design of a semiconductor chip) is more easily transferred than a process competence, which is entwined in the social fabric of a company. Asian companies often learn more from their Western partners than vice versa because they contribute difficult-to-unravel strengths, while Western partners contribute easy-to-imitate technology.

So companies must take steps to limit transparency. One approach is to limit the scope of the formal agreement. It might cover a single technology rather than an entire range of technologies; part of a product line rather than the entire line; distribution in a limited number of markets or for a limited period of time. The objective is to circumscribe a partner's opportunities to learn.

Moreover, agreements should establish specific performance requirements. Motorola, for example, takes an incremental, incentive-based approach to technology transfer in its venture with Toshiba. The agreement calls for Motorola to release its microprocessor technology incrementally as Toshiba delivers on its promise to increase Motorola's penetration in the

Japanese semiconductor market. The greater Motorola's market share, the greater Toshiba's access to Motorola's technology.

Many of the skills that migrate between companies are not covered in the formal terms of collaboration. Top management puts together strategic alliances and sets the legal parameters for exchange. But what actually gets traded is determined by day-to-day interactions of engineers, marketers, and product developers: who says what to whom, who gets access to what facilities, who sits on what joint committees. The most important deals ('I'll share this with you if you share that with me') may be struck four or five organizational levels below where the deal was signed. Here lurks the greatest risk of unintended transfers of important skills.

Consider one technology-sharing alliance between European and Japanese competitors. The European company valued the partnership as a way to acquire a specific technology. The Japanese company considered it a window on its partner's entire range of competences and interacted with a broad spectrum of its partner's marketing and product-development staff. The company mined each contact for as much information as possible.

For example, every time the European company requested a new feature on a product being sourced from its partner, the Japanese company asked for detailed customer and competitor analyses to justify the request. Over time, it developed a sophisticated picture of the European market that would assist its own entry strategy. The technology acquired by the European partner through the formal agreement had a useful life of three to five years. The competitive insights acquired informally by the Japanese company will probably endure longer.

Limiting unintended transfers at the operating level requires careful attention to the role of gatekeepers, the people who control what information flows to a partner. A gatekeeper can be effective only if there are a limited number of gateways through which a partner can access people and facilities. Fujitsu's many partners all go through a single office, the 'collaboration section', to request information and assistance from different divisions. This way the company can monitor and control access to critical skills and technologies.

We studied one partnership between European and US competitors that involved several divisions of each company. While the US company could only access its partner through a single gateway, its partner had unfettered access to all participating divisions. The European company took advantage of its free rein. If one division refused to provide certain information, the European partner made the same request of another division. No single manager in the US company could tell how much information had been transferred or was in a position to piece together patterns in the requests.

Collegiality is a prerequisite for collaborative success. But *too much* collegiality should set off warning bells to senior managers. CEOs or division presidents should expect occasional complaints from their counterparts about the reluctance of lower level employees to share information. That's a sign that the gatekeepers are doing their jobs. And senior management should regularly debrief operating personnel to find out what information the partner is requesting and what requests are being granted.

Limiting unintended transfers ultimately depends on employee loyalty and self-discipline. This was a real issue for many of the Western companies we studied. In their excitement and pride over technical achievements, engineering staffs sometimes shared information that top management considered sensitive. Japanese engineers were less likely to share proprietary information.

There are a host of cultural and professional reasons for the relative openness of Western technicians. Japanese engineers and scientists are more loyal to their company than to their profession. They are less steeped in the open give-and-take of university research since they receive much of their training from employers. They consider themselves team members more than individual scientific contributors. As one Japanese manager noted, 'We don't feel any need to reveal what we know. It is not an issue of pride for us. We're glad to sit and listen. If we're patient we usually learn what we want to know'.

Controlling unintended transfers may require restricting access to facilities as well as to people. Companies should declare sensitive laboratories and factories off-limits to their partners. Better yet, they might house the collaborative venture in an entirely new facility. IBM is building a special site in Japan where Fujitsu can review its forthcoming mainframe software before deciding whether to license it. IBM will be able to control exactly what Fujitsu sees and what information leaves the facility.

Finally, which country serves as 'home' to the alliance affects transparency. If the collaborative team is located near one partner's major facilities, the other partner will have more opportunities to learn—but less control over what information gets traded. When the partner houses, feeds, and looks after engineers and operating managers, there is a danger they will 'go native'. Expatriate personnel need frequent visits from headquarters as well as regular furloughs home.

ENHANCE THE CAPACITY TO LEARN

Whether collaboration leads to competitive surrender or revitalization depends foremost on what employees believe the purpose of the alliance to be. It is self-evident: to learn, one must *want* to learn. Western companies won't realize the full benefits of competitive collaboration until they overcome an arrogance borne of decades of leadership. In short, Western companies must be more receptive.

We asked a senior executive in a Japanese electronics company about the perception that Japanese companies learn more from their foreign partners than vice versa. 'Our Western partners approach us with the attitude of teachers', he told us. 'We are quite happy with this, because we have the attitude of students'.

Learning begins at the top. Senior management must be committed to enhancing their companies' skills as well as to avoiding financial risk. But most learning takes place at the lower levels of an alliance. Operating employees not only represent the front lines in an effective defence but also play a vital role in acquiring knowledge. They must be well briefed on the partner's strengths and weaknesses and understand how acquiring particular skills will bolster their company's competitive position.

This is already standard practice among Asian companies. We accompanied a Japanese development engineer on a tour through a partner's factory. This engineer dutifully took notes on plant layout, the number of production stages, the rate at which the line was running, and the number of employees. He recorded all this despite the fact that he had no manufacturing responsibility in his own company, and that the alliance didn't encompass joint manufacturing. Such dedication greatly enhances learning.

Collaboration doesn't always provide an opportunity to fully internalize a partner's skills. Yet just acquiring new and more precise benchmarks of a partner's performance can be of great value. A new benchmark can provoke a thorough review of internal performance levels and may spur a round of competitive innovation. Asking questions like, 'Why do their semiconductor logic designs have fewer errors than ours?' and 'Why are they investing in this technology and we're not?' may provide the incentive for a vigorous catch-up program.

Competitive benchmarking is a tradition in most of the Japanese companies we studied. It requires many of the same skills associated with competitor analysis: systematically calibrating performance against external targets; learning to use rough estimates to determine where a competitor (or partner) is better, faster, or cheaper; translating those estimates into new internal targets; and recalibrating to establish the rate of improvement in a competitor's performance. The great advantage of competitive collaboration is that proximity makes benchmarking easier.

Indeed, some analysts argue that one of Toyota's motivations in collaborating with GM in the much-publicized NUMMI venture is to gauge the quality of GM's manufacturing technology. GM's top manufacturing people get a close look at Toyota, but the reverse is true as well. Toyota may be learning whether its giant US competitor is capable of closing the productivity gap with Japan.

Competitive collaboration also provides a way of getting close enough to rivals to predict how they will behave when the alliance unravels or runs its course. How does the partner respond to price changes? How does it measure and reward executives? How does it prepare to launch a new product? By revealing a competitor's management orthodoxies, collaboration can increase the chances of success in future head-to-head battles.

Knowledge acquired from a competitor-partner is only valuable after it is diffused through the organization. Several companies we studied had established internal clearinghouses to collect and disseminate information. The collaborations manager at one Japanese company regularly made the rounds of all employees involved in alliances. He identified what information had been collected by whom and then passed it on to appropriate departments. Another company held regular meetings where employees shared new knowledge and determined who was best positioned to acquire additional information.

PROCEED WITH CARE—BUT PROCEED

After World War II, Japanese and Korean companies entered alliances with Western rivals from weak positions. But they worked steadfastly toward independence. In the early 1960s, NEC's computer business was one-quarter the size of Honeywell's, its primary foreign partner. It took only two decades for NEC to grow larger than Honeywell, which eventually sold its computer operations to an alliance between NEC and Group Bull of France. The NEC experience demonstrates that dependence on a foreign partner doesn't automatically condemn a company to also-ran status. Collaboration may sometimes be unavoidable; surrender is not.

Managers are too often obsessed with the ownership structure of an alliance. Whether a company controls 51% or 49% of a joint venture may be much less important than the rate at which each partner learns from the other. Companies that are confident of their ability to learn may even prefer some ambiguity in the alliance's legal structure. Ambiguity creates more potential to acquire skills and technologies. The challenge for Western companies is not to write tighter legal agreements but to become better learners.

Running away from collaboration is no answer. Even the largest Western companies can no longer outspend their global rivals. With leadership in many industries shifting toward the East, companies in the United States and Europe must become good borrowers—much like Asian companies did in the 1960s and 1970s. Competitive renewal depends on building new process capabilities and winning new product and technology battles. Collaboration can be a low-cost strategy for doing both.

APPENDIX. COMPETITION FOR COMPETENCE

In the article 'Do You Really Have a Global Strategy' (*Harvard Business Review*, July–August 1985), Gary Hamel and C.K. Prahalad examined one dimension of the global competitive battle: the race for brand dominance. This is the battle for control of distribution channels and global 'share of mind'. Another global battle has been much less visible and has received much less management attention. This is the battle for control over key technology-based competences that fuel new business development.

Honda has built a number of businesses, including marine engines, lawn mowers, generators, motorcycles, and cars, around its engine and power train competence. Casio draws on its expertise in semiconductors and digital display in producing calculators, small-screen televisions, musical instruments, and watches. Canon relies on its imaging and microprocessor competences in its camera, copier, and laser printer businesses.

In the short run, the quality and performance of a company's products determine its competitiveness. Over the longer term, however, what counts is the ability to build and enhance core competences—distinctive skills that spawn new generations of products. This is where many managers and commentators fear Western companies are losing. Our research helps explain why some companies may be more likely than others to surrender core skills.

Alliance or outsourcing?

Enticing Western companies into outsourcing agreements provides several benefits to ambitious OEM partners. Serving as a manufacturing base for a Western partner is a quick route to increased manufacturing share without the risk or expense of building brand share. The Western partners' distribution capability allows Asian suppliers to focus all their resources on building absolute product advantage. Then OEMs can enter markets on their own and convert manufacturing share into brand share.

Serving as a sourcing platform yields more than just volume and process improvements. It also generates low-cost, low-risk market learning. The downstream (usually Western) partner typically provides information on how to tailor products to local markets. So every product design transferred to an OEM partner is also a research report on customer preferences and market needs. The OEM partner can use these insights to read the market accurately when it enters on its own.

A ratchet effect

Our research suggests that once a significant sourcing relationship has been established, the buyer becomes less willing and able to reemerge as a manufacturing competitor. Japanese and Korean companies are, with few exceptions, exemplary suppliers. If anything, the 'soft option' of outsourcing becomes even softer as OEM suppliers routinely exceed delivery and quality expectations.

Outsourcing often begins a ratchet-like process. Relinquishing manufacturing control and paring back plant investment leads to sacrifices in product design, process technology, and, eventually, R&D budgets. Consequently, the OEM partner captures product-development as well as manufacturing initiative. Ambitious OEM partners are not content with the old formula of 'You design it and we'll make it'. The new reality is, 'You design it, we'll learn from your designs, make them more manufacturable, and launch our products alongside yours'.

Reversing the verdict

This outcome is not inevitable. Western companies can retain control over their core competences by keeping a few simple principles in mind.

A competitive product is not the same thing as a competitive organization. While an Asian OEM partner may provide the former, it seldom provides the latter. In essence, outsourcing is a way of renting someone else's competitiveness rather than developing a long-term solution to competitive decline.

Rethink the make-or-buy decision. Companies often treat component manufacturing operations as cost centres and transfer their output to assembly units at an arbitrarily set price. This transfer price is an accounting fiction, and it is unlikely to yield as high a return as marketing or distribution investments, which require less research money and capital. But companies seldom consider the competitive consequences of surrendering control over a key value-creating activity.

Watch out for deepening dependence. Surrender results from a series of out-sourcing decisions that individually make economic sense but collectively amount to a phased exit from the business. Different managers make outsourcing decisions at different times, unaware of the cumulative impact.

Replenish core competences. Western companies must outsource some activities; the economics are just too compelling. The real issue is whether a company is adding to its stock of technologies and competences as rapidly as it is surrendering them. The question of whether to outsource should always provoke a second question: Where can we outpace our partner and other rivals in building new sources of competitive advantage?

12

Interfirm Diversity, Organizational Learning, and Longevity in Global Strategic Alliances

Arvind Parkhe

On March 6, 1990, West Germany's Daimler Benz ($48 billion in sales) and Japan's Mitsubishi Group ($200 billion in sales) revealed that they had held 'a secret meeting in Singapore to work out a plan for intensive cooperation among their auto, aerospace, electronics, and other lines of business. However, combining operations of the two companies seems remote: Daimler's orderly German corporate structure doesn't mesh well with Mitsubishi's leaderless group management approach' (*Business Week*, 1990b).

This example illustrates an important paradox in international business today. On one hand, global strategic alliances (GSAs) are being used with increasing frequency in order to, *inter alia*, keep abreast of rapidly changing technologies, gain access to specific foreign markets and distribution channels, create new products, and ease problems of worldwide excess productive capacity. Indeed, GSAs are becoming an essential feature of companies' overall organizational structure, and competitive advantage increasingly depends not only on a company's internal capabilities, but also on the types of its alliances and the scope of its relationships with other companies. On the other hand, GSAs bring together partners from different national origins, with often sharp differences in the collaborating firms' cultural and political bases. As in the above illustration, there may also exist considerable diversity in *firm-specific* characteristics that may be tied to each firm's national heritage.

Interfirm diversity can severely impede the ability of companies to work jointly and effectively (Adler and Graham, 1989; Harrigan, 1988; Perlmutter and Heenan, 1986), since many GSA partners—relative newcomers to voluntary cooperative relationships with foreign firms—have yet to acquire the necessary skills to cope with their differences. Not surprisingly, the rapid growth of GSAs is accompanied by high failure rates (Hergert and Morris, 1988; Porter, 1986).[1]

Before probing the nexus between diversity and alliance performance, however, it is fruitful to begin with the recognition that (1) in GSAs, significant interfirm diversity is to be expected, and (2) this diversity can be analytically separated into two types. Type I includes the familiar interfirm differences (interdependencies) that GSAs are specifically created to exploit. These differences form the underlying strategic motivations for entering into alliances; an inventory of such motivations is provided, for instance, by Contractor and Lorange (1988, p.10). Thus, Type I diversity deals with the reciprocal strengths and complementary resources furnished by the alliance partners, differences that actually facilitate the formulation, development, and collaborative effectiveness of GSAs.

Reprinted with permission from *Journal of International Business Studies*, Fourth Quarter, pp.579–601.
Copyright © 1991 Journal of International Business Studies.

Type II diversity, the major focus of this paper, refers to the differences in partner characteristics that often negatively affect the longevity and effective functioning of GSAs. Over the life of the partnership, the dynamics of Types I and II are very different, since the two types are differentially impacted by the processes of organizational learning and adaptation. In the case of Type I, learning through the GSA may enable one partner to acquire the skills and technologies it lacked at the time of alliance formation, and eventually rewrite the partnership terms or even discard the other partner. Thus, the GSA becomes a race to learn, with the company that learns fastest dominating the relationship and becoming, through cooperation, a more formidable competitor. Conversely, organizational learning and adaptation can progressively mitigate the impact of Type II differences, thereby promoting longevity and effectiveness. To summarize, a minimum level of Type I differences are essential to the formation and maintenance (*raison d'etre*) of an alliance, and their erosion destabilizes the partnership. Type II differences, though inevitably present at the initiation of an alliance, may be overcome by iterative cycles of learning that strengthen the partnership.

A large number of previous studies have examined how Type II interfirm differences can play a major role in frustrating the joint efforts of GSA partners. For example, Adler and Graham (1989), found that cross-cultural negotiations are more difficult than intra-cultural negotiations. Several other studies have also established that negotiations between businesspeople of different cultures often fail because of problems related to cross-cultural differences (Adler, 1986; Black, 1987; Graham, 1985; Tung, 1984). Harrigan (1988) studied the influence of sponsoring-firm asymmetries in terms of strategic directions (horizontal, vertical, and relatedness linkages with the venture) on performance. Hall (1984) analysed the effects of differing management procedures on alliances. Still other researchers have examined the influence of variations in corporate culture (Killing, 1982) and national setting Turner (1987) on successful collaboration. This brief overview, while not exhaustive, conveys the basic directions in which research to date has progressed.

Unfortunately, the usefulness of these important studies in an overall assessment of international interfirm interactions is limited, since they examine the impact of selected aspects of interfirm diversity on cooperative ventures in a piecemeal fashion. The academic literature thus remains fragmented at different levels of analysis, with no overarching theme cohesively pulling together the various dimensions of interfirm diversity in systematic theory-building. Therefore, the main contributions of this paper will be to extend current theory (1) by developing and justifying a typology of the major dimensions of interfirm diversity in the context of GSAs; and, (2) by examining diversity's impact on alliance outcomes through a dynamic model rooted in organizational learning theory. For this purpose, the following questions will be addressed. What are the theoretical dimensions of diversity between GSA partners? In what ways and under what circumstances does each dimension, individually or collectively, translate into reduced collaborative effectiveness? To what extent can deliberate learning/adaptation actions by firms deter expensive alliance failures and promote longevity?

A PREFATORY NOTE ON TERMINOLOGY

It is important at the outset to define terminology. Interfirm cooperative relationships have previously been defined by Borys and Jemison (1989), Schermerhorn (1975), Nielsen (1988), and Oliver (1990). However, the conceptual domain of GSAs must include the additional properties of being international in scope, mixed-motive (competitive plus cooperative) in nature, and of strategic significance to each partner, i.e., tied to the firms' current and anticipated core businesses, markets, and technologies (commonly referred to as the corporate mission). Thus, GSAs are the relatively enduring interfirm cooperative arrangements, involving cross-border flows and linkages that utilize resources and/or governance structures from autonomous organizations with headquarters in two or more countries, for the joint accomplishment of individual goals linked to the corporate mission of each sponsoring firm.

This definition delineates GSAs from single-transaction market relationships, as well as from unrelated diversification moves, while accommodating the variety of strategic motives and organizational forms that accompany global partnerships. For example, GSAs can be used as transitional modes of organizational structure (Gomes-Casseres, 1989) in response to current challenges as firms grope to find more permanent structures including, sometimes, whole ownership after the GSA has achieved its purpose. Often, however, longevity is an important yardstick of performance measurement by each parent company (Harrigan, 1985; Lewis, 1990).

It must be clearly noted that longevity is an imperfect proxy for 'alliance success'. Longevity can be associated, for instance, with the presence of high exit barriers. And in some alliances, success can also be operationalized in terms of other measures such as profitability, market share, and synergistic contribution toward parent companies' competitiveness (cf. Venkatraman and Ramanujam, 1986). Yet, achievement of these latter objectives can be thwarted by premature, unintended dissolution of the GSA. Furthermore, objective performance measures (e.g., GSA survival and duration) are significantly and positively correlated with parent firms' reported (that is, subjective) satisfaction with GSA performance and with perceptions of the extent to which a GSA performed relative to its initial objectives (Geringer and Hebert, 1991), so that for many research purposes the use of longevity as a surrogate for a favourable GSA outcome is probably not too restrictive. With the above limitations acknowledged, we focus mainly on the subset of GSAs where longevity (not planned termination) is sought by each partner, but is threatened by problems stemming from Type II interfirm diversity; however, in as much as planned termination represents an important potential alliance outcome involving the deliberate erosion of Type I diversity, it is treated as a special case of a more general diversity/longevity dynamic model later in the paper.

Interfirm diversity refers to the comparative interorganizational differences on certain attributes or dimensions (Molnar and Rogers, 1979) that continually shape the pattern of interaction between them (Van de Ven, 1976). In sum, this paper examines the interorganizational interface at which inherent interfirm diversity between GSA partners often makes effective management of pooled resource contributions problematic.

THE PROBLEM OF DIVERSITY

Just as modern business organizations are complex *social* entities (and therefore studied in the ambit of the social sciences), GSAs represent an emerging *social institution*. As researchers in sociology, marketing, and interorganizational relations theory have long noted, dissimilarities between social actors can render effective pairwise interactions difficult, and vice versa.

Evans' (1963) 'similarity hypothesis', for example, maintains that 'the more similar the parties in a dyad are, the more likely a favorable outcome'. The proposed mechanism is: similarity leads to attraction (sharing of common needs and goals), which causes attitudes to become positive, thus leading to favourable outcomes (McGuire, 1968). Likewise, Lazarsfeld and Merton (1954) identify the tendency for similar values and statuses to serve as bases for social relationships, as a basic mechanism of social interaction. These same principles may explain the characteristics of linkages between organizations (Paulson, 1976). And Whetten (1981, p.17) argues that 'potential partners are screened to reduce the costs of coordination that increase as a function of differences between the collaborating organizations'.

Although the above literature primarily focuses on problems of surmounting communication difficulties and establishing a common set of working assumptions, a broader set of dimensions is crucial in understanding GSA interactions, given the nature of GSAs as defined above. These dimensions are developed next.

DIMENSIONS OF INTERFIRM DIVERSITY IN GSAs

The major dimensions of Type II interfirm diversity in global strategic alliances are described below; Table 1 summarizes this discussion.[2] In a departure from previous studies that have focused on limited aspects of interfirm diversity, Table 1 spans multiple, critical levels of analysis that are indispensable in providing a fuller understanding of the factors that may lead to friction and eventual collapse of the GSA. In addition, the following discussion also includes an analysis of how each diversity dimension can influence ongoing reciprocal *learning* within the partnership, an important consideration in the study of alliance longevity and effectiveness. Table 1 distinguishes between levels of conceptualization and levels of phenomena. Levels of phenomena refer to dimensions of interfirm diversity that can, with arguable intersubjectivity, be observed and measured, for example, operationalized culture in four dimensions (Hofstede, 1983). Conceptual levels deal with ideas and theories about phenomena. Thus, the social behaviour of interfacing managers from each GSA partner firm is an output of the managers' respective societal (meta), national (macro), corporate-level (meso), and operating-level (micro) influences. While the actual behaviours can be observed, appreciating the often significant differences between them requires an abstraction to the underlying conceptual level of analysis. Finally, it is noted that the dimensions in the typology are often interrelated, and therefore cannot be treated as mutually exclusive.

Societal culture

The influence of a society's culture permeates all aspects of life within the society, including the norms, values, and behaviours of managers in its national companies. The cross-cultural interactions found in GSAs bring together people who may have different patterns of behaving and believing, and different cognitive blueprints for interpreting the world (Kluckhohn and Kroeberg, 1952; Black and Mendenhall, 1990). Indeed, Maruyama (1984) argues that cultural differences are at the epistemologic level, that is, in the very structure of perceiving, thinking, and reasoning.

Excellent examples of the deep impact of culture on GSA management can be found in the partners' approaches to problem solving and conflict resolution. In some cultures, problems are to be actively solved; managers must take deliberate actions to influence their environment and affect the course of the future. This is the basis for strategic planning. In contrast, in other cultures, life is seen as a series of preordained situations that are to be fatalistically accepted

Table 1. Interfirm diversity in GSAs: a summary

Conceptual level	Phenomenological level	Dimension of diversity	Sources of tension	Coping mechanisms	Proposition
Meta	Supranational	Societal culture	Differences in perception and interpretation of phenomena, analytical processes	Promote formal training programmes, informal contact, behaviour transparency	1a, 1b
Macro	National	National context	Differences in home government policies, national industry structure and institutions	Emphasize 'rational' (i.e., technological and economic) factors	2
Meso	Top management	Corporate culture	Differences in ideologies and values guiding companies	Encourage organizational learning to facilitate 'intermediate' corporate culture	3
Meso	Policy group	Strategic direction	Differences in strategic interests of partners from dynamic external and internal environments	Devise flexible partnership structure	4
Micro	Functional management	Management practices and organization	Differences in management styles, organizational structures, of parent firms	Set up unitary management processes and structures	5

(Moran and Harris, 1982). Similarly, GSA partners must routinely deal with conflicts in such areas as technology development, production and sourcing, market strategy and implementation, and so on (Lynch, 1989). In some cultures, conflict is viewed as a healthy, natural, and inevitable part of relationships and organizations. In fact, programmed or structured conflict (e.g., the devil's advocate and dialectical inquiry methods) has been suggested as a way to enhance the effectiveness of strategic decision-making (cf. Cosier and Dalton, 1990). But in other cultures, vigorous conflict and open confrontation are deemed distasteful. Embarrassment and loss of face to either party is sought to be avoided at all costs by talking indirectly and ambiguously about areas of difference until common ground can be found, by the use of mediators, and other techniques.

Effective handling of such cultural differences must begin with developing an understanding of the other's modes of thinking and behaving. For example, reflecting on the failed AT&T-Olivetti alliance, AT&T group executive Robert Kavner regretted, 'I don't think that we or Olivetti spent enough time understanding behaviour patterns' (Wysocki, 1990). Avoidance of such preventable mistakes may become increasingly essential, and investments in sophisticated programmes to promote intercultural awareness may become increasingly cost-effective, given the accelerating trend of GSA formation and the often enormous losses stemming from failed GSAs.[3] Ethnocentric arrogance (or cultural naivete) and GSAs simply do not mix well.

Nonetheless, Black and Mendenhall (1990) report from their survey of 29 empirical studies that the use of cross-cultural training (CCT) in US multinationals is very limited. Essentially, American top managers believe that a good manager in New York or Los Angeles will be effective in Hong Kong or Tokyo, and that a candidate's domestic track record can serve as the primary criterion for overseas assignment selection. Such a culturally insensitive approach is particularly unfortunate in light of CCT's proven success in terms of enhancing each of its three indicators of effectiveness: cross-cultural skill development, adjustment, and performance (Black and Mendenhall, 1990, pp.115–20). Clearly, CCT can be a powerful catalyst not only in enhancing intrafirm foreign operations, but also toward overcoming cultural diversity between GSA partners and facilitating ongoing mutual learning that promotes alliance longevity. More formally:

Proposition 1a. Societal culture differences will be negatively related to GSA longevity. However, this relationship will be moderated by formal training programmes that enhance intercultural understanding.

Furthermore, bridging the culture gap between GSA partners may be facilitated by effective communication at all interfacing levels. This suggests the need to improve behaviour transparency at each level, including effective recognition, verification, and signalling systems between the partners.

Proposition 1b. The relationship between differences in societal culture and longevity of the alliance will be further moderated by structured mechanisms that improve behaviour transparency.

National context

A company's national context primarily includes surrounding industry structure and institutions, and government laws and regulations. The great diversity that exists in the national contexts of global companies can hamper effective collaboration. For instance, disparities in the national context differentially impact global companies' ability to enter and operate GSAs. Of central relevance to this paper are national attitudes about simultaneous competition and cooperation. As noted below, however, national differences notwithstanding, important common patterns may be emerging internationally.

Japanese context. In Japan, companies have a long history of cooperating in some areas while competing in others, a practice that can be traced primarily to two factors: direction from the Ministry of International Trade and Industry (MITI), and *keiretsu*, or large industrial groups of firms representing diverse industries and skills. However, driven by recent trends in the competitive and political environments, Japanese companies are increasingly entering into GSAs, in the process forsaking their traditionally close *keiretsu* ties. In the context of this paper, the significant implications can be summed up as follows: (1) traditional Japanese industrial associations are in a state of flux; (2) a gradually diminishing role of the *keiretsu* in the future and a greater focus on the individual company; and (3) greater opportunities to enter into GSAs with Japanese firms.[4]

US context. In the US, the federal government has traditionally viewed cooperation between companies with suspicion, particularly if they competed in the same markets. The environment of strict antitrust regulations spawned companies with little experience in successfully managing interfirm cooperation. More recently, however, in an attempt to help correct structural problems in mature industries and to promote international competitiveness in high-tech industries, the US government has adopted more favourable attitudes toward interfirm cooperation, as reflected in its patent, procurement, and antitrust policies. For example, the National Cooperative Research Act of 1984 holds that cooperative ventures between companies are permissible when such arrangements add to the companies' overall efficiency and benefit society at large.

Though intended primarily to benefit US firms, these changes in American national attitudes and policies regarding interfirm cooperation may also have spillover benefits for non-US firms, in that the latter may have greater opportunities to enter into GSAs with US companies.[5] Recent developments in the US may also mean that the ability of US companies to spot, structure, and manage interfirm cooperative relationships will improve over time.

*European contex*t. In Europe, interfirm cooperation historically has been hampered by fragmented European markets, cultural and linguistic differences, diverse equipment standards and business regulations, and nationalist and protectionist government policies. Only in the past several years has the impending threat of a European technology gap against US and Japanese competition compelled European governments to promote the integration of European firms, such as the European Strategic Programme in Information Technologies (ESPRIT). However, such efforts to build a more dynamic, technologically independent Europe do not diminish the fact that Europe is too small to support the risky, multibillion dollar commitments required in many new industries.[6] As Ohmae (1985) argues, companies also need to establish a strong presence in US and Japanese markets to survive.

Three major points emerge from the preceding discussion. First, firms from the Triad regions are heavily influenced by their unique national contexts. Second, cooperating in GSAs may be rendered difficult by the significant differences in national contexts. Third, while these differences are likely to persist, as seen above, they may be progressively overwhelmed by powerful technological and economic factors.

Proposition 2. Differences in partner firms' national contexts and GSA longevity will be negatively related. The effects of these differences on longevity will be moderated by the technological and economic imperatives facing global firms.

Before concluding this discussion of national contexts, it is essential to broach one question that may have a significant bearing on global firms' future partnering abilities and success patterns. Will experience in managing linkages within a firms' home base provide an advantage in building linkages with foreign organizations (cf. Westney, 1988)? As just seen, Japanese firms have greater domestic experience in interfirm cooperation than US and European firms, though the latter are also accumulating more local experience. But is this experience transferable to GSAs, where partners typically have more widely varying characteristics? Insufficient evidence currently exists to answer this question; however, systematic research may yield important insights into the differential organizational learning patterns of companies weaned in different domestic contexts.

Corporate culture

Corporate culture includes those ideologies and values that characterize particular organizations (Beyer, 1981; Peters and Waterman, 1982). The notion that differences in corporate culture matter, familiar to researchers of international mergers and acquisitions (BenDaniel and Rosenbloom, 1990), is also crucially important in GSAs. Such firm-specific differences are often interwoven with the fabric of the partners' societal cultures and national contexts, as reflected in the phrases: European family capitalism, American managerial capitalism, and Japanese group capitalism.

Harrigan (1988) argues that corporate culture homogeneity among partners is even more important to GSA success than symmetry in their national origins. (She maintains, for example, that GM's values may be more similar to those of its GSA partner, Toyota, than to those of Ford.) However, studies have shown that a corporation's overall organizational culture is not able fully to homogenize values of employees originating in national cultures (Laurent, 1983), indicating the transcending importance of meta- and macrolevel variables relative to corporate culture. Although the relative importance of these dimensions must be determined empirically, it is clear that each dimension can be instrumental in erecting significant barriers to effective cooperation.

For example, strikingly different temporal orientations often exist in US versus Japanese corporations. The former, pressed by investors and analysts, may tend to focus on quarterly earnings reports, while the latter focus on establishing their brand names and international marketing channels, a *sine qua non* of higher order advantage leading to greater world market shares over a period of several years. Thus, Japanese partners may give GSAs more time to take root, whereas their US counterparts may be more impatient.

Significant differences may also exist on the issues of power and control. As Perlmutter and Heenan (1986) assert, Americans have historically harboured the belief that power, not parity, should govern collaborative ventures. In contrast, the Europeans and Japanese often consider partners as equals, subscribe to management by consensus, and rely on lengthy discussion to secure stronger commitment to shared enterprises.

For effective meshing of such diverse corporate cultures, each GSA partner must make the effort to learn the ideologies and values of its counterpart. For managers socialized into their own corporate cultures (Terpstra and David, 1990), openness to very different corporate orientations may be difficult. Yet, new forms of business often necessitate the acquisition of new core skills. Among some US firms, for instance, this may mean a reduced emphasis on equity control and an acceptance of slower payback periods on GSA investments in the interest of future benefits over longer time horizons. Among Japanese firms, this may mean a keener recognition of the demands on US managers to show quicker results, with possible modifications in the goals of the GSA and the means used to achieve those goals. Turner (1987) found some support for the emergence of 'intermediate' corporate cultures—those characterized by priorities and values between those of the sponsoring firms—as GSA partners made mutual adjustments. However, he did not relate his findings to alliance longevity, and his study was limited to UK–Japanese alliances. More empirical work is needed to test the following proposition:

Proposition 3. Corporate culture differences will be negatively related to alliance longevity. This relationship will be moderated by the development of an intermediate corporate culture to guide the GSA.

Finally, corporate culture has a circular relationship with learning in that it creates and reinforces learning and is created by learning; as such, it influences ongoing learning and adaptation within and between GSA partners. Miles and Snow (1978) demonstrate, for example, that a firm's posture (defender, prospector, etc.) is tied closely to its culture, and that shared norms and beliefs help shape strategy and the direction of organizational change. These broad norms and belief systems clearly influence the behavioural and cognitive development that each GSA partner can undergo; in turn, learning and adaptation in organizations often involves a restructuring of these norms and belief systems (Argyris and Schon, 1978).

Strategic directions

As Harrigan (1985) observes, 'asymmetries in the speed with which parent firms want to exploit an opportunity, the direction in which they want to move, or in other strategic matters are destabilizing to GSAs' (p.14). Partner screening at the alliance planning stage tests for strategic compatibility by analysing a potential partner's motivation and ability to live up to its commitments, by assessing whether there may exist probable areas of conflict due to overlapping interests in present markets or future geographic and product market expansion plans. Yet, a revised analysis may become necessary as the partners' evolving internal capabilities, strategic choices, and market developments pull them in separate directions, diminishing the strategic fit of a once-perfect match. Strategic divergence is particularly likely in environments characterized by high volatility, rapid advances in technology, and a blurring and dissolution of traditional boundaries between industries.[7]

One key to managing diverging partner interests may be to build flexibility into the partnership structure, which allows companies to adjust to changes in their internal and external environments. Flexible structures may be attained, for example, by initiating alliances on a small scale with specific, short-term agreements (such as cross-licensing or second sourcing), instead of huge deals that can pose 'lock-in' problems with shifting strategic priorities. In a gradually developed relationship, areas of cooperation can be expanded to a broader base to the extent that continuing strategic fit exists. Alternatively, flexibility can be attained by entering into a general (or blanket) cooperative agreement which is activated on an as-needed basis. For example, RCA and Sharp have a long-established cooperative agreement within which they have worked on a series of specific ventures over the years, including a recent

$200 million joint venture to manufacture complementary metal oxide semiconductor (CMOS) integrated circuits.

> *Proposition 4.* Divergence in the parents' strategic directions will be negatively related to GSA longevity. The relationship between divergence and longevity will be moderated by structural flexibility, that permits adaptation to shifting environments.

Strategy can affect organizational learning, and through learning alliance longevity, in various ways. Since strategy determines the goals and objectives and the breadth of actions available to a firm, it influences learning by providing a boundary to decision-making and a context for the perception and interpretation of the environment (Daft and Weick, 1984). In addition, as Miller and Friesen (1980) show, a firm's strategic direction creates a momentum for organizational learning, a momentum that is pervasive and highly resistant to small adjustments.

Management practices and organization

The wide interfirm diversity in management styles, organizational structures, and other operational-level variables that exists across firms from different parts of the world can largely be traced to diversity along the first four dimensions discussed above. In turn, these differences, illustrated by the Daimler Benz versus Mitsubishi contrast at the outset of this paper, can heighten operating difficulties and trigger premature dissolution of the GSA. An important issue in this regard is the problem of effectively combining the diverse systems of *autonomous* international firms, each accustomed to operating in a certain manner.

Many researchers in international cooperative strategies have tended, perhaps unwittingly, to focus solely on this final dimension of interfirm diversity (e.g., Dobkin, 1988; Hall, 1984; Pucik, 1988). Among the major differences that have been noted are the style of management (participatory or authoritarian), delegation of responsibility (high or low), decision-making (centralized or decentralized), and reliance on formal planning and control systems (high or low). To prevent problems of unclear lines of authority, poor communication, and slow decision-making, GSAs may need to set up *unitary* management processes and structures, where one decision point has the authority and independence to commit both partners. Implementation of this recommendation is difficult in cases where both partners are evenly matched in terms of company size and resource contributions to the GSA (cf. Killing, 1982).[8] Yet, agreement on the streamlining of tough operational-level issues must be reached *prior* to commencement of the GSA.

> *Proposition 5.* Diversity in the sponsoring firms' operating characteristics will be negatively related to longevity of the GSA. This relationship will be moderated by the establishment of unitary management processes and structures.

Though structure is often seen as an outcome of organizational learning, it plays a crucial role in determining the learning process itself (Fiol and Lyles, 1985). This observation can be important in the context of GSAs, where one firm's centralized, mechanistic structure that tends to reinforce past behaviours can collide with another firm's organic, decentralized structure that tends to allow shifts of beliefs and actions. More broadly, different management practices and organizational structures can enhance or retard learning, depending upon their degree of formalization, complexity, and diffusion of decision influence.

Theory and practice are linked in Table 2, which illustrates how significant Type II differences between GSA partners can impact the entire spectrum of alliance activities. For the sake of brevity, Table 2 outlines only a select number of characteristics that are derived from the typological dimensions of Table 1. Yet, a review of Table 2 clearly indicates that: (1) the extent of interfirm diversity in global strategic alliances may be high; and (2) as stressed earlier, the various dimensions of diversity are not distinct and unrelated, but rather share a common core that touches GSAs.

Furthermore, Type I and Type II diversity can undergo distinctly different patterns over time, generating different alliance outcomes. The dynamic model of longevity presented in the next section suggests that a pivotal factor in the interfirm diversity/alliance outcome link is organizational learning and adaptation to diversity by the GSA partners.

LONGEVITY IN GSAs: A LEARNING-BASED DYNAMIC MODEL

Organizational theorists (Lyles, 1988; Fiol and Lyles, 1985) define learning as 'the development of insights, knowledge, and associations between past actions, the effectiveness of those actions, and future actions' and adaptation as 'the ability to make incremental adjustments'. Learning can be minor, moderate, or major. In stimulus–response terms, in minor learning, an organization's worldview (tied to its national and corporate identity) remains the same, and choice of responses occurs from the existing behavioural repertoire. In moderate learning, partial modification of the interpretative system and/or development of new responses is involved. And in major learning, substantial and irreversible restructuring of one or both of the stimulus and response systems takes place (Hedberg, 1981). This conceptualization parallels Argyris and Schon's (1978) single-loop (or low-level) learning that serves merely to adjust the parameters in a fixed structure to varying demands, versus double-loop (or high-level) learning that changes norms, values, and worldviews, and redefines the rules for low-level learning.

Using a contingency theory perspective, we may expect the extent of learning (minor, moderate, or major) necessary for a given level of GSA longevity to be commensurate with the extent of interfirm diversity. Highly similar partners would require relatively little mutual adjustment for sustained collaborative effectiveness. Highly dissimilar partners would need to expend greater (double-loop) efforts and resources toward learning, absent which longevity may be expected to suffer.

Moreover, Type I and Type II diversity may shift dynamically along different phases of alliance development. Regarding the former, Porter (1986) observes that:

> Coalitions involving access to knowledge or ability are the most likely to dissolve as the party gaining access acquires its own internal skills through the coalition. Coalitions designed to gain the benefits of scale or learning in performing an activity have a more enduring purpose. If they dissolve, they will tend to dissolve into merger or into an arm's-length transaction. The stability of risk-reducing coalitions depends on the sources of risk they seek to control. Coalitions hedging against the risk of a single exogenous event will tend to dissolve, while coalitions involving an ongoing risk (e.g., exploration risk for oil) will be more durable (p. 329).

Thus, Type I strategic motivations and organizational learning interact to shape alliance stability and outcome. Similarly, the impact of Type II diversity on alliances can be dynamically altered by organizational learning that itself is an outcome of certain types of deliberate management investments during different phases of alliance development. The pattern of these

Table 2. Selected international differences and impacted areas of GSA management

Characteristic	Value	Country Examples	Description	Impacted Areas of GSA Management
Ownership of assets	Private	'Free World' countries	Factors of production predominantly privately owned	Sourcing strategy; pricing flexibility, quality control technology transfer, profit repatriation
	Public	Eastern bloc countries,[a] Communist China[b]	Factors of production predominantly publicly owned	
Coordination of national economic activity	Market	'Free World' countries	Consumer sovereignty; freedom of enterprise, equilibration of supply and demand of resources and products by market forces	Sourcing strategy; pricing flexibility, quality control, technology transfer, profit repatriation
	Command	Eastern Bloc countries,[a] Communist China[b]	Centralized planning of production quotas, prices, and distribution. Pyramidal hierarchy of control	
Perceived ability to Influence future	Self-determination	USA	Individuals and firms can take actions to influence their environment and improve prospects for the future	Long-range planning, production scheduling
	Fatalistic	Islamic countries	People must adjust to their environment. Life follows a preordained course	
Time orientation	Abstract, lineal,	USA	The clock serves to harmonize activities of group members. Punctuality is important. Time is money	Productivity; joint project deadlines
	Concrete, circular	Argentina, Brazil	Activities are timed by recurring rhythmic natural events such as day and night, seasons of the year	
Communication	Low context	USA	Most information is contained in explicit codes, such as spoken or written words. Articulation ('spelling it out') is important	Initial negotiations, ongoing communications
	High context	Saudi Arabia	Sending and receiving messages is highly contingent upon the physical context and non-verbal communication	
Information evaluation	Pragmatic	UK	Emphasis on practical applications of specific details in light of particular goals	Structure of the GSA management
	Idealistic	Soviet Union	Utilization of abstract frameworks for structuring thinking processes which are moulded by a dominant ideology	

Table 2 (continued)

Characteristic	Value	Country Examples	Description	Impacted Areas of GSA Management
Conflict management style	Confrontation	USA	Openness and directness in work relations is promoted. Conflict resolution is preferred over conflict suppression	Conflict management
	Harmony	Japan	Wa (maintaining harmony in Japanese) is important. Saving face is preferred over direct confrontation and disharmony	
Decision-making	Autocratic	South Korea	Decisions fully formulated before being announced, either individually or with input from experts	Negotiation and bargaining
	Group	Japan	Information is shared with subordinates whose input is sought before decisions are made	
Leadership style	Task oriented	West Germany	Enforcement of rules and procedures. Focus on technological aspects	Decision-making, leadership
	People oriented	Japan	Greater attention to human factors, including morale and motivation. Utilization of group dynamics to reach organizational goals	
Problem solving	Scientific	Most occidental countries	Logic and scientific method are the means of solving new problems. Accurate data are more important than intuition	Decision-making process
	Traditional	Most oriental countries	Solutions to new problems are derived by sifting through past experiences	
Employment duration	Variable	USA	Employees can quit to accept better jobs. Employers can terminate low-performing employees	Human resources management
	Lifetime	Japan	Employees are a 'family' which cannot be abandoned. Termination causes enormous loss of prestige and must be avoided	

Continued on next page.

Table 2 (continued)

Characteristic	Value	Country Examples	Description	Impacted Areas of GSA Management
Power distance[d]	Low	Austria	Relative equality of superiors and subordinates. Greater participation of subordinates in decision-making	GSA structure and communication
	High	Mexico	Distinct hierarchical layers with formal and restricted interactions. Emphasis on ranks. Top-down communication	
Uncertainty avoidance[d]	Low	Denmark	Uncertainties are a normal part of life. Business risks are judged against potential rewards. Flexibility and innovation are emphasized	Choice of projects tackled, information and control systems
	High	South Korea	Business risks lead to high anxiety, leading to mechanisms that offer a hedge against uncertainty: written rules and procedures, plans, complex information systems	
Individualism[d]	Individualistic	Canada	Reliance on individual initiative, self-assertion, and personal achievement and responsibility	Accountability, performance evaluation systems
	Collectivistic	Singapore	Emphasis on belonging to groups and organizations, acceptance of collective decisions, values, and duties	
Masculinity[d]	Masculine	Italy	Machismo attitudes. Valued ideals are wealth, power, decisiveness, growth, bigness, and profits. Compensation in monetary rewards, status, recognition, and promotion is expected in proportion to achievement of ideals	Organizational design, reward systems
	Feminine	Netherlands	Nurturing attitudes. Care of people, interpersonal relations, quality of life, service, and social welfare are valued ideals. Members seek cooperative work climate, security, and overall job satisfaction	

[a] The situation in the Eastern Bloc countries is in a state of flux, with political reform toward democratization and economic reform embracing free markets and private property. However, Western companies rushing to enter into cooperative ventures with these countries are likely to encounter considerable inertia, from past practices (see *Business Week*, 1990a); as such, managers must remain aware of fundamental differences and their implications for alliances.
[b] The international business environment in Communist China has deteriorated considerably following the Tiananmen Square Massacre, forcing corporate strategists to reassess their commitments in the PRC and Hong Kong (see *New York Times*, 1990).
[c] From Kolde (1985).
[d] From Hofstede (1983).

investments may be a function of the configuration of Type II diversity, i.e., the *degree* and *type* of interfirm differences. If the relatively stable dimensions of societal culture, national context, or corporate culture constitute salient interfirm differences, then organizational learning becomes a threshold condition for alliance success, and management attention must be aimed at the relevant dimensions during the earliest phases of alliance development (such as partner screening and pre-contractual negotiations). In cases where significant diversity arises from the relatively more volatile dimensions of strategic direction and management practices and organization, later adaptive learning under new partner circumstances is a necessary precondition for GSA longevity.

It is evident, then, that the magnitude and timing of Type I and Type II diversity shifts contribute to different alliance outcomes. Specifically, when Type I diversity (mutual interdependency) is larger than Type II diversity, *ceteris paribus*, longevity will be high. In this situation, additional alliances between the GSA partners become more likely, and ongoing organizational learning in repeated successful collaborative experiences may further reduce Type II diversity, reinforcing the alliancing process.

But when Type II diversity is larger than Type I diversity, *ceteris paribus*, longevity will be low. This situation can arise in one of two ways: shrinkage of Type I diversity, or escalation of Type II diversity. The first way represents the stepping-stone strategy (planned termination), in which one partner rapidly internalizes the skills and technologies of the other; after the process is completed, that is, when Type I diversity vanishes, little incentive remains for the internalizer firm to remain in the partnership. The second way represents untimely dissolution of the GSA, as a lack of learning and adaptation exacerbates problems of social interaction among managers from the alliance partners. Such unplanned termination is more likely when the partner firms are working together for the first time and have yet to establish a history of prior successful collaborative experiences; differ sharply on one or more of the Type II dimensions; and the efforts and resources committed to learning and adaptation are not commensurate with this diversity.

Thus, the relationship between diversity and longevity is dynamic, and is strongly influenced by the amount of learning and adaptation occurring between the GSA partners. The greater the amount of learning, the greater the negative impact of Type I diversity on longevity, but the smaller the negative impact of Type II diversity on longevity.

IMPLICATIONS AND CONCLUSIONS

The process model of longevity proposed in this paper, drawing upon learning-based management of differences in the properties of the partners, offers rich and exciting opportunities for improved research and practice in GSAs. Only a few of these are touched upon below.

First, there is a need for inductive theory-building (following covariance structure modelling and empirical research) on the relative importance, patterns of interconnectedness, and tension-inducing capacity of the typological dimensions of diversity in a variety of partnering situations, especially in longitudinal studies focusing on the phases of alliance development. Such research will be timely and useful for developing ex post alliance performance generalizations as well as ex ante partner selection criteria. Although preliminary work has been done in both of these areas, as noted above, the research has been fragmented and theory-building in GSAs has been slow, reflecting the lack of systematic conceptualization of a typology of interfirm diversity, much less a dynamic link between diversity and longevity.

The propositions and model developed here draw attention to the crucial aspect of *learning* among interfacing managers of GSA partners; important corollary implications flow from this emphasis. For example, faced with rapid internationalization and even faster growth of interfirm cooperation, how best can global firms quickly enlarge the severely limited cadre of culturally sophisticated, internationally experienced managers (cf. Strom, 1990; Hagerty, 1991)? Since coping with interfirm diversity (e.g., formal training programmes) is not costless, how are (or methodologically should be) the costs and benefits of such coping efforts assessed by managers or researchers? Fledgling attempts toward institutionalizing learning within the company and enhancing the cumulativeness of cooperative experiences with other companies are already evident, such as General Electric Company's establishment of GE International in 1988. Created as a special mechanism to efficiently handle the swift growth of GSAs and facilitate organizational learning, GE International's primary roles are to identify and implement GSAs, to promote enhanced international awareness within GE, and to permit the sharing of international partnership expertise throughout the company.

In conclusion, as global firms' technological, financial, and marketing prowess increasingly becomes tied to the excellence of their external organizational relations, 'GSA sophistication'—the ability to diagnose important differences between partners and fashion a productive partnership by devising novel solutions to accommodate the differences—is likely to become an imperative. GSAs represent a type of competitive weapon, in that they involve interorganizational *cooperation* in the pursuit of global *competitive* advantage. Sharpening the edge of this competitive weapon may require the adoption of multifirm, multicultural perspectives in joint decision-making, a process rendered difficult by the perceptual blinders imposed by culture-bound and corporate-bound thinking (e.g., respectively, the 'ugly foreigner' mentality and the NIH, or not invented here, syndrome).[9] Thus, future research on GSA longevity and performance must take into account the partners' cognition of, and adaptation to, the important dimensions of diversity that is an integral, inescapable part of such alliances.

ACKNOWLEDGEMENTS

This research has been supported by a grant from the School of Business at Indiana University, Bloomington. The author gratefully acknowledges the helpful comments of Charles Schwenk, Janet Near, and the anonymous *JIBS* reviewers.

NOTES

1. Although other factors, such as hidden agendas and conceptually flawed logic of the GSA may also account for a portion of these failures, interfirm diversity remains a prime culprit. Moreover, as noted shortly, dissolution of a GSA does not necessarily constitute failure. When GSAs are used as 'stepping stones' their termination may be viewed by the parents as a success, not a failure.
2. This typology is suggested as a parsimonious framework to be built upon in future research on GSAs, not as the comprehensive final word. For instance, differences in industry-specific considerations and firm sizes can be significant factors in some cases; these factors are not explicitly considered here.

3. GSAs typically involve commitment of substantial resources on both sides, in cash and/or in kind. Failure can result in a loss of competitive position far beyond merely the opportunity cost of the resources deployed in the GSA itself; synergistic gains and expected positive spillover effects for the parent firm may not be realized.
4. However, the speed with which these changes may occur should not be overestimated, in light of the deeply embedded industry structure and institutions in Japan.
5. One example is the GM-Toyota alliance called New United Motor Manufacturing, Inc. (NUMMI). NUMMI was approved despite strenuous objections from Chrysler and others, whose traditional (antitrust-based) arguments were rejected by the US Department of Justice.
6. This is likely to remain true even after taking into account (a) the move toward a more genuine Common Market in 1992, which creates an integrated economy of 320 million consumers, and (b) the increase in the size of the market arising from Eastern Bloc upheavals.
7. For example, the growing inseparability of data transmission and data processing has created hybrid businesses among companies in computers, telecommunications, office products, modular switchgears, and semiconductors. Similarly, auto firms, driven by cost, quality, and efficiency considerations, increasingly invest in electronics, new materials, aerodynamics, computers, robotics, and artificial intelligence.
8. GSAs must ultimately be guided by careful consideration of the respective management practices and organization of the parents, as well as the operational needs of the venture, such as response time to market developments and management information systems that accurately reflect the magnitude and scope of the alliance.
9. This problem may be particularly severe for Japanese companies, whose overseas activities until recently strongly emphasized exports and direct investments in wholly owned subsidiaries. The historically closed nature of Japan's society and corporations makes integrating outsiders—even other Japanese—difficult.

REFERENCES

Adler, N. J. (1986) *International Dimensions of Organizational Behaviour.* Kent, Boston, MA.
Adler, N. J. and Graham, J. L. (1989) 'Cross-Cultural Interaction: The International Comparison Fallacy?' *Journal of International Business Studies*, Fall: 515–537.
Argyris, C. and Schon, D. A. (1978) *Organizational Learning.* Addison-Wesley, Reading, MA.
BenDaniel, D. J. and Rosenbloom, A. H. (1990) *The Handbook of International Mergers and Acquisitions.* Prentice-Hall, Englewood Cliffs, NJ.
Beyer, J. M. (1981) 'Ideologies, Values, and Decision Making in Organizations'. In Nystrom, P. C. and Starbuck, W. H. (eds), *Handbook of Organization Design.* Oxford University Press, New York.
Black, J. S. (1987) 'Japanese/American Negotiation: The Japanese Perspective'. *Business and Economic Review*, **6**: 27–30.
Black, J. S. and Mendenhall, M. (1990) 'Cross-Cultural Training Effectiveness: A View and a Theoretical Framework for Future Research', *Academy of Management Review*, **15**: 113–136.
Borys, B. and Jemison, D. B. (1989) 'Hybrid Arrangements as Strategic Alliances: Theoretical Issues in Organizational Combinations'. *Academy of Management Review*, **14**: 234–249.
Business Week, (1990a) 'Big Deals Run into Big Trouble in the Soviet Union'. 19 March: 58-59.
Business Week, (1990b) 'A Waltz of Giants Sends Shock Waves Worldwide'. 19 March: 59-60.
Contractor, F. J. and Lorange, P. (eds). (1988) *Cooperative Strategies in International Business.* Lexington Books, Lexington, MA.
Cosier, R. A. and Dalton, D. R. (1990) 'Positive Effects of Conflict: A Field Assessment'. *International Journal of Conflict Management*, January: 81–92.
Daft, R. L. and Weick, K. E. (1984) 'Toward a Model of Organizations as Interpretation Systems'. *Academy of Management Review*, **9**: 284–295.
Dobkin, J. A. (1988) *International Technology Joint Ventures. Publishers,* Butterworth Legal, Stoneham, MA.
Evans, F. B. (1963) 'Selling as a Dyadic Relationship—A New Approach'. *American Behavioural Scientist*, **6** (May): 76–79.

Fiol, C. M. and Lyles, M. A. (1985) 'Organizational Learning'. *Academy of Management Review*, **10**: 803–813.
Geringer, J. M. and Lois, H. (1991) 'Measuring Performance of International Joint Ventures'. *Journal of International Business Studies*, **22**: 249–264.
Gomes-Casseres, B. (1989) 'Joint Ventures in the Face of Global Competition'. *Sloan Management Review*, Spring: 17–26.
Graham, J. L. (1985) 'The Influence of Culture on the Process of Business Negotiations: An Exploratory Study'. *Journal of International Business Studies*, **16**: 81–95.
Hagerty, R. (1991) 'Firms in Europe try to Find Executives Who Can Cross Borders in a Single Bound'. *Wall Street Journal*, 25 January: B1, B3.
Hall, R. D. (1984) *The International Joint Venture*. Praeger, New York.
Harrigan, K. R. (1985) *Strategies for Joint Ventures*. Lexington Books, Lexington, MA.
Harrigan, K. R. (1988) 'Strategic Alliances and Partner Asymmetries'. In Contractor, F. J. and Lorange, P. (eds) *Cooperative Strategies in International Business*. Lexington Books, Lexington, MA.
Hedberg, B. (1981) 'How Organizations Learn and Unlearn'. In Nystrom, P. C. and Starbuck, W. H. (eds) *Handbook of Organizational Design*. Oxford University Press, New York.
Hergert, M. and Morris, D. (1988) 'Trends in International Collaborative Agreements'. In Contractor, F. J. and Lorange, P. (eds) *Cooperative Strategies in International Business*. Lexington Books, Lexington, MA.
Hofstede, G. (1983) 'National Cultures in Four Dimensions'. *International Studies of Management and Organization*, **13**:46–74.
Killing, J. P. (1982) 'How to Make a Global Joint Venture Work'. *Harvard Business Review*, May–June.
Kluckhohn, C. and Kroeberg, A. L. (1952) *Culture: A Critical Review of Concepts and Definitions*. Vintage Books, New York.
Kolde, E. J. (1985) *Environment of International Business*. PWS-Kent Publishing Co., Boston.
Laurent, A. (1983) 'The Cultural Diversity of Management Conceptions'. *International Studies of Management and Organization*, Spring.
Lazarsfeld, P. M. and Merton, R. K. (1954) 'Friendship as a Social Process'. In Berger, M., Abel, T. and Page, C. (eds), *Freedom and Control in Modern Society*. Octagon Books, New York.
Lewis, J. D. (1990) *Partnerships for Profit: Structuring and Managing Strategic Alliances*. Free Press, New York.
Lyles, M. A. (1988) 'Learning Among Joint Venture-Sophisticated Firms'. In Contractor, F. J. and Lorange, P. (eds) *Cooperative Strategies in International Business*. Lexington Books, Lexington, MA.
Lynch, R. P. (1989) *The Practical Guide to Joint Ventures and Alliances*. Wiley, New York.
Maruyama, M. (1984) 'Alternative Concepts of Management: Insights from Asia and Africa'. *Asia Pacific Journal of Management*, **1**(2):100–111.
McGuire, W. J. (1968) 'The Nature of Attitudes and Attitude Change'. In Gardner L. and Aronson, G. (eds) *The Handbook of Social Psychology*. Addison-Wesley, Reading, MA.
Miles, R. E. and Snow, C. C. (1978) *Organizational Strategy, Structure and Process*. McGraw-Hill, New York.
Miller, D. and Friesen, P. H. (1980) 'Momentum and Revolution in Organization Adaption'. *Academy of Management Journal*, **23**: 591–614.
Molnar, J. J. and Rogers, D. L. (1979) 'A Comparative Model of Interorganizational Conflict'. *Administrative Science Quarterly*, **24**: 405–424.
Moran, R. T. and Harris, P. R. (1982) *Managing Cultural Synergy*. Gulf Publishing Co., Houston.
New York Times (1990) 'Bush Distressed as Policy Fails to Move China'. *New York Times*, 11 March: 1, 11.
Nielsen, R. P. (1988) 'Cooperative Strategy'. *Strategic Management Journal*, **9**: 475–492.
Ohmae, K. (1985) *Triad Power*. Free Press, New York.
Oliver, C. (1990) 'Determinants of Interorganizational Relationships: Integration and Future directions'. *Academy of Management Review*, **15**: 241–265.
Paulson, S. (1976) 'A Theory and Comparative Analysis of Interorganizational Dyads'. *Rural Sociology*, **41**: 311–329.
Perlmutter, H. V. and Heenan, D. A. (1986) 'Cooperate to Compete Globally'. *Harvard Business Review*, March–April: 136–152.
Peters, T. J. and Waterman, R. H. (1982) *In Search of Excellence*. Warner Books, New York.
Porter, M. E. (ed). (1986) *Competition in Global Industries*. Harvard Business School Press, Boston.
Pucik, V. (1988) 'Strategic Alliances with the Japanese: Implications for Human Resource Management'. In Contractor, F. J. and Lorange, P. (eds) *Cooperative Strategies in International Business*. Lexington Books, Lexington, MA.

Schermerhorn, J. R., Jr. (1975) 'Determinants of Interorganizational Cooperation'. *Academy of Management Journal*, **18**: 846–856.

Strom, S. (1990) *The Art of Luring Japanese Executives to American Firms*. *New York Times*, 25 March: F12.

Terpstra, V. and David, K. (1990) *The Cultural Environment of International Business*. Southwestern-Publishing Co., Cincinnati.

Tung, R. (1984) *Key to Japan's Economic Strength: Human Power*. Lexington Books, Lexington, MA.

Turner, L. (1987) Industrial Collaboration with Japan. Routledge and Kegan Paul, London.

Van de Ven, A. H. (1976) 'On the Nature, Formation, and Maintenance of Relations Among Organizations'. *Academy of Management Review*, **2**: 24–36.

Venkatraman, N. and Ramanujam, W. (1986) 'Measurement of Business Performance in Strategy Research: A Comparison of Approaches'. *Academy of Management Review*, **11**: 801–114.

Westney, D. E. (1988) 'Domestic and Foreign Learning Curves in Managing International Cooperative Strategies'. In Contractor, F. J. and Lorange, P. (eds) *Cooperative Strategies in International Business*. Lexington Books, Lexington, MA.

Whetten, D. A. (1981) 'Interorganizational Relations: A Review of the Field'. *Journal of Higher Education*, **52**: 1–28.

Wysocki, B. (1990) 'Cross-Border Alliances Become Favorite Way to Crack New Markets'. *Wall Street Journal*, 26 March: A1, A12.

13

Towards a Theory of Business Alliance Formation

Jagdish N. Sheth and Atul Parvatiyar

The popularity of business alliances has increased in recent years. Business and academic press have reported thousands of alliances involving many international companies (Ellram, 1992; Ghemawat et al., 1986; Gross and Neuman, 1989; Morris and Hergert, 1987). Its importance is realized by the fact that some of the world's largest companies, including AT&T, Philips, General Motors, Siemens, IBM, Ford, Boeing, Olivetti, General Electric, Xerox, Toyota, Mitsubishi, General Foods, and several others, are involved in these business alliances. A variety of patterns are also observed such as large–small company alliances (Doz, 1988; Hull and Slowinski, 1990), private (profit)—public (nonprofit) partnerships (Lynch, 1989), competitor alliances (Hamel, et al., 1989), and spider-web alliances (Gullander, 1975) wherein an intricate array of interconnections between companies, often across international and industrial boundaries, exist—as in the case of networks and *keiretsu*[1] (Ferguson, 1990; Håkansson and Johanson, 1988).

The scope of these business alliances from specific functional agreements—as in R&D, product development, distribution, logistics, marketing, etc.—to full scope joint venture and/or consortia. This had led to several names and labels for business alliances: for example, joint ventures, R&D consortia. minority participation, cross-licensing, cross-distribution, supply purchasing, franchising, co-manufacturing, cross marketing, buying groups, and so on. Some authors have begun to use 'strategic alliance' as a common term to refer to all types of business alliances (Harrigan, 1986; Ohmae, 1989; Parkhe, 1991). This however, is likely to cause confusion because, as we will show later in this article, not all business alliances are formed with a strategic purpose; furthermore, strategic alliance is a term borrowed from military and political science where it has a specific connotation, namely formal association of sovereign states for the use (or non-use) of military force, intended against specific other sovereign states, whether or not these sovereign states are explicitly identified (Snyder, 1991). As such, the use of 'strategic alliance' in business is best suited for competitive alliances and, in our opinion, it would not be used as a generic term for all alliances. In this article, we will develop a typology of business alliances in order to reduce some terminological confusion.

Given the current popularity of business alliances, a comprehensive theory to explain the purpose, properties and governance of alliances is needed. Although research in this area has been sparse, previous studies in strategic management and international business have developed constructs on the rationale for co-operation (Contractor and Lorange, 1988),

Reprinted from *Scandinavian International Business Review*. Vol. 1, No.3, J. N. Sheth and A. Parvatiyar, 'Towards a Theory of Business Alliance Formation', pp.71–87. Copyright © 1992, with kind permission from Elsevier Science Ltd, The Boulevard, Langford Lane, Kidlington, OX5 1GB, UK.

alliance complexity (Killing, 1988), factors governing degree of co-operation in 50:50 equity joint ventures (Buckley and Casson, 1988), alliance characteristics and hybrid arrangements (Borys and Jemison, 1989), the influence of technological intensity and R&D intent of partners on the choice of alliance governance form (Osborn and Baughn, 1990), and social governance of dyadic networks (Larson, 1992). While these conceptual frameworks and empirical observations have significantly contributed towards understanding some specific aspects of business alliances, what is lacking is a general theory of business alliances. Accordingly, this article is an attempt to develop a theory of competitive and collaborative business alliances. It is based on a fusion of behavioural and economic constructs that underlie and determine formation, governance, properties and the evolution of business alliances.

The theory is based on two constructs: purpose of the business alliance (strategic versus operations) and parties to the business alliance (competitors versus non-competitors). We suggest that most forms of business alliances and their specific properties, governance structures, and evolution over time, can be explained by these two constructs. Furthermore, we can provide a strong rationale for them based on several popular and powerful conceptual frameworks in industrial organization, behavioural sciences, and social sciences.

THEORETICAL BACKGROUND ON EXTERNAL RELATIONS OF FIRMS

It is important at the outset to define business alliances. A business alliance is an ongoing, formal, business relationship between two or more independent organizations to achieve common goals. This definition encompasses any formalized organizational relationship between two or more firms for some agreed purpose. It refers to the external relationships of a firm with other firms where the relationship is more than a standard customer–supplier or labour–management relationship, and more than venture capital investment or other stakeholder relationship, but falls short of an outright acquisition or merger. Evident in our definition, all business alliances have two underlying dimensions: purpose and parties. In this section, we will develop theoretical support for the two underlying dimensions of alliances and in the following sections examine the characteristics of different types of alliances and their effects on governance structures.

The study of a firm's external relationships are grounded in four theories: transactions costs theory (Williamson, 1975, 1985), agency theory (Fama, 1980; Jensen and Meckling, 1976), relational contracting (Macneil, 1980), and resource-dependence perspective (Pfeffer and Salancik, 1978). While the common theoretical constructs in the first three approaches are the notion of contracts and transactions, the resource-dependence perspective is concerned with organizational interdependencies and interorganizational power. An examination of the basic propositions of each theory will help identify the applicable constructs from these theories in understanding the nature and properties of alliances.

The primary concern of agency theory is the optimal incentive structure that will help avoid efficiency losses, given the conflicting interests of a principal and agent (Fama and Jensen, 1983). Since the agency theory presupposes a conflict of interests among interacting parties, it does not provide the appropriate perspective for the information of business alliances. In other words, conflict of interest is not the basis for business alliances, but a potential context which may or may not exist in a specific business alliance.

The resource-dependence perspective is anchored on two themes: that organizations are the primary social actors and the interorganization relations can be understood as a product of interorganizational dependence and constraint (Pfeffer, 1987). This perspective sees the question of who controls the organization as both problematic and critical (Mintzberg, 1973). The issue of control is linked to apprehensions regarding intent (trust) of each party. In essence, the issue of intent or trust can be considered as the underlying dimension of such apprehensions. If the organizations were certain about other actor's actions and intentions and, consequently, trusted each other, the concern for control or internalization of interdependencies would be minimal. Thus, trust is the underlying determinant of managerial action relating to control and acquisition of power. The more the actors trust each other, the less will be the intentional managerial action towards control of external interdependencies.

This notion of trust, as an important dimension of a firm's external relationship, is also supported in Macneil's (1980) relational contracting. There is a tacit assumption of trust of relationship contracting unlike discrete contracts wherein there is no room for tacit assumptions (Macneil, 1980). Other studies on alliances have also included trust as a significant variable in analysis of partner relationship (Buckley and Casson, 1988; Larson, 1992; Schaan and Beamish, 1988).

While recognizing the value of trust, transaction costs theorists have contended the difficulties of operationalizing trust and hence avoided it (Williamson, 1975, 1984, 1985). The basic proposition of transaction cost theory is that properties of transactions determine the governance structure and the institutional arrangements of firms (Reve, 1990; Williamson, 1985). Transaction costs economics provisionally identifies three key dimensions on which the properties of transaction differ: asset specificity (or the degree to which assets are dedicated to transacting with a particular economic partner); uncertainty (that is, ambiguity in transaction definition and performance); and infrequency (transactions that are rarely undertaken). Of the three, asset specificity is considered the most important and most distinctive (Williamson, 1990).

In our opinion, asset specificity and infrequency, which transaction costs theory treat as determinants, are really the consequences of managerial choice of a specific institutional arrangement or alliance form, and therefore they are consequent and not determinant variables. For example, the choice of joint venture or consortia as an institutional arrangement warrants commitment of specific assets to the project, whereas, such degree of asset specificity may not be required in case of co-operative agreements or cartel type alliances. In fact, studies on joint ventures[2] (Harrigan, 1985; Killing, 1983; Stuckey, 1983) have not indicated that joint ventures are not an inherent outcome in those cases where organizations have already committed specific assets to a project. In short, asset specificity seems more an outcome, or a consequence, rather than the cause of business alliances. Given the fact that asset specificity can be a consequence of business alliances, we have decided not to use it as one of the determinants of business alliances.

Similarly, frequency of transactions is a managerially controlled decision which is influenced by the choice of particular institutional arrangements. For example, firms may choose to reduce or expand frequency of transactions based on technical, physical, managerial and financial considerations. One has to just look at the impact of online computerized systems in changing the frequency mix between alliance partners (say between buyers and sellers). As we will show in subsequent sections, frequency of transaction is more a consequence of purpose and parties to business alliances. For example, operational purposes necessitate greater frequency than strategic purposes.

Perhaps the most significant dimension of transaction costs theory which influences the selection of the type of institutional arrangement is uncertainty. It plays a role in the supply of upstream product/service and the need for information by the downstream firm (Arrow, 1974). Uncertainty is the consequence of environment and largely has external origins due to random acts of nature and unpredictable changes in customer preferences (Koopmans, 1957). Uncertainty, unlike asset specificity and infrequency, is not managerial controlled. On the other hand, organizations and managers have to cope and deal with uncertainty. It is, therefore, an independent variable that determines managerial action. Based on the level of uncertainty that has to be coped with, managers will choose an institutional form that helps reduce those uncertainties.

Hence, we can infer from theories on external relationships of firms that there are two primary constructs that affect alliance relationships and their institutional arrangement: uncertainty and trust. The level of uncertainty and the level of trust are likely to impact on alliance characteristics. When there is high trust between partners, autonomy will be accorded to the alliance venture. Low trust amongst partners is likely to lead to high management control. It will also result in a greater degree of internalization of interdependence and use of power as suggested by the resource dependency viewpoint. Similarly, when uncertainty is high, management will like to make assets specific to the transaction so that risk is delineated to the transaction specific assets and partners are also locked in through designated commitment. In case of low uncertainty, partners will be willing to rely on market processes of buyers and sellers or in sharing of assets of the two firms.

MEASUREMENT OF UNCERTAINTY AND TRUST

Uncertainty and trust are not variables but constructs. Therefore, they need to be operationalized in order to link with reality and empirical observation. Trust is a behavioural construct and, therefore, it is often measured by self-assessment and perceptions of individual managers and decision makers involved in business alliances. Unfortunately, we have not yet fully developed a psychometric scale that measures trust with a degree of reliability and validity sufficient to feel comfortable (Andaleeb, 1992). Similarly, measures of uncertainty suffer from problems of ambiguity with respect to definition and observation.

In view of the fact that the traditional measures of trust and uncertainty are subject to measurement errors, we have adopted the econometric approach of identifying measurable indicators that can be good surrogates of each construct. By measuring the purpose of a business alliance as operations versus strategic, we are able to capture the degree of uncertainty. Operations purposes are, by definition, more certain than strategic purposes because the latter are, by definition, anchored to the future.

Trust is a perceived notion regarding a partner's likely behaviour. It is perceived estimation of behavioural 'opportunism' (Williamson, 1975) of the alliance partner. Such perception of opportunistic behaviour is likely to be associated more with partners who are competitors or are perceived as potential competitors. Guarding against competitors in an alliance relationship has thus been the concern of some studies (Hamel et al., 1989). We can, therefore, state that trust is manifested in parties to an alliance, where the competitors are viewed with low trust and non-competitors are generally viewed with greater trust.

Purpose and parties are, therefore, isomorphic dimensions of uncertainty and trust. Purpose and parties are easy to measure and hence, we will use them. In the previous section, we had defined business alliance with the two underlying dimensions of purpose and parties. This can be expressed notationally as:

Business alliance = f(purpose, parties)

The two dimensions can be easily dichotomized for a conceptual understanding of alliance types, its properties and governance structures. It is also possible to represent the dimensions in the form of vectors representing the degree of strategic purpose and the degree of competitive rivalry among alliance partners. The dichotomous categorization of purpose and parties helps us here in highlighting the distinctive properties of each type of alliance and making observations on the distinctive forms of governance structures associated with each type of alliance.

Table 1 provides a typology of business alliances based on the two dichotomies of purpose and party. If a business alliance is formed for operations efficiency among competitors, it is called a cartel. If it is among non-competitors (suppliers, customers, and non-competitive businesses), it is called a co-operative. If a business alliance is formed for strategic purpose among competitors, it is called a competitive alliance. Finally, a business alliance among non-competitors for strategic purpose is called a collaborative venture.

PURPOSE OF AND PARTIES TO BUSINESS ALLIANCES

Several factors drive companies towards entente. Some are related to macroenvironment forces like globalization and integration of markets, rapid changes in technologies, high cost of R&D, increased global competition and shortening of the period of competitive advantage (Badaracco, 1991; Collins and Doorley, 1991; Ohmae, 1989). Others are linked to corporate objectives and vision. The basic question of why companies form alliances can be answered by focusing on the corporate purpose these alliances fulfil. As shown in Figure 1, eight corporate alliance purposes can be broadly identified. Four of these—growth opportunity, diversification, strategic intent and protection against external threat[3]—reflect the future reasons of forming alliances. They are considered strategic because they impact on corporate effectiveness, that is, its future position and competitiveness. The other four alliance purposes—asset utilization, resource efficiency, enhancing core competence and bridging the performance gap—represent the operational purposes of alliance. They are operational because they impact upon corporate efficiency and improve the current position of the firm.[4]

The strategic and operations purposes of alliance may overlap. However, based on the primary purpose, we can safely dichotomize the alliance purpose as predominantly strategic or predominantly operations in nature.

Along with the alliance purpose, also important to our conceptualization are the parties to an alliance and their role definition. The parties to an alliance can comprise of those with whom a company already has ongoing relationships (customers, suppliers or competitors[5]) or those with whom there is potential for a relationship (potential customers, potential suppliers and potential competitors). Potential customers, suppliers and competitors may provide synergistic pay-offs from complementary support and integrative linkages to business. Figure 2 shows at least eight parties with whom companies team up by forming business alliances.

COOPERATIVE INTERNATIONAL COMPETITION 179

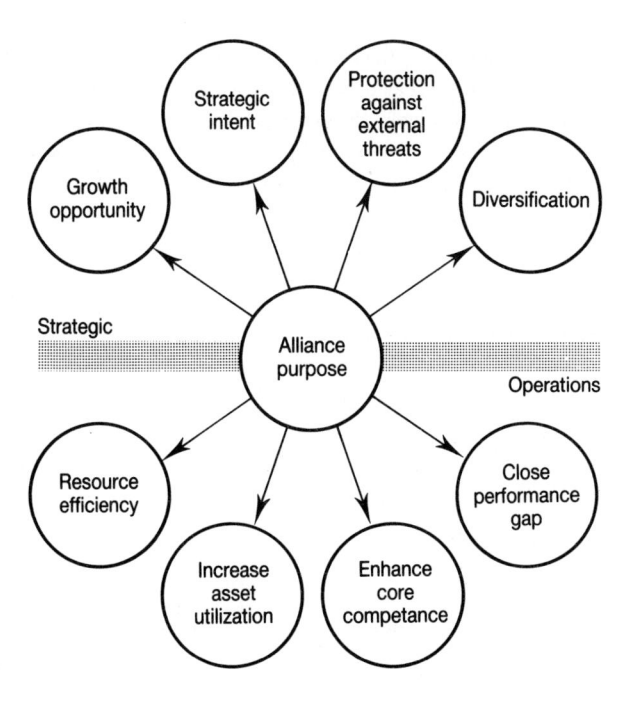

Figure 1. Purpose of Alliance.

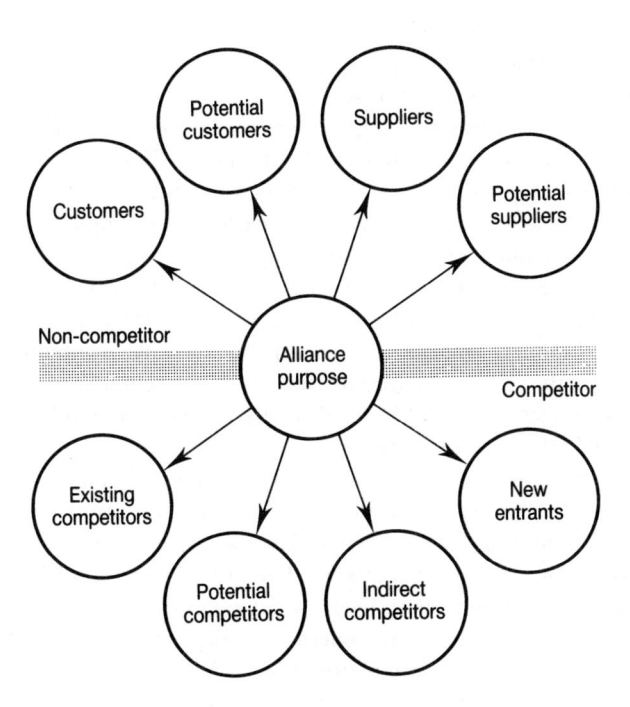

Figure 2. Alliance Parties.

On a broader level, customers, suppliers and complementary consociates (potential suppliers and customers) can be considered as non-competitors in an alliance and existing competitors, new entrants, substitute producers (indirect competitors), and companies with similar future intent (potential competitors) can be grouped as competitors.[6] Thus, we can categorize business alliances as those formed with competitors or those with non-competitors for either strategic or operations purpose. Based on these dichotomies, we can now develop a typology of business alliances.

TYPOLOGY OF BUSINESS ALLIANCES

Given the two dimensions of alliance (purpose and parties) and their dichotomous levels (strategic versus operations, competitors versus non-competitors), we can categorize business alliances into four types: cartels, co-operative collaboratives and competitive alliances. The four alliance types are shown in Table 1.

Table 1. Types of Alliances

	Parties	
	Competitors	Non-competitors
Strategic	Competitive alliances	Collaborative ventures
Operations	Cartels	Co-operatives

Note: Purpose is a surrogate measure of uncertainty and parties is a surrogate measure of trust.

Cartels are formal (or semi-formal) agreements among competitors for operations purposes, for example, controlling the supply of products, fixing prices, or sharing a common infrastructure. Cartels have been known to operate in case of petroleum, diamonds, semiconductor chips and chocolate producers. They are more prevalent in Europe and Asia because existing anti-competitive laws allow these alliances to maintain industry efficiency.

Alliance between non-competitors for operations purposes usually results in *co-operative arrangements*. Partners share costs and facilities with customers or suppliers or other consociates in order to introduce operating efficiency. Modification of the customers' or suppliers' systems or procedures, sharing of relevant information, and multiple level two-way contacts are common in co-operative alliances. Examples of co-operative alliance include the co-operative marketing programme between WalMart and Procter & Gamble, Citibank's credit card and American Airlines frequent flyer programme, IBM and Sears co-operation to market Prodigy, and the warehouse service venture of Lever Brothers and Distribution Centres, Inc. for operation of a high-tech dedicated distribution centre at Columbus, Ohio. The oldest form of co-operative alliances are, of course, the farmers' co-operatives and industrial buying groups.

Competitive alliances are business ventures between strong rival companies that remain competitors outside the relationship. Most of them have well-defined strategic objectives and are designed to serve global or regional markets. They see the virtue of leveraging combined resources and capabilities of each other. Even the largest global companies, including General Motors, Toyota, Siemens, Philips, IBM, General Electric, Mitsubishi, and several others, find the world too large and competition too strong to do it alone. General Motors and Toyota assemble automobiles; Siemens and Philips develop semiconductors; Canon supplies photocopiers to Kodak; France's Thomson and Japan's JVC jointly manufacture VCRs.

Competitive alliances are usually based on reciprocity; partners offering complementary products, facilities, skills and technologies. Generally a partnership among equals, most competitive alliances are related to the core business of the partners. Their form is flexible to suit the need of the project or programme and the relative contributions of the partners.

Collaborative enterprises are formed by non-competitors for strategic purposes. Joint product, market or technology development and joint marketing efforts are the hallmark of collaborative enterprises. Usually the scope of alliance is broad and encompasses many functional areas. The epitome of such collaboration is a fusion of partner objectives and efforts. The most popular form of collaboratives is joint ventures.[7]

Since uncertainty and trust are manifested in alliance purpose and parties, we can observe its incidence in different degrees in each alliance type. Collaborative enterprises are likely to be formed when external uncertainty is high and partners trust each other significantly. When uncertainty is low and partners trust each other, co-operative ventures are most likely to be formed. Competitive alliances would be considered most appropriate when uncertainty is high but partners do not trust each other enough; and cartels will be the likely alliance form whenever there is low external uncertainty and low or medium level of trust.

ORGANIZATIONAL PROPERTIES OF BUSINESS ALLIANCES

Organizational properties of business alliances will vary significantly depending upon the purpose of, and parties to the alliance. In Figure 3, we have listed a number of organizational properties that are directly linked to strategic versus operations purpose, and to competitor versus

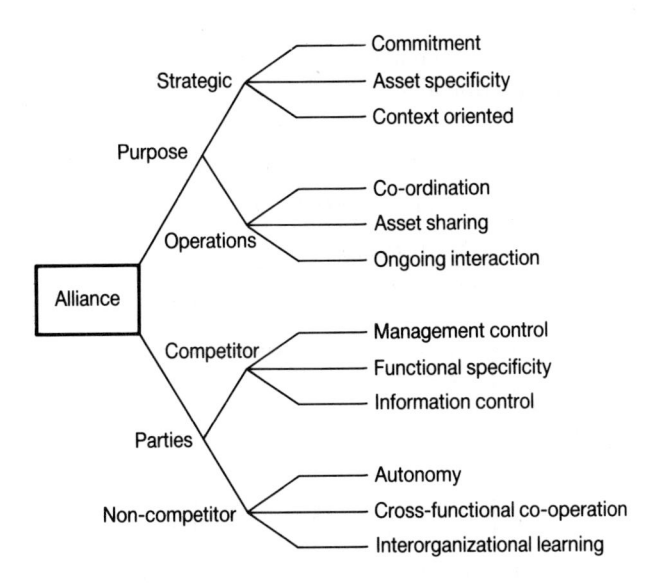

```
Alliance
├── Purpose
│   ├── Strategic
│   │   ├── Commitment
│   │   ├── Asset specificity
│   │   └── Context oriented
│   └── Operations
│       ├── Co-ordination
│       ├── Asset sharing
│       └── Ongoing interaction
└── Parties
    ├── Competitor
    │   ├── Management control
    │   ├── Functional specificity
    │   └── Information control
    └── Non-competitor
        ├── Autonomy
        ├── Cross-functional co-operation
        └── Interorganizational learning
```

Note: The organizational properties of alliances are based on conceptual and empirical research in organizational psychology, interorganizational sociology, and industrial organizations disciplines

Figure 3. An Organizational Map of Alliance Properties.

non-competitor parties to a business alliance. Most of this is based on existing conceptual as well as empirical research.

We know that strategic purposes result in greater commitment, a higher level of asset specificity and are based more on context and case-by-case. Therefore, there is no real learning curve from one strategic alliance to the next. It is, therefore, unwise to rely on one successful strategic alliance as a guide for future alliances. This is the experience of General Electric, AT&T, IBM and Motorola in their global strategic alliances.

On the other hand, operations purposes result in a high degree of co-ordination and asset sharing, on an ongoing basis. This is the experience of Whirlpool in appliances, buying groups in retailing, pharmaceuticals and agriculture, as well as more recently, the joint quality efforts between suppliers and customers.

If competitors are parties to an alliance, we know that there will be a high degree of management control and it will be limited to specific functions and tasks. Neither party will encourage an open-door policy even though each is interested in learning from the other. This is because there is lack of trust in each other.

Finally, if non-competitors get together in a business alliance, mutual trust is high. This encourages a greater degree of autonomy for the alliance, free flow of information, and better cross-functional co-operation between alliance partners.

This description leads us to state the following propositions (see Figure 4).

Proposition 1. Successful strategic alliances (among competitors or non-competitors) will require a high degree of commitment among alliance members and greater asset-specificity dedicated to the alliance. Furthermore, strategic alliances will be context driven and, therefore, each alliance must be organized as a unique business venture to achieve its strategic effectiveness.

Proposition 2. A successful operations alliance (among competitors or non-competitors) will require a high degree of co-ordination and asset sharing on an ongoing basis. Furthermore, operations alliances will require re-engineering of business processes of alliance members to achieve their operational efficiency.

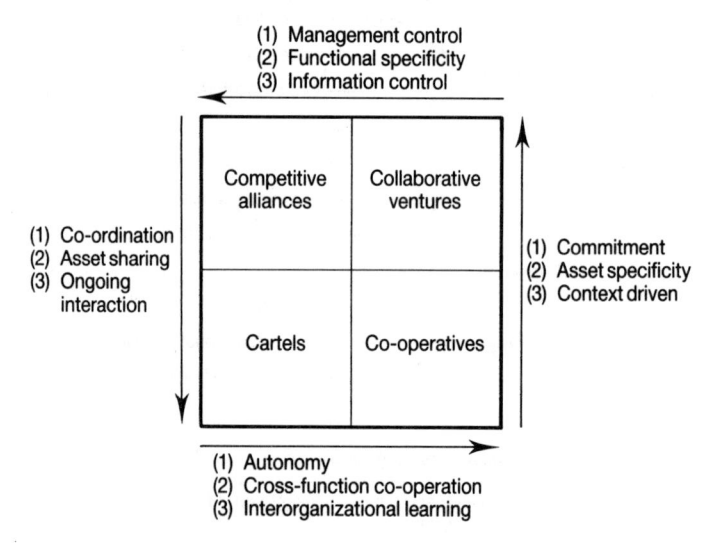

Figure 4. Properties of Alliances.

Proposition 3. A successful competitive alliance (for strategic or operations purpose) will require a high degree of management control and will be limited to specific functions. Furthermore, it must be organized for mutual learning among competitors.

Proposition 4. A successful non-competitive alliance (for strategic or operations purpose) will require a high degree of autonomy to the business alliance and cross-functional co-operation and learning. Furthermore, it must be organized in a way that encourages free flow of communication.

CHARACTERISTICS OF BUSINESS ALLIANCES

Each type of business alliance (cartels, co-operatives, competitive alliances and collaborative ventures) is likely to have its own unique set of behavioural, economic and managerial consequences. It is, therefore, possible to use this profile as a benchmark against which one can judge the performance of a specific business alliance in each category. Table 2 lists ten benchmarks for each business alliance.

Cartels

Operations alliances among competitors are likely to experience low entry barriers, especially in an oligopolistic industry where business processes are standard and regulation allows sharing of resources for efficiency reasons. Conversely, it is relatively easy for a member to exit a cartel if economies of scale and scope justify doing it, rather than sharing in the cartel resources. Therefore, transaction cost theory (Williamson, 1975) and market governance are likely to determine the continuation of cartel alliances.

As a consequence, commitment to the cartel alliance by any member organization is likely to be low, and cross-functional co-operation will be bounded to specific functions, departments and activities as specified in the cartel alliance. At the same time, management control and involvement will be high even though the cartel alliance is allowed to operate at arm's length in a semi-autonomous manner. Finally, communications among the alliance members will be guarded and interorganizational learning will be limited and focused on specific operations areas (R&D, manufacturing, marketing, logistics, customer service, etc.).

Co-operatives

Operations alliances among non-competitors are likely to have low entry barriers because regulatory, emotional and business processes will not inhibit their formation. However, once co-operative alliances are formed, they are likely to generate strong exit barriers due to operational alignment and each member's inability to economically justify their own dedicated resources to replace the shared operations. The governance mechanism will be multilateral or consortia.

While the commitment to the co-operative alliance will be modest, and only limited resources will be dedicated to it, there will be widespread cross-functional co-operation and sharing of information about one another through open communication. Consequently, co-operative alliances will result in widespread interorganizational learning.

Table 2. Characteristics of business alliances

	Characteristics	Cartels	Co-operatives	Competitive alliance	Collaborative ventures
1.	Entry barriers	Low	Moderate	High	High
2.	Exit barriers	Low	High	Moderate	High
3.	Alliance governance	Market transaction	Multilateral	Bilateral	Consortium
4.	Asset specificity	Low	Moderate	High	High
5.	Commitment to alliance	Low	Moderate	High	High
6.	Management control	High	Low	High	Moderate
7.	Autonomy of alliance	Low	Moderate	Low	High
8.	Cross-functional co-operation	Limited	Widespread	Bounded	Widespread
9.	Information	Guarded	Open	Proprietary	Open
10.	Interorganizational learning	Incidental	Widespread	Focused	Widespread

Competitive alliances

Strategic alliances among competitors will experience high entry barriers, especially due to regulatory and emotional roadblocks. The historical rivalries among competitors will make them less comfortable to co-operate in the future. For example, it will be more difficult for General Motors and Ford Motor Company, or Coca-Cola and Pepsi, to get together in an alliance than for them to get together with non-competitors from other industries. Even if they do get together, let us say, at the urging of government policy or customer demands, the competitive alliance will be fragile and likely to dissolve quickly because the exit barriers are likely to be relatively low. The governance mechanism is likely to be bilateral, because it will be extremely difficult to bring together more than two competitors due to the possibility of forming a coalition against any one member. For example, recently the computing industry tried to create a competitive alliance between Honeywell, Bull and NEC, but it failed. Similarly, a consortium of United States memory chipmakers (MCC) failed, probably for the same reasons.

Because the entry barriers are high and exit barriers low in a typical bilateral competitive alliance (GM–Toyota, IBM–Apple, GE–Thomson, Motorola–Hitachi, etc.), it will demand a high degree of commitment to the alliance, and greater allocation of resources on a dedicated basis (asset-specificity). However, management control and involvement will be high, and the autonomy granted to the alliance will be limited. Finally, cross-functional co-operation will be bounded and limited, communication highly guarded and interorganizational learning will be focused to the purpose and nature of the competitive alliance.

Collaborative Alliance

Strategic alliances among non-competitors will experience high entry barriers because strategic purposes may not be convergent or business processes cannot be utilized for future market or technology developments. This is especially true in joint ventures and technology transfers between advanced and developing nations, for example, between the United States and India or Western Europe and Eastern Europe. Similarly, once a collaborative alliance is formed, it will be difficult to leave the alliance. This has been a common experience of many joint ventures, especially in the international context. The common governance structure is to form a trilateral or a small group consortium among non-competitors for future business development. Recent formation of consortia in the telecommunications industry to participate in the worldwide growth opportunity are good examples of this phenomenon.

Commitment to the collaborative alliance will be high and economic and physical resources will be dedicated to the alliance (usually by creating a joint venture). It will be given greater autonomy, and management control and involvement will be limited to financial performance similar to the portfolio management approach. Finally, cross-functional co-operation will be widespread, communication open, and interorganizational learning will be high among the alliance partners.

FUTURE DIRECTIONS

In this article, we have attempted a theory of business alliance formation based on purpose (strategic versus operations) and parties (competitors versus non-competitors) to alliance formation. Underlying these variables are the powerful constructs of uncertainty and trust. The uncertainty construct is anchored to risk assessment and risk sharing, whereas the trust construct is anchored to intent, opportunism and self-interest. Since trust and uncertainty have not been satisfactorily operationalized in organizational psychology, industrial organizations and interorganizational sociology, we have chosen party (competitors versus non-competitors) and purpose (strategic versus operations) as surrogate indicators of trust and uncertainty.

Our future research directions related to business alliances consist of the following:

(1) What are the specific operations and strategic purposes most common in forming alliances? While we believe that most operations alliances (cartels and co-operatives) will be for efficiency improvements, we do not know specific areas of business inefficiency that will motivate organizations to get together for efficiency and productivity. We suspect that, in the past, this efficiency issue was focused on manufacturing operations but, as they have become more efficient, it may be more attractive to form operations alliances for support functions (information systems, human resources, logistics, training, etc.) and in R&D, engineering, and customer service operations of the business.

Similarly, the most common reasons for strategic alliances (competitive or collaborative) historically have been focused on international market opportunities and domestic market protection. Once this is accomplished, the future strategic alliances may focus on reducing the technological, political and economic barriers prevalent in a given industry. Also, we believe that future strategic alliances may be organized for process re-engineering, setting global standards, and development of new industries (for example, ecological business).

(2) Another area of future research is the governance principles of business alliances. What governance mechanisms are appropriate for each type of business alliance and can we develop 'best in practice' benchmarks that can be used to role-model similar types of business alliances? For example, which cartels, co-operatives, collaboratives and competitive alliances are worth emulating for other cartels, co-operatives and competitive alliances?

(3) We know that business alliances like all organizational arrangements are dynamic and evolutionary. What is the evolution of a specific business alliance? Is there a life cycle (birth–death) theory of business alliances? For example, competitor alliances (cartels and competitive alliances) as they develop mutual trust, may behave more like non-competitor alliances

(co-operatives and collaborative alliances). On the other hand, if they do not build mutual trust, they are likely to be dissolved through exit or acquisition process.

Similarly, all operations alliances (cartels and co-operatives) once they achieve business efficiency are likely to focus on strategic purposes and, therefore, evolve into strategic (competitive or collaborative) alliances. On the other hand, alliance members may feel that there is no common strategic goal and, therefore, the operations alliance may be dissolved by group consensus and allowed to die by not renewing the alliance agreement.

NOTES

1. *Keiretsu* is a Japanese term for societies of business or group companies (Anchordoguy, 1990). However, such industrial groups are not exclusive to Japan but also existed in Europe and other Asian countries. Industrial groups like Krupp and Axle-Johnson were dominant in Germany and Sweden not very long ago. Similarly, the Tata, Birla and other industrial groups dominate the private sector in India.
2. Williamson (1985, pp. 118–119) does cite evidence of asset-specificity resulting into backward integration in the case of the aluminium industry based on Stuckey's (1983) summary assessment. However, such evidence is not supported for joint venture arrangements and a true cause-and-effect relationship between asset-specificity and institutional arrangement cannot be supported.
3. Alliance purposes have been broadly stated here. In actuality, they include many inflections. For example, growth opportunity can be sought through new markets or through integration of technologies. Similarly, an alliance may be formed for market diversification, product diversification or technology diversification.
4. Illustrative examples of alliances formed to achieve one or more of these purposes can be found in Konsynski and McFarlan (1990); Bowersox (1990); Anderson and Narus (1991); Johnston and Lawrence (1988); Business International Corporation (1987); and Badaracco (1991).
5. The co-operative and collaborative paradigm of relationship with customers, suppliers and competitors is a shift from transactional or adversarial relationship orientation of the past (see Parvatiyar *et al.*, 1992).
6. The categorization of parties as competitors or non-competitors is based on their role definition, rather than any objective identification method. Role definition as competitor or non-competitor is related to how partners view each other. It is largely based on intent and perspective.
7. The most common forms of collaborative enterprises include joint ventures and consortia. However, many traditional joint ventures fall short of being strategic collaborations, especially when companies do not enter into them as part of an overall strategic plan but limit them to dealing with a specific problem, such as, how to handle a single product or market. That is a tactical, short-term move, and at best a co-operative form of alliance.

Some may view consortia as a competitive alliance, but we consider them as collaborative enterprises because partners do not view their role in this type of venture as that of competitors.

REFERENCES

Anchordoguy, M. (1990) 'A Brief History of Japan's Keiretsu'. *Harvard Business Review*, **90**(4): 58–59.
Andaleeb, S. S. (1992) 'The Trust Concept: Research Issues for Channels of Distribution'. In Sheth, J. N. (ed.), *Research in Marketing*, Vol. II, pp.1–34. JAI Press, Greenwich, CT.
Anderson, J. C. and Narus, J. A. (1991) 'Partnering as a Focused Market Strategy'. *California Management Review*, **33**(3): 95–113.
Arrow, K. (1974) *The Limits of Organization*. W. W. Norton, New York.
Badaracco, J. L. (1991) *The Knowledge Link: How Firms Compete through Strategic Alliances*. Harvard Business School Press, Boston, MA.

Borys, B. and Jemison, D. B. (1989) 'Hybrid Arrangements as Strategic Alliances: Theoretical Issues in Organizational Combinations'. *Academy of Management Review*, **14**(2): 234–249.

Bowersox, D. J. (1990) 'The Strategic Benefits of Logistics Alliances'. *Harvard Business Review*, **90**(4): 36–45.

Buckley, P. J. and Casson, M. (1988) 'A Theory of Co-operation in International Business'. In Contractor, F. J. and Lorange, P. (eds), *Co-operative Strategies and International Business*, pp. 31–53. Lexington Books, Lexington, MA.

Business International Corporation (1987) 'Competitive Alliances: How to Succeed at Cross-Regional Collaboration'. Business International Corporation, New York, NY.

Collins, T. M. and Doorley, T. L. (1991) *Teaming Up for the 90s: A Guide to International Joint Ventures and Strategic Alliances*. Business One Irwin, Homewood, IL.

Contractor, F. J. and Lorange, P. (1988) 'Why Should Firms Co-operate? The Strategy and Economics Basis for Co-operative Ventures'. In Contractor, F. J. and Lorange, P. (eds), *Cooperative Strategies and International Business*, pp. 3–28. Lexington Books, Lexington, MA.

Doz, Y. L. (1988) 'Technology Partnerships between Larger and Smaller Firms: Some Critical Issues'. In Contractor F. J. and Lorange, P. (eds), *Cooperative Strategies and International Business*, pp. 317–338. Lexington Books, Lexington, MA.

Ellram, L. M. (1992) 'Patterns in International Alliances'. *Journal of Business Logistics*, **13**(1): 1–25.

Fama, E. F. (1980) 'Agency Problems and the Theory of the Firm'. *Journal of Political Economy*, **88**, April: 288–307.

Fama, E. F. and Jensen, M.C. (1983) 'Agency Problems and Residual Claims'. *Journal of Law and Economics*, **26**, June: 327–349.

Ferguson, C. H. (1990) 'Computers and the Coming of the US Keiretsu'. *Harvard Business Review*, **90**(4): 55–70.

Ghemawat, P., Porter, M. E. and Rawlinson, R. (1986) 'Pattern of International Alliance Activity'. In Porter, M. E. (ed.), *Competition in Global Industries*, pp.345–366. Harvard Business School Press, Boston, MA.

Gross, T. and Newman, J. (1989) 'Strategic Alliances Vital in Global Marketing'. *Marketing News*, **23**(13): 1–2.

Gullander, S. O. O. (1975) *An Exploratory Study of Inter-firm Co-operation of Swedish Firms*. Unpublished PhD dissertation, Columbia University, New York, NY.

Håkansson, H. and Johanson, J. (1988) 'Formal and Informal Co-operation Strategies in International and Industrial Networks'. In Contractor, F. J. and Lorange P. (eds), *Cooperative Strategies in International Business*, pp. 369-379. Lexington Books, Lexington, MA.

Hamel, G., Doz, Y. L. and Prahalad, C. K. (1989) 'Collaborate with your Competitors—And Win' *Harvard Business Review*, **89**(1): 133–139.

Harrigan, K. (1985) *Strategies for Joint Ventures*. Lexington Books, Lexington, MA.

Harrigan, K. (1986) *Strategic Alliances: Form, Autonomy and Performance*, working paper. Columbia University, New York, NY.

Hull, F. and Slowinski, E. (1990) 'Partnering with Technology, Entrepreneurs'. *Research & Technology Management*, November–December, pp. 16–20.

Jensen, M. C. and Meckling, W. H. (1976) 'Theory of the Firm: Managerial Behaviour, Agency Costs, and Ownership Structure'. *Journal of Financial Economics*, **3**(4): 305–360.

Johnston, R. and Lawrence. P. R. (1988) 'Beyond Vertical Integration—The Rise of the Value Adding Partnership'. *Harvard Business Review*, **88**(4): 94–101.

Killing, J. P. (1983) *Strategies for Joint Venture Success*. Praeger, New York, NY.

Killing, J. P. (1988) 'Understanding Alliances: The Role of Task and Organizational Complexity'. In Contractor F. J. and Lorange, P. (eds), *Co operative Strategies and International Business*, pp. 55–67. Lexington Books, Lexington, MA.

Konsynski, B. R. and McFarlan, F. W. (1990) 'Information Partnerships—Shared Data, Shared Scale'. *Harvard Business Review*, **90**(5): 114–120.

Koopmans, T. (1957) *Three Essays on the State of Economic Science*. McGraw-Hill, New York.

Larson, A. (1992) 'Network Dyads in Entrepreneurial Settings: A Study of the Governance of Exchange Relationships'. *Administrative Science Quarterly*, **37**: 76–104.

Lynch, R. P. (1989) *The Practical Guide to Joint Ventures and Corporate Alliances*. John Wiley & Sons, New York.

Macneil, I. R. (1980) *The New Social Contract: An Inquiry into Modern Contractual Relations*, Yale University Press, New Haven, CT.

Mintzberg, H. (1973) *The Nature of Managerial Work*. Harper & Row, New York.
Morris, D. and Hergert, I. (1987) 'Trends in International Collaborative Agreements'. *Columbia Journal of World Business*, **22**(2): 15–21.
Ohmae, K. (1989) 'The Global Logic of Strategic Alliances'. *Harvard Business Review*, **89**(2): 143–154.
Osborn, R. N. and Baughn, C. C. (1990) 'Forms of Interorganizational Governance for Multinational Alliances'. *Academy of Management Journal*, **33**(3): 503–519.
Parkhe, A. (1991) 'Interfirm Diversity, Organisational Learning and Longevity in Global Strategic Alliances'. *Journal of International Business Studies*, **22**(5): 579–601.
Parvatiyar, A., Sheth, J. N. and Whittington, F. B. (1992) *Paradigm Shift in Interfirm Marketing Relationships: Emerging Research Issues*. Paper presented for the Research Conference on Customer Relationship Management: Theory and Practice, 9–10 April, Emory University, Atlanta, GA.
Pfeffer, J. (1987) 'A Resource Dependence Perspective on Intercorporate Relations'. In Mizruchi, M. and Schwartz, M. (eds), *Intercorporate Relations: The Structural Analysis of Business*, pp. 25–55. Cambridge University Press, Cambridge.
Pfeffer, J. and Salancik, G. R. (1978) *The External Control of Organizations: A Resource Dependence Perspective*, Harper & Row, New York, NY.
Reve, T. (1990) 'The Firm as a Nexus of Internal and External Contracts'. In Aoki, M., Gustafsson, B. and Williamson, O. E. (eds), *The Firm as a Nexus of Treaties*, pp. 133–161. Sage, London.
Schaan, J. L. and Beamish, P. W. (1988) 'Joint Venture General Managers in LDCs'. In Contractor, F. J. and Lorange, P. (eds), *Co-operative Strategies and International Business*, pp. 55–67. Lexington Books, Lexington, MA.
Snyder, G. H. (1991) 'Alliance Theory: A Neoralist First Cut'. In Rothstein, R. L. (ed.), *The Evolution of Theory in International Relations*, pp. 83–103. University of South Carolina Press, Columbia.
Stuckey, J. (1983) *Vertical Integration and Joint Ventures in the Aluminium Industry*. Harvard University Press, Cambridge, MA.
Williamson, O. E. (1975) *Markets and Hierarchies: Analysis and Antitrust Implications*. The Free Press, New York, NY.
Williamson, O. E. (1984) 'The Economics of Governance: Framework and Implications'. *Journal of Theoretical Economics*, **140**, March: 195–223.
Williamson, O. E. (1985) *The Economic Institution of Capitalism*. The Free Press, New York, NY.
Williamson, O. E. (1990) 'The Firm as a Nexus of Treaties: An Introduction'. In Aoki, M., Gustafsson, B. and Williamson, O. E. (eds), *The Firm as a Nexus of Treaties*, pp.133–161. Sage, London.

Part III

Understanding Non-Western Structures

CONTENTS

14. Eastern Asian enterprise structures and comparative analysis of forms of business organization — 191

    RICHARD D. WHITLEY, *Organization Studies* (1990) **11**(1), 47–74

15. The nature and competitiveness of Japan's *Keiretsu* — 213

    ANGELINA HELOU, *Journal of World Trade* (1991) **25**, 99–131

16. The Japanese corporate network: a blockmodel analysis — 244

    MICHAEL L. GERLACH, *Administrative Science Quarterly* (1992) **37**, March, 105–139

17. The worldwide web of Chinese business — 274

    JOHN KAO, *Harvard Business Review* (1993) March–April, 24–36

18. A network approach to probing Asia's invisible business structures — 285

    S. BENJAMIN PRASAD and PERVEZ N. GHAURI, *Proceedings of Southern Management Association* (1993) Atlanta, Georgia, 371–374

14

Eastern Asian Enterprise Structures and the Comparative Analysis of Forms of Business Organization

Richard D. Whitley

INTRODUCTION

The economic success of Japanese firms over the past 40 years has emphasized the viability of alternatives to United States management structures and practices, as well as highlighting the limited generality of the business strategy–structure relationships identified by Chandler (Alford, 1976; Kagono *et al.*, 1985, pp.99–110; Maurice *et al.*,1986). Whereas it may have seemed reasonable in the 1960s and 1970s to regard Japanese organizational practices and forms as temporary stepping stones on the path to 'modern', i.e. US practices, their continuation and growing success in US and European markets render such dismissal increasingly untenable.

The failure of competitive pressures to generate isomorphic management structures and practices throughout successful firms in world markets (cf. DeMaggio and Powell, 1983) is further emphasized by the distinctive nature of firms in other East Asian societies which also compete effectively. Not only does the archetypal Japanese company (see e.g., Clark, 1979, pp.221–222) differ considerably from the integrated and diversified managerial bureaucracy celebrated by Chandler (1977) in his account of the rise of big business in the USA (cf. DuBoff and Herman, 1980), but successful South Korean business groups (*chaebol*) and expatriate Chinese family businesses also manifest major differences from both the US and the Japanese models. Thus international competition seems quite consonant with a variety of forms of business organization established in different societies. Indeed, as Orru *et al.* (1988) suggest, isomorphism between management structures seems much greater within individual East Asian societies than between them, largely because of specific institutional structures and pressures which lead to particular kinds of firms being successful in those contexts. Similar points are made by Maurice *et al.* (1980, 1986) in their comparisons of British, French and German manufacturing firms.

The development of distinctive types of enterprise structure and practice in different national contexts which appear equally successful and competitive in world markets suggests

Reprinted with permission from *Organization* Studies, Vol. 11, No. 1, pp.47–74.
Copyright © 1990 EGOS.

that not only do institutional variations affect management systems in business organizations, but there is also no dominant technical rationality in economic markets which inexorably leads to a single way of organizing and controlling economic resources. Instead, there are a variety of successful 'recipes' institutionalized in different societies that function equally efficiently in their particular contexts. This implies that the generalization of a single national pattern of business development and organization to all industrially advanced societies is untenable. Rather, the processes by which such recipes develop and function successfully in different societal contexts require analysis in a comparative study of forms of business organization. In this paper, I suggest a way of identifying and classifying different enterprise structures as an initial step towards such a study.

The comparative analysis of business recipes presumes that social institutions and structures significantly influence the sorts of competitive business structures that develop in different societies. In a general sense, of course, this is axiomatic since all organizations and ways of co-ordinating economic activities are socially constructed and so are dependent up their social context (Sorge, 1983; Stinchcombe, 1983, pp.136–144). However, the extent to which this dependence affects the technical efficiency of organizational forms remains a matter of some dispute with some writers claiming a convergence of successful structures across societal boundaries so that the relationships between certain variables remain stable (Hickson et al., 1974, 1979; cf. Child and Tayeb, 1983). Others claim that distinctive cultures and social structures are so important in determining what sorts of managerial practices are successful in particular contexts that they are not generalizable to other contexts (e.g. Hofstede, 1980, 1983).

This dispute raises a number of complex theoretical and epistemological issues, such as the possibility and desirability of a general theory of formal organizational structures (cf. Sorge, 1983; Maurice, 1979; Rose, 1985), but the critical ones here concern the significance of the nation state and/or 'culture' as the basic unit of analysis and the identification of dominant enterprise structures within such units which are relatively specific to them The nation state is a crucial focus for the comparative analysis of forms of business organization, I suggest, because major social institutions, such as legal, financial and educational systems vary between them, and these variations affect the sorts of enterprise structures that become dominant in them (Maurice et al., 1986; Zysmar, 1983). It is also, of course, the key unit for attempts of political and bureaucratic elites to achieve economic development, and different state policies and structures affect enterprise development, as the contrast of South Korea and Taiwan demonstrates (Lau, 1986; Wade, 1988). The nation state is especially important in East Asia because of the relatively high levels of cultural homogeneity in Japan, Korea and China, including expatriate Chinese (Jacobs, 1985; Pye, 1985; Redding, 1989; Silin, 1976).

Dominant institutions of nation states, then, are crucial influences on the kinds of entrepreneurs and managers who gain control over economic resources and the practices and procedures they develop for dealing with business problems. They also structure the sorts of managerial practices that are effective in contrasting situations, especially where cultural homogeneity is high. Relatively high levels of work group autonomy in deciding how clerical tasks are to be carried out, for example, presume considerable employer–employee trust which can be generated by particular employment practices in particular societies (Rohlen, 1974, 1979). Similarly, high levels of bank borrowing are less risky in countries where industrial enterprises are closely linked to banks than where the financial system is capital market based (Abegglen and Stalk, 1985, pp.161–167; Cable and Dirrheimer, 1983; Cable and Yasuki, 1985).

The identification of the dominant business 'recipe' in a country implies that these institutions are sufficiently pervasive and influential to restrict the range of feasible enterprise structures that become established. A limited number of ways of organizing economic activities become institutionalized as distinctive systems that function effectively in particular contexts. Such recipes include the structure of relations between authority hierarchies and patterns of development, as well as their 'internal' organization. They are thus distinctive configurations of market-hierarchy relations which become established and function effectively in different societal contexts. The dominant Japanese economic actor in the post-war period, for example, has been identified by Clark (1979, pp.221–222) as combining a low degree of functional self-sufficiency with considerable long-term interdependence with industry partners and membership in inter-sector groups (Futatsugi, 1986; Hamilton et al., 1989) as well as particular employment practices. While variations between large Japanese firms do exist (Abegglen and Stalk, 1985, pp.189–190), there is clearly a distinctive system for organizing and controlling economic activities in Japan which works well in that context. Although some of its features may be translatable to other societies (cf. Trevor, 1988), the recipe as a whole is not because it is interdependent with particular contextual institutions (cf. Lincoln et al., 1986; Lincoln and McBridge, 1987). Crucial components, such as the authority and trust system, cannot be directly transferred to other East Asian enterprise structures, as the experience of Japanese–Korean joint ventures clearly demonstrates (Liebenberg, 1982; cf. Jacobs, 1985).

In summary, the relatively isomorphic enterprise structures in export industries in different East Asian societies reinforce the significance of what Maurice (1979) termed the 'societal effect' in structuring business organizations. This implies that successful ways of organizing economic activities in market societies reflect key structures and institutions of those societies, and would have developed differently in different contexts. It also suggests that managerial structures and practices need to be studied in relation to their societal contexts if we are to understand how they function effectively. Such a comparative study requires a common unit of analysis and some ways of comparing and contrasting crucial characteristics of such units across societies. In the next section of this paper, I discuss some of the issues involved in standardizing the unit of analysis for comparing forms of business organization, and then outline some of the major ways in which dominant forms in Japan, South Korea and Taiwan vary. These differences can be summarized under three separate headings: (a) enterprise specialization and development, (b) authority, loyalty and the division of labour, and (c) enterprise interdependence and co-ordination. They constitute the basis for eight dimensions on which enterprise structures can be systematically compared across societies. These are: the narrowness of economic activities co-ordinated by authority structures, the degree to which firms develop stable relationships with suppliers and other industry partners, preferences for evolutionary or discontinuous growth strategies, the importance of personal authority relations, the degree of employer–employee commitment and loyalty, role specialization and individuation, the extent of inter-industry risk sharing and co-ordination of strategies and, finally, the extent to which state agencies and banks plan and co-ordinate firms' activities. Together, these dimensions form distinctive configurations that develop in particular social contexts.

FIRMS AS AUTHORITATIVE UNITS OF ECONOMIC ACTION

In market societies which decentralize control over resources to holders of property rights and their agents, the key economic actor is the firm because it exercises considerable discretion over the acquisition, use and disposition of human and material resources. The comparison of enterprise structures and practices involves the analysis of how these entities are differentiated and interconnected in different societies and how their controllers pursue particular objectives. The nature of firms as relatively autonomous decision-making entities, and the ways in which their interrelationships are organized, vary between societies, because of the influences of the state, the financial system and other major social institutions which are societally specific. Thus, the relatively weak position of the central civil service in the USA and the capital-market-based financial system have affected the development of large, integrated and diversified managerial bureaucracies there (Zysman, 1983, pp.266–273), just as the quite different institutional environments of firms in France and Germany have resulted in different patterns of enterprise structures (Bauer and Cohen, 1981; Maurice et al., 1986).

In considering how we are to identify the basic units of economic action in different societies, I suggest that the key criterion is the extent to which they integrate, co-ordinate and control resources through an authority system. Firms, in this view, function as economic actors by authoritatively directing and organizing economic activities in the pursuit of their controllers' goals. Authority relations provide the basis for continued and systematic co-ordination of activities, and so the integrated transformation of resources into productive services (Penrose, 1980, pp.15–25; cf. Whitley, 1987). It is through this system that firms 'add value' to human and material resources and function as relatively separate units of economic decision-making. Although the degree of central direction of activities varies, as does the basis of authority relations, it is this co-ordinated control of a varied set of resources which distinguishes firms from co-operative networks and informal alliances. In this view, then, federations of firms agreeing market shares and pricing policies on an *ad hoc* and informal basis (cf. Daems, 1983) do not constitute discrete, separate enterprises.

This emphasis on the centralized authoritative control over resources as the key property of units of economic action focuses attention on the entity responsible for major financial, personnel and strategic decisions. In the case of French industrial groups and Korean *chaebol*, for instance, the critical issue in determining whether it is the group as a whole which is the basic unit of analysis for comparison purposes is the location of these sorts of decisions. If the *President-Directeur Général* of a French industrial group is at the apex of an authority hierarchy which combines all member firms and has the final responsibility for assessing their performance, allocating funds and making senior managerial appointments, as Bauer and Cohen (1981, pp.132–136) claim was the case for Riboud when BSN took over Gervais-Danone, then the group is the dominant unit of economic activity rather than its components.

On the other hand, comparing the pre-war Japanese family controlled business groups (*Zaibatsu*) with the post-war intermarket groups it is clear that while the former did function as distinct units of economic action through the central holding company (Morikawa, 1976; Yasuoka, 1976), this is not true of the latter (Clark, 1979, pp.73–87; Goto, 1982; Kiyonari and Nakamura, 1980). Even when the leading firms in vertically associated groups of sub-contractors (*keiretsu*) exercise strong contractual pressure on suppliers, they do not do so through systematic authority relations but rather through a combination of market power and long-term relations of mutual obligation and commitment (Clark, 1979, pp. 62–64; Kono, 1984, pp.136–138). Thus, for post-war Japan, the extensive reliance on subcontracting, and long-term commitments between distinct economic entities, mean that the dominant unit of authoritative resource control is the single, or related, industry company rather than the diversified industrial group (Clark, 1979, pp.60–62). It also means, of course, that 'firms' are less discrete and isolated entities than those found in Anglo-Saxon societies.

The identification of firms as distinct units of economic action with the authoritative co-ordination of human and material resources also emphasizes their interdependence with general relations of subordination in the wider society. Clearly, the ways in which resources are directed in firms reflects dominant conceptions of hierarchical relations in different cultures so that, for instance, reliance on purely formal, legal–rational modes of authority is unlikely to prove successful in patrimonial societies (cf. Jacobs, 1985; Pye, 1985). Thus authority patterns in Chinese family businesses reproduce more general patterns of superior–subordinate relations institutionalized in Chinese civilization and culture throughout the expatriate community (Redding, 1989; Silin, 1976).

EAST ASIAN FORMS OF BUSINESS ORGANIZATION

In the cases of Japan, South Korea, Taiwan and Hong Kong, the dominant economic actors can be identified as: the large Japanese company—whether in a business group or not—the Korean *chaebol*, and the Chinese family business. These constitute the major systems of co-ordination and control of economic activities within these countries, which are quite different from each other. While not all large firms exhibit all the features to be discussed, and in the case of Taiwan large firms are much less important than in Japan and Korea, and their average size is smaller (Myers, 1986), key characteristics of the dominant system of organizing economic activities in each country can be reconstructed from accounts of the major actors in different sectors. These reconstructions deal with: (a) the nature of the activities being co-ordinated by authoritative structures and the dominant logic underlying their development, (b) how those activities are co-ordinated and controlled, and (c) how economic actors are interconnected with each other and related to major social institutions such as the state and financial agencies.

The large Japanese company

One of the most striking features of large enterprises in Japan, when compared with those in the USA and UK, is their concentration on a limited range of business activities and the homogeneity of skills and resources (Clark, 1979, pp. 55–64). Their specialization in particular industries and sectors is relatively high, with many activities being carried out by sub-contractors. Toyota, for example, sub-contracts much of its specialized maintenance work (Cusumano, 1985, p.312). This low degree of functional self-sufficiency and narrowness of business boundaries means that managers have a much more homogeneous set of skills and experiences than those in large US firms, and this facilitates co-ordination within them (Aoki, 1987; Clark, 1979, p.63; Imai and Itami, 1984). This preference for restricting the heterogeneity of activities co-ordinated by authority hierarchies is also manifested by the relatively low degree of industrial diversification in Japan, especially across sectors, and the tendency to spin off subsidiaries in new industries as separate companies when they are successful (Kono, 1984, pp.78–80; Dore, 1986, pp.61–63). The industrial specificity of enterprises is thus quite high and both encourages, and is encouraged by, high levels of employee identification with particular industries since unrelated diversification would require new, more heterogeneous skills.

This high degree of specialization and narrowness of business activities controlled by them clearly implies considerable interdependence between firms. As already mentioned, high levels of sub-contracting are characteristic of the Japanese economy, with many major sub-contractors of large manufacturers themselves sub-contracting work to tertiary contractors (Dore, 1986, pp.176–178). This extensive use of sub-contractors involves much greater trust and sense of mutual obligation between the parties than simple spot market transactions. This means that Toyota and Nissan, for example, share technical information with their suppliers, develop long-term commitments to their major contractors, exchange managerial staff with them and, occasionally, shareholdings (Cusumano, 1985, pp. 186–193, 248–261; Shimokawa, 1985). While large firms do change sub-contractors in Japan, contractual commitments are longer-term and based more on the mutual recognition of interdependence and trust than just being *ad hoc*, impersonal bargains (Dore, 1986, pp.77–83) . Specialist firms are embedded in elaborate networks of mutual commitments which reduce their autonomy and ability to change suppliers, customers and industry quickly. Thus strategic decision-making in Japanese companies is quite constrained by comparison with US ones and is more driven by their capabilities and current commitments to other firms in the industry and related activities than by opportunities in unrelated sectors and markets (Imai and Itami, 1984; Kagono *et al.*, 1985).

Another distinctive characteristic of large Japanese enterprises is their high degree of managerial autonomy from shareholders. Especially since the growth of inter-company shareholdings in the 1960s (Aoki, 1987; Dore, 1986, pp.67–72; Futatsugi, 1986), managerial elites in Japan are remarkably isolated from the 'market for corporate control' (Lawriwsky, 1984, pp.165–177) and can afford to ignore short-term capital market pressures (Abegglen and Stalk, 1985, p.177; Kagono *et al.*, 1985, p.28). This autonomy helps to explain why growth goals, and, in particular, the objective of increasing market share, are so important. Additional factors encouraging growth are the importance of employer size for individual prestige and the strong relationships between firm size and employee wages and fringe benefits as well as bigger firms having easier access to credit (Clark, 1979, pp.93–97). The risks involved in specializing in a particular line of business to such an extent are reduced in the Japanese system by sharing them with sub-contractors, trading companies and other members of business groups in quasi-market relationships (Hamilton *et al.*, 1989; Imai and Itami, 1984). The relatively narrow scope of economic activities controlled by enterprises, and the extensive reliance on 'relational contracting' (Dore, 1986, pp.77–85), enables firms to add productive capacity in the same industry at relatively low long-term cost.

The low degree of shareholder control and influence means that personal authority derived from ownership is unimportant in dominant economic actors in Japan, except perhaps in new firms dominated by the founder. Instead, hierarchical position and the competence implied by holding superior posts appear to be the major grounds for eliciting obedience and conformity to instructions (Clark, 1979, pp.212–219). This presumption of managerial competence and acceptance of superior–subordinate relationships is reinforced by the high level of formal education of most managers—and indeed of most employees—in large businesses and the strong correspondence between managerial labour markets and the prestige hierarchy of tertiary education institutions (Dore, 1973, pp.293–295). Acceptance of managerial authority is also linked to the considerable dependence of semi-permanent 'members' (Rohlen, 1974, pp.18–20) of large enterprises upon the success of their employer. As their own prestige, earnings and benefits directly depend on enterprise growth it is not surprising that they accept authority hierarchies, particularly since the boundaries between strata within organizations are much less marked than in many western firms and income differentials are lower (Abegglen and Stalk, 1981, pp.191–198; Dore, 1973, pp.94–113; Lincoln and Kalleberg, 1985). Commitment to overall enterprise objectives and awareness of its competitive position are obviously easier when markets and skills are homogeneous and direct competitors are readily identified.

Loyalty and commitment to organizational goals are also encouraged by the well-known employment practices of many large firms in Japan (cf. Lincoln and McBridge, 1987). Perhaps the most discussed is the long-term commitment to 'permanent' employees which means that redundancies among them are a sign of managerial incompetence and sometimes a cause for top managers to resign (Dore, 1986, pp.88–119). Coupled with this commitment is a reliance on seniority-based promotions and salary increases, which obviously ties male employees to the company and makes it unlikely that they will leave (Rohlen, 1974, 1979). Because inter-firm mobility of males over 25 years old is low and because the existing workforce is, in effect, a long-term cost or asset, Japanese firms invest heavily in training and frequently move staff to new jobs and tasks. Compared to Anglo-Saxon businesses, internal mobility and the development of multiple skills within firms is high in Japan (Abegglen and Stalk, 1985; Clark, 1979; Koike, 1987). These skills are specific to individual firms and are not readily transferable, nor do they form the basis of distinct occupational identities as in the West.

This lack of skill-based horizontal identities is reinforced by the enterprise union system in Japan which clearly focuses loyalties on firms rather than class or expertise (McMillan, 1985, pp.165–185). The importance of this in the views of top managers can be judged by the lengths that Nissan went to in 1953 to break the industry-wide union and establish one for the enterprise (Cusumano, 1985, pp.149–164). Additionally, in Japan many officials in these unions are junior managers who expect to receive promotion after leaving their union posts (Clark, 1979, p.218; Rohlen, 1974, pp.184–190).

Another characteristic of large Japanese firms which has frequently been remarked upon is the relatively decentralized system of initiating decisions and the emphasis on obtaining a consensus before acting (Kagono *et al.*, 1985, pp.42–43; Rohlen, 1979). The relatively high levels of employer–employee commitment and loyalty facilitate, and are reinforced by, considerable decentralization of much managerial decision-making and sharing of information with all employees (Lincoln *et al.*, 1986). While scarcely functioning as a worker-controlled co-operative, large Japanese firms do seem to involve middle managers in developing plans and decisions more than elsewhere and the development of group agreement is an important part of the decision-making process (Clark, 1979, pp.126–133; McMillan, 1985, pp.160–161). This importance of group consensus and commitment is also reflected in the priority of group goals and tasks over individual ones. Individual duties, roles and responsibilities are much less sharply delineated and significant in Japanese firms than in US ones (Kagono *et al.*, 1985, pp.106–117; Lincoln *et al.*,1986). Instead, work groups have considerable autonomy over how tasks are to be carried out and group performance is more important than specific individual achievements. This is reflected in the evaluation of managers who are expected to boost group morale and performance rather than just direct tasks from above (Rohlen, 1974). Section heads who remain aloof from the groups and whose behaviour results in transfer requests are likely to be moved and/or demoted.

Turning now to consider intermarket connections between Japanese firms, many large Japanese companies have long-term links with firms in other industries through joint membership of intermarket business groups (Goto, 1982; Hamilton *et al.*, 1989; Miyazaki, 1980). Three of the largest of these groups stem from the pre-war *zaibatsu* groups of Mitsui, Mitsubishi and Sumitomo while others, such as Fuyo, Sanwa and Dai-ichi Kangin, are organized around large 'city' banks in a comparable way to the German bank-based groupings (Clark, 1979, pp.73–87). Typically, members of these groups own some of each others' shares, regularly exchange information and advice in weekly 'presidents' club' meetings, sometimes exchange managerial personnel and directors and often borrow from the same bank or other financial intermediaries. They usually include banks, insurance companies, general trading companies and firms from most of the major industries so that they compete with one another as loosely-connected, diversified associations. However, unlike the quasi-vertically integrated *keiretsu* usually dominated by the final assembler of consumer products, these business groups are structured in a more egalitarian manner with no single component controlling the network. While they have acted on occasion to support a member firm in severe difficulties, and, in the case of Mitsui, encouraged the dismissal of the president of the Mitsukoshi department store in the 1970s (Abegglen and Stalk, 1985, pp.185–186), the collective mobilization of group resources for a joint goal has been a rare occurrence in the past 40 years and the post-war business groups are not at all integrated business entities (Dore, 1986, pp.79–80). Rather, they seem to function as informal mutual support groups, helping to reduce risks and provide opportunities for new ventures by pooling knowledge and expertise (Kiyonari and Nakamura, 1980).

Finally, connections between the large Japanese firm and banks and state agencies tend to be closer than those in Anglo-Saxon countries, although not much more than those in some continental European countries (Miyazaki, 1980; Zysman, 1983). The high reliance on bank loans to financing growth in Japan is well known and banks develop long-term commitments to their major customers which sometimes lead to an exchange of personnel, as when Fukio Nakagawa went to Toyota from the Mitsui Bank in 1950 to monitor a financial re-organization (Cusumano, 1985, p.74). These close relations are developed by firms outside business groups as well as within them, and reflect higher levels of interdependence than those found in capital-market-based financial systems such as those in the USA and UK.

The role of state agencies in the economic development of Japan has, of course, been emphasized in most accounts of Japanese industrialization (e.g. Johnson, 1982; Wade, 1988). The high prestige of the central bureaucracy and its commitment to development goals have led to close links between large firms and key ministries, especially the Ministry of International Trade and Industry. While the dominant role of MITI may be less marked now than in the 1950s and 1960s, firms still participate in MITI-organized cartels and capacity reduction exercises as well as more informal co-ordination processes (Dore, 1986, pp.128–147), and MITI is heavily involved in the promotion of new industries, co-operative R&D initiatives, etc. (Abegglen and Stalk, 1985, pp.138–144). Generally, the role of the state in formulating and implementing an industrial policy is much more accepted in Japan than in the USA and the UK and helps to spread the risks of major new investments (Eads and Yamamura, 1987; Zysman, 1983).

One of the most important characteristics of the large Japanese company as the dominant economic actor in Japan is the degree to which many of these features form a coherent and mutually supportive pattern (Clark,1979, pp.221–222). The low level of self-sufficiency is encouraged by risk sharing with sub-contractors and other members of business groups. It is also interdependent with the high degree of homogeneity of markets and skill which, together with distinctive employment practices, help to generate high levels of commitment to the enterprise as a whole. This commitment in turn facilitates some decentralization of decision-making and flexible control systems which rely on considerable trust between vertical strata Homogeneity also encourages growth goals within industrial sectors and when coupled with a supportive financial and political system, long-term commitments to particular sectors. This configuration is not, of course, perfectly closed and immune to change but does consist of interdependent elements which are unlikely to change without some major external shock.

The South Korean *chaebol*

In contrast to the relatively specialized and narrowly focused large Japanese company, the South Korean *chaebol* co-ordinate a variety of resources and are much more self-sufficient in terms of the activities they control directly. Sub-contracting is thus much less marked than among Japanese firms. However, they tend to focus on related business fields and vertical integration rather than on unrelated diversification (Levy,1988; Orru *et al.*,1988). Similar to the pre-war Japanese *zaibatsu*—and they share the same Chinese characters (Jones and Sakong, 1980, p.259) they also limit themselves to distinct business sectors rather than competing with each other in all major areas. Thus Hyundai is heavily committed to shipbuilding and vehicles but not to electrical machinery, unlike Samsung and Lucky-Goldstar. The largest *chaebol* do, though, all include general trading companies which were established shortly after the state began to encourage them in 1975 (Cho, 1987, pp.50–59). They also own minority shareholdings in the state controlled banks and insurance companies (Orru *et al.*, 1988).

A further marked difference between Korean *chaebol* and Japanese firms is the strong connection between ownership and control in the former businesses. Despite government pressure to float their companies on the stock market, most *chaebol* remain firmly controlled by their founder and his family with equity funds being restricted to under a third of the shares in a few of the constituent firms (Orru *et al.*, 1988). Furthermore, many of the shares held by non-family members are owned by financial institutions largely controlled by the dominant family. In general, then, managerial independence from dominant shareholders is much less than in Japan, if not virtually negligible. This has not, though, inhibited the pursuit of growth goals, on the contrary, the leading *chaebol* have grown considerably over the past 20 or so years with considerable encouragement from the Korean state (Jacobs, 1985, pp.144–146; Michell, 1988, pp.95–98). However, this growth has been less focused on a single industrial sector than is the case for most large Japanese firms and appears more discontinuous.

The strong influence of family ownership in the direction of the *chaebol* is reflected in the highly centralized decision-making process (Liebenberg, 1982; Yoo and Lee, 1987). Authority stems direct from ownership and the founder, or his son, is involved in all major decisions, and, indeed, many minor ones (Orru *et al.*, 1988). Furthermore, most of the major subsidiaries are headed by family members so that although a considerable number of highly educated managers are employed in these large enterprises, and bureaucratic control systems are quite highly developed, personal, particularistic attributes and connections are more important than formal rules and procedures and many managers delegate upwards (Yoo and Lee, 1987). Hierarchical relations are more patrimonial and paternalistic than legal–rational (cf. Jacobs, 1985, pp.1–33; Pye, 1985, pp.83–87).

This paternalistic ethos encourages relatively long-term employer–employee commitment in these large enterprises and a seniority-based promotion system which rewards loyalty, although less so than in large Japanese firms. Labour turnover, in general, appears higher in Korea than in Japan or Taiwan, although it varies considerably between sex and age groups as well as between the *chaebol* and small businesses (Amsden, 1985; Michell, 1988, pp.109–110). As in Japan, the larger firms demonstrate their success by providing more fringe benefits and higher wages than small ones, and it is more difficult to move between the *chaebol* than between the latter. A further influence on authority patterns in Korea noted by Liebenberg (1982) is military service and the pervasive sense of being a threatened society. According to many of the Japanese managers interviewed by Liebenberg, Korean companies are run in comparable ways to military units and authority is unquestioned by middle managers.

Seniority-based reward systems and the large-scale recruitment of school leavers and college graduates by the *chaebol* are associated with extensive job rotation and on-the-job training, as in Japan (Yoo and Lee, 1987). However, this training is not very closely linked to job assignments or future promotion opportunities. Also similar to Japanese firms, job specifications are often not very detailed or tied to individual tasks, and formal rules and procedures tend to be interpreted rather flexibly. Because authority is relatively personal, obeying superiors' decisions and meeting their goals are more important than following formal rules. Thus, Korean *chaebol* exhibit a mixture of Japanese and more patrimonial employment practices which reflect limited levels of trust and do not encourage initiative (Liebenberg, 1982).

As relatively self-sufficient and broadly based, integrated businesses, Korean *chaebol* have not developed elaborate networks of interdependent relations with sub-contractors, customers, and other firms. In this sense they are more similar to the diversified, autonomous Anglo-Saxon firm than to Japanese ones and are able to pursue relatively independent strategies. However, even more than Japanese companies, they are heavily dependent upon the major banks for loans and these banks are state controlled. Thus the *chaebol* are much more directly linked to state agencies and dependent on their priorities than are Japanese firms and their growth patterns reflect the preferences of, and opportunities provided by, politicians and planners (Jones and Sakong, 1980, pp.269–285). Indeed, Jacobs (1985, pp.14–32) claims that the state as a whole in South Korea still functions as an essentially patrimonial system and dominates the economic system. Certainly the leaders of the *chaebol* are closely connected to members of the political and bureaucratic elites and have received preferential treatment in many instances (Kim, 1979, pp.70–80). Failure to support state policies or the ruling political party can prove costly if not fatal, as when Yolsan collapsed after showing support for the opposition in 1979 (Cumings, 1987). While not embedded in complex networks of mutual obligation with other firms in the same and related sectors, then, Korean *chaebol* are highly dependent upon banks, state agencies and political connections. They are therefore much less autonomous than large conglomerates in Anglo-Saxon countries.

The Chinese family business

The expatriate Chinese family business (CFB) is the dominant unit of economic action in Taiwan, Hong Kong and most South East Asian countries, although it is not important in the exporting industries of Singapore which are dominated by subsidiaries of western multi-national firms (Redding, 1989; Yoshihara, 1988). Despite some variations in particular features between societies, such as a greater tendency to change employers in Hong Kong than in Taiwan (Amsden, 1985; Sit and Wong, 1988), the basic structure and mode of operating of the Chinese family business seem remarkably similar in Thailand, Indonesia, the Philippines, Malaysia, Hong Kong and Taiwan (Limlingan, 1986; Redding, 1989).

The scope of economic activities authoritatively co-ordinated by each CFB is typically quite specialized, with extensive reliance on sub-contractors. However, the owner and/or his family sometimes diversify into quite unrelated areas by establishing another business run by a trusted member of the family together with salaried managers. Such diversification is often opportunistic and imitative, as in the growth of the plastic and electronics industries in Taiwan (Myers, 1986, p.55). Usually such businesses are not integrated through an authority system and often they have little connection with each other. Each one is owned by the dominant family and any co-ordination there may be is achieved through personal control over their finances.

The heavy reliance on sub-contracting and the emphasis on personal authority and basis of trust in the CFB means that they are embedded in elaborate networks of personal obligation and are highly interdependent with other firms. However, these connections are often not long-term ones and commitments between contractors are unstable compared with those in Japan (Sit and Wong, 1988). Personal knowledge and/or reputation for reliability and speed are essential for gaining contracts (Ward, 1972) but do not necessarily lead to repeat orders or long-term associations. Since firms are essentially family possessions and most sub-contractors are outsiders, commitments cannot be expected to be long-lived in Chinese cultures (Redding, 1989). Networks of interdependent firms, then, are based on personal contacts and reputations, and so these are crucial to CFB survival, but are not very stable and often change. This 'molecular' system of co-ordination (Redding and Tam, 1985) is highly flexible and enables rapid changes of products and markets as is evidenced by the successful development of the wigmaking, plastic flower and toy industries in Hong Kong.

Turning to the internal system of co-ordination and control, one of the most striking features of the Chinese family business (CFB) is its highly personal nature. The firm is typically regarded as a family possession and its major function is to increase family wealth and prestige. Thus control is strongly associated with ownership and is highly centralized (Redding and Wong, 1986; Silin, 1976). Frequently, family members fill top management positions and it is relatively rare for managers without strong personal ties to owners to become trusted members of top management. Partly as a result, many managers and skilled manual workers leave to start their own businesses and both the establishment and failure rates of new firms are high. In contrasting dominant growth processes in Hong Kong with those in Japan, Tam (1989) characterizes the former as essentially centrifugal with firms frequently spinning off new businesses as ambitious employees learn about the industry and technology and then seek to establish their own source of family wealth and prestige.

This high degree of personal control limits the effective size of such businesses and the use of formal control systems. As Silin (1976) showed in his account of Taiwanese firms, a manager's formal status and position are much less significant as an indicator of power and responsibility than his relationship to the owner. Authority was essentially dyadic and diffuse between managers and the owner with little delegation to intermediate levels of management or differentiation of authority between particular sections. Similarly, formal rules and procedures were less important in guiding behaviour than personal wishes and objectives. Since the owner was *de facto*, morally superior to and worthier than his subordinates, their duty was to anticipate his decisions and follow his way of thinking. However, this loyalty to the individual was contingent upon continued business success and so, according to Silin (1976, pp.127–131), was 'rational' rather than emotional as in Japan. Trust and commitment in the CFB, then, are not as great as in large Japanese companies and while a paternalistic ethos of looking after the workforce is frequently expressed (Redding, 1989), it does not usually extend to a working lifetime commitment on either side. Equally, seniority-based promotion and reward systems are more evident in the CFB than in many Anglo-Saxon firms, but less so than in Japan. As might be expected, role and responsibility specifications are rarely formally and precisely spelled out or allocated to distinct individuals (Pugh and Redding, 1985). Job overlaps and multiple role incumbency are quite common among managers and again demonstrate the flexibility of the CFB relative to formal bureaucratic administrative systems (Hamilton and Kao, 1987; Silin, 1976).

The identification of firms with families leads to a reluctance to rely on bank loans or sell shares on the stock market. Typically, finance for expansion is obtained from personal contacts and family connections. In Taiwan, long-term bank loans to private businesses grew considerably at the end of the 1970s (Myers, 1986) but according to Gold (1986, p.108) this was primarily to a relatively small number of well-established large firms who do not dominate the Taiwanese economy in the same way as do the Japanese and Korean. The bulk of the small and medium-sized businesses borrow from the unofficial 'curb' market at high interest rates when they need more capital than their personal contacts can raise. Thus indebtedness and dependence on the formal banking system are much less significant than in South Korea or Japan (Levy, 1988).

Dependence on the state also tends to be lower in Taiwan and Hong Kong despite the banks and several major industries being state owned and controlled in the former country. The Taiwanese state is 'developmentalist' in the same way that the Japanese and Korean ones are (Cumings, 1987; Haggard, 1988; Johnson, 1982, pp.18–23), but is much less inclined to intervene in particular firms' decisions, beyond a general commitment to export industries after 1958, than the Korean state. Although Formosa Plastics was set up in 1958 at the behest of government officials, most new export industries in Taiwan have been developed without active state involvement and direction and have been dominated by relatively small, labour-intensive firms (Myers, 1986, pp.54–56). Central co-ordination of firms' policies and strategies is, then, relatively unusual in Taiwan and, of course, even more so in Hong Kong so that investment risks have typically been borne by entrepreneurs and their families, thus reducing commitment to highly capital intensive industries and R&D expenditures. In summary, then, the CFB is typically highly interdependent with sub-contractors and trading agents in a complex network of personal connections and obligations but does not usually form part of large intermarket groups like the Japanese business groups, nor does it manifest high levels of dependence on state agencies and politicians in Taiwan and Hong Kong.

THE COMPARATIVE ANALYSIS OF ENTERPRISE STRUCTURES

These differences between dominant forms of business organization in East Asian societies and their patterns of development suggest a number of dimensions for comparing and contrasting types of enterprise structure which becomes established in different societal contexts. Together they constitute a set of characteristics for identifying distinctive 'recipes' that function effectively in different societies. These recipes institutionalize different ways of dealing with the following concerns: first, how similar and complementary are the resources and activities being authoritatively co-ordinated, how are other necessary resources and activities to be integrated with these and how have enterprises changed and developed? Second, how are authority relations within each enterprise structure organized, loyalties mobilized and work allocated? Third, how are enterprises related to each other and integrated with major social institutions? The major dimensions linked to each of these concerns will now be discussed.

Enterprise specialization and development

This aspect of enterprise structure deals with three separate dimensions. First, the extent to which business activities are specialized around distinctive capabilities of skill, knowledge and experience. Second, the degree of relational contracting with suppliers and other industry partners. Third, preferences for incremental evolutionary strategies as opposed to discontinuous, radical ones.

A major difference between East Asian business recipes concerns their varied degree of business specialization and functional self-sufficiency. As we have seen, dominant economic actors in Japan and expatriate Chinese communities are much narrower in the activities they co-ordinate through authority relations than are Korean *chaebol* and most large western firms. They restrict themselves to activities in which their specialized skills and knowledge provide distinctive capabilities and advantages and then rely on quasi-market relationships to co-ordinate complementary but dissimilar, i.e. requiring different capabilities, activities (cf. Richardson, 1972). Such relational contracting is an especially effective alternative to authoritative co-ordination of economic activities in societies where strong social control mechanisms are institutionalized to govern contracts. The importance of these intermediate forms of co-ordinating transactions in Japan, Korea, Taiwan and Hong Kong emphasizes a further variable characteristic of enterprise structure: the degree to which businesses are embedded in networks of interdependent activities as distinct from functioning largely independently (Imai and Itami, 1984). In Anglo-Saxon countries, dominant economic actors are much more strongly bounded and separated as authoritative co-ordination systems engaging in short-term market transactions with each other.

High levels of specialization of resources and activities are associated with considerable homogeneity of the skills and experiences of employees and encourage their identification with particular fields of business activity. This homogeneity reduces co-ordination costs and facilitates loyalty to common objectives, especially when reinforced by a union system based on specialized enterprises, as in Japan. It is reflected in the sorts of manager who become members of the dominant coalition of large businesses and their attitudes to business development.

Business specialization and skill homogeneity encourage growth strategies derived from existing competences and capabilities where these are decided by internally promoted managers, and so focus on increasing the market share in existing and related business areas (Imai and Itami, 1984). Because the large Japanese firm is committed to maintaining its existing 'permanent' workforce, and relies on high levels of employee loyalty to achieve productivity increases and flexibility, unrelated diversification requiring new skills and managerial techniques is unlikely to be undertaken. Where, on the other hand, economic actors operate in a variety of markets and integrate a variety of activities through managerial hierarchies, relative success in a single market or industry is less important than overall profitability. Here strategic choices are governed more by perceptions of opportunities in a variety of domains than by primary commitment to any particular one. In order to co-ordinate resources and evaluate performance across markets in such diversified businesses, standardized financial procedures and measures are more important than in specialized ones, and so accounting and finance skills tend to be more highly valued in diversified enterprise systems (Abegglen and Stalk, 1985, pp.178–179; Kagono *et al.*, 1985).

High levels of industrial specialization can, of course, be risky when markets and technologies are unstable, and diversification is often seen as a means of reducing such risk (Kay, 1984, pp.94–100; Richardson, 1972). In the case of the Japanese system, the long-term commitment to core employees increases this risk and restricts the feasibility of major diversification strategies, as does the institutionalization of relational contracting and moral obligations to industry partners. However, the much greater flexibility within authority hierarchies, facilitated by the high levels of mutual employer–employee commitment, and between businesses because of the sub-contracting system, enables Japanese firms to deal with change more effectively than the large, integrated and diversified Anglo-Saxon enterprise. Specialization here restricts choice of sector, and hence the ability to reallocate capital resources, but can enable rapid responses to external changes because of the externalization of most complementary but dissimilar activities, as the continued existence of the Japanese textile industry demonstrates (Dore, 1986). Just as the heavy reliance on bank loans in Japan is much less risky, in practice, than many Anglo-Saxon commentators have claimed (cf. Abegglen and Stalk, 1985, pp.149–179), so too specialization in core skills and knowledge can be highly effective when integrated with particular employment policies, growth strategies, relational contracting and a generally supportive institutional environment.

Variations in enterprise specialization and development are thus linked to differences in skill and experience homogeneity, in the degree of interdependence with industry partners and the extent of co-operation with contractors and preferences for growth within specialist sectors as opposed to diversification across sectors. Broadly, we can contrast enterprise structures which integrate a narrow range of activities and skills, and co-ordinate complementary activities through various kinds of contractual relationships, with those that authoritatively integrate a much wider set of resources, including those activities which are complementary for core functions, but dissimilar to them in terms of the skills and knowledge required to perform them effectively. The former tend to deal with uncertainty by being highly flexible and evolutionary in their patterns of strategic change, while the latter engage in much more discontinuous changes by reallocating resources to new activities as opportunities arise (cf. Kagono et al., 1985, pp.57–87).

Authority loyalty and the division of labour

This heading covers a further three dimensions. First, the importance of personal authority relationships and commitment to the individual leader, as opposed to impersonal and formal relations of subordination. Second, the degree of employer–employee commitment and loyalty to the enterprise as a whole, together with the employment policies that manifest and reproduce this. Third, the degree of work specialization and the emphasis on individual performance.

A key feature of enterprise systems is the degree to which authority is closely dependent on personal, particularistic connections or is relatively impersonal and linked to formal rules and procedures. Allied to this feature is the scope of authority relationships. Are they highly specific to particular responsibilities and activities or are they more diffuse and cover a wide range of tasks and concerns including extra-organizational ones? In general, the more paternalistic and personal are the relations of subordination, the more they tend to be broad in scope and not restricted to specific areas of work. Thus, the authority of the boss in the Chinese family business is wide-ranging and not precisely delimited, in contrast to more formal and narrowly specified forms of authority (Redding, 1989; Silin, 1976). Formal positions and responsibilities are less significant in highly personal authority systems than the nature of relationships with the owner.

A strong connection between ownership and control of economic activities is often associated with highly personal authority systems. Both in South Korea and Taiwan, direct owner control of enterprises is linked to personal and paternalist authority relations as well as to considerable centralization of control of decision-making. Owner-controlled businesses often exhibit strongly personal authority relations and high degrees of centralization, but this association is especially marked in these societies because of the tendency to infuse leadership with the moral qualities of individuals which inhibits delegation in 'Confucian' cultures (Pye, 1985; Silin, 1976; Yoo and Lee, 1987).

It is also due to the lack of formal trust mechanisms in Chinese and Korean societies for regulating relationships with non-kin groups and strangers, which means that personal loyalties are crucial in maintaining control. As Silin (1976, p.37) puts it: 'aside from kinship, no coherent model or set of organizing principles exists to govern interpersonal relations within the Confucian conceptual system'. As a result, most central management posts are filled by family members or by those with long standing and highly personal ties to the owner and superior–subordinate relations are often characterized by distrust and limited communication. This extends to the formal information and control system so that official channels are often bypassed in order to find out what is 'really' going on (Silin, 1976, pp.80–85).

A further aspect of authority relations in enterprise structures is the preferred managerial style. In particular, the extent to which supervisors are expected to be superior and more competent in all aspects of their work than subordinates varies considerably between the Japanese management system and others (Silin, 1976). While a major responsibility of the Japanese manager is to facilitate group performance and improve morale rather than demonstrate his superior expertise (Rohlen, 1979), in Taiwan, and other societies dominated by the Chinese family business, superiors are expected to be aloof, omnipotent and omniscient (Redding and Richardson, 1986; Redding and Wong, 1986; Silin, 1976). The distance between superior and subordinates and the extent to which the former are responsible for maintaining commitment and morale, then, vary considerably between enterprise systems (Liebenberg, 1982).

An important aspect of the internal organization of economic actors is the way in which employees are integrated into the organization and the employment practices by which commitment is elicited. Both the degree to which employers and employees are committed to each other on a long-term basis, and the ways in which such commitment is reinforced, vary considerably between enterprise structures. A further point about long-term commitments in East Asian businesses is their limited scope of application. In all three types considered here, core employees receive much better benefits and security than relatively unskilled and uneducated workers, young employees and women (Clark, 1979; Redding, 1989; Rohlen, 1974). For this privileged group of 'permanent' employees, the level of mutual commitment is high when compared to enterprise structures which rely primarily on the external labour market to recruit staff and operate market-based wage systems (Dore, 1973, pp.264–279; McMillan, 1985, pp.175–185).

In addition to relatively long-term commitments being made to male graduates and highly skilled manual workers (Koike, 1987), many large firms also link financial rewards to loyalty and organizational success. The importance of the regular bonus payments to Japanese incomes is well known and the Chinese New Year bonuses play a similar though less marked, role in the Chinese family business. A related means of increasing employee integration into the enterprise is to provide a finely graded hierarchy of posts, which enable rewards to be clearly identified and frequently allocated, and keep differentials relatively low (Dore, 1973, pp.94–115).

These employment practices and policies encourage considerable flexibility and mobility between tasks of the 'permanent' labour force as well as enterprise loyalty. Because employees' opportunities and identities are focused on individual organizations, rather than on more general occupational groupings based on certified expertise, they are more willing to change roles and acquire new, enterprise specific skills. Even where loyalty and commitment are less 'emotional' than in Japan, willingness to adapt to new technologies seems to be high in enterprise systems which reward loyalty and institutionalize organization-oriented wage systems rather than market-oriented ones (Dore, 1973, pp.384–402; Redding, 1989; Silin, 1976). Where, on the other hand, loyalties are more focused on externally acquired and certified skills, and employment practices are more market governed, internal flexibility and mobility is more constrained (Maurice et al., 1980).

These variations in commitment and employment practices are also related to the allocation and control of specific tasks to individuals and groups. The degree of the division of labour between individuals and the importance of formal job specification for determining roles and responsibilities are, in general, less in East Asian enterprise structures than in the USA and group tasks are often more important than individual ones (Lincoln et al., 1986). Where loyalties are more focused on the organization than on externally certified competences, tasks are not so tied to the specific skills of individuals and can be allocated on a broader, less tightly controlled basis to work groups. Similarly, if rewards are based more on long-term performance in a variety of roles within one narrowly focused enterprise, rather than on achievements in one job held for two or three years in a diversified structure, willingness to cooperate in group activities is likely to be higher and employees' emphasis on individual professional expertise lower. This relatively fluid division of labour and focus on group achievements is encouraged by the greater emphasis in some enterprise structures on group performance standards and reward systems.

The allocation of tasks and roles to individuals as a major feature of enterprise structures, then, is linked to the flexibility and mobility of employees between tasks, to their development of multiple, enterprise specific skills and to their willingness to co-operate in groups and the use of group based performance standards and reward systems. Highly specialized tasks limit flexibility and skill development within the enterprise and require more elaborate and formal means of co-ordinating them. They also tend to be associated with individually based reward systems and often inhibit co-operation across skill and role boundaries (Maurice et al., 1986).

Enterprise interdependence and co-ordination

Turning now to consider how enterprises are interconnected and their activities co-ordinated in different societies, there are two distinct features to be analysed. First, there is the extent to which dominant economic actors form alliances and groups across major sector boundaries— in addition to interdependencies within industries—that are relatively long term and help to reduce risks and uncertainty. Second, there is the extent to which strategies and plans are co-ordinated and orchestrated around more general objectives, typically by state agencies, and risks are shared by other collective structures. The first can be termed the degree of intersector horizontal co-ordination and the second the degree of vertical co-ordination.

The horizontal co-ordination of strategies and activities across industrial sectors varies considerably between bank-based Japanese business groups and the relatively independent and discrete Anglo-Saxon corporation operating in an impersonal and fairly remote market environment. In the former instance, enterprises exchange shareholdings, directors, information and sometimes senior managerial personnel, while in the latter they have few, if any, long-term ties to other businesses, except perhaps an overlapping directorship with a financial institution. Co-ordination across sectors here is achieved either by capital markets and the market for corporate control or by state agencies and plans. Thus the extent of long term horizontal linkages with businesses in other sectors is limited in capital-market-based financial systems (Zysman, 1983, pp.57–80). It is also low when the dominant economic actor authoritatively integrates a broad variety of capabilities and activities and yet is dependent on state agencies and banks, as in South Korea. Horizontal co-ordination in Taiwanese business groups and Hong Kong family businesses is achieved through common ownership and family membership, but such diversified groups do not dominate their economies in the same way that the Japanese ones do (Hamilton and Kao, 1987), and in general the Chinese family business does not seem to engage in long-term alliances and co-ordinated activities across sectors. It is either achieved through direct ownership of different businesses, or by opportunistic joint ventures with trusted partners who have personal relationships of long standing with the owner, or else not at all (Redding, 1989).

Vertical co-ordination of enterprise policies and activities is typically accomplished by the state, although banks may also play a part, as in J. P. Morgan's involvement in the restructuring of US railroads and US Steel (Chandler, 1977, pp.181–186, 361). It may be associated with considerable horizontal co-ordination, as in the case of Japan or not, as in South Korea. Typically linked to 'developmental' and 'plan rational' state policies (Johnson, 1982, pp.18–30), such co-ordination can vary considerably in degree between the direct manipulation of opportunities and threats exemplified by South Korea (Jones and Sakong, 1980, pp.79–127), and the more distant and indirect encouragements for exporters used by Taiwan (Cumings, 1987; Haggard, 1988; Johnson, 1987). It also varies in specificity to particular firms and industries, as opposed to broad economy-wide measures. Additionally, the way in which such co-ordination is achieved varies from direct administrative action, such as tax investigation and foreign exchange control, through manipulation of the credit system and financial incentives to state-sponsored meetings and information exchange. Finally, the purposes and focus of state co-ordination can vary from the implementation of broad, long-term industrial policies to relatively *ad hoc* and opportunistic attempts to influence individual investment decisions.

High levels of vertical co-ordination increase enterprise dependence on state agencies, and thereby reduce managerial autonomy, but also, of course, reduce enterprise risks and uncertainty. Thus while many Japanese business leaders complain about the power of MITI, they also take advantage of its co-ordinating role and support for particular initiatives (Dore, 1986, pp.28–132). By linking enterprise policies with each other and with overall state goals, such vertical co-ordination facilitates long-term planning and encourages investments that might otherwise be regarded as too risky. Similarly, it can reduce the costs of reducing capacity and changing priorities, as in the case of the Japanese textile industry (Dore, 1986).

Where, on the other hand, there is little vertical co-ordination of enterprise plans, economic actors are more autonomous and independent, but, equally, are also more isolated and have to bear risks on their own. Thus, major long-term commitments in fields where there is considerable uncertainty about outcomes are less likely to be made and risk reduction becomes a major strategic concern. Integration of critical resources and activities under central authoritative control, together with diversification of activities, is one way of dealing with this concern. Another is to focus on narrow specialist activities and rely on extensive subcontracting relationships policed by reputational networks, for flexibility and rapid responses to change, as in the Chinese family business. The large diversified corporation represents an attempt to control uncertainty by extending authority relations to potential threats, while the latter structure focuses on flexibility as the prime way of coping with an uncertain and threatening environment.

Overall, then, there are eight major ways of comparing and contrasting dominant economic actors in different societal contexts. First, there is the extent to which they specialize in particular business areas and are based on specific capabilities of skill, knowledge and experience. Second, they vary in their commitment to industrial partners and investment in relational contracting. Third, their patterns of growth and preferences for evolutionary as distinct from discontinuous strategies differ. Fourth, the significance of personal and particularistic authority relations within enterprise structures varies, as does, fifth, the extent of employer–employee commitment and the major ways of eliciting employee loyalty. Sixth, the division of labour and responsibilities differs in its specificity and degree of separation of individual roles and tasks. Seventh, economic actors vary in the extent of their inter-sector horizontal co-ordination and, eighth, in their dependence on forms of vertical co-ordination. These eight dimensions are listed in Table 1 together with their application to the three distinct East Asian configurations discussed earlier. For comparative purposes I also apply them to the modern US corporation as discussed by Chandler (1977) and others.

Table 1. East Asian enterprise structures

	Large Japanese enterprises	Korean *chaebol*	Chinese family businesses	US diversified corporation
Enterprise specialization and development				
Business specialization	High	Low	High	Low
Relational contracting	High	Low	Medium	Low
Evolutionary strategies	High	Medium	Medium	Low
Authority, loyalty and the division of labour				
Personal authority	Low	High	High	Low
Enterprise loyalty	High	Medium	Medium	Low
Role individuation	Low	Low	Low	High
Enterprise co-ordination				
Horizontal co-ordination	High	Low	Medium	Low
Vertical co-ordination	High	High	Low	Low

This table indicates that there are a number of different combinations of these eight characteristics of dominant economic actors that are viable in terms of competing successfully in world markets when established in particular social contexts. Thus the Japanese combination of high levels of business specialization, high levels of relational contracting and enterprise loyalty with considerable horizontal co-ordination between enterprises is by no means the only alternative to the managerially integrated and diversified US corporation. However, some combinations do seem unlikely to be either stable entities or economically successful. For example, highly specialized economic actors are unlikely to become established without some commitment to co-operative arrangements with sub-contractors and other industry partners and some means of ensuring trust over the medium term, just as high levels of relational contracting are improbable without some specialization. Similarly, evolutionary strategic changes are more likely when actors are relatively specialized in their capabilities. Opportunistic diversification into new sectors which require new skills is unlikely to be successfully integrated into such enterprises. Business specialization facilitates high levels of enterprise loyalty as well, although, of course, it is not sufficient on its own to produce this. In turn, it is facilitated by high levels of horizontal and vertical co-ordination, although these are not necessary conditions of business specialization. Other relationships between these dimensions depend on the characteristics of their societal contexts such as the education and training system, the organization of labour markets and the financial system as well as general features of the cultural and political systems.

CONCLUSIONS

The economic success of different sorts of economic actors in different East Asian societies, together with their high degree of similarity within those societies, suggest that: (a) there are a variety of forms of business organization which are competitive in world markets; (b) these vary in certain basic characteristics because of the institutional environment in which they become established, and (c) to a considerable extent, they are societally specific in that they would not function as effectively in different societal contexts. These points, in turn, emphasize the need for a comparative analysis of dominant economic actors across societies, which would examine the processes by which different kinds of enterprise structure became established and successful in different contexts, and the ways in which they operate effectively.

The dominant economic actors in Japan, South Korea, Taiwan and Hong Kong exhibit considerable variation in the range of economic activities they co-ordinate and develop through an authority system, in the way activities are co-ordinated and controlled and loyalties generated and, finally, their interdependence and co-ordination across sectors. These variations suggest eight distinct dimensions by which different types of enterprise structure can be compared and contrasted. These in turn are related to a number of subsidiary characteristics. Together, these dimensions describe distinctive business 'recipes' which become established and function effectively in different contexts. The factors that affect these processes include both specific institutional structures, such as the political and financial systems, as well as more diffuse and general phenomena such as cultural conventions, patterns of dependence and the foundations of social identities.

REFERENCES

Abegglen, J. C. and Stalk, G. (1985) *Kaisha, the Japanese Corporation*. Basic Books, New York.
Alford, B. (1976) 'Strategy and Structure in the UK Tobacco Industry'. In Hannah, L. (ed.) *Management Strategy and Business Development*. MacMillan, London.
Amsden, A. H. (1985) 'The Division of Labour is Limited by the Rate of Growth of the Market: the Taiwan Machine Tool Industry in the 1970s'. *Cambridge Journal of Economics*, **9**: 271–284.
Aoki, M. (1987) 'The Japanese Firm in Transition'. In Yarmamura, K. and Yasuba, Y. (eds) *The Political Economy of Japan I: the Domestic Transformation*. Stanford University, Stanford.
Bauer, M. and Cohen, E. (1981) *Qui Gouverne les Groups Industriels?* Seuil, Paris.
Cable, J. and Dirrheimer, M. J. (1983) 'Hierarchies and Markets. An Empirical Test of the Multidivisional Hypothesis in West Germany'. *International Journal of Industrial Organization*, **1**:46–52
Cable, J. and Yasuki, H. (1985) 'International Organisation, Business Groups and Corporate Performance. An Empirical Test of the Multidivisional Hypothesis in Japan'. *International Journal of Industrial Organization*, **3**: 401–420.
Chandler, A. D. (1977) *The Visible Hand*. Harvard University Press, Cambridge, Mass.

Child, J. and Tayeb, M. (1983) 'Theoretical Perspectives in Crossnational Organisational Research'. *International Studies of Management and Organisation*, **12**: 23–70.
Cho, D. S. (1987) *The General Trading Company*. D. C. Heath, Lexington, Mass.
Clark, R. (1979) *The Japanese Company*. Yale University Press.
Cumings, B. (1987) 'The Origins and Development of the Northeast Asian Political Economy'. In Deyo F. C. (ed.) *The Political Economy of the New Asian Industrialism*, pp.44-83. Cornell University Press, Ithaca, NY.
Cusumano, M. A. (1985) *The Japanese Automobile Industry: Technology and Management at Nissan and Toyota*. Harvard University Press, Cambridge, Mass.
Daems, H. (1983) 'The Determinants of the Hierarchical Organisation of Industry'. In Francis, A. *et al.* (eds) *Power, Efficiency and Institutions*, pp.35–53. Heinemann, London.
DeMaggio, P. J. and Powell, W. W. (1983) 'The Iron Cage Revisited: Institutional Isomorphism and Collective Rationality in Organisational Fields'. *American Sociological Review*, **48**: 147–160.
Dore, R. (1973) *British Factory–Japanese Factory*. Allen and Unwin, London.
Dore, R. (1986) *Flexible Rigidities*. Stanford University Press, Stanford.
DuBoff, R. B. and Herman, E. S. (1980) 'Alfred Chandler's New Business History: A Review'. *Politics and Society*, **10**: 87–110.
Eads, G. C. and Yamamura, K. (1987) 'The Future of Industrial Policy', In Yamamura, K. and Yasuba, Y. (eds) *The Political Economy of Japan I: The Domestic Transformation*, pp.423–468. Stanford University Press, Stanford.
Futatsugi, Y. (1986) *Japanese Enterprise Groups*. Kobe University, School of Business Administration.
Gold, T. B. (1986) *State and Society in the Taiwan Miracle*. Sharpe, Armonk, N.Y.
Goto, A. (1982) 'Business Groups in a Market Economy'. *European Economic Review*, **19**:53–70.
Haggard, S. (1988) 'The Politics of Industrialisation in the Republic of Korea and Taiwan'. In Hughes, H. (ed.) *Achieving Industrialisation in East Asia*, pp.260–282. Cambridge University Press, Cambridge.
Hamilton, G. and Kao, C. S. (1987) 'The Institutional Foundation of Chinese Business: the Family Firm in Taiwan'. Programme in East Asian Culture and Development, Working Paper Series, No. 8, University of California at Davis; Institute of Governmental Affairs.
Hamilton, G., Zeile, W. and Kim, W. J. (1989) 'The Network Structures of East Asian Economies'. In Clegg S. and Redding, G. (eds) *Capitalism in Contrasting Cultures*. de Gruyter, Berlin.
Hickson, D., Hinings, C. R., McMillan, C. J. and Schwitter, J. P. (1974) 'The Culture-Free Context of Organisational Structure: a Tri-national Comparison'. *Sociology*, **8**:59–80.
Hickson, D., McMillan, C. J., Azumi, K. and Horvath, D. (1979) 'Grounds for Comparative Organisation Theory: Quicksands or Hard Core?' In Lammers, C. J. and Hickson, D. J. (eds) *Organisations Alike and Unalike*, pp.25–41. Routledge and Kegan Paul, London.
Hofstede, G. (1980) *Culture's Consequences*. Sage, London.
Hofstede, G. (1983) 'The Cultural Relativity of Organisational Practices and Theories'. *Journal of International Business Studies*, **14**: 75–89.
Imai, K. and Itami, H. (1984) 'Interpretation of Organisation and Market. Japan's Firm and Market in Comparison with the US'. *International Journal of Industrial Organisation*, **2**: 285–310.
Jacobs, N. (1985) *The Korean Road to Modernisation and Development*. University of Illinois Press, Urbana.
Jamieson, I. (1978) 'Some Observations on Socio-Cultural Explanations of Economic Behaviour' *Sociological Review*, **26**:777–805.
Johnson, C. (1982) *MITI and the Japanese Miracle*. Stanford University Press, Stanford.
Johnson, C. (1987) 'Political Institutions and Economic Performance: The Government–Business Relationship in Japan, South Korea and Taiwan'. In Deyo, F. C. (ed.) *The Political Economy of The New Asian Industrialism*, pp.136–164. Cornell University Press.
Jones, L. and Sakong, I. (1980) *Government Business and Entrepreneurship in Economic Development: The Korean Case*. Harvard University Press, Cambridge, Mass.
Kagono, T., Alonaka, I., Sakakibara, K. and Okumara, A. (1985) *Strategic vs. Evolutionary Management*. North Holland, Amsterdam.
Kay, N. (1984) *The Emergent Firm*. Macmillan, London.
Kim, K. D. (1979) *Man and Society in Korea's Economic Growth*. Seoul National University Press, Seoul.
Kiyonari, T. and Nakamura, H. (1980) 'The Establishment of the Big Business System'. In Sato K. (ed.) *Industry and Business in Japan*, pp.247–284. M. E. Sharpe, New York.

Koike, K. (1987) 'Human Resource Development and Labour-Management Relations'. In Yamamura, K. and Yasuba, Y. (eds). *The Political Economy of Japan I: The Domestic Transformation*, pp.289–330. Stanford University Press, Stanford.
Kono, T. (1984) *Strategy and Structure of Japanese Enterprises*. Macmillan, London.
Lau, L. J. (ed.) (1986) *A Comparative Study of Economic Growth in South Korea and Taiwan*. ICS Press, San Francisco.
Lawriwsky, M. L. (1984) *Corporate Structure and Performance*. Croom Helm, London.
Levy, B. (1988) 'Korean and Taiwanese Firms as International Competitors: the Challenges Ahead'. *Columbia Journal of World Business* (Spring): 43-51.
Liebenberg, R. D. (1982) *'Japan Incorporated' and 'The Korean Troops': A Comparative Analysis of Korean Business Organisations*. Unpublished MA Thesis, Dept. of Asian Studies, University of Hawaii.
Limlingan, V. S. (1986) *The Overseas Chinese in Asean: Business Strategies and Management Practices*. Vita Development Corporation, Pasig, Metro Manila.
Lincoln, J. R. and Kalleberg, A. L. (1985) 'Work Organisation and Workforce Commitment: A Study of Plants and Employees in the US and Japan'. *American Sociological Review*, **50**: 738–760.
Lincoln, J. R. and McBridge, K. (1987) 'Japanese Industrial Organisation in Comparative Perspective'. *Annual Review of Sociology*, **13**: 238–312.
Lincoln, J. R., Hanada, M. and McBridge, K. (1986) 'Organizational Structures in Japanese and US Manufacturing'. *Administrative Science Quarterly*, **31**:338–364.
Maurice, M. (1979) 'For a Study of "The Societal Effect": Universality and Specificity in Organisation Research'. In Lammers, C. J. and Hickson D. J. (eds) *Organisations Alike and Unlike*, pp.42–60. Routledge and Kegan Paul, London.
Maurice, M., Sorge, A. and Warner, M. (1980) 'Societal Differences in Organizing Manufacturing Units'. *Organisation Studies*, **1**: 59–86.
Maurice, M., Sellier, F. and Silvestre, J. (1986) *The Social Bases of Industrial Power*. M.I.T. Press, Cambridge, Mass.
McMillan, C. (1985) *The Japanese Industrial System*. de Gruyter, Berlin.
Michell, T. (1988) *From a Developing to a Newly Industrialised Country: The Republic of Korea, 1961–82*. ILO, Geneva.
Miyazaki, Y. (1980) 'Excessive Competition and the Formation of *Keiretsu*'. In Sato, K. (ed) *Industry and Business in Japan*. pp. 53–73. M. E. Sharpe, New York.
Morikawa, H. (1976) 'Management Structure and Control Devices for Diversified *Zaibatsu* Business'. In Nakagawa K. (ed) *Strategy and Structure of Big Business*. University of Tokyo Press, Tokyo.
Myers, R. H. (1986) 'The Economic Development of the Republic of China on Taiwan'. In Lau, L. J. (ed.) *Modes of Development*. ICS Press, San Francisco.
Orru, M., Biggart, N. and Hamilton, G. (1988) 'Organisational Isomorphism in East Asia: Broadening the New Institutionalism'. Program In East Asian Culture and Development, Research Working Paper Series No. 10, Institute of Governmental Affairs, University of California, Davis.
Penrose, E. T. (1980) *The Theory of the Growth of the Firm*. Blackwell, Oxford.
Pugh, D. S. and Redding, G. (1985) 'The Formal and the Informal: Japanese and Chinese Organisation Structures'. In S. R. Clegg et al. (eds) *The Enterprise and Management in East Asia*. University of Hong Kong, Centre for Asian Studies.
Pye, L. (1985) *Asian Power and Politics: the Cultural Dimensions of Authority*. Harvard University Press, Cambridge, Mass.
Redding, G. R. (1989) *The Spirit of Chinese Capitalism*. de Gruyter, Berlin.
Redding, G. R. and Richardson, S. (1986) 'Participative Management and its Varying Relevance in Hong Kong and Singapore'. *Asia Pacific Journal of Management*, **3**: 76–98.
Redding, G. and Tam, S. (1985) 'Networks and Molecular Organisations: an Exploratory View of Chinese firms in Hong Kong'. In Mun, K. C. and Chan T. S. (eds) *Perspectives in International Business*. Chinese University Press, Hong Kong.
Redding, G. R. and Wong, G. Y. Y. (1986) 'The Psychology of Chinese Organisational Behaviour'. In Bond, M. (ed) *The Psychology of the Chinese People*, pp. 267–295. Oxford University Press, Oxford.
Richardson, G. (1972) 'The Organisation of Industry'. *Economic Journal*, **82**: 883–896.
Rohlen, T. P. (1974) *For Harmony and Strength: Japanese White-Collar Organisation in Anthropological Perspective*. University of California Press, Berkeley, Cal.

Rohlen, T. P. (1979) 'The Company Work Group'. In Vogel, E. F. (ed.) *Modern Japanese Organisation and Decision-Making*, pp.185–209. Tuttle, Tokyo.

Rose, M. (1985) 'Universalism, Culturalism and the Aix Group: Promise and Problems of a Social Approach to Economic Institutions'. *European Sociological Review*, **1**: 65–83.

Shimokawa, K. (1985) 'Japan's *Keiretsu* System: The Case of the Automobile Industry'. *Japanese Economic Studies*, Summer: 331.

Silin, R. H. (1976) *Leadership and Values. The Organisation of Large Scale Taiwanese Enterprises*. Harvard University Press, Cambridge, Mass.

Sit, V. F. S. and Wong, S. L. (1988) *Hong Kong Manufacturing: Growth and Challenges of an Export-Orientated System Dominated by Small and Medium Industries*. Unpublished report, Centre for Asian Studies, University of Hong Kong.

Sorge, A. (1983) 'Cultured Organisations'. *International Studies of Management and Organisations*, **12**: 106–138.

Stinchcombe, A. L.(1983) *Economic Sociology*. Academic Press, New York.

Tam, S. (1989) 'Centrifugal Versus Centripetal Growth Processes: Contrasting Ideal Types for Conceptualising the Developmental Patterns of Chinese and Japanese firms'. In Clegg, S.and Redding, G. (eds) *Capitalism in Contrasting Cultures*. de Gruyter, Berlin.

Trevor, M. (1988) *Toshiba's New British Company*. Policy Studies Institute, London.

Wade, R. (1988) 'The Role of Government in Overcoming Market Failure: Taiwan, Republic of Korea and Japan'. In Hughes, H. (ed.) *Achieving Industrialization in East Asia*, pp.129–163. Cambridge University Press, Cambridge.

Ward, B. E.(1972) 'A Small Factory in Hong Kong: Some Aspects of its Internal Organisation'. In Willmott, W. E. (ed.) *Economic Organisation in Chinese Society*. Stanford University Press, Stanford.

Whitley, R. D. (1987) 'Taking Firms Seriously as Economic Actors: Towards a Sociology of Firm Behaviour'. *Organisation Studies*, **8**: 125–147.

Yasuoka, S. (1976) 'The Tradition of Family Business in the Strategic Decision Process and Management Structure of *Zaibatsu* Business: Mitsui, Sumitomo and Mitsubishi'. In Nakagawa, K. (ed.) *Strategy and Structure of Big Business*. University of Tokyo Press, Tokyo.

Yoo, S. and Lee, S. M. (1987) 'Management Style and Practice in Korean *Chaebols*'. *California Management Review*, **29**: 95–110.

Yoshihara, K. (1988) *The Rise of Ersatz Capitalism in South East Asia*. Oxford University Press, Oxford.

Zysman, J. (1983) *Governments, Markets and Growth: Financial Systems and the Politics of Industrial Change*. Cornell University Press, Ithaca.

15

The Nature and Competitiveness of Japan's *Keiretsu*

Angelina Helou

What is at issue is the comparative performance of a Japanese economic institution, the *Keiretsu*.[1] But the initial task is to identify such an institution and to introduce its specific characteristics. Accordingly, the institution's competitiveness would imply first an understanding of the nature of its mechanics, i.e. as a matter of priority or as a pre-condition to an interest in the competitive performance of its products (tangible or intangible) in the market-place.

At best, a definition of the Japanese *Keiretsu*, from the viewpoint of an outside observer, is the perception of it as a type of concept or simply a certain pattern of relationships. Ultimately then, it would be a matter of interest in the performance of the individual firm within such a concept and in the contextual influence which would have a bearing on its behaviour;[2] and, more significantly, would also be an interest in its behaviour as a 'related' versus a more 'independent' economic entity.[3]

As a pattern of relationships, the Japanese *Keiretsu* itself has not been set or developed in a vacuum. It functions within a wider (designed) context—that of the Japanese national economy, with a particular industrial philosophy serving as an underlying force.[4] Thus the Japanese *Keiretsu*, or an individual firm, each, in turn, fits in according to a designed market order. This is indicative that the role of the 'visible' hand (in a general Japanese economic setting) is more apparent than that of the 'invisible' hand.[5]

In a primary sense, a *Keiretsu* individual firm becomes competitive due to the induction of economic powers from the *Keiretsu*'s own milieu and its indigenous interactive tendencies. In turn, this milieu itself is a sphere of economic power and can maintain interactive tendencies in the manner it does thanks to its own existence within a national economic context which, on account of its own setting and behavioural patterns, tends to nurture and sustain the *Keiretsu*'s development with implicit recognition of its instrumental role in the achievement of the country's industrial policy objectives.[6]

What, at this point, may then be deduced is that the competitive nature of the Japanese individual firm is, in an effective manner, the subject-matter of the principle of 'Japanese relativity' and its appreciation of inter-relatedness in economic behaviour. Thus, if a certain economic unit (e.g. a firm) is to function in the optimum manner, it has to exist and be maintained in an expedient relative status, in principle contrasted with its standing and behaviour under *laissez-faire* economics. Accordingly, the *modus operandi* in the Japanese case represents a

This article was first published in the *Journal of World Trade*, Vol. 25, No. 3 (June 1991) and is reproduced here by kind permission of its publisher. Copyright © 1991 Werner Publishing Company Ltd.

state of interactive behaviour among economic units and a state of interdependence between each and the whole.

Theoretically also, the *Keiretsu* may be thought of precisely in terms of a 'Japanese methodology', i.e. as opposed to an organizational form. Such an impression (or even viewpoint) may, in turn, be interpreted to be reflective of the nature of the Japanese's own precepts and principles of industrial organization and economic management which stem from a Japanese industrial rationality and economic mind.[7]

Simply then, a *Keiretsu*, although it is subject to being treated as an organization, may also be essentially interpreted as originating from a state of mind and can take effect, in some form, in any market where the Japanese have economic interests and exercise efforts to establish economic institutions.

A basic premise is, therefore, a matter of institutional design and engineering. The standard architecture of Japanese homes bears a sharp contrast with that in any western country. Given this simple fact, should not the principle of their economic engineering also bear striking differences? If they inherently do, the point does not prevent an appreciation of the resulting structures; the underlying tendencies also deserve more than an equal appreciation—for forms are not as dynamic and mobile as philosophies and ideas.

Focusing specifically on the question of competitiveness, interest, in general, reflects on the prevalence of a certain level of international recognition of a *Keiretsu's* attributes. Pragmatically the first Japanese reaction to this effect (domestically) would be to duly maintain and reinforce the competitive setting.[8] It would then seek to transplant outside Japan, convinced by the idea that a state of international recognition implies a tendency towards necessarily positive international acceptance.[9]

Yet an approach towards looking into the 'internalities' of the *Keiretsu* competitive standing remains to be defined. The question here lends itself to two main interpretations: (a) theoretical, i.e. on the basis of an admission that the Japanese economic and organizational theory and thought are fundamentally different from western ideas; and (b) by direct focus on outstanding comparative results of the Japanese *Keiretsu* as an organization.[10] (In both instances, however, one needs to account for the fact that the criteria for defining and assessing institutional competitiveness differs between the Japanese and the non-Japanese.)

The question that is to be addressed here is the competitiveness of the Japanese style of organization. Competitiveness, in this context, also means: understanding the composite nature that is being brought into shape under such a style; the reference to the key factors which enforce the performance of the different parts involved and that of the whole; and a value judgement as to whether or not the Japanese method or style (*Keiretsu*) is necessarily at odds with non-Japanese economies, which renders the total question of competitiveness the subject for a good debate.[11]

Furthermore, a Japanese *Keiretsu* (style) is maintained, and run, by the existence of an effective 'core' (its substance). Such a simple frame of reference applies to the total organisation of the economy, of an industry, of an industrial group and of an individual firm.[12]

In principle, the core represents a solid composition of a number of parts, in varying types and proportions depending on different situations. It is being maintained by a condition (or criterion) the Japanese normally interpret as 'cohesion'. The crux of the matter is, therefore, their tendencies in terms of what may be identified as the 'economics of cohesion'.[13]

Simply then, understanding the Japanese *Keiretsu* is to understand the Japanese way of bringing parts together and finding out what is involved in their own concept of 'economic cohesion'. *Is it then by understanding what is a 'core' in the Japanese economic setting that one is likely to unveil a clue to the nature of the competitiveness of the economic institutions?*

I. KNOWN DEFINITIONS

A popular synonymity prevails between the two concepts of industrial groups and *Keiretsu*.[14] It also generally claimed that a *Keiretsu* represents a post-World War II image of a pre-war predecessor—the *Zaibatsu*.[15] Against these general views is the existence of identifiable industrial groups, on their own merit, in Western economies.[16] Thus there is an element of ambiguity in the total impression, overshadowing (if not shunning) direct focus on a Japanese *Keiretsu* as a separate entity or concept.

Categorically, however, these entities (*Keiretsu*) tend to fall into two general types. The main criteria for such distinctions have been implicitly that of control and the direction of inter-firm ties assumed. One type is commonly introduced as the horizontally tied type representing such industrial groups as Mitsubishi, Mitsui Sumitomo, Dai-Ichi Kangyo Bank (DKB), Fuyo and Sanwa.[17] The second, with vertical tendencies, concentrates on enterprises centred by a large parent company, i.e. with a good number of medium-and small-sized firms under its aegis and where the principle of vertical links applies, based, in particular, on industrial division of labour and technological criteria.[18] Although there exists a distinct and in-depth meaning characteristic of both the Japanese horizontal and vertical tendencies, there is also a tendency to see little distinction in their disposition in general, underlying the fact that both horizontal and vertical principles apply universally. Undoubtedly the two principles are universal but their understanding, manner and purpose in application, do differ between Japanese and non-Japanese approaches.

What is further to be emphasized in the case of Japan is that the two distinct patterns which exist are not, in effect, exclusive. A *Keiretsu* formed through horizontal ties accommodates enterprises that are being formed through vertical integration. Separately, enterprises which are of the latter type but comparatively independent, are often inclined to establish certain links with one horizontally held industrial group or the other.[19] Thus linkages among Japanese firms represent an economic effort that is both strategic and tactical.[20]

Yet, in relation to the two cases, popular emphasis has repeatedly been on certain ties which exist and which sharply mark their type.[21] But concrete bridges do exist and may differ by type; so do certain ties among member-firms in a Japanese *Keiretsu*. Bridges and ties exist, however, for a purpose, e.g. for the flow of traffic. Thus the emphasis is then on two aspects: structure of the links; and the flow (i.e. for which such a structure is being created and maintained).

Basically, in the background, is the Japanese perception of the rationale of an enterprise—cluster as an economic phenomenon. This has manifested itself in the organization of the pre-war *Zaibatsu*, in the form of the *Keiretsu* and, perhaps, will do so in some other form in the foreseeable future:[22] it is general Japanese strategy when constructing economic institutions and envisaging their operational systems.

Such a phenomenon implies dynamism. The *Keiretsu*, due to the very nature of its composition and behaviour (internally and in relation to its market), is inherently of a changing rather than static order. In simple terms, it takes the form of a system encompassing a number of sub-systems—and the principle of the system's dynamics runs through all.

Thus it would be conceivable to reckon on the existence of good possibilities towards changes and modifications in the kind of ties involved (horizontal and vertical), i.e. as opposed to assuming that these ties are of a given and rigid character.

Again the principle of 'Japanese relativity' becomes vivid. Enterprise clusters, as economic phenomena, are relative to periods or stages in the industrial history of the country. This, interestingly enough, puts the given definition of a *Keiretsu* in an historical perspective. The notion also creates an interest in the manner in which the defined types evolve and in forms that would duly be acquired.

Thus a specific interest would focus on the changing nature of a cluster (i.e. as opposed to a general interest in its form on the whole). The central point would then be the nature of its 'core' and, more specifically, that of its dynamics. The frame of reference here is the Japanese-type pursuit of 'cohesion-economics'. At a different level, it is the general understanding that a *Keiretsu* is more a result of a Japanese methodology as contrasted with being seen as a form of organization. So, as a matter of principle, methods are innately subject to continuous revision and change.[23]

More precisely, however, a primary criterion underlying the Japanese understanding of cohesion-economics is their own concept of 'cost'. The nearest definition of the term implies two trends: one towards the optimum use of inputs (involving their methods towards this end) and the other, the optimization of results—both numerically and qualitatively.[24] Cohesion-economics, as a Japanese concept, tends therefore to identify with their understanding and practice of 'cost-economics'. A *Keiretsu* then, of any type, represents a pragmatic manifestation of these hypotheses of 'concentrate' of economic thought.

A. Established pattern(s)

A prototype of a *Keiretsu*, built by horizontal links, is normally seen among those industrial groups with a comparatively strong *Zaibatsu* lineage.[25] An answer to why this is so maintains sufficient points of interest to merit being pursued on its own. In terms of priority, however, the question that is addressed here focuses on the identifiable features of the 'model', attempting to read through its nature and its standing within the country's industrial dynamics.

An overall, and perhaps indispensable feature, rests on quantitative indices, e.g. scope, size and economic power.[26] Counting, for instance, the subsidiaries and affiliates of key *Keiretsu* firms, as well as their branch offices, domestic and overseas, their magnitude tends to be representative more of an economy than an institution.[27] Such a view is supplemented, in particular, by the 'closed nature' or boundaries drawn among these groups.

A different feature is a common tendency to bring together representatives of *Keiretsu* firms, at different levels, for joint consultation, policy-making and the monitoring of activity developments. A good example is the Presidents' Association, constituted of top executives of key *Keiretsu* companies.[28] Also *ad-hoc Keiretsu* missions and study groups are continuously formed to provide feed-back to the activities of the standing committees and more permanent bodies.[29]

A third general feature is based on the central role played by major *Keiretsu* institutions—that of general trader (*sogo shosha*) and bank.[30] The former (as a matter of *Keiretsu* policy) is attributed with a special organizing function and leads in bringing the group's firms together in joint ventures, domestically or overseas.[31] Such a role became significant due, in part, to the trader's own economic nature and, particularly, in the light of its comparative superiority in research and information technology.[32]

In turn the position of a *Keiretsu* bank is particularly strategic. This can be seen on account of: its own position within the nucleus of a *Keiretsu* financial institution; the general tendency of Japanese industrial enterprises towards a comparatively high level of capital gearing; the Japanese's shareownership pattern reflecting on a concentration with institutional shareholders—financial in particular.[33] Thus a *Keiretsu* bank assumes a catalystic role, i.e. in terms of pooling resources, it maintains a control power on the basis of provision of funds and shareownership, and provides guidance to corporate investment behaviour and opportunities.

A further general feature takes the form of a drive towards a general objective: *Keiretsu* cohesion. Exhibited in such a drive is a keen sense of industrial competitiveness carried in line with concurrent industrial policy objectives, and in the form of a tense race with a *Keiretsu* counterpart.[34]

A more scrutinizing approach would, however, be interested in examining the type and nature of inter-firm ties witnessed in the case of a *Keiretsu*, with a simultaneous interest to reveal and formulate the nature of a related resource strategy. This brings forth the concept of the *Keiretsu* as a nexus of relationships. But the network is being built in order to accommodate certain patterns in the flow of resources which, in turn, lean towards promoting the development and level of competitiveness of the *Keiretsu* enterprises. (Relationships between patterns in resources' flow and the promotion of cohesion–cost-economics–within a *Keiretsu*, are assumed here to be very close; the two tendencies, in principle, concur.)

(i) *Specific ties*

The point, at this level, is to look further than the identification of the kind of inter-firm *Keiretsu* ties that exist and to become more interested in accompaniments, ramifications and trigger effects.[35] Instant examples are seen in interlocked shareownership and in the Japanese practice of industrial division of labour or specialization.[36] (Whereas the former type of ties are a popular target in literature and foreign concern over the *Keiretsu*, the latter, applied with special effectiveness within a *Keiretsu*, have been either ignored as a good source of inter-firm links or taken for granted. These two fundamental tendencies are, however, seen here to be characteristically reinforcing, rather than separate and exclusive.)

Mutual share ownership and the Japanese principles of industrial specialization may actually then be seen as the two sides of the same coin. As twinned aspects (at least implicitly), in a *Keiretsu* economic strategy, the one relates, in particular, to the Japanese way of thinking in finance and the other, specifically, to their understanding of industrial productivity. Thus *Keiretsu* firms are held together by a counterfaced financially industrial criterion.

(a) *Interlocked shareholding.* A common indicator of the magnitude (and change over time) of the practice binding 'key' group companies is the average ratio of reciprocal shareownership; a comparative synopsis to this effect is provided in Table 1.[37] What should be simultaneously considered is the vertical shareholding pattern between *Keiretsu* industrial enterprises and their subsidiaries and related smaller companies. Thus, as a matter of strategic location on its own merit, any one of the key industrial companies becomes empowered on the basis of a duly acquired stability, i.e. being in a state of balance or the subject of the general network of mutuality, and resting on an in-depth base constituted of a layered pyramid of enterprises.[38]

A contrasting norm with the Japanese mutual shareholding practice is to issue corporate stocks in open capital markets, i.e. where individuals (and institutions) seek subscription in anticipation of dividends and striking profitable deals. The tendency thus implies a comparatively high level of corporate stock circulation and comes to represent a field of behaviour which determines the general style of corporate management and even the life-cycle of enterprises.[39]

Explicitly, profitability and a high level of dividends become primary targets and good criteria for efficient corporate management or a condition underlying turnover of corporate executives; the same phenomena have been accountable for the creation and activation of the takeover market.

Mutual shareholding, Japanese style, prompts the pursuit of investment expansion (i.e. as opposed to high margins of profit). This is duly based on an order of stability which may be identified as a 'corporate balance'.[40] Investment expansion, in turn, is to be seen in a 'mutual' perspective working with a state of stability for cause and effect.

Table 1. Development of interlocked shareholding ratios of Japan's leading six industrial groups

Group	1953	1957	1973	1975	1981	1987
Mitsui	6.2	11.0	17.4	17.3	18.2	17.1
Mitsubishi	1.3	16.4	26.8	29.4	25.2	27.8
Sumitomo	7.0	21.2	27.0	26.8	26.2	24.2
Fuyo	—	—	13.6	13.9	14.6	15.6
DKB	—	—	—	—	15.4	12.5
Sanwa	—	—	—	14.5	11.7	16.5

Sources: Robert J. Ballon, Iwao Tomita and Hajime Usami, *Financial Reporting In Japan*, Tokyo: Kodansha International Ltd., 1976. Iwao Nakatani, 'The Economic Role of Financial Corporate Grouping', in M. Aoki (ed.) *The Economic Analysis of the Japanese Firm*, North Holland, Amsterdam, 1984. 'Six Industrial Groups in Japanese Economy', *The Oriental Economist*, December 1982; and 'Intimate Links Within Japan's Corporate Groups', *Tokyo Business Today*, January 1989.

Also mutuality in stock ownership induces reciprocity in management and interlocked directorship. Communality in management talent is also exhibited in joint committees and conferences at different corporate levels.[41] Effectively the managerial behaviour and attributes here rest on the Japanese practice of life-employment while neither the market forces of labour, shares, or corporate takeovers, disturb a managerial function.

A *Keiretsu* has, then, a management pool which is also fed by separate *Keiretsu* information resources and know-how pools.[42] Its individual enterprises are involved but at the same time they have access to the different common resources. Thus each one of them has an advantage as it is covered by a certain quantum of management expertise beyond that which it could maintain or afford itself, in an individual capacity, and is so positioned that it has the channels (various links) to enable it to resort and utilize the general management capacities.

Against the preceding picture the following advantageous tendencies can be envisaged: (a) given the wide, and potentially widening, scope of the *Keiretsu* managerial world and resources management of individual enterprises, it would be possible to concentrate more on the internalities of their own companies; they could also apply themselves to funnelling know-how; (b) management cost per firm would be reduced on account of the distilled know-how being received, the low turnover of managerial staff (if at all) and the effective application of know-how; and (c) there would be a state of general diffusion of know-how given the fact that it would not be comparatively rare nor restricted to a minority.

If the Japanese interlocked shareholding does not itself totally and directly contribute to the creation of a *Keiretsu* common managerial pool in the manner described above, there is sufficient reason to argue its validity as a basic condition to the effectiveness of the Japanese management science. Simply then, although the practice stands in terms of the purely pragmatic matter of inter-firm ties, it serves to prompt further inter-firm links with a consequential degree of cohesion. Thus, in brief, the ownership tendency is at the same time, a typical tendency in Japanese management.

From a different perspective the practice of interlocked shareholding could be evaluated, specifically, by focusing on the status and behaviour of *Keiretsu* financial institutions. In the first instance, these institutions represent a distinct inter-related structure. They themselves as a 'set', reflect on a concentration of shareownership in a *Keiretsu's* mutual shareholding network; they also keep a heavy proportion of the corporate stocks issued to the public.

A relationship between the two conditions, in terms of cause and effect, remains an open question. It may be speculated that what results is an empowered position, serving as a lever, in relation to other *Keiretsu* affiliates and subsequently as a springboard for an effective role in the finance market both domestically and overseas.[43]

Simply stated, the Japanese banks' position in the *Keiretsu's* interlocked shareholding structure together with their role in stockownership of Japanese enterprises in general (i.e. as stable stockholders) combine to constitute a good base for maintaining and developing their links with industrial enterprises. This also gives a clue towards understanding and interpreting the development of the competitive power of Japanese banks and other financial institutions.[44]

Interpreted differently, interlocked shareholding could be seen as a means (or method) by which the Japanese can pool financial resources and provide stable channels to accommodate the flow of these resources. Thus the practice represents a major component of their finance strategies and the nature of their finance management.

Different glimpses of the general sphere of understanding would reveal for example: (a) specific patterns of relationships and inter-relatedness among the financial institutions of the *Keiretsu*; (b) the supplementary financial role of the *Keiretsu's sogo shosha*; and (c) the highly geared capital structure of *Keiretsu* enterprises.[45] A crucial question is whether these features could be maintained if it were not for the fundamental practice of interlocked shareholding.

To the individual *Keiretsu* firms, financial resources, as a matter of principle, become guaranteed. Their costs are mainly fixed (interest payments) allowing and prompting the introduction of long-term strategies to cover regularity in financial expenses which accordingly assume a structured position in the enterprise's activities. (The alternative carries with it a cost of capital under scarcity, change or interruption in the production-flow on account of capital shortage or scrutiny and a tendency to earmark profits for distribution to shareholders interested mainly in the amounts of the dividends received, i.e. a general state which tends to inhibit or restrict the flow of funds towards the promotion of operational activities proper.)

In a nutshell, what the argument amounts to is to propose that interlocked shareholding, as witnessed in a Japanese *Keiretsu*, represents a ground base for their kind of managerial science in general, and to that of their finance management in particular. Thus, it would be too controversial to assume that the tendency is monopolistic or contravenes the principle of free market forces. This assumption would be alien to the Japanese setting not because they cling to monopolistic tendencies, but because in their economic rationality mutual shareholding is more of a technique than an objective.

Therefore, there is more attached to the practice of their corporate culture than to be seen purely as means of transacting in corporate shares. The practice itself is not absolute; its full use and implications are dependent on other Japanese economic tendencies.

(b) *Industrial ties.* As an economic phenomenon the Japanese style of interlocked shareholding is supported by the Japanese's own concept of industrial division of labour. The first is the key to understanding their finance strategies and activities. The latter, in turn, is the key to understanding their industrial performance. Are the two practices inseparable?

A *Keiretsu*, in the sense described above, contributes to the optimization of the two phenomena. It provides a workshop for their application although there is room to believe that a *Keiretsu* itself endures, and is what it is, due to the existence of the two fundamental conditions.

What the standing is of the *Keiretsu* itself in the performance of the Japanese economy, takes the form of a separate question. Yet it is of some significance to introduce it at this point, with the understanding that such a question may go further and address the specific corresponding standing of interlocked shareholding and industrial specialization. (In other words, to function appropriately towards national industrial and economic objectives, both interlocked shareholding and industrial division of labour are to be accommodated or manifested in a Japanese *Keiretsu.*)

One aspect of Japanese industrial specialization represents functional concentration by firms.[46] A state of interdependence or inter-firm ties duly formed, works to guarantee markets by one firm to another. This tendency contributes towards the development and sophistication of the separate firm's own type of activity which, in turn, increases the degree of interdependence.

For example, a *Keiretsu* manufacturer concentrates on production, relying on the *Keiretsu* general trader for marketing and trade. Each provides a certain amount of guarantee in terms of sponsorship and stable markets. This, in turn, leads to mutuality in functional sophistication. This tendency is multiplied because other institutions, besides the manufacturer and the general trader, are, at the same time, being involved.[47]

Functional interdependence and the manner in which it works and contributes to the development of the different enterprises would also crucially lead to a situation when certain *Keiretsu* enterprises acquire key positions (big brother) among other *Keiretsu* firms.[48] The key role expresses itself here in, for instance, *Keiretsu* decision-making and effecting the desired degree of cohesion.

The key position of enterprises may, from a different perspective, be identified as a condition based on the existence of 'pools' of resources.[49] Thus each one of them becomes a resource reference on its own merits. (For instance, a bank would represent a resource reference in finance, a general trader a reference of multiple nature, and manufacturers representing, in particular, a good number of intangibles.)[50]

What may need to be underlined here is that the *Keiretsu* separate pools of resources gain comparative advantages, not only because of how they stand and develop internally, but also because of their typical potential exhibited within their immediate universe. For example, due to the general industrial principle of interrelatedness within a *Keiretsu*, especially as each of its enterprises maintains a comparative advantage because of access to the resources of the other, there is potential for the development of internal resourcefulness and more potential in terms of readiness in resources transfusion.

(ii) *Resource strategy*

The impression of an established model of a *Keiretsu* so far has been primarily based on its standing as a structure made up of certain types of ties and links. As significant an approach is to envisage the *Keiretsu* as a matter of Japanese 'economics of resources'.[51] Ties and links exist for a purpose. One assumption (if not a real fact) is that such a purpose is the maintenance and use of resources. A skill in creating and maintaining ties, coupled with one in pooling and use (or distribution) or resources becomes, therefore, the *raison d'être* of a Japanese *Keiretsu*.

Pooling represents one principle. Such a principle is applied along with principles in methods of distribution. The tendencies also cover technologies and Japanese know-how in resource utilization. Thus, distinctively, in relation to a *Keiretsu*, there is a Japanese method of pooling resources, resource distribution and resource utilization at destination.

A pragmatic analysis of these three areas becomes necessary in order to understand the economic dynamics of the *Keiretsu*, i.e. as separate from understanding its structure. (It is quite valid to raise the question at this point as to whether dismantling the *Keiretsu* structure would mean a change in the nature of its economic dynamics or whether the Japanese are smart enough to manipulate, and so modify, the nature of the *Keiretsu* structure while maintaining, if not enforcing, its economic dynamics.)

For example, finance units are pooled from where financial technology is at best; circulation takes effect on the basis of expert knowledge with industrial criteria; and utilization is scrutinized, i.e. knowing what the resource is meant for and being conscious of the process of its circulation; for money does not end up in the *Keiretsu* enterprise but tends to return to the pools from which it originated.[52]

Resource economics applies in the case of raw materials, labour (as a resource), finance, technology and other fields. The main principles in each case include a tendency to pool precepts in allocation and principles for resource utilization.[53] What the total implies is a keen interest in the related units, meticulous follow-up of its movement, interest in the manner in which it combines with its own kind and with other different resources, and the manner in which it is being handled at all stages. This may sum up—in terms of a Japanese perception of cost—its implications and control.[54]

Here there is a certain difference between an interest in cost as an economic factor in the general sense and the Japanese tendency in 'cost-economics'. For example, what generally matters in relation to an interest in cost in the first instance is a reduced level in order to maximize profit. In contrast the Japanese understanding is more representative of a science and skills in handling the different components and in pursuing their movement. A frame of reference is the achievement of cohesion and what the Japanese normally refer to as 'harmony'.

Although the term tends to assume mystical characteristics, in the real sense it implies a state reflecting the optimum manner of combining production factors. It is a state of making the best use of the minimum while implicitly or explicitly aiming for high quality levels of results.

In effect, a *Keiretsu*, in terms of its links and ties and general interest in cohesion, may, as a framework, be seen as a prerequisite to the effective application of Japanese cost-economics. Yet the *Keiretsu* as an institution may, however, have prompted the development of the Japanese science of cost. Overall there is a sense of purpose as well as techniques, and institutions available for the 'internalization of resources'. In other words the *Keiretsu* structure and setting provides an accommodating framework as well as the necessary means.

What may, in general, be commented at this stage, is that an understanding of the institutional structure and build-up of an established *Keiretsu* and the nature of its resources economics, provides a good example of the organizational pattern and economic principles adhered to in the management of the Japanese economy at large. Simply, this type of a *Keiretsu* represents, in effect, a synopsis of the mechanism and operational principles of such an economy. Also, in as much as a *Keiretsu* enterprise may not receive due appreciation in isolation from an understanding of the general scope and nature of the *Keiretsu*, the latter, as a whole, may in turn not be given due appreciation in isolation from an understanding of the setting and principles of the operation of the national economy.

In a more precise perspective the Japanese *Keiretsu* as a concept (or method of economic organization) applies in a more specific manner and in comparative confinement to a Japanese manufacturing enterprise. How the limit and scope the enterprise's system would develop accordingly, remains an open scenario.[55] Furthermore, it is also in line to see the *Keiretsu* (as so meant) applicable at a more micro level, e.g. to the unit (or microcosm) of the same enterprise.

B. Manufacturing enterprises

Compared with established models, a Japanese industrial enterprise identified as a *Keiretsu*, represents a new phenomenon. It is a new enterprise in the sense that its development and growth only took effect since World War II. It has also been rarely treated or identified separately as an industrial group, i. e. if compared with industrial enterprises in the West.[56] Yet it is a *Keiretsu* in the pure sense of Japanese economic understanding.

Japanese companies that are presently sizeable and economically powerful, by world standards, have become identified recently as *Keiretsu* and have attracted interest on the basis of such a criterion.[57] They feature, in turn, a typical structure built primarily, however, through vertical integration and specifically in the way the principle applies in terms of the kind of integration witnessed in the production process.

The state of fundamental equilibrium which applies among different industrial firms but which are members of an established *Keiretsu*, manifests itself here in a different manner. Equilibrium (i.e. gravity) is the responsibility of Headquarters—the central or parent firm. This, at face value, represents a condition that is similar to a parent company and its satellites headquartered in Western economies.

But judging the position of the Japanese industrial enterprise by the criteria of its cost-economics would reveal fundamental differences. It is, in the first instance, a *Keiretsu*—a network of ties, i.e. given the nature of these ties with an emphasis on Japanese tendencies in the division of labour in production activities. (Featured to this effect, in particular, is a notable practice among Japanese manufacturers in spinning off departments into separate firms which concentrate on specific production operations.[58])

Secondly, a tendency to pool resources exhibits itself clearly and distinctly at a parent Headquarters.[59] The parent firm also functions as a conduit of resources between the marketplace (domestic and international) and firms under its aegis. Interest would then particularly arise in the related efficiency of the Headquarters, i. e. the nature of its own mechanics.

What the enterprise therefore is (its mechanics), at first impression, is a structure of ties or a constitution of some sort and secondly, a mode of production integration. The two conditions tend to be interchangeable and stand as prerequisites to one another. It is specifically in the dynamics of production integration that the Japanese cost-economics principles manifest themselves. What is then the role of the parent firm in such a context?

What is not to be underestimated, however, is that the Headquarters' efficiency and mechanics are but a matter of the dynamics of the total system; it is relative to its contribution to each component and effect on the latter's efficiency. In turn, a unit's dynamism provides a feed-back to that of Headquarters'.

'Relativity', as a criterion for optimum performance, comes in sight again. Also the state of inter-relatedness among different units, as well as applied in relation to the co-ordination of inputs in the production process as such, simply makes the *Keiretsu*. The impression here especially stands, as a *Keiretsu* is being interpreted as a Japanese methodological tendency, i.e. essentially meant to accommodate the Japanese-type of resources economics.[60]

(i) *General constitution*

Headquarters is, therefore, assumed to represent the core of the general system.[61] This implies, in the first instance, that the constitution of the general enterprise represents the structure of a parent firm and that of the congregation of related companies. But there are basic contrasts between the separate constitutions of the primary firm and that of each of the related companies. The distinctiveness here, however, is meant to make and to contribute towards the cohesion of the system—the *Keiretsu*.

The central firm is generally distinctive by its typical policies and position as a large company, in contrast with the Japanese medium- and small-sized firms.[62] For example, its employment policy is distinct, it procures funds from separate institutions, and its leadership maintains an active role in determining the fate of the economy.

The medium- and small-sized firms, in contrast, apply different employment policies and resort to other sources of funds. By adopting different practices, however, they tend to supplement those of the central company and prompt a reciprocal relationship which works to promote the viable structure of the general system which both types constitute. But the complementary conditions of that kind amongst the number of companies covered, throws light only on one aspect of the *Keiretsu's* constitution. In a separate perspective are the different types of ties that are specifically created in line with, and in the course of, production activities proper. This may simply be exemplified by the existence of designed standards and also by the flow of resources (technology, finance, labour) to feed into and control the general production process.

(ii) *Production integration*

The integrated constitution of the Japanese industrial enterprise, meaning ties among different firms involved in the production process, and also the core (Headquarters) assuming a gravitating power, provide a general impression of the *Keiretsu*. There is more, however, to be read in relation to the system's internalities, i.e. to its production function.

Production integration is introduced here as a key term or a frame of reference. It is meant to be reflective of the internal phenomenon—the production flow. This simply involves the integration of inputs into the process resulting in the finished product. But production integration of a *Keiretsu*, in the implied sense, is made possible on account of the kind of constitution it maintains.

Assuming, at this point, that the *Keiretsu*, as a concept, represents the essentials of the Japanese-type organization tendencies, then a point of strong interest is how to make it effective. One possible answer is by the method used to combine inputs and in the choice of proportion and variances at any one time. (Inputs include basic machinery, labour, raw material and parts, know-how as incorporated in designs and standards, and above all the maintaining of a balance among them during the flow process.)

Overall, a state of synergy in relation to *Keiretsu* production activities applies in two ways: within the parent enterprise itself, and between the parent company and its satellites. It is further expected that a certain level of synergy applies within each production centre contributing to the nature of ties among the total which, in turn, contributes towards the general state of synergy of the system on the whole.

In essence, the principle of synergy works at all levels, due to the Japanese art and skill in combining parts and inputs together. Whereas this could be interpreted in terms of a general sense of organization (more of an art) it could also be seen more pragmatically in terms of a Japanese sense of cost.[63]

There is sufficient evidence in Japanese literature and economic behaviour to put emphasis on the latter assumption. The country has always insisted on emphasizing its need for raw materials resources—a need which inevitably conditioned its methods of production organization. A more specific factor that has been emphasized recently was the scarcity of oil and the subsequent turn of Japanese companies towards rationalization. More recently still has been the rising scarcity of labour and the trend towards computer-integrated manufacturing (CIM). This is a technology which has expanded the conventional robot-focused factory automation field to a new realm of sophistication. (CIM refers to the use of computer networks to create integrated systems incorporating development, design, material orders, production inspection and sales.[64])

Resource- (or cost-) economics then is being expressed with Japanese art and skill in synthesizing inputs; but attention is paid to each minimal unit not only due 'scarcity', so resource-economics seems also to be built on the basis of the Japanese sense of 'supernatural' values.[65] Yet this tendency on the whole is being made effective because it takes place within a context which also represents both a combination of the Japanese senses of pragmatism and spirituality.[66]

The appropriate mention at this stage is that a Japanese industrial enterprise, such as a *Keiretsu*, manifests the principles of simplification (division of labour) and cohesion; and the limits with respect to each are unforeseeable.

In retrospect, institutional competitiveness in relation to Japanese *Keiretsu* (of both types) balances on the existence of an 'integrated core'. The synopsis of the established model is in the nature of inter-relatedness among key group-enterprises and in the manner in which this inter-relatedness is being reinforced by the specific roles of the bank and the *sogo shosha*.

Competitiveness in the case of the second model (the industrial enterprise) is in the nature of the synergy exhibited, especially in the production process proper. This is specifically manifested by the Japanese choice of inputs and in their methods and manner of integration.

To an outsider what is involved tends to be seen as a matter of organization. There is much truth in this view. But there is also truth in qualifying the general effort as an expression of the Japanese 'economics (or science) of cost'.

Thus a primary approach towards understanding the Japanese *Keiretsu* would assume an interest in understanding the different conditions underlying the state of integration which, at the same time, implies avoiding emphasis on any one of these conditions; for they tend to exist and influence inter-relatedly.

Further, an understanding of any one *Keiretsu* may not be obtained without reference to the existence of the other. Japanese *Keiretsu(s)*, in general, operate within a national *Keiretsu*—the organization and economic behaviour of the domestic economy at large. A total impression of any one *Keiretsu* necessitates an understanding of each type.

II. CRUCIAL ISSUES

There is some dilemma between Japanese attitudes towards the *Keiretsu* (of all types) as the *sine qua non* of Japanese-type industrial/economic organization and the non-Japanese view of specifically monopolistic attributes exhibited inhibiting market entry and restricting free competition.

But the essential problem is basically a matter of a *Keiretsu* as an economic concept. More pragmatically it is also a matter of 'direct' targeting, i.e. of what is crucially 'odd' in relation to a *Keiretsu*. In both respects the problem tends to bear a good degree of ambiguity and is, undeniably, complex.

However, the separation between an emphasis of the *Keiretsu* as an organization (or a Japanese structure of interlocking ties) and a view that the term is but a methodology originating from a Japanese-style economic mind, provides a more strategic standpoint to outside observers in order to assess the kind of economic institutions the Japanese tend to acquire domestically and overseas. This implies that there are preliminaries to be investigated and assumed before an outright projection of the *Keiretsu* is to be made.

Thus the main issue would be brought to the realm of logic and theoretical analysis of economic organizational thought to allow a new field sufficient room to emerge and be observed. At the same time it creates specific interests towards subjecting related institutions to testing and comparison—in a universal perspective but on equal grounds. The assumption here is that Japanese economic institutions are a result of their own economic theories and it is necessary for these theories to be more explicit and also acknowledged.

A. Opposition of views

In a more realistic sense the issue rests on: first, the highly critical views of the West (the United States and Europe) as regards the *Keiretsu*; and second, on corresponding responses from the Japanese side. Yet there is still the good question, from either side, as to why the other is not getting the message. The duel seems to be on-going and each party is either not seeing or missing crucial targets.

In brief, the non-Japanese side developed the issue on the basis of their assumption of the closed nature of the Japanese market, pointing specifically to the impact of non-tariff barriers, for which the *Keiretsu* are considered highly accountable. However, it may not be dismissed that in the first place what prompted the issue was a general consciousness of the position of Japanese manufacturers as active (or highly competitive) exporters.

In a total perspective, therefore, two main problems are to be addressed: (a) what the state of organization of the Japanese market is as an importer; and (b) to find clues to the competitiveness of Japanese manufacturing enterprises as exporters. (Whether there is a relationship between these two areas of interest remains an open but interesting question.)

The first concern implies making a general effort towards analysing the structure of Japanese industry or the fabrics of the country's industrial organization in which industrial groups (*Keiretsu*) popularly represent an outstanding feature. Thus the main task remains a matter of understanding the composite nature of the *Keiretsu* and locating or identifying what shuns or restricts market entry.

In relation to the second, understanding why Japanese companies are competitive is basically understanding also the nature of the country's industrial structure and industrial organization, i.e. the nature of the enterprise's base and grass roots, as a priority as opposed to an interest in its products and markets.

If, then, it is possible that the competitiveness of a Japanese enterprise is a result of Japanese industrial organization, how convinced would they be to bring about changes, i.e.without convincingly undermining or eroding, in their view, the ground of their own competitive power?

Retrospectively, the general conflict at one stage centred on the balance of trade, addressing specifically a consistently achieved surplus balance on the Japanese side. But the focus is being eventually shifted more and more to diagnosing problematic conditions in the make-up and constitution of Japanese economic and industrial institutions. The interest of the contestants is changing from products (the Japanese with non-Japanese) to respective economic institutions.[67]

In simple terms, then, the issue of market entry is becoming concerned with the entry of non-Japanese institutions into the Japanese market, its adjustment and free performance. The same concern, though not as developed, is beginning to involve the question of entry of a Japanese firm to local markets and, in turn, the nature of the problems that are likely to develop relative to its own adaptive behaviour and performance.

An interest in the competitiveness of a Japanese industrial firm as an exporter has also acquired a wider scope. It is covering a growing curiosity over what makes Japanese economic institutions so capable of transforming themselves into structures built on a world-scale. It is not only their competitive status, as seen in their domestic constitution, that matters; it is also the nature of related structures that are being established and operating in host economies.

Competitiveness, as applied to the new state of affairs, transcends 'bilateralism' as manifested in comparative trading transactions between one country and another. The two main criteria become flexibility in production technology and the nature of the communication systems and skills utilized. How competitive Japanese institutions are on the basis of these criteria, represents, then, a major question.

At a glance it may be seen that Japanese *Keiretsu* allow ample room for production flexibility manoeuvring, given the nature of their organization and of their 'economics of resource'. Much truism is to be read in such an assumption. It may also serve as a guide to detecting production flexibility in relation to separate components and conditions of a *Keiretsu* structure and resource strategy.

For example, there is stability in basics such as labour structure and funding channels. Resources in a *Keiretsu*, e.g. financial and R & D, are available for any one firm of comparatively unlimited means.[68] Thus, accommodating factors to a production process are there with a long-term perspective. The same horizon, in turn, applies to the flow of resources. Stable conditions and assurance of resources have thus established a kind of general set-up for production manoeuvring.

Flexibility also results from the enterprise's degree of concentration on production activities proper, especially on the basis of stable conditions and the level of assurance of resources. The tendency also, given the nature of the training of the Japanese labour force, prompts technical propagation which, in a sense, manifests itself in the quality of products and in greater division of labour in the production function itself.

In turn, communication capacities and skills of a *Keiretsu* represent, in a way, a common resource, since such facilities have been specifically developed and made available by the *sogo shosha*. (The latter's communication complex is backed by the world-wide spread of its branches and subsidiaries. It is also effectively supported by its heavy commitment towards research and information technology.)

In a separate perspective, communication facilities and expertise are provided by the network of sales subsidiaries and the spread of the different channels of Japanese (but independent) manufacturing enterprises.[69] But their access to the *sogo shosha's* are also open and in many instances their own sales subsidiaries are linked with one trader or the other, particularly in the form of joint ventures.

Yet conditions in relation to both the Japanese position in production flexibility and in communication capabilities and potential, have been subject to interpretations arguing the existence of the kind of rigidity and economic power which deter the operating of free market principles.

The point, however, is that although there are realities in relation to the two sides of the general debate, what remains obscure is a common understanding regarding the ultimate criteria. The possibility of an agreement of the sort is likely to avail itself once it is being recognized that the issue is between two different economic systems and industrial organization styles and with separate common grounds. It is therefore a matter of accepting the existence of two criteria and not one. The degree to which the two are, or may become, compatible, rests on value judgements.

B. The Japanese stand

It is too simplistic to sum up the Japanese attitude towards the issue of the *Keiretsu* as a defensive posture (or in terms of their present reaction to what outsiders see in the nature of such an institution) for there are more established dimensions in the background which, although not so pronounced by the Japanese themselves, do weigh heavily in their judgement of their own economic organization and achievements.

Firstly, there is a strong historical background representing the developments and counting the achievements of the *Zaibatsu*, as especially reflected during the period between the two world wars.[70] Although the economic progress witnessed by the country then led to the venture of World War II, and its own economic devastation in the aftermath, this did not erase from the Japanese mind the value of the principles underlying the *Zaibatsu* type economic organization with its various lineages and ties to other aspects of their societal structure.[71] Simple proof of this is the promptitude of *Zaibatsu* enterprises to re-group as soon as the early 1950s.

Secondly, there is the outstanding level of economic growth that picked-up during the 1960s when the role of the Japanese *Keiretsu* (focusing on the horizontally integrated manufacturers) maintained a special significance as a locomotive power.[72] The same decade, with a different perspective, prepared the ground and prompted the development of Japanese vertically integrated manufacturers.

Thirdly, the same framework (*Keiretsu*) tends to be credited with the success of the kind of rationalization effort that pulled the domestic economy from the recession caused by the series of oil crises of the 1970s.[73] The same structure is further seen to feed into and contain effectively the 'technological paths' which the Japanese economy converged into during the 1980s.[74] The advantage of the *Keiretsu* was further confirmed during this period in the light of the need for closely co-ordinated efforts and for special resources and a careful watch over their use.[75]

A fourth but more specific point, reflects on the requirements of the high-tech industries and especially electronics and its diffusion in the national economy.[76] Here, the need for the existence of a solid 'core' in organization (whether in the horizontally or vertically integrated *Keiretsu*) becomes more insistent and more varied in content, with wider ramifications. Ideally, a strong national build-up of basic research, of which the resourcefulness of the *Keiretsu* means good potential and comparative advantages on a national scale.

In other words, the same outlook would also include a greater need for the centralization of resources, or at least provide further confirmation of the need of the *Keiretsu* pattern in resources strategy. Whereas the necessary solid core would act as a magnet for new resources procurement (nationally and internationally), it also would empower the search for and development of new resources.

A fifth argument is presented in the light of the country's current interest in industrial internationalization. A *Keiretsu* has the economic power and the know-how to internationalize.[77] It also maintains the communication links for the maintenance and control of international operations (the international position and related expertise of a *Keiretsu*'s *sogo shosha* is central to this effect). The same is eventually developing with respect to the role of a *Keiretsu* bank.

In turn, the vertically integrated *Keiretsu*'s power in internationalization is implied to be the nature of the technological impetus of its domestic base, i.e. specifically that of its production core. More explicitly, it is seen in relation to the nature of flexibility maintained by its constitution and its production organization, which provide a certain reach to distant markets and maintain opportunities to accommodate the creation of local interests.[78]

Upon reflection, however, the very critical point to the Japanese with respect to the *Keiretsu* may not be a matter of the past and its achievements (whether or not examples of these achievements were witnessed during the early 1920s, the 1960s or in the rationalization efforts of the 1970s) for all such achievements have taken place mainly on domestic grounds, i.e. with the domestic base and its organization representing the primary standpoint or sphere of operation.

By contrast, the country's current industrial strategy tends to rest on two conditions: (a) the promotion of high-tech industries (particularly the related software supplements); and (b) the development of an international industrial sector prompted by an increasing emphasis on the industrial export and institutional transfers.

Under both conditions there is, for the Japanese, more to be done fundamentally, outside Japan, which undermines the comparative utility and standing of the domestic base as witnessed in the past. For example, recent trends (or drives) in resources outflow are meant for long-term investment purposes as in the form of local manufacturing operations or for feeding basic research projects.[79] The outward reach of the domestic base and, in turn, the nature of the contribution and effect of the local (and would-be established) sector, are both trends which are most likely to trigger changes in what exists domestically. In other words, the kind of anchor required abroad would have to exercise weight on the domestic base; it also calls for attention and specific interest in its own kind and its growth.

(i) *High-tech criteria*

In the case of the promotion of the high-tech sector, an explicit primary condition is the development of basic research. Beyond a certain level such activities call for individualistic effort and concentration (i.e. singular brain-work). Also the promotion of high-technology prompts further division of labour and specialization, leading to a more popular utilization of small-scale enterprises, i.e. versus the large.[80]

The general tendency also prompts an increasing industrial application of automation and computers.[81] This, in turn, would have its impact on existing Japanese managerial attributes. For instance, less manpower, engineers and specially skilled labour would run an automated factory whose labour force would mainly consist of 'steel-collar workers' (or robots). Such a structure would need a corresponding type of brain-work, applied in a more individualistic depth than in the past.

In total there is a great difference in results from a mind that works on the development of imported basic research and one that concentrates on the pursuit and development of basic research. There is also a strong difference between a mind that works inter-relatedly with another (joint effort) to manage operations, from one which is required to apply its efforts to concentrating on technical expertise and on the control of an automated industrial setting.

However, innovative minds (needing facilities that abundant resources, as seen within the power and scope of a *Keiretsu*, would provide) by nature need and treasure isolation and freedom to work. The level of intangible remuneration in their case would eventually create a contrast with the tangible type of pay applied so far to Japanese labour.[82] The type of need also is more inclined to be separate (if not genuinely apt to reject) the kind of know-how resources generated by mutuality of effort and consensus.

These new conditions and requirements provide an ultimate standpoint from where to question the nature of the 'core' (or cohesion) that would be needed to be developed by a Japanese *Keiretsu* in order to remain competitive. If, upon simple reflection, the new tendencies lead to or necessitate the creation of several cores (under one umbrella) the next questions would then be what was the nature of the new structure and what was now the internal make-up of a transformed *Keiretsu*.

Actually these questions are being introduced to the Japanese, who are ardent defenders of the *Keiretsu*, and to the non-Japanese, who are highly critical. Possible answers based on the natural development of events, as necessitated by the present high technology, causes both reactions, in their rather outmoded prevailing forms. (The current state of centralization of the Japanese economy on the promotion and deployment of high technology is irreversible. The effect on industrial organization seems to be beyond control. A Japanese *Keiretsu*, as a good tool for both effective promotion and control, is, in relation to the behaviour of high technology, under very testing times.)

(ii) *Internationalization*

What the Japanese are also currently after is the internationalization of their manufacturing industries. Their efforts have been preceded, due to their understanding of the internationalization process, by a strategy focusing on a worldwide distribution of Japanese products or achievement of a certain national level of exports.[83] Whether the current effort is mainly due to world market problems encountered or relates to changes within the Japanese manufacturing institutions, is a valid question in both respects.[84]

In relation to current efforts there is a difference in 'crafting' a manufacturing unit in the Japanese domestic industrial order and a Japanese operation in a foreign market economy. *Keiretsu* institutions normally support a manufacturing affiliate in its investment activities (an advantage *par excellence* compared with overseas activities based only on its own resources).

But the ground (economic environment and industrial setting) is not Japanese. This fact would, in due course, have repercussions on the nature of inter-firm relationships maintained amongst *Keiretsu* institutions domestically, as well as on the nature of their overseas inter-relationships.

There is also a difference between the type of cohesion maintained by a production system which converges on the production of finished products and their export, and the type of make-up and manner of operation of one that would eventually acquire a number of 'appendages' as a result of local manufacturing operations.[85]

Seeing internationalization as an activity specifically promoted by the existence of good communication systems, the Japanese enterprises maintain a comparative advantage in the 'hardware' aspect as well as the existence of typical institutions (*sogo shosha*) with expediency and expertise.[86] Thus the preliminaries needed towards internationalizing their industries, as well as the capacity and certain level of know-how in establishing international linking channels, are in their favour.

What remains quite uncertain, if not obscure, is how know-how in sifting and correlating international information on the basis of which a strategic flow of resources would take effect and be promoted within their international enterprises and on the basis of which effective management (i.e. internationally tinted) would be provided. The point here is to introduce the problem but not to investigate its reasons nor provide a direct answer. In simple terms it is rather to propose its possibility.

What the preceding suggestions, in a nutshell, assume, is that the very mechanics of the *Keiretsu* (which is the cradle of Japanese competitive power) have been exposed, under the era of high technology and internationalization, to triggers of change which, due to the very nature of their causes, tend to be beyond measurement or confinement at present.

This is not to suggest that the accommodation of the new strategies under the *Keiretsu*, would eventually lead to the undermining of their competitive edge, nor to assume that the Japanese may not as expediently transform the *Keiretsu* organization to correspond with these strategies.

What is left for the Japanese, however, is the problem of convincing the world market (and themselves at some stage) that their economic and organizational theory is valid and is so even under crucial conditions.

NOTES

1. In effect the problem is paradoxical involving a growing interest in the nature of competitiveness of the *Keiretsu* and at the same time a strong criticism of their presence in the Japanese economy (specifically as a deterrent to free market principles and market entry).
2. In other words the contest is between a Japanese firm as an affiliate of a *Keiretsu* complex, with one in the same industry but standing on its own. One point is the impact of the existence of the *Keiretsu* on the latter, i.e. on its performance compared with what its condition would be, in markets where the *Keiretsu*(s) are absent. Limited studies have been attempted to provide certain answers. One example is Iwao Nakatani's *The Economic Role of Financial Corporate Grouping*, in Masahiko Aoki, (ed.) *The Economic Analysis of the Japanese Firm*. North-Holland, Amsterdam, 1984.
3. The Japanese economic understanding of the value of 'relatedness' in its various aspects (versus simply individual performance as a matter of general economic principle) appears, then, as a field for in-depth investigation and study.
4. A *Keiretsu* as a concept is therefore incorporated within the country's concept of industrial policy. The latter involved 'movement' (development) and industrial structure. The first aspect covered a sequential trend in the promotion of designated priority industries; secondly, the focus on industrial structure targeted the promotion of enterprises and patterns in inter-firm ties and relationships. The idea of the

implied principles and targets may be read in the Ministry of International Trade and Industry's (MITI) Industrial Structure Council's periodical publications: *Japan's Industrial Structure—A Long Range Vision*, various issues. Also, Chalmer Johnson, *The Institutional Foundation of Japanese Industrial Policy*, in Claude E. Barfield and William A. Schambra, (eds.) *The Politics of Industrial Policy*, The American Enterprise Institute for Public Policy Research, Washington D.C., 1986. See also citation in footnote 40, *infra*.

5. The 'visible' hand is seen at two levels: in the process of formulating industrial policy (joint effort of bureaucrats, private business executives and professionals) and implementation of policy under bureaucracy and executive personnel. It is also the group-industrial ethics within the firm. Thus a definition of the 'visible' hand does not simply mean the role of national policy to combat market failure. It covers Japanese group tendencies and efforts as in government business relationships, among firms and within a firm. For a general background refer to: R. S. Ozaki, *How Japanese Industrial Policy Works*, in Chalmer Johnson (ed.) *The Industrial Policy Debate*. Institute for Contemporary Studies, San Francisco, 1984. Also, C. J. McMillan, *The Japanese Industrial System*. Walter de Gruyter, Berlin, 1985, Chapter 4. 'I believe that to foster dynamic growth of the industrial society of today we must combine Adam Smith's invisible hand of the market force with what I would call a visible hand of policy.': MITI's Vice-Minister, Shinji Fukukawa, 'A New Industrial Structure—MITI's Policies Towards the 21 Century'. Speaking of Japan, January 1987, p. 10.

6. Japanese *Keiretsu* (particularly the top six) served as 'greenhouses' to nationally set industrial objectives. Their leadership participated in determining these objectives; their executives participated with MITI (among other government departments) in the implementing stages, and lastly, they maintained the services institutions e.g. *sogo shosha* (general traders) and banks, which provide equipment. 'For many Japanese the *Keiretsu* system has been central to the country's rise as a world class manufacturing nation, and encourages the long-term thinking and technological prowess for which Japan is widely praised.' Staff editors, 'Keiretsu—What They Are Doing? Where They Are Heading?' *Tokyo Business Today*, September 1990, p. 26. See also, Toshimosa Tsuruta, 'The Rapid Growth Era', in Ryutaro Komiya, Masahiro Okuna and Kotaro Suzumura, *Industrial Policy of Japan*, Academic Press, New York, 1988. Specifically the author's reference to the 'one-set' development pattern of industrial groups expounded by Miyazaki Yoshikazu, *The Economic Mechanism of Post-War Japan*, Shin Hyoron Sha, Tokyo, 1966.

7. Industrial rationality and economic mind which, as experience shows, tend to centre on techniques and methods, imbued by a perception of the value of a balanced flow of resources meaning, in a way, balanced attention to each unit involved and concern in the state of their unity over, for instance, a production or a time horizon. See also footnote 63, *infra*.

8. This has been manifested in efforts to strengthen group cohesion and converge towards the promotion of new industries and technologies. In a different perspective, efforts were made to sophisticate enterprise headquarters. (See also notes 34 and 73.)

9. Approaches overseas by Japanese industries applied predominantly (at least at the early stage) through *Keiretsu's* efforts. Available data reveal that the top six tend to conduct their own respective research on overseas markets; affiliates of each go abroad in a 'related' or joint manner; and, in due course, their respective organizational prototype takes form locally, i.e. in a country or region. Manufacturing enterprises (the *Keiretsu*) on their own tend towards establishing local 'clusters'. Examples are the cases of large textile firms in Asia (Toray and Teijin) and the current endeavours of Japanese auto-makers in the United States and Europe.

10. 'Internalities' as an object for investigation here would then be preceded by an implicit understanding of the assumption that the Japanese economic system is different from other non-Japanese systems and that the Japanese economic institutions are but typical results or constituents. Such an approach allows for caution and keener interest in details along the line of investigation and also more consideration of the principle of relativity.

11. The Japanese are said to be group-oriented, but their group orientation, as it affects Japanese industrial behaviour, requires careful interpretations. It is neither a collectivism with strong ideological overtones nor communalism that leans towards peace and the warm comfort of the *status quo*. Rather, it operates most effective at the level of a firm and an enterprise group. R. S. Ozaki (*op. cit.*, note 5, p. 52). 'When we consider all the ramifications, however, we can see that the existence of these corporate groups relates in a basic way to the very nature of Japanese capitalism. So we should be ready for a far-reaching debate over their merit and demerit'. Ken'Ichi Imai, 'The Legitimacy of Japan's Corporate Groups' *Economic Eye*, Autumn 1990, p. 16. Yet the main question remains: if the *Keiretsu* represent implanted organizational

orientations and methods, and these in a different Japanese economic setting, would it be 'neutral', would it live or possibly be transplanted to take root?

12. 'Core' industries (priority industries) typified post-World War II industrial Japan; each industry in turn maintained its 'core' (or lead) enterprises. Also each industrial group had its enterprise nucleus (or key companies). The individual key enterprise each had its primary production and control 'core'.

13. In their terminology such an understanding is often referred to as 'harmony'. In a 'hard' or tangible sense 'cohesion' is an industrial situation or condition in the realm of economic performance, be it the economy, the industry, the firm or a unit within the firm. (See also note 24.)

14. Japanese definitions of *Keiretsu* tended to cover predominantly the leading six industrial or known economic groups. It is only recently (and still hesitantly) that a large industrial enterprise is identified as a *Keiretsu* in the sense that it represents an industrial group as such, as normally understood in Western countries. (See also notes 17 and 56.)

15. See Yoshikazu Miyazaki, 'Excessive Competition and the Formation of *Keiretsu*', in Kazuo Sato,(ed.) *Industry and Business in Japan*, Croom Helm, London, 1980. 'Although the term *Zaibatsu* is currently used, especially in mass media, the economic phenomena referred to is basically different from that of the pre-war situation. The standard technical name is *Keiretsu* (alignment).' Robert J. Ballon, Iwao Tomita, Hajime Usami, *Financial Reporting in Japan*, Kodansha International Ltd., Tokyo, 1976, p. 43.

16. For a general impression of the differences defining industrial groups in Western countries and Japan, refer to Peter Mathia and M. M. Postan (eds.) *The Cambridge Economic History of Europe—The Industrial Economies: Capital, Labour, and Enterprise*, Cambridge University Press, Cambridge, 1978, parts I and II, Vol. III. Also *European Economic Review*, Special issue: Market Competition, Conflict and Collusion Vol. 19, No. 1, 1982; and, Pierre Grou, *The Financial Structure of Multinational Capitalism*, BERG, Heidelberg, 1985.

17. Member firms are of different industries but brought together through various means, e.g. interlocked shareholding, interlocked directorship and co-ordination by key institutions, as in the *Keiretsu's* general trader and bank. (See also notes 26 to 28.)

18. Examples are seen, particularly in the motor and other industries, in the machinery sector with a Japanese enterprise system involving co-ordinated efforts and alignment among firms specialized in each of the different parts that form a total production system. The phenomena are seen at face value in terms of sub-contracting activities. A reference is made to, for instance, a Japanese automotive manufacturer maintaining 168 primary sub-contractors, 4700 secondary and 1600 tertiary. Takashi Yokokura, 'Small and Medium Enterprises', in Ryutaro Komiya, Masahiro Okuno, Kotaro Suzumura (*op. cit.*, note 6, p. 526.) A Japanese view sees in the subcontracting system 'an intermediate form (an intermediate organization) between use of the market (market purchase) and use of organization (in-house manufacturing), or as a form of quasi-integration.' Nakamura Tsutomu, *Small Business and Big Business*. Toyo Keizai Shin Posha, Tokyo, 1983, exemplified in Takashi Yokokura, *ibid*.

19. For example, Matsushita Electric Industrial maintains loose ties with Sumitomo Group, Toyota Motor with Mitsui and Nissan with the Fuyo Group.

20. This is to say that there are fundamental inter-firm links among Japanese enterprises and those that are created for specific purposes and their nature, or even existence, differs over time. Whether the general tendency is inseparable from, and also inherent in, Japanese economic culture, remains a good question.

21. Literature and common knowledge of the *Keiretsu* tended to concentrate on a general concern as to how the different firms involved become bound together. Thus the focus tended to be on the identification of ties. In contrast, the economics of the *Keiretsu*, as a viable system (historically and prospectively) represents a subject matter at the inception stage.

22. An interesting, relevant and foreseeable form is the Japanese multinational enterprise.

23. There is a subtle relationship between bringing about and accommodating change and at the same time recreating different levels (or situations) in cohesion. Is then the *Keiretsu* a tool, an accommodating framework, or a reflection of the 'subtle' process?

24. This is within the context of the Japanese comparative concentration on 'supply economics'. Also, although the implication is that as attention is paid to details in the organization of inputs, quality of finished products would become consequential or up to standard, it being understood that the qualitative aspect, in the Japanese conception maintains a deeper interpretation than that common in the West. For instance a worker's mind is expected to function beyond given standards, i.e. to think about what he is doing, be alert for possible short-cuts to improve production so that products could be made better and cheaper. Refer to Jon P. Alston, *The American Samurai–Blending American and Japanese Managerial Practices*,

Walter De Gruyter, Berlin, 1986, p. 271. Also, in recent years, the qualitative aspect of emphasis became more permeating as an objective to cover the total composition and behaviour of the production system to insure increases in its flexibility. 'Emphasis is shifting from improvement of the production process, not only in quantitative terms to facilitate large-scale mass production as in the past, but also to improvement in qualitative terms so that the production system will be characterized by 'flexibility, efficiency and rapid responsiveness, in consideration of the product cycle and wide-variety low volume production.' See Economic Planning Agency, *Economic Survey of Japan*, 1988–1989, pp. 62–78.

25. Mitsubishi, Mitsui, and Sumitomo, as their organizational features are more recognized and established, tend to serve as models to be copied by the more recently formed groups: Dai-lchi Kangyo Bank (DKB), Fuyo and Sanwa.

26. For one thing the large Japanese companies tend to be concentrated among the six industrial groups. Studies of these groups show that in 1987 the proportion of the capital of their 163 leading companies, to the grand total of all non-financial Japanese enterprises, represented 40.7%; the figure for their total assets was 32%. The same year (1987) the number of firms belonging to the six was approximated at 12 000. This is indicative of the scope and economic power of the six if companies other than their 163 leading enterprises, were also included in the above calculations. Refer to the results of the Fair Trade Commission, 'Survey on the Status of the Corporate Groups', summarized in *Economic Eye*, Autumn, 1990. But there are, in terms of scope and power, good elements and aspects that may not be possibly quantified as in the six's group representation in the national economic decisions arena, and in that power that rests on a group's (or collective) infrastructure.

27. Scope is one thing here. What also counts is the level of complementary activities that exist within a group which is indicative of a state of self-sufficiency. Group firms cover top manufacturers, financial institutions, general traders, research institutions, and other firms in various industries such as real estate, warehousing and transport.

28. For example, the presidents of the key companies of the Sumitomo Group (21 in number) form the *Hakusui Kai* (Presidents' Club) who tend to meet and confer regularly mapping and reviewing the group's strategies. Refer to 'Sumitomo Group', *The Oriental Economist*, February 1985. Other industrial groups also are overseen by presidents' associations of their respective key companies which tend to slightly vary in number and industrial activities. Interestingly enough, however, the pattern of composition among the six (especially with respect to the 'set' in financial institutions) tend generally to correspond. Refer to *The Japan Economic Journal*'s Series on 'Analysis of Standing of Six Major Groups', Mitsubishi Group, *The Japan Economic Journal*, 30 August 1977; Mitsui Group, 6 September 1977; Sumitomo Group, 13 September 1977; Fuyo Group, 20 September 1977; DKB Group, 27 September 1977, and Sanwa Group, 4 October 1977. See also Appendix A.

29. Outstanding in this context is the active role of this type of mission in getting to assess conditions and views in foreign countries and international markets. This serves the trade/investment purposes of the respective groups and beyond that feeds the formulation of economic policies at the national level. For example, at one stage, the DKB and Mitsui Groups concluded economic co-operation agreements with China. Their missions to that country, with those of other groups led, in effect, to the 1978 long-term trade agreement between the two countries. See, 'Industrial Groups', *Industrial Review of Japan*, 1979. 'Dai-lchi Kangyo Group', *The Oriental Economist*, April, 1982. For content of the Agreement refer to 'The China–Japan Long-Term Trade Agreement, 16 February 1978', *International Legal Materials*, 1 January 1979.

30. History, structure, scope (diversification) and international spread and involvement of a Japanese general trader (*sogo shosha*) represents a field study on its own. What is of significance here is the fact that an institution of this kind is a key *Keiretsu* affiliate and specifically entrusted with a co-ordinating role. For a general definition of the Japanese *sogo shosha* refer to: Alexander K. Young, *The Sogo Shosha: Japan's Multinational Trading Companies*, Westview Press, Boulder, 1979. Also, M. Y. Yoshino and Thomas B. Lifson, *The Invisible Link: Japan's Sogo Shosha and the Organisation of Trade*, Cambridge: The MIT Press, 1986. In turn leading Japanese banks (given the fact that they were not dismantled as institutions by the Supreme Commander of the Allied Power (SCAP) but remained comparatively intact) plus the country's post-World War II drive towards industrialization, played a central role in enterprise re-grouping simply (other things being equal) to establish themselves an industrial base. An end result is the status of the 'groups' and concomitantly their own present world position. The principle of interaction and concomitant advantage remains the same but the environment has been extended beyond the domestic scene.

31. A noted tendency is that *Keiretsu* manufacturers normally establish local manufacturing (and even sales companies) overseas in partnership with their group *sogo shosha*. The latter is normally active in

undertaking feasibility studies, locating sources of funds, assuming responsibility in supplying basic machinery and raw materials, and consequently marketing the finished products. 'Like Adam Smith's "invisible hand" of the market, and like Alfred Chandler's "visible hand" of the vertically integrated firm, the *sogo shosha* provides a system of governance, channelling money, information, ideas, raw materials, products, services and other economic goods into a coherent system of activity. The subtle and ever-changing dynamics of power between a *sogo shosha* and its client firms, and the utility to both of the co-ordinating function performed by the *sogo shosha*, challenge us to rethink many assumptions of the nature and boundaries of the firm and look at the basic organization of economic activity with new eyes.' M. Y Yoshino and Thomas B. Lifson, *op. cit., supra* footnote 30, p.6.

32. Simply, on account of the level of its diversification, the general trader is a 'risk absorber'. Also innate to the 'multiple' character acquired, i.e. in products handled, functions applied and worldwide branches, subsidiaries and offices, the *sogo shosha* tends to utilize sophisticated communication systems and market research facilities. Its institutional attributes in these respects become accessible to other group affiliates. This puts them in a position whereby their comparative cost is reduced not only because of their access to communication and information facilities and knowledge beyond their own singular reach, but also because their own decision-making process becomes duly more specialized, accurate and strategic. In effect the two aspects: high level of diversification and sophisticated communication and information systems, make a *sogo shosha* a typical *Keiretsu* on its own. Yet such a *Keiretsu* functions within the industrial group proper; it is also accessible to any other *Keiretsu*, i.e. Japanese manufacturers. A glimpse of the international dimension of the *sogo shosha* (and therefore necessary scope of communication links and market research) may be based on the number of overseas affiliates maintained. The lead six maintained, in 1981, a total of 1170 affiliates overseas. The range was between 280 affiliates for Mitsui and Co. and 125 for Nissho Iwai Corp. See *The Oriental Economist*, January 1982, p. 32.

33. Each group maintains a 'set' of financial institutions (e.g. Sumitomo Bank, Sumitomo Trust and Banking Co., Sumitomo Mutual Life Insurance Co. and Sumitomo Marine and Fire Insurance Co. See Sumitomo Corporation, *The Sumitomo Group*, Tokyo). Group enterprises tend to rely mainly on the group bank to supply them with credit, to guarantee credit from other sources and to offer advice and guidance on fund procurement from Japan or overseas. Studies show that the ratio of group member firms borrowing from group financial institutions, to their total debt, averaged 22.3% in 1981 in the case of the three *Zaibatsu*-based, and 19% in the case of the other three groups. Refer to Akira Negishi, 'The Business Groups and the Distribution System and the Antimonopoly Law in Japan', *Kobe University Law Review*, No. 18, 1984, pp. 34–35. Notably, both the trust banks and insurance firms provide long-term credit to industrial enterprises and are also active in the management of their pension funds. They complement the comparatively short-term (but renewable) lending by group banking and the activities of all tend to be co-ordinated.

34. That is the creation of higher level of co-ordination and consensus among member firms as a means towards the introduction of new and sophisticated products and industries. Each *Keiretsu* tends to tune its efforts to excel to this effect, i.e. comparatively with one another. See 'Industrial Groups—Long Recession and Int'l Problems Lead Groups to Bolster Internal Solidarity', *Industrial Review of Japan*, 1979. It is also common understanding that group cohesion is intended to prevent foreign takeovers, specifically through the medium of interlocked shareholding. (Cohesion is thus meant to promote industrial competitiveness; it is also meant to guarantee an uninterrupted course of development of group enterprises, i.e. in terms of hindering, if not shunning, takeovers.)

35. This is to assume that there is a general economic rationale for each type of link which itself has a role in a wider context. (Refer also to note 21.) This does not mean that the state of affairs should be overlooked, as it tends to be, because of the nature of the country's institutional setting at a wider level. A reference to this effect focused on the legal structure of the country: 'Only under a legal structure of this kind is it possible for business grouping of the Japanese description to exist and function'. See Hiroshi Okumura, 'Japanese Business Groupings Face World Criticism', *The Oriental Economist*, December 1982, p. 34.

36. Interlocked shareownership has been popularly targeted as a typical practice, i.e. to a point that a Japanese *Keiretsu* has been narrowly identified in terms of this kind of ownership. In effect, however, interlocked shareholding, in the case of Japan, represents more of a Japanese economic and managerial conceptualization or phenomenon which throws light on the state of its intractability. 'It is common for companies to hold each other's stock. For this reason, Japanese capitalism is often referred to as "trust capitalism" or "no-capitalist management capitalism".' See Takeshi Hayashi, *The Japanese Experience in Technology—From Transfer to Self-Reliance*, United Nations University, Tokyo, 1990, p. 173. Other sources went further to see the 'seed' of interlocked shareownership implanted in the country's economic culture

as before the post-World War II period; it eventually 'sprouted'. '... it may be quite necessary for us to understand that any political power as strong as that of G. H. Q. cannot upset an historical premise to bring about a fundamentally new structure in society; meanwhile an inside process cannot go its own way for itself, in some cases, without an aid of an outside power'. See, for example, Kenji Tominomori, 'Big Business Groups and Financial Capital in Post-War Japan', *Hokudai Economic Papers 1979–80*, Vol. IX. p. 26. A confirmation of the author's view is (as reflected in Table 1) the development of interlocked shareholding ratios of the comparatively established groups (Mitsui, Mitsubishi and Sumitomo), between 1952–1973, and the maintenance of a less variable rate since then.

37. A 'key' group company is a constituent member of the Presidents' Association. Refer to Appendix A for 'key' member firms in each group.

38. That is, a 'balance' created by horizontal linkages with member group firms and also on account of a broad base of smaller firms due to the nature of Japan's industrial organizational tendencies which propagate because the central firm becomes economically empowered by group membership. 'Stability' here may not be seen in a static form. The characterization is assumed in a developmental manner due to forces empowering the firm by interactions, both horizontally and vertically. Refer to note 18 for an example of a manufacturer's constitutional structure by firm. In effect the pattern applies as a general rule to large Japanese manufacturing enterprises which, by their majority, tend to concentrate in industrial groups. (See also note 26.)

39. Sources of managerial power, purpose of corporate control, rights and powers of shareholders—all have become subject-matter of controversial debates. Refer to a special issue of the *Journal of Law and Economics*, Vol. XXVI (2), June 1983, covering a conference sponsored by the Hoover Institution on Corporation and Private Property. See also James A. Brickley and Christopher M. James, 'The Take-Over Market, Corporate Board Composition and Ownership Structure: The Case of Banking', *The Journal of Law and Economics*, Vol.XXX (I), April 1987.

40. In one perspective stability is seen in terms of a state of the phenomenon of institutional shareholding among key firms (in a horizontal manner) as the large Japanese enterprise normally represents the main shareholders of smaller companies. Both types of transactions shun or limit the placement of shares on the open market. 'Expansion' in the sense of promoting institutional share-ownership (mutual or vertical); it may also be seen as expressed by merger behaviour of Japanese companies—a tendency implicitly promoted by MITI's and the country's industrial policy. 'The merger and re-organization policy has been a powerful tool of the post-war Japanese industrial policy and has been considered indispensable for industrial restructuring and adjustment... Classifying 63 major merger cases between 1953–1973, mergers between firms belonging to the same group were found to account for 33 cases; over half the number.' See Akira Iwasaki, 'Mergers and Reorganization', in Ryutaro Komiya, Masahiro Okuna and Kataro Suzumura (*op. cit.*, note 6, pp. 497 and 503.) Refer also to Chalmer Johnson (*op. cit.*, note 4.) The key then to understanding the criteria for corporate stability in the Japanese economic mind is not only dwelling on their practice in interlocked shareholding but becoming further interested in the ground principles and tendencies of institutional (versus the individual) shareholding in general. Featured to this effect is the comparatively 'ceremonial' role of shareholders' meeting, or assembly, in Japan's corporate life and management. Refer to Akio Takeuchi 'Shareholders Meeting Under the Revised Commercial Code', *Law In Japan* Vol. 20:173,1981. In turn, stability/balance as an objective maintains a wider ramification than a straightforward pursuit of profit margins, high dividends and a corporate market value. In respect of the first, institutional grass roots and structures of intricate ties are to be created, maintained, and behaviour-monitored. Pursuit of the second implies high risks and instability, i.e. as a part of the nature of the economic game.

41. The ratio of member firms having executives from other member firms within the same group to total number of member firms of each business group, as of 1981, averaged 77.7% for the three ex-*Zaibatsu* groups and 68% for the other three groups; the figure for the six was 72.8%. Refer to Akira Negishi (*op.cit.*, note 33). One advantage is the reduction in the cost of information and know-how. Another is the gain in effective managerial coverage; the management scope and know-how thus available to one firm is beyond its own individual possibilities.

42. In one respect there is the kind of pool(s) created by 'deliberations' of executives at different levels (e.g. presidents, production managers, engineers, public relations and marketing managers). Sources of information and know-how may be seen as originating from the in-depth specialization of key enterprises and simply from *Keiretsu* institutions created to provide the kind of intangible services, e.g. Mitsubishi Economic Research Institute, Mitsui Inter-Company Research Institute, Fuyo's Geothermal Energy

Development Committee, Fuyo Data Processing and System Development Ltd. and Sanwa's Toyo Information System. Refer to 'Fuyo Group Rising to Challenge', *The Oriental Economist*, February 1982, and 'Sanwa Group Moves to Gain in Size and Power', *The Oriental Economist*, September 1982.

43. This leads to the speculation (if not a statement of fact at present) that a long-term competitive state of Japanese banks in the world market implies a long-term international strategy of other *Keiretsu* affiliates. A *Keiretsu* domestic 'niche' (its general 'milieu') is thus necessarily to be extended overseas. The latter's international strategy itself is also dependent on the long-term international competitiveness of its finance institutions. (Refer to note 30.)

44. In essence, it is in the nature of our industrial base and the nature of its interlinking and interchanges with the *Keiretsu* finance-inter-related and inter-fed complex. The competitiveness of any institution (whether in the domestic market or in the international) within the *Keiretsu* is a result of its own 'open' boundaries in the *Keiretsu* economic society. More specifically, the operation of each financial institution is being empowered by the 'openness' and nature of interchange with one another as a *Keiretsu* set and as their very 'set' acquires due bargaining power in relation to finance markets. Refer to Appendix A for a quick appreciation of the 'sets' in finance. Statistical evidence is also strong as regards the comparative standing of financial institutions as top holders of corporate shares issued to the public. See The Research and Statistics Department/The Bank of Japan, *Economic Statistics Annual 1989*, The Bank of Japan, Tokyo, March 1990, p. 212.

45. Refer to note 43. *Sogo shosha* provides a significant financial cushion and supplements that of the *Keiretsu* finance structure proper. It mainly supplies *Keiretsu's* medium and small firms and specifically plays a key role in financing *Keiretsu's* overseas joint ventures, i.e. as an equity partner and even more as a provider of loans. Refer to Kiyoshi Kojima, and Terutomo Ozawa, *Japan's General Trading Companies—Merchants of Economic Development*. Development Center Studies Paris, (OECD), 1984. Also *Keiretsu* industrial enterprises, compared with 'independent' firms, tend to retain a higher level of liabilities in their capital structure, i.e. relying more on indirect funding and their 'direct' approach is normally ushered and supported by *Keiretsu* financial institutions. For a rough idea concerning comparative equity ratios of Japanese enterprises refer to *The Oriental Economist*, Japan Company Handbook—Newest Data on Big Listed Companies. Toyo Keizai Shinposha, Tokyo, semi-annually.

46. Although it is quite obvious that manufacturers would concentrate on manufacturing, the trader on commerce and the bank on finance, what is featured in the Japanese case is a comparatively deeper concentration on the main function of the one enterprise while there is a more 'strategic' dependence on the other providing a supplementary function. The 'depth' of concentration is further spelled out by vertical industrial specialization and division of labour among smaller firms. (Refer to note 57.)

47. Concentration on separate areas of economic activities (e. g. finance or marketing) allows in-depth pursuit of development in each respective area. The total effort induces a general spirit (a group force) which serves as a lever or driving power. The conception of stable relationships and relativity of one institution to another, serves as an underlying factor. 'Interdependence is thus key to a thriving group life, it flourishes in times of prosperity but it works best in time of need.' See R. J. Ballon, I. Tomita, and H. Usami (*op. cit.*, note 15, p. 50.)

48. This is more in line with the idea of a frame of reference, leader of a task force, or a general resort as opposed to a competitive winner or an absolute leader.

49. Or custodians of resources which are, in principle, available to group member firms.

50. For instance the manufacturer here represents a source of technology and know-how. The main outflow tends to be internalized, i.e. in the sense that it is, in principle, shared among member companies in the same enterprise system. Two conditions reflect on the nature of the source: concentration of Japanese R&D in the private sector and internationalization of industrial training. (Further the enterprises type of specialization and interdependence reflects on the nature of the source.)

51. 'Basically a *Keiretsu* is a web of relationships ranging from tight to loose, among companies working together' (Ken Ichi Imai, *op. cit.*, note 11). The point is to reverse the starting point by assuming a basic interest in the nature of Japanese resources management principles which prompted the designing of the *Keiretsu* as an institution. Refer also to notes 2 and 58 *supra*.

52. For instance a *Keiretsu* manufacturer tends to deposit its main funds with the *Keiretsu* financial institution. There is also the specific handling of corporate pension funds by the group institutions. In a different perspective is the 'regular' outflow of funds to financial institutions in the form of interest payment on loans and, in a more limited and less regular manner, the payments of dividends. Further, *Keiretsu* financial institutions are guaranteed a certain level of funds by their corporate clients in the form of 'compen-

sating balances'. See R. J. Ballon, I. Tomita and H. Usami (*op. cit.*, note 15, pp. 93–94). Accordingly a Japanese firm is expected to use 20 to 50% of borrowed money in the form of time or other deposits with the financial institution.

53. In other words the Japanese tend to concentrate on factor procurement, mobility and co-ordination. Thus, in their case, there are separate areas in resource economics: economics of procurement, of mobility and of coordination. This position seems to be synonymous with systems-thinking in institutional engineering.

54. Supply economics with its focus on cost; interest in cost as related to high productivity—the latter seen in the context of 'economics of cohesion'.

55. The issue is highlighted as Japanese *Keiretsu* attempt to establish, operate and control production facilities outside Japan. It is also an interesting question in the light of the current Japanese intensive application of microelectronics to industry and the consequent rise of the 'economies of scope', i.e. versus the economies of scale. Refer to Takashi Kiuchi, 'The Microelectronic Revolution', *LTCB Economic Review*, No. 95, December 1988.

56. Singled out recently as 'production *Keiretsu*' with more attention paid to the nature of industrial ties, i.e. as compared to one on interlocked shareholding. Emphasis is gaining, in a different perspective, on industrial cohesion or supply economics as applied internally with a new related identification emerging under '*Keizen*' (i.e. as a Japanese method of industrial organization). Refer to Yoshihiko Shimizu, Mikio Tsutsui, Yu Inaba and Masakuni Umesawa, 'Production Keiretsu: A New Export From Japan', *Tokyo Business Today*, September 1990. (Also note 16.)

57. The best examples are cases in the machinery sector, e.g. motor vehicles, electronics and general machinery. Typically revealed in relation to these industries is the high level of sub-contracting practices. For instance studies show that the percentage of small- and medium-sized firms that are sub-contractors in the transport industry is 88%, in electrical machinery 85% and in general machinery 84% . Refer to Takashi Yokokura (*op. cit.*, note 18, p. 525). 'Throughout the world's auto industry, the term "*keiretsu*" may not be well-known. But the concept is familiar and most commonly referred to as "design in". Far from being applicable only in Japan the production *Keiretsu* concept has universal applicability. Auto executives and economists alike increasingly realize that manufacturers that do not develop close, long-term relationships with suppliers will not be able to compete.' See Y. Shimizu, M. Tsutsui, Y. Inaba and Masakuni Umesawa (*op. cit.*, note 56, p. 31). 'The web of relationships is close-knit and durable which allows the car-maker to spread risks since the suppliers are able and willing to be partners in the product development process'. See Michael L. Dertouszo, Richard K. Lester and Robert M. Solow, and the MIT Commission on Industrial Productivity, *Made in America: Regaining the Productive Edge*, The MIT Press, Cambridge, 1989, p. 100.

58. This tendency represents one step into a necessary interest in the 'internalities' (industrial) of the Japanese enterprise or in the composite nature of its mechanism in more detail . 'The Japanese emphasis placed on industrial engineering, basic production principles and the organization of work has received only scant attention in Western countries.' See C. J. McMillan (*op. cit.*, note 5, p. 226). More recently attention is being called to the 'micro', (internal) structure of the Japanese firm. See Masahiko Aoki, 'Towards an Economic Model of the Japanese Firm', *Journal of Economic Literature*, March, 1990.

59. The concept here maintains fundamental differences from the understanding of the nature and role of a headquarters in Western enterprises. In the Japanese case, due to their typical tendencies towards industrial specialization, the parent enterprise as a whole (not a division or a department) is usually identified as the Headquarters. Reference needs to be made here to capacity and comparative bargaining power, in finance, level of qualitative labour due to life-time employment and internal skill training and level of R&D on account of a Japanese tendency to concentrate such activities in the private sector—the large enterprises in particular. Refer also to notes 49 and 50 *supra*.

60. Refer to notes 7, 12, 13, 23, 51, 53 and 54.

61. It feeds into and is fed by the 'numerous' and 'specialized' departments or sub-systems of the total enterprise. The principle has been identified, in one source, in reference to the organization of work in Japanese companies: 'The practical shape of the organization of the Japanese company is therefore a chain of the cooperative work group from the bottom to the top or from the top to the end ... The management method of the Japanese company is again designed to support the chain of the co-operative work groups throughout the company'. Masumi Tsuda, 'Management System of Japanese Company in Practice', *Hitotsubashi Journal of Social Studies*, Vol. 17, No. 1, April 1985, pp. 14–15.

62. The defined character of each type and nature of separation between the two, is representative of Japan's industrial society which has been fundamentally influenced and determined by the country's industrial policy/industrial structure tutology. Witness to this is the series of laws introduced defining the field and fate of medium and small companies, merger policy and the effectiveness of what is normally uncodified but comes under the practice of 'administrative guidance'.

63. Cost minimization is synonymous with resource utilization. The dynamics of inter-relatedness is synergy. Perfection in synergy (which means bringing parts together) would be expected to create a certain force (level of productivity) on account of, in particular, the combined behaviour and science of interchange. Thus cost is minimized in two ways. At the level when a certain art of resource utilization is applied and when the combined resources start to function, a high level of productivity is witnessed. Simply, resource utilization plus high level of productivity reflect on cost. The 'art' here may best be seen in the Japanese 'modern' concept of *Kaizen*. An authority of the art stated that *Kaizen* includes those actions which make the best use of the resources at hand (people, machines, facilities, technology and so forth) and within that framework there is an attempt to improve little by little. Refer to Masaaki Imai, 'Kaizen Wave Circles the Globe', *Tokyo Business Today*, May 1990. Also a previous, and more comprehensive analysis by the same author in Imai Miazaki, *Kai Zen (Ky'Zen) The Key to Japan's Competitive Success*, Random House, New York, 1986.

64. Refer to 'CIM—The Manufacturing/Information Wave of the Future', *Tokyo Business Today*, 1990. Also Economic Planning Agency, *Economic Survey of Japan 1988/1989*. The trend is a part of moves of the Japanese machinery industry in general which is currently testing assembly automation, referred to as FA, and the flexible manufacturing system complex (FMSC). It is estimated that if such automation can be successfully implemented labour productivity could be enhanced by 30 to 40%. See Takeshi Hayashi (*op. cit.*, note 36). Scarcity of labour focuses mainly on software engineers. According to MITI's estimates, Japan needs 600 000 more software engineers than it has and that the shortage will reach one million by year 2000. (See *Tokyo Business Today*, July 1990, p. 9.) What is, for instance, implied in the total picture is increases in the level and scope of integration (synergy) and a necessarily corresponding change in labour's skill, meaning development in the depth and breadth of know-how to handle new types of work and new 'scope' in the work situation.

65. There is a tendency on the part of the Japanese to see life in matter; a god existed in everything. Kato Ichiro, Robotic Engineering, Waseda University, is quoted as saying that Japanese workers utilize robots as fellow workers, not as mere lifeless pieces of equipment. Refer to Oyama Shigeo, 'Semiconductors and the Japanese Mind', *Japan Quarterly*, January–March 1989, p. 89.

66. Sense of pragmatism as, for instance, expressed through their economics of resources and concentration on the present; the sense of spirituality is reflected in their views of 'total' Nature and the incorporation of each part in the whole. Yet spirituality, in their case, is not in relation to Heaven above: it is the real Universe.

67. At one level the problem is generally expressed in terms of investment friction. Deeper, however, it becomes a matter of institutional adjustments which makes it necessary to examine the mechanics of an economic institution as well as, in the Japanese case, its 'boundaries'.

68. The individual firm, in one respect, has various options: from its source, within the context of the *Keiretsu* and on the basis of the latter's potential reach (and bargaining power) to external sources; and secondly, though various existing options the 'unlimited' qualification applies also to the operational dynamism of the central 'pools' of resources, i.e. as represented by *Keiretsu* financial and service institutions and R&D joint ventures.

69. Large Japanese manufacturers tend to maintain a good-sized complex of sales subsidiaries which, in the history of establishment, preceded their local manufacturing operations. These subsidiaries (either alone, jointly with each other or with the parent manufacturer) are largely accountable for local manufacturing facilities. For example, Matsushita Trading Company, headquartered in Japan, and a subsidiary of Matsushita Electric Industrial, covers roughly 26 main sales subsidiaries in 22 countries. Refer to *Matsushita Electric*, Matsushita Electric Industrial Co. Ltd. Osaka.

70. Refer to Hidemasa Morikawa, 'The Organizational Structure of Mitsubishi and Mitsui: Zaibatsu 1868–1922—A Comparative Study', *Business History Review*, Vol. XLIV, 1970. Also, Keiichiro Nakagawa (ed.) *Strategy and Structure of Big Business*, University of Tokyo Press, Tokyo, 1977.

71. One feature of such lineage is the 'partnership' with national bureaucracy, i.e. Japanese-type of business/government relationships witnessed in the post-World War II period in the sphere of, for example, economic planning, form of industrial policy and manner of implementation and in the existence and

operation of the numerous 'deliberative' councils. (The general principle and corresponding patterns of relationship have also been applied in Japan since the *Meiji* period.)

72. Refer to note 6.

73. This should be seen in terms of efforts in energy-saving by Japanese vertical *Keiretsu* and efforts of 'industrial groups' to establish their own energy development and sourcing schemes, e.g. Mitsubishi Petroleum Development Company and Fuyo Petroleum Development. Further, each 'group' converged its strategies towards switching their industrial structures towards knowledge intensification and development of high-tech industries in line with developments in national industrial policy. Refer to Economic Planning Agency, *Economic Survey of Japan 1983/1984* on resource-saving techniques. 'The engine that will propel the industrial structure of Japan to a higher level of creative knowledge-intensification in the 1980s will be technological innovation... This calls for the development of urgently needed large-scale system technologies such as energy-related technology and large-scale projects'. See, MITI, *The Industrial Structure of Japan in the 1980s—Future Outlook and Tasks*. MITI, Tokyo, 1981, p.3. What is to be noted, in the general context is the related level of need for investment funds and the precedent, in resource potential and investment capacity and behaviour, of the *Keiretsu*.

74. 'Technological paths' seen in terms of 'objectives' which in general have been covered under such terms, as 'microelectronic revolution' or 'softnomics' (the latter term refers to changes in the economy representing a rising ratio of the cost of non-material inputs, or non-material inputs plus labour costs, to the cost of all inputs. In other words, it refers to a new way of economic management corresponding to the coming of a 'softnomical' society, i.e. a society placing increasing emphasis on the application of microelectronics in manufacturing industries and the increasing role of the service sector. The term, 'softnomics' was introduced, at an early stage, in the *Report of the Study Group on the Structural Transformation of the Economy and Policy Implication*, 7 June 1983, commissioned by the Research and Planning Division of the Ministry of Finance. Refer to Hiroshi Takeuchi, 'Softnomization of Society', *The Oriental Economist*, December 1983. Also Economic Planning Agency, *Economic Survey of Japan 1985/1986*, p.159. In retrospect, the 'path' is largely determined by R&D expenditure and the level of investment in services—both aspects have the potential environment and institutional framework (or network) within the context of the *Keiretsu*.

75. A fundamental prerequisite of the 'new' technological/industrial phase is a certain capacity to integrate, i.e. integrative effort at various levels. This implies selectivity of the resources or inputs needed; it also requires a level of apprehension or cost-consciousness, given, especially, the comparative degree of resources scarcity to be encountered. Cohesion-economics and the economics of cost exhibited as a principal attribute of a *Keiretsu* offer a good answer. Refer to notes 13, 51 and 63.

76. High-technology here has been defined as 'a technology that is R&D-intensive and system-oriented'. See Ken 'Ichi Imai, 'Industrial Policy and Technological Innovation', in Ryutaro Komiya, Mahsairo Okuna, Kotaro Suzumura (*op. cit.*, note 6, p.206). Refer also to Takashi Kiuchi, 'The Microelectronics Revolution', *LTCB Research Economic Review*, No. 95, December 1988, and Economic Planning Agency, *Economic Survey of Japan 1988/1989*, Chapter 2: 'Sophisticated Life-Style and Sophisticated Production'.

77. Internationalization, as recent trade in Japan's economic activity, tends to be seen in different perspectives. A general outlook focuses on the country's thrust overseas, since the late 1970s, in terms of direct investments. The same is also 'thinly' seen in terms of the country's sudden rise in capital export. Recent estimates of the level of Japan's long-term capital export put the total at $136 billion; it is also estimated that Japan would have a net creditor position of well over $1 trillion by the middle of l990 and possibly $1.5 trillion. Refer to Yoshio Suzuki, 'The Sun is Still High', *Tokyo Business Today*, September 1990. Yet, essentially, internationalization ties in with the Japanese concept of 'softnomics'; it implies the transfer of industries and industrial processes abroad. It also means the creation of international links to serve as conduits for know-how towards the promotion of technological innovations. Against the general picture stands specifically the financial resourcefulness and know-how of the *Keiretsu* institutional network and coverage of information resources. There is also the expediency (due to institutional co-operation) to transform industrial activities and to transfer such activities.

78. Technological impetus may simply be represented by the drive towards knowledge intensification and pursuit of higher value added production activities. This implies 'shedding' operations and the operations to be shed tie with regional diversification. Secondly the 'constitution' of the *Keiretsu* in this case is flexible and an overseas operation would simply fit in among the numerous medium and small affiliates held. There is, however, a potential kind of sensitivity that may develop in relation to the transfer of operations overseas, on account of the increasingly sophisticated and integrative tendencies of the domestic production system, or core. In one respect it makes the local operation more subject to Japanese practices; in

another it makes the domestic system more sensitive towards accommodating the 'alien' elements these operations may create and impart.

79. At one level a tendency under Japan's current technology/industrial policy is the promotion of joint international R&D activities. 'A policy line to which MITI attaches great importance is that of developing basic research in basic technologies... MITI is also giving priority to furthering international joint research.' See, Shinji Fukukawa, 'A New Industrial Structure—MITI's Policies Towards the 21st Century', *Speaking of Japan*, January 1987, p.9. The tendency has recently materialized in establishing (under MITI's direction and support) the International Superconductivity Technology Center (ISTEC) and attached Superconductivity Research Laboratory in 1988. The latter accommodates 46 Japanese companies and encourages participation by foreign companies and researchers. Refer to Shoji Tanaka, 'Leading the Search for Superconductors', *Journal of Japanese Trade and Industry*, No.3, 1989. Individual Japanese companies themselves comply with such a national tendency by funding research projects overseas and in particular, by establishing their own local R&D operations. For example, the MIT Industrial Liaison Program has 45 Japanese companies as participants and beneficiaries. At $30 000 per year, companies like NEC, Canon and Hitachi and other high-tech heavyweights obtain priority access to MIT research projects. Separately, NEC established its own Research Institute in New York USA in 1988. Refer to Thomas Murtha, 'Japan's Soft Approach to R&D', *The Oriental Economist*, October 1984, p. 26 and Kenkichi Takahashi, *A Shift Towards R&D Oriented Business Strategy*, Digest of Japanese Industry and Technology, No. 254, 1989, p.45.

80. 'The present innovation in high technology differs from the production formula for a small number of different products formerly prevailing and follow the formula featuring the production of small quantities of various products to a trend towards demand for high quality goods and diversification... There, essence of the current trend in high-tech innovation is advanced control technology featuring free use of microelectronics and it is spreading to all fields of industry in a "technology inducing technology manner"'. See Economic Planning Agency, *Economic Survey of Japan 1983/1984*, p. 92. Also, Takashi Kiuchi, *The Microelectronics Revolution* (*op. cit.*, note 76, p. 2).

81. Refer to note 64. Also Economic Planning Agency, *Economic Survey of Japan 1988/1989*, Chapter 2.

82. For a general impression of tendencies towards changes in Japanese labour practices and anticipated developments under the influence of increasing application of technology refer, for example, to Shuhei Aida, 'Economic and Social Effects of Factory Automation', *Modes en Developpement*, Vol. 14, Nos. 54–55, 1986. Also Mine Manabu, 'The Social Impact of Microelectronics in Japan', *International Labour Review*, Vol. 125, No. 4, July-August 1986; and Taichi Sakaiya, *New Role Model for the Work Force*, in Keizai Koho Center, *Economic Views From Japan*, Tokyo Keizai Koho Center, 1986.

83. In effect the export level represented, at an initial stage of the Japanese enterprise growth, a built-in structure within its production system. This is one reason why a reduction in exports from Japan has been always feared because it would lead to operations below capacity and contribute to increases in cost. Yet this very built-in export structure, to the Japanese, represented a step in internationalization.

84. Internationalization at this stage relates undoubtedly to trade friction. But more fundamentally it ties in with a new stage of development in the production system and corresponding requirements towards transformation under the country's new industrial strategies. Thus, in one sense, the built-in export structure of the past is eventually becoming outmoded. In another, the nature of production core that is emerging is becoming more and more exclusive but with a new need for 'external' operations to lend vitality to the continuity of the kind of feedback required.

85. An appendage here is a local operation (or a certain economic tie with a foreign economic environment) which tends to be 'outstanding', i.e. against a background of the typical nature of Japanese institutional composition and operational behaviour.

86. Another aspect of the 'hardware' infrastructure (or capital) is the level of Japanese financial resources with the world-wide spread and reach of their financial institutions . It may also be seen in the 'stock' and potentially so, of basic machinery and parts that could be shipped from Japan or from a Japanese source.

Appendix A
Member companies of president associations of six major industrial groups (Fiscal, 1987)

Industry	Mitsui (Nimokukai; 24 firms; started in October 1961)	Mitsubishi (Kinyokai; 29 firms; started in c.1955)	Sumitone (Hakusuikai; 20 firms; started in April 1951)	Fuyo (Fuji) (Fuyokai; 29 firms; started in February 1967)	Sanwa (Sansuikai; 44 firms; started in February 1967)	Dai Ichi Kangyo (Sankinkai; 47 firms; started in January 1978)
Banking and insurance	Mitsui Bank Mitsui Trust & Banking Mitsui Mutual Life Insurance[a] Taisho Marine & Fire Insurance	Mitsubishi Bank Mitsubishi Trust & Banking Meiji Mutual Life Insurance[a] Tokio Marine & Fire Insurance	Sumitomo Bank Sumitomo Trust & Banking Sumitomo Life Insurance[a] Sumitomo Marine & Fire Insurance	Fuji Bank Yasuda Trust & Banking Yasuda Mutual Life Insurance[a] Yasuda Fire & Marine Insurance	Sanwa Bank Toyo Trust & Banking Nippon Life Insurance[a]	Dai Ichi Kangyo Bank Asahi Mutual Life Insurance[a] Fukoku Mutual Life Insurance[a] Nissan Fire & Marine Insurance Taisei Fire & Marine Insurance
Trading	Mitsui & Co.	Mitsubishi Corp.	Sumitomo Corp.	Marubeni Corp.	Nichimen Corp. Nissho Iwai Corp. Iwatani International	C. Itoh & Co. Kanematsu-Gosho Ltd Nissho Iwai Corp. Kawasho Corp.
Primary industries	Mitsui Mining Hokkaido Colliery & Steamship		Sumitomo Forestry Sumitomo Coal Mining			
Construction	Mitsui Construction Sanki Engineering	Mitsubishi Construction[a]	Sumitomo Construction	Taisei Construction	Ohbayashi Corp. Zenitaka Corp. Toyo Construction Sekisui House	Shimizu Corp.
Foodstuffs	Nippon Flour Mills	Kirin Brewery		Nisshin Flour Milling Sapporo Breweries Nichirei Corp.	Itoham Foods Suntory Ltd.	
Textiles	Toray Industries	Misubishi Rayon		Nisshinbo Industries Toho Rayon	Unitika Teijin Ltd.	Asahi Chemical Industry
Paper pulp	Oji Paper	Mitsubishi Paper		Sanyo-Kokusaku Pulp		Honshu Paper

Appendix A (continued)

Chemicals	Mitsui Toatsu Chemicals Mitsui Petrochemicals	Mitsubishi Kasei Mitsubishi Gas Chemical Mitsubishi Petrochemical Mitsubishi Plastics Mitsubishi Monsanto Chemical[a]	Sumitomo Chemical Sumitomo Bakelite	Showa Denko Kureha Chemical Nippon Oil & Fats	Tokuyama Soda Sekisui Chemical Ube Industries Hitachi Chemical Tanabe Seiyaku Fujisawa Pharmaceutical Kansai Paint	Denki Kagaku Kogyo Kyowa Hakko Kogyo Nippon Zeon Asahi Denka Kogyo Sankyo Co. Shiseido Co. Lion Corp.
Oil		Mitsubishi Oil		Toa Nenryo Kogyo	Cosmo Oil	Showa Shell Sekiyu
Rubber					Toyo Tire & Rubber	Yokohama Rubber
Glass Stone, etc.	Onoda Cement	Asahi Glass Mitsubishi Mining & Cement	Nippon Sheet Glass Sumitomo Cement	Nihon Cement	Osaka Cement	Chichibu Cement
Iron and steel	Japan Steel Works	Mitubishi Steel	Sumitomo Metal Industries	NKK	Kobe Steel Nisshin Steel Nakayama Steel Works Hitachi Metals	Kawasaki Steel Kobe Steel Japan Metals & Chemicals
Non-ferrous metals	Mitsui Mining & Smelting	Mitsubishi Metal Mitsubishi Cable Industries Mitsubishi Aluminium[a]	Sumitomo Metal Mining Sumitomo Light Metal Sumitomo Electric Industries		Hitachi Cable	Nippon Light Metal Furukawa Co. Furukawa Electric
Machinery		Mitsubishi Kakoki	Sumitomo Heavy Machinery	Kubota Ltd Nippon Seiko	NTN Toyo Bearing	Niigata Engineering Iseki & Co. Ebara Corp.
Electric machinery	Toshia Corp.	Mitsubishi Electric	NEC Corp.	Hitachi Ltd. Oki Electric Industry Yokogawa Electric	Hitachi Ltd Iwatsu Electric Sharo Corp. Kyocera Corp. Nitto Denki Corp.	Hitachi Ltd Fuji Electric Yasukawa Electric Works Fujitsu Ltd. Nippon Columbia

Appendix A (continued)

Electric Machinery	Toshia Corp.	Mitsubishi Electric	NEC Corp.	Hitachi Ltd. Oki Electric Industry Yokogawa Electric	Hitachi Ltd Iwatsu Electric Sharo Corp. Kyocera Corp. Nitto Denki Corp.	Hitachi Ltd Fuji Electric Yasukawa Electric Works Fujitsu Ltd. Nippon Columbia
Transportation equipment	Mitsui Engineering & Shipbuilding Toyota Motor[b]	Mitsubishi Heavy Industries Mitsubishi Motors	Nissan Motor	Hitachi Zosen Shin Meiwa Industry Daihatsu Motor	Kawasaki Heavy Industries Ishikawajima-Harima Heavy Industries Isuzu Motors
Precision machinery		Nikon Corp.	Canon Inc.	Hoya Corp.	Asahi Optical
Retail	Mitsukoshi			Takashimaya Co.	Seibu Department Store[a]
Finance				Orient Leasing	Nippon Kangyo Kakumaru Securities Orient Finance
Real estate	Mitsui Real Estate Development	Mitsubishi Estate	Sumitomo Realty & Development	Tokyo Tatemono	
Transportation, communications, etc.	Mitsui-O.S.K. Lines Mitsui Warehouse	Nippon Yusen Mitsubishi Warehouse	Sumitomo Warehouse	Tobu Railway Keihin Electric Express Showa Line	Hankyu Corp. Nippon Express Yamashita-Shinnihon Steamship	Nippon Express Kawasaki Kisen Shibusawa Warehouse
Services					Korkuen Co.

[a] Unlisted companies.
[b] Toyota Motor is an observer, not a full member, in the Mitsui group.
Source: 'Intimate Links within Japan's Corporate Groups', *Tokyo Business Today*, January, 1989.

16

The Japanese Corporate Network: A Blockmodel Analysis

Michael L. Gerlach

In response to Japan's continuing competitive performance and to its ongoing trade frictions with important trading partners, researchers have become increasingly interested in recent years in the distinctive patterns of its overall industrial organization (e.g., Aoki, 1988; Hamilton and Biggart, 1988; Lawrence, 1991; Fruin, 1992; Gerlach, 1992). Located at a level intermediate between the internal managerial practices of the Japanese firm and the national and international forces that define Japan's macroeconomy and industrial policies, the Japanese corporate network is marked by an elaborate structure of institutional arrangements that have organized its companies within complex patterns of cooperation and competition. The result, in the words of two observers, is 'a thick and complex skein of relations matched in no other industrial country' (Caves and Uekusa, 1976, p.59).

Among the widely noted characteristics of intercorporate relationships in Japan is the existence of highly visible clique-like patterns based on intercorporate alliances, or *keiretsu*. Diversified groupings of firms descended from the prewar *zaibatsu*, or family-centred holding companies, involve firms that often share the same names and logos (e.g., Mitsubishi and Sumitomo) and organize relationships among financial institutions, trading companies and industrial producers (Hadley, 1970; Orru et al., 1989; Gerlach, 1992). Large industrial concerns (e.g., Toyota Motors and Hitachi) are in turn positioned at the apex of their own vertically linked groupings of smaller affiliated supplier and distribution firms (Aoki, 1988; Asanuma, 1989; Fruin, 1992).

Despite the apparent significance of densely clustered corporate groupings, however, basic questions remain about the overall structure of Japanese business networks. To what extent do nominal groupings correspond to empirical patterns of network structure using standard network methods? Are these groupings the main basis for network structure in Japan, or are other forms of intercorporate relationship equally important? In particular, do Japanese banks and other financial institutions play the same kind of central role in networks of directorships, stock ownership, and corporate control as they do in the US. If so, are ties to common financial institutions the main source of structural coherence in enterprise groupings, or are direct ties among affiliated industrial firms equally important? Furthermore, how do these patterns interact with the business interests of firms in the network—by, for example, linking competi-

---

Reprinted from 'The Japanese Corporate Network: A Blockmodel Analysis', by Michael L. Gerlach, published in *Administrative Science Quarterly*, Vol. 37, March 1992, pp. 105–139, by permission of *Administrative Science Quarterly*.
Copyright © 1992 by Cornell University.

tors or vertically related suppliers and customers through common structures of intercorporate coordination and control?

Most studies of Japan's corporate network have proceeded by first identifying nominal groupings of firms based on some criterion for classification. One commonly used measure is formal participation in one of the executive councils that bring together executives of affiliated companies in regular monthly meetings for the purpose of social and strategic interaction (Kosei Torihiki Iinkai, 1983; Gerlach, 1992). Other researchers have instead relied on classifications provided by public data sources, which are based on considerations such as the history of relationships and contemporary patterns of interaction (Nakatani, 1984; Orru et al., 1989). These nominal groupings are then used as the basis for describing characteristics of or relationships among those firms that are of theoretical interest. Structurally oriented researchers have used them to measure relatively precisely the characteristics of the relationships among firms in the same *keiretsu* and to compare the coherence of different groupings (Hadley, 1970; Futatsugi, 1976; Orru et al., 1989; Gerlach, 1992). Econometrically oriented researchers have used patterns of affiliation as the basis for tracing performance differences among Japanese firms in order to infer the functions groups play for member firms (Caves and Uekusa, 1976; Nakatani 1984; Cable and Yasuki, 1985).

To the extent that these studies rely on the *a priori* classification of firms into specific groups, however, they may overstate the importance of clique patterns in the Japanese corporate network. The existence of frequent connections among a subset of group firms, for example, may be an artifact of high overall levels of exchange among all companies in the network rather than an indication of truly differentiated clusters of firms. Some observers have recently suggested that corporate groupings are less important in the Japanese economy than is usually believed and represent primarily socially defined epiphenomena that have only limited significance in actual patterns of interaction among Japanese firms (Komiya, 1990; Miwa, 1990). Conversely, prior classification of groups may understate the importance of non-clique bases for network structure. In so far as they are based on what Burt (1980) has termed a 'cohesion' logic resting on the presumption of dense sets of intensive ties among actors, they ignore patterns of interaction in which firms are linked not directly but through the sharing of common relationships in the overall network that exist independent of nominal groupings.

In order to overcome these limitations, this study follows an alternative approach. In contrast to clique-based models, which partition networks based on social proximity resulting from direct relationships, such as friendship or informal association, the Japanese corporate network as a whole is taken as the starting point for analysis. Based on a logic of structural equivalence, the analytic models developed here partition networks based on actors' common patterns of relations with all other actors in the network, whether those actors are directly linked or not (Lorrain and White, 1971; White et al., 1976; Burt, 1980). These methods can detect cohesive cliques where they are an important element of network structure, thereby permitting empirical verification of nominal classifications of groupings, but they can also determine a variety of other structures of theoretical interest, including patterns of network stratification (e.g., bank centrality) and sectoral differentiation (Burt, 1983; DiMaggio, 1987).

This study represents one of the first attempts to apply standard network techniques to the overall Japanese corporate network. Although the structural analyses described below are exploratory, they prove capable of demonstrating relatively precisely the significance of different sets of network patterns across several types of intercorporate relations among large firms in the Japanese economy. Role positions within the network are shown to be strongly differentiated among firms based on *keiretsu* affiliations and sectoral variations among financial and industrial firms. In addition, the results also reveal some interesting interactions among these patterns not readily apparent in previous studies of Japanese industrial organization.

THE JAPANESE CORPORATE NETWORK IN COMPARATIVE PERSPECTIVE

Intercorporate relationships have been approached from a variety of perspectives, each representing an implicit theory about network structure. In this section, I consider three different underlying patterns in this structure as they apply to the Japanese corporate network: (1) intercorporate alliances, including Japanese *keiretsu* groupings, based on relatively dense networks of historically determined relationships among companies; (2) financial centrality, based on the stratification of network structure by economic sector and focusing on the special role of financial institutions in the network as a result of their role in capital allocation processes; and (3) industrial interdependence, based on business corporations' need to manage uncertainty in their environment through various mechanisms of coordination with competitors and business partners.

Although each perspective imposes a different pattern on network structure, the resulting predictions are generally complementary and there are reasons to believe that each is an important organizing principle in the Japanese economy.

Two sources of interaction are also considered. First, where intercorporate alliances and financial centrality are both important, I consider how roles within *keiretsu* structures become differentiated among financial and industrial firms. Second, where intercorporate alliances or financial centrality interact with industrial interdependency, I point to ways that firms in particular industries manage their business relationships through the strategic use of *keiretsu* groupings and key banking relationships.

Intercorporate alliances

The existence of durable cliques, or interest groups, organized around major banks, elite families, or regions of the country has long been of interest to American researchers. Several writers have suggested that the US economy is composed of a number of major and minor groupings, each with a large commercial bank at its control centre (Perlo, 1957; Allen, 1978; Kotz, 1978). Yet while there is some evidence of identifiable groupings in the earlier part of the century, these have proven difficult to detect or replicate in studies relying on more recent data (Useem, 1984; Mintz and Schwartz, 1985). Additional doubts are raised by findings from research on broken directorship interlocks on the durability of relations in the American corporate network. In contrast to the prediction that firms with enduring strategic interests will seek to reconstitute directorship ties that are discontinued through retirement from other companies' boards of directors, evidence indicates that the majority of directorship ties among companies are not reconstituted (Palmer, 1983; for similar evidence from Canada, see Ornstein, 1984). This suggests that the American directorship network is characterized by a relatively fluid pattern of ties.

The case for the existence of coherent intercorporate alliances would seem to be considerably stronger in Japan. Japanese enterprise groupings, unlike interest groups in the US, maintain a well-defined identity, with membership roles reported in the Japanese business media. Affiliated firms frequently share common names and engage in a variety of groupwide business and social activities that facilitate their collective identification. In addition to holding monthly executive councils, firms in the same *keiretsu* have been involved in joint cooperation in a wide variety of business activities, including the development of atomic energy in Japan in the 1950s, overseas oil exploration projects in the 1960s, and the installation of groupwide information networks since the beginning of the 1980s.

The salience of these forms can be traced to a complex nexus of historical and institutional considerations (Hamilton and Biggart, 1988; Gerlach, 1992). Contemporary patterns of alliance in Japan reflect distinctive path-dependent trajectories that represent considerable carryover from the prewar period. Control over *zaibatsu* subsidiaries before and during the Second World War was exercised by a small set of holding companies, while control over the holding companies themselves was located in a set of prominent families. At the end of the war, for example, the Sumitomo family held 83% of the shares in the Sumitomo holding company, which in turn was the major shareholder in and sent several directors to each of its key subsidiary companies (Hadley, 1970; Miyazaki, 1976). With Japan's defeat and the subsequent arrival of US Occupation forces came attempts at reforms of the Japanese economy. The most important measures from the point of view of the *zaibatsu* were the dissolution of the holding companies, the elimination of family assets held in the *zaibatsu*, the removal of many top executives from first-line subsidiaries, and the breakup of a number of leading *zaibatsu* companies.

Despite the role of the Occupation forces in introducing reforms into the Japanese economy during the early postwar period, however, it appears in retrospect that these were far from the kind of universal overhaul of the Japanese economic system that its initiators had intended. Family ownership connections to the holding companies and holding-company connections to the direct subsidiaries were eliminated by postwar reforms, but these proved to be only a portion of the networks of connections that held together the various elements constituting each group, and important connections to the past remained. A new generation of executives was selected to replace those who had been forced out, but these people came from middle management in the old subsidiaries and had developed and maintained ongoing personal connections with managers in other subsidiaries extending back to the wartime and prewar years.

In addition, despite the role of the holding company in the subsidiaries' capital structures, equity interlocks among the subsidiaries themselves also sometimes existed. Unlike family and holding company positions, these shareholdings were not eliminated after the war and served as a convenient preexisting structure for the emergence of interlocking ownership patterns during the postwar period. At the time of dissolution, for example, Sumitomo Bank held 40% of the shares of Sumitomo Trust & Banking, as well as 7% of the shares of Sumitomo Metal Mining and Sumitomo Metal Industries (Hadley, 1970). Other *zaibatsu* subsidiaries held significant positions in the Sumitomo Bank itself, as well as in Sumitomo Metal Industries, Sumitomo Metal Mining, Sumitomo Electric, Sumitomo Chemical, Sumitomo Machinery, and Nippon Electric—all of the major subsidiaries that were to constitute the core of the newly formed Sumitomo group. According to an executive in the Sumitomo group at the time, 'If one looks for stable and trustworthy stockholders, one naturally turns to former Honsha subsidiaries. It is not that any specific plan was followed in going ahead with interlocking ownership. It would be more correct to say that things happened in this way out of the desire, among brother-companies, to help each other' (*Oriental Economist*, April 1955). The family metaphor was also used by another executive: 'Because one's parents are dead, one is not prevented from continuing as before with one's brothers and sisters. What could be more natural than the brothers and sisters of a family helping each other to keep going as a group?' (*Oriental Economist*, January 1959).

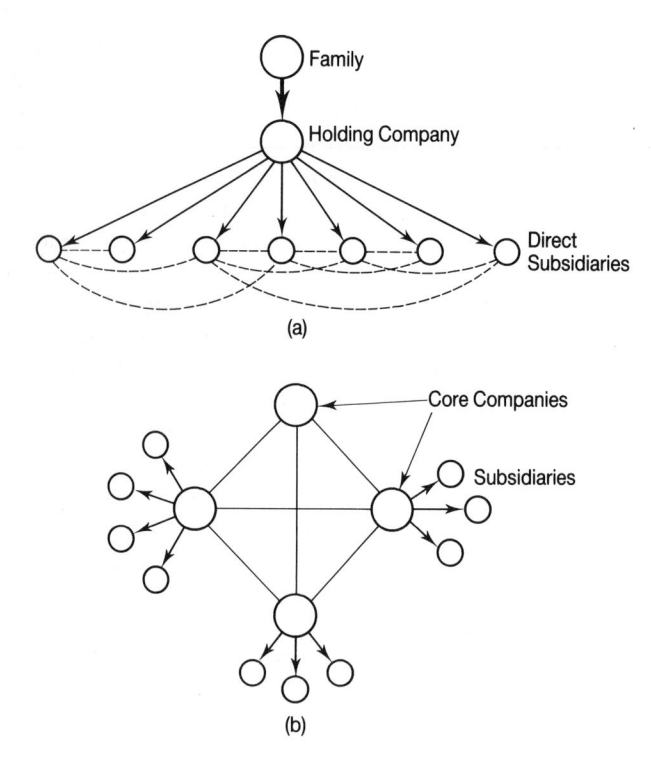

Figure 1. (a). Prewar *Zaibatsu* Ownership and Control Patterns. (b) Postwar *Keiretsu* Ownership and Control Patterns.

The changes in group structure brought about by the postwar reforms are depicted schematically in Figure 1(a), (b). The prewar structure of the *zaibatsu*, organized around key families and the group holding company, is shown in Figure 1(a). With the dissolution of this structure, many of these subsidiary companies grew into substantial enterprises in their own right and formed the nucleus around which the present-day *keiretsu* are based. When the former subsidiary firms began meeting again in the early 1950s they comprised nearly all of the old first-line subsidiaries, each now an 'independent' operation. In addition to consolidating direct relationships with other subsidiaries, these companies have created networks of subsidiaries and satellite firms around their periphery, as seen in Figure 1(b).

Over the course of time, structures of cooperation have become institutionalized features of the Japanese industrial landscape. Six major *keiretsu* now exist in Japan: the Mitsui, Mitsubishi, Sumitomo, Fuji, Sanwa, and Dai-Ichi Kangyo groups. Although various differences exist in the coherence of these six groupings, they have nevertheless demonstrated generally similar patterns of membership and activities. Each includes a major commercial bank at its centre, a large life insurance company, one or more general trading companies, and one or more manufacturing firms in virtually all important industrial sectors. Each has used monthly presidents' councils as a forum for interaction among member companies' top executives, and each has devoted energies to symbolically signifying these relationships through groupwide projects that closely follow each other into new fields. By 1980, the year of this study, 187 firms in Japan participated formally in a group presidents' council, and hundreds of other firms maintained informal affiliations (Gerlach, 1992).

In structural terms, alliances are an important component of intercorporate organization to the extent that networks show patterns of strong clustering around socially significant and historically durable ties among companies. Below, I use blockmodels to analyse these clusters from two directions. First, the overall network is partitioned into discrete groupings of firms based on common patterns of relationships throughout the network. Because the resulting model of network structure is derived inductively regardless of nominal group identity, this provides an index of the relative importance of alliances versus other components of network structure. Second, the blocks themselves are analysed in terms of the density of relationships within and across clusters of firms. A strong-form argument for the importance of alliance structures would predict not only that group firms will cluster together in the same blocks but that most of the ties sent to and from that block are with blocks dominated by same-group members.

Financial centrality

Research on interlocking directorships in the United States while raising doubts about the significance of durable interest groups in the contemporary American corporate network, has provided strong support for a second dimension of network structure: financial centrality. Studies have consistently shown that financial institutions, and especially major commercial banks, are the primary senders of directorship ties in the interlock network. Mintz and Schwartz (1985) argued that this is a direct product of firms' need to maintain relationships with commercial banks in order to ensure continued access to their most critical resource, capital. As a result of their central position in the network, they argued, banks have become the 'primary mechanisms for collective decision making within the business sector', whether through direct intervention in specific decisions or, more generally, through the enforcement of more general 'rules of corporate conduct' (Mintz and Schwartz, 1985, p.117).

Financial institutions would appear to play at least as important a role in the Japanese economy. Modern banking and life insurance companies were introduced in Japan in the 1870s as an organizational import from the West. The Japanese government encouraged the banking system in various ways but left the actual function of financing Meiji-period development largely to private financial institutions. These banks, particularly the large-scale city banks, emerged in close conjunction with the development of manufacturing operations. The inchoate *zaibatsu* of the Meiji period each started its own bank for the purpose of funding the activities of its group companies. As Lockwood (1968, p.222) has pointed out. 'Big banks and trust companies were securely tied into each major combine by intercorporate stockholding, interlocking directorates, and the "interrelated solvency" of these institutions and their combine affiliates. They held the deposits of affiliated companies (as well as individual depositors) and were at the same time their chief source of capital'.

Those banks that had begun independently, such as Dai-Ichi Kokuritsu Bank (the forerunner of the contemporary Dai-Ichi Kangyo Bank), found it necessary to develop close relationships with a subset of reliable client firms that relied on them for the bulk of their external capital needs. Even the smaller, specialized *zaibatsu* (e.g., Nissan) developed their own internal financial arms for the same purposes. This supporting role is evidenced in the term that described them, *kikan ginkō*, or 'organ banks'. In the 1930s, as Japan was rapidly expanding to meet its wartime needs, banks increasingly replaced the holding companies and the *zaibatsu* families as the main sources of working capital for the group companies. In total, four-fifths of all debt financing and two-fifths of all external corporate funds came from banks during this period (Goldsmith, 1983).

The close connections between financial institutions and their clients that have characterized the Japanese postwar period, therefore, were already well in place by the end of the war. These were reinforced when banks managed to escape postwar dissolution and furthermore benefited by the freezing of bank deposits held by the *zaibatsu* families, releasing the banks' deposit liabilities. Industrial firms themselves were growing rapidly and had extremely high external capital requirements that could not be met by the relatively undeveloped equity market, so they turned increasingly to the banks. The postwar period was marked by a dramatic increase in reliance on bank borrowing, with stock financing declining from two-fifths of total funds in 1934–1936 to less than one-tenth in 1946–1953 and loans and discounts increasing from less than one-tenth in 1934–1936 to considerably over one-half in 1946–1953 (Goldsmith, 1983, pp.142–143).

In addition to serving as a major supplier of loans, Japanese banks maintain an additional source of influence over their client companies not enjoyed by US commercial banks: the ability to take equity positions in other companies on their own account. Banks in the US are restricted by provisions of the Glass–Steagall Act from direct ownership of nonfinancial corporations and are therefore limited to managing portfolios for pension funds and other ultimate beneficiaries. Japanese banks, in contrast, have been allowed to hold up to 10% of the total equity issued by a nonfinancial firm until 1987, when new restrictions took effect, and up to 5% thereafter. These banks typically maintain holdings of several percent in those client firms that are important borrowers.

To the extent that financial centrality characterizes the Japanese economy, this will be reflected empirically in several ways. First, financial institutions will differ systematically from industrial corporations in their roles within the network, as determined by partitioning of the overall network. Second, analysis of relationships among the blocks themselves will show that blocks dominated by financial firms are disproportionately linked to the remainder of the network. In particular, these blocks should be heavily involved in the sending of ties of coordination and control through directorship and ownership interlocks. Mintz and Schwartz (1985) have shown that, although firm centrality in directorship networks varies across centrality measures, financial institutions are the most central actors in directorship networks whether it is the absolute numbers of ties or a derived centrality score that is used. Mariolis and Jones (1982) demonstrated that the absolute number of ties, which is the measure used here, tends to be somewhat more stable and reliable than other centrality measures.

Financial centrality may also interact with alliance structures in interesting ways. If financial institutions are more central in the network than industrial firms, roles within *keiretsu* groupings will be differentiated correspondingly. Instead of a nonhierarchical structure in which every group firm is linked to all others directly through reciprocal interlocks, banks and other financial institutions will be first among equals, holding the most central position in their own group and sending ties to other firms in the group that are often unreciprocated. Figure 2(a) recreates the relationships among the core firms shown earlier in Figure 1(b), with directional arrows and industrial classifications attached. In this structure, all members have co-equal statuses. Figure 2(b), in contrast, indicates a structure in which affiliated firms are linked primarily through their sharing of common banks and in which the directional flow of directorship, equity, and other linkages moves primarily from financial to nonfinancial corporations in the group. To the extent this latter structure holds, it suggests patterns with similarities to the hierarchical structure of the prewar *zaibatsu*, albeit with banks rather than families and holding companies located at the apex.

Industrial interdependency

A third potential source of network structure is firms coordinating their business activities with competitors and trading partners in order to manage nonfinancial resource flows. Researchers in both resource dependence and transaction costs approaches emphasize the problem of organizational action in a world of interorganizational exchange and argue that managers and organizations craft a variety of control and influence mechanisms to reduce external uncertainty. One means of managing this interdependence is through the exchange of directors, allowing for the exchange of information and creation of interfirm commitments in order to develop 'a stable collective structure of coordinated action' (Pfeffer and Salancik, 1978, p.161). Alternatively, firms may use partial equity ownership positions as a means of gaining control over problematic exchanges and establishing 'credible commitments' toward cooperation while at the same time maintaining a degree of formal and legal independence (Williamson, 1985; Pisano, 1989; Powell, 1990).

There are strong reasons to believe that this structural dimension, like those discussed above, will be important in the organization of the Japanese corporate network. Japanese firms are on the whole less likely than their American counterparts to integrate their business activities through mergers and acquisitions (Gerlach, 1992), but they have forged a wide variety of forms of cooperation among themselves. These relationships are clearest in the managing of vertical interdependencies that exist among major manufacturers and their primary suppliers. In addition to coordinating activities through formal production associations and regularly scheduled planning meetings, lead manufacturers also often take a partial ownership position in and send directors to those core suppliers that have proven effective over time (Asanuma, 1989).

Less clear are the network relationships that exist among competitor firms themselves. I consider here three possible patterns. First, coordination may take place directly through extensive ties of dispatched directors and intercorporate shareholding similar to those that exist

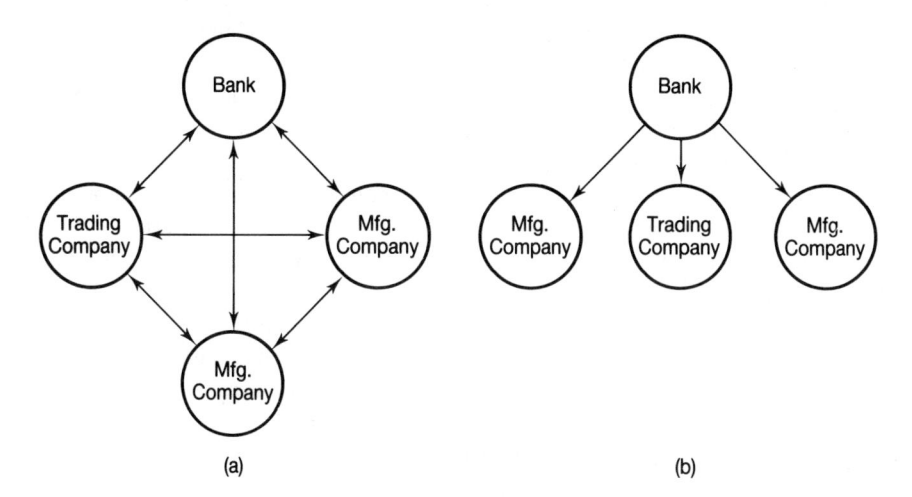

Figure 2. The *Keiretsu* as (a) a Nonhierarchical Clique; (b) a Bank-Centred Clique.

among large firms and their smaller satellites. In this case, a dense network of relationships linking large industrial firms directly to each other will exist. Although research has generally failed to find strong direct interlocking among horizontal competitors in the US (Pennings, 1980; Zajac, 1988), these relationships may be more prevalent in Japan. In particular, the relative weakness of antitrust enforcement in Japan may allow firms in the same industry to send ownership or directorship ties under circumstances that would be problematic or proscribed elsewhere.

A second means of coordinating horizontal interdependency is indirectly, through the sharing of common positions in the overall network. To the extent that banks are central in the Japanese corporate network, they may use their positions in order to subject client firms to collective constraints that affect those firms' own business activities and thereby reap monopoly profits through the elimination of market competition among their borrowing firms (Kotz, 1978). Hilferding has suggested as follows:

> In general [a bank] can only stand to lose from competition among enterprises which are its customers. Hence the bank has an overriding interest in eliminating competition among the firms in which it participates. Furthermore, every bank is interested in maximum profits, and, other things being equal, this will be achieved by the complete elimination of competition in a particular branch of industry (Hilferding, 1910, quoted in Bowman, 1989: 57).

Despite the logical appeal of this argument, there are reasons to believe that the opposite pattern is more common in Japan. Miyazaki's (1976) influential account of Japan's postwar groupings argued that Japanese banks and industrial firms are connected through a network pattern defined by a diversification of relationships. Instead of seeking to control single industries, banks seek instead to manage a broad stable of client firms. This is summarized in the pattern of affiliation that he has dubbed the 'one-set principle', or the practice among the *keiretsu* of striving to have in its core membership one company involved in each major industry, but only one company. The working rules of membership captured in this phrase are twofold. First, corporate groups need to develop key external relationships by being involved in all major industries—'from soup noodles to missiles', as Mitsubishi's trading company puts it. Second, in order to avoid disruptive competition among firms in the same group, no more than one company in the same industry, ideally, should be a member. In this way, interdependencies are managed not through control over single markets but through the spreading of risk across weakly correlated economic sectors.

The importance of each of these bases for network structure can be analysed empirically in terms of both the overall positions of industrial firms in the network and the patterns of relationships within and between specific clusters of industrial firms. The possibility that vertically or competitively interdependent firms are linked directly to each other can be evaluated by measuring the extent to which blocks of industrial firms are senders and receivers of ties to blocks constituted by firms in related or the same industries. If firms manage their industrial interdependencies indirectly, however, through the sharing of common positions in the network (e.g., by ties to the same bank), they will cluster together in the same structurally equivalent blocks even if they do not have direct ties to each other. A third view, that Japanese network structure is characterized by attempts to diversify industrial relationships, will be supported by the finding that blocks instead comprise industrially disparate enterprises.

Like financial centrality, industrial interdependency is likely to interact with alliance membership in interesting ways. The empirical issue becomes determining the industrial composition of the firms making up corporate cliques. Although a degree of diversification in membership is implied by the existence of both financial and industrial firms in the formal membership of major *keiretsu* groupings, a more detailed analysis of industrial firms themselves might demonstrate membership patterns differentially oriented toward particular industrial sectors. These might, for example, reflect historical residues, such as the emergence during the early Meiji period of the Sumitomo group out of the mining business and the Mitsubishi group out of the shipping industry. In so far as interdependencies can be managed not only through direct linkages among industrial firms but through the indirect sharing of group affiliations and banking relationships, a blockmodelling approach is an especially promising means of getting at this issue.

METHOD

The above discussion suggests that intercorporate relations in Japan may reflect overlapping network structures that coexist in complex interaction. This potential richness in underlying network structure should, ideally, be matched by the richness of the data and by analytic methods capable of mapping different structures simultaneously. Nevertheless, choices must inevitably be made on which network actors and variables to include. In a practical sense, it is impossible to map the network structure of an entire economy, as the number of actors involved and the variety of their linkages is overwhelming. In order to limit the size of the database, while at the same time emphasizing ties among those firms likely to be most central in the Japanese corporate network, this study focuses on 60 of Japan's top industrial and financial enterprises. Included in the sample are Japan's largest 40 industrial companies, measured by sales for the year 1980. Also included are Japan's 20 largest financial institutions, as measured by assets in 1981. These are the top ten commercial banks (or 'city banks'), the top five trust banks, and the top five nonlife insurance companies. Life insurance companies are excluded from the analysis because, as mutual corporations, they do not have publicly traded shares.

Three different intercorporate relations are considered in the analysis: bank borrowing, equity ownership, and dispatched directors. Availability of data is one advantage to the study of Japanese network structure. In the US the difficulty of gaining access to detailed information on financial and other relationships has led to a reliance on some forms of interorganizational relationships, notably interlocking directorships, while other relationships remain under-researched. Although directorship interlocks are considered important traces of financial and other business relationships, researchers have also recognized that these interlocks are often loosely connected to financial or other relationships among firms (Mizruchi, 1982; Palmer, 1983; Mintz and Schwartz, 1985). To the extent that these ties only partially overlap, important information about network structure is lost when only one type of tie is considered.

In many ways, Japan poses fewer difficulties in data collection, despite the obvious problems of translation from Japanese-language sources. Data are widely available on a variety of important network variables, including not only directorship interlocks but also companies' major creditors and shareholders. The Ministry of Finance requires that all publicly traded corporations provide in their annual securities reports detailed information on their borrowing positions with important banks, as well as lists of their major shareholders. This range of data allows for determination of network structure based on multiple interests firms have in each other. Each of the three network variables employed here is likely to have a distinctive role in the Japanese corporate network.

Bank borrowing. Banks have long been an important source of external capital for Japanese firms, which have historically maintained far higher debt-to-equity ratios than their American counterparts. In a comparative analysis of firms in the US and Japan from 1966 to 1978, for example, Flaherty and Itami (1984) found that banks provided over half of the external capital of the Japanese firms, double the proportion of that provided by banks to American firms. While the share of external capital coming from banks declined somewhat during this period, so too did the use of bank capital by US corporations, maintaining a nearly two-to-one ratio. As a result, although the net worth of Japanese companies has increased in recent years, it remains on average far below that found in other advanced industrialized countries.[1]

Equity shareholding. Students of Japanese industrial organization have long argued that corporate ownership in Japan is generally dominated by firms' trading partners and affiliated companies, and these investors are interested in a set of goals more complex than straightforward capital market returns (Futatsugi, 1982; Okumura, 1983). In the words of one observer, 'Unlike Western institutional shareholders, which invest largely for dividends and capital appreciation, Japanese institutional shareholders tend to be the company's business partners and associates; shareholding is the mere expression of their relationship, not the relationship itself' (Clark, 1979, p.86). The increase in securities-based financing in Japan in recent years suggests that equity capital is now taking on added significance as itself a major source of external capital.

Directorship interlocks. Although interlocking directorships have long been considered a primary element of structure in the American corporate network, there are reasons to believe that their role in Japan is less important, at least among major Japanese corporations. The boards of directors of large Japanese companies are generally dominated by inside directors (Clark, 1979; Gerlach, 1992), so networks of interlocks among large firms tend to be sparse. Where these interlocks do exist, however, they generally indicate the existence of a business relationship. Gerlach and Lincoln (1992), for example, found that nearly two-thirds of all outside directors in their sample of large Japanese firms came from companies that had an identifiable banking, equity, or trading relationship with the receiving firm, and in over half of these cases the sending firm had two or more different types of relationships.

These three network variables were coded for the 60 firms in the sample for the base-year 1980. Data on firms' top-ten banks and top-ten shareholders were translated from a Japanese annual, *Keiretsu no kenkyū* (1980 volume). This source compiles lists of the important suppliers of debt capital for all major Japanese companies, as well as their leading shareholders. Those top-ten shareholders and top-ten creditors that were also among the 60 industrial and financial institutions in the sample were identified and coded with 1s in the sending (row) cell that corresponded to the receiving (column) firm. Intercorporate directorships were identified through another Japanese language annual, *Kaisha nenkan* (1980 volume). This publication provides information on firms' outside directors and the current or former affiliations of those directors.

It is important in studying directorship interlocks in Japan to know both current and former company affiliations of directors, because many 'inside' directors have actually moved in mid-career from another company, such as the receiving company's bank. Unlike in the US, these 'dispatched directors' (*haken yakuin*) take on full-time managerial positions in their new firm while at the same time retaining ongoing contacts with their former employer (Gerlach, 1992). As with the equity and debt data, companies sending directors to other companies in the sample were coded with 1s in the row position. The results of this coding were three 60×60 matrices across three different types of directional ties.

Only directional interlocks were used in this study, for the following reasons. Prior studies on US and Canadian directorship networks (Palmer, 1983; Ornstein, 1984; Palmer et al., 1986) have shown that directional interlocks are more stable than indirect interlocks and more likely to convey information and serve the purpose of informal coordination. In addition, while the meaning of indirect directorship interlocks seems relatively straightforward (i.e., two companies are linked through the sharing of the same director from a third company or organization), it is not clear what indirect interlocks mean for equity or debt relationships. Rather than mix forms of interlock in the three types of ties, I decided instead to focus solely on the more readily interpretable direct interlocks.

In choosing a method for analysing these network data, the following factors were considered. First, as noted above, the method should be able to discern both direct or dyadic relationships, as well as indirect and hierarchical relationships through common third parties. If, for example, industrial companies are coordinated not through direct ties between each other but through their sharing a common bank, it is important that we be able to pick up these patterns. In addition, the method should be able to handle several types of ties simultaneously, since data were collected on three different network variables and the primary concern was in the nexus of key business relationships. Furthermore, the method should be able both to partition networks into structurally related groupings and to show relationships within and between those groupings that are easily interpretable with respect to the underlying data they represent.

Blockmodelling is perhaps the only approach yet available that is capable of addressing each of these varied objectives (Di Maggio, 1987). In a number of studies, blockmodelling has been used to derive empirically meaningful patterns of relationships that are verified in ethnographic and sociometric descriptions of the same social system (Breiger et al., 1975; White et al., 1976; Faust, 1988). Furthermore, it does so without imposing on the structure *a priori* categories or attributes of actors. Based on the criterion of structural equivalence, blockmodelling focuses the researcher's attention on overall patterns of relationships in a network. Subsets of actors within the network (blocks) are determined based on the similarity of their relationships with actors in other blocks, regardless of the presence or absence of ties directly among themselves.

Detailed analyses of relationships within and between blocks also provide a parsimonious model of global social structure. Fully developed cliques are operationalized as blocks of actors that share similar relationships with other actors in the network (the structural equivalence criterion) and, moreover, send ties to other actors within the same block. Patterns of hierarchy are based on structurally asymmetric positions of dominance, with blocks of actors sending unreciprocated ties of equity, directorships, etc., to other blocks of actors. Empirically derived blocks can also be used to test hypotheses regarding the basis for position in the network, for example, membership in the same *keiretsu* or coordination of companies in related industries through common ties to the same banks.

The analyses were carried out in four separate steps. First, the set of three 60×60 matrices were stacked and analysed together to derive spatial mappings of overall network structure. The intention at this point was to present general patterns rather than to try to isolate differences among debt, equity, and directorship relationships. In the second step, the stacked matrices were then used to create structurally equivalent blocks by CONCOR partitioning. As with the spatial mapping, the main interest here was in discerning patterns of overall structural equivalence in the corporate network. In the third step, relationships within and between blocks were analysed based on their absolute and relative densities. In addition to considering the separate density matrices for debt, equity, and directorship ties, the equity and directorship matrices were also merged to show global patterns of relationships among structurally equivalent blocks. Finally, the subset of blocks comprising industrial firms were analysed for composition, with special attention paid to the issue of whether the blocks derived through CONCOR partitions clustered along the lines of competitive firms in the same industry, firms in vertically interdependent industries, or firms that were *keiretsu* affiliates. All analyses, including calculation of correlations, distances, and CONCOR partitions, were carried out with UCINET, a widely used package of network analysis programs (MacEvoy and Freeman, 1987).

RESULTS

A spatial mapping of the overall corporate network

Among the different ways of portraying network structure the first method presented here is the most straightforward: a two-dimensional map of network distances. This map, shown in Figure 3, represents a multidimensional scaling of the Euclidean distances (Burt, 1980) among the 60 companies based on the stacked matrices of the original three network variables. This serves as a spatial representation of the proximity of companies based on the similarities of their relationships to other companies across the three network variables.

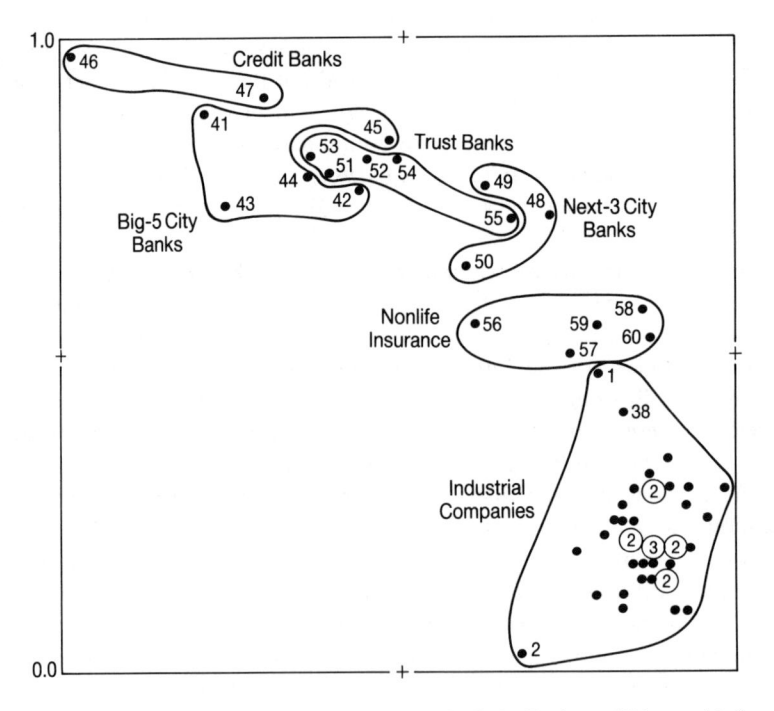

Figure 3. Spatial Map Derived from Stacked Matrices for Debt, Equity, and Directorship Interlocks.

This map shows striking differences in the network positions held by financial and industrial companies. Each of the 40 industrial companies is grouped together in the lower right-hand side of the map in closely corresponding positions. A few industrial firms lie somewhat to the periphery of this cluster [these are Nippon Steel (2), Toyota Motors (1), and an affiliated company of Toyota, Nippondenso (38)], but the more significant pattern is the close spatial positions overall among the industrial firms.

The financial institutions are more widely dispersed indicating greater variation in their network structures. At the far extreme from the industrial cluster are the two long-term credit banks, the Industrial Bank of Japan (46), in the upper left-hand corner of the map, and the Long-Term Credit Bank (47). Also close to these two banks but distant from the industrial firms are the five major city banks of Dai-Ichi Kangyo (41), Fuji (42), Sumitomo (43), Mitsubishi (44), and Sanwa (45). Four of the five trust banks also show network relationships resembling those of the major city banks—Mitsubishi Trust (51), Sumitomo Trust (52), Mitsui Trust (53), and Yasuda Trust (54). A somewhat smaller trust bank, Toyo Trust (55) shows patterns most closely related to those of the three smaller city banks of Tokai (48) Taiyo-Kobe (49), and Mitsui (50). The group of financial institutions showing patterns most similar to the industrial firms are the five nonlife insurance companies of Tokio (56), Yasuda (57), Taisho (58), Sumitomo (59), and Nichido (60).

The structural differentiation between industrial and financial firms evident in this spatial mapping is attributable in part to the fact that industrial companies do not send one of the three types of ties used in the analysis, i.e., debt. As shown below, however, this differentiation remains even when equity and directorship measures are analysed apart from bank loans. Significant variation in the network positions of financial and industrial corporations—a basic tenet of theories of financial centrality—turns out to be a pervasive feature of Japanese intercorporate structure.

Blockmodels of network structure

There is further evidence of structural differentiation in the Japanese corporate network when the network is clustered into discrete blocks of structurally equivalent firms. These blockmodels, which serve as the basis for the remaining set of analyses, also show a number of interesting relationships not apparent in the overall mapping.

A widely used blockmodelling algorithm, CONCOR, was used to partition the stacked matrix based on the receiving of ties (Breiger *et al.*, 1975). Selection of the number of partitions in CONCOR is at the discretion of the researcher. An eight-block model (resulting from seven partitions of the stacked matrix) was chosen for representation below, based on the following considerations. First, among the 60 firms in the sample, six major industrial sectors are strongly represented (automobiles, oil, electrical, steel, chemicals, and shipbuilding), along with two financial sectors (banking and insurance). If sharing the same or related industrial product lines is an important consideration in block composition, an eight-block model should minimize interindustry overlap without unnecessarily fragmenting same-industry firms. Second, since there are six major bank-centred industrial groupings in Japan, as noted earlier, to the extent group affiliation is an important determinant of block membership, it was predicted that an eight-block model would allow each group its own separate block, leaving two additional blocks for 'independent' industrial firms and/or financial institutions.

Table 1 reports the results from the eight-block model. Not surprisingly, given results from the spatial mapping, the first partition of the network (not shown here) primarily separated financial institutions from industrial firms along the vertical axis shown in the spatial map, creating two distinct clusters, with only a few firms crossing over. This structural differentiation is further clarified by six additional CONCOR iterations, leading to an eight-block model. The first three blocks in this resulting model are made up entirely of the 20 financial institutions, while the remaining five blocks comprise the 40 industrial firms. The ordering of blocks in CONCOR is arbitrary, so the three financial blocks and the five industrial blocks were grouped together for ease of presentation. There are no zeroblocks, indicating that all firms in the sample shared ties with others in the network.

Blocks A and B both comprise several large city banks, one long-term credit bank, and two trust banks. Block C includes the smallest of the ten city banks in the sample (Mitsui) and the five nonlife insurance companies. This reinforces the finding in Figure 2 that nonlife insurance

Table 1. Block membership, stacked matrices for debt, equity, and directorship ties (eight-block level)

Company no.	Company name (main product line)	*Keiretsu*[a]
Block A—Financial institutions		
41	Dai-Ichi Kangyo Bank	DKB
44	Mitsubishi Bank	Mitsubishi
47	Long-Term Credit Bank of Japan	—
48	Tokai Bank	—
49	Taiyo-Kobe Bank	—
51	Mitsubishi Trust Bank	Mitsubishi
53	Mitsui Trust Bank	Mitsui
Block B—Financial institutions		
42	Fuji Bank	Fuji
43	Sumitomo Bank	Sumitomo
45	Sanwa Bank	Sanwa
46	Industrial Bank of Japan	—
52	Sumitomo Trust Bank	Sumitomo
54	Yasuda Trust Bank	Fuji
55	Toyo Trust Bank	—
Block C—Financial institutions		
50	Mitsui Bank	Mitsui
56	Tokio Marine and Fire	Mitsubishi
57	Yasuda Fire and Marine	Fuji
58	Taisho Marine and Fire	Mitsui
59	Sumitomo Marine and Fire	Sumitomo
60	Nichido Fire and Marine	—
Block D—Industrial corporations		
2	Nippon Steel	—
7	Mitsubishi Heavy Ind. (shipbuilding)	Mitsubishi
15	Maruzen Oil	—
26	Mitsubishi Chemical	Mitsubishi
28	Kawasaki Heavy Ind. (shipbuilding)	DKB
Block E—Industrial corporations		
13	Honda Motors	(Mitsubishi)
16	Kirin Breweries	Mitsubishi
19	Mitsubishi Oil	Mitsubishi
22	Isuzu Motors	DKB
27	Taiyo Fisheries	—
31	Fujitsu (electronics)	DKB

Table 1 (*continued*)

Company no.	Company name (main product line)	*Keiretsu*[a]
Block F—Industrial corporations		
1	Toyota Motors	Mitsui
4	Nippon Oil	—
8	Toshiba Corp. (electronics)	Mitsui
11	Kawasaki Steel	DKB
12	Mitsubishi Electric	Mitsubishi
17	IHI Heavy Ind. (shipbuilding)	DKB
25	Showa Oil	DKB
29	Nippon Kogyo (mining)	—
35	Sony (electronics)	(Mitsui)
36	Toray Industries (textiles)	Mitsui
38	Nippondenso (auto parts)	(Mitsui)
Block G—Industrial corporations		
3	Nissan Motors	Fuji
6	Hitachi Limited (electronics)	Fuji/Sanwa/DKB
9	Nippon Kokan (steel)	Fuji
14	Kobe Steel	Sanwa/DKB
23	Toa Nenryo (oil)	Fuji
34	Snow Brand (dairy)	—
40	Nippon Suisan (fish products)	—
Block H—Industrial corporations		
5	Matsushita Electric	(Sumitomo)
10	Sumitomo Metal Ind. (steel)	Sumitomo
18	Toyo Kogyo (automobiles)	(Sumitomo)
20	NEC (electronics)	Sumitomo
21	Daikyo Oil	—
24	Sanyo Electric	(Sumitomo)
30	Kubota (farm machinery)	Fuji
32	Sumitomo Chemical	Sumitomo
33	Asahi Chemical	DKB
37	Komatsu (construction machinery)	(Sumitomo)
39	Matsushita Denko (building materials)	(Sumitomo)

[a] Defined by participation in a group presidents' council. *Keiretsu* affiliations in parentheses refer to companies that do not participate in a formal group council but have relied on the commercial bank of a *keiretsu* as their reference bank (*torihiki ginkō*) for a minimum of 20 years, from 1959 to 1979.

companies show structurally similar patterns, while the major banks are less easy to differentiate. The remaining five blocks (D–H) are constituted by the 40 industrial firms in the sample.

Table 1 also shows the *keiretsu* affiliations of block members at the eight-block level, as well as companies' main product lines in those cases in which they were not readily apparent in the company name. Group affiliations were determined using two criteria. The first, social criterion was participation in a group presidents' council. These councils have their membership lists reported in a variety of publications, including *Keiretsu no kenkyū*. The second criterion was informal, historical association with a *keiretsu*. This was defined as a company's reliance on the commercial bank of a *keiretsu* as the reference bank (*torihiki ginkō*) for a minimum of 20 years, from 1959 to 1979. Companies that satisfied only the second criterion have their affiliations denoted in parentheses. Reference bank affiliations were established from volumes of *Kaisha nenkan* for the years 1960 to 1980.

An initial interpretation of block composition suggests that the industrial blocks demonstrate a close correspondence to *keiretsu* affiliation, while the financial blocks do not. Among the financial firms, Block A comprises the commercial and trust banks in the Mitsubishi group but also an assortment of other banks, including two from other groups (DKB and Mitsui). Both the commercial and trust banks from the Sumitomo and Fuji groups reside in Block B but so, too, do the Sanwa bank and two independent banks. Block C, as noted above, is essentially a non-life insurance company block that cuts across *keiretsu*. Among the industrial firms, Blocks D and E combine companies in the Mitsubishi and Dai-Ichi Kangyo groups, along with several independent companies. Block F is made up predominantly of Mitsui- and Dai-Ichi-Kangyo-affiliated companies, while Block G combine firms in the Fuji and Sanwa groups. The cleanest *keiretsu* pattern is found for Block H, which is constituted almost solely by Sumitomo-affiliated companies.

Companies' main product lines were determined from the 1980 volume of *Japan Company Handbook*, which gives a breakdown of the share of companies' sales in different industrial sectors. The overall diversification levels of Japanese firms is relatively low (Clark, 1979; Goto, 1981), and the outputs for most of the industrial firms in the sample were in the same or closely related industrial sectors. Initial impressions here suggest substantial diversity in the product lines of firms constituting the same blocks. The industrial blocks appear to comprise companies in various industries, many of them horizontally and vertically unrelated. A more rigorous analysis of block composition by *keiretsu* and industrial affiliation is carried out below.

Patterns of relationships among blocks

The main interest in evaluating patterns of relationships among the blocks derived above was in discerning underlying structures of intercorporate coordination and influence. This task is made more difficult by the uncertainty in the corporate network literature concerning the precise meaning of interlocks. An unresolved issue remains the extent to which these represent mechanisms by which the sending firm controls the receiving firm (e.g., Kotz, 1978; Palmer, 1983) and the extent to which it is the receiving firm that co-opts the sending firm (Pfeffer and Salancik, 1978). In many cases it is likely that influence flows in both directions, as companies sacrifice a degree of decision-making discretion in return for access to capital or business partners. Nevertheless, there are reasons to believe that for the kind of relationships considered here the primary direction of influence flows from sending to receiving firms. Japanese corporate law, as in the US, grants the board of directors ultimate authority over the decision-making process of the firm. To the extent that the sending firm sits on the board of the receiving firm in a directional interlock, it gains a corresponding voice in the strategic oversight of that company that is not reciprocated (Mintz and Schwartz, 1981, p. 146). In addition, it enjoys a disproportionate share of inside information (Richardson, 1987). The same argument applies to equity ties. As in the US, shareholders in Japan vote on the composition of the board of directors itself, as well as on other major decisions affecting the firm, such as dividend policies and fundamental changes in by-laws and articles of incorporation. The receiving firm is granted no such right of influence over its own shareholders. These structural asymmetries in influence are likely to become especially apparent when major disagreements over policies arise between two companies.

EQUITY

Block	Financial			Industrial				
	A	B	C	D	E	F	G	H
A	10	4	17	29	29	31	20	9
B	0	7	14	29	21	12	37	31
C	12	5	10	27	11	20	10	15
D	14	17	3	0	3	2	0	0
E	0	0	0	0	0	0	0	0
F	10	3	3	0	0	2	0	0
G	0	18	0	0	0	0	0	0
H	0	16	3	0	0	0	0	2

DIRECTORSHIPS

Block	A	B	C	D	E	F	G	H
A	0	0	2	9	17	5	2	0
B	0	2	0	3	2	0	8	10
C	2	0	3	0	3	3	0	0
D	0	0	0	0	3	0	0	2
E	0	0	0	0	0	0	0	0
F	0	0	0	0	0	2	0	0
G	0	0	0	0	0	0	0	0
H	0	1	0	0	0	0	0	2

DEBT

Block	A	B	C	D	E	F	G	H
A				46	48	55	35	23
B				49	24	20	61	52
C				0	0	9	0	2
D								
E								
F								
G								
H								

Figure 4. Density Matrices for Equity, Directorship, and Debt Networks.

Figure 4 presents the density matrices for the debt, equity, and directorship networks, representing the proportion of potential ties among all member firms of the sending and receiving blocks that are actually constituted. Each cell contains the percentage of rows by columns ($m \times n$) for which the row actor sent a choice to the column actor. These matrices have in turn been divided into quadrants to facilitate comparisons among the financial and industrial blocks. Representation of the debt matrix has been restricted to the upper-right-hand quadrant (ties sent from the three financial blocks to the five industrial blocks). All other values in the debt matrix were zero, as is to be expected, since lending ties flow predominantly from financial suppliers of capital to industrial users of capital.

The three different types of ties demonstrate substantial differences in both their overall densities and the specific patterns that they take. Among the three networks, equity relationships demonstrate the most complete interlocking. Densities among blocks of 10% or more are apparent in three of the four matrix quadrants (financial sending to financial, financial sending to industrial, and industrial sending to financial). The density of ties is especially high in the upper-right-hand quadrant, in which financial blocks send ties to industrial blocks. In the fourth quadrant, where industrial blocks send ties to industrial blocks, interlocks are largely absent, showing up in only four of the 25 cells.

Densities among blocks in the directorship matrix are far lower than for equity. Only in the quadrant in which financial blocks send ties to industrial blocks are any densities over 10%, and then only in two cells. The low densities for directorship interlocks support the view, discussed earlier, that the predominance of inside directors in large Japanese companies has limited the extent of directorship interlocking among these firms. By contrast, the high densities for equity ties suggest that interlocking equity shareholding is widespread among Japanese companies and is an important source of Japanese corporate network structure.

Within the debt matrix, the two bank blocks (A and B) send to nearly all of the ties and to all five of the industrial blocks. In one cell (Block B sending to Block G), fully 61% of the potential ties are constituted, and in no cell is the share of ties constituted less than 23%. The third financial block (C), which is composed primarily of nonlife insurance companies, is far less active in lending to large industrial firms. This block, however, serves as a major shareholder in many industrial firms, as the equity matrix demonstrates.

Of interest to financial centrality, resource dependency, and transaction costs perspectives is the possibility that equity or directorship positions are used by financial institutions to gain influence over those companies to which they lend. Figure 5 shows a scatterplot of the cell densities of debt and equity ties flowing from the three financial blocks to the five industrial blocks. The nonlife insurance block again shows a pattern distinct from the two bank blocks, with debt ties minimal at the same time that equity ties are substantial. The two bank blocks, in contrast, demonstrate a general tendency for debt and equity cell densities to be positively associated, as indicated by the best-fit line. These results appear to support the view that the densities of different types of ties tend to move in the same direction in the overall network.

The separate density matrices were then aggregated and analysed together as a means of revealing global patterns of relationships, specifically relationships of intercorporate influence. In this respect, the debt matrix poses special problems in interpretation. Since lending ties log-

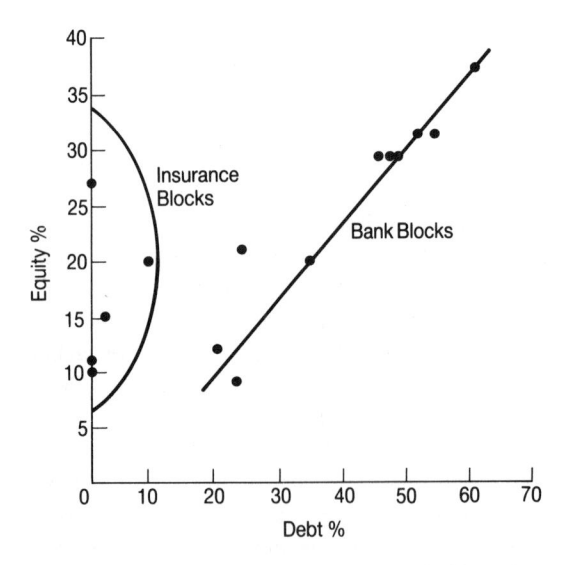

Figure 5. Cell Densities for Debt and Equity Networks.

ically (and empirically) flow only from financial to industrial firms, and since these densities are very high, including these in the overall density matrix would strongly bias the overall matrix in the direction of debt flows, even if equity and directorship matrices alone show other patterns. Equity and directorship ties, in contrast, could in principle flow in both directions. Although a strong case can be made that the various restrictive covenants that banks are able to impose on their borrowers are an important form of intercorporate control (Herman, 1981; Mintz and Schwartz, 1985), a decision was made to exclude debt ties from the aggregated matrix in order to emphasize those network connections that could potentially be reciprocal. If unidirectional flows of influence from financial to industrial blocks were detected in the equity-directorship matrix, these should apply *a fortiori* to the full three-network model.

From the separate equity and directorship matrices, a combined density matrix was created, shown in Figure 6. This was based on Boolean addition of the two matrices out of which it is built, i.e., the density of the submatrices created by the Boolean union of the two tie matrices. Once again, the vast majority of ties exist in the three quadrants involving financial institutions, either as sender of ties, receiver of ties, or both. Direct ties among the industrial blocks themselves are weak or nonexistent.

DENSITY MATRIX

Block	Financial			Industrial				
	A	B	C	D	E	F	G	H
A	10	4	19	37	45	36	22	9
B	0	10	14	32	24	12	45	42
C	14	5	13	27	14	23	10	15
D	14	17	3	0	3	2	0	2
E	0	0	0	0	0	0	0	0
F	10	3	3	0	0	2	0	0
G	0	18	0	0	0	0	0	0
H	0	17	3	0	0	0	0	4

MEAN DENSITY IMAGE MATRIX

Block	A	B	C	D	E	F	G	H
A	1	0	1	1	1	1	1	1
B	0	1	1	1	1	1	1	1
C	1	0	1	1	1	1	1	1
D	1	1	0	0	0	0	0	0
E	0	0	0	0	0	0	0	0
F	1	0	0	0	0	0	0	0
G	0	1	0	0	0	0	0	0
H	0	1	0	0	0	0	0	0

HIGH DENSITY IMAGE MATRIX

Block	A	B	C	D	E	F	G	H
A	0	0	1	1	1	1	1	0
B	0	0	0	1	1	0	1	1
C	0	0	0	1	0	1	0	0
D	0	1	0	0	0	0	0	0
E	0	0	0	0	0	0	0	0
F	0	0	0	0	0	0	0	0
G	0	1	0	0	0	0	0	0
H	0	1	0	0	0	0	0	0

Figure 6. Boolean Density and Image Matrices for Stacked Equity and Directorship Networks.

A simplified image of the density matrix can be constructed by placing 1s in those cells with high densities and 0s in those cells with low densities (White et al., 1976). These are also reported in Figure 6, based on two different cutoff-density criteria. The Mean Density Image Matrix uses the commonly used measure of overall mean density as its cutoff point, while the High Density Image Matrix limits 1s to those cells that exceed twice the overall mean density. The latter, of course, is a more stringent condition and shows solely those ties within and between blocks in which substantial interlocking takes place. The mean density for the matrix was 8.5%, so the high density cutoff point was 17%.

In the Mean Density Image Matrix, every cell in the upper-right-hand quadrant is filled, indicating that the three financial blocks are senders of ties to all industrial blocks. In the upper-left-hand quadrant, the financial blocks send ties to themselves, in the three diagonal cells, and to three of the six remaining financial cells. In the lower two quadrants industrial blocks send ties to financial blocks in five of the 15 cells but to none of the industrial blocks, including to themselves. Financial institutions, once again, appear as the predominant senders of influence ties among the large firms in the sample.

CONTACT

	Financial			Industrial				
Block	A	B	C	D	E	F	G	H
A	1	0	1	1	1	1	1	1
B	0	1	1	1	1	1	1	1
C	1	1	1	1	1	1	1	1
D	1	1	1	0	0	0	0	0
E	1	1	1	0	0	0	0	0
F	1	1	1	0	0	0	0	0
G	1	1	1	0	0	0	0	0
H	1	1	1	0	0	0	0	0

DOMINANCE

Block	A	B	C	D	E	F	G	H
A	0	0	0	0	1	0	1	1
B	0	0	1	0	1	1	0	0
C	0	0	0	1	1	1	1	1
D	0	0	0	0	0	0	0	0
E	0	0	0	0	0	0	0	0
F	0	0	0	0	0	0	0	0
G	0	0	0	0	0	0	0	0
H	0	0	0	0	0	0	0	0

COALITION

Block	A	B	C	D	E	F	G	H
A	1	0	1	1	0	1	0	0
B	0	1	0	1	0	0	1	1
C	1	0	1	0	0	0	0	0
D	1	1	0	0	0	0	0	0
E	0	0	0	0	0	0	0	0
F	1	0	0	0	0	0	0	0
G	0	1	0	0	0	0	0	0
H	0	1	0	0	0	0	0	0

Figure 7. Contact, Dominance, and Coalition Matrices for Stacked Equity and Directorship Networks.

Further refinement in the relationships among the blocks is offered by the High Density Image Matrix. Here the total number of 1 cells is reduced from 26 to 14 as a result of the more stringent criterion. This reduction is not evenly distributed, however, since the greatest change comes in the quadrant of ties among financial institutions. While 33% (five of 15) of the interlocks are eliminated from financial to industrial blocks and 40% (two of five) from industrial to financial, 83% (five of six) are eliminated among the financial to financial interlocks. This confirms the fact that the densest sets of relationships in the network are not those among financial institutions but those between financial and industrial firms.

Figure 7 reports three other matrices derived from the Mean Density Image Matrix.[2] The first is a Contact Matrix, in which a 1 appears for a pair of blocks whenever either sends a tie to the other. This matrix makes perhaps even more starkly clear than previous matrices the predominant role of financial institutions as senders and/or receivers of ties. Industrial firms are connected in the overall network, but they are connected through financial institutions rather than directly to each other. Financial institutions, in contrast, are connected both to industrial firms and to each other.

The second derivative matrix is a Domination Matrix, in which a 1 appears in the row block if a row block sends an equity or directorship tie to the column block but receives no tie in turn. These represent relationships of relatively unreciprocated influence. In all cases, the dominant block is a financial block, and in all but one case, the dominated block is an industrial block. The third derivative matrix is a Coalition Matrix, wherein a 1 appears in a cell whenever row and column blocks send ties reciprocally to each other. In contrast to the Domination Matrix, the Coalition Matrix denotes relationships of mutual influence. Block coalitions are apparent both between financial and industrial blocks and in each of the three financial blocks' ties to itself (own-block ties are, by definition, coalitions). In contrast, none of the industrial blocks is linked through coalition relationships with any of the other industrial blocks, including itself.

Quadrant block	Receiving	
Sending	Financial institutions	Industrial companies
Financial institutions, Blocks A–C	9.3	25.6
Industrial companies, Blocks D–H	6.1	0.4

Figure 8. Quadrant Densities for Stacked Equity and Directorship Networks (Weighted by Cell Size).

The relatively dense set of ties flowing from financial to industrial corporations is reinforced by consolidating the blocks in each of the quadrants and calculating overall quadrant densities, weighted by number of potential ties in each cell. The results of this consolidation are shown in Figure 8. In total, 25.6% of the potential ties from financial institutions in the sample to industrial corporations are constituted, as opposed to 9.3% of the ties among the financial institutions themselves, 6.1% of the ties from industrial to financial corporations, and only 0.4% of the ties among the industrial firms themselves. Once again, it is evident that the primary ties in equity and directorship networks among large companies in Japan are those from financial to industrial corporations. If debt networks were added to this analysis, these differences in patterns of flows would be further emphasized.

These results help to address the predictions about network structure presented earlier, as well as providing some interesting additional information. The prediction that large industrial firms will be substantially tied directly to each other based on membership in the same *keiretsu* or in the same industry is not supported. Directorship interlocks are infrequent anywhere in the network, while ownership interlocks flow primarily between financial and industrial firms, and secondarily among financial firms themselves, but rarely among the industrial firms in the sample. There is some evidence of multiplexity—financial blocks sending large numbers of debt ties to another block also sending large numbers of equity ties. There is also some evidence suggesting the existence of reciprocal coalitions, wherein financial and industrial blocks send ties to and from each other.

Although the results indicate that the large industrial firms in the sample are not tied together through direct directorship and ownership interlocks, the overall significance of financial firms in the network and the prevalence of financial–industrial ties is consistent with the view that an important source of coherence for cliques of large industrial firms in Japan is the sharing of common banking relationships. This is reinforced by more detailed analysis of the financial–industrial blocks. In the case of Blocks E and F, the highest network densities are with Block A, while Blocks G and H have the highest densities with Block B. In all four cases, the predominant *keiretsu* identity of the industrial block is also reflected in the block membership of its affiliated banks—Mitsui group industrial firms tend to link with the Mitsui bank block, Sumitomo with Sumitomo, and so on. Moreover, this is the case across all three types of ties measured in this study.

Analysis of industrial block assignments

As Burt (1983) has pointed out, firms in the same or in related economic sectors can be constrained through the sharing of similar positions in network space, even where they do not directly interact. This possibility is tested here through what will be termed structural equivalence linkages. This approach views each pair of industrial companies as a potential dyadic linkage. Linkages are considered to be constituted if the pair occupies a similar position in the network, as measured by assignment to the same block. The proportion of the potential structural equivalence linkages that are actually constituted among firms categorized along some dimension of theoretical interest can then be compared to a hypothetical distribution based on random block assignments. Applying this approach to the industrial blocks derived earlier, three possible sources of block assignment are considered here: competitive interdependence among firms in the same industry, vertical interdependence among firms in industries in which substantial trade is likely to exist, and *keiretsu* affiliation.

In order to determine the significance of competitive interdependencies in block composition, industrial firms were categorized by their primary line of business (see Table 1). Among the sample of 40 industrial firms, the primary businesses of thirty proved to overlap with at least one other firm: eight companies make consumer and industrial electronics products, six are oil producers, five manufacture automobiles, five produce steel products, three are shipbuilders, and three are chemical companies.

Overlaps among firms in each of these six industries represent potential structural equivalence linkages that are constituted when another firm in the same industry is assigned to the same block. Table 2 presents the results from this analysis. All six industries had horizontally competitive firms assigned to the same block, but in only one industry (electronics) were more than two competitors in the same block. Among the other five industries, each had only one potential linkage constituted through the criterion of common block assignment. The 36 remaining potential linkages among firms in the same industry were not constituted, indicating a rate of assignment to the same block of 12%. Even when the electronics industry is included in the total, the rate of assignment of competitors to the same block still only reaches 16%. In comparison, a random distribution across the five industrial blocks leads to an expected assignment rate, assuming equally sized blocks, of 20%. Block assignments (i.e., occupancy of common network positions) do not appear to be based, therefore, on industrial overlap.

Table 2. Structural equivalence linkages among horizontal competitors.

		Distribution of ties	
Industry	No. of companies	Same block	Other block
Electrical	8	6	22
Oil & gas	6	1	14
Automobiles	5	1	9
Steel	5	1	9
Shipbuilding	3	1	2
Chemicals	3	1	2
Total	30	11	58

Another possibility is that structurally equivalent ties in the network may be used instead to manage interdependencies resulting from vertical supply relationships rather than horizontal competition. Firms whose main product lines might be important inputs for other firms' production were identified as follows: steel and autoparts for automobile companies, steel for shipbuilding, steel for construction and agricultural machinery, oil products for chemicals, chemicals for textiles, and electrical supplies for building materials. Using the same procedure as above, dyads of firms that were potentially vertically linked were considered constituted if they were assigned to the same block. The results, reported in Table 3, again do not indicate disproportionate links among interdependent firms. Of the 84 potential vertical linkages, 17, or 20%, involve common block assignment, the same proportion as would be expected under a hypothetical random distribution rate.

Table 3. Structural equivalence linkages among vertically interdependent companies

		Distribution of ties	
Industry pair	No. of companies	Same block	Other block
Autos/autoparts	5/1	1	4
Autos/steel	5/5	4	21
Steel/shipbuilding	5/3	3	12
Steel/heavy machinery	5/2	2	8
Chemicals/oil	3/6	3	15
Chemicals/textiles	3/1	0	3
Electrical/materials	8/1	4	4
Total	30	17	67

In addition to competitive and vertical interdependencies, structural equivalence may also be determined by membership in the same intercorporate alliance. Table 4 provides a more rigorous analysis of the patterns of *keiretsu* affiliation and block membership discussed earlier.

Following a procedure similar to that used above to classify competitive and vertically related firms, structural equivalence linkages are defined as industrial firms in the same *keiretsu* falling within a common block. Independent firms were excluded from the analysis, as were two firms with multiple group memberships (Hitachi and Kobe Steel, in Block G). The results indicate that, among the remaining firms, 49 of 80 potential structural equivalence linkages among firms with shared *keiretsu* affiliations, or 61% were constituted by assignment to the same block, as compared with a hypothetical random distribution across the five blocks of 20%. These figures would be even higher if it were not for splitting among blocks of firms in two groups, Dai-Ichi Kangyo and Mitsubishi. Excluding these two *keiretsu* results in a near-perfect block assignment of 93%.

Table 4. Structural equivalence linkages among *keiretsu* affiliates

Keiretsu	No. of companies	Distribution of ties Same block	Other block
Mitsui	5	10	0
Fuji[a]	4	3	3
Sanwa[b]	0	0	0
Sumitomo	8	28	0
Mitsubishi	6	4	11
Dai-Ichi Kangyo[b]	7	4	17
Total	30	49	31
Excluding Mitsubishi and DKB	17	41	3

[a]Hitachi excluded due to multiple memberships.
[b]Hitachi and Kobe Steel excluded due to multiple memberships.

That the DKB group demonstrates the most dispersed network patterns is not surprising. DKB is the newest, largest, and most loosely organized of the six major *keiretsu*. The Dai-Ichi Kangyo Bank itself was formed out of a merger of two large banks in 1971, and the first group-wide presidents' council meeting did not take place until 1978. In addition, unlike most of the other groups, this bank is the only financial institution from the group represented among the top 20, limiting the number of ties between financial and industrial corporations from which network position could be determined. The results for Mitsubishi group firms are more perplexing. Although across-block dispersion is not as great as for DKB, it is still higher than for the other four groups. This is despite the reputation of Mitsubishi as, along with Sumitomo, the most cohesive of the major *keiretsu*. It is possible that ties by Mitsubishi group industrial firms to independent financial institutions (notably the Industrial Bank of Japan) interacted with ties to their own financial institutions in determining these block assignments. In addition to these major group affiliations, several other interesting patterns are also evident. The core companies in the smaller prewar Nissan *zaibatsu*, Nissan Motors and Hitachi Ltd., both show up together in Block F. This is despite extensive efforts by the Occupation forces in the early postwar period to break up this *zaibatsu* due to its heavy involvement in Japan's war effort. Block G represents both a Sumitomo and a regional block. Kubota and Asahi Chemical, which sit on the presidents' councils of other groups, were headquartered in Osaka, where most Sumitomo group companies (including Sumitomo Bank) have their historical origins. Among the 11 companies in this block, all but three (NEC, Toyo Kogyo, and Daikyo Oil) had their headquarters located in Osaka. Most other firms in the sample, in contrast, were Tokyo-based.

Overall role differentiation among industrial firms themselves suggests patterning by historical alliances rather than by the immediate functional requirements of competitive or vertical interdependence. If anything, block membership appears to be defined by industrial diversification rather than by industrial overlaps, supporting the one-set hypothesis discussed earlier. However, two caveats to this conclusion should be noted. First, industrial firms in Japan have a variety of alternative means of coordinating their activities, including group presidents' councils, industry associations, and government-led cooperative projects. The lack of direct or indirect ties among industrially interdependent firms in the sample need not imply that these relationships do not exist in Japan, only that among very large firms they do not take place through the types of ties considered here.

Second, in so far as the sample is based on company size, the kind of vertical relationships among large manufacturers and medium-sized suppliers that dominate certain industries, such as automobiles and electronics, are underrepresented. It is of interest, therefore, to find that among the two sets of parent-satellite company relationships in the sample, both show structurally equivalent positions. Toyota and its affiliated supplier Nippondenso were both located in the Mitsui block (Block F), while Matsushita Electric and Matsushita Denko were both located in the Sumitomo/Osaka block (Block H). Although it is impossible to generalize from two cases, this is consistent with the view that satellite companies in Japan tend to hold similar relationships with financial institutions as their parent companies.

DISCUSSION AND CONCLUSIONS

The main findings in the empirical analyses are the following. First, financial institutions in Japan share network positions that are relatively similar among themselves but highly differentiated from those of industrial enterprises. This is evident in the spatial mapping of the overall network, in the composition of the partitions produced by CONCOR, as well as in the analysis of the relationships within and between blocks. Second, an important basis for this differentiation is the central position held by financial institutions in the network. The vast majority of directorship and equity ties are sent by the financial rather than the industrial blocks. Third, these ties are directed primarily to the industrial blocks rather than to other financial institutions. Conversely, to the extent that industrial firms send ties, it is to financial institutions, while ties to other industrial firms are almost entirely absent. Fourth, among the industrial firms in the sample, structurally equivalent positions are held by firms in diverse industries. Contrary to predictions that the same industrial blocks might comprise a disproportionate share of competitively or vertically interdependent firms, the majority of block members cut across market sectors. Fifth, block composition among the industrial firms reflects marked patterns of clustering based on alliances of affiliated firms, or *keiretsu*. Ties of social and historical relatedness among specific companies prove to be of fundamental importance in the structure of the Japanese corporate network.

Together, these results indicate that the Japanese corporate network represents a relatively well-ordered structure of relationships among highly differentiated firms and that understanding the precise contours of this structure requires consideration of a set of complex and overlapping structures. The finding that industrial firms share similar positions in the network based on *keiretsu* ties is striking, given that analyses started from the level of network relationships were coded without regard to formal affiliations. The existence of other forms of coordination among these firms, such as group presidents' councils, only reinforces the importance of alliance forms in the Japanese corporate network. Unlike the relatively fragmented, loosely organized ties typically discerned in the American corporate network, the reality in Japan appears far closer to one of coherent and enduring cliques among affiliated financial institutions and industrial firms.

Although financial institutions prove to be central in the Japanese corporate network, as they have in the US, these patterns appear to interact with *keiretsu* groupings in ways that alter the nature of each. On the one hand, the absence of direct ties among large industrial firms suggests that the primary focus of group coherence in the major groupings, at least where these take the form of ownership and directorship interlocks, is relationships between industrial enterprises and their financial suppliers. To the extent that ties flowing from financial institutions predominate, these groupings will be characterized as hierarchical cliques among structurally differentiated firms in which banks hold a special role. On the other hand, the existence of *keiretsu* groupings would seem to provide Japanese financial institutions with a stable client base of the kind that the more loosely structured American network does not. If so, then the most appropriate model for financial centrality in the Japanese economy is not that of a fully integrated network in which central banks are tied to the economy as a whole, as exists in the US (Mintz and Schwartz, 1985), but of banks as coordinators of specific subsets of affiliated firms.

The additional finding that blocks of structurally equivalent firms comprise both *keiretsu* affiliates and industrially disparate firms is consistent with recent theories concerning the strategic rationale behind Japan's corporate group structure. From one perspective the *keiretsu* are seen as an attempt to spread industrial risk and reduce performance variability among group members (Nakatani, 1984; Aoki, 1988; Sheard, 1991). According to this argument, the high levels of firm-specific capital that are associated with Japan's internal labour markets expose Japanese employees to severe risks associated with an undiversified portfolio of employment opportunities. This creates strong incentives for managers to stabilize their external business relationships and to create implicit insurance arrangements with other companies, should their companies face financial difficulties. A somewhat different perspective emphasizes the strategic advantages of interindustry synergies in diversified groupings. I have argued (Gerlach, 1992) that the fact that it is Japan's largest firms that historically have participated in these groups is a reflection less of their higher need for implicit insurance arrangements—these companies are better able to diffuse risks across a diverse range of business lines than are smaller and more focused firms—than of the broader scale and scope of activities of these firms and the correspondingly greater potential benefits to complementary coordination. In reality, Japan's diversified group structure probably represents an attempt by member firms to gain the benefits both of sharing downside risks and creating strategic complementarities for upside gains.

Follow-up research could usefully proceed in several directions. Most basically, it would be helpful to compare the results obtained here with those resulting from analytic methods in the network repertoire that are tailored to address specific concerns, such as the detection of network cliques and the measurement of actor centrality. It is also important to expand the size and range of the network considered. The results reported here are the product of relationships among Japan's largest corporations. To the extent that the Japanese industrial landscape is made up of a wide variety of medium and smaller enterprises that serve as satellite operations for major manufacturers, broadening the variety of actors studied may affect underlying network structures and dynamics. Since parent companies frequently send directors to and hold substantial equity positions in supplier firms, including these relationships in network data would certainly increase the proportion of direct linkages among industrial firms, perhaps substantially. As more firms are added, network structure is also likely to take on the characteristics of an increasingly finely stratified social order, with larger industrial firms acting as simultaneous receivers of some ties (from financial institutions) and senders of others (primarily to satellite companies) and smaller industrial firms serving primarily as receivers of ties.

Finally, and most important, it is essential to develop better theories of the sources of institutional variation in corporate network structure. As Hamilton and Biggart (1988) have persuasively argued, economic organization varies considerably across countries and there is no *a priori* reason why they should converge on a common form. The distinctive trajectory of Japan's network structure is the product of a complex set of interacting forces. Historical legacy is one critical determinant, as Japan's contemporary groupings reflect substantial carryover from the prewar period. Despite attempts by the Allied Occupation to dissolve the *zaibatsu*, commercial banks retained longstanding personal and business ties to other affiliated companies and remained as their primary suppliers of capital. Japan's regulatory environment has also played a role in reinforcing these relationships. Commercial banks in Japan have been allowed to forge close client bases, including through the direct holding of ownership positions in their leading customers, while restrictions in the US (imposed by the Glass–Steagall and other legislative acts) have limited commercial banks to the management of holdings for ultimate beneficiaries, subject to various fiduciary obligations. Over the course of time, these relationships have become institutionalized as standard models of how economic organizations 'should look' (DiMaggio and Powell, 1983), as reflected in similarities in patterns of membership and in common reliance on strategic coordination mechanisms. It remains to be seen whether internal demands or external pressures from Japan's trading partners will force the initiation of changes sufficiently fundamental to overcome these collective forces of institutional inertia.

ACKNOWLEDGEMENTS

Data collection and analyses for this paper were made possible through funding from the University of California Pacific Rim Program, the National Science Foundation (SES-8912498 and SES-9147040), and the Japan Society for the Promotion of Sciences. Special thanks are owed to James Lincoln, Marshall Meyer, and three anonymous *ASQ* reviewers for detailed comments on an earlier draft of this paper. Portions of the paper were also presented at the social networks session of the ASA, August 1991.

REFERENCES

Allen, M. P. (1978) 'Economic Interest Groups and the Corporate Elite Structure'. *Social Science Quarterly*, **58**: 597–615.
Aoki, M. (1988) *Information, Incentives, and Bargaining in the Japanese Economy*. Cambridge University Press, Cambridge.
Asanuma, B. (1989) 'Manufacturer–Supplier Relationships in Japan and the Concept of Relation-Specific Skill'. *Journal of the Japanese and International Economies*, **3**: 1–30.
Bowman, J. R. (1989) *Capitalist Collective Action*. Cambridge University Press, Cambridge.

Breiger, R. L., Boorman, A. S., and Arabie, P. (1975) 'An Algorithm for Clustering Relational Data with Application to Social Network Analysis Comparison with Multidimensional Scaling'. *Journal of Mathematical Psychology*, **12**: 328–383.

Burt, R. S. (1980) 'Models of Network Structure'. In Inkeles, A., Smelser, N. J. and Turner, R. H. (eds), *Annual Review of Sociology*, **6**: 79–141. Annual Reviews, Palo Alto, CA.

Burt, R. S. (1983) *Corporate Profits and Cooptation*. Academic Press, New York.

Cable, J. and Hirohiko, Y. (1985) 'International Organisation, Business Groups, and Corporate Performance: An Empirical Test of the Multidivisional Hypothesis in Japan'. *International Journal of Industrial Organisation*. **3**: 401–420.

Caves, R. and Uekusa, M. (1976) *Industrial Organization In Japan*. Brookings Institution, Washington, DC.

Clark, R. C. (1979) *The Japanese Company*. Yale University Press, New Haven, CT.

DiMaggio, P. (1987) 'Structural Analysis of Organizational Fields: A Blockmodel Approach.' In Staw, B. M. and Cummings, L. L. (eds), *Research in Organizational Behaviour*, Vol. 10, 335–370. JAI Press, Greenwich, CT.

DiMaggio, P. and Powell, W. (1983) 'The Iron Cage Revisited: Institutional Isomorphism and Collective Rationality in Organizational Fields'. *American Sociological Review*, **48**: 147–160.

Faust, K. (1988) 'Comparison of Methods for Positional Analysis'. *Social Networks*, **10**: 313–341.

Flaherty, M. T. and Itami, H. (1984) 'Finance'. In Okimoto, D. I., Sugano, T. and Weinstein F.B. (eds), *Competitive Edge: The Semiconductor Industry In the US and Japan*, pp.134–176. Stanford University Press, Stanford, CA.

Fruin, M. (1992) *The Japanese Enterprise System: Competitive Strategies and Cooperative Structures*. Oxford University Press, Oxford.

Futatsugi, Y. (1976) *Gendai, Nihon No Kigyō Shūdan Dai-kigyō, bunseki o mezashite*. Toyo Shinposha, Tokyo. (Published in translation in 1986 as *Japanese Enterprise Groups*. School of Business, Kobe University, Kobe, Japan.)

Futatsugi, Y. (1982) *Nihon No Kabushiki Shoyū Kōzō (Japan's Stockholding Structure)*. Dobunkan Shuppan, Tokyo.

Gerlach, M. L. (1992) *Alliance Capitalism: The Social Organization of Japanese Business*. University of California Press, Berkeley.

Gerlach, M. L., and Lincoln, J. R. (1992) 'The Organization of Business Networks in the US and Japan'. In Eccles, R. and Nohria, N. (eds). *Networks and Organization Theory*. Harvard Business School Press, Boston.

Goldsmith, R. A. (1983) *The Financial Development of Japan, 1868–1977*. Yale University Press, New Haven, CT.

Goto, A. (1981) 'Statistical Evidence on the Diversification of Japanese Large Firms'. *Journal of Industrial Economics*, **29**: 271–278.

Hadley, E. (1970) *Antitrust in Japan*. Princeton University Press, Princeton.

Hamilton, G. G. and Biggart, N. W. (1988) 'Market, Culture, and Authority: A Comparative Analysis of Management and Organization in the Far East'. *American Journal of Sociology*, **94**: S52–S94.

Herman, E. S. (1981) *Corporate Control, Corporate Power*. Cambridge University Press, Cambridge.

Komiya, R. (1990) *The Japanese Economy: Trade, Industry and Government*. University of Tokyo Press, Tokyo.

Kosei Torihiki Iinkai (Japanese Federal Trade Commission) (1983) 'Kigyo Shudan No Jittai Ni Tsuite'. (On the State of Affairs of Enterprise Groups). Japanese Federal Trade Commission, Tokyo.

Kotz, D. M. (1978) *Bank Control of Large Corporations in the United States*. University of California Press, Berkeley.

Lawrence, R. Z. (1991) 'Efficient or Exclusionist? The Import Behaviour of Japanese Corporate Groups' *Brookings Papers on Economic Activity*, **1**: 311–330. Brookings Institution, Washington, DC.

Lockwood, W. W. (1968) *The Economic Development of Japan: Growth and Structural Change*. Princeton University Press, Princeton.

Lorrain, F. and White, H. C. (1971) 'Structural Equivalence of Individuals in Social Networks'. *Journal of Mathematical Sociology*, **1**: 49–80.

MacEvoy, B. and Freeman, L. (1987) *UCINET 3.0*. Mathematical Social Science Group, School of Social Sciences. University of California at Irvine.

Mariolis, P. and Jones, M. H. (1982) 'Centrality in Corporate Interlock Networks: Reliability and Stability'. *Administrative Science Quarterly*, **27**: 571–584.

Mintz, B. and Schwartz, M. (1981) 'Interlocking Directorates and Interest Group Formation'. *American Sociological Review*, **46**: 851–869.
Mintz, B. and Schwartz, M. (1985) *The Power Structure of American Business*. University of Chicago Press, Chicago.
Miwa, Y. (1990) *Nihon No Kigyō to Sangyō Soshiki (Japanese Enterprise and Industrial Organization)*. Tokyo Daigaku Shuppan-kai, Tokyo.
Miyazaki, Y. (1976) *Sengo Nihon No Kigyō Shūdan (Enterprise Groups in Postwar Japan)*. Nihon Keizai Shimbunsha, Tokyo.
Mizruchi, M. (1982) *The American Corporate Network: 1904–1974*. Sage, Beverly Hills, CA.
Nakatani, I. (1984) 'The Economic Role of Financial Corporate Groupings'. In M. Aoki (ed.) *The Economic Analysis of the Japanese Firm*, pp. 227–258. North Holland, Elsevier Science, Amsterdam.
Okumura, H. (1983) *Shin Nihon No Rokudai Kigyō Shūdan (Japan's, Six Major Enterprise Groups)*. Daiyamondo-sha, Tokyo.
Ornstein, M. D. (1984) 'Interlocking Directorates in Canada: Intercorporate or Class Alliance?' *Administrative Science Quarterly*, **29**: 210–231.
Orru, M., Hamilton, G. G. and Suzuki, M. (1989) 'Patterns of Inter-firm Control in Japanese Business'. *Organization Studies*, **10**: 549–574.
Palmer, D. (1983) 'Broken Ties: Interlocking Directorates and Intercorporate Coordination'. *Administrative Science Quarterly*, **28**: 40–55.
Palmer, D., Friedland, R. and Singh, J. V. (1986) 'The Ties that Bind: Organizational and Class Base of Stability in Corporate Interlock Networks'. *Annual Sociological Review*, **51**: 781–796.
Pennings, J. M. (1980) *Interlocking Directorates*. Jossey-Bass, San Francisco.
Perlo, V. (1957) *The Empire of High Finance*. International, New York.
Pfeffer, J. and Salancik, G. R. (1978) *The External Control of Organizations*. Harper and Row, New York.
Pisano, G. P. (1989) 'Using Equity Participation to Support Exchange: Evidence from the Biotechnology Industry'. *Journal of Law, Economics, and Organization*, **5**: 109–126.
Powell, W. (1990) 'Neither Market nor Hierarchy: Network Forms of Organization'. In Staw, B. M. and Cummings, L. L. (eds), *Research in Organizational Behaviour*, Vol. 12, pp.295–336. JAI Press, Greenwich, CT.
Richardson, R. J. (1987) 'Directorship Interlocks and Corporate Profitability'. *Administrative Science Quarterly*, **32**: 367–386.
Sheard, P. (1991) 'The Role of Firm Organization in the Adjustment of a Declining Industry in Japan: The Case of Aluminum'. *Journal of the Japanese and International Economies*, **5**: 14–40.
Useem, M. (1984) *The Inner Circle*. Oxford University Press, New York.
White, H. C., Boorman, S. A. and Breiger, R. L. (1976) 'Social Structure from Multiple Networks, I: Blockmodels of Roles and Positions'. *American Journal of Sociology*, **81**: 730–780.
Williamson, O. E. (1985) *The Economic Institutions of Capitalism*. Free Press, New York.
Zajac, E. J. (1988) 'Interlocking Directorates as an Interorganizational Strategy: A Test of Critical Assumptions'. *Academy of Management Journal*, **31**: 428–438.

17

The Worldwide Web of Chinese Business

John Kao

Most discussion of today's global economy centres on three power houses: North America, Europe, and Japan. In turn, economists usually divide Asia into Japan, a People's Republic of China that is rapidly changing and on the rise, and the industrialized 'dragons' of South Korea, Taiwan, Hong Kong, and Singapore. Yet this standard economic definition doesn't match Pacific Rim realities. In fact, Chinese businesses—many of which are located outside the People's Republic itself—make up the world's fourth economic power.

The very definition of 'China' is up for grabs. What we think of as Chinese now encompasses an array of political and economic systems that are bound together by a shared tradition, not geography. For many generations, emigrant Chinese entrepreneurs have been operating comfortably in a network of family and clan, laying the foundations for stronger links among businesses across national borders. And Chinese-owned businesses in East Asia, the United States, Canada, and even farther afield are increasingly becoming part of what I call the *Chinese commonwealth*.

Not based in any one country or continent, this commonwealth is primarily a network of entrepreneurial relationships. From restaurants to real estate to plastic-sandal makers to semiconductor manufacturing—from a staff of five or six family members to a plant floor of thousands—the Chinese commonwealth consists of many individual enterprises that nonetheless share a common culture.

It is the kind of global network many Western multinationals have tried to create in their own organizations. Now these same Western companies are casting about for Asian joint venture partners, looking for ways to tap into the increasingly powerful Chinese network. For most multinationals, Asian based or not, it's time to take the commonwealth seriously.

To begin with, countries with Chinese-based economies have astonishingly large capital surpluses. Taiwan, one of the smallest countries in the world, has the largest foreign exchange reserves. Singapore, a country of 2.7 million people, has foreign exchange reserves exceeding $34 billion. Then there are the private and informal capital markets of Chinese family and clan associations, in which financial resources are deployed for new venture activities without the intervention of commercial banks, professional venture capital companies, or government investment agencies.

Reprinted by permission of *Harvard Business Review*. 'The Worldwide Web of Chinese Business', by John Kao, March–April 1993, pp. 24–36. Copyright © by the President and Fellows of Harvard College; all rights reserved.

In addition, the Chinese entrepreneurial network and Japan represent two very different integrating forces in Asia. Unlike the Japanese, the Chinese commonwealth has, in computer terms, an 'open architecture'. It represents access to local resources like information, business connections, raw materials, low labour costs, and different business practices in a variety of environments. In contrast to the Japanese *keiretsu*, the emerging Chinese commonwealth is an interconnected yet potentially open system—and in many respects, provides a new market mechanism for conducting global business.

Thus it is now possible to reach markets in the People's Republic of China through Chinese entrepreneurs in Taiwan. Outsiders may be able to access Southeast Asian markets through the Hong Kong and Singaporean business communities. And ultimately, both Chinese and non-Chinese entrepreneurs may come to take advantage of opportunities in North America and Europe through the Chinese network in those regions.

Many of these Chinese entrepreneurial connections, of course, still involve few outsiders. The traditional small size and family orientation of Chinese businesses certainly have hampered their growth. The Beijing Stone Group, whose stated goal was to become 'China's IBM' (until co-founder Wan Runnan fled the People's Republic in 1989), offers one example of how Chinese business practices have evolved in the past 20 years—and the difficulties these companies still face. Other companies like the Acer Group in Taiwan and the Pico Group in Singapore have successfully blended the old with the new.

The new Chinese management model, like the commonwealth that underpins it, is grounded in both traditional Chinese values and Western practices that encourage flexibility, innovation, and the assimilation of outsiders. Such a shift in values has meant not only a transformation in how Chinese businesspeople view themselves and their work but also the expansion of the emerging network. And over time, a new ideology of economic self-interest, one that truly does transcend politics and the clannish constraints on traditional Chinese business, may lead to even greater integration of the commonwealth.

THE SHAPING POWER OF CONFUCIAN TRADITION

For more than 2 000 years, Chinese culture has stressed the importance of social order. From the sixth to fifth century B.C., Confucius codified the ties of individual, family and society that define a person's proper place and position. Given China's long history of political upheaval, natural disasters, waves of emigration, and, above all, economic scarcity, these well-defined relationships have often helped keep social chaos at bay.

Based on a study of Chinese entrepreneurship I have conducted over the past two years, in which my research team has surveyed or interviewed more than 150 entrepreneurs both inside and outside of China, it is clear that the Confucian tradition is remarkably persistent. For most Chinese entrepreneurs, Westernized as they may be, the enterprise is still a means for exerting control—and for achieving security in a disordered world.

My research interviews reveal a consistent pattern of personal disruption and hardship, including loss of country, wealth, home, or a family member. In my survey, 90% of the entrepreneurs who were first-generation emigrants had experienced war; 40% had gone through a political disaster like the Cultural Revolution; 32% had lost a home; and 28% had weathered economic disasters that resulted in significant loss of wealth.

In ancient China, farmers in a largely agrarian economy focused on surviving storms, droughts, and locusts. More recently, business has become a key to survival for Chinese emigrants, especially during the Chinese diaspora of the past century. Enterprising entrepreneurs work long hours and save wherever they can, accumulating capital in a world they still consider unsafe.

This survivor mentality and the Confucian tradition of patriarchal authority inform the values of the typical Chinese entrepreneur—one who seeks to control his own small dynasty. In fact, China's history of political and social turmoil has led to a relentless practicality, which can be summarized in the following 'life-raft' values:

- Thrift ensures survival.
- A high, even irrational, level of savings is desirable, regardless of immediate need.
- Hard work to the point of exhaustion is necessary to ward off the many hazards present in an unpredictable world.
- The only people you can trust are family—and a business enterprise is created as a familial life raft.
- The judgement of an incompetent relative in the family business is more reliable than that of a complete stranger.
- Obedience to patriarchal authority is essential to maintaining coherence and direction for the enterprise.
- Investment must be based on kinship or clan affiliations, not abstract principles.
- Tangible goods like real estate, natural resources, and gold bars are preferable to intangibles like illiquid securities or intellectual property.
- Keep your bags packed at all times, day or night.

These underlying values probably account for certain archetypal business choices of first-generation Chinese: real estate, shipping, and import–export companies. Such industries generally require a limited span of control and can be managed effectively by a small group of insiders who can be members of the same family. Even Chinese enterprises that have grown quite large tend to maintain immature organizational patterns—for example, management 'spokes' around a powerful founder 'hub' or a management structure with only two layers. Of the entrepreneurs I surveyed, 70% noted that they still operated around one of these two simple structures.

In such imperial organizations, Chinese entrepreneurs manage traditional enterprises much as a Chinese emperor would his empire. Not surprisingly, the assets of the business usually are passed on only to family members. My research interviews indicate that many Chinese entrepreneurs still consider imperial organizations crucial to their success, regardless of the entrepreneurs' age or generational identity. As one old Chinese saying puts it, 'Better to be the head of a chicken than the tail of a large cow'.

The founder of Formosa Plastics in Taiwan, Y. C. Wang, still controls this successful chemicals and plastics company, which now employs more than 30 000 people. Wang directs the company through an inner circle of fewer than 10 professional managers who are not family members. These executives, in turn, work with an administrative group of about 200 other managers.

The purpose of this administrative group is to channel and distil information into a series of daily reports, which reach Wang either in person or by fax. And Wang's son, an operations manager, occupies a plush office at corporate headquarters—much as the princes in an imperial bureaucracy lived in different wings of the palace.

There are plenty of other recent examples of dynastic 'succession'—from former prime minister Lee Kuan Yew, whose son, Lee Hsien Loong, became Singapore's Minister of Trade and Industry to Wee Cho Yaw, the founder of Singapore's United Overseas Bank, who installed his son, Wee Te Cheong, as deputy president not long ago. As original founders like Hong Kong's Li Ka Shing of Cheung Kong Holdings, Malaysia's Robert Kuok of the Shangri-La Hotel and other ventures, and Indonesia's Liem Sioe Liong of the Salim Group approach the end of their careers, control of these global companies will probably remain in family hands as well.

But dynastic aspirations may explain why companies that appear as cosmopolitan as Wang Laboratories in Lowell, Massachusetts still maintain an imperial model at their core—and often fall apart. Fred Wang, whom his father An Wang finally called an inadequate manager, seemed quite capable when he was promoted to president of Wang. Still, the American management group that surrounded Fred Wang didn't fully accept his inherent right to run the company.

In Asia, the executives in a professional management group would have accepted unquestioningly a family member as leader. They might have wondered if it was too early for that person to achieve power, but they would not have contested the basic promotion. At Wang Laboratories, such East–West value differences led to many additional conflicts and contributed to the company's eventual decline.

By its very nature, the life raft of a familial business is unstable for key outsiders. Based on my research, a non-Chinese professional manager can't expect the same level of trust he or she would have as a family member in the company. Outsiders can never know family insiders as well as they know each other. And non-Chinese professionals often have to work doubly hard to understand the reasons underlying certain decisions.

Anyone who routinely deals with successful Chinese businesspeople soon realizes that while 90% of a given entrepreneur's decisions may be brilliant, the other 10% often make no business sense. The typical Chinese entrepreneur may keep a poor manager on because 'he's family'; sit on decisions that involve outsiders; conceal information because 'she's not family'; avoid necessary confrontations; and in many respects, behave toward subordinates like a guilt-provoking parent.

Most telling, however, is how quickly traditional organizations hit snags when they expand beyond the limits of family control. In a 1990 *Fortune* survey of Pacific Rim businesses, only one Chinese enterprise made the list of the top 150 based on size. As these companies start to grow, the conventions of traditional Chinese business, especially caution toward outsiders, become a clear competitive disadvantage.

In the classic story of a Chinese dynasty's fall, a weak emperor, along with a weak group of imperial managers, can no longer satisfy the people and loses the 'mandate of heaven'. In today's global economy, the need for continual innovation may provide a new earthly mandate for organizational change.

BREAKING WITH TRADITION

'In Chinese culture, you have to respect your father and mother', notes James Yen, the president of Advanced Microelectronic Products in Taiwan. 'This respect kills creativity. If you have to respect what your father says, then you tend to kill your own thinking'.

Along with the adherence to traditional Chinese values across generations, my research also reveals that the 'life raft' has expanded. The emergence of an economically powerful commonwealth is due to a number of changes over the past three decades, including a break with traditional life-raft values.

The sons, daughters, and grandchildren of first-generation entrepreneurs have assimilated to a far greater extent. People of Chinese descent are now born all over the world; they are multicultural and have lived and been educated in a manner different from their parents. While second- and third-generation Chinese still respect the family enterprise, these younger entrepreneurs have absorbed other values as well, particularly if they live in Western countries like the United States. (See Appendix 'The American Connection').

D. Y. Yang of Winbond in Taiwan, who considers his computer chip company to be Chinese, says, 'A Chinese company depends less on data and more on intuition, feelings, and people'. At the same time, he notes that no blood relatives, including his children, are part of Winbond. 'You have to depend on the system to work. Of course you have to respect the family business structure, but since this is a high-tech company, individual contributions are important'.

The commonwealth's new breed of entrepreneurs have shifted from a survivor mentality to a focus on self-actualization, a goal that reflects Western philosophies and practices. In my research, respondents cited these 'soft' factors most often as crucial for improving their businesses in the future: managing growth, nurturing creativity, developing more open communication and confrontation skills, and encouraging professionalization of the organization and smooth assimilation of outsiders.

For example, the Acer Group in Taiwan markets its own brand of computer clones in more than 70 countries and is one of the largest personal computer companies in the world. Acer's employees are encouraged to own shares of company stock, the company's emphasis on decentralization, doing its own R&D, and creating its own brand name have become highly praised models for other enterprises in Taiwan. Yet CEO and cofounder Stan Shih attributes many of the company's greatest strengths—especially the stability of its senior managers—to traditional Chinese culture.

The Pico Group in Singapore is an other amalgam of traditional and Western management styles. Pico includes 300 operating companies in 25 countries, which focus on everything from design and fabrication of exhibits to marketing services to leisure businesses like game centres and Broadway shows. Pico's 2 500 employees receive bonuses and stock options and can participate in profit-sharing plans. Managers can direct the investment of any surplus from their operating units.

Yet Pico was founded by three brothers; and three of its four main business groups still are run by family members. The executive director of the fourth group, which focuses on the new business area of entertainment, is a long-time family friend. In fact, all of Pico's top managers, half of whom were educated abroad, started out as family friends rather than raw hires.

In contrast, the Beijing Stone Group introduced what co-founder Wan Runnan called a 'modern Western concept' of business from the very beginning. Stone, which in 1984 started in a two-room office that was formerly a collective's vegetable shop, grew much larger than any enterprise in the People's Republic of China during the 1980s. It included more than 40 companies, from computer equipment manufacturers to CAD product designers to technical typesetters—with subsidiaries in various parts of the People's Republic, as well as in Hong Kong, Australia, Japan, and the United States.

By 1989, just before Wan fled the country for his open espousal of democratic principles, Beijing Stone had developed the sophisticated matrix organizational structure favoured by many Western multinationals. Wan's charismatic leadership style alone made Stone look like a Western company. He and the other founders established a strong corporate culture and compensation policies keyed to performance—with salaries much higher than those offered by other companies in the People's Republic but with fewer automatic benefits like free housing.

While Wan Runnan paid the price for moving too fast in the People's Republic of China, Chinese entrepreneurs are now on the cutting edge when it comes to establishing new democratic processes. china itself has yet to evolve a true model of Chinese democracy; its traditional institutions always have been based on the imperial mode, be they the government, business enterprises, or the family. Yet new business practices often lead to new ways of thinking about political and social organization. Witness the rejuvenating effects of the most recent spate of economic reforms in the People's Republic of China.

CAPITAL AS THE SPRINGBOARD

The explosion of high-technology industries in Asia and the political opening of China in the 1980s have reinforced and will continue to expand today's Chinese commonwealth. But perhaps the most important development that has consolidated the commonwealth is how rich many Chinese communities have become.

In Indonesia, one individual of Chinese descent, Liem Sioe Liong, is reputed to generate 5% of the country's gross domestic product through the Salim Group. And *Institutional Investor* has estimated that the private wealth of Southeast Asia's 40 million ethnic Chinese exceeds $200 billion.

Because of the unprecedented availability of capital, a sophisticated Chinese plutocracy has emerged on the world scene. In effect, these plutocrats are the guardians of large scale entrepreneurship within the Chinese commonwealth, whether it has to do with building a highway or creating a satellite broadcasting service from virtually a standing start.

Billionaire Li Ka Shing's Star TV in Hong Kong broadcasts entertainment and information services to an Asian market of 2.7 billion. Gordon Wu's Hopewell Holdings, oversees construction of the highway, which runs from Hong Kong to Guangzhou through the province of Guangdong in southern China.

Since the 1970s, the growing wealth of Chinese communities clearly has fuelled significant levels of investment across national borders. In fact, cross-border investments alone are responsible for turning the de facto network of loose family relationships into today's Chinese commonwealth. While the invisible or unofficial capital market of family, friends, and clan affiliations is on the rise, the opportunities provided by official banking and government sources also have increased.

For example, Thailand's Charoen Pokphand Group, an agribusiness conglomerate headed by ethnic Chinese, was one of the first companies to make large investments in the People's Republic of China. Or take the development funds provided by the Taiwanese government or the Monte Jade Association, which help finance joint ventures and encourage the flow of market information between expatriate high-tech entrepreneurs and their homeland.

Chinese entrepreneurs have become the first or second most prominent source of foreign investment in countries such as Thailand, the Philippines, and Vietnam. These entrepreneurial links are forged through extensive networks of ethnic Chinese: Taiwanese to Thai-Chinese, Hong Kong Chinese to mainland Chinese; American Chinese to Vietnamese Chinese.

Of the entrepreneurs I surveyed, 52% noted that more than half of their domestic working relationships were with Chinese principals—and 39% of their international working relationships were with other Chinese, a percentage that's much higher than one would expect in a multinational. In general, foreign direct investment in the People's Republic reportedly has reached more than $30 billion, most of which has come from Chinese business-people in Hong Kong and Taiwan.

But most significant for the emergence of the commonwealth, these investment patterns across borders, forged through cultural links, have become more visible. For example, Western media recently have paid much more attention to Vancouver's expatriate Hong Kong Chinese, who have invested significantly in Canadian real estate and business in preparation for Hong Kong's return to China in 1997.

Of course, the entrepreneurial network that I have been calling the Chinese commonwealth is not a unified interest group or unofficial 'nation'. According to an old saying, 'The Chinese are like a bowl of loose sand'. The sudden wealth of expatriate Chinese communities and the new possibilities for business afforded by them still come down to a global patchwork of many small enterprises that, in some cases, have little or no respect or love for one another.

Yet entrepreneurs who are motivated primarily by economic self-interest generally don't let personal animosity get in the way of shrewd business decisions. And with new large-scale business opportunities bankrolled by Chinese money come a range of new financial intermediaries. While these outside deal brokers, bankers, and lawyers are not exactly welcome in the traditional entrepreneur's orbit, they are nevertheless part and parcel of dealing on a broader financial canvas.

'KNOWLEDGE ARBITRAGE' IN A NEW ECONOMY

Inevitably, capital abundance leads to greater business flexibility and mobility. The ability to transfer funds is equivalent to the ability to transfer corporate flags across national boundaries. And making such transfers is much easier when the enterprise is not tied to immovable assets. Thus the Chinese entrepreneur—who may still believe in the importance of tangible goods and a closed circle of family to manage them—now finds himself or herself in an expanding social network, trafficking the most intangible of assets.

Many of today's Chinese business-people have successfully made the shift from the role of trader in a relatively small market to that of international arbitrageur. In other words, they've moved from the perspective of individuals clinging to a life raft to a view from above that takes in the whole ocean.

According to the usual definition of arbitrage, Chinese entrepreneurs have been quick to exploit fully the financial anomalies in Chinese markets. Obviously, the Chinese commonwealth encompasses a wide array of disparate growth rates, investor psychologies, and approaches to valuation. The significant capital markets within the network include Hong Kong, Singapore, Taiwan, the United States—and, most recently, the People's Republic of China—yet each of these markets often value assets in completely different ways.

For example, at its height in 1989, the average price/earnings ratio of a share on the Taiwan Stock Exchange was more than seven times greater than the average p/e ratio on the New York Stock Exchange. That meant a US company with an established marketing and sales arm in Taiwan could, after satisfying residency and regulatory requirements, go public in Taiwan, thereby raising 'cheap capital'. Companies like Wang and Qume were among those attempting such strategies.

But when it comes to the new opportunities available to entrepreneurs in the Chinese commonwealth, I would like to expand the strict definition of arbitrage. Given the strength of the entrepreneurial network, Chinese business-people are well positioned to take advantage of other market differences—a process I call *knowledge arbitrage*. Precisely because of its scale and diversity, the Chinese commonwealth now includes fundamental differences in labour costs and product markets. Given varying levels of technology development and resources in different countries, an engineer from Taiwan can start a company in Silicon Valley, which then carries out low-cost manufacturing on an Indonesian island—with Chinese financing organized by the government of Singapore.

Labour-cost differences, in fact, offer some of the most dramatic opportunities for knowledge arbitrageurs. For example, making shoes in Taiwan started in the 1950s as a low-cost commodity manufacturing industry that took advantage of the country's low labour costs and Confucian work ethic to produce cheap shoes like plastic sandals for export. Gradually, manufacturers developed higher priced running shoes and other products, and labour costs began to skyrocket in Taiwan.

At the same time, business links were forged between Taiwan and the People's Republic of China, not through official channels but through grey-market mechanisms. Typically, a cash-rich Taiwanese entrepreneur would create at low cost a 'paper' company in Hong Kong, using it as a trans-shipment point for goods and services between Taiwan and the cash-starved mainland.

Then, in 1987, Taiwan's shoe companies suddenly began to relocate their operations to the People's Republic. Manufacturing equipment was transferred through Hong Kong to the mainland, and key personnel from Taiwan moved as well. The Taiwanese Shoe Association estimates that up to 80% of Taiwan's shoe companies have moved to the People's Republic of China in search of labour cost advantages.

Another form of knowledge arbitrage involves differing consumer trends in the Chinese commonwealth. Knowledge arbitrageurs who bridge Chinese communities in diverse countries can link products with markets in innovative ways. For example, the Quanta Group in Taiwan, a leader in the consumer business, established itself by representing Western companies in Chinese markets. Under David and John Sun, two brothers who were educated in the United States, the company brought McDonald's and Disney merchandise outlets to Taiwan in the early 1980s.

In many respects, of course, the political opening of the People's Republic of China now represents the ultimate arbitrage for entrepreneurs in the commonwealth. China offers a huge pool of low-cost labour and untapped natural resources to countries like Singapore, in which labour costs have steadily risen and resources have always been restricted.

And China's 1.1 billion population of new consumers, who have had little access to outside products for decades, are hungry to buy. The recent run on Avon cosmetic packs and Bausch & Lomb optical products in the People's Republic are just two examples of a wildly shifting consumer focus.

Of course, whether social change can keep pace with China's rapid economic change remains to be seen. The Chinese Communist Party still controls the country's social machinery and numbers its membership at some 50 million people. Yet the People's Republic, where gunfire echoed in the streets a scant four years ago, is also a country where its citizens now can watch MTV and count their stock certificates while munching on Big Macs. Such contradictions—and opportunities—abound for today's Chinese commonwealth and all who can tap into it.

THE FUTURE OF THE FOURTH POWER

There's an old Chinese saying that goes 'the shrewd rabbit has three holes'. Taiwanese entrepreneur Steve Tsai has interpreted this to mean having one business base in the People's Republic to represent the future, one in Taiwan to capitalize on the present, and another 'hole' in the United States to serve as insurance. By his account, Chinese entrepreneurs want to be where the action is but where the risks are not—and show little inherent loyalty to home.

Steve Tsai's 'shrewd rabbit' metaphor is a good representation of how Chinese entrepreneurs view the world today, their position in it, and how they still may need to change. 'Doing business is like driving a car', says P. T. De of San Sun Hats. 'In the United States, everything has rules and regulations, and you just follow the rules, and it's easy. In Taiwan, even if the light is red, somebody can get through it. If it's green, there still aren't rules to tell you how to go'.

Obviously, what I've been calling the Chinese commonwealth contains no official clearing-house for coordinating joint ventures or operating as a united economic community. Singapore with its sophisticated technological infrastructure, Hong Kong with its capital markets and trading infrastructure, and Taiwan with its incredible foreign exchange reserves are all major power centres. Yet to the extent that Chinese communities remain apolitical, they can't act on their own behalf in most host countries, including the United States.

Still, Chinese-owned trade shows, electronic databases, consulting firms, periodicals on entrepreneurship, investment banks, business schools, and other institutions will expand the reach of the commonwealth in the future. In 1991, Singapore held the First World Chinese Entrepreneurs Convention, which brought together 800 Chinese businesspeople from some 35 countries. The entrepreneurs themselves have begun to recognize the commonwealth for what it is: a new global power base.

At the same time, the Chinese commonwealth is no longer exclusively Chinese. By participating in such a pervasive economic network, potential partners of Chinese entrepreneurs can obtain not only greater access to Chinese-based markets at much lower costs but also access to world markets in general.

Such East–West connections will be particularly important to small and medium-size companies looking for ever-more efficient ways of internationalizing at an earlier stage in their development. Chinese entrepreneurs also have a great deal to gain from outside joint-venture partners especially large ones: for example, new brand names, market information, and professional management structures.

Yet paradoxically, the continued evolution of the commonwealth depends on most of its entrepreneurs continuing to opt for a small-business management model. Through a global network, many small units can come up with a variety of solutions at an acceptable level of risk. While Chinese entrepreneurs are moving clearly toward a new management model, one that encourages growth and an openness to outsiders when a business is ready to take off, most Chinese companies have incentives to remain small, familial organizations. Such a trend is based partly on Chinese cultural biases and partly on what now appears to pay off in the world at large.

In other words, the Confucian tradition of hard work, thrift, and respect for one's social network may provide continuity with the right twist for today's fast-changing markets. And the central strategic question for all current multinationals—be they Chinese, Japanese, or Western—is how to gather and integrate power through many small units. The evolution of a worldwide web of relatively small Chinese businesses, bound by undeniably strong cultural links, offers a working model for the future.

APPENDIX: THE AMERICAN CONNECTION, BY FRANK B. GIBNEY

For Chinese students, intellectuals, and entrepreneurs, the United States is the quintessential open society Despite past exploitation of coolie labour on Western railroads and the bigotry of immigration laws, successive generations have found the individualist ideals of America as appealing as its pop culture. While Asia watchers often don't consider its impact, the 'American connection' is an essential force behind today's growing Chinese entrepreneurial network.

The influence of US values and business practices on Chinese communities around the world is most obvious where the connection is weakest. As experienced victims of racial persecution, the Chinese of the Pacific Basin have good reason to welcome big friends like the United States. Especially in Southeast Asia, Chinese have been victimized time and again by people who envy their industry and success. The vivid images of ancestors slaughtered in racial massacres do not fade easily—all the more reason for overseas Chinese to appreciate America's continued political and military presence in the region.

Protective action is a way of life. During the 1960s, tens of thousands of Chinese were killed in racial massacres in both Malaysia and Indonesia. Even now, Malaysia, in particular, has codified discrimination against its Chinese entrepreneurs. Its laws insist on *bumiputra*—Malay ownership of corporations. Mindful of ever-smouldering racial tensions, middle-class Chinese in the South Pacific tend to adopt local names and customs. While visiting Jakarta a few years ago, I discovered that local Chinese business-people, although Christians, prudently fast with Moslem employees during Ramadan.

It is also true that Chinese entrepreneurs and technocrats have been quick to make themselves useful to the governments of Moslem Indonesia and Malaysia. The two largest Indonesian conglomerates, Salim and Astra, are owned and operated by Chinese. Still, for those living in Southeast Asia, implied threats remain.

While the influence of American democratic principles is most necessary in countries where Chinese are actively discriminated against, education and emigration have fuelled the deepest changes in Chinese values. To most overseas Chinese, American education represents a continuing ideal; and for many, emigration has become increasingly attractive. Since the 1965 changes in US immigration laws, high percentages of new Asian immigrants have been Chinese. But even before that time, political repression in Taiwan as well as in the People's Republic of China drove thousands of Chinese students to study and work in the United States.

America has become the educator of the Pacific Rim. Unlike the exclusionist universities of Japan, where foreigners will not have an easy time finding teaching jobs at Tokyo University, American education is determinedly internationalist. No one has benefited more from US higher education and technological training than the overseas Chinese.

In 1990, a year when more than 160 000 students from East Asia were enrolled in US colleges, one-fourth of all American doctorates in electrical engineering were awarded to students from Taiwan. For years, the National Science Foundation has been impressed by overseas Chinese performance in graduate sciences, math, and engineering. While the machines in Chinese entrepreneurial factories often come from Japan, the technology they use is American. In fact, English is the *lingua franca* of Asian R&D.

Clearly, a healthy interdependence has formed between overseas Chinese entrepreneurs and many Americans over the years. While happy to do deals with the Japanese, Chinese businesspeople are understandably nervous about the market-share drives of government-assisted Japanese companies. Nor are they necessarily comfortable with the master–serf relationship between the Japanese *keiretsu* and their clients and suppliers. Even with trade patterns shifting somewhat for fear of increasing US protectionism, almost one-quarter of East Asia's exports go to the United States. The American consumer, it is truly said, has been the engine of growth for the Asian Pacific region.

The economic connection, however, goes far beyond mere buying and selling. Taiwan's booming economy was jump-started by the off-shore production of American corporations, and this pattern has been repeated in Singapore and other Pacific Basin countries. By working to match the instructions of US marketers closely, Chinese producers have developed a symbiotic relationship with US business interests.

Of course, most Chinese entrepreneurs have little political power to back them up. Some large Taiwanese and Singaporean companies, many of them government related, can count on support from their economic bureaucrats. But the Chinese entrepreneurial network as a whole is too diverse and protean to allow for the massive government help Japan and Korea give their *keiretsu* and *chaebol* corporate groups. Spontaneous US alliances tend to fit Chinese family businesses much better.

And in this, American ideals of democracy and pluralism, as well as US technology, provide vital leavening for the capitalist development economies that virtually have become East Asia's trademark. More important, as we look to Asia's future in a post-Cold-War world, US concern for human rights, still backed by the greatest political and military power in the region, should remain a strong counter to the dictatorial impulses of the ageing communist bureaucrats in Beijing, as well as to the 'soft authoritarianism'—to use a Japanese political science phrase—of military leaders in both Indonesia and Thailand.

18

A Network Approach to Probing Asia's Invisible Business Structures

S. Benjamin Prasad and Pervez N. Ghauri

Toyota Motors has often been characterized rightly as the source of most of the contemporary manufacturing methods that industrial firms in the United States and Western Europe have adopted but with limited success. On the one hand, Toyota's Ohno System is regarded as the foundation for manufacturing efficiency accomplished by such means as JIT and QCC, and a model of managerial effectiveness attained through a huge network of suppliers and subcontractors. From the Japanese perspective such a network is functional; from the point of view of the Western firms it is dysfunctional and exclusionary. A more balanced view of this seeming paradox is possible if we were to juxtapose Asian structures and the Scandinavian network perspective.

The purpose of this paper is to briefly sketch the network approach as a framework which would enrich one's understanding of Japan's *keiretsu* and South Korea's *chaebol*, as well as 'group' business relationships in India and other Asian nations. Khambatta and Ajami (1992) characterize *keiretsu* as large groups of industrial companies and banks with scores of firms supplying raw materials, components, and financing of operations (p.304); Lee *et al.* (1989) describe *chaebols* as conglomerate groups (e.g., Hyundai and Samsung) that have been the backbone of industrialization. Group companies in India, such as Tatas and Birlas are also conglomerates more similar to *chaebols* than to *keiretsu*—looser versions of *zaibatsu*.

Such an understanding would augment theory-building efforts in the field of international business, and provide insights especially to Western firms as they map out entry, re-entry, or expansion strategies in the burgeoning Asian region. The paper is organized as follows: (1) Underpinnings of interfirm networks; (2) Asian business structures; (3) Implications for Western companies; and (4) Summary and conclusion.

UNDERPINNINGS OF INTERFIRM NETWORKS

Interfirm networks can be defined as two or more firms involved in relationships that, in the long run, crystallize into relational structures. These structures are often based on unwritten rules and they are not akin to contractual relationships that typify linkages among entities in the United States. Interfirm networks have been examined from different perspectives; for example, Thorelli (1986) has focused on the political implications of resource flows through such a network; Johanson (1987) has developed a taxonomy of networks differentiated by the structures of the linkages and the dynamics of the interactions; Jarillo (1988) has focused on the forms of the interactions among network members; Sekaran and Snodgrass (1990) have offered a culture-based perspective of business networks.

The network approach holds that firms are linked with each other through different types of bonds forming a network. Through the networks, firms adapt to each other in regard to production, purchasing, marketing and even research and development (R&D). Each firm develops or attains a position in its network over time (Johanson and Mattsson, 1988). The position describes a firm's relations to its network. Relationships can be tightly or loosely structured. A tight structure generates high interdependencies with well-defined positions of the firms; the loose structure implies weak bonds and less clearly defined positions.

From a theoretical perspective, there are two mainstreams of thought regarding networks. The Scandinavian view supports the notion that leading firms take pivotal (nodal) positions in the network while the American view maintains that networking, in the sense of strategic partnering, is a second-tier cooperative activity induced by specific weaknesses of a firm's business units. To amplify, taking a nodal position, Daimler–Benz developed a network with United Technology; in contrast, General Motors forged a strategic partnership in 1984 with Toyota, apparently because of some weakness of its Chevrolet Division. Our focus is on the first perspective.

Research evidence (Ghauri, 1990; Hallén *et al.*, 1991) suggests that (a) firms tend to build and maintain these networks as tools of long-term competitive strategy; (b) contemporary networks

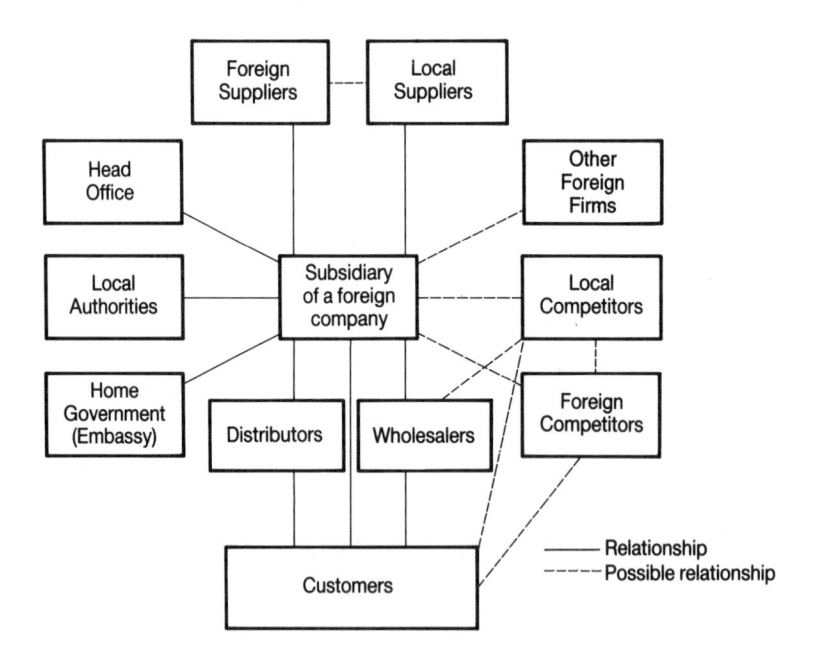

Figure 1. Broadening Horizons of Networks. (*Source*: Ghauri, 1989, p.264.)

extend beyond supplier-firm and envelope relationships among suppliers, distributors, customers, and even public organizations and rivals (see Figure 1); and (c) in the information technology industry in particular (Hagedoorn and Schakenraad, 1992) 'the leading companies create flexible networks that enable them to capitalize on economies of scope' (p.166).

In sum, the interfirm network, as briefly noted above, manifests three main features: (i) long-term relationships involving a larger number of stakeholders than mere producer–supplier or producer–distributor linkages, (ii) a deliberate, rather than emergent, bonding as a tool of long-term competitive strategy, (iii) initiatives flowing from the leading, not necessarily the largest, firm in the network.

Do the existing business structures in Asia exhibit these salient characteristics? Our short answer is *Yes*. Having said so, we hasten to add that such a recognition will certainly enable one to avoid the pitfalls of '*keiretsu*phobia'—the fear of Asian networks (Kinsley, 1991). In the following section our intent is not to explain the Japanese corporate network, but to sketch the origin and scope of the *keiretsu*-type business networks with which Western firms in the Asian region would have to interface.

ASIAN BUSINESS STRUCTURES (NETWORKS)

Keiretsu, as industrial networks, are said to have had their inception in the ancient relationships that existed between feudal lords in Japan and their samurai. Japan's industrial sector before World War II was organized around a handful of *zaibatsu* which 'had their own bank at the centre'. Before the war, a handful of families (Mitsui, Mitsubishi, Sumitomo and so on) owned the majority of the stock of large corporations in key industries. To varying degrees, all main subsidiary companies of the *Zaibatsu* were systematically placed in a pyramid-shaped control structure, and at the apex was the holding company—a family company. The *zaibatsu* were perceived as cartels, monopolies and trusts and hence deemed antethetical to the American legal framework. These 'formal clusters, or *zaibatsu*, were officially dissolved, in part because of their central role in Japan's military efforts, and in part because they conflicted with American anti-monopoly ideals' (Wright, 1989, p.20).

'Although the *Zaibatsu* were legally dissolved, the relationships continue[d]... due to the dependence of all companies on a closely knit network of allied banks for their financing' (Ouchi, 1981, p.17). The Mitsui, Mitsubishi, and the Sumitomo groups were '*zaibatsu* groups each of which was owned by a holding company before World War II, [but] dissolved by the American Occupation Authorities' (Sasaki, 1982, pp.11–12). Since then, big business in Japan has taken the more flexible form of *keiretsu*, distinguished by their webs of cross-holdings.

These webs have been characterized by western authors variously as: enterprise groupings (Eiteman and Stonehill, 1979, p.632); loosely linked confederations (Christopher, 1983); bank-centred or industrially-linked business groups (Kotler *et al.*, 1985); stable, strategically coordinated alliances (Ferguson, 1990); industrial clusters of related and supporting industries (Porter, 1990); power rings in a strategy group (Ross, 1991); ultimate vertically integrated megacompany, diabolic organisms (Kinsley, 1991) and corporate network. In sum, as Dore (1987) notes, *keiretsu* tend to be 'networks of preferential bilateral trading relationships,[and] networks of relational contracting'. As Helou (1991) puts it, 'a *keiretsu* [individual] firm becomes competitive due to the induction of economic powers from the *keiretsu*'s own milieu and its indigenous interactive tendencies. In turn, this milieu itself is a sphere of economic power...' (p.100).

Two categories of the *keiretsu* in Japan have been identified: (i) a group in which member companies operating in multi-industries, considered equal, have had close relationships with financing institutions whose core is a main bank, and (ii) a group which is independent of a main bank, but where the relationships are hierarchical—a manufacturing giant at the apex and several small suppliers at the bottom, so to speak. The first type is often referred to as *financial keiretsu* and the second, *production keiretsu*. These are purely Western designations. Whether financial or production type, *keiretsu* conduct business transactions among the members and hence exclude non-members, the outsiders. The term 'outsiders' for one *keiretsu* includes other *keiretsu* as well as foreign companies.

Keiretsu are clearly close-knit industrial networks in Japan just as there are industrial groups in Western countries. The salient features of the *keiretsu* suggest that, by design, the group fosters a strong sense of mutual dependence for the benefit of the members whose economic fortunes would otherwise suffer. 'In Japan, relationships between firms are paramount and promote efficiency and innovation... For us, all value is in the product; relationships take a back seat' (Lewis, 1991).

As alluded to earlier, many elements of the relational structure of the Japanese *keiretsu* are also evident in other Asian countries. In South Korea, there are several industrial conglomerates—*chaebols*. One major difference between the *chaebols* and *keiretsu* is in ownership and control. Member firms in the *keiretsu* are said to own minority equity in each other and are led by the lead bank or the lead firm in the network. In the case of *chaebols*, a family and its members own the companies in multi-industries. Furthermore, a circular type of corporate ownership is said to dominate the *chaebol* structure: company A holds significant proportion of shares or equity in company B which holds equity in company C which holds equity in company A.

The Korean entrepreneurial families have been powerful entities since World War II and during the Park regime (1961–1973), it was said that the families fostered close relationships with President Park Chung Hee. The presence of the *chaebols* has been so overwhelming that the government in the 1980s struggled to contain the power of the *chaebol* founding families that control much of South Korea's economy. A capsule profile of the four largest *chaebols* in South Korea (Table 1) shows the scope of these industry groups. Samsung was the earliest and Daewoo the latest to come into existence. All four can be characterized as conglomerates since ownership is held by the family and control resides therein. Some have their origin in the trading activity resembling the *zaibatsu*; however, all are now engaged in many key industries including electronics. Whether or not the *chaebols* can count on their past success depends on a few imponderables.

Business group formation activities in India clearly predate *keiretsu* and *chaebols*. The British East India Company lost its franchise—the China monopoly—in 1833 and the net consequence was its concentration on India, and in introducing the 'managing agency system'— 'a rather unusual type of industrial organization' (Brimmer, 1955). The system has been characterized as 'hybrid business organizations' (Prasad, 1990). At the time, there were ample business opportunities for managing agents, initially British managers and later on Indian executives, especially in large-scale textile manufacturing and light engineering who emerged as managing agents. For nearly 60 years (1850–1910), the managing agency system functioned as the dominant model of industrial organization in India. In his seminal work, Lokanathan (1935) pointed out that the managing agents came to control and manage a large number of similar (industrial) undertakings. Thus, the managing agency system acted as the organizational mechanism that could fill the capital and management needs of the then emerging large-scale industry in India.

Table 1. A brief profile of four *chaebols*

Chaebol by rank	Founded (in/by)	Total no. of major firms	Stake held by founder's family (%)	Industry scope to include
Samsung	1938/Lee Byung-Chull[a]	48	53.2	Electronics, shipbuilding, food-processing
Hyundai	1947/Chung Ju-Yung[b]	42	67.8	Engineering and construction, heavy industries, automotive
Lucky-Goldstar	1967/Koo In-Hwoi[c]	62	38.3	Electronics, chemicals, machinery, etc.
Daewoo	1967/Kim Woo-Choong To Dae Do[d]	24	50.4	Electronics, automotive, steel, etc.

[a] Japan educated Lee started a rice mill in 1936 in Korea (then under Japanese rule) and was also trading in dried fish; by the end of WWII, Samsung entered into real estate and transportation. After the Korean war, Lee re-established Samsung in sugar, textiles, banking and trading. In the 1970s, in concert with the industrialization effort by the government, Samsung entered shipbuilding, petrochemicals, precision engineering and electronics. In 1989, Samsung's major business segments as a percentage of total revenue were: trading (33%), service (25%) and electronics (23%).
[b] Chung set up an engineering and construction firm in 1947 and Hyundai Motor in 1967, initially to assemble Ford cars. In 1983, Hyundai entered electronics to produce semiconductors despite a lack of experience in technology-based industries In 1989, electronics accounted for 32% of Hyundai's revenue.
[c] Koo founded Lucky Chemical to make personal care products such as facial creams, tooth powder etc. He also formed Goldstar in 1958 to make electric appliances. In 1989, electronics accounted for 48% of the group's revenue.
[d] Daewoo combines the two founding partners' names. Debuting as a textile exporter, this group has garnered a variety of competences to make cars for GM, aerospace parts for Boeing, General Dynamics, Daimler–Benz and others.
Source: Compiled from corporate profiles in *Hoover's Handbook of World Business*, 1992. Detailed discussion of these Korean conglomerates can be found in Steers *et al.* (1985).

In the early part of the 20th century, the fledgling entrepreneurial families (such as Birlas, Mafatlals and Tatas[1]) began to emulate the managing agency system model. Even though the managing agency system was outlawed in 1969, the point to be noted here is that the entrepreneurial families such as the Birlas and the Tatas could expand their business activities and stretch their management acumen and competence, by means of complicated contractual managing agency agreements, beyond the scope of their own businesses. Many, if not all, of the outside firms managed by existing companies, were part of the group. In addition, joint ventures were not uncommon. One of the most well-known joint venture companies in India has been Voltas—a joint venture of Tata and Volkart Brothers Company of Switzerland. The case of Voltas, a marketing company within the Tata Group, illustrates how capital allocation to member firms within the Voltas network had been based on relational, rather than cost–benefit, considerations. In short, even though it might seem to outsiders that the financial support extended by Voltas to the affiliated companies—member firms in the Group—

was clearly non-rational, it is not atypical of managerial behaviour group companies, particularly in Asia. Capital losses at times are not considered more important than loss of bonding.

IMPLICATIONS FOR WESTERN COMPANIES

The notion of obligations to member firms stemming from the bonding process in the network historically has been a potent force in the survival of these industrial structures—Japan's *keiretsu*, Korea's *chaebol* and India's groups. The role played by the founding families varies in degree—more prominent in *chaebols* and in several of India's larger group companies, than perhaps in financial *keiretsu*. Some contrasts among the three Asian business structures are identified in Table 2. Of course, for a fuller understanding of the prevailing subtle differences, one would have rely on social-anthropological inquiries.

Table 2. Some contrasts among Asian business structures

	Keiretsu (Japan)	*Chaebol* (South Korea)	Groups (India)
Role of the lead bank	Pivotal	Secondary	Secondary
Dominant type of relationship	Relational contracting	Familial[a]	Contractual managing[b]
Intergroup rivalry	High	Moderate	Moderate
Network functional control	Lead firm (bank, trading or industrial firm)	Founding family	Founding family

[a] Children of founding families are known to intermarry.
[b] A well-established industrial group would, for a fee, take a fledgling enterprise into its management fold.

In general, the dominant type of relationship that prevails among network members is significant for foreign firms as they deliberate entry-level foreign direct investment (FDI) decisions if not in Japan or South Korea, at least in India (and China). That is to say, interfacing with firms in Asia has been tantamount to facing family management style and family dominated management values. It should not be inferred from our analysis that the traditional Asian networks are immune from change. They are not, and we would add that organization culture and values of these structures may not change as much as the form.

In particular, we focus here on three implications to Western companies (US mid-size multinational firms). Growth potential in the West (US as well as Western Europe) in the 1990s is likely to be miniscule; it is clearly high in the Asian region, except perhaps in Japan. Western managers could avoid '*keiretsu*phobia' by seriously considering the following elements as an integral part of their FDI decision matrix.

First, learning more about the relational structures. Even though one needs a contract, the contract should be viewed as a codification of the relationship a Western firm has established. Building up relations gradually implies a certain competence which Cavusgil and Ghauri underscore as 'negotiation skills'.

Second, the presence of *keiretsu*, *chaebol*, group, or other parallel structures should not be viewed as negative elements in a country. In a temporal sense, these relational structures have been, despite some misuse, the backbone of industrialization. It is the current industrial tempo that opens up opportunities for investment in Asia in stark contrast to Eastern Europe.

Third, whether or not a US firm is eyeing a business opportunity in Japan or South Korea, the organizational structural influence flowing from these successful nations is likely to have permeated other regions in Asia. Once one recognizes the Asian logic, it will be less difficult to discern the comparisons and contrasts in individual Asian nations. Managers have ample opportunities to acquire such knowledge and skills in the United States.[2]

SUMMARY AND CONCLUSION

In this essay an attempt was made to provide an organizational characterization of the *keiretsu*—the post-*zaibatsu* reconstituted structures. Seen as networks, they are not unique to Japan. Current concern in the United States is clearly about the production *keiretsu*,[3] as in the auto or memory chip business. These enduring structures are seen by Japan's critics as the invisible impediment—the insurmountable non-tariff barrier. Leaving aside the important geoeconomic question of how the Western nations can proceed in reducing Japan's trade surplus, we explored ways in which management and business scholars could enlarge the network approach in order to fathom the depths of Asian business networks.

The underpinnings of interfirm networks could enrich the theorems that are advanced to augment the geocentric, or global, capabilities particularly of US multinational firms. From a strategic perspective, those firms are in 'Stage II' of their organizational life cycle. An evaluation of entry strategies in the Asian region is likely to find that Japanese foreign direct investment (FDI) has already taken root there. Broadly interpreted, FDI is the flow of a bundle of capital, technology and management. Our discussion suggests a fourth vital element, namely, *keiretsu*—'originating from a state of mind' (Helou, 1991). In the emerging Asian countries such as Indonesia, Malaysia and Thailand, Japanese firms have not only invested large sums of financial capital, but there is growing evidence that they have also fostered *keiretsu*-type networks. In India, as we noted, the group model is still vibrant, except perhaps in the computer engineering industry.

In conclusion, Western firms eager to capitalize on the growing business opportunities in the Asian region may have to rethink their international production and marketing strategies against the backdrop of the *keiretsu*—or the group-type networks.

NOTES

1. Jamsedji Tata was a descendant of the Zoroastrian group that migrated from Persia and settled in Bombay. Jamsedji started a textile trading company in 1868, then entered into manufacturing textiles and later embarked upon a mission to industrialize India. Most of his industrial projects prior to World War II involved infrastructure building efforts: a hydroelectric power plant, a forum for technical and scientific education and a steel mill, to cite a few. In collaboration with a Swiss trading company, it set up a joint venture, Voltas. The managerial behaviour of Voltas is illustrative of the relational structure of group companies in India.

2. There are many opportunities for the novice managers if they wish to learn about Asian nations, Japan in particular. *Working with Japan* (Intercultural Training Resources, Inc., 1991) is a six-part video series that provides practical recommendations for western managers.

3. In response to the *Business Week* (24 September 1990) cover story and editorial comment (p.162) on Mitsubishi, US Representative Helen Delich Bentley (R-Md.) retorted: 'As the world can plainly see now, the web of deception that is Japan runs throughout the business culture—from manufacturing *keiretsu* all the way up to banks, securities firms, politicians, and the omnipotent Ministry of Finance' (*Business Week*, 23 September 1991, p.8).

REFERENCES

Brimmer, A. F .(1955) 'The Setting of Entrepreneurship in India'. *Quarterly Journal of Economics*, **69**: 41–74.
Christopher, R. (1983) *The Japanese Mind*. Simon and Schuster, New York.
Dore, R.(1987) *Taking Japan Seriously*. Stanford University Press.(Particularly Ch. 9, pp.169–192.)
Eiteman, D. K. and Stonehill, A. I. (1979) *Multinational Business Finance*, Addison Wesley, Reading, MA.
Ferguson, C. H. (1990) 'Computers and the Coming of the US *Keiretsu*.'. *Harvard Business Review*, July–August: 55–70.
Ghauri, P. N. (1989) 'Global Marketing Strategies: Swedish Firms in South East Asia'. In Kaynak, K. and Lee, L. H. (eds),*Global Business: Asian Pacific Dimensions*, pp.261–274, Routledge, New York.
Ghauri, P. N. (1990) 'Emergence of New Structures in Swedish Multinationals'. *Advances in International Comparative Management*, **5**: 227–243.
Hagedoorn, J. and Schakenraad, J. (1992) 'Leading Companies and Networks of Strategic Alliances in Information Technologies'. *Research Policy*, **21**: 163–190.
Hallén, L., Johanson, J. and Seyed-Mohamed, N. (1991) 'Interfirm Adaptation in Business Relationships'. *Journal of Marketing*, **55**: 29–37.
Helou, A. (1991) 'The Nature and Competitiveness of Japan's *Keiretsu*'. *Journal of World Trade*, **25**: 94–131.
Jarillo, J. C. (1988) 'On Strategic Networks'. *Strategic Management Journal*, **9**: 31–42.
Johanson, B. (1987) 'Beyond Process and Structure: Social Exchange Networks'. *International Studies of Management and Organization*, **17**: 3–23.
Johanson, J. and Mattsson, L.G. (1988) 'Marketing Investments in Industrial Networks'. *International Journal of Research in Marketing*, **2**: 185–195.
Khambatta, D. and Ajami, R. (1992) *International Business: Theory and Practice*. Macmillan, New York.
Kinsley, M. (1991) '*Keiretsu*phobia', *The New Republic*, 1 July: 4.
Kotler, P., Fahey, L. and Jatusripitak, S. (1985) *The New Competition: What Theory Z Didn't Tell You about Marketing*. Prentice-Hall, Englewood Cliffs, NJ.
Lee, S. M., Yoo, S. and Lee, T. M. (1989) 'Korean *Chaebols*: Corporate Values and Strategies'. *Organization Dynamics*, **xx**: 36–50.
Lewis, J. D. (1991) 'IBM and Apple: Will they Break a Mould'. *The Wall Street Journal*, 27 July: C6.
Lokanathan, P.S. (1935) *Industrial Organization in India*. George Allan and Unwin, London.
Ouchi, W. G. (1981) *Theory Z*. Addison Wesley, New York.
Porter, M. (1990) 'Why Nations Triumph'. *Fortune*, 12 March: 94–108.
Prasad, S. B. (1990) 'Agency Theory: Historical Antecedents of a Hybrid Management System'. *Advances in International Comparative Management*, **5**: 137–148.
Ross, D. N. (1991) '*Keiretsu*: Global Managers Unseen Rival's. *Advances in International Comparative Management*, **6**: 233–255.
Sasaki, N. (1982) *Management and Industrial Structure in Japan*. Pergamon Press, London.
Sekaran, U. and Snodgrass, C. (1990) 'Understanding the Dynamics of Culture in Networking: A Framework and an Initial Test'. *Advances in International Comparative Management*, **5**: 91–115.
Steers, R., Shin, Y. K. and Ungsoh, G. (1985) The *Chaebols*. Harper and Row, New York.
Thorelli, H.B. (1986) 'Networks: Between Markets and Hierarchies'. *Strategic Management Journal*, **7**(1): 37–51.
Wright, R. W. (1989) 'Networking—Japanese Style. *Business Quarterly*, **57**(2): 19–25.

Part IV

Developing Global Managers

CONTENTS

19. Human resource planning in Japanese multinationals: a model for US firms? 295
    ROSALIE TUNG, *Journal of International Business Studies* (1984) **15**(2), 139–149

20. The cross-cultural puzzle of international human resource management 308
    ANDRÉ LAURENT, *Journal of Human Resource Management* (1986) Spring, 91–102

21. Developing leaders for the global enterprise 317
    STEPHEN H. RHINESMITH, JOHN N. WILLIAMSON, DAVID M. EHLEN AND DENISE S. MAXWELL, *Training and Development Journal* (1989) April, 25–34

22. Toward a comprehensive model of international adjustment: an integration of multiple theoretical perspectives 327
    J. STEWART BLACK, MARK MENDENHALL and GARY ODDOU, *Academy of Management Review* (1991) **16**, 291–317

23. Managing globally competent people 350
    NANCY J. ADLER and SUSAN BARTHOLOMEW, *Academy of Management Executive* (1992) **6**(3), 52–65

24. Initial examination of a model of intercultural adjustment 365
    BARBARA PARKER and GLENN M. McEVOY, *International Journal of Intercultural Relations* (1993) **17**, 355–379

19

Human Resource Planning in Japanese Multinationals: A Model for US Firms?

Rosalie Tung

INTRODUCTION

Since the Industrial Revolution, nations have focused on technological innovations and developments to gain superiority in the world economic arena. Although technology is essential to a firm's competitiveness in the international environment, the successful operation of a multinational corporation is contingent upon the availability of other resources besides technology. These include capital, know-how, and manpower. In this paper, the argument is made that human resource or manpower is a key ingredient to the efficient operation of a multinational corporation (MNC). Without a highly developed pool of managerial and technical talent, all the other aforementioned resources could not be effectively and efficiently allocated or transferred from corporate headquarters to the various subsidiaries in the world. Given this premise, it is essential for the MNC to pay greater attention to human resource planning within the organization.

Although US multinationals have emphasized the traditional aspects of human resource planning, such as, the selection of people who possess skills in the various functional disciplines of administration, accounting, finance, marketing, and so on, by and large they have operated on the assumption that an effective manager in the United States will also be a high performer in a foreign country. This is not necessarily true. In a study by Tung (1981), it was found that the failure rates among US expatriates were high; that is, the incidences where expatriates had to be recalled to headquarters or dismissed from the company because of their inability to perform effectively in a foreign country were numerous. More than half of the firms surveyed ($n = 80$) had failure rates of between 10 to 20% and some 7% of the respondents had recall rates of 30%.

This is consistent with the findings of Henry (1965) which showed that approximately 30% of overseas assignments in American multinationals had been mistakes. These failures are costly to the company, time-wise, money-wise, and man resource-wise. Because of the inability of these personnel to operate effectively abroad, the company's foreign operation may stagnate and, worse yet, lose existing market share to its competitors. Given this possibility, multinational corporations should devote more attention to the area of human resource planning to maximize efficient performance overseas. Human resource planning is viewed here as part of the overall planning and control process in a firm.

This paper compares the human resource development programmes between a sample of US and Japanese MNCs. In general, it appeared that the Japanese MNCs sent abroad individuals who were more adept at living and working in a foreign environment (Tung,1982). The contention is made that while the international competitiveness of American MNCs may be weakening because of the narrowing technological gap between the United States and Japan, a more important reason for the difference could be that Japanese MNCs traditionally place heavier emphasis on international markets, and thus devote considerably more attention to selection and training of their people for overseas assignments, which in turn translates into better performance abroad. In the United States, because of the large size of its domestic market, international sales have often been relegated to a secondary position in the company's overall corporate picture. This is often reflected in the attitude that what sells well in Peoria, Illinois, for example, will also have a ready market abroad. This attitude is then carried over into staffing policy—an effective manager in the United States will perform well in a foreign environment, regardless. In a time of increasing global competition, this strategy does not fare well, and there are many tales of misadventures among US MNCs that have pursued such a policy.

In contrast, Japanese MNCs have done an excellent job in this regard. This is all the more remarkable in light of the fact that the Japanese, by culture and history, do not readily mix with *gaijins* (foreigners). Because of the homogeneity of Japanese society and its relative isolation from the outside world (with the exception of China) until the mid-nineteenth century, its people are by nature less adept at living and working in a foreign environment. Through self-discipline and meticulous preparation, however, the Japanese who have been sent abroad to establish foreign subsidiaries have succeeded in making Japan a most formidable force in the global economic arena. Although much of this success could be attributed to the quality and competitiveness of Japan's products, the ingenuity of its workforce also played a very major role in ensuring that its products are effectively marketed in foreign countries.

This paper will examine in some detail the human resource planning programmes adopted by Japanese multinationals to prepare expatriates for overseas assignments.

HUMAN RESOURCE DEVELOPMENT PROGRAMMES: US VERSUS JAPANESE

In Tung (1982), the staffing policies and human resource planning programmes for a sample of US ($n = 80$) and Japanese ($n = 35$) MNCs were compared. The most salient findings of the study are summarized below.

Sources of manpower

The Japanese MNCs surveyed used parent country nationals more extensively in their top and middle management positions in all their foreign operations. This finding could be attributed to one of several reasons. First, the stage of evolution of Japanese multinationals may be significant. Second, the Japanese system of management requires constant consultation and communication between the parent headquarters and the overseas subsidiary. Hence, it may be difficult for foreigners to operate within the system. Third, because many of the senior executives in Japanese corporations do not speak English, and conversely most foreigners do not speak Japanese, there is a language barrier. Besides language, there are conceptual barriers; the control mechanisms in Japanese organizations are usually implicit, rather than explicit (Pascale and Athos, 1981). Hence, it may be difficult for foreigners to have an implicit understanding of the company's philosophy, which is central to smooth operations in industrial organizations. Fourth, until recently, Japanese MNCs had problems in recruiting competent local nationals to work for their overseas subsidiaries. Fifth, because of the systems of lifetime employment and seniority, there is perhaps a psychological reluctance among the Japanese to hire foreigners (Tung, 1984b). The Japanese are beginning to see the advantages associated with the use of host country nationals, and many of the manufacturing companies have embarked on a policy of localization.

In contrast, the subsidiaries of US MNCs in industrialized regions of the world were generally staffed by host country nationals at all levels of management, while subsidiaries in less developed countries were usually staffed by parent country nationals or third country nationals (nationals who are neither citizens of the United States nor the country of foreign operation). This difference in staffing policy among US MNCs is logical, as one would expect the more developed nations to have a larger pool of personnel that would possess the necessary manpower and technical skills to staff management-level positions.

Most of the US MNCs surveyed appeared to realize the advantages associated with hiring host country nationals, such as, familiarity with local culture, good public relations, knowledge of the language, and reduced costs. Although this policy of employment of local nationals is commendable and should be continued, there are two reasons why American MNCs cannot rely solely upon this source for staffing of overseas operations. First, although local nationals can effectively manage their fellow countrymen and relate well to domestic clients, they may have problems in communicating with corporate headquarters. These may stem from their inability to comprehend the overall goals and objectives of corporate headquarters, rather than lack of command of the English language. Hence, many American MNCs recognize the need to send over a number of expatriates who can serve as liaison persons between the foreign subsidiary and corporate headquarters in the United States. This will facilitate the communication and control processes in the firm.

Second, with the increasing cooperation among nations in the fields of commerce, there will be a greater need for individuals who can interact effectively with foreign clients and nationals. Consequently, American MNCs cannot simply dismiss the issue, but should try to improve their present selection criteria and training programmes for expatriate assignments.

Failure rates and reasons for failure

As noted earlier, the statistics for American MNCs were fairly dismal. Seven percent of the MNCs surveyed had failure rates of between 20 to 40%; 69% had failure rates of between 10 and 20%; and the remaining 24% had failure rates of below 10%. This contrasted with the very low failure rates among the sample of Japanese MNCs studied. Seventy-six percent of the firms had failure rates of below 5%; 10% had failure rates of between 6 to 10%; and 14% had failure rates of 11 to 19%. The reasons for the lower failure rates among Japanese MNCs were the focus of a subsequent study, which findings will be presented in a later section.

With regard to reasons for failure for the US sample, lack of relational skills (that is, the inability of the individual to deal effectively with clients, business associates, superiors, peers, and subordinates) and the family situation factors emerged as the two primary reasons for failure in overseas assignments. These reasons were different from those given by Japanese MNCs. In the Japanese sample, the principal reasons for failure were inability to cope with the larger responsibilities associated with an overseas assignment and the manager's inability to adapt to a different physical or cultural environment. Most Japanese MNCs did not perceive the family situation factor as having a major impact on the incidences of failure abroad.

Selection criteria

Despite the recognition among American personnel administrators that the family situation factor and lack of relational skills are often responsible for the expatriate's inability to function effectively in a foreign environment, they did not place sufficient emphasis on these criteria, but instead based their selection decision primarily on the criterion of technical competence.

Although the Japanese MNCs did not specifically administer any test to determine the candidate's relational abilities, these were clearly taken into consideration in the overall assessment of the person's suitability for an overseas position. Furthermore, the Japanese MNCs recognize the importance of such skills for success abroad, as evidenced by the fact that 57% of the firms surveyed had specialized training programmes to prepare candidates for overseas work.

Training programmes

In the US sample, only 32% of the respondents indicated that their company had formalized training programmes to prepare candidates for overseas work. For those firms that sponsored training programmes, most used environmental briefings that are designed to provide the trainee with factual information about a particular country's sociopolitical history, geography, stage of economic development, and cultural institutions. When used alone, such environmental briefings are inadequate for preparing trainees for assignments that require extensive contact with the local community overseas (Textor, 1966; Harrison and Hopkins, 1967; Lynton and Pareek, 1967).

In contrast, a full 57% of the Japanese MNCs studied had training programmes to prepare candidates for overseas work. Besides environmental briefings, most of the Japanese firms emphasized language training. In the case of US MNCs, because English is the universal language of international business transactions, there is not much of a problem if the expatriate does not speak the local language. In contrast, most Japanese MNCs mentioned language skills as one of the most important criterion in selection. In the words of one Japanese executive, 'If the expatriate does not speak English, how can he adapt?' (Tung, 1984b). If the expatriate cannot converse with people in the host country, it is impossible for the individual to adjust to the foreign country, much less perform his job in the new environment.

Relationship between selection, training, and incidences of success

For the US sample, it was found that the use of appropriate criteria for selecting candidates as identified in the contingency framework for human resource planning in Tung (1981) significantly reduced the incidences of expatriates' inability to function effectively in a foreign environment ($p \leq 0.01$). The contingency framework essentially states that for positions involving longer durations of stay in a foreign country and requiring more extensive and intensive contacts with members of a local community, such as, CEO and functional head, the selection criteria should emphasize relational skills and the family situation factors. No significant relationship was found between the selection criteria and incidences of failure in the Japanese sample. This latter finding could be attributed to the different system of human resource planning used in Japanese MNCs, which will be discussed later.

For both the US and Japanese samples, it was found that the use of rigorous training programmes could significantly improve the expatriate's performance in an overseas environment, thus minimizing the incidences of failure. Given this finding, it appears all the more important for US multinationals to provide more comprehensive training for their expatriates.

In an attempt to gain a better understanding of the reasons for the lower failure rates of Japanese MNCs, in-depth interviews were conducted with a sample of 18 Japanese MNCs engaged in different industries, including financial institutions, general trading companies, and manufacturers of industrial and consumer products, such as, automobiles, electronics, textiles, and so on. Each interview averaged $2\frac{1}{2}$ hours and was conducted in English. All the persons interviewed for the study were either fluent in English or were assisted by individuals who had good command of English, hence, language did not pose a problem. The interviews were conducted by the researcher with the chief of international operations or personnel division in each company. For the 18 Japanese multinationals, the failure rate nowhere exceeded 5%. In addition, an interview was conducted with the Director of the Institute for International Studies and Training which provides three month and one-year training programmes to expatriates of Japanese MNCs to prepare them for overseas assignments. These in-depth studies provide a better understanding of the human resource planning programme in Japanese MNCs.

REASONS FOR LOWER FAILURE RATES AMONG JAPANESE MNCs

The reasons for the lower failure rates of Japanese MNCs appear to be severalfold, each of which will be examined below.

Overall qualification of candidates

In Japan, there is a heavy emphasis on education. In the report of the US National Commission on Excellence in Education published in early 1983, it was found that the average high school graduate in Japan received an equivalent of four more years of education than his/her American counterpart. The entrance examinations to the elite universities in Japan are tough, and admission is based entirely on the results of scholastic aptitude tests. Because one's status in society is determined to a large extent by the company to which one belongs, college graduates exercise extreme caution in selecting the company that they will work for. In the words of one senior Japanese executive, 'To choose a job is almost as important as selecting a woman for his wife. In fact it is more important'. In the event of an inappropriate spouse, the individual can always choose divorce. In the case of one's job, however, it is difficult to quit and seek some position elsewhere unless 'one sacrifices himself, both financially and status-wise'.

Similarly, the well-established companies meticulously choose their prospective employees from among the large pool of new college graduates every year. The hiring decision is based primarily on performance in the aptitude tests administered by the respective companies. Nippon Steel Corporation (the largest steel manufacturer in the world) chooses only the top 80 candidates from 1 000 applicants. These are the career staff who will be protected under the system of lifetime employment. Consequently, only the elite are selected. The same procedure holds true for the other well-established Japanese companies. Once inducted into the company, these candidates are given a very extensive training programme which spans several years. Hence, in the words of another senior Japanese executive, 'Practically anybody that is admitted into the company is qualified for an overseas assignment'. This may be an overstatement because technical competence alone does not necessarily guarantee high performance abroad. When technical competence is combined with the other factors, however, it could become a very powerful force, and would, in turn, account for their high performance overseas.

Commitment to one's company

A second reason for the lower failure rate among Japanese MNCs could be the basic difference between personnel systems in the United States and Japan. Given the traditional Japanese loyalty to one's company and the low mobility of employees, the expatriate 'has to endure' and do his best even if he does not like the overseas situation. Poor performance abroad would constitute a loss of face, and given the importance of face-saving in the Japanese context, the expatriate will do his utmost to uphold his track record in a foreign country. Furthermore, under the system of lifetime employment a Japanese expatriate feels that he must not disrupt the foreign operation because it will not be good for his future career in the company.

Longer duration of overseas assignments

A third reason for the lower failure rate among Japanese multinationals is the differences in time perspective adopted by US and Japanese MNCs in the areas of overall planning and control. Given the longer-term orientation of Japanese firms with regard to human resource planning, the average duration of an overseas assignment is generally more extended. Although the exact duration of an overseas stay varies according to position and country of assignment, the average span is five years. This is consistent with the findings of a survey conducted by the *Japan Economic News* (24 June 1982) on 612 expatriates, which showed that the average duration of an overseas assignment was 4.67 years. This contrasts with the much shorter duration of overseas assignments for most American multinationals, where it is common to rotate individuals once every two to three years.

This variation stems from the overall difference in time perspective between American and Japanese MNCs. The former are generally more short-term oriented and tend to focus on immediate profitability and return on investments this year. Japanese firms, on the other hand, tend to be longer-term oriented, and are more concerned about market share and growth. This difference in time perspective has often been a source of friction in joint cooperative agreements between US and Japanese firms (Tung, 1984a). Americans are unique in this regard; their European counterparts, like the Japanese, tend to possess longer-term perspectives in decision making and planning. In general, the performance of European managers is judged not so much by short-term fluctuations in their company's earnings, but by the long-term profitability. Hence, they can concentrate more on courses of action that are beneficial to the long-term interests of the company (Ball, 1980). It should be emphasized that long-term and short-term goals may often be in conflict—for example, reducing expenditure in R&D will result in increased short-term profits, but may be detrimental to the long-term goals of the company. Because of the control procedures used in most US firms, many managers tend to focus on the short-run objectives at the expense of long-term goals.

The longer duration of overseas assignments means that the Japanese expatriate has more time to adjust to the foreign country. Most of the 18 Japanese MNCs indicated that they did not expect the expatriate to perform up to full capacity until the third year of assignment. In the first year, they allow the individual to adjust to the foreign culture. In the second year, the expatriate 'tries to be active', but corporate headquarters make allowances because this is still viewed as part of the basic period of adjustment. In the third year, the expatriate begins to function up to his usual capacity. Some Japanese executives feel that the duration of certain overseas assignments should be extended to 10 years, because the company could then have a full seven years to enjoy the fruits of their labour in the initial two to three years. Of course, this proposal would not apply to the Middle East and some of the developing countries where the living conditions are harsh, from the Japanese perspective.

In contrast, the frequent rotation of personnel in the overseas operations of American MNCs often does not give the expatriate sufficient time to get acquainted with a foreign environment. For example, it was reported that when an American food manufacturer sent its marketing manager to Japan for 18 months, the individual spent the first six months in adjusting to Japan and the last six months planning for his reentry back to the United States. Consequently, there were only six months in which the individual was really contributing to the organization in Japan. Because of his preoccupation with the problems of entry to and exit from Japan, the company lost approximately 98% of its market share to a major European competitor over the 18-month period.

Support system in corporate headquarters

Besides the shorter time perspective of American MNCs, another possible reason for the generally briefer duration of overseas assignments could be the fact that the expatriates themselves are anxious to return to corporate headquarters as soon as possible for fear that they may be forgotten in a foreign country, and hence passed up for promotion in the corporate organizational hierarchy. These fears are justified to a large extent because of the revolving door policy at the top management level in American corporations—an expatriate who has been away for an extended number of years may find himself a 'stranger' to the members of the board. Although there are some Japanese expatriates who voice a similar concern, it is mentioned only infrequently. In general, most Japanese multinationals provide a comprehensive support system or network for the expatriate to set his mind at ease once he is overseas.

This support mechanism covers a fairly broad spectrum of activities. First, many of the larger MNCs have a division whose sole purpose is to look after the needs of expatriates. For example, Nissan Motors has an Overseas Section within the company's human resource division. Similarly, two divisions in the Bank of Yokohama—the International Department and the Personnel Department—provide both 'mental and financial support' to their expatriates. Second, the superior–subordinate relationship or mentor system in Japanese organizations implies certain obligations and responsibilities. In the words of a Japanese expatriate, 'My boss will continue to be my boss for a long time. I know he will take care me'. Third, due to the Japanese organization's greater concern for the total person, when expatriates go overseas alone because of the problem of their children's education, the company will try to find excuses for the expatriates to make frequent business trips to Japan. Fourth, at any point in time there is usually a fairly large contingent of Japanese expatriates that have already settled in a given country. Because of the strong group orientation among the Japanese, these 'early settlers' will provide assistance to the new arrivals.

Evaluation of performance

Given the longer-term orientation of most Japanese firms, the control mechanisms used are often different from that of US MNCs. This is reflected primarily in terms of criteria used for evaluation of an individual's performance. In Japanese organizations, the evaluation is generally based on a person's capabilities in the long run; Japanese managers are usually more understanding of circumstances that may temporarily affect an employee's level of performance. For example, in the first one to two years of an expatriate's assignment overseas, even though the individual is not performing up to his usual capacity, most managers make allowances for such behaviour. In the words of a Vice President of Marubeni Trading Company who has lived in the United States for the past 25 years as a Japanese expatriate, 'I would say that even though the individual's performance may not be what the company wants, if he is doing his best, which is 100%, we would like to think that way, not that he is just doing 75%'.

Selection for overseas assignments

Although the Japanese multinational may not administer specific tests to determine the candidate's relational abilities prior to an overseas assignment (such tests are unavailable in the Japanese context), it does carefully review every aspect of the employee's qualifications before making a final decision. This is possible because of the differences between US and Japanese personnel systems. First, it is general practice that recommendations for an overseas assignment are made by the division chief in consultation with the overseas subsidiary and the personnel department in corporate headquarters. In Japan, the latter wields considerable power over various aspects of the company's operations, is highly centralized, and reports directly to the office of the president. Because of the strong group orientation and the after-hours socializing among the male career staff 5 days a week, the immediate supervisor in a Japanese company is thoroughly familiar with an individual's family background, general preferences, qualifications, and so on. In the words of a senior Japanese executive, 'Each person knows the other very well. We know what the other person's mother looks like, etc., etc. The boss knows your family situation'. This is very different from the US context, where most employees would like to separate their professional lives from their personal affairs. Given such knowledge, the Japanese supervisor would generally not make unreasonable recommendations.

Second, most Japanese companies keep very detailed personnel profiles or inventories on all their career staff. These are compiled from the annual or semiannual performance evaluations that are completed by the individual, his immediate supervisor, and the chief of his division. Every year, the employee is asked to write a self-description of himself, detailing his aspirations and career plans. Furthermore, the personnel department of some companies conducts 45- to 60-minute interviews with each career staff as part of the annual evaluation programme.

Because corporate headquarters oversees all assignments for overseas positions, it is able to control for the overall quality of expatriates sent abroad.

Third, most of the candidates considered for an overseas assignment (excluding those who have been selected to study abroad) have generally been with the company for 10 years, during which time they have been carefully indoctrinated with the company's philosophy and overall objectives, thus facilitating the implementation of corporate strategy. The 10-year period also provides the company ample opportunity to assess each individual's capabilities and qualifications. Consequently, although Japanese MNCs may not administer specific tests prior to the actual selection of an individual for an overseas assignment, they generally have sufficient information to assess the candidate's suitability for a position abroad.

Training for overseas assignments

Because of the system of lifetime employment and longer-term perspective, most Japanese firms feel safe to invest in their employees' future by spending huge sums of money to carefully groom and train them for an overseas assignment. In Tung (1982), it was reported that a full 57% of the Japanese MNCs surveyed sponsored some formal training programme to prepare their expatriates for overseas assignments. This is consistent with the finding of the *Japan Economic News* survey (24 June 1982), which showed that 70% of the 267 largest companies in Japan offered some preparatory courses for their expatriates. The detailed description of the human resource development programmes of all 18 MNCs will not be reported here (see Tung, 1984b); instead, the highlights of the training programmes offered by most of the MNCs are outlined below.

Language training

Because most Japanese MNCs consider language a very important criterion for overseas assignment, practically all the companies sponsored intensive language training programmes, ranging from three months to one year, for their expatriates. To promote fluency in a foreign language, many Japanese companies invite Caucasians to live in the same dormitories as the trainees so that the latter will have ample opportunity to practice their language skills and to gain a better understanding of the foreign country.

General training for career staff

A career staff in a Japanese company typically does not receive his first major promotion until 10 years after he joins the company. The initial 10 years could be viewed as one extensive training period wherein the individual is trained in the various aspects of the company's business.

Field experience

Many of the Japanese MNCs surveyed send select members of their career staff as trainees for one year to their overseas subsidiaries. As trainees, their primary mission is to observe closely and hence learn about the foreign operations of the company's business. This kind of training prepares them for eventual overseas assignments, which are viewed as part of their career development. This is part and parcel of the longer-term planning perspective adopted by most Japanese firms.

Graduate programmes abroad

Many of the Japanese MNCs surveyed send between 10 to 20 career staff every year to attend graduate business, law, or engineering programmes overseas. The company pays for the tuition and all expenses in addition the employee's regular salary. Many companies indicated that these graduate programmes may sometimes take as long as four years. In the first year, the trainee is immersed in intensive English-language training in the foreign country, followed by two years of the MBA programme and a year of field experience. In the graduate programmes, the prospective expatriate is exposed to foreign principles of management that will come in handy when he is eventually assigned overseas.

In-house training programmes

Besides language training, the expatriates take courses in international finance and international economics and are given environmental briefings about the country of assignment.

Outside agencies

Besides in-house training programmes, there are a number of institutes that prepare expatriates for overseas assignments. One such agency is the Institute for International Studies and Training which was established under the auspices of the Ministry of International Trade and Industry, and is a joint venture among business, government, and academic circles. The institute offers a three-month and a one-year programme. The shorter programme is designed for specialists and covers courses in English and international business transactions. The one-year programme is designed to 'foster generalists and internationally-minded businessmen. Trainees enrolled in this programme have to master English plus one other foreign language and receive intensive training in area studies. Under both programmes, the trainees live in dormitories located at the foot of Mount Fuji. According to the Director of the Institute, classes run from 9:00 a.m. to 4:00 p.m. In the evenings, the trainees have to attend extracurricular activities, such as presentations by ambassadors and business people from foreign countries. Because the trainees have to do their homework to prepare for the following day's class meetings, most of them study until 2:00 a.m. Besides the use of visiting professors from foreign countries, there is an exchange programme so that students from other nations can live under the same roof as the Japanese trainees. Again, the purpose here is to provide ample opportunities for the trainees to practice their language skills and learn more about a foreign country. There is an optional overseas training programme held in the United States after the completion of the one-year programme.

The tuition for the one-year programme is 1.5 million yen (or approximately $6 500 US at the exchange rate of 230 yen to the dollar). When textbooks, room and board, heating surcharge in winter months, and the overseas training programme are added to the tuition fee, these amount to a staggering $26 956 per trainee. This is paid by the company. In addition, the employee receives his regular salary. Besides the Institute for International Studies and Training, there are a number of other agencies in the country that provide similar services.

Role of the family

In the case of US MNCs, a principal reason for failure is the family situation factor. In Japan, wives are generally more 'obedient and dependent'. In the words of an American who is a student of Japanese history, 'Japanese women think of their roles as wife and mother as jobs. So she is a failure if she cannot stand it. An American wife, on the other hand, thinks she has an independent life'. Again, given the emphasis on face-saving, a Japanese woman would not want to 'fail' in her role as a wife by constantly complaining about the problems encountered in living in a foreign country.

From the foregoing, it appears that a multitude of factors account for the lower failure rates among Japanese MNCs, which in turn contribute to the increasing competitiveness of Japanese firms in the international context.

IMPLICATIONS FOR US MULTINATIONALS

Based on the comparative analysis of the human resource planning programmes between US and Japanese MNCs and the cursory review of the reasons for the lower failure rates among Japanese MNCs, the following implications for American firms can be drawn.

Training

In the US sample (Tung, 1982), it was found that the more rigorous the selection and training procedures used, the less the incidences of poor performance in a foreign country. Given the recognition that lack of relational skills is often responsible for failure overseas, US MNCs should emphasize this criterion in their selection decision for certain categories of overseas job assignments and certain countries, in accordance with the contingency paradigm proposed by Tung (1981). Furthermore, US MNCs should sponsor training programmes to prepare expatriates for their overseas assignments. While US MNCs may contend that their Japanese counterparts can afford to invest in their people because of the system of lifetime employment, an argument could be made that the high failure rates among American MNCs are also very costly. The cost of sending an average American family overseas is estimated at around $150 000 to $250 000 per annum. This includes base pay, cost-of-living differentials, and other adjustments. When these six-figure salary/fringe benefits are combined with lost market opportunities, they could be equally as staggering, if not more so, than the costs borne by the Japanese MNCs to train their expatriates.

Longer-term orientation

US firms should develop a longer-term perspective with regard to overall planning and control. In the area of expatriate assignments, this would translate into longer durations of stay overseas. Short stints abroad are not conducive to high performance because the expatriate barely has time to adjust before he is transferred to another location. Although there is a genuine concern among American expatriates that prolonged absence from corporate headquarters may negatively affect their chances of promotion in the corporate organizational hierarchy, the implementation of some supportive mechanisms (akin to that in Japanese companies) may alleviate these fears. This requires a fundamental reorientation in overall planning and control procedures.

A longer-term orientation among American companies may also engender a greater commitment and loyalty among their employees, and hence an increased willingness to face temporary inconvenience for the company's overall goals. This has a positive impact on other aspects of the company's operation.

Provision for spouses and children

Although it may be difficult to change the attitudes of spouses and children, an American MNC could try to cope with the situation by including the spouse in the selection procedure and by providing training programmes for the spouse and children. In Tung (1982), it was found that those US MNCs that interviewed both candidate and spouse to determine suitability for an overseas position experienced significantly lower incidences of failure among their expatriates. The family situation may, of course, be compounded by several factors. First, the wife may feign preference for a foreign country because she feels that it has a positive impact upon her husband's future career. This problem may be partially overcome through rigorous training programmes.

Second, the provision of training programmes for the spouse and children are costly. Here again, however, the argument could be made that the costs of failure to the company are also very high. Furthermore, the training programme provided for the family need not be as rigorous as the one given the expatriate. This will help reduce costs. Third, with the increase in the number of dual career families, American wives are becoming less mobile. This latter problem is not unique to overseas assignments alone but to relocations within the United States as well. Consequently, the companies should develop procedures to deal with this problem, which is beyond the scope of this paper.

In conclusion, if American MNCs could emulate the positive aspects of the human resource development programmes of their Japanese counterparts, the incidences of ineffective or poor performance overseas could be reduced, thus helping to maintain US competitiveness in the international arena. When the technological gap between the United States and Japan is narrowing, American MNCs cannot rely solely on technology to gain the competitive edge in international markets. Rather, the focus should be shifted to the area of human resource planning, because companies and technology are, after all, managed and operated by humans. In the final analysis, the international competitiveness of American MNCs has to depend on the ingenuity of its people, especially the people they send overseas as representatives or embodiment of corporate headquarters.

REFERENCES

Ball, R (1980) 'Europe Outgrows Management American Style'. *Fortune*, 20 October :147–148.
Harrison, R. and Hopkins, R. L. (1967) 'The Design of Cross-Cultural Training'. *Journal of Applied Behavioural Science*, **3**(4): 431–460.
Henry, E. R. (1965) 'What Business Can Learn from Peace Corps Selection and Training'. *Personnel*, July–August: 17–32.
Lynton, R. P. and Pareek, U. (1967) *Training for Development*. Dorsey Press, Illinois.
Pascale, R. and Athos, A. (1981) *The Art of Japanese Management: Applications for American Executives*. Simon and Schuster, New York.
Textor, R. B. (ed.) (1966) *Cultural Frontiers of the Peace Corps*. MIT Press, Cambridge, MA.
Tung, R. L. (1981) 'Selection and Training of Personnel for Overseas Assignments'. *Columbia Journal of World Business*, Spring: 68–78.
Tung, R. L. (1982) 'Selection and Training Procedures of US, European, and Japanese Multinationals'. *California Management Review*, Fall: 57–71.
Tung, R. L. (1984a) *Business Negotiations with the Japanese*. Lexington Books, D. C. Heath, Lexington, MA.
Tung, R. L. (1984b) *Key to Japan's Economic Strength: Human Power*. Lexington Books, D. C. Heath, Lexington, MA.

20

The Cross-Cultural Puzzle of International Human Resource Management

André Laurent

INTERNATIONAL HUMAN RESOURCE MANAGEMENT: A FIELD IN INFANCY

As noted by Tichy (1983), the human resource field appears to be in a process of gradual and uneven transformation, where different companies may be experiencing different phases of transition: 'endings', 'inbetween', 'new beginning'. Against this background, what can be said as to the status of the emerging field of International Human Resource Management which is the topic of this symposium.[1] Is there such a field?

Interestingly, the international dimension of HRM was apparently not retained among the important themes resulting from the previous HRM Symposium held at the University of Michigan two years ago. While the 'importance of cultural phenomena' was selected (Tichy, 1983), this theme was framed more in terms of corporate cultures than in terms of national cultures and international implications.

The organizers of the Fontainebleau symposium must be credited for creative leadership in launching a symbolic event that calls the attention of both executives and researchers on an emerging reality that is neither systematically managed nor extensively researched.

Recent labels like 'Human Resource Management' or newer ones like 'International Human Resource Management' obviously do not emerge by accident. Even though they often precede our understanding of what they mean, they are social productions that reflect some shared awareness of something important that has not been given enough attention in the past. When the new label is coined, it has the power of inviting people to wonder what it means and to inquire into the underlying reality which the label may be attempting to describe. In the field of organization studies, the concept of organizational culture seems to share a very similar history.

From a more practical point of view, there are some indications suggesting that we are not all caught into some collective illusion. Many organizations are indeed confronted with the issues of managing human resources internationally. 'Human Resource Managers' in such organizations are entitled to expect 'Professors of HRM' to provide some useful insight on such processes. Yet these new international processes are so complex and so poorly defined and

[1] International Human Resource Management Symposium, Fontainebleau, 20–23 August 1985.

Reprinted with permission from *Human Resource Management*, Spring 1986, Vol. 25, No. 1, pp. 91–102.
Copyright © 1986 by John Wiley & Sons, Inc.

ill-understood at the moment that superficiality remains the mark of most current treatments, including the one attempted during this symposium. As an illustration of this primitive state of affairs, would it be unfair to suggest that in many cases during this symposium, participants have made a point of finishing their sentences with the four magic and official words: 'within an international context'. It remains to be assessed whether the former part of the sentences would have differed in the absence of that ending. If the field of HRM is in a stage of adolescence, International HRM is still at the infancy stage. The intent of this paper is to contribute to the framing of this new domain in building upon the author's inquiry into the cultural diversity of management conceptions across nations.

HRM PRACTICES AS INSTITUTIONALIZED PREFERENCES FOR THE MANAGEMENT OF PEOPLE

Managers in organizations hold particular sets of assumptions, ideas, beliefs, preferences, and values on how to manage people toward the attainment of some organizational goals. Over time these various ideas get translated into particular policies, systems, and practices which in turn may reinforce or alter the original ideas. Furthermore, organizational members have sets of expectations related to those practices which may again reinforce or alter the existing policies. Through this complex process of mutual interaction between various actors' ideas and actions, certain preferred ways of managing people tend to emerge in some organized fashion which we may then call Human Resource Management.

As different organizations have developed different ways of managing their human resources that seem to have been more or less successful, this observation has reinforced the intuition that more strategic thinking was required in this area and that some competitive advantage could be acquired through some form of excellence. Future historians of work organizations may well have a hard time understanding why it took so long to realize the strategic importance of the management of human resources.

If HRM policies and practices reflect managers' assumptions about how to manage people, it becomes very critical to understand such assumptions in order to correctly interpret the meaning of particular policies and practices.

NATIONAL DIFFERENCES IN MANAGEMENT ASSUMPTIONS: A RESEARCH INQUIRY

In the past few years, we have been interested in systematically exploring management assumptions in an attempt to enrich our understanding of management and organizational processes. The initial research objective was not to explore national differences but to bring into focus some of the implicit management and organizational theories that managers carry in their heads (Laurent, 1981).

As it is very difficult to inquire into beliefs that individuals take for granted, our research strategy has consisted in writing up a large number of possible assumptions about the management of organizations which we inferred from discussing organizational issues with managers. These assumptions were expressed in the form of statements within a standard questionnaire that would seek from respondents their degree of agreement/disagreement with such statements.

Typical survey statements read as follows:

- The main reason for having a hierarchical structure is so that everyone knows who has authority over whom.
- Most managers seem to be more motivated by obtaining power than by achieving objectives.
- It is important for a manager to have at hand precise answers to most of the questions that his subordinates may raise about their work.
- In order to have efficient work relationships, it is often necessary to bypass the hierarchical line.
- Most managers would achieve better results if their roles were less precisely defined.
- An organizational structure in which certain subordinates have two direct bosses should be avoided at all costs.

Successive groups of managers participating in executive development programmes at INSEAD (The European Institute of Business Administration) were surveyed. These managers came from many different companies and many different countries.

When their responses were analysed, it appeared that the most powerful determinant of their assumptions was by far their nationality. Overall and across 56 different items of inquiry, it was found that nationality had three times more influence on the shaping of managerial assumptions than any of the respondents' other characteristics such as age, education, function, type of company... etc.

One of the most illustrative examples of national differences in management assumptions was reflected in the respondents' reaction to the following statement:

'It is important for a manager to have at hand precise answers to most of the questions that his subordinates may raise about their work'.

As indicated in Figure 1, while only a minority of Northern American and Northern European managers agreed with this statement, a majority of Southern Europeans and South-East Asians did. The research results indicated that managers from different national cultures vary widely as to their basic conception of what management is all about (Laurent, 1983).

Conceptions of organizations were shown to vary as widely across national cultures as conceptions of their management did. Across a sample of 10 Western national cultures, managers from Latin cultures (French and Italians) consistently perceived organizations as social systems of relationships monitored by power, authority, and hierarchy to a much greater extent than their Northern counterparts did.

American managers held an 'instrumental' view of the organization as a set of tasks to be achieved through a problem-solving hierarchy where positions are defined in terms of tasks and functions and where authority is functionally based. French managers held a 'social' view of the organization as a collective of people to be managed through a formal hierarchy, where positions are defined in terms of levels of authority and status and where authority is more attached to individuals than it is to their offices or functions (Inzerilli and Laurent, 1983). Once these results were obtained, the question arose as to whether the corporate culture of multinational organizations would reduce some of the observed national differences and therefore bring some more homogeneity in the picture.

A new research study was designed to test this hypothesis. Carefully matched national groups of managers working in the affiliated companies of a large US multinational firm were surveyed with the same standard questionnaire. The overall results gave no indication of convergence between national groups. Their cultural differences in management assumptions were not reduced as a result of working for the same multinational firm. If anything, there was slightly more divergence between the national groups within this multinational company than originally found in the INSEAD multicompany study. These findings were later replicated with smaller matched national samples of managers in several American and European multinational corporations.

The overall research findings led to the conclusion that deep-seated managerial assumptions are strongly shaped by national cultures and appear quite insensitive to the more transient culture of organizations.

Further exploration was conducted with different methods of inquiry in order to better assess the validity of the findings. In one research study, a large US-based multinational corporation was approached because of its high professional reputation in human resource management. This corporation has implemented for years a standardized worldwide system for the multiple assessment of managerial potential and performance. Open-ended interviews were conducted across a number of affiliated companies in an attempt to identify what managers perceived as being important to be successful in their career. This led to a list of 60 criteria mentioned by managers as being most important for career success. Matched national groups of managers were later asked, in a systematic survey, to select among these 60 criteria those they saw as most important for career success within the firm.

For the American managers, the single most important criterion in order to have a successful career with the company was 'Ambition and Drive'—a pragmatic, individualistic, achievement-oriented, and 'instrumental' reading of the assessment system. The French managers saw things quite differently. For them the single most important criterion was 'Being labelled as having high potential' a more 'social' and political reading of the same system. The degree of consensus on what it takes to be successful was significantly higher within the American

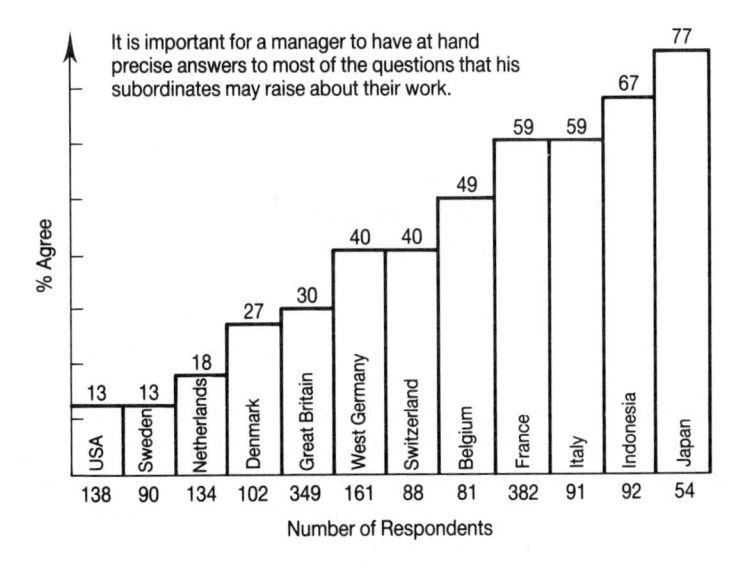

Figure 1.

Affiliate—culturally closer to the designers of the HRM system—than it was in the British, Dutch, German, and French Affiliates.

In spite of the convergence effects that could be expected from a similar and global administrative system of assessment and reward, managed by the US Headquarters on a worldwide basis, a remarkable degree of cultural diversity was observed again across countries in managers' perceptions of the determinants of career success. In a later part of the study, the same national groups of managers were asked to list what they thought were the features of a well-functioning organization, the attributes of effective managers, and the most important things that effective managers should be doing.

The analysis of some of the results can be summarized as follows:

- German managers, more than others, believed that creativity is essential for career success. In their minds, the successful manager is the one who has the right individual characteristics. Their outlook is rational: they view the organization as a coordinated network of individuals who make appropriate decisions based on their professional competence and knowledge.
- British managers hold a more interpersonal and subjective view of the organizational world. According to them, the ability to create the right image and to get noticed for what they do is essential for career success. They view the organization primarily as a network of relationships between individuals who get things done by influencing each other through communicating and negotiating.
- French managers look at the organization as an authority network where the power to organize and control the actors stems from their positioning in the hierarchy. They focus on the organization as a pyramid of differentiated levels of power to be acquired or dealt with. French managers perceive the ability to manage power relationships effectively and to 'work the system' as particularly critical to their success.

From the perspective of these various results, international human resource management may only be international in the eyes of the designers.

DISCUSSION

Naive parochialism has plagued the field of Management and Organization Studies for a long time. The societal and cultural context of theories and practices has long been ignored or overlooked by both researchers and practitioners (Hofstede, 1980). Management approaches developed in one particular culture have been deemed valid for any other culture. Models of excellence (Peters and Waterman, 1982) are still being presented with virtues of universality.

A comparative analysis across national cultures brings the startling evidence that there is no such thing as Management with a capital M. The art of managing and organizing has no homeland.

Every culture has developed through its own history some specific and unique insight into the managing of organizations and of their human resources. At the same time, any single cultural model may become pathological when pushed to its extreme, an illustration of the fact that every culture has also developed specific and unique blindspots in the art of managing and organizing. There lie the still largely undiscovered opportunities and threats of international management.

The emerging field of Human Resource Management is not compelled to fall into the trap of universalism. It has the opportunity and the challenge to integrate cultural relativity in its premises. In fact, and given the global context of international business, this field has no choice but to take into full consideration the international dimension of the organizational world.

Comparative research shows that managers from different national cultures hold different assumptions as to the nature of management and organization. These different sets of assumptions shape different value systems and get translated into different management and organizational practices which in turn reinforce the original assumptions. Among such practices, human resource management practices are likely to be most sensitive to cultural diversity as they are designed by culture bearers in order to handle other culture bearers. Thus the assumptions and values of the local designers are likely to be amplified by the expectations of the natives to create a cultural product that may be highly meaningful and potentially effective for the home country but possibly meaningless, confusing, and ineffective for another country.

If we accept the view that HRM approaches are cultural artifacts reflecting the basic assumptions and values of the national culture in which organizations are imbedded, international HRM becomes one of the most challenging corporate tasks in multinational organizations.

With varying degrees of awareness, such organizations are confronted all the time with strategic choices that need to be made in order to optimize the quality and effectiveness of their very diverse human resources around the world. In order to build, maintain, and develop their corporate identity, multinational organizations need to strive for consistency in their ways of managing people on a worldwide basis. Yet, and in order to be effective locally, they also need to adapt those ways to the specific cultural requirements of different societies. While the global nature of the business may call for increased consistency, the variety of cultural environments may be calling for differentiation.

Faced with such a high degree of strategic complexity in managing human resources internationally, corporations have become increasingly seduced by a new and highly attractive dream called corporate culture, that would encapsulate on a worldwide basis their own genuine and unique ways of managing people. What if our corporate culture could act as a 'supra-culture' and be expected to supersede some of the annoying specificities of the different national cultures in which we operate?

Indeed different organizations from the same country develop different organizational cultures over time and there is no doubt that the recent recognition of the importance and reality of organizational cultures represents a step forward in our understanding of organizations and of their management. However, and in spite of the interest of the concept, it would probably be illusionary to expect that the recent and short history of modern corporations could shape the basic assumptions of their members to an extent that would even approximate the age-long shaping of civilizations and nations. Indeed the comparative research reported above indicates that the corporate culture of long established large multinationals does not seem to reduce national differences in basic management assumptions across their subsidiaries.

Our tentative interpretation of this finding is that a conceptualization of organizational cultures in terms of basic assumptions (Schein, 1985) may be searching for the reality of organizational culture at a deeper level than it really is. To a certain extent, it may be useful to interpret the current appropriation of the concept of culture in the field of organization studies as a modern attempt at increasing the legitimacy of management in business firms by calling upon a higher order concept of almost indisputable essence. Who can deny the existence of an IBM culture?

Instead of locating the roots of organizational culture at the deepest level of basic assumptions, an alternative and possibly more realistic view would be to restrict the concept of organizational culture to the more superficial layers of implicit and explicit systems of norms, expectations, and historically-based preferences, constantly reinforced by their behavioural manifestations and their assigned meanings. Under this view, organizational members would be seen as adjusting to the behavioural requirements of organizational cultures without necessarily being so deeply immersed into their ideological textures.

Consistent with the previous arguments on the deep impact of national cultures upon organizational theories and practices, our proposed interpretation of the concept of organizational culture probably reflects the Frenchness of the author through his eagerness to differentiate 'actors and systems' (Crozier and Friedberg, 1977).

Thus on the international scene, a French manager working in the French subsidiary of an American corporation that insists on an open-door policy may very well leave his office door open—thus adjusting to the behavioural requirements of the corporate culture—without any modification whatsoever of his basic conception of managerial authority. In the French subsidiary of a Swedish firm, whose corporate values include an almost religious reliance upon informality, French shopfloor employees were recently observed as addressing their managers by their first names and using the intimate *tu* form within the boundaries of the firm. The same individuals immediately reverted to *Monsieur le Directeur* and the more formal *vous* form whenever meeting outside the firm.

Similarly the degree of ingeniosity and creativity that can be observed in order to recreate private space and status out of open space offices probably expresses some of the same dynamics whereby organizational members may very well play the expected game without abdicating their own personal values.

Deep-rooted assumptions could then be better understood as the historical result of broader cultural contexts like civilizations and nations. Organizations would only select from the available repertory of their larger cultural context a limited set of ideas that best fit their own history and modes of implementation. This would be called their organizational culture and would strongly reflect national characteristics of the founders and dominant elite of the organization (Hofstede, 1985).

STEPS TOWARD THE INTERNATIONAL MANAGEMENT OF HUMAN RESOURCES

In dealing with other cultures than their home-based culture, international organizations need to recognize more explicitly that they are dealing with different 'fabrics of meaning' (Geertz, 1973). Therefore, whatever can be the strength, cohesiveness, or articulated nature of their corporate cultures, the same HRM policy or practice is likely to be attributed quite different meanings by different cultural groups. Behavioural adjustment may occur at a superficial level and provide the designer from Headquarters with an illusory feeling of satisfaction in front of apparent homogeneity across subsidiaries. The dances will appear similar while their actual meaning may be quite different and thus lead to very different outcomes than anticipated. Fortunately, in many other cases, the dances will also be different enough across subsidiaries so as to effectively remind Headquarters that the rest of the world is different from 'home'.

In the Italian subsidiary, the introduction of a Management-by-Objectives system may be experienced as follows: 'We used to be rewarded for our accomplishments and punished for our failures. Why should we now sign our own punishment even before trying?' For the Indonesian affiliate company, the inclusion of negative feedback in performance appraisal interviews may mean 'an unhealthy pollution of harmonious hierarchical relationships'. The introduction of a matrix-type multiple reporting relationship system may be experienced as a horrible case of divided loyalty in the Mexican subsidiary. Unlike many others, the subsidiaries of Swedish multinational corporations may complain that they do not receive enough 'help' from Headquarters. Participative management may mean very different things to Scandinavians and North Americans.

To a large extent, Human Resource Managers who operate internationally know these things and multinational organizations have accumulated wisdom from experience and developed skills to handle cultural diversity. Yet, more often than not, such organizations must have learned by accident or out of necessity how to cope with cultural differences. Only on rare occasions have they explicitly and consciously set out to develop a truly multinational identity by building upon cultural differences in their human resources. How many headquarters genuinely believe that they can learn from their foreign subsidiaries? How many implement such a rare belief by internationalizing headquarters' staff and top management? It may be that recent trends toward multinational cooperative ventures and networks (Lorange, 1985), characterized by a lesser degree of centralized power, will accelerate such development processes.

A truly international conception of human resource management would require a number of critical and painful steps that have not occurred yet in most instances:

- an explicit recognition by the headquarter organization that its own peculiar ways of managing human resources reflect some assumptions and values of its home culture.
- that as such these peculiar ways are neither universally better or worse than others, they are different and they are likely to exhibit strengths and weaknesses particularly when travelling abroad.
- an explicit recognition by the headquarter organization that its foreign subsidiaries may have other preferred ways of managing people that are neither intrinsically better nor worse but that could possibly be more effective locally.
- a willingness from headquarters to not only acknowledge cultural differences but also to take active steps in order to make them discussable and therefore usable.
- the building of a genuine belief by all parties involved that more creative and effective ways of managing people could be developed as a result of cross-cultural learning.

Obviously such steps cannot be dictated or easily engineered. They have more to do with states of mind and mindsets than with behaviours. As such, these processes can only be facilitated and this may represent a primary mission for executives in charge of international human resource management. They may also represent some of the prerequisites and foundations for the development of forward-looking international corporate cultures.

Such cultures could then provide the impetus and the proper framing to address important strategic issues in the area of international HRM such as: how much consistency and which similarity in policies and practices should be developed? How much variety and differentiation and what adaptation should be encouraged? Which policies should be universal and global? Which ones should be local? Which HRM practices should be designed at the centre? Locally? By international teams? Which processes can be invented to reach agreement on objectives and allow variable paths to achieve them? Which passports should key managers have in the headquarter organization and in the main subsidiaries? Home office nationals? Country nationals? Third nationals? How much and which expatriation should occur? How to manage the whole expatriation process? How to properly assess management potential when judgment criteria differ from country to country? How to orchestrate the management of careers internationally? All of these issues require strategic choices that cannot be left to an obscure function as they need to be fully integrated in a global vision of the firm and as they feed and shape that vision.

The challenge faced by the infant field of international human resource management is to solve a multidimensional puzzle located at the crossroad of national and organizational cultures. Research is needed on the various strategies that international firms are using as their own attempts at solving the puzzle.

REFERENCES

Crozier, M. and Friedberg, E. (1977) *L'Acteur et le Systeme: Les Contraintes de L'Action Collective*. Editions du Seuil, Paris.

Geertz, C. (1973) *The Interpretation of Cultures: Selected Essays*. Basic Books, New York.

Hofstede, G. (1980) 'Motivation, Leadership and Organization: Do American Theories Apply Abroad?' *Organizational Dynamics*, Summer: 42–63.

Hofstede G. (1985) 'The Interaction between National and Organizational Value Systems'. *Journal of Management Studies*, **22**(4): 347–357.

Inzerilli, G. and Laurent, A. (1983) 'Managerial Views of Organization Structure in France and the USA'. *International Studies of Management and Organization*, **XIII**(1/2), 97–118.

Laurent, A. (1981) 'Matrix Organizations and Latin Cultures. A Note on the Use of Comparative Research Data in Management Education'. *International Studies of Management and Organization*, **X**(4): 101–114.

Laurent, A. (1983) 'The Cultural Diversity of Western Conceptions of Management'. *International Studies of Management and Organization*, **XIII**(1/2): 75–96.

Lorange, P. (1985) 'Human Resource Management in Multinational Cooperative Ventures and Networks'. Paper presented at the International Human Resource Management Symposium, Fontainebleau, 20–23 August.

Peters, T. J. and Waterman, R. H. (1982) *In Search of Excellence*. Harper & Row, New York.

Schein, E. H. (1985) *Organizational Culture and Leadership*. Jossey-Bass Publishers, San Francisco.

Tichy, N. M. (1983) 'Foreword'. *Human Resource Management*, **22**(1/2), 3–8.

21

Developing Leaders for the Global Enterprise

Stephen H. Rhinesmith, John N. Williamson, David M. Ehlen and Denise S. Maxwell

A major new organizational form has emerged in the 1980s. The 'Global Enterprise' is rapidly coming to dominate competitive behaviour in many industries around the world. It operates basically without the constraints or traditions of national boundaries and seeks to compete in any high-potential marketplace on earth.

The global enterprise is a consequence of several new and sophisticated forces that have come to shape the world economy over the last decade, including:

- aggressive and massive financial accumulation and relatively free-flowing resource transfer;
- well-defined and highly efficient communication channels and information transfer and control systems;
- technology development and application that seek both leading-edge and low-cost positions in product creation and production;
- clear recognition of the potential for mass markets, mass customization and global brands.

EVOLUTION OF THE GLOBAL ORGANIZATION

A business goes through four conceptually distinct and progressively more complex stages as it evolves from a successful domestic organization to a global corporation:

- *Domestic enterprise.* This business operates solely within its own country—using domestic suppliers and producing and marketing its services and products to customers at home.

- *Exporter.* This is a successful national business that sells or markets its products and services in foreign countries, but operates primarily from its sense of domestic competitiveness and advantage. This firm has little information about marketplace conditions outside its national boundaries and will most often operate through independent agents or distributors. The exporter tends to be opportunistic and transitional in form, as trends and events that it does not anticipate or understand affect its success.

- *International or multinational corporation.* This organization supplements its international sales and distribution capability with localized manufacturing. Such organizations often turn over their foreign operations to locals. Import/export activities move freely within the infrastructure of the multinational corporation; technology and manufacturing may be as equally distributed as sales and logistics. The parent company operates with a centralized view of strategy, technology, and resource allocation, but decision making and customer service shift to the local or national level for marketing, selling, manufacturing, and competitive tactics. Many multinational firms are more accurately characterized as multidomestic, because each national or regional operation acts quite independently of the enterprise's other operations.

- *Global enterprise.* This organization is an extension of the international or multinational corporation. It is constantly scanning, organizing, and re-organizing its resources and capabilities so that national or regional boundaries are not barriers to potential products, business opportunities, and manufacturing locations.

    Such an organization is always looking for potential products or businesses. It delivers them in the best markets from the lowest cost positions and with the most appropriate management resources, largely without regard to where dollars, people, resources, and technology reside. The mindset of the Global Enterprise is to reach and penetrate marketplaces before local or international competitors are equipped to exploit the opportunities.

When an organization moves from an international to a global perspective an essential shift takes place—a shift from the tight control of a bureaucracy to an entrepreneurial, flexible, rapid-response capability that is totally comfortable with cross-cultural influences and conditions.

The global enterprise, as Kenichi Ohmae describes it in his book, *Triad Power*, is one that becomes an 'insider' in any market or nation where it operates, much as a domestic enterprise operates in a local market. The difference is a global strategic perspective, with cross-cultural integration and a highly localized sense of customers and competitors.

For many international organizations, one of the central executive-suite issues of the late 1980s and into the 1990s is how to organize, integrate, and manage their activities to become global players. That will become particularly true for the large US firms that are just now beginning to understand that an export mentality—or having offshore divisions or businesses—does not necessarily mean they are equipped to compete effectively on a global basis.

Increasingly, the issue of global strategy deals with a series of differentiation and integration decisions. On one hand, companies have a clear need for a sense of global strategic intent, or for broad-based resource, technology, and marketing allocation schemes. At the same time, they need a sense of localized customer focus and competitiveness that deals with regional or local conditions as well as culture, behaviour, and values.

Interestingly, most of the current writing and thinking about global organizations focuses on marketing resource allocation, technology transfer, and organizational configuration as they relate primarily to information-flow, strategy, and control requirements. Little attention is given to the management and human-development needs that arise in the evolution from a domestically-postured business to one that operates from a true global perspective.

GLOBAL LEADERSHIP-DEVELOPMENT AGENDA

What are the leadership-development requirements of an organization that is moving through those phases to a global outlook? How can it successfully develop its human resources to meet the changing, emerging, and increasingly complex conditions?

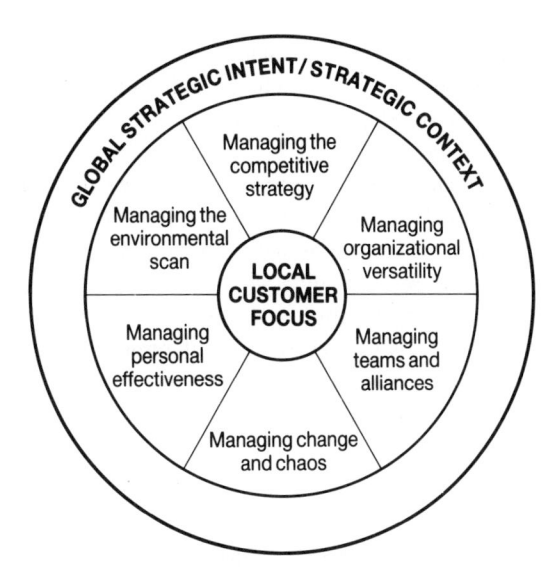

Figure 1. The Leadership Agenda. (© 1989, Wilson Learning Corporation.)

The 'leadership agenda' (Figure 1) shows the leadership-development requirements that face a company as it evolves toward a global perspective. Several premises lie behind the agenda:

- The customer is the centre or focus of development and training. In other words, the primary focus of training and development is serving customers increasingly well and with competitive advantage.
- The company's global strategy 'wraps around' the training and development approaches; the organization's essential sense of competitiveness and strategic intent is embedded in all training programmes and interventions.
- The six leadership-development clusters have a contemporary management viewpoint. The clusters are organized around requirements for global competitive success rather than traditional skill or behaviour sets.

Let us define briefly what each of the leadership-clusters comprises and then seek to organize them against the framework of the evolving enterprise.

Managing the environmental scan

This cluster represents the systematic process of assessing and understanding the major internal and external influences on the enterprise's ability to achieve competitive advantage. In a larger sense, the cluster focuses on changing the frame of reference from a local or national orientation to a truly global perspective. It involves understanding influences, trends, and directions in technology, financial resources, marketing and distribution practices, political and cultural influences, and international economics.

Operationally, information systems and data-collection processes need to be reframed and revised to enable the organization to collect and utilize, in a timely and strategic way, the information required to proactively manage the business. That often requires an extensive reorganization of the company's data- and information-collection capacities. The process must ensure that the information to be collected is useful, and that the necessary systems, analytical processes, and human-resource-development schemes are in place to support the business's strategic information requirements.

For many organizations, that task appears complex. For others, it simply means augmenting and enhancing the systems already in place, or taking a new look at the company's strategic intent and articulating the information that is necessary to support the current strategy.

Whatever the degree of revision, it requires an understanding of today's critical success factors—those few things that must go right for the business to prosper—and the appropriate data about them. That often means narrowing, not enlarging, the information agenda and being careful about specifying information and data sets that are crucial to the firm's success.

Managing the competitive strategy

The focus of this cluster is understanding and developing competitive strategies, plans, tactics that operate outside the confines of a domestic marketplace orientation. Again much of the requirement deals with changing the basic frame of reference or point of view from which competitive activities and strategies are addressed. Several new dimensions need to be addressed and internalized. One of the first 'new understandings' is that the competitive environment operates in a greatly expanded and increasingly complex manner. Market strategy can be complicated by new issues and problems arising from unknown new competitors, the possibility of new entrants or players, and the implications of legislation such as tariffs and quotas.

In another sense, the resources and assets of the enterprise need to be looked at in dramatically expanded ways. For instance, the role of the enterprise's brand positioning has to be considered in terms of global strategic presence, as well as local marketing and competitive conditions.

The internationalization of taste, modified by local culture and values, supports the practice of mass customization and segmentation, but always from the perspective of the global brand, product offering, or business franchise. The issues of quality, resource efficiency, and cost leadership are becoming elements of marketing as well as financial strategy. And innovation and creativity have strong strategic implications as the organization confronts different competitors in virtually every local marketplace.

A customer-back business definition—with the organizational responsiveness and value-adding activities that support changing tastes and needs—still must be the fundamental driving force behind the organization's sense of competitiveness. Being close to customers remains a crucial element of success in the global model.

Such marketing tactics as pricing and promotional plans, which historically have operated on a local basis, must have a strategic or global coherence, as well as a localized sense of advantage and competition.

Managing organizational versatility

The advent of the global organization will bring dramatic new changes and learning requirements for individuals; other changes will be reflected in the architecture of the organizational models for tomorrow's successful global enterprises.

The most basic shift will take place as an organization moves from the classical, bureaucratic-control model to one that is characterized by flexible and responsive structures, adaptive and sometimes temporary operating systems, control mechanisms driven by information networks, and decision-making and behaviour processes that are entrepreneurial, rapid response, and risk-oriented.

Unstable business environments and irregular competitive and customer changes will contribute to a state of continuous organization and re-organization of resources, technologies, marketing and distribution systems, and human networks. Such changes will be necessary for adapting to the new success factors that will be critical for the business.

The underlying issue and challenge will be one of rapid and continuous response to opportunities and threats in terms of resource allocation, strategies, and human behaviour. Certainly those needs seem straightforward, but the new approaches and systems may seem foreign to the conventional thinking that characterizes management practice in today's successful international enterprises.

Managing teams and alliances

The central operating mode for the global enterprise will be the creation, organization, and management of multinational teams and alliances—groups that represent diversity in functional capabilities, experience levels, and cultural values.

The effective global manager will need to understand how to organize and lead multinational teams; deal with issues of collaboration and cross-cultural variances; and develop processes for coaching, mentoring, and assessing performance across a variety of attitudes, beliefs, and standards. That requires the ability to effectively lead and direct a diverse group of people, most of whom will have values, beliefs, behaviours, business-practice standards, and traditions that are likely to be culturally different from those of the manager or leader.

Success in the global model will also come from the ability to create links across traditional organizational and national boundaries. Strategic partnerships will be formed to 'achieve higher performance and/or lower costs through joint, mutually dependent action of independent organizations or individuals', according to John Henderson of MIT. The basis for such alliances will be a mutually-shared purpose that transcends cultural differences.

In that sense, the requirements of global leadership extend well beyond traditional management practices, to reflect sensitivity to cultural diversity and perspective, and understanding of different—and sometimes conflicting—social forces without prejudice. Often, a manager will be required to operate in an unfamiliar and uncomfortable organizational setting.

Within the architecture of cross-cultural teams, managers need to recognize and focus on the subtle requirements for organizational loyalty and commitment, despite the presence of different cultural values and beliefs. At the same time, they must manage in the context of continuous change and diversity.

Managing change and chaos

Continuous change—not stability—is the dominant influence in global business activities today. That demands not only new skills, but also new realities, and even new comfort zones for global managers, who must realize and understand that global management will operate largely in the face of continuous change. The traditional role of making order out of chaos will shift to one of continuously managing change and chaos in ways that are responsive to customers and competitive conditions.

The idea that change—not stability—will be the regular and understood frame of reference for global management underlies the need for training, development, and understanding for managers who operate in international or global enterprises.

Only recently has the subject of change been given legitimate status in managerial training and learning activities. The real nature of the training and development need remains vague and largely undefined.

The concepts and metaphors that describe the management of change are increasingly visual. Peter Vaill of George Washington University describes it as learning how to 'navigate in perpetual whitewater'. Others see it as the process of continuous learning and improvement, of dealing with the personal requirements of constantly changing environments, and of viewing success as the process of improving (changing) faster than competitors—learning more quickly about opportunities and responding more completely when information and strategy point the way.

A significant learning opportunity in the domain of managing change is contextual: creating the mindsets, metaphors, beliefs, and attitudes that support and define the impact of irregular and chaotic change at a personal level. That means developing self-management and personal growth practices that can provide the stability, energy, and managerial confidence that are crucial to effectively handling such conditions.

Managing personal effectiveness

The personal growth and adaptation requirements for many US managers, as they move toward operating in global enterprises, will be far-reaching, primarily because US-based managers generally lack the experience, diversity, and globe-trotting skills of so many of their offshore counterparts.

Personal adaptation to the changing conditions, cultures, and operating requirements of the global enterprise represents a significant and largely unfunded training need. Development of global managers in most businesses is done *ad hoc*, rather than as a systematic and orderly movement toward the skills, perceptions, and attitudes of effective global management.

In many respects, the global leader will need to have a cosmopolitan perspective new to many US firms. A working knowledge of international relations and foreign affairs will be required, as well as a careful and complete sensitivity to the diversity of cultures, beliefs, social forces, and values, and a commitment to treating that diversity largely without prejudice.

Global managers will also have to manage accelerated change in their own lives, family relations, living conditions, and perhaps even economic constraints. A true world view and sense of world citizenship will be a valuable frame of reference.

At the same time, managers must remain grounded in their skills, capacities, and personal sense of energy and balance, often under the continuing impact of destabilizing organizational and personal influences. That will be particularly true as they move across cultures. Even aspects of their life as mundane as personal living requirements will be challenging and at times difficult.

We believe the effective manager will emerge as a kind of global citizen, always anchored in a nationalistic framework, but embodying the openness, adaptability, and personal versatility necessary to live under new and often unpredictable conditions.

Many of the attitudes, skills, and perceptions of global adaption can be provided in well-structured learning and training experiences. But complete growth will come only when training and personal on-the-job experiences are integrated to reflect a thoughtful, institutionalized development process. For most global managers, that process can and will be a lifelong journey.

The six development clusters represent the essence and focus of the leadership development and training necessary to support the global enterprise. They may lack definitive clarity in today's operating climate, but they point to the direction in which attention and resources must be applied if the successful international organization of today is to make the transition to global enterprise.

The 'global management matrix' (Table 1) summarizes the focus of leadership attention as an organization increases in complexity from a domestic to a global entity.

THE AMERICAN LEADERSHIP CHALLENGE

It is somewhat ironic that conventional wisdom about the inability of US firms to compete effectively in the global marketplace usually focuses on inadequate spending in technology, plants, and equipment. The real vulnerability may lie in the lack of attention to training and developing key managers in the approaches, concepts, and experiences required to be effective global managers and leaders.

It is equally ironic that the presumed strength of US firms is the level and quality of management and leadership training—either in academic or corporate settings. Our managers are believed to be better trained than their offshore counterparts. The reality as it relates to the global organization may be just the opposite.

US businesses increasingly recognize the need for achieving a global marketplace perspective. However, they do not have the training and experience needed for developed and seasoned management teams capable of operating at the same skill level as companies from such countries as Japan and Germany. Such nations have been forced by the nature of their competitive positions to compete nationally—and even globally—over the last 10, 20, or more years. Until recently, the United States has had the luxury of being able to remain domestic.

We in the United States are an insular society. That quality is present in our schools, our government, our corporations, and our values and beliefs. To change the pattern in a fundamental way may take years, if not a generation. During that process, we may well be managerially unprepared to meet the requirements for global competitiveness.

What will it take to change and effectively compete?

First, we need to recognize that the new game will not be played or driven by the US business model. To cling to traditional US views of competitiveness and marketplace success will increasingly threaten an organization's ability to compete in the years ahead.

That shift in thinking will be particularly difficult for those American enterprises that have done little in the last 30 or 40 years to educate and train their managers to organize and manage the firm's resources from a multicultural or international perspective. Feeding that deficiency is the failure of the American educational system to provide students with international business skills and cross-cultural knowledge to bring to organizations.

We also need to modify certain barriers, misconceptions, and beliefs, if American enterprise is going to grapple with the question of managerial competitiveness. Some of the barriers

Table 1. The global management matrix

Leadership development clusters	Corporate type			
	Global enterprise	International or multinational corporation	Exporter	Domestic enterprise
Managing the environmental scan. How do we determine what must go right?	Global trends, conditions, and resources.	Multidomestic trends, environmental conditions, and strategic resources.	Offshore market trends and conditions; domestic strategic resources.	Domestic market trends, resources, and environmental conditions.
Managing the competitive strategy. How do we allocate and align resources?	Integrate holistic strategies.	Proliferate successful domestic market model with cultural adaption.	Extend domestic success to offshore markets.	Penetrate and segment markets.
Managing organizational versatility. How do we organize for success today and tomorrow?	Create free-flowing resource-allocation schemes.	Adapt systems and processes to international competitive conditions.	Respond to emerging foreign-market opportunities.	Respond to local competitive and market changes.
Managing teams and alliances. How do we connect with others for advantage?	Create global strategic partnerships—inter- and intra-organizational links.	Develop multinational alliances and ventures; manage cross-cultural work teams.	Manage cross-cultural distribution links.	Manage cross-functional teams.
Managing change and chaos. How do we thrive in times of unpredictable change?	Proactively create destabilized conditions for advantage.	Respond and adapt to destabilizing change by flexibly reallocating resources across national markets.	Adapt to destabilizing change by entering or withdrawing from foreign markets.	Flexibly protect ourselves against unpredictable change.
Managing personal effectiveness. How do we change and grow successfully as individuals?	Transcend cultural differences.	Work effectively in cross-cultural situations.	Understand cross-cultural needs.	Understand self and associates.

© 1989, Wilson Learning Corporation and Rhinesmith and Associates Inc.

appear in research by André Laurent, who has studied multinational corporations and has made several key observations:

- Multinational companies do not and cannot submerge the individuality of different cultures. As strong as corporate culture is, people never give up their own backgrounds and preferences. People can adapt, but in periods of crisis or uncertainty, they will retreat to their own sets of beliefs and cultural values.
- Contact with other nationality groups can even promote determination to be different. It is interesting that many people withdraw when confronted with cultural differences, and reinforce their determination not to adjust and not to give up their own values.
- It is useless to present new kinds of management theory and practice to individuals who are culturally unable or unwilling to accept it. For example, performance reviews are difficult in most multinational corporations because of differences in personal style. Americans tend to be open, direct, and blunt; Asians tend to be much more indirect, oblique, and subtle in giving feedback. Thus, something as apparently basic and common as a performance-appraisal system probably cannot be implemented uniformly on a global basis.

Several other key paradigms about cross-cultural awareness that affect our ability to re-think the new game are worth observing:

- The 'we are all alike' syndrome is one that many of us have experienced when we have visited a foreign land and come back with the initial perception that all people are very much alike—we are just one, big human race.
- The second stage of understanding comes when we begin to uncover differences—some subtle, some specific. Then we realize that although people have some significant similarities, we can also have strong differences.
- Third comes the realization that we are really both different and similar, and that in an organization, a leadership and management model must address both common and uncommon threads, as well as diverse behaviours and beliefs.

The prevailing attitude of senior executives in American companies seems to be a point of view that suggests, 'If we can get our enterprise's corporate culture and values right—no matter where it operates around the globe—then the issue of strategy and local behaviour will be predictable and appropriate'.

They are saying that the template for values, beliefs, and behaviours of the enterprise must necessarily come from the values, beliefs, behaviours, and attitudes of the parent corporation. We believe that holding on to that viewpoint means starting from the wrong place.

The difficult task for senior management today is to flip-flop the traditional thinking that suggests that values, beliefs, and behaviours need to be highly standardized from a central, corporate perspective, and that strategies and resource-allocation schemes can be played out from a local point of view. We believe the opposite reflects today's reality and is the fundamental operating condition for an organization that wants to achieve true global status.

We believe that in the 1990s the challenge for most enterprises as they move toward the global model will lie in successfully managing international teams. And US corporations have done little in the last 30 or 40 years to educate, train, and provide experience for managers to manage a multicultural workforce.

Meeting that challenge will be expensive in terms of both resources and time. US firms need to get on with the task of building a new model for leadership development in a global community—a model that derives not from the traditional management skill base of planning, staffing, and control, but rather from a recognition of a whole new array of leadership requirements:

- The capacity to manage, live with, and operate under conditions of continuous change and turmoil.
- The recognition that global advantage is transitory and that the role of managers and global leaders will be to continuously assess and adjust resources, technologies, organizational structure, and human beings to reflect simultaneously a centralized view of strategy and a localized view of customers and cultures.
- An acknowledgment that the US business model is not necessarily the best point of departure for evaluating the implications and meaning of global-marketplace trends and opportunities. A fundamental shift in thinking needs to take place in setting assumptions and beliefs about the role enterprises can play in the global marketplace. US businesses have to move from a perspective that considers the rest of the world from a US viewpoint, to a more global outlook that views the home country in the context of the world marketplace.
- A heightened awareness of strategic marketing and global competitiveness. On one hand, brands, technologies, and franchises need to be played out from the advantage of scale and clout that only a global point of view can provide. At the same time, businesses need to recognize and acknowledge the 'close to the customer' conditions that operate locally or inside major national marketplaces.
- The development of skills and capabilities to lead multinational teams in flexible and responsive ways. Human resources need to reflect the same capacity for adaptation and flexibility as technology and financial resources. The new organizational model that emerges will shift from the traditional bureaucratic control scheme that drives so many large enterprises today to a contemporary entrepreneurialism characterized by flexibility, resource fluidity, and continuously changing beliefs and attitudes about competitiveness. It will embody a willingness to shed old assumptions and beliefs quickly, and a recognition that home base is really the globe.
- The understanding that managers, particularly in the United States, need cross-cultural and expatriate experiences early on and continually throughout their careers.

The challenge for all of us involved in both management and the development of management is to begin to change the context in which we think about our human-development responsibilities. We clearly need to discard traditional models and views and begin to think from a global rather than a domestic paradigm. In the process, we must challenge and change many of our views about hiring, training, controlling, offering incentives, and measuring our managers.

It is a long-term assignment, probably three to five years for most large enterprises simply to get moving; in all likelihood, it will take a full generation to implement the approach.

By that time, we will have a whole new game to worry about.

22

Toward a Comprehensive Model of International Adjustment: an Integration of Multiple Theoretical Perspectives

J. Stewart Black, Mark Mendenhall and Gary Oddou

The internationalization of the world's markets has led to a significant increase in the cross-cultural interactions between businesspeople, and in the business world, the use of expatriate managers in this 'global village' has led to large numbers of Americans living and working overseas and having to adjust not only to a new work culture, but also to new ways of living. Unfortunately, research shows that many Americans do not succeed in their overseas assignments. Between 16 and 40% of all American employees sent overseas return from their assignments early, and each premature return costs a firm roughly $100 000 (Baker and Ivancevich, 1971; Black, 1988; Copeland and Griggs, 1985; Misa and Fabricatore, 1979; Tung, 1982). In addition to these costs, approximately 30 to 50% of American expatriates, whose average compensation package is $250 000 per year, stay at their international assignments, but are considered ineffective or marginally effective by their firms (Copeland and Griggs, 1985).

Scholars have only focused their research efforts on the problem of expatriate adjustment and effectiveness since the late 1970s. Previous to that time, some research had been conducted on Peace Corps volunteers and foreign exchange students, but little work was done on expatriate managers (see Church, 1982, for a review). The past decade has seen an increase in research on cross-cultural adjustment; however, to date, little theoretical work has been conducted in the area of international adjustment of expatriates—the existing literature consists mostly of anecdotal or atheoretical empirical efforts to understand the phenomenon (Adler, 1983; Kyi 1988; Mendenhall and Oddou, 1985; Schollhammer, 1975).

Conversely, the literature in the area of domestic (US/Canada) transfers and adjustment is much richer theoretically; researchers in this area have increasingly focused their efforts on understanding how an individual adjusts to a new organizational setting either after a transfer or upon initial entry into the firm (Ashford and Taylor, 1990; Feldman, 1976; Feldman and Brett, 1983; Jones, 1986; Latack, 1984; Louis, 1980a; Nicholson, 1984; Pinder and Schroeder, 1987; Van Maanen and Schein, 1979). To date, scholars in the area of international human resource management have not utilized the domestic adjustment literature in order to formulate theories or models that would assist them in understanding the international adjustment process.

Perhaps this has not occurred because although the theories of adjustment of employees to new organizational settings in the domestic context may have some application to adjustment in the international context, there seem to be substantial differences between domestic and international (or cross-cultural) adjustment. For example, most domestic adjustments do not involve significant changes in the nonwork environment; living in Los Angeles versus New York may be quite different in many ways, but the language, cultural, economic, social, and political contexts are significantly familiar. This is not the norm for international adjustments. Moving from the United States to a foreign country often involves changes in the job the individual performs and the corporate culture in which responsibilities are executed; it can also involve dealing with unfamiliar norms related to the general culture, business practices, living conditions, weather, food, health care, daily customs, and political systems—plus facing a foreign language on a daily basis.

Because the work as well as the nonwork contexts usually change during an international adjustment, not only are unique variables involved, but it also seems possible that different relationships among the variables may also exist. Thus, given (1) the substantial contextual differences between domestic and international adjustment, (2) the relevance of the issue to today's organizations, and (3) the lack of theoretical work in the area of international adjustment, it is appropriate to move toward a theoretical framework and research agenda concerning international adjustment.

This article has three basic objectives. The first is to review the literature on international adjustment, delineating the important variables that scholars have found to influence international adjustment. The second is to review the theoretical literature on domestic adjustment, exploring what it suggests about international adjustment. The third is to integrate what is known and what seems logically compelling from both literatures into a theoretical framework of international adjustment, deriving propositions in an effort to establish a basic research agenda for the future.

REVIEW OF THE INTERNATIONAL ADJUSTMENT LITERATURE

Although international adjustment has received increased scholarly attention, the majority of the writing has been anecdotal in nature, and few scholars have rigorously investigated the phenomenon, empirically or theoretically (Adler, 1983; Black and Mendenhall, 1990; Kyi, 1988; Schollhammer, 1975). Thus, this section summarizes the findings of this empirical research to ascertain if any themes or dimensions exist. Many articles have reviewed parts of the empirical cross-cultural adjustment literature; therefore, we begin by *reviewing the review articles* of the field. Recent empirical articles, which postdated the review articles, are also included.

Five dimensions (or themes) emerged as components of the cross-cultural adjustment process: (1) predeparture training, (2) previous overseas experience, (3) organizational selection mechanisms, (4) individual skills, and (5) nonwork factors. The first three dimensions describe issues that exist before expatriates leave their home countries, and the remaining two deal with issues that become relevant after the expatriates arrive at their foreign assignments.

Predeparture training

Three review articles have covered the relationship between predeparture training and subsequent cross-cultural adjustment (Black and Mendenhall, 1990; Fiedler *et al.*, 1971; Mitchell *et al.*, 1972). Black and Mendenhall (1990) subsumed within their review the findings of the previous two, and they also reviewed more comprehensively the entire cross-cultural training effectiveness literature. Additionally, they critiqued the methodology of the studies they reviewed and found that 48% included control groups and nearly half of these studies included both the use of control groups and longitudinal designs. These and other studies that had slightly less rigorous designs found support for a positive relationship between cross-cultural training and cross-cultural adjustment, cross-cultural skill development and job performance. They concluded their review of the literature by stating: 'Thus, the empirical literature gives guarded support to the proposition that cross-cultural training has a positive impact on cross-cultural effectiveness' (Black and Mendenhall, 1990, p.120).

Previous overseas experience

It is logical to assume that previous experience living overseas—especially in the same foreign country to which a person is currently assigned—should facilitate adjustment, even though some culture shock will still occur. Church (1982, p.549) found in his review of the empirical literature in this area that 'empirical findings support the importance of accurate prior cultural experience or prior exposure... for sojourner adjustment'. Black (1988) discovered that previous overseas work experience was related to work adjustment for expatriates, but not to general adjustment. Torbiorn (1982) found that specific length of previous overseas experience was not related to higher levels of adjustment; thus, quantity of previous overseas experience does not seem to necessarily relate to current overseas adjustment. Overall, though, previous overseas experience does seem to facilitate the adjustment process. Exactly how that happens or what factors inhibit or magnify the impact of previous experience has yet to be comprehensively determined by scholars in the field.

Organizational selection criteria and mechanisms

In their review of the empirical expatriate selection literature, Mendenhall *et al.* stated that 'MNCs [multinational corporations] consistently overlook key criteria that are predictive of overseas success in their recruiting and screening of potential overseas workers' (1987, p.334). Many researchers have noted that American MNCs, despite the evidence that a variety of skills are necessary for success in an overseas assignment, focus only on one selection criterion: technical competence. (For a review, see Mendenhall *et al.*, 1987; also see Hays, 1974; Miller, 1973; Tung, 1981.)

Why firms focus on only one important skill necessary for overseas success is reflected in a statement by a respondent in Baker and Ivancevich's (1971, p.40) study: 'Managing [a] company is a scientific art. The executive accomplishing the task in New York can surely perform as adequately in Hong Kong' This attitude among managers making selection decisions may reflect why Tung (1981) discovered that only 5% of the firms in her sample administered tests to determine the degree to which candidates possessed cross-cultural skills. In a 1987 study, Moran, Stahl, and Boyer, Inc., found that only 3% of the American firms in their sample selected expatriates from multiple candidates, and that technical job-related experience and technical job skills were the two most important criteria used in selecting candidates for overseas posts. Thus, the trend of a unidimensional selection practice among American MNCs, first delineated in the early 1970s, has continued throughout the 1980s as well.

Individual skills

Many researchers have investigated the skills necessary for an executive to be effective in a cross-cultural setting. (For reviews see Brein and David, 1971; Church, 1982; Mendenhall and Oddou, 1985; Stening, 1979.) These skills have been categorized by Mendenhall and Oddou (1985) into three dimensions: (1) the self-dimension, which encompasses skills that enable the expatriate to maintain mental health, psychological well-being, self-efficacy, and effective stress management; (2) the relationship dimension, which constitutes the array of skills necessary for the fostering of relationships with host nationals; and (3) the perception dimension, which entails the cognitive abilities that allow the expatriate to correctly perceive and evaluate the host environment and its actors.

Nonwork factors

The first nonwork factor that the empirical literature suggests is important to international adjustment is *culture novelty*, or what Mendenhall and Oddou (1985) referred to as *culture toughness*. Some countries' cultures seem to be more difficult to adapt to than others. Church (1982, p.547) referred to this phenomenon as *cultural distance* and noted that 'empirical studies have generally supported this view' that the more culturally distant or different a host culture is from a person's own, the more difficult it is for him or her to adjust. Mendenhall and Oddou, in their 1985 review, reached the same conclusion. Torbiorn (1982) noted that cultural novelty has its largest impact on expatriates during the first two years of their assignments; after that, the impact of cultural novelty diminishes somewhat.

The second major nonwork factor concerns the adjustment of the spouse and family of the expatriate. Although the expatriate may possess the necessary skills for successful international adjustment, if his or her spouse does not possess these same skills, an aborted assignment may ensue simply because the spouse or family members cannot adjust to the new culture. Past reviews have consistently supported the importance of this nonwork factor (Church, 1982; Mendenhall and Oddou, 1985), and a study by Black and Stephens (1989) provides further support for this conclusion on the basis of a positive and significant relationship between the adjustment of expatriates and spouses for a large sample of American expatriates on assignment in several different countries.

Summary of the international adjustment literature

Thus, based on a review of the international adjustment literature three categories of predeparture variables (i.e., previous experience, predeparture training, and candidate selection) and two postarrival variables (i.e., individual skills and nonwork factors) have been identified. It should also be noted that the international adjustment literature has been primarily focused on the degree of overall adjustment to the new culture. Figure 1 provides a rough sketch of how these various categories of variables are conceptually related to international adjustment.

REVIEW OF THE DOMESTIC ADJUSTMENT LITERATURE

Domestic adjustment also involves the basic process of adjusting to a new setting; therefore, this literature may provide important insights for constructing a theoretical framework for international adjustment. Consequently, the following sections briefly review four areas of research that are related to individual adjustment (Ashford and Taylor, 1990): (1) organizational socialization, (2) career transitions and sense making, (3) work role transitions, and (4) relocation/domestic transfers. The relevance of each of these areas of theory and research will be discussed in a later section.

Organizational socialization literature

According to Van Maanen and Schein (1979, pp.211–212), 'Organizational socialization refers minimally...to the fashion in which an individual is taught and learns what behaviours and perspectives are customary and desirable within the work setting as well as what ones are not'. Much of the research on this topic can be divided into two general areas: (1) socialization stages and (2) socialization tactics and individual responses to socialization efforts.

Many scholars have proposed that socialization occurs in stages. Although slight variations exist among the stage models, Fisher's (1986) three-stage model captures most of what has been discussed in this area. The first stage is often referred to as *anticipatory socialization* (Brief *et al.*, 1979; Feldman, 1976; Louis, 1980b). In this stage, individuals make anticipatory adjustments to the organization through means such as organizational choice, organizational

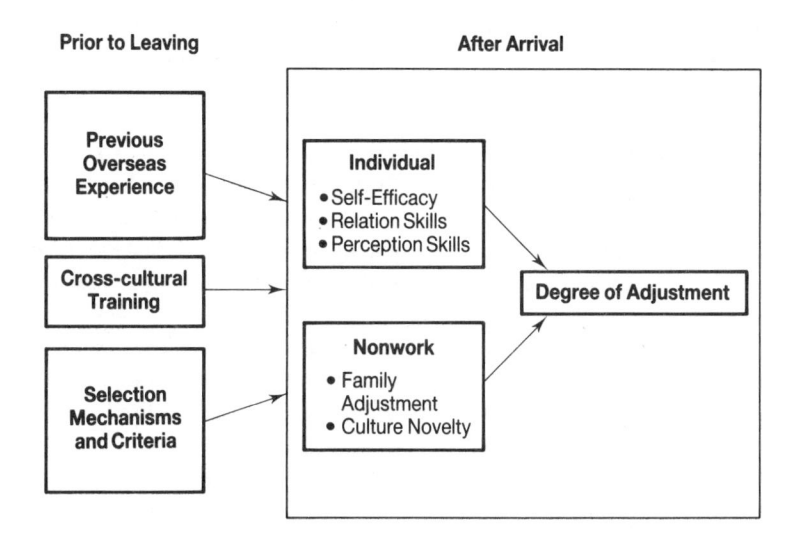

Figure 1. Relationships Based on International Adjustment Literature.

selection, and expectation formulation. Essentially, the more complete and accurate the anticipatory socialization, the greater the ease and speed of adjustment to the new organization (Fisher, 1986).

The second stage of socialization has been referred to as the *encounter stage* (see Fisher, 1986, for a review). During this phase the individual begins to master the tasks of the job and the relationships with others involved in working in the new organization. At this point, expectations are confirmed or disconfirmed. In general, accurate individual expectations, low role ambiguity, and low role conflict facilitate a person's adjustment to the organization during the encounter stage.

The final stage has been referred to as the *role management* stage by Feldman (1976). During this stage the individual moves toward becoming a fully accepted member of the organization. Adjustments to the organization, such as adopting organizational norms or values, are more incremental in nature at this point.

The second major area of investigation relating to organizational socialization concerns the tactics that organizations use to socialize newcomers and the responses of newcomers to these efforts. Van Maanen and Schein (1979) provided one of the most detailed theoretical discussions of the various tactics organizations use and the expected reactions from newcomers. Though space does not permit a complete review of their theoretical arguments, in general, they suggested that institutional tactics lead to custodial responses by newcomers and that individual tactics lead to innovative responses. With the exception of the relationship between two specific tactics and individual responses, Jones (1986) found general empirical support for Van Maanen and Schein's (1979) arguments. Jones (1986) also found that individuals with high levels of self-efficacy were less influenced by institutional socialization tactics to respond in a custodial manner than individuals with low levels of self-efficacy.

Career transitions and sensemaking literature

This area of study is perhaps best codified in two articles by Louis (1980a, b), who proposed a typology of transitions and a process of how individuals adjust to transitions. Louis's (1980b) typology includes both interrole and intrarole transitions. Louis cited five interrole transitions (i.e., when a new and different role is taken): (1) entry/reentry, (2) intracompany, (3) intercompany, (4) interprofession, and (5) exit. *Entry/reentry* role transitions describe the changes in roles when a person moves from one context to another, such as from school to work or from being single to being married. When a person moves from one division to another within the same company, where co-workers, procedures, and the physical setting are likely to change, this describes an *intracompany* role transition. Similarly, if an individual experiences the same type of changes, but moves from one company to another, this refers to an *intercompany* transition. *Interprofessional* transitions occur when individuals change from one profession to another (e.g. dentist to teacher, attorney to Boy Scouts of America leader). Finally, *exit* roles describe the transitions of individuals who voluntarily or involuntarily leave one organization or context and enter another (e.g. stopping work for parenthood, being fired, joining another organization).

Intrarole transitions, in contrast, describe those situations in which a person takes a new orientation toward an old role. Louis described four intrarole transitions: (1) intrarole adjustment, (2) extrarole adjustment, (3) role/career-stage transition, and (4) life-stage transition. An *intrarole* adjustment represents the changes an individual makes toward his or her role over the duration of time. An *extrarole* adjustment describes the changes a person makes in one role as a result of a new role or changes in an old role. For example, an individual might decide to work fewer hours as a result of getting married due to apparent value changes. Both of the preceding transitions might well be unconscious changes the individual makes. A *role/career-stage* transition represents the changes an individual experiences as a result of progressing through the career life cycle. Finally, when a person experiences the psychological changes of moving from adolescence to adulthood, he or she is going through a *life-stage* transition. In moving through the above roles, then, an individual acts and reacts differently throughout the process. However, there are certain commonalities to the experience and the adjustment process. Louis (1980a) described the adjustment process in terms of three constructs—change, contrast, and surprise—and sensemaking.

Constructs in the adjustment process

Change occurs when there is an objective difference in a major feature between the new and old settings. The more such changes occur, the greater the person's unfamiliarity with the new situation, and the greater his or her difficulty in adjusting. These types of changes can be represented by hierarchical or functional differences between the old and new (Schein, 1971) or by status differences. *Contrast*, however, describes changes that are noticed internally and are 'perceived products of the individual's experience in the new setting and role (i.e., features identified as figures against the background of a total field)' (Louis, 1980, p.331). The important distinction between change and contrast is that change relates to an external perspective, whereas contrast describes an internal perspective. The third construct, *surprise*, represents the difference between a person's expectations, which might be conscious or unconscious, and what actually occurs.

Sensemaking in the adjustment process

In Louis's model, the pertinent question relates to how an individual makes sense out of his or her new experience. How does the individual cope? To a certain extent, the individual unconsciously acts out of programmed scripts. This is particularly true when the situation confronted is perceived as similar to previous experiences. In other cases, the individual must think and use rational means to understand the situation, and this occurs at a conscious level. Research has indicated that a person uses rational means to sort out confusion when confronted with a novel situation or with a surprise (e.g., unmet exepectations) (Abelson, 1976; Langer, 1978). Festinger's (1956) theory of cognitive dissonance explains the action: when what is expected does not happen, individuals must rationalize it through reanalysis, or what Louis referred to as a 'need ... for a return to equilibrium' (1980a, p.337).

In summary, when an individual changes roles, certain elements in the total situation bring about confusion. The transition is compounded or simplified by the number and importance of novel or unexpected elements in the situation and by the person's internal reaction to those surprises. Discrepant events require explanations, which are developed, and attributions are made based primarily on an individual's familiarity with past events and his or her expectations about the present situation. Based on this, modifications in the person's expectations are made for future events, and the cycle continues.

The inputs for an individual's attempt to understand the novel or unexpected situation come from several sources: past experiences, a set of cultural assumptions, and input from associates. Unfortunately, these sources are often inadequate because the person does not have enough history in the new context or isn't acquainted with enough or the right people to help interpret the discrepancies or novelties in the novel context.

Work role transition literature

In 1984, Nicholson's article, 'A Theory of Work Role Transitions' and Dawis and Lofquist's work, *A Psychological Theory of Work Adjustment*, provided a codification of theoretical ideas on the topic of work role transitions. Although these two works are by no means the only ones on work role transitions, they are key theoretical exemplars and include most of the variables and underlying theoretical arguments of other works in the area. Both works focused on variables that predict how an individual will adjust to the work role change, or *mode of adjustment*, as both Nicholson (1984) and Dawis and Lofquist (1984) called it. Dawis and Lofquist (1984) argued that individuals can adjust by changing the environment in the new situation to more readily correspond to or match their needs and abilities and labelled this mode of adjustment as *active*. They also argued that individuals can adjust to the new situation by changing themselves and labelled this mode of adjustment as *reactive*.

Although Dawis and Lofquist (1984) acknowledged that individuals may not use one or the other of these modes of adjustment exclusively, their theory and research focused primarily on work factors that would predict active or reactive modes of adjustment. In many ways, their notions of active and reactive adjustment are similar to Van Maanen and Schein's (1979) concepts of role innovation and custodial response, respectively. Nicholson (1984) extended these ideas to a two-by-two matrix. Adjustment made by changing neither self nor the situation he termed *replication*. Adjustment made by changing self but not the situation he termed *absorption*. Adjustment made by changing the situation but not self was called *determination*. Finally, adjustment made by changing both self and the situation was termed *exploration*.

According to Dawis and Lofquist (1984), the first set of antecedents of mode of adjustment is the flexibility of the work environment which moderated the mode of adjustment. Nicholson (1984) referred to this notion as *role discretion*, and both sets of scholars argued that greater role discretion leads to modes of adjustment that focus on adjustment through changing the situation rather than changing aspects of the individual. Additionally, Nicholson (1984) concluded that low role novelty leads to modes of adjustment focused on changing the situation and high role novelty leads to modes focused on changing aspects of the individual.

The second set of antecedents of mode of adjustment were addressed by Nicholson (1984), who termed it *induction–socialization processes*. These were essentially the same socialization tactics and predictions made by Van Maanen and Schein (1979), although Nicholson addressed only three of the six sets of tactics. In agreement with Van Maanen and Schein (1979), Nicholson argued that socialization tactics that are sequential and serial and that involve divestiture lead individuals to change aspects of themselves, whereas socialization tactics that are random and disjunctive and that involve divestiture lead individuals to change aspects of their work role.

Nicholson (1984) believed that shifts in role discretion also affect a person's mode of adjustment. Essentially, Nicholson argued that upward shifts in role discretion lead to modes of adjustment focused on individuals making changes in themselves, whereas downward shifts lead to modes focused on individuals changing aspects of the work role. Nicholson also argued that two individual variables also affect mode of adjustment. He asserted that low desire for feedback and low need for control lead to adjustment by changing neither aspects of the work role nor the individual and that high desire for feedback and high need for control lead to adjustment by changes in both aspects of the work role and of the individual.

Although not addressed by Nicholson (1984), Dawis and Lofquist (1984) also defined the degree of adjustment as well as mode of adjustment. They defined degree of adjustment as the gap between the extent to which the work environment meets the needs of the individual (termed *satisfaction*) plus the gap between the extent to which the individual's abilities meet the demands of the work role (termed *satisfactoriness*). The narrower the total gap, the more adjusted the individual was considered to be. Dawis and Lofquist (1984) argued that role ambiguity, role novelty, and role conflict would inhibit the degree of work adjustment because these work variables reduced the ability of the individual and the organization to appropriately match rewards with individual needs and individual abilities with role demands.

Relocation literature

Many researchers have studied the topic of employee relocation by examining both the effect that relocation has on a number of personal, work, and family outcomes and the factors that affect adjustment after relocation. Studies that have examined the antecedents of adjustment after relocation are the most relevant to the focus of this article. In her review of the literature, Brett stated that 'the studies are typically descriptive and atheoretical' (1980, p.104). However, Brett (1980) added a theoretical perspective to the topic and asserted that one of the primary processes in relocation adjustment is that of reasserting control through reducing uncertainty. The underlying notion was that the greater the disruption of prior routine caused by the relocation, the greater the resulting uncertainty, and the longer it would take before the uncertainty would be reduced to a comfortable level. Brett (1980) argued that role conflict, role ambiguity, role novelty, and work environment novelty—because these factors tend to increase uncertainty—would be negatively related to adjustment after relocation (i.e., these factors inhibited a smooth and quick adjustment).

On the basis of essentially this theoretical premise (Brett, 1980), Pinder and Schroeder (1987) found that role clarity and social support from supervisor and co-workers facilitated adjustment, and role novelty inhibited adjustment after a relocation transfer. Thus, this area of research suggests that job factors (e.g., role ambiguity, role conflict, role novelty) or organizational factors (e.g., organization culture novelty) that increase uncertainty will inhibit adjustment, whereas job factors (e.g., role clarity) or organization factors (e.g., social support) that reduce uncertainty will facilitate adjustment.

Summary of the domestic adjustment literature

The socialization and work role adjustment literatures, in general, have focused on mode of adjustment as the outcome of interest, whereas the relocation and sensemaking literatures have focused on the degree of adjustment. The research on socialization, relocation, and surprise and sensemaking suggests that individuals make anticipatory adjustments before they actually encounter the new situation; it also suggests the importance of accurate expectations to facilitate adjustment. Further, the socialization literature emphasizes the importance of proper selection criteria and mechanisms relative to effective socialization. Regarding the period after individuals enter the new situation, the work role transition literature and the relocation literature emphasize the importance of job-related variables as antecedents of degree of adjustment. The socialization literature and the work role transition theory, particularly Nicholson (1984), stress the importance of organizational socialization tactics as antecedents to mode of adjustment. The surprise and sensemaking and relocation literatures emphasize the importance of organizational culture or work environment novelty and the social support of co-workers and supervisor as important antecedents of degree of adjustment. Figure 2 provides a rough sketch of how these various factors fit together as antecedents of both mode and degree of adjustment within the domestic context.

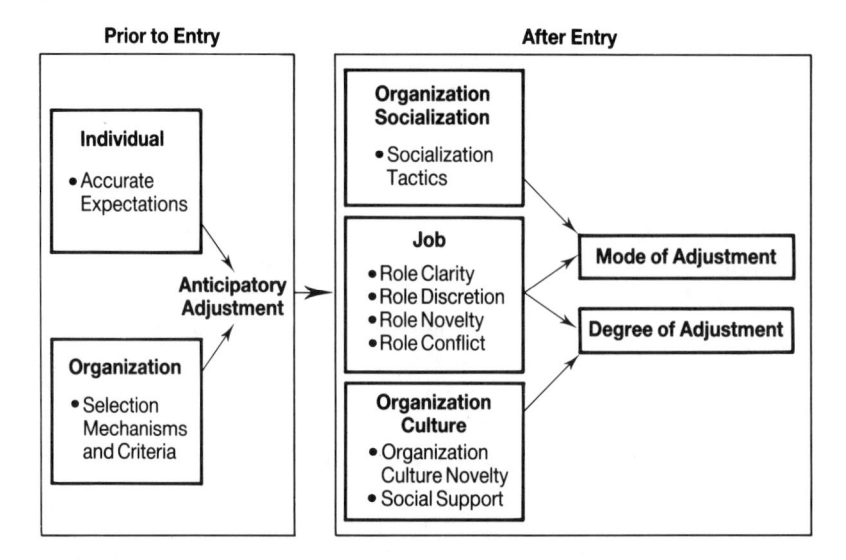

Figure 2. Relationships Based on Domestic Adjustment Literature.

THEORETICAL FRAMEWORK AND RESEARCH AGENDA

The domestic and international adjustment literatures have at least one common and underlying thread: in both literatures an individual leaves a familiar setting and enters an unfamiliar one. Because the new setting is unfamiliar, it upsets old routines and creates psychological uncertainty. Scholars from both literatures either argue or imply that individuals generally have a desire to reduce the uncertainty inherent in the new setting, especially concerning new behaviours that might be required or expected and old behaviours that would be considered unacceptable or inappropriate. Thus, if information concerning these issues is available before people actually enter the new situation, anticipatory adjustments can be made. Once they are actually in the new situation, individuals continue to reduce the uncertainty and discover what behaviours and attitudes are appropriate or inappropriate. Thus, to the extent that various factors either increase or decrease uncertainty, they either inhibit or facilitate adjustment.

However, because international adjustments usually entail greater disruptions of old routines (e.g., work, social, and nonwork routines) than domestic adjustments, the magnitude of uncertainty is usually higher in international versus domestic adjustments. Thus, it should not be surprising that although each literature points to some common important antecedents, each one focuses on unique variables as well. In general, the domestic adjustment literature has focused on pre- and postentry adjustment variables, especially those related to the job and the organization, and mode and degree of adjustment, whereas the international adjustment literature has focused on individual and nonjob variables and on degree of adjustment. We argue that a more comprehensive understanding of international adjustment can be gained by integrating both literatures rather than simply extrapolating from the domestic adjustment literature or from only relying on the extant cross-cultural adjustment literature. Figure 3 represents a schematic integration of both literatures and a more comprehensive theoretical framework of international adjustment than is provided by either the domestic or international literature alone.

Perhaps the easiest way to discuss this framework and the propositions it suggests is to move through Figure 3, from top to bottom and left to right. It should be noted that we will derive propositions from the framework, which primarily involve concepts, rather than hypotheses, which primarily involve measures (Whetten, 1989). The framework includes both the degree of adjustment and the mode of adjustment as outcomes.

Facets of degree of international adjustment

In early studies on adjustment in cross-cultural settings, researchers conceptualized degree of adjustment as a unitary construct (e.g., Gullahorn and Gullahorn, 1962; Oberg, 1960; Torbiorn, 1982). It is interesting to note that early research in the area of job satisfaction and organizational commitment also conceptualized those variables as global, unitary phenomena; however, each has gradually been conceptualized and operationalized as a multifaceted construct (Black, Gregersen, 1989; Reichers, 1985; Smith et al., 1969; Wanous and Lawler, 1972).

Research in the 1980s (Black, 1988; Black and Stephens, 1989) suggests that there are at least three specific facets of international adjustment: (1) adjustment to work, (2) adjustment to interacting with host nationals, and (3) adjustment to the general environment. Both factor analyses and mean-level differences within subjects regarding these possible facets suggest that international adjustment may not be a unitary construct. Because adjustment appears to be multifaceted, it follows logically that different antecedents to adjustment may have different impacts on each facet of adjustment. There is preliminary evidence that global antecedents are most strongly related to global facets and specific antecedents are most strongly related to specific facets. For example, Black (1988) found that although job variables (e. g., role ambiguity and role conflict) were related to work adjustment, they were not related to general adjustment. Thus, regarding the various propositions derived from the framework presented, we would expect that the specific variables within the 'job' factors and the 'organization culture' factors, would be most strongly related to degree of work adjustment compared to their relationship with degree of interaction or general adjustment. Likewise, we would expect that the specific variables within the 'nonwork' factors would have their strongest relationship with general and interaction adjustment rather than with work adjustment (see legend to Figure 3).

Although the domestic adjustment literature has focused primarily on work adjustment, degree of domestic adjustment might also be conceptualized as multifaceted. In fact, the work, interaction, and general facets of international adjustment might also be descriptive of domestic adjustment. At this point, there is little evidence to accept or reject this multifaceted

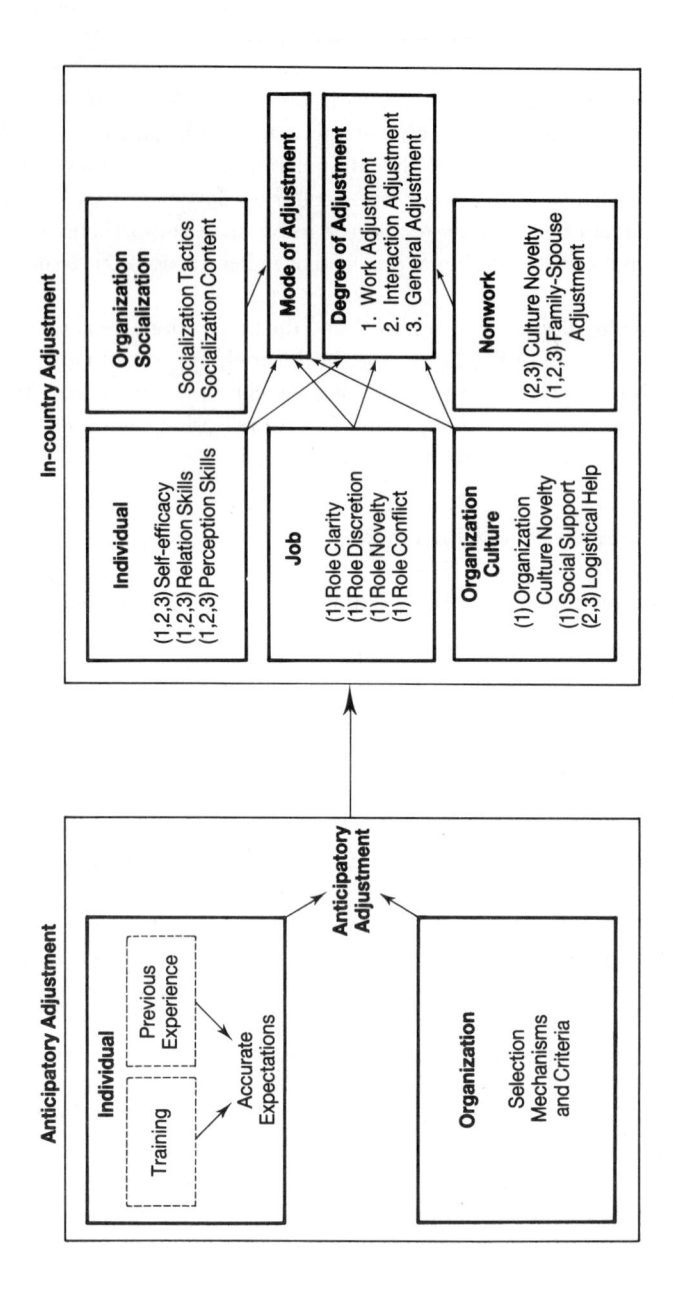

Figure 3. Framework of International Adjustment. (Numbers in parentheses indicate the numbered facet(s) of adjustment to which the specific variable is expected to relate.)

concept of domestic adjustment. However, there is logical reason to believe that it is less relevant to domestic adjustment in comparison to international adjustment.

For example, although a person might argue that adjusting to interacting with people from New England is difficult when that individual is from southern California, there is a substantial difference in degree, if not kind, between that interaction and interacting with people from China, whose language, religion, political system, values, daily customs, family structure, economic system, and general world view are significantly different from those in the United States. The same argument could be made regarding general adjustment. To the extent that these facets of adjustment are at least differences in substantial degree between domestic and international adjustment, it raises the probability that the different facets of international adjustment could have greater differential influences on outcome variables relative to domestic adjustment.

For example, general and interaction adjustment might be much stronger predictors of organizational commitment, intent to leave, or turnover in the case of international adjustment versus domestic transitions. Although we have argued that the multifaceted conceptualization of international adjustment is an important change for future research in this area, and perhaps more important than in the domestic adjustment literature, the lack of systematic empirical evidence leaves the question open for future research.

PROPOSITIONS FOR FUTURE RESEARCH

Anticipatory adjustment

Perhaps one of the greatest contributions gained by examining the domestic adjustment literature for understanding international adjustment concerns the notion of anticipatory adjustment. The basic premise is that if appropriate anticipatory adjustments are made, the actual adjustment in the new international setting will be easier and quicker.

Individual factors

The notion of anticipatory adjustment can be separated into specific factors related to the individual. Work in the socialization, surprise and sensemaking areas suggests that the accuracy of the expectations held by individuals is a key to effective anticipatory adjustment and actual adjustment. The more accurate expectations individuals can form, the more uncertainty they will reduce and the better their anticipatory adjustment will be. The better the anticipatory adjustment, the fewer surprises and negative affective reactions or less culture shock individuals will experience, the more appropriate behaviours and attitudes they will exhibit, and the smoother and quicker their adjustment will be. However, in the case of international adjustments, there are several distinct areas about which individuals might form expectations: (1) the job, (2) the organizational culture, (3) the host-country nationals, (4) the general culture, and (5) daily life in the foreign country (Black, 1988; Bochner, 1982; Brislin, 1981). Based on the previous discussion about facets of adjustment, we would expect, for example, that accurate expectations concerning the job would be most strongly related to the 'work' facet of international adjustment.

Proposition 1. Accurate expectations will be positively related to anticipatory adjustment and to degree of international adjustment and specific types of expectations will have their strongest relationship with conceptually similar facets of degree of international adjustment.

On the basis of the international adjustment literature, it seems reasonable to argue that previous international experience may be an important source of information from which accurate expectations can be formed (Church, 1982). Based on the underlying notion of uncertainty reduction described above, we would expect that several previous international adjustment experiences would provide more information from which uncertainty could be reduced and accurate expectations formed. Additionally, if the previous experiences were in the same (or a similar) culture to the one the individual will enter, they would be a better source from which accurate expectations could be made than previous experiences in a dissimilar culture. Similarly, if the previous experiences were work related, they would facilitate the formation of accurate work expectations, and if the previous experiences were not work related (e.g., study abroad as a student), they would facilitate the formation of nonwork expectations (Church, 1982; Stening, 1979). Although studies of adjustment after a domestic relocation transfer by Pinder and Schroeder (1987) failed to find a significant correlation between the number of previous domestic transfers and adjustment, studies of cross-cultural adjustment by Torbiorn (1982) and Black (1988) provide some support for the following proposition. This difference may stem from the greater number of adjustments that are involved in a cross-cultural adjustment versus a domestic adjustment and, consequently, the number of lessons that may be learned from previous international experiences and applied to the current international transition.

Proposition 2. Previous work-related experiences will facilitate the formation of accurate work expectations, and previous nonwork experiences will facilitate the formation of accurate nonwork expectations.

Just as frequent and relevant previous experiences can facilitate the formation of accurate expectations, so too can predeparture cross-cultural training. Essentially, cross-cultural training provides individuals with useful information for reducing uncertainty associated with the impending international transfer and for forming accurate expectations about living and working in the prospective host country. It is important to note that such training does not necessarily need to be company-sponsored; it could be self-initiated. (This may be important for future empirical research because most US firms do not provide predeparture cross-cultural training.) Additionally, this training need not immediately precede the international transfer, though we would expect more recent training would have the strongest effect (Black and Mendenhall, 1990; Brislin and Pedersen, 1976). (For a more detailed discussion of what types of cross-cultural training would be expected to be more or less effective, see Black and Mendenhall, 1990.)

Proposition 3. Predeparture cross-cultural training will be positively related to accurate expectations.

Organization factors

During the anticipatory phase, perhaps the most important organization factors are the selection criteria and mechanisms. Research in the socialization area suggests that the closer the selected individual matches the needs of the firm, the easier the individual's adjustment after entering the firm. It has already been mentioned that most US MNCs use one dimension (domestic job track record) in selecting individuals for overseas assignments and most do not select the candidate from a pool of competitive or comparable candidates. Thus, we would expect expatriates who have been selected on the basis of a wide array of relevant criteria and from a pool of candidates will experience the easiest and quickest cross-cultural adjustment.

Proposition 4. Individuals who have been selected based on a wide array of relevant criteria will experience easier and quicker cross-cultural adjustment compared to individuals who have been selected on the basis of only job-related criteria.

Proposition 4A. US MNCs that select expatriates based on a wide array of relevant criteria and from a pool of candidates will have lower rates of failed expatriate assignments and lower rates of ineffective expatriates than firms that do not employ these selection criteria or mechanisms.

IN-COUNTRY ADJUSTMENT

Integrating the domestic and international adjustment literatures with the notion of in-country adjustment is somewhat more complicated than was the case for anticipatory adjustment. This is because we must consider both mode of adjustment and degree of adjustment in examining the process of in-country adjustment.

Individual factors

The following three categories of individual factors relating to in-country adjustment were presented in the review article by Mendenhall and Oddou (1985): (1) self-oriented, (2) others-oriented, and (3) perceptual-oriented. One of the underlying issues of the various self-oriented skills discussed by Mendenhall and Oddou (1985) was the ability to believe in oneself and one's ability to deal effectively with the foreign surroundings, even in the face of great uncertainty. This idea is quite similar to what Bandura (1977) and others have consistently referred to as self-efficacy. According to the research on self-efficacy, individuals with higher levels of self-efficacy tend to persist in exhibiting new behaviours that are being learned, even when those efforts are not successful, longer than do individuals with less self-efficacy. The more individuals attempt to exhibit new behaviours in the foreign situation, the more chances they have of receiving feedback, both positive and negative. These individuals can then use this feedback to reduce the uncertainty of what is expected of them and how they are doing, and they can correct their behaviour to better correspond to the expectations. This process, in turn, would facilitate degree of adjustment. There may be an interaction effect between self-efficacy and need for feedback (e.g., self-efficacy has the greatest impact on adjustment for individuals with high needs for feedback, Nicholson, 1984), but it would be self-efficacy that would drive the person to persist in exhibiting new behaviours which, in turn, would facilitate degree of adjustment.

Proposition 5. Self-efficacy will have a positive relationship with degree of adjustment.

Proposition 5A. Self-efficacy will have its strongest relationship with adjustment for individuals who also have a high need for feedback.

Relational skills also provide an important means of increasing the cues individuals receive about what is expected and how they are doing regarding those expectations. Consequently, these skills can reduce the uncertainty associated with the foreign environment. The greater individuals' relational skills, the easier it is for them to interact with host nationals (Mendenhall and Oddou, 1985). The more individuals interact with host nationals, the more information they can receive about what is and isn't appropriate in the host culture and how they are doing. Black (1988) found a positive relationship between percentage of time spent with host nationals and general cross-cultural adjustment.

Proposition 6. Relational skills will be positively related to degree of in-country adjustment.

Perceptual skills also provide a significant means of understanding what is appropriate and inappropriate in the host country; these skills, therefore, can reduce the uncertainty associated with the foreign environment. The greater individuals' perceptual skills, the easier it is for them to understand and correctly interpret the host culture (Mendenhall and Oddou, 1985).

Proposition 7. Perceptual skills will be positively related to degree of in-country adjustment.

The integration of the domestic adjustment literature provides a set of propositions regarding the relationship between individual factors and mode of adjustment that are new to the area of international adjustment. For example, Nicholson (1984) suggested that a high desire for control would lead to a mode of adjustment characterized more by adjustment through changing the situation rather than through changing the individual. Nicholson acknowledged that this concept is similar to internal locus of control or high self-efficacy. Thus, we would expect that individuals with high levels of self-efficacy would be more likely to utilize 'role innovation' as a means of adjustment than individuals with low levels of self-efficacy.

Proposition 8. High levels of self-efficacy will be associated with modes of adjustment that are directed at changing the environment (e.g., the work role), whereas low levels of self-efficacy will be associated with modes of adjustment characterized by changing the individual.

Job factors

The domestic adjustment literature, in particular, points to the importance of job factors for both degree and mode of adjustment. Regarding job-related variables after arrival in a host culture, theory and past research indicate that role clarity reduces the amount of uncertainty associated with the work situation, which, in turn, would facilitate adjustment at work (Black, 1988; Nicholson, 1984; Pinder and Schroeder, 1987). Theorists of domestic adjustment (Brett, 1980; Dawis and Lofquist, 1984; Nicholson, 1984) also have argued that role discretion allows individuals to adapt their work role and setting to themselves rather than adapting themselves to the situation. Accordingly, greater role discretion makes it easier for individuals to utilize previous behaviour patterns, which, in turn, reduces uncertainty in the new situation and facilitates adjustment in the novel setting.

Proposition 9. Role clarity and role discretion will be positively associated with international adjustment, especially work adjustment.

In contrast to the positive impact of role clarity and role discretion on work adjustment, conflicting signals about what is expected of individuals in a new work setting (e.g., role conflict) would be expected to increase uncertainty and inhibit adjustment. In a new cultural setting, conflicting signals can generate a high degree of uncertainty because individuals must first understand the messages and then decide which messages to follow or ignore. Once the conflicting messages are sorted out, individuals must then execute appropriate behaviours in the new work role. Additionally, role novelty, which is essentially the degree to which the current role is different from past roles, would increase the uncertainty associated with the job. Consequently, we would expect role novelty to have a negative relationship with adjustment (Black, 1988; Nicholson, 1984; Pinder and Schroeder, 1987). The work by Louis (1980a, b) suggests that one important source of role novelty might be the number of boundaries being traversed in the transfer (e.g., functional, hierarchical, inclusionary).

Proposition 10. Role conflict and role novelty will be negatively associated with international adjustment, especially work adjustment.

Although little empirical work has been conducted concerning Propositions 9 and 10, there seems to be preliminary evidence to support the facilitating effect of role clarity and role discretion and the inhibiting effect of role conflict and role novelty (Black, 1988; Black and Gregersen, 1989).

On the basis of the theoretical work by Nicholson (1984), we can speculate not only about the relationship between job factors and degree of adjustment but also about the relationship between certain job factors and mode of adjustment. Nicholson (1984, p.178) argued that 'high discretion roles...make it impossible simply to conform to job specifications, role descriptions, or practices of previous incumbents'. Therefore, high role discretion would lead to modes of adjustment characterized by efforts to change the situation.

Proposition 11. International transfers that involve high role discretion will be associated with individuals utilizing modes of adjustment characterized by efforts to change the situation (e.g., the work role), whereas international transfers that involve low role discretion will be associated with individuals utilizing modes of adjustment characterized by efforts to change themselves.

Nicholson (1984, p.178) also stated that low novelty in job demands would be associated with modes of adjustment focused on changing the work role because the similarity of the current role compared to the past role would provide 'little scope or pressure for change in the person's job-related skills or professional identity'.

Proposition 12. International transfers that involve low role novelty will be associated with individuals utilizing modes of adjustment characterized by efforts to change the situation (e.g., the work role), whereas international transfers that involve high role novelty will be associated with individuals utilizing modes of adjustment characterized by efforts to change themselves.

Organizational culture factors

Based on an integration of both the domestic and international adjustment literatures, three specific organizational culture factors emerge as important in the international adjustment process. First, just as job novelty was expected to increase uncertainty associated with the work role, organizational culture novelty would be expected to increase the uncertainty associated with the work environment in which the work role was carried out (Church, 1982; Mendenhall and Oddou, 1985; Stening, 1979). The greater the difference between the organizational culture of the subsidiary organization in the foreign country compared to the organization in the home country, the more difficult the international adjustment would be.

Proposition 13. High organizational culture novelty will be negatively associated with degree of international adjustment, especially work adjustment.

An organizational culture that included social support from co-workers and superiors in the subsidiary firm overseas would serve to provide newcomers (transferees) with information about what was acceptable and unacceptable in the new organizational setting. This would reduce uncertainty and thereby facilitate cross-cultural adjustment (Pinder and Schroeder, 1987).

Proposition 14. Social support from organizational members will be positively associated with degree of international adjustment, especially work adjustment.

Organizations differ in the degree and types of logistical support they provide employees involved in international transfers (Tung, 1984). Logistical support regarding housing, schools, grocery stores, and so on, could potentially reduce uncertainty associated with these significant issues (Baker and Ivancevich, 1971; Copeland and Griggs, 1985; Tung, 1988) and thereby facilitate adjustment (Torbiorn, 1982). Because most logistical support deals with nonwork issues, we would expect logistical support to have a stronger relationship with interaction, and especially general adjustment, rather than with work adjustment.

Proposition 15. Logistical support from the organization will be positively associated with degree of international adjustment, especially interaction and general adjustment.

Organizational socialization factors

The theoretical and empirical literature on organizational socialization has mainly focused on the relationship between organizational socialization tactics and mode of adjustment (Fisher, 1986; Jones, 1986; Van Maanen and Schein, 1979). As mentioned previously, Jones (1986) found support for a significant relationship between institutional socialization tactics and low role innovation as individuals' mode of adjustment and between individual socialization tactics and high role innovation as the mode of adjustment.

Proposition 16. Institutional socialization tactics will be associated with low role innovation, and individual socialization tactics will be associated with high role innovation as modes of adjustment during international transfers.

Although the theoretical arguments regarding socialization tactics presented by Van Maanen and Schein (1979) have influenced both theoretical thinking (e.g., Nicholson, 1984) and empirical work (e.g., Jones, 1986; Zahrly and Tosi, 1989), Fisher (1986), in her review of the literature, argued that in addition to socialization tactics the content of the socialization (or what individuals learn) is important. Thus, in one sense content messages can be communicated both through socialization methods and socialization content. For example, the implicit message of collective socialization tactics (based on Van Maanen and Schein, 1979) is that the roles into which the collective group are about to enter are sufficiently fixed so that it is possible to 'process' or socialize the group collectively. This, in turn, influences individuals to respond in a custodial manner (i.e., they do not try to change the definition or content of the role). Theoretically, however, it is possible for the content of the information communicated during the collective socialization process to encourage the group members to innovate and change things. For example, we expect that collective socialization tactics combined with content that encouraged group members to conform would lead to a custodial mode of adjustment, but collective socialization tactics combined with content that encouraged group members to change things would lead to more innovative modes of adjustment.

Proposition 17. Institutional socialization tactics and congruent content will be associated with low role innovation, and individual socialization tactics and congruent content will be associated with high role innovation as modes of adjustment during international transfers.

Nonwork factors

Whereas the role of organizational socialization factors stems from the domestic adjustment literature, the role of nonwork factors is derived from the international adjustment literature. In the same way that job novelty and organizational culture novelty were argued to increase uncertainty, so too would the general culture novelty of the host country (Church, 1982; Mendenhall and Oddou, 1985; Stening, 1979). The greater the difference between the culture of the host country compared to the home country, the more difficult would be the international adjustment. Because policies and procedures of the US parent company could dilute the impact of the novelty of the host culture, culture novelty is likely to be most salient in nonwork interactions and activities; therefore, we expect it to have its strongest impact on interaction and general adjustment.

Proposition 18. High culture novelty will be negatively associated with degree of international adjustment, especially interaction and general adjustment.

Bhagat (1983) has argued that nonwork variables can have a spillover effect on employees' adjustment. Perhaps the most important nonwork variable in the international adjustment of US expatriates is the adjustment of family members, especially the spouse, because most US expatriates are married (Black, 1988; Black and Stephens, 1989). We would expect that the uncertainty that could result from poor cross-cultural adjustment of a spouse would inhibit the expatriate's adjustment. In fact, in her survey of US MNC executives, Tung (1981) found that these executives believed that a spouse's inability to adjust to the foreign host culture was the number one reason for expatriate failures. Black (1988) and Black and Stephens (1989), in studies of two separate samples of US managers and spouses, found significant relationships between expatriate and spouse cross-cultural adjustment.

Proposition 19. Family adjustment, especially spouse adjustment, will be positively related to employee international degree of adjustment.

WHAT DID WE LEARN?

In conclusion, it is perhaps helpful to summarize what has been gained by this attempt to provide a theoretical framework of international adjustment. After a careful examination of the last two decades of research on international adjustment, it is clear that most of the work has been anecdotal or atheoretical in nature. Most empirical studies have tried to determine if certain factors were related to international adjustment without a theoretical map of which ones would be expected to be related or why. Given the early stage of development of the international literature in general, and the international adjustment literature in particular, this is perhaps understandable. However, it seems that the lack of an emphasis on theory in the area of international adjustment has perhaps inhibited the field from making as rapid or systematic advances as might otherwise have been possible. Based on the haphazard path of past empirical work over the past two decades, attempts to provide theoretical guidance are important at this stage of the literature's development.

Although the purpose of this paper has been to move toward a more comprehensive theoretical framework of international adjustment and not to provide a framework for both domestic and international adjustment, it is useful to examine some of the differences between the two. Although the fundamental theoretical process is similar between domestic and international adjustment, there are sufficient enough differences that lead to different variables moving from 'figure' to 'ground' and vice versa for each type of adjustment. For example, because of the generally greater magnitude and breadth of changes involved in international compared to domestic changes, it is expected that predeparture training, especially cross-cultural training (Black and Mendenhall, 1990), would be an important variable (i.e., figure) in international adjustment and much less important (i.e., ground) in domestic adjustment. Likewise, there is preliminary evidence that previous experience is important in international adjustment (Black, 1988) and not in domestic adjustment (Pinder and Schroeder, 1987). Additionally, there is evidence that the adjustment of the spouse is significantly related to the adjustment of the employee during international transfer (Black, 1988; Black and Stephens, 1989); this, in fact, seems to be the primary reason for failed international adjustments (Tung, 1981). In contrast, there is less evidence that the adjustment of the spouse has such a significant impact on the employee during domestic transitions.

We would also expect that culture novelty would be a more important variable during international compared to domestic transitions. Because there is greater variance in culture novelty between, as opposed to within, cultures (Hofstede, 1980), we would expect culture novelty to have a greater impact on adjustment during international transitions. Given the ease of misunderstandings and their serious consequences in a cross-cultural situation (Mendenhall and Oddou, 1985), we might also expect that perceptual skills would be a more important variable during international compared to domestic adjustment transitions. Similar arguments might be made for selection criteria or relational skills; however, the lack of sufficient empirical evidence in the areas of international and domestic adjustment leaves some of these 'figure' and 'ground' distinctions open to future research.

CONCLUDING COMMENTS

We believe that in addition to pointing out differences and some similarities between international and domestic adjustment that this investigation also provides general guidance for future research in both areas. In the past, scholars in the international adjustment area have relied primarily on the international adjustment literature, neglecting the domestic adjustment literature. We have argued that an integration of the two literatures provides a more comprehensive theoretical framework for understanding international adjustment and for guiding future research. For example, without integrating the domestic adjustment literature, issues such as anticipatory adjustment, job factors, and organizational factors might continue to be neglected as important predictors of the degree of international adjustment. An important agenda for future international adjustment research would be to attempt more longitudinal studies in order to examine the influence of anticipatory variables relative to in-country variables on in-country adjustment.

Also, few researchers (cf. Black, 1988) have included an examination of job variables; yet, certainly job variables are theoretically critical antecedents of in-country work adjustment. Additionally, without the integration of the domestic literature, researchers in the area of international adjustment might continue to neglect the issue of mode of adjustment and the individual and organizational factors that likely influence mode of adjustment. Little is known about how employees adjust to international transitions in terms of the extent to which they try to change themselves or their environment and the predictors of these different modes of adjustment. This would seem to be an important research agenda for the future.

The integration of the two literatures may also provide direction for future research on domestic adjustment. In the past, the domestic adjustment literature has focused on anticipatory adjustment and work-related issues, and perhaps it has underemphasized nonwork factors. Although nonwork factors may not play as important a role for domestic adjustment compared to international adjustment, they may add significantly to understanding the process. An important addition to the domestic adjustment research agenda may be the investigation of the role of organizational culture novelty. In light of the present importance of strong organizational cultures (i.e., widely shared and firmly held values), one research agenda from a domestic adjustment perspective would be to determine if similar organizational cultures involved in a domestic transfer (which should be related to a strong organizational culture) are positively related to degree of adjustment and if dissimilar organizational cultures are negatively related to degree of domestic adjustment.

Additionally, future empirical work in both areas may benefit from not only examining the methods of socialization but also from examining the content of the messages that are implicitly and explicitly communicated during the socialization process. As was mentioned previously, the international adjustment literature has neglected the issue of mode of adjustment and the role that organizational socialization tactics play. Although this is not true of the domestic adjustment literature, both literatures have neglected the issue of socialization content. Theoretically, socialization content may play as important, or perhaps even more important, a role than socialization tactics. This would seem to be an additional, important research agenda for scholars in both areas.

In conclusion, we believe that although the fundamental process of uncertainty reduction is a common theoretical thread between domestic and international adjustment, there are sufficient contextual differences that some antecedent variables move from figure to ground and vice versa in each type of adjustment. Additionally, the impact of adjustment on other outcome variables such as commitment, intent to leave, or turnover may be different for domestic and international adjustment. This would seem to be a fruitful area for future research. Finally, we believe that a comparison of domestic and international adjustment has contributed to a more comprehensive theoretical framework of international adjustment, but future comparisons and integration are needed to further refine and make more comprehensive theories of international and domestic adjustment.

REFERENCES

Abelson, R. (1976) 'Script Processing in Attitude Formation and Decision Making'. In Caroll, J. S. and Payne, J. S. (eds), *Cognition and Social Behaviour*, pp.33–46. Erlbaum, Hillsdale, NJ.
Adler, N. (1983) 'Cross-Cultural Management Research: The Ostrich and the Trend'. *Academy of Management Review*, **8**: 226–232.
Ashford, S. J. and Taylor, M. S.(1990) 'Understanding Individual Adaptation: An Intergrative Approach'. In Rowland, K. and Ferris, J. (eds), *Research in Personnel and Human Resource Management*, vol. 8 pp. 1–41. JAI Press, Greenwich, CT.
Baker, J. C. and Ivancevich, J. M. (1971) 'The Assignment of American Executives Abroad: Systematic, Haphazard, or Chaotic?' *California Management Review*, **13**(3): 39–44
Bandura, A. (1977) *Social Learning Theory*. Prentice-Hall, Englewood Cliffs, NJ.
Bhagat, R. S.(1983) 'Effects of Stressful Life Events on Individual Performance and Work Adjustment Progress Within Organizational Settings: A Research Model'. *Academy of Management Review*, **8**: 660–671.
Black, J. S. (1988) 'Work Role Transitions: A Study of American Expatriate Managers in Japan'. *Journal of International Business Studies*, **19**: 277–294.
Black, J. S. and Gregersen, H. B. (1989) 'Antecedents of Adjustment and Turnover in Overseas Assignments'. *Proceedings of the Eastern Academy of Management*: 158–160.
Black, J. S. and Mendenhall, M. (1990) 'Cross-Cultural Training Effectiveness: A Review and Theoretical Framework for Future Research'. *Academy of Management Review*, **15**: 113–136.
Black, J. S. and Stephens, G. K. (1989) 'The Influence of the Spouse on American Expatriate Adjustment in Overseas Assignments'. *Journal of Management*, **15**: 529–544.
Bochner, S. (1982) *Cultures in Contact: Studies in Cross-Cultural Interaction*. Pergamon Press, New York.
Brein, M. and David, K. H. (1971) 'Intercultural Communication and Adjustment of the Sojourner'. *Psychological Bulletin*, **76**: 215–230.
Brett, J. M. (1980) 'The Effect of Job Transfers on Employees and their Families'. In Cooper, C. L. and Payne, R. (eds), *Current Concerns in Occupational Stress*, pp. 99–136. Wiley, New York.
Brief, A. P., Aldag, R. J., Van Sell, M. and Melone, N. (1979) 'Anticipatory Socialization and Role Stress Among Registered Nurses'. *Journal of Health and Social Behaviour*, **20**: 161–166.
Brislin, R. W. and Pedersen, P. (1976) *Cross-Cultural Orientation Programmes*. Gardner Press, New York.
Brislin, R. W. (1981) *Cross-Cultural Encounters*. Pergamon Press, New York.
Church, A. T. (1982) 'Sojourner Adjustment'. *Psychological Bulletin*, **9**: 540–572.
Copeland, L. and Griggs, L. (1985) *Going International*. Random House, New York.
Dawis, R. V. and Lofquist, L. H. (1984) *A Psychological Theory of Work Adjustment*. University of Minnesota Press, Minneapolis.
Feldman D. (1976) 'A Contingency Theory of Socialization'. *Administrative Science Quarterly*, **21**: 433–452.
Feldman, D. C. and Brett. J. M. (1983) 'Coping With New Jobs: A Comparative Study of New Hires and Job Changers'. *Academy of Management Journal*, **26**: 258–272.
Festinger (1956) *A Theory of Cognitive Dissononce*. Stanford University Press, Stanford, CA.
Fiedler, F., Mitchell, T. and Triandis, H. (1971) 'The Culture Assimilator: An Approach to Cultural Training'. *Journal of Applied Psychology*, **55**: 95–102.
Fisher, C. (1986) 'Organizational Socialization: An Integrative Review'. *Research in Personnel and Human Resource Management*, **4**: 101–145. JAI Press, Greenwich, CT.
Gullahorn, J. R. and Gullahorn, J. E. (1962) 'An Extension of the U-Curve Hypothesis'. *Journal of Social Issues*, **3**: 33–47.
Hays, R. D. (1974) 'Expatriate Selection: Insuring Success and Avoiding Failure'. *Journal of International Business Studies*, **5**(1): 25–37.
Hofstede, G. (1980) *Culture's Consequences*. Sage, Beverly Hills, CA.
Jones, G. R. (1986) 'Socialization Tactics, Self-Efficacy, and Newcomers' Adjustment to the Organization'. *Academy of Management Journal*, **2**: 262–279.
Kyi, K. M. (1988) 'APJM and Comparative Management in Asia'. *Asia Pacific Journal of Management*, **5**: 207–224.
Lagner, E. (1978) 'Rethinking the Role of Thought in Social Interactions'. In Hervey, J. H., Ickes, W. and Kid, R. F. (eds). *New Directions in Attribution Research*, pp. 35–58. Erlbaum, Hillsdale, NJ.

Latack, J. C. (1984) 'Career Transitions within Organizations: An Exploratory Study of Work, Nonwork, and Coping'. *Organizational Behaviour and Human Decision Processes*, **34**: 296–322.

Louis, M. R. (1980a) 'Career Transition: Varieties and Commonalities'. *Academy of Management Review*, 5: 329–340.

Louis, M. R. (1980b) 'Surprise and Sense Making: What Newcomers Experience in Entering Unfamiliar Organizational Settings'. *Administrative Science Quarterly*, **25**: 226–251.

Mendenhall, M., Dunbar, E. and Oddou, G. R. (1987) 'Expatriate Selection, Training, and Careerpathing: A Review and Critique'. *Human Resource Management*, **26**: 331–345.

Mendenhall, M. and Oddou, G. (1985) 'The Dimensions of Expatriate Acculturation: A Review'. *Academy of Management Review*, **10**: 39–48.

Miller, E. K. (1973) 'The International Selection Decision: A Study of Some Dimensions of Managerial Behaviour in the Selection Decision Process'. *Academy of Management Journal*, **16**: 239–252.

Misa, K. F. and Fabricatore, J. M. (1979) 'Return on Investment of Overseas Personnel'. *Financial Executive*, **47**(April): 42–46.

Mitchell, T. R., Dossett, D., Fiedler, F. and Triandis, H. (1972) 'Cultural Training: Validation Evidence for the Cultural Assimilator'. *International Journal of Psychology*, **7**: 97–104.

Moran, Stahl, and Boyer, Inc. (1987) *International Human Resource Management*. Moran, Stahl, and Boyer, Inc, Boulder, CO.

Nicholson, N. (1984) 'A Theory of Work Role Transitions'. *Administrative Science Quarterly*, **29**: 172–191.

O'Brien, G. E., Fiedler, F. E. and Hewett, T. (1970) 'The Effects of Programmed Culture Training Upon the Performance of Volunteer Teams'. *Human Relations*, **24**: 209–231.

Oberg, K. (1960) 'Culture Shock: Adjustment to New Cultural Environment'. *Practical Anthropologist*, **7**: 177–182.

Pinder, C. C. and Schroeder, K. G. (1987) 'Time to Proficiency Following Transfers'. *Academy of Management Journal*, **30**: 336–353.

Reichers, A. (1985) 'A Review and Reconceptualization of Organizational Commitment'. *Academy of Management Review*, **10**: 465–476.

Schein, E. H. (1971) 'The Individual, the Organization, and the Career: A Conceptual Scheme'. *Journal of Applied Behavioural Science*, **7**: 401–426.

Schollhammer, H. (1975) 'Current Research in International and Comparative Management Issues'. *Management International Review*, **13**(1): 17–31.

Smith, P. C., Kendall, L. M. and Hulin, C. L. (1969) *The Measurement of Satisfaction in Work and Retirement: A Strategy for the Study of Attitudes*. Rand McNally, Chicago.

Stening, B. W. (1979) 'Problems of Cross-Cultural Contact: A Literature Review'. *International Journal of Intercultural Relations*, **3**: 269–813.

Torbiorn, I. (1982) *Living Abroad*. Wiley, New York.

Tung, R. (1981) 'Selecting and Training of Personnel for Overseas Assignments'. *Columbia Journal of World Business*, **16**(2): 68–78.

Tung, R. (1982) 'Selecting and Training Procedures of US, European, and Japanese Multinational Corporations'. *California Management Review*, **25**(1): 57–71.

Tung, R. (1984) *Key to Japan's Economic Strength: Human Power*. Lexington Books, Lexington, MA.

Tung, R. (1988) *The New Expatriates: Managing Human Resources Abroad*. Ballinger, Cambridge, MA.

Van Maanen, J. and Schein, E. (1979) 'Toward a Theory of Organizational Socialization'. In Staw, B. M.(ed.), *Research in Organizational Behaviour*. vol. 1, pp. 209–264. JAI Press, Greenwich, CT.

Wanous, J. P. and Lawler, E. E. (1972) 'Measurement and Meaning of Job Satisfaction'. *Journal of Applied Psychology*, **56**: 95–105.

Whetten, D. (1989) 'What Constitutes a Theoretical Contribution?' *Academy of Management Review*, **14**: 490–495.

Zahrly, J. and Tosi, H. (1989) 'The Differential Effect of Organizational Induction Process on Early Work Role Adjustment'. *Journal of Organizational Behaviour*, **10**: 59–74.

23

Managing Globally Competent People

Nancy J. Adler and Susan Bartholomew

Top-level managers in many of today's leading corporations are losing control of their companies. The problem is not that they have misjudged the demands created by an increasingly complex environment and an accelerating rate of environmental change, nor even that they have failed to develop strategies appropriate to the new challenges. The problem is that their companies are incapable of carrying out the sophisticated strategies they have developed. Over the past 20 years, strategic thinking has far outdistanced organizational capabilities.[1]

Today, people create national competitiveness, not, as suggested by classical economic theory, mere access to advantageous factors of production.[2] Yet human systems are also one of the major constraints in implementing global strategies. Not surprisingly therefore, human resource management has become 'an important focus of top management attention, particularly in multinational enterprises'.[3]

The clear issue is that strategy (the *what*) is internationalizing faster than implementation (the *how*) and much faster than individual managers and executives themselves (the *who*). 'The challenges (therefore) are not the 'whats' of what-to-do, which are typically well-known. They are the 'hows' of managing human resources in a global firm'.[4]

How prepared are executives to manage transnational companies? How capable are firms' human resource systems of recruiting, developing, retaining, and using globally competent managers and executives? A recent survey of major US corporations found only 6% reporting foreign assignments to be essential for senior executive careers, with 49% believing foreign assignments to be completely immaterial.[5]

Which firms are leading in developing globally competent managers and executives, and which remain in the majority and lag behind? That majority, according to a recent survey of 1500 CEOs, will result in a lack of sufficient senior American managers prepared to run transnational businesses, forcing US firms to confront the highest executive turn-over in history.[6]

This article recommends changes in global human resource management at two levels: individual and systemic. First, from an individual perspective, it recommends skills required by individual managers to be globally competent, highlighting those which transcend the historic competencies required of international and expatriate managers. Second, from a systems perspective, it recommends a framework for assessing globally competent human resource systems. It then shows that the majority of North American firms have much room for improvement in developing both globally competent managers and globally effective human resource systems.

Reprinted with permission from *Academy of Management Executive*, Vol. 6, No. 3, pp. 52–65.
Copyright © 1992 Academy of Management Executive.

By contrast, it describes the approaches of some of the world's leading firms that distinguish them from the majority. There is no question that world business is going global; the question raised in this article is how to create human systems capable of implementing transnational business strategies. Based on their research, the authors support the conclusion of the recent *21st Century Report* that 'executives who perceive their international operations as shelves for second-rate managers are unsuited for the CEO job in the year 2000, or indeed any managerial job today'.[7]

TRANSNATIONALLY COMPETENT MANAGERS

Not all business strategies are equally global, nor need they be. As will be described, a firm's business strategy can be primarily domestic, international, multinational, or transnational. However, to be effective, the firm's human resource strategy should be integrated with its business strategy. Transnational firms need a transnational business strategy. While superficially appearing to be a truism, transnational firms also need a transnational human resource system and transnationally competent managers.

As summarized in Table 1, transnationally competent managers require a broader range of skills than traditional international managers. First, transnational managers must understand the worldwide business environment from a global perspective. Unlike expatriates of the past,

Table 1. Transnationally Competent Managers

Transnational skills	Transnationally competent managers	Traditional international managers
Global perspective	Understand worldwide business environment from a global perspective	Focus on a single foreign country and on managing relationships between headquarters and that country
Local responsiveness	Learn about many cultures	Become an expert on one culture
Synergistic learning	Work with and learn from people from many cultures simultaneously	Work with and coach people in each foreign culture separately or sequentially
	Create a culturally synergistic organizational environment	Integrate foreigners into the headquarters' national organizational culture
Transition and adaptation	Adapt to living in many foreign cultures	Adapt to living in a foreign culture
Cross-cultural interaction	Use cross-cultural interaction skills on a daily basis throughout one's career	Use cross-cultural interaction skills primarily on foreign assignments
Collaboration	Interact with foreign colleagues as equals	Interact within clearly defined hierarchies of structural and cultural dominance
Foreign experience	Transpatriation for career and organization development	Expatriation or inpatriation primarily to get the job done

transnational managers are not focused on a single country nor limited to managing relationships between headquarters and a single foreign subsidiary. Second, transnational managers must learn about many foreign cultures' perspectives, tastes, trends, technologies, and approaches to conducting business. Unlike their predecessors, they do not focus on becoming an expert on one particular culture. Third, transnational managers must be skilful at working with people from many cultures simultaneously. They no longer have the luxury of dealing with each country's issues on a separate, and therefore sequential, basis. Fourth, similar to prior expatriates, transnational managers must be able to adapt to living in other cultures. Yet, unlike their predecessors, transnational managers need cross-cultural skills on a daily basis, throughout their career, not just during foreign assignments, but also on regular multicountry business trips and in daily interaction with foreign colleagues and clients worldwide. Fifth, transnational managers interact with foreign colleagues as equals, rather than from within clearly defined hierarchies of structural or cultural dominance and subordination. Thus, not only do the variety and frequency of cross-cultural interaction increase with globalization, but also the very nature of cross-cultural interaction changes.

The development of transnationally competent managers depends on firms' organizational capability to design and manage transnational human resource systems. Such systems, in turn, allow firms to implement transnational business strategies. Before investigating firms' capability to implement transnational business strategies, let us briefly review a range of global business strategies along with each strategy's requisite managerial skills.

THE GLOBALIZATION OF BUSINESS: STRATEGY, STRUCTURE, AND MANAGERIAL SKILLS

Since World War II, industry after industry has progressed from dominantly domestic operations toward more global strategies. Historically, many firms progressed through four distinct phases: domestic, international, multinational, and transnational.[8] As firms progress towards global strategies, the portfolio of skills required of managers undergoes a parallel shift.

Domestic

Historically, most corporations began as domestic firms. They developed new products or services at home for the domestic market. During this initial domestic phase, foreign markets, and hence international managerial skills, were largely irrelevant.

International

As new firms entered, competition increased and each company was forced to search for new markets or resign itself to losing market share. A common response was to expand internationally, initially by exporting to foreign markets and later by developing foreign assembly and production facilities designed to serve the largest of those markets. To manage those foreign operations, firms often restructured to form a separate international division. Within the new international division, each country was managed separately, thus creating a multidomestic nature. Because the foreign operations were frequently seen as an extension—and therefore a replication—of domestic operations, they generally were not viewed as state of the art.

During this international phase, a hierarchical structure exists between the firm's headquarters and its various foreign subsidiaries. Power and influence are concentrated at corporate headquarters, which is primarily staffed by members of the headquarters' national culture. It is during this phase that firms often send their first home country managers abroad as expatriates. Cross-cultural interaction between expatriate managers and local subsidiary staff thus takes place within a clearly defined hierarchy in which headquarters has both structural and cultural dominance.

During this phase, international management is synonymous with expatriation. To be effective, expatriate managers must be competent at transferring technology to the local culture, managing local staff, and adapting business practices to suit local conditions. Specifically, international expatriate managers require cultural adaptation skills—as does their spouse and family—to adjust to living in a new environment and working with the local people. They must also acquire specific knowledge about the particular culture's perspectives, tastes, trends, technologies, and ways of doing business. Learning is thus single country focused—and culturally specific—during the international phase.

Multinational

As competition continues to heighten, firms increasingly emphasize producing least-cost products and services. To benefit from potential economies of scale and geographic scope, firms produce more standardized products and services. Because the prior phase's multi-domestic structure can no longer support success, firms restructure to integrate domestic and foreign operations into worldwide lines of business, with sourcing, producing, assembling, and marketing distributed across many countries, and major decisions—which continue to be made at headquarters—strongly influenced by least-cost outcomes.

During the multinational phase, the hierarchical relationship remains between headquarters and foreign subsidiaries. In addition, with the increased importance of foreign operations to the core business, headquarters more tightly controls major decisions worldwide. However, headquarters' decisions are now made by people from a wider range of cultures than previously, many of whom are local managers from foreign subsidiaries posted on temporary 'inpatriate' assignments at corporate headquarters. These 'inpatriates' are not encouraged to express the diversity of national perspectives and cultural experience they represent. Rather, they are asked to adapt as the firm implicitly and explicitly integrates them into the organizational culture which is still dominated by the values of the headquarters' national culture. While multinational representation increases at headquarters, cultural dominance of the headquarters' national culture continues, remaining loosely coupled with structure.

For the first time, senior managers, those leading the worldwide lines of business, need to understand the world business environment. Similarly for the first time, senior managers must work daily with clients and employees from around the world to be effective. International and cross-cultural skills become needed for managers throughout the firm, not just for those few imminently leaving for foreign postings. Expatriates and 'inpatriates' still require cultural adaptation skills and specific local knowledge, but these are not the dominant international skills required by most managers in a multinational firm. For the majority, learning needs grow beyond local context to encompass a need to understand the world business environment.

In addition, multinational managers need to be skilled at working with clients and employees from many nations (rather than merely from a single foreign country), as well as at standardizing operations and integrating people from around the world into a common organizational culture.

Transnational

As competition continues to increase and product lifecycles shorten dramatically, firms find it necessary to compete globally, based simultaneously on state-of-the-art, top quality products and services and least-cost production. Unlike the prior phase's emphasis on identical products that can be distributed worldwide, transnational products are increasingly mass-customized—tailored to each individual client's needs. Research and development demands increase as does the firm's need for worldwide marketing scope.

These dynamics lead to transnational networks of firms and divisions within firms, including an increasingly complex web of strategic alliances. Internationally, these firms distribute their multiple headquarters across a number of nations. As a result, transnational firms become less hierarchically structured than firms operating in the previous phases. As such, power is no longer centred in a single headquarters that is coincident with or dominated by any one national culture. As a consequence, both structural and cultural dominance are minimized, with cross-cultural interaction no longer following any pre-defined 'passport hierarchy'. It is for these firms that transnational human resource strategies are now being developed that emphasize organizational learning along with individual managerial skills.

To be effective, transnational managers need both the culturally specific knowledge and adaptation skills required in international firms, and the ability to acquire a worldwide perspective and to integrate worldwide diversity required in multinational firms. As a consequence, one of the transnational manager's primary skills is to exercise discretion in choosing when to be locally responsive and when to emphasize global integration.

Moreover, the integration required in transnational firms is based on cultural synergy—on combining the many cultures into a unique organizational culture—rather than on simply integrating foreigners into the dominant culture of the headquarters' nationality (as was the norm in prior phases). Transnational managers require additional new skills to be effective in their less hierarchical, networked firms: first, the ability to work with people of other cultures as equals; second, the ability to learn in order to continually enhance organizational capability. Transnational managers must learn how to collaborate with partners worldwide, gaining as much knowledge as possible from each interaction, and, transmitting that knowledge quickly and effectively throughout the worldwide network of operations. This requires managers who both want to learn and have the skills to quickly and continuously learn from people of other cultures.[9]

TRANSNATIONAL HUMAN RESOURCE SYSTEMS

The development of such 'transnationally competent managers', as discussed previously, depends upon firms' capability to design and manage transnational human resource systems. The function of human resource systems, in general, is to recruit, develop, and retain competent managers and executives. Beyond these core functions, we add utilization: human resource systems facilitate the effective 'utilization' of those managers who have been recruited, developed, and retained. Therefore, a transnational human resource system is one that recruits, develops, retains and utilizes managers and executives who are competent transnationally.[10]

Three Dimensions of a Transnational Human Resource System

For a transnational human resource system to be effective, it must exhibit three characteristics: transnational scope, transnational representation, and transnational process. We will describe each briefly, and then discuss their implications for recruiting, developing, retaining, and using human resources.

Transnational Scope

Transnational scope is the geographical context within which all major decisions are made. As Bartlett and Ghoshal have stated, global management is a 'frame of mind', not a particular organizational structure.[11] Thus, to achieve global scope, executives and managers must frame major decisions and evaluate options relative to worldwide business dynamics. Moreover, they must benchmark their own and their firm's performance against worldclass standards. They can neither discuss nor resolve major issues within narrower national or regional context. An example is Unilever's 'Best Proven Practices'. This British–Dutch consumer products firm identifies superior practice and innovations in its subsidiaries worldwide and then diffuses the outstanding approaches throughout the worldwide organization.[12]

Transnational Representation

Transnational representation refers to the multinational composition of the firm's managers and executives. To achieve transnational representation, the firm's portfolio of key executives and managers should be as multinational as its worldwide distribution of production, finance, sales, and profits. Symbolically, firms achieve transnational representation through the well balanced portfolio of passports held by senior management. Philips, for example, maintains transnational representation by having 'the corporate pool'. This pool consists of mobile individuals representing more than 50 nationalities, each having at least five years of experience and ranked in the top 20% on performance, and all financed on a corporate budget.[13]

Transnational Process

Transnational process reflects the firm's ability to effectively include representatives and ideas from many cultures in its planning and decision-making processes. Firms create transnational process when they consistently recognize, value, and effectively use cultural diversity within the organization; that is, when there is 'no unintended leakage of culture specific systems and approaches'.[14] Transnational process, however, is not the mere inclusion of people and ideas of many cultures; rather, it goes beyond inclusion to encompass cultural synergy—the combination of culturally diverse perspectives and approaches into a new transnational organizational culture. Cultural synergy requires 'a genuine belief…that more creative and effective ways of managing people could be developed as a result of cross-cultural learning'.[15] To create a transnational process, executives and managers must be as skilled at working with and learning from people from outside their own culture as with same culture nationals.

TODAY'S FIRMS: HOW TRANSNATIONAL?

A survey was conducted of 50 firms headquartered in the United States and Canada from a wide variety of industries to determine the extent to which their overall business strategy matched their current human resource system, as well as identifying the extent of globalization of their human resource strategies. The results paint a picture of extensive global business involvement. Unfortunately, however, similar involvement in recruiting, developing, retaining, and using globally competent managers is lacking.

Global strategic integration

The 50 firms made almost half of their sales abroad, and earned nearly 40% of their revenues and profits outside of their headquarters' country (the United States or Canada). Similarly, almost two fifths of the 50 firms' employees worked outside the headquarters' country. Yet, when these firms reviewed their human resource systems as a whole, and their senior leadership in particular, they could not reveal nearly as global a portrait.

For example, in comparing themselves with their competitors, the 50 firms found themselves to be more global on overall business strategy, financial systems, production operations, and marketing. However, they found their human resource systems to be the least global functional area within their own organization. Moreover, unlike their assessment in other functional areas, they did not evaluate their human resource systems as being more global than those of their competitors.

Similarly, the senior leadership of the surveyed firms was less global on all three global indicators—scope, representation, and process—than each firm's overall business performance. For example, an average of only eight countries were represented among the most senior 100 executives in each firm. Half of the companies reported fewer than four nationalities among the top 100 executives. Firms therefore have less than a quarter of the international representation in their senior leadership (8%) as they have in their global business performance (i.e., sales, revenues, and profits: 47%). Similarly, of the same top 100 executives in each firm, only 15% were from outside of North America. This represents less than half the internationalization of the senior executive cadre (15%) as of business performance (40%). Moreover, using experience, rather than representation, yields similar results. Of the same 100 leaders, almost three quarters lacked expatriate experience, with only a third reporting any international experience at all. Not surprisingly, less than one in five spoke a foreign language. On no measure of international experience is the senior leadership of these North American firms as international as the business itself.

Transnational human resource integration

Firms' organizational capability to implement transnational business strategies is supported by transnational human resource management systems. As discussed, such systems should exhibit all three dimensions—transnational scope, transnational representation, and transnational process. These three global dimensions are clearly important for each of the four primary components of human resource systems—recruiting, developing, retaining, and utilizing globally competent people. Each will therefore be discussed separately. Unfortunately, the results of this study indicate that firms' human resource management systems have not become global either as rapidly or as extensively as have their business strategies and structures.

Recruiting

For recruiting decisions, transnational scope requires that firms consider their business needs and the availability of candidates worldwide. Similar to the firm's strategic business decisions, some recruiting decisions must enhance worldwide integration and coordination, others local responsiveness, and others the firm's ability to learn.[16] Local responsiveness requires that firms recruit people with a sophisticated understanding of each of the countries in which they operate; this includes recruiting host nationals. Worldwide integration requires that recruiting be guided by worldclass standards in selecting the most competent people from anywhere in the world for senior management positions. Individual and organizational learning requires that people be selected who are capable of simultaneously working with and learning from colleagues from many nations: people who are capable of creating cultural synergy.

Transnational representation in recruiting requires that firms select managers from throughout the world for potential positions anywhere in the world. In a literal sense, it requires that talent flows to opportunity worldwide, without regard to national passport.

Transnational process in recruiting requires that firms use search and selection procedures that are equally attractive to candidates from each target nationality. Selection criteria, including the methods used to judge competence, must not be biased to favour any one culture.

Similarly, incentives to join the firm must appeal to a broad range of cultures. The antithesis of transnational process was exhibited by one US firm when it offered new college recruits from the Netherlands one of the same incentives it offers its American recruits: free graduate education. The Dutch candidates found this 'benefit' amusing given that graduate education in the Netherlands—unlike in the United States—is already paid for by the government and thus free to all students.

Rather than encouraging high potential candidates, this particular incentive made Dutch students hesitate to join a firm that demonstrated such parochialism in its initial contact with them.

The 50 surveyed firms reported that their recruitment and selection activities were less than transnational in terms of scope, representation, and process. In selecting future senior managers, the 50 firms ranked an outstanding overall track record as the most important criterion, with foreign business experience, demonstrated cultural sensitivity and adaptability, and a track record for outstanding performance outside the home country ranked as somewhat, but not highly, important. Moreover, foreign language skills were not considered at all important. Similarly, while considering three out of four transnational scope and process skills to be somewhat important for promotion to senior management (understanding world issues and trends;

working effectively with clients and colleagues from other countries; and, demonstrating cultural sensitivity), none was considered highly important. Once again, foreign language skills were not considered important for promotion. Similarly, on transnational representation, only a third of the 50 firms stated that they 'recruit managers from all parts of the world in which ... [they] conduct business'.

Development

In managerial development, transnational scope means that managers' experiences both on-the-job and in formal training situations prepare them to work anywhere in the world with people from all parts of the world; that is, it prepares them to conduct the firm's business in a global environment. Transnational firms search worldwide for the best training and development options and select specific approaches and programmes based on world-class standards.

To achieve transnational representation, training and development programmes must be planned and delivered by multinational teams as well as offered to multinational participants. To be transnational, programmes cannot be planned by one culture (generally representatives of the headquarters' nationality) and simply exported for local delivery abroad. By contrast, using a transnational approach, American Express created a multinational design team at headquarters to develop training approaches and programmes which were subsequently localized for delivery around the world. At no time did American cultural values dominate either the process or the programmes.

Transnational process in development requires that the approaches taken effectively include all participating cultures. Thus, the process cannot encourage greater participation by one nationality to the exclusion of other nationalities. Ericsson and Olivetti provide examples of a transnational development approach. Each company created a management development centre in which both the staff and executive participants come from all regions of the world. To minimize the possibility of headquarters' cultural dominance, neither company located its management development centre in the headquarters' country—Sweden or Italy—but rather both chose another more culturally neutral country.[17]

For transnational firms, foreign assignments become a core component of the organizational and career development process. 'Transpatriates' from all parts of the world are sent to all other parts of the world to develop their worldwide perspective and cross-cultural skills, as well as developing the organization's cadre of globally sophisticated managers. Foreign assignments in transnational firms are no longer used primarily to get a job done in a foreign country (expatriation) or to socialize foreign country nationals into the home country headquarters' culture ('inpatriation'), but rather to enhance individual and organizational learning in all parts of the system ('transpatriation'). Using a 'transpatriation' approach, Royal Dutch Shell, for example, uses multifunctional and multinational experience to provide corporate wide, transnational skills. Shell's 'aim is that every member of an operating company management team should have had international experience and that each such team should include one expatriate ... [Similarly, at IBM], international experience is [considered] indispensable to senior positions.[18]

In the survey, the 50 firms reported that their training and development opportunities were less than transnational on all three dimensions of human resource strategy: scope, representation, and process. Fewer than one in four of the firms reported that the content of their training programmes was global in focus, that they had representatives of many nations attending each programme, or that their programmes were designed or delivered by multinational training teams. Only 4% reported that cross-cultural training was offered to all managers. However, the firms did report offering a greater number of general development opportunities worldwide than specific international training programmes. A third of the firms provide equivalent development opportunities for managers worldwide and 42% provide such opportunities for managers of all nationalities.

In reviewing foreign assignments, the 50 firms reported using expatriates primarily to 'get the job done abroad', not to develop the organization, nor to develop the individual manager's career. Given their emphasis on getting the immediate job done, it is not surprising that they did not report consistently selecting the 'stars' (either high potential junior managers or very senior, top-performing executives) for expatriate positions. To increase globalization in their development programmes, the surveyed executives strongly recommended 'transferring different nationalities to different countries several times in their career' and 'making it clear to these employees that international assignments are important to career development'. However, to date, the majority of the surveyed firms do not have such recommended programmes in place.

Similar to recruitment, training and development approaches currently are not nearly as global as are overall business strategies. To reduce the gap between the relative globalization of firms' strategies and their less-than-global human resource systems, firms must learn how to recognize, value, and use globally competent managers. As one surveyed executive summarized, closing the gaps begins by having 'the key organizational development activity... focused on allowing people of different nationalities to meet and to get to know each other, and, through these linkages, to meet the needs of the company."

Retaining

Transnational scope in retaining managers means that decisions about career paths must consider the firm's needs and operations worldwide. Performance incentives, rewards, and career opportunities must meet world-class standards such that the firm does not lose its most competent people. Firms must benchmark excellence in their human resource systems against their most significant global competitors in the same ways that they assess the relative competitiveness of their research and development, production, marketing, and financial systems.

Transnational representation requires that organizational incentives and career path opportunities be equally accessible and appealing to managers from all nationalities. Firms with transnational human resource systems do not create a glass ceiling beyond which only members of the headquarters' nationality can be promoted.

Transnational process requires that the performance review and promotion systems include approaches which are equally appropriate to a broad range of nationalities. The process by which promotion and career path decisions are made should not be innately biased towards any one culture, nor should it exclude particular cultures. The underlying dynamic in transnational process is not to institute identical systems worldwide, but rather to use approaches which are culturally equivalent. Shell for example, ensures this transnational orientation by having managers' 'career home' be in 'a business function rather than a geographical place'.[19] As one surveyed senior executive summarized, firms considered to be outstanding in transnational human resource management are 'flexible enough in systems and practices to attract and retain the best people regardless of nationality'.

Utilizing

Transnational scope in utilization means that managers' problem solving skills are focused on the firm's worldwide operations and competitive environment, not just on the regional, national, or local situation. To assess the competitive environment in transnational human resource management, the 50 surveyed firms identified leading North American, European, and Asian companies. The top North American firm was perceived to be IBM, followed by General Electric, and Citicorp. The surveyed firms identified Royal Dutch Shell as the leading European firm, followed by Nestlé and Philips, along with British Petroleum and Unilever. Sony was selected as the leading Asian firm, followed by Honda, Toyota, and Mitsubishi. Yet, in reviewing the pattern of responses, a significant proportion of the surveyed firms do not appear to be benchmarking excellence in global human resource management at all, and an even greater number appear to be geographically limiting their perspective to a fairly narrow, parochial scope. For instance, almost a fifth of the surveyed firms (all of which are North American) could not name a single leading North American firm. Even more disconcerting, more than a third could not identify a single excellent European firm, and half could not name a single excellent Asian firm.[20]

Beyond scope, transnational representation in utilization means that managers and executives of many nationalities are included in the firm's critical operating and strategic planning teams. Managers from outside of headquarters are not 'out of sight and out of mind'; rather they are integrated into the worldwide network of knowledge exchange, continual learning, and action. For example, as Unilever's director of management development explains:

> In recent years, I have had several product group directors ... [want] an expatriate on the board of the local company. Not just because they haven't got a national, not just because it would be good for the expatriate, but because it would be good for the company to have a bit of challenge to the one-best-way of doing things.21

Transnational process in human resource utilization means that the organization culture does not inherently bias contributions from or towards any particular cultural group. The human resource system recognizes the firm's cultural diversity and uses it either to build culturally synergistic processes that include all cultures involved or to select the particular process that is the most appropriate for the given situation.

ILLUSIONS AND RECOMMENDATIONS

From the prior discussion, it is clear that transnational human resource systems are both fundamentally important for future business success and qualitatively different from prior approaches to human resource management. Equally evident is the fact that North American firms' human resource systems are not nearly as global as their business operations on any of the three fundamental human resource dimensions: transnational scope, transnational representation, and transnational process. Competitive demands appear to have 'outrun the slow pace of organizational change and adjustment ... [with] top management beginning to feel that the organization itself is the biggest barrier to competitive and strategic development'.[22] It is telling that in most cases the respondents found the survey itself to be important and yet very difficult to complete, primarily because their firms did not systematically collect or keep data on any aspect of global human resource management.

The remaining question is why. There appears to be a series of illusions—of mind traps— that are preventing firms from acting in a global manner, including recognizing the mental gap between their current human resource approaches and those necessary to succeed in a highly competitive transnational business environment. Many of the surveyed executives recognized that their firms simply 'lack global thinking' and 'lack global business strategies', largely due to the 'massive US imprint on human resource practices'. According to many of the American executives, firms must 'stop thinking that the world begins and ends at US borders', 'stop having a US expatriate mentality', and begin to 'realize that the world does not revolve around us'. This pattern of responses suggests the following seven illusions.

(1) *If business has gone well, it will continue to go well.* No, today is not like yesterday, nor will tomorrow be a projection of today. Business has fundamentally changed, and human resource systems must undergo similar transformational changes to stay relevant, let alone effective. As Kenichi Ohmae has pointed out, 'Today and in the twenty-first century, management's ability to transform the organization and its people into a global company is a prerequisite for survival because both its customers and competitors have become cosmopolitan'.[23]

(2) *We have always played on a level playing field and won.* No. The North American economies (and therefore North American firms) have had an advantage: they were the only developed economies left intact following World War II and were thus 'the only game in town'. Today, Asia, Europe, and the Americas each have highly competitive firms and economies, none of which will continue to prosper without being excellent at including people and business worldwide. As Ohmae has observed, 'The key to a nation's future is its human resources. It used to be its natural resources, but not any more. The quality and number of its educated people now determines a country's likely prosperity or decline'; so too with global firms.[24]

(3) *If we manage expatriates better, we will have an effective global human resource system.* No. Doing better at what was necessary in the past (expatriate management) is not equivalent to creating systems capable of sustaining global competitiveness today. Whereas the temptation is to attempt to do better at that which is known (in this case, the simple expatriation of managers), the real challenge is to excel at that which is new. Transnational firms need transnational human resource systems to succeed. Better managed expatriate transfers will only improve one small aspect of existing human resource management, not create an overall transnational system.

(4) *If we're doing something, we must be doing enough.* No. Focusing on only one of the three transnational dimensions—scope, representation, or process—is not enough to transform domestic, international, or multinational human resource approaches into truly transnational systems. Bringing a 'foreigner' onto the board of directors, for example, gives the illusion of globalization, but is insufficient to underpin its substance.

(5) *If 'foreigners' are fitting in at headquarters, we must be managing our cultural diversity well.* No. This is a multinational paradigm trap. In multinationals, foreigners must adapt to the headquarters' culture, including learning its native language. Multinationals typically see

cultural differences 'as a nuisance, a constraint, an obstacle to be surmounted'.[25] In transnational firms, all managers make transitions, all managers adapt, and all managers help to create a synergistic organizational culture which transcends any one national culture.

(6) *As national wealth increases everyone will become more like us.* No. To the extent that the world is converging in its values, attitudes, and styles of doing business, it is not converging on a single country's national pattern, even that of the world's wealthiest nation. 'The appealing "one-best-way" assumption about management, the belief that different cultures are converging at different paces on the same concept of organization, is dying a slow death'.[26] Moreover, transnational firms need to create transnational cultures that are inclusive of all their members, not wait for the world to converge on a reality that looks like any particular firm's national culture, even one that looks 'just like us'.

(7) *If we provide managers with cross-cultural training, we will increase organizational capability.* No. Increased cognitive understanding does not guarantee increased behavioural effectiveness, nor is enhanced individual learning sufficient for improved organizational effectiveness. Simply increasing the number of cross-cultural training programmes offered to individual managers does not ensure that they will actually use the skills on a regular basis, nor that the firm as a whole will benefit from the potentially improved cross-cultural interaction. To benefit, the individual must want to learn that which is not-invented-here and the organization must want to learn from the individual. To enhance organizational capability, managers must continually work with and learn from people worldwide and disperse that knowledge throughout the firm's worldwide operations.

Despite the seemingly insurmountable challenges, firms are beginning to address and solve the dilemmas posed by going global. To date, no firm believes it has 'the answer', the solution to creating a truly transnational human resource system. However, a number of firms are currently inventing pieces of the solution which may cohere into just such a system. For example, as John Reed, CEO of Citicorp, describes:

> There are few companies in the world that are truly global... Our most important advantage is our globality. Our global human capital may be as important a resource if not more important, than our financial capital. Look at the Policy Committee, the top thirty or so officers in the bank. Almost seventy-five percent have worked outside the United States; more than twenty-five percent have worked in three or more countries. Half speak two or more languages other than English. Seven were born outside the United States.[27]

Perhaps then, a primary role of transnational human resource executives today is to remain open to fundamental change and to continue to encourage the openness and experimentation needed to create truly global systems.

ACKNOWLEDGEMENTS

The authors would like to thank the Ontario Centre for International Business for generously funding this research. See 'Globalization and Human Resource Management', (Nancy J. Adler and Susan Bartholomew) in *Research in Global Strategic Management: Corporate Responses to Global Change*, Alan M. Rugman and Alain Verbeke (eds), Vol. 3 (Greenwich. Conn.: JAI Press, 1992) for further details of the research design and results of the study.

NOTES

1. Christopher A. Bartlett and Sumantra Ghoshal, 'Matrix Management: Not a Structure, a Frame of Mind' *Harvard Business Review*, July–August 1990: 138.
2. See Michael E. Porter. *The Competitive Advantage of Nations* (New York The Free Press, 1990).
3. Paul A. Evans, Yves Doz, and Andre Laurent, *Human Resource Management in International Firms* (London: Macmillan Press, 1989), pp.xi–1.
4. Ibid.; see also Gunnar Hedlund, 'Who Manages the Global Corporation? Changes in the Nationality of Presidents of Foreign Subsidiaries of Swedish MNCs During the 1980s', Working Paper (Institute of International Business and the Stockholm School of Economics, May 1990).
5. See Donald C. Hambrick, Lester B. Korn, James W. Frederickson, and Richard M. Ferry, *21st Century Report: Reinventing the CEO* (New York: Korn/Ferry and Columbia University's Graduate School of Business, 1989), pp.1–94.
6. Ibid.
7. Ibid., p.57.
8. See Nancy J. Adler and Fariborz Ghadar, 'International Strategy from the Perspective of People and Culture: The North American Context', in Alan M. Rugman (ed.), *Research in Global Strategic Management: International Business Research for the Twenty-First Century; Canada's New Research Agenda*, Vol. 1, (Greenwich, Conn.: JAI Press, 1990), pp.179–205; and 'Strategic Human Resource Management: A Global Perspective', in Rudiger Pieper (ed.), *Human Resource Management in International Comparison* (Berlin, de Gruyter, 1990), pp.235–260.
9. See Gary Hamel, Yves Doz and C. K. Prahalad, 'Collaborate With Your Competitors and Win', *Harvard Business Review*, **89**(1), 1989:133–139.
10. For a review of international human resource management, see Nancy J. Adler, *International Dimensions of Organizational Behaviour*, 2nd ed. (Boston: PWS Kent 1991); Peter J. Dowling 'Hot Issues Overseas', *Personnel Administrator*, 34(1), 1989: 66-72; Peter J. Dowling and R. Schuler, *International Dimensions of Human Resource Management* (Boston: PWS Kent, 1990); Peter J. Dowling and Denise E. Welch, 'International Human Resource Management: An Australian Perspective', *Asia Pacific Journal of Management*, 6(1), 1988: 39–65; Yves Doz and C. K. Prahalad, 'Controlled Variety: *A Challenge for Human Resource Management in the MNC'. Human Resource Management*, 25(1), 1986: 55–71; A. Edstrom and J.R. Galbraith, 'Transfer of Managers as a Coordination and Control Strategy in Multinational Firms', *Administrative Science Quarterly*, **22**, 1977: 248–263; Evans, Doz, and Laurent (1989), op. cit.; Andre Laurent, 'The Cross-Cultural Puzzle of International Human Resource Management', *Human Resource Management*, 25(1), 1986: 91–101; E. L. Miller, S. Beechler, B. Bhatt, and R. Nath, 'The Relationship Between the Global Strategic Planning Process and the Human Resource Management Function', *Human Resource Planning*, 9(1), 1986: 9–23: John Milliman, Mary Ann Von Glinow, and Maria Nathan, 'Organizational Life Cycles and Strategic International Human Resource Management in Multinational Companies: Implications for Congruence Theory', *Academy of Management Review*, 16(2), 1991: 318–339; Dan A. Ondrack, 'International Human Resources Management in European and North American Firms', *Human Resource Management*, 25(1), 1985: 121–132; Dan A. Ondrack, 'International Transfers of Managers in North American and European MNEs', *Journal of International Business Studies*, 16(3), 1985: 1–19; Vladimir Pucik, 'The International Management of Human Resources', in C. J. Fombrun, N. M. Tichy, and M. A. Devanna (eds), *Strategic Human Resource Management* (New York: Wiley, 1984); Vladimir Pucik and Jan Hack Katz, 'Information, Control and Human Resource Management in Multinational Firms', *Human Resource Management*, 25(1), 1986: 121–132; Rosalie Tung, *The New Expatriates: Managing Human Resources Abroad* (New York: Harper & Row 1988), and 'Strategic Management of Human Resources in Multinational Enterprises', *Human Resource Management*, 23(2), 1984: 129–143; among others.
11. Op. cit., 1990.
12. Unilever's 'Best Proven Practice' technique was cited by Philip M. Rosenzweig and Jitendra Singh, 'Organizational Environments and the Multinational Enterprise', *Academy of Management Review*, 16(2), 1991: 354, based on an interview that Rosenzweig conducted with Unilever.
13. See Paul Evans, Elizabeth Lank, and Alison Farquhar, 'Managing Human Resources in the International Firm: Lessons from Practice', in Paul Evans, Yves Doz, and Andre Laurent, 1989. op. cit., p.138.

14. Kenichi Ohmae, *The Borderless World: Power and Strategy in the Interlinked Economy* (New York: Harper Business, 1990), p.112.
15. Andre Laurent, op. cit., 1986, p.100.
16. See C. K. Prahalad and Yves Doz, *The Multinational Mission: Balancing Local Demands and Global Vision* (New York: Free Press, 1987); also, for a discussion of global integration versus local responsiveness from a business strategy perspective, see Michael E. Porter, 'Changing Patterns of International Competition', *California Management Review*, **28**(2), 1986, 9–40; and Christopher A. Bartlett, 'Building and Managing the Transnational: The New Organizational Challenge', in M. E. Porter (ed.) *Competition in Global Industries* (Boston: Harvard Business School Press, 1986), pp.367–401, who explicitly developed the concepts, along with initial work and elaboration by: Christopher A. Bartlett and Sumantra Ghoshal, *Managing Across Borders: The Transnational Solution* (Boston: Harvard Business School Press 1989); Yves Doz, 'Strategic Management in Multinational Companies', *Sloan Management Review*, **21**(2), 1980: 27–46; Yves Doz, Christopher A. Bartlett, C. K. Prahalad, 'Global Competitive Pressures and Host Country Demands: Managing Tensions in MNCs', *California Management Review*, **23**(3), 1981: 63–73; and Yves Doz and C. K. Prahalad, 'Patterns of Strategic Control Within Multinational Corporations', *Journal of International Business Studies*, **15**(2), 1984: 55–72.
17. See Evans, Lank and Farquhar, op. cit., 1989, p.119.
18. Ibid., 130–131, p.139.
19. Ibid., p.141.
20. An even more disconcerting display of ignorance was that four surveyed firms listed 3M, Citicorp, Ford and General Motors as European firms, and in another four responses Dupont, Eastman Kodak, Coca-Cola, and Wang were identified as leading Asian firms.
21. Evans, Lank, and Farquhar, op. cit., p.122.
22. Paul Evans and Yves Doz, 'The Dualistic Organization', in Evans, Doz and Laurent, op. cit., 1989, p.223; based on the earlier work of Doz, 'Managing Manufacturing Rationalization Within Multinational Companies', *Columbia Journal of World Business*, **13**(3), 1978: 82–94; Prahalad and Doz, op. cit., 1987.
23. *Beyond National Borders* (Homewood, Illinois: Dow Jones-Irwin, 1987), p.93.
24. Ibid., p1.
25. Evans, Lank and Farquhar, op. cit., p.115.
26. Ibid., p.115.
27. Noel Tichy and Ram Charan, 'Citicorp Faces the World: An Interview with John Reed', *Harvard Business Review*, November–December, 1990: 137.

24

Initial Examination of a Model of Intercultural Adjustment

Barbara Parker and Glenn M. McEvoy

The rapidly expanding global reach of many organizations has increased interest in the issue of employee adjustment to foreign cultures (Abe and Wiseman, 1983; Black *et al.*, 1991; Hammer *et al.*, 1978). The topic has gained significance for two primary reasons. First, increased interdependence of national economies has led organizations of every size to internationalize, and inexperience abroad often leads them to expatriate employees for learning purposes (Kobrin, 1984). Second, increasing evidence shows that inadequate adjustment to international assignments is costly both to organizations and individuals in terms of turnover, absenteeism, early return to the home country, and lower performance (Black, 1988; Copeland and Griggs, 1985: Tung 1982).

Prior studies have focused primarily on either individual background variables (Black and Gregersen, 1991; Hawes and Kealey, 1981; Ruben and Kealey, 1979; Stoner *et al.*, 1972) or situational variables (Gomez-Meija and Balkin, 1987; Tung, 1982) hypothesized to influence adjustment abroad. Situational variables have included some that were within direct organizational control (e.g., predeparture training) and some that were not directly controllable (e.g., the degree of cultural novelty or cultural toughness), creating interpretation difficulty for the findings. We argue below that a model of adjustment using three categories of antecedents—individual, organizational, and contextual—is more logically defensible and pragmatically useful than prior models.

Further, few prior studies have been of a large enough scope to consider the question of which variables have the greatest impact on adjustment abroad. In effect, the research at present succeeds at demonstrating the complexity of the intercultural adjustment process but is less successful at suggesting how this complexity might be understood and managed.

We believe that part of past confusion over the nature of the adjustment process is due to the fact that adjustment was considered a unitary concept by some researchers, and a multidimensional concept by others (Church, 1982; Torbiorn, 1982). Therefore, the present study assessed Black's (1988) recent view of intercultural adjustment as containing three related but conceptually distinct facets: work adjustment, interaction adjustment, and general living adjustment.

Overall, the three objectives of our study were to: (a) develop a conceptual model of intercultural adjustment that integrates and organizes prior empirical studies by individual, organizational, and contextual variables; (b) attempt to replicate Black's (1988) findings regarding the multidimensionality of the adjustment concept; and (c) test selected portions of the model of intercultural adjustment using a sample of 169 employees working in a total of 12 different countries.

THE LITERATURE OF INTERCULTURAL ADJUSTMENT

Intercultural adjustment is 'the degree of psychological comfort with various aspects of a host country' (Black and Gregerson, 1991, p. 463). Recent research initiated by Black (1988) and confirmed in subsequent empirical investigations with colleagues (Black, 1990; Black and Gregerson, 1991; Black and Stephens, 1989) suggests that adjustment abroad contains multiple related factors. According to Black, the factor most often considered important to employers is work adjustment, including adjustment to job responsibilities, supervision, and performance expectations.

However, in the intercultural setting, one also might expect to face new challenges associated with living in a new environment (general living adjustment, including adjustment to housing, food, shopping, etc.) and dealing with people from differing cultures (interaction adjustment, including adjustment to socializing and speaking with host country nationals both on and off the job). Accordingly, Black and his colleagues argue—based on factor analyses results and mean-level differences observed within subjects—that adjustment abroad includes a total of three conceptually distinct factors (Black *et al*, 1991). Of course, it is important that such findings be replicated by independent researchers, and that is one goal of the research reported in this paper.

Broadly speaking, our review of the literature suggests that there are three major categories of factors influencing the degree of intercultural adjustment: individual, organizational, and contextual. While many believe personality characteristics are important to individual expatriate success, there is little agreement as to which of many personality characteristics is the most important to study. Factors like honesty, integrity, sincerity, patience, open-mindedness, or persistence (Baker and Ivancevich, 1971; Hays, 1974; Kobrin, 1984) may inspire confidence and trust and thus improve interaction adjustment with others while personality traits of maturity, self-knowledge, and confidence, or a sense of humour (Ivancevich, 1968; Tung, 1982) may be important to work adjustment if they encourage the broad perspective often required in overseas assignments. Examples of frequently studied individual antecedents to work adjustment abroad also include anticipatory behaviour (Black and Gregerson, 1991; Torbiorn, 1982), demographic characteristics such as gender or age (Adler, 1987; Zeira and Banai, 1985), motivation to go abroad, predeparture knowledge of the host country, and prior international experience (Black, 1990; Ivancevich, 1968). This category of antecedent is directly within organizational control through the selection process. That is, if research demonstrates a relationship between prior international experience and adjustment overseas, then the organization can use such experience as one selection criterion in expatriate screening.

Examples of organizational practices researched or discussed in the adjustment literature include compensation and benefits, length of overseas assignments, promotion and career development policies, predeparture and repatriation training, contact with the home office, assignment of mentors back home, and so forth (Black *et al.*, 1991; Earley, 1987; Gomez-Meija and Balkin, 1987; Tung, 1982). Again, factors within this category are directly controllable by the organization and, if a relationship is found to exist, they suggest potentially useful ways for organizations to improve overseas adjustment.

The last category of adjustment antecedent—contextual—differs from the first two because variables in this category largely are beyond direct organizational control. It includes spouse or family adjustment (Black and Gregerson, 1991; Torbiorn, 1982; Tung, 1982) as well as culture toughness or culture novelty of the host country (Mendenhall and Oddou, 1985).

While potentially influencible by the organization (e.g., through predeparture orientation for the spouse and family, or by reducing the degree of novelty through longer assignments overseas), these variables generally have indirect effects on expatriate adjustment. Thus, finding a strong relationship between contextual factors and intercultural adjustment would suggest that adjustment is for the most part beyond the direct control of the organization.

To facilitate the literature review below, we outline in Figure 1 the overall model of expatriate adjustment we are proposing. It includes a multidimensional concept of intercultural adjustment as well as antecedents and consequences hypothesized to be related to adjustment.

Antecedents

Individual
Prior international experience
Work preparation/experience
   Education; Host language fluency
Demographic characteristics
   Gender; Nationality; Age
   Physical appearance; Health
Personality
   Extraversion; Open-mindedness;
   Empathy; Flexibility/adaptability
Self-efficacy
Perception and relation skills
Predeparture knowledge of host country
Motivation to go abroad
Free time spent with host country expatriates (vs. other expatriates)

Organizational
Compensation and benefits
Repatriation/career practices
   Promotion opportunities
Length of assignment
Extent of home office contact
   Mentor assignment
Relocation assistance
Work assignment
   Role clarity; Job challenge
Expatriate/repatriate training
Organizational culture
Organization size

Contextual
Urban/rural location
Family/spouse adaptation
Culture novelty

Adjustment
Work
General Living
Interaction

Consequences

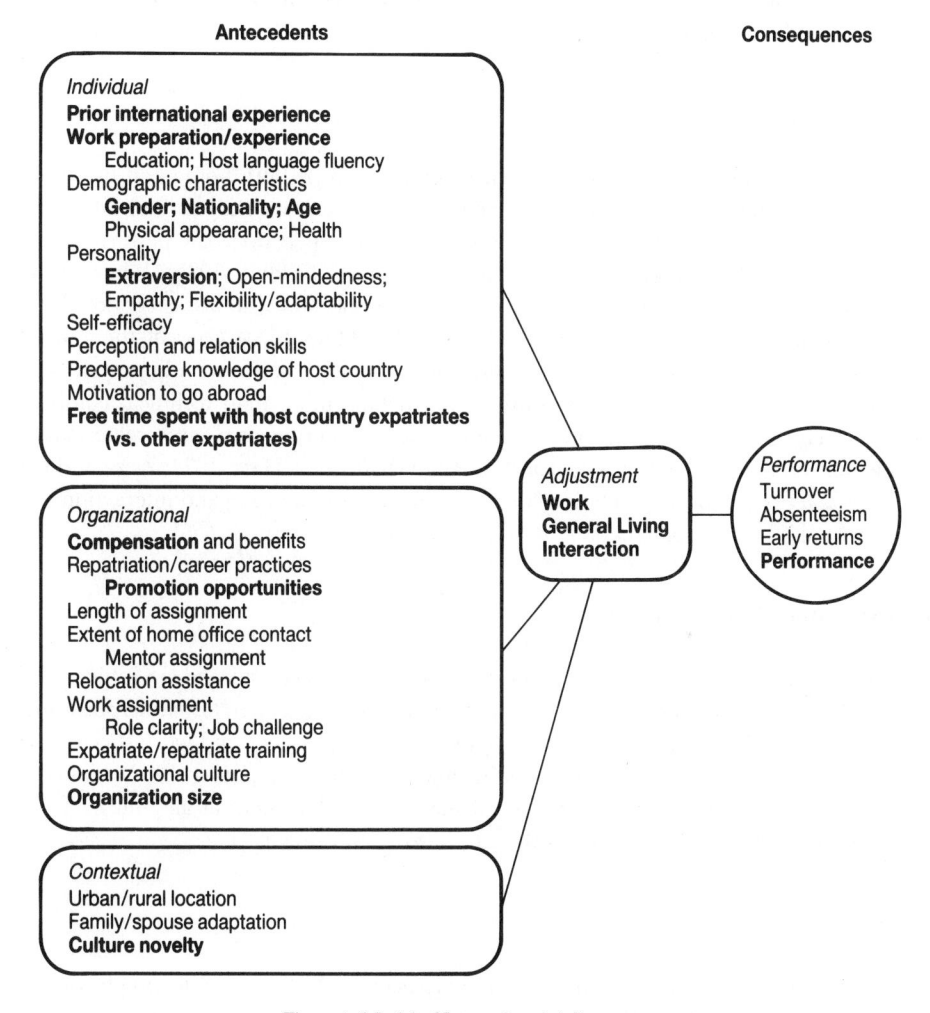

Performance
Turnover
Absenteeism
Early returns
Performance

Figure 1. Model of Intercultural Adjustment.
(Portions of this model tested in this study are identified by bold print.)

INDIVIDUAL BACKGROUND VARIABLES

The literature on individual background variables affecting adjustment can be organized around four major categories: prior international experience, work preparation/experience, demographic characteristics, and personality. The effect each might be expected to have on intercultural adjustment will be discussed in turn.

Prior international experience

Although there is inconsistency in the empirical findings relating to prior international experience, it is reasonable to assume that such experience reduces culture shock and allows quicker and more complete adjustment (Black, 1988; Black et al., 1991; Church, 1982). Since the prior international experience need not be one involving work (e.g., it could be extensive personal travel), one might expect that such experience would have a significant effect on general living and interaction adjustment, but little effect on work adjustment.

Work experience/preparation

Technical competence in assigned work is frequently rated by both home and host-country managers as the most important selection criterion for sending workers abroad (Miller, 1973; Zeira and Banai, 1985). Further, organizations often equate past domestic performance with future international work performance (Mendenhall and Oddou, 1985). Thus, selection research finds that organizations typically expatriate employees who are exceptionally well-qualified technically for their assigned work (Adler, 1987; Hays, 1974). Overall, then, this literature suggests the likelihood of a link between work experience and work adjustment abroad.

It should be noted that work preparation can include more than technical competence alone. it may, for instance, include development of interpersonal and relational skills (Mendenhall and Oddou, 1985) as well as host language fluency (Hays, 1974; Zeira and Banai, 1985). In such cases, a positive relationship between work preparation and interaction adjustment might also be anticipated.

Demographic characteristics

The relationship between personal characteristics and work success abroad is a subject of some debate. There is little agreement as to whether factors like age, gender, physical appearance or health, or nationality at birth aid or impede expatriate adjustment and work success (Adler, 1987; Church, 1982; Ivancevich, 1968; Stening and Hammer, 1989; Tung, 1982). Unlike work preparation or experience, demographics—if they affect adjustment at all—may have their greatest impact on adjustment factors other than work adjustment.

Gender

While North American men perceive foreigners (especially Asians) as preferring to work with other men, research suggests that in Asia and elsewhere local nationals increasingly view women working abroad in their work roles rather than in gender roles (Adler, 1987; Thal and Cateora, 1979). This being the case, a relationship between gender and work adjustment is not anticipated. However, relational skills have been suggested as precursors of adjustment to interaction with host-country nationals (Mendenhall and Oddou, 1985), and further appear to be present to a greater extent in women than in men (Adler, 1987), suggesting that there may be a relationship between gender and interaction adjustment.

Nationality

Early research on adjustment with foreign students noted that the nationality of the student seemed to be related to successful adjustment, particularly when used to estimate the degree of difference between home and host-country cultures (Church, 1982). Subsequently, several studies of expatriate adjustment and work abroad found that Americans failed more frequently than others in international assignments, becoming ineffective at work or returning early from the international posting (Black and Stephens, 1989; Earley, 1987; Stening and Hammer, 1989; Tung, 1988b). This high comparative failure rate suggests that nationality, in particular US versus non-US, may be related to intercultural adjustment.

Age

Based on a review of adjustment studies of foreign students, Peace Corps volunteers, businesspeople, and others, Church (1982) speculated that more mature expatriates may adjust better to other cultures. This speculation is theoretically plausible when one considers that job satisfaction is an important part of the work adjustment concept (Black *et al.*, 1991; Dawis and Lofquist, 1984) and that older workers are generally more satisfied with their job than younger workers (Brush *et al.*, 1987).

Personality and perceptual acuity

Some studies of workers abroad look at personality and perceptual acuity variables in an attempt to explain adjustment, and often adjustability itself has been viewed as a critical success variable (Ivancevich, 1968; Ratiu, 1983; Tung, 1982). Mendenhall and Oddou (1985), for example, noted that perceptual accuracy may be critical in sensing and interpreting cues in a foreign environment.

Frequently cited personality characteristics include broad- or openmindedness and cultural empathy (Abe and Wiseman, 1983; Hays, 1974; Kobrin, 1984; Ratiu, 1983), creativity and a sense of humour (Stoner, Aram and Rubin, 1972), integrity and sincerity (Habir and Conway, 1986; Ivancevich, 1968), and stress tolerance (Mendenhall and Oddou, 1985; Stening and Hammer, 1989). While personality traits such as open mindedness might be expected to relate to one or more facets of adjustment, research along these lines will be limited until operational definitions of such constructs develop. The personality trait of extroversion, though less frequently studied in expatriate adjustment research, is one of the most consistently useful dimensions in personality research (Digman, 1990). Extroversion is positively related to sociability and interpersonal involvement, and therefore we anticipate that it is also related to interaction adjustment abroad.

Other individual variables

Other individual factors that have been suggested include self-efficacy, perceptual and relational skills, motivation to go international, predeparture knowledge of host country, and percent of work and nonwork time spent with host-country nationals (Black, 1990; Black *et al.*, 1991; Habir and Conway, 1986). These factors are also worthy of future research.[1]

ORGANIZATIONAL VARIABLES

Whereas the research cited above has focused on individual explanations for expatriate adjustment abroad, other research suggests that adjustment may be more directly related to certain organizational policies and practices bearing on the expatriation/repatriation process (Gomez-Meija and Balkin, 1987; Habir and Conway, 1986; Tung, 1988a). Organizational policies and practices that have been suggested as critical include predeparture orientation and training, promotion opportunities and general repatriation procedures upon return to the home country, relocation assistance, compensation and benefits practices, work assignments and role clarity/conflict issues, and the extent of contact with the home office while abroad (Black *et al.*, 1991). Black (1988), for example, found that about 25% of expatriates left their parent companies within one year of return from the international posting, suggesting a possible flaw in repatriation policies and procedures.

Compensation policies

Compensation policies and practices may affect certain types of adjustment abroad. Expatriates—especially those from the US—often are well compensated for their work, both in direct pay and in perquisites such as home leave, income tax equalization, housing allowances, and cash premiums for 'hardship' posts. One estimate of the direct costs for American expatriate employees is three times the domestic salary plus relocation costs (Kobrin, 1988); another is two to five times what it would cost to employ a local national for the same work (Guptara, 1986). Added income or benefits, in addition to enhancing work adjustment, may free the expatriate and his or her family from some of the potential life-style difficulties that might otherwise be encountered in a foreign posting, such as helping the international worker purchase accustomed high-value consumer goods or permitting the individual and family to travel beyond the country of work to relieve stresses associated with living in that culture. Higher compensation should therefore enhance general living adjustment. At the same time, it may also encourage the expatriate to live so differently from the host-country nationals (i.e., in isolated expatriate communities) that interaction opportunities, and hence interaction adjustment, are impeded.

---

1. It should be noted here that many other potential personality and individual variables exist that may be predictive of cross-cultural adjustment. In the interest of parsimony, no attempt has been made to be fully exhaustive in listing these variables.

Repatriation practices

For American expatriates, the short-term benefits of better compensation plans may be offset by poor career and promotional opportunities upon repatriation. For example, a study of management succession in US companies found that international experiences and perspectives were not considered important to promotion in 114 of the 123 sampled firms. Conversely, interviews with Japanese, European, and Australian executives revealed that the international assignment was considered an important—perhaps *the* only important—avenue to organizational advancement (Tung, 1988a). Furthermore, neither returned US expatriates nor their personnel managers believe an international assignment is a step up on the career ladder (Gomez-Meija and Balkin, 1987; O'Boyle, 1989). This may explain some of the research cited earlier suggesting that US expatriates may be less well adjusted than their counterparts from other countries.

Organization size

The size of the employing organization is not a policy or practice choice in the same sense that expatriate compensation and repatriation orientation would be but it is within organizational control, and larger size may have a positive effect on intercultural adjustment. The likelihood of greater resources in larger organizations suggests they have other employees with adjustment experience to guide and counsel the new expatriate. In this sense, organization size may be a proxy for other organization practice variables, such as mentoring, that may be more directly related to adjustment but which are difficult to measure in a particular study.

Other organizational variables

Many other organizational factors have yet to be studied. For example, organizational culture offers a fruitful area for future research. We might expect that an organizational culture consistent with the host country's culture would positively affect adjustment. Similarly, another organizational practice that has drawn research attention in the adjustment literature is length of the international assignment. Length of time abroad could have an influence on one or more of the adjustment variables. US organizations typically send workers abroad for a limited time such as two to three years, whereas nationals from Western Europe and Japan often are posted abroad for six to eight years (McClenahen, 1987). Again, this difference in organizational expatriation policy may explain the differences some authors perceive in US versus non-US expatriate failure rates.

CONTEXTUAL VARIABLES

As noted above, this category of variables contains those that are basically beyond direct organizational control. For example, Church (1982) noted that Peace Corps volunteers seemed to have significantly more difficulty adjusting to rural assignments than to more urban ones. In a similar vein, Church noted that there was some support for an association hypothesis which suggests that more informal contact with host-country nationals leads to better expatriate adjustment. Contextual variables are included in the model to suggest that there may be antecedents of adjustment that managers can do nothing about, and in order to begin to understand what percentage of the variance in intercultural adjustment may be controllable and what percentage uncontrollable.

Family/spouse adjustment

Family adaptability to the international assignment frequently is viewed as an important influence on the worker abroad. For example, family-related problems and spousal maladjustment are two reasons cited for expatriate failure (Tung, 1982), but the exact nature of these relationships has been difficult to assess, since most reports of family adjustment problems are provided by the expatriate rather than the spouse, and hence may be biased and self-serving (Black and Gregerson, 1991). If a spouse or child objects to living conditions in the host country, the worker abroad, regardless of his or her personal ability to adapt, is likely to experience tensions in general adjustment. If the spouse's objections also extend to relationships with host nationals, interaction adjustment might also be lower for the worker abroad. Thus, the worker abroad may terminate the assignment even though work adjustment could be high because family maladjustment interferes with general and interaction adjustment.

Culture novelty

Depending on the expatriate's country of origin, some cultures are likely to be more difficult to adjust to than others. Known variously as 'cultural distance' (Church, 1982) or 'culture toughness' (Mendenhall and Oddou, 1985), research generally supports the view that the more different the host-country culture is from the home country culture, the more difficult the adjustment process is likely to be, especially during the first two years of an expatriate's posting (Black et al., 1991). While the effects of culture novelty are likely to be more pronounced in relation to interaction and general living adjustment, they may also show up in work adjustment due to the presence of host country nationals in the work setting.

ADJUSTMENT AND WORK PERFORMANCE

The model in Figure 1 also suggests several possible consequences of intercultural adjustment. Organizations are interested in expatriate adjustment because the failure to adjust may result in high turnover and absenteeism, early return to the home country, and possibly lower levels of work performance (Black, 1988; Copeland and Griggs, 1985; Tung, 1982). One of these potential relationships, that between adjustment and work performance, is explored in the empirical research reported below. The literature reviewed above is summarized in Figure 1. In order to explore this model, the following specific research hypotheses were developed:

(1) Prior international experience is positively associated with each facet of intercultural adjustment.
(2) Work experience/preparation is positively associated with work adjustment, but not with general living or interaction adjustment.

(3) Gender is not related to work adjustment, but men exhibit higher levels of general living adjustment and women higher levels of interaction adjustment.
(4) Americans are less well adjusted to international postings than are expatriates from other countries.
(5) There is a positive relationship between age and work adjustment, but not with interaction or general living adjustment.
(6) Personality traits associated with extroversion are positively related to interaction adjustment, but not to work or general living adjustment.
(7) The amount of time spent with host-country nationals is positively related to interaction and general living adjustment, but not related to work adjustment.
(8) Better-compensated expatriates exhibit higher levels of work and general living adjustment, but lower levels of interaction adjustment.
(9) Perceived promotability upon repatriation is positively related to work adjustment, but not to interaction or general living adjustment.
(10) Organizational size is positively associated with all three facets of intercultural adjustment.
(11) Culture novelty is negatively related to all three facets of intercultural adjustment.
(12) Job performance is positively related to work adjustment, but not to interaction or general living adjustment.

Method

Sample

The names of expatriates were randomly selected from printed sources that varied from country to country and included expatriate club membership rosters, Chamber of Commerce directories, organizational employment lists, and other published directories. Each individual received a cover letter, explaining study purposes and inviting participation, together with a three-page questionnaire. A total of 250 questionnaires were distributed to individuals working in business, government, and educational settings in 12 countries; 169 usable questionnaires were returned, for a total response rate of just over 63%. While most responses were from the individuals addressed, in a few cases the questionnaire had been passed along to others in the same company (usually a job replacement) or copied and returned by the respondent and by colleagues in other countries. We estimate that the latter practice resulted in about 10% of questionnaires returned. Respective sample sizes in the business, government, and education sectors were 67, 20, and 82. The 169 respondents thus assembled were living and working in 12 different countries. Seventy-four were located in Western Europe, 60 in Asia, and 35 in North or South America. While people from 21 nations responded to the questionnaire, US respondents outnumbered all others and were 62% of the sample ($n=103$). Average age was 36 years old, 65% of respondents were married, and 51% had children. Just over 57% of the sample were men.

The average reported age of expatriates for this study is lower than usual for expatriate business managers (see Black and Stephens, 1989) and the number of women in this study is higher than usual for a business sample (Adler, 1987). These differences may be partially attributed to the research design, since the sample included teachers (a traditional field for women) and non-US nationals who are usually sent abroad earlier in their careers (Tung, 1988a).

Measures

Adjustment. Black's 14-item scale (reported in Black and Stephens, 1989) was used to measure three types of adjustment: work adjustment, general living adjustment, and interaction with host-country nationals. Following Black, respondents were asked to report the degree of adjustment they felt toward specific job responsibilities at work (work adjustment), to conditions such as housing and food (general living), and to talking with and socializing with host nationals (interaction adjustment). Scale end points were anchored with 1 = 'not adjusted at all' and 7 = 'very well adjusted'. Black's scale contained three, seven and four questions respectively in each of the three adjustment factors, and the same questions were used here.

Responses on the 14 items used here were factor analysed using principal components extraction and varimax rotation in an effort to test the robustness of Black's assertion that adjustment consists of three conceptually distinct facets (Black, 1988; Black and Stephens, 1989). Results shown in Table 1 are supportive of Black's three-factor solution; no other factors with eigenvalues of one or greater were identified by the factor analysis. Based on the factor analysis for this study, and still following Black, each of the three adjustment subscales were formed by summing items loading on each factor. Coefficient alpha reliabilities for these scales were 0.75 for work adjustment, 0.74 for general living adjustment, 0.86 for interaction adjustment. These alphas are consistent with those reported by Black and Stephens (1989).

Individual factors. Prior international experience and work preparation were each assessed with single item objective-type questions: 'How many months have you lived abroad, including the present assignment?' (mean = 44.3 months) and 'How many years of experience do you have in this type of work?' (mean = 10.2 years).

The questionnaire included several demographic questions. Those examined empirically in this study were nationality, gender, and age. Nationality was measured with the question 'Of what country were you a citizen at birth?' Then, non-US respondents were coded 1 and US respondents were coded 0. Age was measured with the question 'How old were you on your last birthday?'

The Myers–Briggs Type indicator (MBTI) is a self-report inventory consisting of four scales, one of which is Extroversion–Introversion (E–I). Form F of the MBTI used here was published in 1962 and has been used subsequently in hundreds of reported studies (see Carlyn, 1977). The E–I index measures a person's orientation to life: extroverted types are primarily oriented to the outer world of people, action, and objects and tend to get involved with whatever is happening around them, while introverted types are more inwardly oriented and thus more detached from the world around them. The E–I scale is scored such that scores of less than 100 indicate extroversion, while higher scores reflect introversion.

MBTI scores can be converted to continuous scores; doing so for the E–I dimension as was done here shows scores of less than 100 to be extrovert scores and scores of more than 100 as introvert scores. Carlyn's (1977) review of empirical research on the MBTI shows continuous E–I measures to be internally consistent, stable, and content valid. The MBTI is typically administered only by those trained in the instrument's use, and individual feedback on MBTI scores is recommended. Honouring this recommendation limited MBTI use to settings where

Table 1. Factor analysis of 14-item adjustment scale

Scale item	1	2	3
Living conditions in general	0.80		
Housing conditions	0.81		
Food	0.73		
Shopping	0.73		
Cost of living	0.62		
Entertainment/recreation facilities and opportunities	0.57		
Health-care facilities	0.51		
Socializing with host nationals		0.82	
Interacting with host nationals in general		0.85	
Interacting with host nationals outside of work		0.89	
Speaking with host nationals		0.60	
Specific job responsibilities			0.79
Performance standards/expectations			0.88
Supervisory responsibilities			0.83
Eigenvalues:	5.98	1.66	1.51
Percent of variance explained:	42.80	11.90	10.80

Note: Loadings less than 0.40 are not reported.

the researchers were on site and able to provide feedback. As a result, the MBTI was administered to only a limited sample in this study ($n = 56$). Hence, results related to MBTI scores should be viewed as exploratory.

Respondents were asked to rate the extent to which they agreed they spent most of their free time with other expatriates rather than with host-country nationals. Response options for this single-item measure ranged from 1 = 'strongly disagree'; to 5 = 'strongly agree'.

Organisational factors. Income was measured by asking respondents to check one of 11 category ranges reflective of 1987 salary in approximate US dollars, starting with less than $10 000 and proceeding up to over $75 000.

Four questions measured promotional opportunities: 'I expect to advance in my firm when I repatriate'; 'Working abroad is a step up for me with the company'; 'Working abroad is necessary for career advancement in my company'; and 'Success in this job leads to promotions in the firm'. The promotional opportunities score was the average of the four items (alpha = 0.91).

As an indicator of organization size, respondents were asked how many people were employed by their organization in the host country.

Contextual factors. Hofstede's (1980) four dimensions of culture (power distance (PWR), individualism/collectivism (IND), masculinity/femininity (MAS), and uncertainty avoidance (UA)) were used to measure culture novelty. Average country scores reported by Hofstede—together with information on nationality and country of assignment provided by respondents—were used to calculate absolute difference scores. For example, where Hofstede reported an individualism score of 91 for the US and 46 for Japan, the absolute difference on the individualism score for an American living in Japan (or a Japanese living in the US) would be 45. The other three difference scores for an American in Japan were 14 (PWR), 46 (UA), and 33 (MAS), resulting in a total difference score of 138. Following this method, culture novelty difference scores were calculated for each person in the sample by comparing nationality to country of current assignment. Culture novelty ranged from a low of 22 (a Canadian in the US) to a high of 169 (a British citizen in Singapore).

Work performance. Specific antecedent variables were expected to relate to each of the three forms of adjustment, but in turn the three forms of adjustment were expected to explain some part of the variance in work performance. Respondents were asked to assess their own performance on four items proposed by Earley (1987): overall performance, ability to get along with others, ability to complete assignments on time, and quality of performance. Scales were anchored with 1 = 'poor' to 5 = 'excellent'. The measure used was the average of the four performance assessments (alpha = 0.93).

Analyses

Zero-order correlation coefficients, both Pearson and point-biserial, between variables were used to test most hypotheses. In addition, regression analyses were used to compare the effects of individual, organizational, and contextual variables on each of the three forms of adjustment. In the latter case, standardized beta weights are reported to facilitate comparability. Regression analysis also was used to examine how much variance in work performance was explained by the three forms of adjustment.

Results

Table 2 reports the means, standard deviations, and correlations for the 15 major variables in the study. The first seven hypotheses explored relationships between adjustment and individual variables; Hypotheses 8–10 explored relationships with organizational variables; Hypothesis 11 looked at the environmental variable of culture novelty. Results for these sets of hypotheses will be discussed in turn.

Individual factors and adjustment

Hypothesis 1 stated that international experience would be positively related to all three forms of adjustment, and the results show this to be the case. However, only the correlation between international experience and general adjustment was statistically significant ($r = 0.24$). Hypothesis 2 stated that work experience would be positively related to work adjustment but not to the other forms of adjustment. The pattern of results in Table 2 supports this hypothesis, but the results are not statistically significant.

The data in Table 2 show that neither gender nor age was significantly correlated with any of the three facets of intercultural adjustment, disconfirming Hypotheses 3 and 5. Nationality was positively correlated with general adjustment but negatively correlated (at roughly the same magnitude) with interaction adjustment, thus generally providing no support for Hypothesis 4.

Personality characteristics and traits showed a stronger relationship to adjustment than did demographic characteristics and work experience. As was suggested by Hypothesis 6,

Table 2. Means, standard deviations, and correlations for intercultural adjustment, antecedents, and performance

Variables	Mean (σ)	1	2	3	4	5	6	7	8	9	10	11	12	13	14
1. Work adjustment	5.98 (1.11)														
2. General adjustment	5.32 (0.94)	0.34**													
3. Interaction adjustment	5.13 (1.28)	0.32**	0.34**												
4. Extrovert/introvert[a]	102.2 (26.01)	−0.07	−0.12	−1.21*											
5. Gender (71F; 96M)[b]	0.57	−0.14	−0.02	−0.06	−0.09										
6. Age	36.4 (9.38)	0.06	−0.03	−0.02	0.12	0.21**									
7. Nationality[c] (103US)	0.38	−0.07	0.15*	−0.13	−0.07	0.02	−0.19**								
8. Work experience (mos)	121.5 (100)	0.06	−0.03	−0.01	0.04	0.26**	0.79**	−0.19*							
9. Intl. experience (mos)	44.36 (28.7)	0.05	0.24**	0.11	0.07	0.06	0.12	0.18*	0.02						
10. Time w/expatriates	3.27 (1.43)	−0.02	−0.15*	−0.30**	0.03	−0.08	0.05	−0.04	0.05	−0.17*					
11. Promotability of work	3.72 (2.1)	0.21**	−0.11	0.02	−0.14	−0.05	−0.17*	0.05	−0.19*	−0.14	−0.05				
12. Compensation	5.56 (4.31)	0.19*	−0.10	−0.03	−0.01	0.32**	0.22**	−0.09	0.25**	0.02	0.05	0.22**			
13. Culture novelty	77.92 (46.81)	−0.07	0.25**	−0.27**	0.03	−0.06	−0.14	0.35**	−0.16*	0.11	0.17*	−0.09	−0.31**		
14. Number of employees	618 (438)	−0.06	−0.13	−0.11	−0.08	0.15	−0.03	0.16	0.11*	−0.02	−0.07	−0.03	0.19*	−0.08	
15. Performance	4.37 (1.34)	0.23**	−0.08	0.08	−0.25**	−0.07	0.05	−0.22**	0.11*	−0.09	0.06	0.27**	0.15*	0.21**	−0.01

[a]100 is the division point between extrovert (<100) and introvert (>100); $n = 56$.
[b]Coded 0 = female, 1 = male.
[c]Coded 0 = US, 1 = non-US.
Note. $N = 157$–169; *$p < 0.05$; **$p < 0.01$

extraversion (scores of less than 100, as compared with introversion, which is scores greater than 100) was significantly correlated with interaction adjustment ($r = -0.21$), but not significantly correlated with work or general adjustment. Similarly, time spent with other expatriates (as opposed to with host-country nationals) correlated negatively with both general adjustment ($r = -0.15$) and interaction adjustment ($r = -0.30$), supporting Hypothesis 7.

Organizational factors and adjustment

Hypothesis 8 suggested there would be a positive relationship between compensation and work adjustment, and this relationship was confirmed by Table 2 results ($r = 0.19$). Compensation also was expected to be positively correlated with general adjustment and negatively correlated with interaction adjustment, but these relationships were not found. Hypothesis 9 argued that promotability of the work would correlate positively with work adjustment but not with general or interaction adjustment, and this hypothesis was confirmed. Contrary to expectations stated in Hypothesis 10, organizational size was not associated with any type of intercultural adjustment. Overall, organizational variables of compensation and promotability correlate moderately, but positively, with work adjustment.

Contextual factors and adjustment

The four dimensions of culture were totalled for the culture novelty score shown in Table 2. This aggregate measure of culture novelty showed mixed results. As was suggested by Hypothesis 11, interaction adjustment was significantly lower when culture novelty was high ($r = -0.27$). Conversely, and contrary to expectations, general living adjustment was positively associated with culture novelty. That is to say, the expatriates sampled here reported greater general living adjustment when culture differences with the home country were highest. This counter-intuitive result was explored by rerunning the regression analysis with the four component parts of culture novelty (individualism, power distance, uncertainty avoidance, and masculinity) disaggregated, but to no effect.[2]

Comparing individual, organizational, and contextual effects on adjustment

The manner in which individual, organizational, and contextual variables combine to explain intercultural adjustment was explored by means of regression analyses. In as much as age and work experience were highly correlated, age was not included in the regression equation. Since extraversion data had been collected from only a small part of the sample, this variable also was excluded from the analysis. Table 3 reports the results of a forced entry regression analysis of the three adjustment factors on individual (except age and extraversion), organizational, and contextual variables.

The results suggest that work adjustment is affected by gender, by compensation level, and by promotability of the work; general living adjustment is affected by international experience, time spent with other expatriates (vs. host-country nationals), and culture novelty; and

---

2. Similar regression analyses were generated for the other two forms of adjustment; results are available from the first author.

interaction adjustment is affected by time spent with expatriates and by culture novelty. The standardized beta weights shown in Table 3 demonstrate that when controlling for the effects of all other variables in the equation, neither demographic characteristics (except for gender) nor organization size account for any variance in intercultural adjustment. At the same time, these results show that gender, time spent with other expatriates, organizational practices associated with promotion and compensation, and the contextual factor of culture novelty all affect at least one of the facets of intercultural adjustment.

Table 3. Results of multiple regression analyses of adjustment abroad

Independent variables	Dependent variables[a]		
	Work adjustment	General living adjustment	Interaction adjustment
Gender	−0.21**	−0.03	−0.06
Work experience	0.09	0.01	−0.01
Nationality	−0.05	0.06	−0.07
International experience	0.03	0.20**	0.11
Time w/expatriates	−0.04	−0.17*	−0.26***
Promotability of work	0.16*	−0.14	−0.08
Compensation	0.21**	−0.03	−0.06
Culture novelty	−0.05	0.22**	−0.22**
Organization size (no. of employees)	−0.05	−0.12	−0.10
R^2	0.11	0.16	0.17
Adjusted R^2	0.07	0.12	0.12
F	2.34**	3.40***	3.48***

[a] $n = 169$.
*$p < 0.05$; **$p < 0.01$; ***$p < 0.001$.

Adjustment and work performance

Hypothesis 12 anticipated that work adjustment would positively affect work performance, and this expectation is supported by the results of both the zero-order correlation analysis reported in Table 2 ($r = 0.23$) and the regression analysis shown in Table 4. However, Table 4 also indicates an unexpected and negative relationship between work performance and general living adjustment. In other words, better work performance is associated with lower general living adjustment after controlling for the effects of variations in work adjustment.

Table 4. Multiple regression of performance on three forms of adjustment abroad

Independent variables	Performance[a] (DV)
Work adjustment	0.29***
General living adjustment	−0.18*
Interaction adjustment	0.06
R^2	0.08
Adjusted R^2	0.07
F	7.35***

[a] $n = 169$.
*$p < 0.05$; ***$p < 0.001$.

DISCUSSION

This paper presents a model of the process of intercultural adjustment and reports a preliminary investigation into some of the relationships suggested by the model. While the model suggests that organizations can exercise some direct control over individual and organizational variables affecting adjustment, the results reported above suggest that one non-controllable, contextual variable—culture novelty—explains as much variance in two facets of adjustment as do the more controllable variables. Thus, organizations need to be aware that some portion of expatriate adjustment may be beyond their direct control.

On the other hand, knowledge that culture novelty is a significant predictor of adjustment suggests that organizations may revise their international staffing policies to select third-country nationals for whom the country of assignment is not that different culturally from their own. Further, the results suggest that training to reduce the effects of culture novelty may also be useful when culture differences are great. If findings from this study are confirmed by subsequent research, they would further demonstrate the need for firms to take steps toward transnationalizing their work forces (Adler and Bartholomew, 1992).

Methodologically, this study successfully replicated the Black (1988) and Black and Stephens (1989) three-factor solution to the contempt of intercultural adjustment. There do indeed appear to be three conceptually distinct facets of expatriate adjustment that are worthy of independent study. It would be quite helpful, for example, to know which aspect of expatriate adjustment is most related to early returns from international assignments, or to high turnover rates upon repatriation. Further research along such lines is clearly needed.

Correlates of adjustment

Several specific relationships were supported by the research. Work adjustment appears to be affected primarily by organizational variables such as compensation level and perceived opportunities for promotion upon repatriation, but it also was shown that women in this sample tended to report higher work adjustment than did men. General living adjustment appears to be primarily a function of individual variables such as prior international experience and the amount of time spent with host-country nationals, as well as the degree of culture novelty. Thus, organizations can facilitate general adjustment through selection practices and by encouraging present expatriates to socialize more with host-country nationals and less with other expatriates. This could be accomplished through housing policies that encourage expatriates to live outside of expatriate communities or through job designs that require regular interaction with host-country nationals.

The finding that greater degrees of culture novelty were associated with greater, rather than lesser, general living adjustment is highly counterintuitive, and the finding frankly surprised us. Disaggregating the culture novelty score into its four component parts of individualism, power distance, uncertainty avoidance, and masculinity and rerunning the regression analysis for general living adjustment did nothing to ameliorate this surprise, but overall these results indicate a clear need for additional research to explore the culture novelty construct and its component parts.

If the relationship observed for overall culture novelty is corroborated in other research, it may be due to the anticipatory effects of clarifying expectations about living in another culture. Black et al. (1991) have discussed the effects of anticipatory adjustment and, based on a review of the literature, speculate that each facet of adjustment may be facilitated by improving the accuracy of expectations dealing with that particular facet. Most of the literature on other countries details the differences in food, housing, shopping, transportation, and the like. Expatriates can read this and prepare in advance for the culture shock to general living, possibly by lowering expectations or by arranging for the shipment of familiar creature comforts typically unavailable in the host country (e.g., cosmetics or tea). At the same time, the generally available literature on other countries is much less likely to specify the problems that expatriates will encounter on their specific jobs or in interacting with host-country nationals and therefore expatriates may be less likely to anticipate and prepare for such difficulties.

As expected, interaction adjustment was negatively related to time spent with other expatriates and with culture novelty, and higher levels of extroversion were associated with higher levels of interaction adjustment. In other words, extroverted personalities who spend more time with host-country nationals in a country that is not very different from their own exhibit the greatest degree of interaction adjustment. Again, organizations control some of the variables leading to interaction adjustment through selection, placement, and training practices.

Not surprisingly, self-rated job performance was most closely associated with work adjustment. After controlling for the effects of work adjustment, general living adjustment was also related to job performance, but negatively (see Table 4). Perhaps within any given level of work adjustment, poorer adjustment to general living conditions results in more commitment to the work itself (evidenced possibly by more time spent at work) and hence a higher level of self-perceived job performance. Conversely, the relationship may function in the opposite direction with greater work commitment leading to poorer adjustment to general living conditions. The latter is particularly plausible for those for whom work is the central life interest, for those who might be abroad without families, or for those who view life abroad as a stepping stone assignment to endure. Relationships between work and nonwork interests are generally viewed as complex (Cummings, 1982), with the cross-cultural context adding another layer of complexity. Clearly, more research is needed to substantiate this relationship.

Nationality and adjustment

Tung (1982; 1988b) identified poor adjustment for the expatriate as the number two reason for early recalls, and the high reported failure rate among US expatriates has apparently caused some firms to reduce their US expatriate work force (Kobrin, 1988; Tung, 1987). If Americans are viewed as failure prone in international work, firms from any country may forgo opportunities to hire highly qualified Americans for global positions. Without these experiences, employees may indeed become less adept interculturally and this could result in US firms whose domestic employees are less well positioned to develop long-run competitive strategies for an increasingly global business world.

Our sample provided no evidence to show that US expatriates were less well adjusted than non-US expatriates. In spite of limitations associated with comparing US to non-US expatriates, these are useful findings for firms that have hesitated to send US expatriates abroad for fear that they will not adjust. Further, these results suggest that adjustment to the international assignment may be more culture-general than nation-specific and may allay organizational fears that Americans will fail to adjust and return early from their expatriate assignments. In view of some amount of cultural convergence and much greater awareness of individual variation within nations, additional research on nationality is important.

Study limitations

One limitation of the study is the problem of common source-common method variance. With the exception of culture novelty and MBTI measures, all other data were collected via a single questionnaire from individual respondents. In this study, the problem was alleviated somewhat by inclusion of many objectively measured variables (e.g., years of experience, nationality, gender, compensation) and by placing related questions in different sections of the questionnaire to help reduce response set bias. Our self-reported measure of job performance is particularly susceptible to bias, and future research clearly needs to use more objective indices of performance before any solid conclusions about the relationship between adjustment and performance can be drawn.

A second limitation to our study was the sampling technique applied. Since part of the population of interest is not easily identified, we were forced to rely on sampling techniques that are difficult to replicate from one country to the next, thus reducing the generalizability of study findings. This limitation is not unusual in cross-cultural research and will be alleviated somewhat as additional business/government/academic research partnerships form to describe the expatriate population and otherwise explore international staffing issues.

A third limitation of the sample was our decision to restrict MBTI use to the small subset of our overall sample to whom we could provide feedback. This precluded using the personality trait of extraversion in our overall regression analysis, and thus may have biased the overall conclusions about the relative impact of individual versus organizational and contextual variables on interaction adjustment.

A final limitation to this study relates to the process aspects of adjustment. Our results indicate that different antecedents may influence each of the three facets of expatriate adjustment, but cross-sectional research such as this is limited in its ability to distinguish cause and effect and to determine the nature of the underlying processes at work. Therefore, we recommend longitudinal research supplemented with qualitative data-gathering approaches for future studies of the intercultural adjustment process. This will both help organizations determine how best to facilitate adjustment to the international adjustment and produce a richer view of how expatriates adjust or fail to adjust in the international assignment.

The conceptual model developed here integrates prior research to capture some of the complexity associated with intercultural adjustment abroad. Further, the partial test of our model described here identified relationships among variables to enhance practice and lead to future research. Both expected and unexpected results from this study suggest that the level of complexity ordinary to organizations is increased in a cross-cultural context where other factors also can be expected to vary. In view of increasing internationalization, and despite the limitations associated with this type of research, there is an increased need for studying complex relationships such as those included in this initial examination of a model for intercultural adjustment.

ACKNOWLEDGEMENTS

The authors wish to thank colleagues abroad who assisted in data collection, and to thank two anonymous reviewers whose comments made substantial contributions to this paper's revision.

REFERENCES

Abe, M. and Wiseman, R. (1983) 'A Cross-Cultural Confirmation of the Dimensions of Intercultural Effectiveness'. *International Journal of Intercultural Relations*, **7**: 53–69.

Adler, N. J. (1987) 'Pacific Basin Managers: A Gaijin, not a Woman'. *Human Resource Management*, **26**: 169–91.

Adler, N. J. (1991) *International Dimensions of Organizational Behaviour* (2nd ed.). PWS-Kent, Boston.

Adler, N. J., and Bartholomew, S. (1992) 'Managing Globally Competent People'. *Academy of Management Executive* **6**: 52–65.

Baker, J. C. and Ivancevich, J. M. (1971) 'The Assignment of American Executives Abroad: Systematic, Haphazard or Chaotic?' *California Management Review*, **13**: 39–44.

Black, J. S. (1988) 'Work Role Transitions: A Study of American Expatriate Managers in Japan'. *Journal of International Business Studies*, **19**: 277–294.

Black, J. S. (1990) 'Factors Related to the Adjustment of Japanese Expatriate Managers in America'. *Research in Personnel and Human Resource Management*, Supp. 2, pp. 109–125, JAI Press.

Black, J. S. and Gregerson, H. B. (1991) 'The Other Half of the Picture: Antecedents of Spouse Cross-Cultural Adjustment'. *Journal of International Business Studies*, **22**: 461–477.

Black, J. S., Mendenhall, M., and Oddou, G. (1991) 'Toward a Comprehensive Model of International Adjustment: An Integration of Multiple Theoretical Perspectives'. *Academy of Management Review*, **16**: 91–317.

Black, J. S. and Stephens, G. K. (1989) 'The Influence of the Spouse on Expatriate Adjustment and Intent to Stay in Assignments'. *Journal of Management*, **15**: 529–544.

Brush, M. J., Moch, M. K., and Pooyan, A. (1987) 'Individual Demographic Differences and Job Satisfaction'. *Journal of Occupational Behaviour*, **8**: 139–155.

Carlyn, M. (1977) 'An Assessment of the Myers-Briggs Type Indicator'. *Journal of Personality Assessment*, **41**: 461–473.

Church, A. T. (1982) 'Sojourner Adjustment'. *Psychological Bulletin*, **91**(3): 540–572.

Copeland, L. and Griggs, L. (1985) *Going International*. Random House, New York.

Cummings, L. L. (1982) 'Organizational Behaviour'. *Annual Review of Psychology*, **33**: 541–579.

Dawis, R. V. and Lofquist, L. H. (1984) *A Psychological Theory of Work Adjustment*. University of Minnesota Press, Minneapolis.

Digman, J. M. (1990) 'Personality Structure: Emergence of the Five-Factor Model'. *Annual Review of Psychology*, **41**: 417–440.

Earley, P. C. (1987) 'Intercultural Training for Managers: A Comparison of Documentary and Interpersonal Methods'. *Academy of Management Journal*, **3**: 685–698.

Gomez-Meija, L. and Balkin, D. (1987) 'The Determinants of Managerial Satisfaction with the Expatriation and Repatriation Process'. *Journal of Management Development*, **6**: 7–17.

Guptara, P. (1986) 'Searching the Organization for the Cross-Cultural Operators'. *International Management*, **41**: 40–42.

Habir, A. D. and Conway, B. (1986) 'The Successful Expatriate: How to Cope in Indonesia'. *Euro-Asia Business Review*, **5**: 47–51.

Hammer, M. R., Gudykunst, W. B. and Wiseman, R. L. (1978) 'Dimensions of Intercultural Effectiveness: An Exploratory Study'. *International Journal of Intercultural Relations*, **2**: 382–393.

Hawes, F. and Kealey, D. J. (1981) 'An Empirical Study of Canadian Technical Assistance'. *International Journal of Intercultural Relations*, **5**: 239–258.

Hays, R. D. (1974) 'Expatriate Selection: Insuring Success and Avoiding Failure'. *Journal of International Business Studies*, **5**: 40–46.

Hofstede, G. (1980) *Culture's Consequences: International Differences in Work-Related Values*. Sage Publications, Beverly Hills, CA.

Ivancevich, J. M. (1968) 'The American Manager Representing Large US Industrial Corporations: A Study of Selected Staffing Steps and Job Attitudes'. *Dissertation Abstracts*, **29**: 3726. (University Microfilms, No. AAD69-0763).

Kobrin, S. J. (1984) '*International Expertise in American Business.*' Institute of International Education, New York.

Kobrin, S. J. (1988) 'Expatriate Reduction and Strategic Control in American Multinational Corporations'. *Human Resource Management*, **27**: 63–75.

McClenahen, J. (1987) 'Why U.S. Managers Fail'. *Industry Week*, **235** (Nov. 16):71–74.

Mendenhall, M. and Oddou, G. (1985) 'The Dimensions of Expatriate Acculturation: A Review'. *Academy of Management Review*, **10**: 39–47.

Miller, E. L. (1973) 'The International Selection Decision: A Study of Some Dimensions of Managerial Behaviour in the Selection Decision Process'. *Academy of Management Journal*, **16**: 239–252.

O'Boyle, T. (1989) 'Little Benefit to Careers Seen in Foreign Stints'. *Wall Street Journal*, B1 (Dec. 11), B4.

Ratiu, I. (1983) 'Thinking Internationally: A Comparison of How International Executives Learn'. *International Studies of Management and Organization*, **13**: 139–150.

Ruben, B. D. and Kealey, D. J. (1979) 'Behavioural Assessment of Communication Competency and the Prediction of Cross-Cultural Adaptation'. *International Journal of Intercultural Relations*, **3**: 15–47.

Stening, B. W. and Hammer, M. R. (1989) 'The Cultural Context of Expatriate Adaptation: American and Japanese Managers Abroad'. *Proceedings of the Academy of Management*, 121–125.

Stoner, J. A. F., Aram. J. D. and Rubin, I. M. (1972) 'Factors Associated With Effective Performance in Work Assignments'. *Personnel Psychology*, **25**: 303–318.

Thal, N. L. and Cateora, P. R. (1979) 'Opportunities for Women in International Business'. *Business Horizons*, December: 21–27.

Torbiorn, I. (1982) *Living Abroad*. Wiley, New York.

Tung, R. L. (1982) 'Selection and Training Procedures of US, European, and Japanese Multinationals'. *California Management Review*, **25**(1): 57–71.

Tung, R. L. (1987) 'Expatriate Assignments: Enhancing Success and Minimizing Failure'. *Academy of Management Executive*, **1**: 117–126.

Tung, R. L. (1988a) 'Career Issues in International Assignments'. *Academy of Management Executive*, **2**: 241–244.

Tung, R. L. (1988b) *The New Expatriates: Managing Human Resources Abroad*. Ballinger, Cambridge, MA.

Zeira, Y. and Banai, M. (1985) 'Selection of Expatriate Managers in MNCS: The Host-Environment Point of View'. *International Studies of Management and Organization*, **15**(1): 33–51.

Index

Acer Group 278
Adaptation 40–1
Administrative heritage 87
Advantage exploitation 81
Advantage seeking 81
Aerospace industry 123–4
Agency theory 175
Aggarwal, R. and Ghauri, P.N. 57
Alliances. *See* Business alliances
AMC 117, 123
API Systems Inc. 122
Apple 148
Argyris, C. and Schon, D.A. 165
Asahi Chemical 268
ASEAN 76
Asian business structures
  implications for Western companies 290–1
  interfirm networks 285–7
  network approach 285–92
Asset specificity 176
AT&T 44, 117, 119, 121, 160
Atlas Copco 74
Automatic washing machine 26–8
Ayoub, Sam 25

Baker, J.C. and Ivancevich, J.M. 329
Bank borrowing 254
Banking industry 121
Bartlett, C.A. 33, 37, 73, 74
Bartlett, C.A. and Ghoshal, S. xi, 47, 52, 53, 62, 85–99, 355
Bauer, M. and Cohen, E. 194
Beamish, P.W. *et al.* ix, x, xxii
Beijing Stone Group 275, 278
Berlin, Sir Isaiah 24
Black, J.S. 337, 374, 380
  and Mendenhall, M. 160
  and Stephens, G.K. 380
Blockmodelling 255
  analysis of industrial block assignments 266–9
  network structure 257–60
  patterns of relationships in 260–6
Boorstin, Daniel 22
Borys, B. and Jemison, D.B. 156
Bouvier, P.L. 65
Branch plan effect 19
Bridgestone
  acquisition of Firestone 107–8
  change in top management 106
  comparative performance 109
  emergence as major player 108
  expanding diversification 112

expansion as regional multinational 100–2
financial data 103
milestones in history of 101
planning for FDI in US 104–6
tire industry 100–14
Bridgestone Bekaert Steel Cord Company Ltd 112
Bridgestone Boshingomo Company Ltd 112
Bridgestone Cycle Company Ltd 112
Bridgestone Imperial Company Ltd 113
Bridgestone Liquefied Gas Company Ltd. 112
Bridgestone Machinery Company Ltd 112
Bridgestone Sports Company Ltd 113
British Petroleum 360
Business alliances
  characteristics of 183–5
  definitions 175
  formation 174–88
  future directions 185
  managing 321
  organizational properties 181–3
  ownership structure 152
  parties in 178–9
  purpose of 151, 178–9
  reasons for entering into 147–9
  scope of 174
  success factors 182–3
  theory 174–88
  typology of 179–81
Buyback arrangements. *See* Joint ventures

CAD/CAM 25, 43
Canon 146, 148
Capital costs 42–3
Career development process 358, 359
Carlyn, M. 374
Cartels 180, 183
Caterpillar 47
Centralization 34, 41, 53
Centre-centre stucture 58
Chandler, A.D. 191
Chandler, A.D. Jr., and Daems, H. 82
Charoen Pokphand Group 279
Cheating 129, 130
Chinese business 274–84
  American connection 283–4
  breaking with tradition 277–9
  capital as springboard 279–80
  dynastic succession 277
  family businesses 191, 195, 200–2, 205
  future directions 282–3
  knowledge arbitrage 280–2

Chinese Communist Party 281
Chinese culture 275–7
Chinese New Year bonuses 205
Church, A.T. 371
Citicorp 360
Clark, R. 193
Coalition Matrix 265
Coca-Cola 22, 45
Collaboration 178, 181, 184
  between competitors 146–54
  collegiality in 150
  proceeding with care 152–3
  reasons for 147–9
  safeguards against unintended informal transfers of information 149–50
  skills contribution in 149
  success factors 149
  transparency limitation 149–50
Commitment 133–4, 300
  psychology of 134
Communication(s) 9, 21
Company enthusiasm 81
Comparative advantage 42
Compensation policies and practices 370
Competence
  competition for 153–4
  vs. technology 149
Competition for competence 153–4
Competitive advantage 35–6, 41–5, 47
Competitive alliances 178, 180–1, 184
Competitive benchmarking 152
Competitive collaboration 146–54
Competitive risks 38
Competitive strategy 320
Competitiveness
  analysis 31
  Japanese *Keiretsu* 214, 224, 226
Computer-integrated manufacturing (CIM) 224
CONCOR blockmodelling algorithm 257–8
CONCOR partitioning 255–6
Confucian tradition 275–7
Consumer preferences 26–8
Contac 600 30
Contact Matrix 265
Contractual risks 39
Control systems 79
Cooperation
  and commitment trust 131–4
  concept of 126–8
  in international business 126–45
Cooperative international competition xiv–xv
Co-operatives 126, 178, 180, 183
Coordination 127
  interfirm 128
  under duress 127
Corporate culture 75, 81, 162–3

Cosmopolitanism 31
Creative analysis 27–8
Credibility problem 131
Cross-cultural human resource management 308–16
Cross-cultural training (CCT) 160, 359
Cultural control 75
Cultural differences 71, 121
Cultural distance 330, 372
Cultural synergy 354
Culture gap 160
Culture novelty 330
Culture toughness 330, 372
Currency risks 39
Customization 31

Daewoo 148
Dai-Ichi Kangyo 248, 257, 268
Dai-Ichi Kokuritsu Bank 249
Daimler–Benz 155, 286
Data-collection processes 319
Data transfer 26
Davidson, W.H. and Haspeslagh, P. 72, 74
Dawis, R.V. and Lofquist, L.H. 334, 335
Debt networks 261
Decentralization 34, 41, 141
Dekker, Wisse 119
Development programmes 358
Directorship interlocks 254–5
Directorship networks 261
DKB 268
DMS Laboratories 122
Do-it-yourself punishment 130
Domestic adjustment
  career transitions and sensemaking literature 332–5
  constructs in 333
  literature review 331–6
  organizational socialization literature 331–2
  sensemaking in 333–4
  work role transition literature 334–5
Domestic companies 317, 352
Domination Matrix 265
Doz, Y., Bartlett, C.A. and Prahalad, C.K. 37
Drucker, Peter 31
Dual career system 78
Dunlop Holdings 121

Eastern Asian enterprise structures 191–212
  authority loyalty 204–6
  bonus payments 205
  commitment and employment practices 204–6
  comparative analysis 202–9
  core employees 205
  division of labour 204–6
  forms of business organization 195–202

horizontal co-ordination 206–9
interdependence and co-ordination 206–9
long-term commitments 205
personal authority systems 204–6
preferred managerial style 205
specialization and development 202–4
vertical co-ordination 206–9
wage systems 206
East-West ventures 117
Economic convergence 31
Economic nationalism 31
Efficiency perspective 37–8
Eguchi, Teiji 106
Electrolux 60
ELGI Ltd. xi, xii
Emery, F.E. and Trist, E.L. 67, 69, 71
EMI 45
Empirical testing 88
Employees, shareholding 80
Entry/reentry role transitions 332
Environment
   Type 1 67
   Type 2 67
   Type 3 67
   Type 4 67
Environmental scan 319–20
EPG profiles 9
   forces toward and against 9–11
Equity networks 261
Equity shareholding 254
Esselte 74
Ethnic markets 25
Ethnocentrism 5–7, 66–7, 160
   costs, risks and pay-offs 11–12
   regression to 12
   see also EPG profiles
Europe, interfirm cooperation 161
European Common Market 26
European Strategic Programme in Information Technologies (ESPRIT) 161
Evans, F.B. 157
Expatriate managers 353
Exporters 317
Exports 19
External consistency 45
External relationships 175–7
Externality problem 127
Extrarole adjustment 333

Failure in global imagination 26–8
Family/spouse adjustment 306, 330, 372
Faucheux, C. and Laurent, A. 64
FCS Industries 122
Feldman, D. 332
Financial centrality, Japan 249–51
Financial institutions, Japan 249–51, 257

Firestone Tyre & Rubber Company 100, 101, 105–8, 111
Firm-specific factors 19
Firms as authoritative units of economic action 193–5
Fisher, C. 331
Flexible manufacturing systems 43
Forbearance 128–31, 141
   incentive 129–30
Ford, Henry 23, 52
Foreign assignments 300–5, 350, 358, 359
Foreign direct investment (FDI) x
Formosa Plastics 202, 276
Franko, L.G. 54, 71
Frequency of transactions 176
Fuji 248, 257
Fujitsu 146, 148
Fukuda Industries Company Ltd 112

Gault, Stanley 111
General Electric x, 117, 122, 360
General Motors 29, 146, 148, 152, 162, 286
Geocentrism 5, 6, 8–9, 13, 68–72
   costs, risks and pay-offs 12
   forces and obstacles toward 10–11
   see also EPG profiles
Ghauri, P.N. 57
Gibney, Frank B. 283
Global business management 85
Global companies 86
Global competition 69, 80
Global cooperation 117–25
Global corporation 21, 24, 32
Global effectiveness xi
Global efficiency x, xi
Global enterprise
   evolution of 317–19
   mindset of 318
   use of term 318
Global imagination, failure in 26–8
Global integration 34
Global management matrix 323
Global managers, developing xvii–xx
Global mentality 80
Global Organizational Model 52–3
Global standardization 25
Global strategic alliances (GSAs) 155–73
   longevity 157, 162, 165–9
   management practices and organization 164–5
   terminology 156–7
Global strategic integration 356
Global strategic partnerships (GSPs) 117–25
   culture 123
   future directions 124–5
   governance 122–3

Global strategic partnerships (GSPs) *cont*
  management 124
  mission 121–2
  obstacles 120–1
  organization 123
  signs of success 121–4
  strategy 122
  use of term 118
Global Strategies Conference 89
Global strategy xiii–xiv, 33–50
  concept of 34
  goals 37–41
  mapping means and ends 35–6
  organizing framework 35, 45–6
  prescriptions in perspective 45–8
  prescriptions on how to manage 34
  use of term 33
Global village 327
Globalization 32
Goldsmith, Sir James 110
Goodyear 100, 104, 109–11
Government intervention 17
Group Bull 152
Groupe Michelin 100, 104, 109, 110

Hamel, G. 153
Hamel, G. and Prahalad, C.K. 33, 34
Hamilton, G.G. and Biggart, N.W. 271
Harmonization process 66
Harrigan, K.R. 162, 163
Hattori, Kunio 106
Hax, A.C. amd Majluf, N.S. 37
Head office 52
Head office/subsidiary relationship 57–61
Headquarters
  control 68
  orientation toward subsidiaries 6
  role of x
Hedlund, G. 74
  and Åman, P. 54, 55
  and Kverneland, A. 69
Helou, A. 287
Henderson, John 321
Henry, E.R. 295
Heterarchical MNC 72–7
  centres 73, 74
  coalitions with other companies 77
  conception 74
  critical characteristic 76
  human resource management 78–81
  integration 75
  organization structure 78
  strategy 72
High Density Image Matrix 264–5
High–tech industries, Japanese *Keiretsu* 228–9
Hitachi Ltd. 268

Hofer, C.W. and Schendel, D. 37
Hofstede, G. 375
Honda 43, 148, 153, 360
Honeywell 152
Hong Kong 202, 203, 281
Hoover Ltd. 26–8
Host–country orientation 7–8
Hout, T. *et al.* 33, 34, 47
Human resource development programmes, US versus Japanese 296–307
Human resource integration, transnational 357–60
Human resource management 78–81, 350
  globalization strategies 356
  in Japanese MNCs 295–307
  individual perspective 350
  institutionalized preferences 309
  international 308–9, 314–16
  national differences in 309–12
  systems perspective 350
Human resource systems
  illusions and recommendations 360–2
  transnational 354–6
Human systems 350
Hyden, H. 66
Hypermodern MNC 64–84
Hyundai 199

IBM 44, 45, 118, 360
ICL 146
Incentives 359
Indian business group formation activities 288–90
Induction-socialization processes 334
Industrial Bank of Japan 257
Industrial companies, Japan 257
Industrial interdependency, Japan 251–3
Industry-specific factors 19
Information systems 319
Innovation 31, 40–1
Integrated network model 69
Integration-responsiveness framework 37
Intercompany transition 332
Intercorporate alliances, Japan 246–9
Intercultural adjustment 365–84
  age factor 369
  and work performance 372–3, 379–80
  comparison of individual, organizational and contextual effects 378–9
  compensation policies and practices 370
  contextual variables 367, 371–2, 375–6, 378
  correlates of 380–1
  definition 366
  demographic characteristics 368
  factors influencing degree of 366
  family/spouse adjustment 372

gender factor in 368–9
individual variables 366, 368–70, 374–8
literature review 366–7
method of study 373–6
model of 367
nationality in 369, 381–2
organization size effect 371
organizational variables 366–7, 370–1, 375, 378
personality and perceptual acuity in 369
prior international experience in 368
repatriation practices 371
results of study 376–9
work experience/preparation in 368
work performance 376
Interfirm cooperation, Europe 161
Interfirm diversity
  dimensions of 158–65
  Type I 155, 157, 165, 169
  Type II 156–8, 165, 169
Interfirm networks, Asian 285–7
Internal consistency 45
Internalization
  across national boundaries 18
  benefits of 17
  costs of 18
International adjustment 327–49
  anticipatory adjustment 340–2
  facets of degree of 338–9
  family/spouse 330
  future research 339–41
  in-country adjustment 341–6
  individual factors 339–40, 341–2
  job factors 342–3
  literature review 328–31
  nonwork factors 330, 345
  organizational factors 340–1, 343–4
  organizational selection criteria and mechanisms 329–30
  organizational socialization factors 344–5
  predeparture training 329
  previous overseas experience 329
  research agenda 336–9
  skill requirements for 330
  summary of findings 345–6
  theoretical framework 336–9
International assets x
International corporate structure, evolution 86–7
International corporation 86–7, 317–18, 352–3
International management
  concept of ix
  subject matter of ix
  use of term ix, x
International operations, theory of 15–20
International Organizational Model 52
International organizational structures, mean agreement scores 90
International transfers 79
Interprofessional transitions 332
Intracompany role transition 332
Intrarole transitions 331
Ishibashi, Kanichiro 104, 106
Ishibashi, Shojiro 101

Japan Synthetic Rubber Company 112
Japanese companies 23, 29, 43, 46, 52, 161, 162, 191, 195–8
  financial centrality 249–51
  financial institutions 249–51, 257
  industrial companies 257
  industrial interdependency 251–3
  intercorporate alliances 246–9
  major industrial groups 241–3
  see also Japanese MNCs
Japanese corporate network 244–73
  in comparative perspective 246–53
Japanese family controlled business groups 194
Japanese firms 193
Japanese *Keiretsu* 213–43, 248, 252, 253, 259, 260, 267–8, 287–8
  and internationalization 229–30
  as economic concept 225
  as separate entity or concept 215
  communication capacities and skills 226–7
  competitiveness 214, 224, 226
  definition 213–14
  established pattern(s) 216–21
  general constitution 223
  high-tech industries 228–9
  industrial ties 220
  interlocked shareholding 217–20
  internalities of 214
  Japanese attitude towards issue of 227–30
  known definitions 215–25
  management pool 218
  manufacturing enterprises 222–5
  opposition of views with the West 225–7
  production flexibility 226
  production integration 223–5
  relativity as criterion for optimum performance 223
  resource economics 221–2, 224
  resource pooling 221, 222
  resource strategy 221–2
  specific ties 217–20
  understanding of 214–15
Japanese MNCs
  commitment to company 300
  duration of overseas assignments 300–1
  evaluation of performance 302
  failure rates and reasons for failure 297–8
  family situation factor 305

Japanese MNCs *cont*
  human resource planning in 295–307
  implications for United States MNCs 305–6
  overall qualification of candidates 299–300
  reasons for lower failure rates 299–305
  relationship between selection, training and incidences of success 298–9
  selection criteria 298
  selection for overseas assignments 302
  sources of manpower 296–7
  support system in corporate headquarters 301–2
  training for overseas assignments 303–5
  training programmes 298
Japanese *zaibatsu* 248, 251, 287
Jarillo, J.C. 286
Jeelof, Gerrit 119
Johanson, B. 286
Johanson, J. and Vahlne, J-E. 67
Joint ventures 71, 75, 77, 78, 126, 176
  avoiding recurrent negotiation 138
  backward integration 136
  breakdown 141
  buyback arrangements 136
    in collaborative R&D 140
  collusion 140, 142
  configuration 135–7
  dominant partner 143–4
  economic theory 134–41
  forward integration 136
  hedging against intermediate product price movements 139
  interlocking networks 143
  internalizing implementation of counterthreats 141
  international aspects 142–3
  local and global symmetry 137
  long-term arm's-length contracts 137–9
  management training 139
  multistage arrangement 136
  operational integration 142
    between upstream and downstsream activities 139
  operations motivated by lack of confidence 137–9
  parallel ventures 143
  quality uncertainty in 139–40
  R&D 140, 142
  symmetry properties 137
  technology transfer 139
JVC 146, 149

Kavner, Robert 160
Khambatta, D. and Ajami, R. 285
Kissinger, Henry 32
Knowledge
  arbitrage 280–2
  production of 18
Knowledge-based products 18
Kodak 146
Koestler, A. 65, 66
Kogut, B. 33, 34, 47
Komatsu 30, 31, 47
Korea 203
Kubota 268

Lane, H. and DiStefano, J. x
Laurent, A. 64, 325
Lazarsfeld, P.M. and Merton, R.K. 158
Leadership
  agenda 319
  American challenge 323–6
  development 319–23
  United States 323–6
Learning capacity, enhancing 151–2
Learning objective 47
Learning opportunities 40–1
Levitt, T. 34
Liem Sioe Liong 279
Life-stage transition 333
Li Ka Shing 279
Local network 59
Local preferences 25
Local servicing 19
Location policies 19
Location strategies 15–17
Lockwood, W.W. 249
Lokanathan, P.S. 288
Long-Term Credit Bank 257
Louis, M.R. 332, 333
Lundgren, S. and Hedlund, G. 69

McCulloch, W. 76
McDonalds 22, 281
Macroeconomic risks 38
Madison Avenue 117
Maisonrouge, Jaques 12
Make-or-buy decision 154
Management development activities 81
Management ethos 75
Management style 75
Managers
  retaining 359–60
  subsidiary 74
  supply problem 72
  transnationally competent 351–2
Managing change and chaos 321–2
Marginal price 31
Mariolis, P. and Jones, M.H. 250
Market globalization 21–32
Market imperfections 17–19
Market research 29

Market segments 24, 25
Market servicing 15
Marketing concept 29
Marketing departments 29
Mascarenhas, B. 47
Matrix organization 74–5
Matsushita Denko 269
Matsushita Electric 269
Maurice, M. 193
Maurice, M. et al. 191
Mean Density Image Matrix 264
Mendenhall, M. and Oddou, G. 330
Mendenhall, M. et al. 329
Mendenhall,M. and Oddou, G. 341
Microelectronics and Computer Cooperative 118
Microprocessors 30
Microsoft 118
Middle Eastern countries 25
Minebea xi–xii
Ministry of International Trade and Industry (MITI) 198
Mino, Akio 107
Mintz, B. and Schwartz, M. 250
Mitsubishi 155, 248, 257, 268, 287, 360
Mitsui 248, 257, 269, 287
Miyazaki, Y. 252
MNCs x, xi, 21, 24, 32, 86, 87, 317–18, 353–4
   based in small countries 51–63
   characteristics of 4
   degree of multinationality 5
   evolution 3–14
   growth of 18
   home country attitudes 5–7
   legalistic definition 7
   states of mind or attitudes to 5
   structural development 51–63
Model T 23
Monarchical MNC 73
Money, special qualities of 25
Monte Jade Association 279
Morgan, J.P. 207
Morita, Akio 105
Motorola 146, 149, 150
Multinational compaies. See MNCs
Multinational Organizational Model 52
Multinationalism and polycentrism 7–8
Mutual forbearance 129
Myers-Briggs Type indicator (MBTI) 374–5, 382

Nation-specific factors 19
National competitiveness 350
National context 160–2
National Cooperative Research Act 1984 161
National differences 24, 25, 34, 41–3
   in human resource management 309–12

National markets 15
   division of 19–20
NEC 44, 147, 152
Negandhi, A.R. ix, x, xxii
Negandhi, A.R. and Prasad, S.B. xvii
Nestlé 360
Network structure, blockmodels of 257–60
Nevin, John 105, 108
New York Stock Exchange 280
Nichido 257
Nicholson, N. 334
Nielsen, R.P. 156
Nimzowitsch, Aron 64
Nippon Electric 247
Nippon Steel Corporation 300
Nippondenso 269
Nissan Motors 43, 46, 196, 268, 301
Nobel Industries 61
Non-nationals in senior posts 12–13
Non-western structures xvi–xvii
NUMMI venture 152

Ogilvy, J. 65, 76, 80
Ohmae, K. 85, 161, 318
Ohno System 285
Oliver, C. 156
Olivetti 121, 160
Olsen, M. 82
Operating risks 39
Organizational behavioural orientation x
Organizational typology 85–99
Organizational versatility 320–1
Orru, M. et al. 191
Outboard Marine Corporation 30, 31
Outsourcing agreements 153–4
Overseas assignments 300–5, 350, 358, 359
Ownership of production 17–19

Partner screening 163
People's Republic of China. See Chinese business
Pepsi-Cola 22
Perlmutter, H. 34, 66, 68, 69, 72
Personal effectiveness 322–3
Philippines 60–1
Philips 146, 360
   GSP portfolio 119–20
Pico Group 278
Pinder, C.C. and Schroeder, K.G. 335
Pirelli & Company 100, 121
Policy risks 38
Polycentrism 5–7, 67–8
   and multinationalism 7–8
   costs, risks and pay–offs 12
   see also EPG profiles
Porter, M.E. 37, 165
Portfolio model 37

Poynter, T.A. 47
Prahalad, C.K. 37, 153
Pratt & Whitney 122
Procter and Gamble 33, 40
Production facilities, location of 15–17
Promotion systems 359
Protectionism 71

Quality and reliability 23
Quality uncertainty in joint ventures 139–40

Radical problem-orientation 77
Ratchet effect 153–4
RCA 163
R&D, location of 16
Recourse to the law 129–30
Recruiting decisions 357–8
Reed, John 362
Region-specific factors 19
Regional centres 60–1
Regional headquarters 58
Relocation literature 335
Renault 123
Repatriation practices 371
Reputation building 132–3
Reputation effects 131
Resource risks 39
Retaining managers 359–60
Returns to scale 16
Revlon 29
Reward and punishment systems 79–80
Rewards in manager retention 359
Risk management 38–40, 81
Risk sharing 130
Rockefeller, John 52
Role/career–stage transition 333
Role management 332
Rolls–Royce 122
Rover 148
Royal Dutch Shell 358, 360

Salim Group 279
Sandvik 60
Sanwa 248, 257
SAS 76, 80
Scale economies 43–5
Scarcity 24–5
Schermerhorn 156
Schultz, T.W. xviii
Scope economies 43–5
Sekaran, U. and Snodgrass, C. 286
Semiconductor Research Cooperative 118
Semicontractual risks 39
Shareholding by employees 80
Sharp 163
Siemens 146, 148

Silin, R.H. 201
Similarity hypothesis 157
Simmonds, K. 74
Singapore 60, 274
Singapore Economic Development Board 89
SKF Steel 80
Skill requirements for international adjustment 330
SmithKline Corporation 30, 31
Social institution 157
Social interaction 158
Societal culture 158–60
Societal effect 193
Sony 360
South Korea 192, 204
South Korean business groups 191
South Korean *chaebols* 199–200, 288
Spatial mapping 256–7
Specialization 72
Spouse. *See* Family/spouse adjustment
Stage model 51
Standardization 23–4
STET 122
Stopford, J.M. and Wells, L.T. 51, 54, 57, 71
Strategic alliance 174
Strategic directions 163–4
Strategic management 37
Strategic risks 40
Strategic trade–offs 47–8
Strong cheating 129
Subsidiaries 18, 19, 54, 58, 67, 68
    headquarters orientation toward 6
Subsidiary managers 74
Sumitomo 248, 257, 287
Sumitomo Bank 247
Sumitomo Chemical 247
Sumitomo Electric 247
Sumitomo Machinery 247
Sumitomo Metal Industries 247
Sumitomo Metal Mining 247
Sumitomo Trust & Banking 247
Sun, David and John 281
Swedenborg, B. 56
Swedish firms 54–7
    FDI 56, 57
    foreign operations 55
    international growth 55–7
Swedish Match 61

Taisho 257
Taiwan 192, 202–4, 274, 275, 281
Taiwan Stock Exchange 280
Taiwanese Shoe Association 281
Takahashi, Takami xi
Team management 321
Technology 32

developments 80
force of 21–2
law of 22–4
vs. competence 149
Technology transfer 26
  joint ventures 139
Teradyne Corporation 30
Tetra Pak 61
Third country nationals (TCNs) 69
Thompson, J.D. 71
Thomson 146, 149
Thorelli, H.B. 286
Toder, E.J. 46
Tokenism 12
Tokio 257
Torbiorn, I. 330
Toshiba 146, 149, 150
Toyota 46, 146, 152, 162, 196, 269, 285, 360
Trade unions 29
Training
  cross–cultural (CCT) 160, 359
  for overseas assignments 303–5
  in Japanese MNCs 298–9
  in United States 298–9, 305
  in United States MNCs 305
  joint ventures 139
  opportunities 358–9
  predeparture 329
Transaction costs theory 176–7
Transnational corporations 354
  H1-H5 92–3
Transnational MNCs 73
Transnational Organizational Model 53–4
Transnational solution 52
Transnational structures, H1–H5 88
Transnationally competent managers 351–3
Trust 176, 182
  measurement of 177–8
TRW 124
Tung, R.L. 295, 296, 298, 381
Tyre industry
  Bridgestone FDI 100–14
  company sales figures 105
  comparative company performance 109
  worldwide market share 110

UCINET program 256
Uncertainty 177
  measurement of 177–8
Unidata 121
Unilever 8, 360

Uniroyal Goodrich Tire Company 110
United Auto Workers 29
United States 32, 161
  and Chinese business 283–4
  leadership challenge 323–6
  relationship between selection, training and
    incidences of success 298–9
United States companies
  corporate culture 161–2
  management structures 191
United States MNCs
  commitment to company 300
  duration of overseas assignments 300–1
  evaluation of performance 302
  failure rates and reasons for failure 297–8
  family situation factor 305
  family/spouse provision 306
  implications from comparison with Japanese
    MNCs 305
  longer-term perspective 305–6
  selection for overseas assignments 302
  sources of manpower 297
  support system in corporate headquarters
    301–2
  training 305
United Steel-workers of America 29
Utilization 360

Vaill, Peter 322
Van Maanen, J. and Schein, E. 331, 332, 334
Vernon, R. 39
Volvo 80
Vulnerability 129

Wang, Y.C. 276
Weak cheating 129
Weiss, Paul 13
Welch, John F. Jr. 29
Western markets 29–30
Westney, D.E. 42
Williamson, O.E. 68
Window dressing 12–13
World homogenization 32
World-oriented concept 8–9
Wu, Gordon 279

Yang, D.Y. 278
Yasuda 257
Yeiri, Akira 106
Yen, James 277
Yoshida Kagyo KK (YKK) 33